THE NEW OXFORD HISTORY OF ENGLAND

General Editor · J. M. ROBERTS

Seeking a Role

THE UNITED KINGDOM,
1951–1970

BRIAN HARRISON

CLARENDON PRESS · OXFORD

OXFORD
UNIVERSITY PRESS

Great Clarendon Street, Oxford OX2 6DP

Oxford University Press is a department of the University of Oxford.
It furthers the University's objective of excellence in research, scholarship,
and education by publishing worldwide in

Oxford New York

Auckland Cape Town Dar es Salaam Hong Kong Karachi
Kuala Lumpur Madrid Melbourne Mexico City Nairobi
New Delhi Shanghai Taipei Toronto

With offices in

Argentina Austria Brazil Chile Czech Republic France Greece
Guatemala Hungary Italy Japan Poland Portugal Singapore
South Korea Switzerland Thailand Turkey Ukraine Vietnam

Published in the United States
by Oxford University Press Inc., New York

First published 2009

British Library Cataloguing in Publication Data
Data available

Library of Congress Cataloging in Publication Data

Harrison, Brian Howard.
Seeking a role: the United Kingdom, 1951–1970/Brian Harrison.
p. cm.
Includes bibliographical references and index.
ISBN 978-0-19-820476-3 (acid-free paper) 1. Great Britain—Social life and customs—20th century. 2. Great Britain—Social conditions—20th century. 3. Great Britain—Foreign relations—1945–1964. I. Title.
DA589.4.H37 2009
941.085'5—dc22 2008046116

Typeset by Laserwords Private Limited, Chennai, India
Printed in Great Britain
on acid-free paper by
Clays Ltd, St Ives plc

ISBN 978-0-19-820476-3

1 3 5 7 9 10 8 6 4 2

Preface

This is the first of two volumes on British history since 1951. The second, *Finding a Role?*, similarly structured, will appear a year hence. It will carry the story forward in detail to 1990, and more cursorily from then to the present. Each book is self-contained, but in *Finding a Role?* the reader will see how some of the tendencies traced here developed after 1970.

Reading prefaces is probably a minority taste, but writing them is a pleasure, for they enable debts to be properly acknowledged at last. Many are incurred while writing a book of this kind, and the brevity of acknowledgement cannot reflect their scale. But first, the regrets. Two are irreparable: I wish that John Roberts, who in 1993 encouraged me to set out on what turned out to be a longer journey than he expected, were alive to cheer me on at the end. I also wish that my respected colleague of more than thirty years, Andrew Glyn, could also have been with him. Our political divergence never marred a happy and (to me) fruitful relationship—so much so, that a year before his death he cheerfully volunteered to read two draft chapters and made discussing them as enjoyable for me as were the many tutorials he gave to our pupils.

My journey would have lasted even longer if a two-year Radcliffe Fellowship in 1994–6 had not freed me to make a good start; and without the two-year emeritus fellowship (2004–6) awarded me by that admirable institution, the Leverhulme Trust, it would have been much more difficult to get my thoughts together at the end. Much to my surprise, the Rockefeller Foundation gave me a second chance to stay for a month (March 2007) at their Study and Conference Center, Bellagio, where I had spent a memorable month in 1980; in such a superb and stimulating environment I had no excuse for not introducing still more coherence. Two Americans, Rob Hume and Tom Minsker, showed extraordinary generosity in making their indexing package available to me, and extraordinary patience in guiding me through it. The warmth in personal relations generated by such individual acts of kindness helps to scale down the huge damage the USA's reputation incurred worldwide with its friends after 2003.

Books of this kind rest on complex support networks of people whose courteous assiduity and patience frequently go unacknowledged. My demands on, and my debt to, the Bodleian Library staff, especially those at the reserve desk in the Upper Reading Room, have been accumulating for half a century. It is one of the world's most beautiful and congenial places in which to work. If I have rarely footnoted my frequent resort to two admirable Oxford University Press reference works—the *Oxford English Dictionary* and the *Oxford Dictionary of*

National Biography—this is because I now resort to them as a matter of course. For decades in Corpus Christi College, Oxford, Mary Davidson, Jean Bateman, and the late Phyllis Beckley carefully and uncomplainingly kept the newspapers for me; and on the computing side David Cooper, Marion Ellis, Martin Campbell, and Tony Brett cheerfully endured what must often have been (for them) painful encounters. The late Abe Aboody, of the typesetters Alliance International (Pondicherry), showed at a late stage how Indian generosity and charm still prolong an Anglo-Indian cultural affinity that reaches far back.

Two anonymous readers took considerable trouble with large sections (one of them with the whole) of this book and its successor while in draft. David Coleman and Alex May, selflessly generous with their time and expertise, undertook to read whole chapters; and the heavy commitments of Andrew Callingham, John Davis, Dick Holt, Alvin Jackson, Mel Johnson, Peter Savill, and John Watts did not prevent them from responding generously when asked to advise on topics where I was especially ignorant. I acknowledge my many other debts in the footnotes.

Among the Fellows of Corpus Christi College, my history colleagues Thomas Charles-Edwards and John Watts have been extraordinarily tolerant—as has my wife Vicky, who must have been thankful when the final text was sent off, though she never said so. I have already dedicated my *Transformation of British Politics* to her, and she will I'm sure forgive me if my dedication now moves on. While I was a teaching fellow of Corpus Christi College (from 1967 to 2000) a sequence of College lecturers in history, by sharing my teaching responsibilities, helped to keep my research and writing going. I am enormously grateful to them. They are a distinguished bunch—or were, as two are now dead: David Englander and Tim Mason. The others are still very much alive: Ian Britain, Martin Ceadel, Martin Conway, Matthew Fforde, Martin Francis, Stephen Howe, Paul Johnson, Ross McKibbin, Joshua Sherman, Andrew Thompson, and Bernard Wasserstein. I dedicate to them and to their memory this book and its successor.

B.H.

August 2008

Contents

Plates

All sixteen plates are collected in a single sequence on art paper in the middle of the book. The page references supplied here identify where in the text each plate is relevant.

1 The Festival of Britain in 1951, buildings on London's South Bank: Skylon, Dome, Festival Hall. (p. xv)
© TopFoto

2 Lord Montagu of Beaulieu kneeling on the floor scrubbing it with inexpert movements in 1952. (p. 18)
© Mirrorpix

3 The *Daily Mirror* labelled Harlow 'pram town' after an early analysis showed that this new town of the 1950s 'had an age structure resembling that of a developing country—20 per cent of the population under five, 40 per cent under 15' (quoted from Ted Swift in J. Morton (ed.) *Harlow: Story of a New Town* (1980), 123). (p. 135)
© Harlow Town Museum

4 Harold Macmillan speaking at the opening ceremony in March 1952 for six houses built in seven weeks. (pp. 161, 413)
© Hulton Archive/Getty Images

5 Troops equipped with sandbags on Canvey Island during flooding, 21 Feb. 1953. (p. 125)
© Picture Post/Getty Images

6 Coronation photo (2 June 1953), showing the Queen and Bishop Ramsey of Durham. (pp. 49, 181)
© Hulton Archive/Getty Images

7 A crowd of children rushes to get into a sweetshop as it opens on the day sweet rationing ended, 5 Feb. 1953. (pp. 332, 337)
© Hulton Archive/Getty Images

8 A crowd of 700 West Indian immigrants in the customs hall at Southampton, 27 May 1956. (p. 82)
© Picture Post/Getty Images

9 Pagodas at Orfordness, Suffolk, used for vibration testing. (p. 97)
© Ian Boyle/Simlon.co.uk

Illustrations

Abbreviations

ASLEF	Associated Society of Locomotive Engineers and Firemen
BBC	British Broadcasting Corporation
BHS	B. R. Mitchell, *Abstract of British Historical Statistics* (Cambridge, 1988)
BLS	Department of Employment and Productivity, *British Labour Statistics: Historical Abstract 1886–1967* (1971)
BPF	D. E. Butler *et al.*, *British Political Facts* (8 edns. 1963–2000)
BST	A. H. Halsey (ed.), *British Social Trends since 1900* (London and Basingstoke, 1988)
CND	Campaign for Nuclear Disarmament
CPGB	Communist Party of Great Britain
CPRS	Central Policy Review Staff
CVCP	Committee of Vice-Chancellors and Principals
DEA	Department of Economic Affairs
DHSS	Department of Health and Social Security
DIY	do it yourself
DT	*Daily Telegraph*
Econ	*Economist*
EEC	European Economic Community
EFTA	European Free Trade Association
ENSA	Entertainments National Service Association
FT	*Financial Times*
G	*Guardian*
GEC	General Electric Company
HC Deb.	*House of Commons Debates*
HL Deb.	*House of Lords Debates*
HMC	Headmasters' Conference
IAPS	Incorporated Association of Preparatory Schools
Ind.	*Independent*
IOS	*Independent on Sunday*
ITV	Independent Television
LSE	London School of Economics

NATO	North Atlantic Treaty Organization
NERC	Natural Environment Research Council
NHS	National Health Service
NUS	National Union of Students
NS	*New Statesman*
O	*Observer*
ODNB	*Oxford Dictionary of National Biography*, online version
PLP	Parliamentary Labour Party
RSPB	Royal Society for the Protection of Birds
SDP	Social Democratic Party
Spec	*Spectator*
ST	*Sunday Times*
STel	*Sunday Telegraph*
T	*Times*
TBS	A. H. Halsey (ed.), *Trends in British Society since 1900: A Guide to the Changing Social Structure of Britain* (London and Basingstoke, 1972)
TCBH	*Twentieth Century British History*
TCBST	A. H. Halsey (ed.), *Twentieth-Century British Social Trends* (London and Basingstoke, 2000)
TGWU	Transport and General Workers Union
TLS	*Times Literary Supplement*
TRHS	*Transactions of the Royal Historical Society*
TUC	Trades Union Congress
UGC	University Grants Committee
WEA	Workers' Educational Association
WVS	Women's Voluntary Service

Introduction

It was raining when the Festival of Britain's South Bank site first opened to the public on 4 May 1951; the afternoon, said *The Times* next day, 'could hardly have been less propitious'. And yet the perceptive eye could already discern through the fog strange shapes and surfaces: the bravura of the Skylon without visible means of support, the sheer scale of the huge Dome of Discovery, and the bold modernity of the Royal Festival Hall [Plate 1]. Alan Bennett, 'a raw provincial schoolboy, famished for colour . . . was captivated', relishing its abundant moulded metal chairs, and excited at the 'incredibly light and mildly perilous' staircases built without risers: 'to stand on one of the platforms cantilevered over the Thames was a small thrill'.[1] At the end of the month Battersea Park temporarily became London's equivalent of Copenhagen's Tivoli Gardens; its striped pavilions and fairground rococo seemed so committed to pure enjoyment that many wondered how such things could ever have emerged from a government department. In little more than a week the Festival Gardens were arranging a special programme for their millionth visitor, Mrs May Whiteman, wife of a totalizator engineer, with her 3-year-old daughter Brenda. The Festival buildings when illuminated at night seemed specially magical to a people accustomed to wartime scarcity and postwar fuel shortages. A commemorative Festival postage stamp was issued—only the tenth special issue since the first (for the British Empire exhibition in 1924)—and a special coin was struck. Care was taken to make the Festival nationwide, with specialist exhibitions not only elsewhere in London but also in Glasgow, Belfast, and Dolhendre in North Wales. A sea-travelling exhibition on HMS *Campania* boasted a miniature South Bank, a land-travelling exhibition displayed aspects of industrial design and production, and communities throughout the country mounted their own miniature arts festivals. Christopher Ede pioneered in Britain a display of *son et lumière* (not officially invented until the following year and in France) by organizing a pageant at Hampton Court with 2,000 performers. The number of foreign visitors to Britain was rising fast in the late 1940s, and 1951 saw 90,000 more than in the previous year. When it closed on 30 September, the South Bank had attracted nearly 8,500,000 visitors,

[1] A. Bennett, 'The Festival of Britain 1951', published in the 'Interior Worlds' supplement (Dec. 2000) to *World of Interiors*. Mr Bennett kindly referred me to this source. Copyright Interior Worlds/The World of Interiors and Alan Bennett.

and the Festival Gardens on closing four days later had attracted almost as many.[2]

The millennium dome of 2000 highlighted how easily such ventures fail: success in 1951, as in 1851, had never been inevitable. The idea for the Festival had originated in 1943 in the Royal Society of Arts, sponsors of the 1851 exhibition, and overcame many hurdles thereafter: the prolonged hunt for a main site in London; the quest for government support amidst great economic uncertainty; the distractions offered by general elections in 1950 and 1951, international crises and setbacks; and sustained hostility from prominent Conservatives and from Beaverbrook's *Daily Express*. Add to these the industrial disputes which ensured that on opening day the site was not quite ready; to quote the *Spectator* on 12 May, there had been a 'long history of labour trouble. (A high proportion of the manpower is Irish)'. The Festival's ultimate success owed much to the Attlee governments' powerful driving force after 1945: its combination of reason, democracy, and belief in progress through planning. Central to its success was that major politician Herbert Morrison. Allied with his customary clutch of middle-class progressive intellectuals, he confidently applied the interventionist, scientific, internationalist, and advanced aesthetic ideas called up by the interwar depression. The public received a taste of Ferranti's Manchester-based digital computer through the simple demonstration computer 'Nimrod', which took on all comers for 'nim', a game resembling noughts and crosses. Overseas influences were prominent: refugee architects from Hitler, Scandinavian designers, and (to design the Festival's symbol itself) Abram Games, son of a Latvian immigrant, one of the decade's several brilliant poster designers. The Festival united a spirited, forward-looking, science-based outlook with modernistic architectural evangelism and a belief in adult education through recreation. New approaches to the landscaping of buildings were first advertised on a grand scale, and architects subsequently famous—Hidalgo Moya, architect of the Skylon, and Leslie Martin, who led the design team for the Royal Festival Hall, to name only two—seized their moment.

Yet the Festival from the outset also looked backwards. King George VI, in what now seems a high-toned inaugural address, referred to the tragic losses and ongoing burdens imposed by two world wars, but claimed that 'under God's providence', and 'with the spirit of our ancestors renewed in us', prosperity could return. Archbishop Fisher somewhat nervously embraced the notion of national festivity, and warned against celebrating 'in a kind of spiritual emptiness devoid of aspiration or inspiration'.[3] Amidst the concrete and glass, the Shot Tower was preserved to symbolize the South Bank's continuity with

[2] For foreign visitors see I. Ebong's valuable Edinburgh Ph.D. thesis, 'The Origins, Organisation and Significance of the Festival of Britain, 1951', 559. Exhibition visitor figures from *T* (1 Oct. 1951), 4; (5 Nov. 1951), 2.

[3] Ebong, 'Origins', 277–8.

the old London, together with English pubs, London buses, and traditional crafts and styles. A revived Victorianism and a somewhat nostalgic respect for folk art and crafts interpenetrated the Festival's uncompromising modernism, with Nicolette Gray promoting Victorian typefaces and Constance Howard reinvigorating embroidery in the art schools.[4] A note even of national self-mockery was struck, most notably in the cartoonist Rowland Emett's copper-and-mahogany working steam engine 'Nellie', which was among the Festival Gardens' most popular attractions. The ensuing decades were pervaded by this tripartite combination of a selective respect for traditions, often only recently invented, with anxiety about the present, and very tentative hopes for the future.

The period from 1951 to 1970 possesses a certain unity. At home it saw the rise of corporatism, almost taken for granted in 1951, to further heights in the 1960s. The term seems first to have been used in the USA antithetically to 'individualism', and in the interwar democracies was regularly employed pejoratively to denote the authoritarian power structure behind Italian Fascism. In the UK by the 1950s, however, it was being employed in a weaker, and decidedly democratic, participatory, and non-pejorative sense to denote the system of economic planning then in vogue: this involved the voluntary and continuous interaction between governments, employers' organizations, and trade unions. By 1970 the system was being questioned, but the doubts were not yet shaping government policy. Abroad, these were years of all-pervading cold war. With Stalin's death in 1953 the clouds slowly lifted, but they soon descended again. There was much indecision in Britain about how to respond, together with much wishful thinking and nostalgia. Should kinship, sentiment, and wartime loyalties make the Commonwealth the national anchor? Or were shifting economic relationships gradually enhancing the appeal of a European alignment? Or should Britain try to get the best of both worlds by pursuing the so-called 'special relationship' with the USA? And should the UK strive to remain in the top international league, or should realities be faced and a virtue be made of necessity? The dilemmas were painful and decisions were taken reluctantly or not at all. Hence the title of this book. Addressing a West Point student conference about American affairs on 5 December 1962, Dean Acheson—chief architect of postwar American foreign policy and adviser to four presidents—claimed that 'Great Britain has lost an empire and has not yet found a role'. He saw no future for a Britain which clung to the USA and presided over a Commonwealth with 'no political structure, or unity, or strength': Britain was ineffectual as broker between America and Russia, and her future lay in Europe. His remarks, lent impact by his Anglophile leanings,

[4] For Gray see N. Whiteley, *Pop Design: Modernism to Mod* (1987), 36. For Howard see obituary in *Ind.* (28 July 2000), 6.

prompted what Lady Violet Bonham Carter called 'a ridiculous explosion of Jingo rage',[5] but he never apologized for them—nor was apology needed, for the UK's search for a role had already begun, and by 1970 the role had yet to be found.

The area discussed in this book—England, Wales, Scotland, and Northern Ireland—lends the period unity at another level. The United Kingdom was relatively cohesive between 1951 and 1970: with its unity as with its corporatism, doubts were mounting only towards the end of the period. The movements stirring for nationalism in Wales and Scotland and for civil rights in Northern Ireland will therefore be discussed, but they will not require separate chapters. Chapter 8 will briefly discuss them, but here as elsewhere in this book the focus will rest less upon a single political chronology than upon the far less familiar and usually distinct chronologies of non-political change, whose long-term effects are often no less revolutionary for being gradual and even sometimes unrecognized while in progress. In no society do politicians and government administrators dominate day-to-day life, and least of all in a parliamentary democracy not involved in major war. Indeed, many of the politicians' concerns in these years seem much less important in retrospect than they seemed at the time. To subordinate their timetable paradoxically but silently acknowledges their achievement in these years: for them, no news is usually good news. Winston Churchill, Harold Macmillan, and Harold Wilson must of course feature, but so must many lesser known and sometimes anonymous people: those who caused the National Trust and the Royal Society for the Protection of Birds (RSPB) to grow so fast in the second half of the twentieth century, for example; or the consistent and unflamboyant labours of the sociologist Peter Townsend, who for decades drew attention to the plight of neglected minorities; or Lady Denman and Margaret Pyke, whose powerful partnership in the Family Planning Association quietly but continuously pushed forward the humanitarian frontier, though Iain Macleod claims a supporting role in their story's later stages. In demographic change, more than anywhere else, the British people, and not the politicians, spontaneously set the pace; the social workers, lawyers, doctors, tax authorities, administrators, moralists, and politicians were left to cope—slowly, often censoriously and clumsily—with the consequences of events whose impulse originated elsewhere. This period of British history—exempt, by comparison with earlier generations, from war and poverty—frees us to focus upon what happened rather than on what the authorities intended to happen, for to a large extent the British people after 1951 made their own history, and great indeed were the changes that they collectively brought about.

[5] D. Brinkley, *Dean Acheson: The Cold War Years 1953–71* (New Haven, 1992), 176. *Daring to Hope. The Diaries and Letters of Violet Bonham Carter 1946–1969*, ed. M. Pottle (2000), 262 (diary, 11 Dec. 1962).

At pp. 547–78 a threefold chronology of events from 1951 to 1970 outlines the separate chronologies that the fields of inquiry require and sets them side by side, but the political narrative can usefully be outlined briefly here. From 1945 the powerful interventionist impetus launched by the Second World War gained impact from the Attlee governments' socialist rhetoric. Yet the numerous problems those governments had to tackle, complex and simultaneous, wore down their leading members; they were worn down still further after 1948 by a resurgent Conservative Party led by Winston Churchill. The National Government's handling after 1931 of the depression, however, together with its appeasement of the Fascist powers, remained a powerful enough memory to leave the Conservatives still on the defensive even after they had narrowly won the general election in 1951. Churchill, like his three successors as prime minister—Eden (1955–7), Macmillan (1957–63), and Douglas-Home (1963–4)—sought to maximize the advantage over Labour by pursuing cautious consensus policies at home, and by combining a traditionalist, patriotic image with a pragmatic acceptance of the need to modernize. It was ironic that the Conservatives' most serious lapse during the period, the Suez crisis of 1956, should occur in their supposed area of greatest strength: colonial and foreign policy. Skilful leadership thereafter, however, and the quick refurbishment of the Anglo-American alliance, ensured that the Conservative electoral victory of 1955 was followed by a larger victory in 1959, though the margin even then between victory and defeat was small. Still more remarkable in its pragmatism was Macmillan's realization by 1960 that Britain's destiny now lay in the European Economic Community (EEC), though the first attempt at entry was rebuffed by de Gaulle in 1963. Meanwhile the Labour Party responded constructively to its threefold defeat, and by 1964 seemed credible as a party of government, provided that it could fend off the mounting Liberal challenge. Harold Wilson's skilfully balanced centrist stance as Labour leader from 1963 enabled Labour narrowly to win the general election of 1964, and much less narrowly his government's second election two years later. There followed the major setback in 1967 of an unplanned devaluation, followed by the decision to make a second (again failed) bid to enter the EEC. Wilson's pursuit of modernization was less inhibited than the Conservatives', and exploited his party's link with the trade unions. Corporatism was now approaching its apogee, and although its failures in the late 1960s seemed serious, and help to explain Wilson's lost election in 1970, they did not immediately prompt a wholesale retreat towards the free market. Wilson's successor as prime minister, Edward Heath, was cast in Macmillan's mould: not till the late 1970s did a new variant of Conservatism come to the fore.

Against this background, this book travels through the seven fields of inquiry which each receive a chapter. The fields are as follows: Britain's international situation, broadly conceived; its changing environment; its social and ethnic structure; its rapidly changing family structure and its interaction with public welfare; its evolving economy; its educational, cultural, and intellectual life; and its political institutions. Even the last of these (Chapter 8) is concerned, not with a political narrative, but with analysing how Britain's political institutions were changing. Many of the threads are drawn together in Chapter 9 on 'the sixties' as a concept. The fields also govern the structure of Chapter 1, whose purpose is twofold: to launch the book by delineating its overall sevenfold shape, but also to convey what Britain was like in 1951. Several recurring themes cut across most chapters and receive sustained discussion in one of them: secularization, professionalization, and specialization, for example; the gradual fragmentation of the British elite; the growing salience and pervasiveness of the media; the vitality of voluntarism; the combination of a new diversity of lifestyles and privacy with pressures towards standardization and conformity; and the individual's experience of combining atomization with new patterns of community.

There are in addition eight cross-cutting motifs which, because they receive no sustained discussion, are at risk of getting lost in the text, though not in the index. There is first the equivocal legacy of the Second World War, which united on the one hand pride at having 'stood alone' in 1940, and at having later emerged on the victorious side, with a slowly growing recognition of the long-term drawbacks this entailed. The second motif highlights the continuing tension between the UK's hermetic and receptive tendencies after 1945. The hermetic tendency combined cultural narrowness with geographical breadth: through trade, immigration, defence, and a shared language it reflected long-standing English-speaking links with Commonwealth and USA. The receptive tendency, by contrast, worked with the economic and touristic grain and pointed towards Europe. Third, there is the motif of almost continuously growing private affluence conjoined with persistent anxiety in public debate about the economy. This links to a fourth motif: the complex interaction between time-saving technology and the pace of daily living. Flowing out of this is the fifth motif: the strain imposed on structures and values religious in origin by a growing and secularized materialism. The latter consists not just in accumulating material objects, but in the humanitarian and often rationalistic priority lent to physical health and fitness. The sixth motif juxtaposes the major social changes in social relationships since 1951 with the UK's unusually stable political framework. Seventh, there is the constraint on politicians' power stemming from their need continuously to seek consensus for what they see as necessary changes, sometimes statist in nature, whilst operating within a strongly voluntarist culture. Interacting with this is the final motif, which grows out of the book's title, whereby potential roles for the UK are produced and tried on for size. These motifs will not receive dedicated chapters or even sections of chapters, but each of Chapters 2–9 will conclude by highlighting how the chapter has illuminated them, for their occasional breaking above the surface of events reflects their continuous presence beneath, which is advertised in the index's subject-entries. As for the index's biographical entries, they briefly identify the personalities discussed.

The concluding chapter's brief 'retrospect' has four objectives. It helps further to integrate discussion of the recurring motifs with which earlier chapters conclude. Its long backward look, reaching further back even than 1940, reinforces Chapter 9's drawing together of the threads; only by this route can the skills and myths be clarified which brought continuity and cohesion to a society simultaneously beset by rapid socio-economic change and international decline. The chapter also analyses the competing roles devised for the UK during the 1950s and 1960s, and it outlines the UK's strengths and weaknesses when launching itself into the dangerous decades of the 1970s and 1980s.

CHAPTER 1

The United Kingdom in 1951

1. THE UNITED KINGDOM AND THE WORLD

By the 1940s the Foreign Office had long abandoned 'splendid isolation' as a strategy for the UK, but nations draw closer for many reasons other than diplomatic: traders, tourists, communicators, writers, and thinkers promote international contacts far broader and more continuous. The UK in 1951 was at once more and less insular than later: more insular because the Second World War and postwar currency restrictions prompted by the dollar shortage precluded overseas travel for its civilian population, and cheap international air travel did not yet exist for the masses. The well-to-do Susan Brown, conversing on a bus in the north of England with Joe Lampton about going abroad soon after the war, was unknowingly taking a risk: for Joe, 'to talk about holidays abroad is one of the almost infallible marks of the stuck-up, the high-and-mighty, who are no better than they should be'. The war had drawn even the boundary between northern and southern Ireland more firmly, and the nearest most British people came to foreign countries was when holidaying on a British beach.[1] Margaret Thatcher first went abroad when 26, for her honeymoon: not till she became party leader did she visit Germany. So the UK, united in war against outsiders, came to view itself as a large cohesive family whose values included fair play, moderation, common sense, decency. This national self-image was nourished by wartime commentators such as J. B. Priestley and George Orwell, and postwar by cartoonists such as Giles, who focused on private life, and by Ealing Studios films which propagated a distinctively British sense of humour. The national incompetence in foreign languages could not yet be justified, as later, by the fact that English had become a world language. Even educated people then took some pride in speaking foreign languages with an English accent; as for the rest, Orwell claimed in 1941 that 'nearly every Englishman of working-class origin considers it effeminate to pronounce a foreign word correctly'.[2] Equally

[1] J. Braine, *Room at the Top* (first publ. 1957, paperback edn. 1991), 133. The novel's action takes place in *c.*1946. See the statistics in Hulton Press, *Patterns of British Life* (1950), 114.

[2] G. Orwell, 'The Lion and the Unicorn' (1941) in his *Complete Works*, ed. P. Davison, xii (1998), 399; cf. his 'The English People' (1947, though largely written in 1943–4), ibid. xvi (1998), 202.

restricted were British tastes in food. 'As a rule they will refuse even to sample a foreign dish', he wrote in 1944 of working-class people; 'they regard such things as garlic and olive oil with disgust, life is unlivable to them unless they have tea and puddings'.[3]

But if, uniquely in the twentieth century, the civilian generation reaching maturity in the 1940s lacked contact with 'abroad', the UK had become in other respects less insular by 1951. Men in two world wars had at every social level experienced more overseas travel than they desired, often (especially in the Second World War) in exotic parts. War correspondents demonstrated how the media could transcend national boundaries, and radio had coordinated resistance movements throughout Europe. The number of foreign-language services more than quadrupled during the war, and output in European languages rose from eighty-three hours per week in six languages during September 1939 to 321 hours in twenty-two languages five years later; nor did the British Broadcasting Corporation (BBC) succeed completely in shutting out the overseas commercial station, Radio Luxemburg.[4] The war had also reinforced the UK's Anglo-American and Commonwealth connections, and almost immediately afterwards the cold war required young men to engage in a 'national service' that often took them overseas. Such involuntary war-related overseas travel was perhaps culturally less broadening than travel from choice, but the UK still saw itself as a great power with worldwide responsibilities, and had been encouraged in this through its role in the winning coalition throughout both world wars. In 1951 *Our Island Story* and *Our Empire Story*, titles of Henrietta Marshall's widely read Edwardian history books for children, still evoked national pride. Ernest Bevin, Foreign Secretary from 1945 to 1951, did not hesitate to claim 'great power' status for Britain,[5] even if it was already becoming common to acquiesce, privately and somewhat ruefully, at being number three in the international pecking order.

London in 1951 was still a distinctively British city alive with Cockney traditions. By later standards it contained few tourists or immigrants, but the war had diversified its population. 80,000 refugees from Greater Germany and Spain entered Britain between 1932 and 1939, many of them Jews, though some were in transit elsewhere. And because Irish emigrants had become less welcome in the USA, four-fifths in 1946–51 went to Great Britain; in 1951 627,000 people in England and Wales had been born in Ireland.[6] In the same year there were, at a low estimate, 33,000 Italians in Great Britain—some

[3] Orwell, 'The English People', 202.

[4] A. Briggs, *The History of Broadcasting in the United Kingdom*, iii. *The War of Words* (1979), 485; see also 12, 18–19.

[5] e.g. in *H[ouse of] C[ommons] Deb[ates]* 16 May 1947, c. 1965.

[6] M. J. Proudfoot, *European Refugees 1939–52: A Study in Forced Population Movement* (Evanston, Ill., 1956), 27. S. Glynn, 'Irish Immigration to Britain, 1911–1951: Patterns and Policy', *Irish Economic and Social History*, 8 (1981), 51, 56.

postwar economic migrants, some former prisoners of war, but also some statistically invisible Italians who in fighting Fascism had assumed British nationality. Poles had also been arriving in Britain for generations, and were among the largest wartime and postwar immigrant groups; in 1951 over 160,000 people in Britain had been born in Poland.[7] Then in June 1948 the converted troopship the SS *Empire Windrush* brought the first 492 immigrants from Jamaica, launching the first large-scale economic migration from the non-white Commonwealth.

There was as yet no notion of 'multiculturalism'. Often thankful to find refuge and livelihood, and sometimes justifiably fearful of becoming visible, these immigrants had other priorities. Besides, each group saw itself as separate and was often itself internally fragmented by location of origin, time of arrival, political or religious allegiance, and even diet. Each national group at any one time constituted only a small minority of the UK's total population, and few were visually identifiable. Their motives and loyalties, too, were diverse. Relatively free to choose the time and place of immigration, the migrant may in moving owe much to prior connections in his destination country, and he is more likely to be young, male, and in need of work. He has not burnt his boats: he can return for visits to the former home that may be his ultimate desired destination. The refugee, by contrast, usually arrives in a hurry, with few clear plans or prior connections, and comprises a more balanced sample by age and sex of the society that has been left behind; no permanent home other than the destination country can be envisaged. A new start is inevitable, a determined struggle to recoup a status lost in translation.[8] Entrepreneurship is often the way forward, with philanthropy as the eventual route to full integration, but survival must, at least initially, be unobtrusive, individualist, and family-centred. Jewish immigrants to Britain by 1951 fell into both refugee and economic migrant categories, depending on place of origin and time of arrival, but most other European immigrants arrived or stayed for economic reasons.

All this is not to say that the newcomers lacked impact. The economic migrant possesses the most efficient of all aids to assimilation: a skill or an expertise to sell, for in the destination country his prize assets are an alertness to cultural contrast and the incentive to exploit it. Hence the immigrants' role in diversifying British food. Poles, Italians, and Hungarians may have aimed at first to cater for compatriots, often in London, but they gave good value, and gradually attracted British custom. Victor Sassie, born in Barrow-in-Furness the son of an Italian-born ship's joiner, went native when visiting Budapest in

[7] N. di Blasio, 'Italian Immigration to Britain: An Ignored Dimension', *ATI: Association of Teachers of Italian Journal*, 29 (Autumn 1979), 25. K. Sword, *Identity in Flux: The Polish Community in Britain* (1996), 75.

[8] This discussion owes much to S. E. Hale, 'The Geography of Vietnamese Secondary Migration in Britain' (Swansea Ph.D. thesis 1991), 37–9.

the 1930s, and returned to England to found his 'Budapest' restaurant in London in 1939; then after wartime service with British Intelligence, he launched in Soho the 'Gay Hussar' restaurant, soon popular with Labour Party leaders.[9] Chinese immigrants, prominent in the interwar laundry trade, were by the late 1940s already finding in the Chinese restaurant a reason for spreading out from the seaports and settling all over Britain. It catered for tastes in oriental food acquired by servicemen during the war, and in its staffing relied increasingly on refugees from Communism; interwar Britain had thirty to forty Chinese restaurants, but about a hundred by 1951.[10]

Jewishness is an elusive concept, but the UK's Jewish population was seemingly at its peak in the early 1950s, with 430,000 as the outside estimate.[11] The qualities shared by the entrepreneur and the scholar—commitment, specialization, postponed gratification, perception of opportunity—were notably combined among those German-Jewish refugees who so profoundly influenced British postwar scholarship and publishing, especially art publishing. The immigrants Paul Hamlyn, André Deutsch, Peter Owen, Max Reinhardt, and George Weidenfeld all launched their own publishing houses. Hamlyn, born in 1926 the son of a German-Jewish paediatrician, arrived with his family in 1933, and at 22 was selling from a barrow in Camden market books that were eventually to reach a mass market. Deutsch, son of a Hungarian-Jewish dentist who reached Britain in 1939, set up as a quality publisher in 1945. The Hungarian-Jewish publisher Bela Horovitz, who moved from Vienna to Oxford, operated at a still more elevated level, re-establishing in Britain the quality art publisher Phaidon. In 1949 the Jewish immigrant Eva Itzig, who had fled Germany in 1938, joined her third husband Walter Neurath in founding Thames & Hudson, thus creating the firm which became the world's leading publisher of art and illustrated books.[12] The Warburg Institute, transported from Germany to London in 1933 and incorporated into London University in 1944, helped the UK to comprehend the wealth of European art and culture. There such distinguished London-based German-Jewish refugee scholars of art and architecture as Ernst Gombrich, Edgar Wind, and Nikolaus Pevsner could flourish in the 1940s. The UK gained equally rich immigrant harvests in such academic areas as physics, criminology, and chemistry. Academic or commercial entrepreneurs live by their wits, and both the pursuit of custom and rising income widen their patterns of settlement. By 1951 early twentieth-century Jewish immigrant families were moving across London from

[9] Obituary, *DT* (9 June 1999), 29.

[10] J. L. Watson, *Emigration and the Chinese Lineage: The Mans in Hong Kong and London* (Berkeley and Los Angeles, Calif., 1975), 73. See also K. H. C. Lo, *The Feast of My Life* (1993), 173.

[11] S. Waterman and B. Kosmin, *British Jewry in the Eighties* (1986), 7.

[12] Obituaries of Hamlyn, *G* (3 Sept. 2001), 18; Deutsch, *DT* (12 Apr. 2000), 31; Eva Neurath, *Ind.* (3 Jan. 2000), 5.

the East End to Golders Green and on to affluent suburbs further north and west.

It seemed sad indeed that a decidedly hot war against the totalitarianism of the right was almost immediately followed by a 'cold' war against the totalitarianism of the left. The UK was in the front line for both, though only later was it widely recognized that left-totalitarianism was as distasteful as its precursor: at the time, the USSR had many British sympathizers, which made resisting Communism all the more complex and fiercely fought. In 1946 the government resumed the assumption of the 1920s that there would be no major war for a decade, but the postwar international situation was ominous. Volunteer servicemen were insufficient to preserve order in destabilized and ex-enemy territories, to provide imperial garrisons and trained reserves, and soon to build up North Atlantic Treaty Organization (NATO) frontline forces.[13] So in 1947 peacetime conscription for twelve months was introduced, and was extended to eighteen months in 1949 and two years in 1950—all under a Labour government whose radical, nonconformist, and humanitarian pioneers would have been astonished. Only once before had the UK experienced peacetime conscription, for a few prewar months in 1939. There was a long-standing, deeply rooted British distaste for standing armies, and the government had difficulty in getting its legislation through. By 1951 national servicemen made up more than a third of servicemen in the RAF and more than a half of those in the army. In that year total numbers in the British army and navy were far larger than at the empire's apogee in 1920—almost twice as many, if the RAF is included.[14]

Shrewd nineteenth-century observers had long predicted that Russia and America would become superpowers. Given that the USSR had been so central to Hitler's defeat, and given that Stalin so successfully concealed long-term Soviet weakness, power lent glamour within postwar Britain to all things Russian or all things American, according to political taste. Yet neither publicly nor privately did the UK confess its waning world status: the pursuit of great-power status helped prompt the Attlee governments to accelerate worldwide nuclear proliferation by responding to Bevin's insistence: 'we've got to have this thing . . . We've got to have the bloody Union Jack on top of it.'[15] Yet vanity or delusion were not the sole motives: the danger from Stalin's huge conventional armaments seemed imminent and America's commitment to defence against them then seemed all too precarious. The USA and USSR in the 1940s failed to internationalize control of these terrible weapons at a time when theirs was

[13] R. Broad, *Conscription in Britain 1939–1963: The Militarization of a Generation* (2006), 75.

[14] J. T. Fensome, 'The Administrative History of National Service in Britain, 1950–1963' (Cambridge University Ph.D. thesis 2001), 218. *BLS* 300–1.

[15] In the cabinet committee on atomic energy, 25 Oct. 1946, as recalled by Sir Michael Perrin in 1982, quoted in P. Hennessy (ed.), *Cabinets and the Bomb* (Oxford, 2007), 48.

a duopoly, thus freeing the UK to set precedents for France, then China, and then many others.

Some refugees from Fascist totalitarianism understandably identified with its most avowed and energetic foe: Soviet totalitarianism. Others, some influential, responded by fiercely espousing anti-totalitarian British liberal traditions. The cold war was the context for the key postwar decisions on UK foreign policy. By dividing Germany, it had temporarily sidelined the German problem only to create what seemed a still more dangerous new alignment. This left the UK with difficult choices between rather few options. Could the UK go it alone, relying purely on British and Commonwealth political and economic resources? These were at first sight considerable. British governments had learnt from the loss of the American colonies in the 1780s, and by hearkening to colonial settlers elsewhere had rendered the second British empire more secure. The British empire had grown by 100,000 square miles per year throughout the nineteenth century, and was still growing in the twentieth: in 1951 *Whitaker's Almanack* assigned it a larger land mass (14,435,060 square miles) than thirty years earlier, and (due to natural increase) a much larger population (539,870,000). True, there were only 50,225,000 people in the UK, a mere 2 per cent of the world's population, occupying a mere 0.0018 per cent of the world's land mass:[16] but after the 1930s, air transport seemed at last to be realizing the Conservative statesman Joseph Chamberlain's Edwardian dream, drawing scattered British territories closer together. Neither major British political party was instinctively hostile to empire: its critics were at this time primarily concerned with how to maintain it in the medium term, even if its independence and fragmentation seemed the long-term destination. And to the Attlee governments—with their progressive, planning, internationalist, and humanitarian instincts—the Commonwealth even seemed attractive as ally, beneficiary, and testing ground.

There were, admittedly, discreet changes of nomenclature: by the late 1940s the term 'empire' was confined to the UK and the non-self-governing territories, whereas the term 'Commonwealth' was reserved for the self-governing elements, with the phrase 'British Commonwealth and empire' applied to the whole.[17] The newly independent India and Pakistan (but not Burma, which left the Commonwealth in 1948) pioneered the Commonwealth's evolution into a multicultural grouping whose purposes contrasted markedly with empire, though the significance of this transition was at first disguised by the somewhat cloudy idealism which clung to the Commonwealth concept. Culturally

[16] A. G. L. Shaw (ed.), *Great Britain and the Colonies 1815–1865* (1970), 2. *Whitaker's Almanack* (1951), 196 shows a world population (1949) of 2,377,400,000 occupying 51,375,000 square miles, to which England, Wales, Scotland and Northern Ireland contribute 93,053 square miles. British population from *BHS* 9–10.

[17] See Ivor Thomas's interesting letter in *TLS* (9 Oct. 1948), 569.

and intellectually, the Commonwealth carried much further the progressive aspects of empire—for example, in its collaborative research on agriculture, medicine, forestry, social anthropology, history, and comparative government. Furthermore, the eighteenth century, by expelling the French from America and India, had accidentally endowed the UK with a world language. Late-Victorian British universities (though not Oxford and Cambridge) had been powerfully moulded in structure and syllabus by German models, sometimes by way of America, but German influences waned between the wars, and Oxbridge collegiate patterns were exported to Commonwealth and even to elite American universities. It was the English-speaking cultural network which dominated twentieth-century British universities, and in the mid-1940s there were in London about fifty private societies—commercial, cultural, and social—primarily concerned with the empire.[18] Sentimental ties with the white Commonwealth had been reinforced by wartime collaboration, and these were underpinned by family connection. The Conservative leader Anthony Eden used to say that 90 per cent of Britain's mail from abroad came from beyond Europe; many years later the Labour leader Harold Wilson thought it worth publicly emphasizing that 'I have forty-three close relatives in Australia, descendants of my four grandparents, more than four times as many as I have in Britain.'[19]

The Commonwealth brought the UK considerable economic assets. Given the wars' hugely damaging impact on Germany and Japan, the UK economy seemed in relatively good shape. Protection in the 1930s had strengthened Commonwealth trade links which postwar Conservative protectionists favoured extending. In the background lay the so-called 'Overseas Sterling Area'. It had originated, though without yet being so designated, in those countries (not all in the Commonwealth) known as the 'sterling bloc'; they had chosen to link their currencies' exchange value to sterling rather than to gold or the dollar after Britain had in 1931 abandoned the fixed gold price of sterling in its foreign-exchange transactions. When in 1939 Britain's introduction of exchange control ended the free world-wide movement of assets, most of the bloc clung even more tightly to Britain in the Sterling Area, which after 1944 collaborated with the other leading currencies to stabilize world trading conditions. The war had by then seriously depleted British reserves, and the postwar holdings in sterling of Egypt and India went into decline, though these were counterbalanced by rising balances in oil-rich Middle-Eastern countries. British economic policy until the late 1960s assumed the Sterling

[18] D. Goldsworthy, *Colonial Issues in British Politics 1945–1961: From 'Colonial Development' to 'Wind of Change'* (Oxford, 1971), 189.

[19] E. Shuckburgh, *Descent to Suez: Diaries 1951–1956* (1986), 18 (Eden). Wilson speech of Dec. 1974 before the EEC summit, defending Commonwealth food imports: H. Wilson, *Final Term: The Labour Government 1974–1976* (1979), 258.

Area's continued existence,[20] and viewed a strong pound as integral to Britain's international financial standing.

Colonies and Commonwealth were economic assets in other respects. Independence for South Asia did not threaten Britain's links with the former colonies of white settlement, nor was it seen as precipitating further departures; instead, it was widely viewed as an unavoidable and unique development that demanded compensation elsewhere. Such compensation seemed all the more necessary to reduce the UK's need for dollars and to gain diplomatic freedom of manœuvre by comparison with the USA. Bevin sought to extend British postwar influence in North-East Africa and the Middle East, and briefly in 1945–6 it looked as though the imperial mansion might boast a new annexe in Somalia and Libya.[21] African nationalism was not yet aroused, and frontiers in Malaya, Gibraltar, and Suez were firmly defended. The motive was not merely strategic, but to defend oil supplies, and to acquire food and raw materials without spending precious dollars; these too might be acquired through trading. In areas of British political control, indigenous self-respect could be upheld by governing through local elites. Colonial markets for British exports were much more important after 1945 than before 1939.[22] The Attlee governments' so-called 'ground nuts scheme' involved pouring capital into Tanganyika in order to meet the British housewife's pressing need for fats; yet British debts were simultaneously piling up in India. In the early 1950s Britain supplied over half the imports into Australia, New Zealand, and British West Africa; as for exports, Britain absorbed three-quarters of New Zealand's, two-thirds of British West Africa's, and two-fifths of Australia's.[23] As late as the mid-1950s Britain was the largest user of the Suez Canal, in which she was the largest single shareholder, and in 1955 she owned a third of the 14,666 ships passing through it.[24]

The UK's European options in 1951 seemed less attractive. Despite the UK's immense goodwill towards the USSR in the war's later stages, the Attlee governments never seriously considered a Communist political alignment: the Labour Party's link to trade union leaders was integral, and they had no reason to love Communists. Inheriting Liberal traditions, interwar Labour had

[20] For the best concise account of the Sterling Area's operation in these years see J. D. B. Miller, *Survey of Commonwealth Affairs: Problems of Expansion and Attrition 1953–1969* (1974), 267–307.

[21] As discussed in K. O. Morgan, *Labour in Power 1945–51* (Oxford, 1984), 191, 241; J. Gallagher, *The Decline, Revival and Fall of the British Empire: The Ford Lectures and Other Essays* (Cambridge, 1982), 145.

[22] J. Darwin, *Britain and Decolonisation: The Retreat from Empire in the Post-War World* (London and Basingstoke, 1988), 140.

[23] Sir William Nicoll in A. May (ed), *Britain, the Commonwealth and Europe: The Commonwealth and Britain's Applications to Join the European Communities* (Basingstoke, 2001), 33.

[24] A. Horne, *Macmillan: 1894–1956* (1988), 395.

worsted the Marxists in a fierce battle for supremacy on the left. British debts to the USA were so great by 1945, the Soviet economy was so shattered, its decision-making procedures and objectives so obscure and controversial, that only left-wing mavericks thought a Soviet alignment feasible for Britain. How feasible, then, would a social-democratic and liberal European alignment have been—with the countries which later formed the EEC? Given that during the Second World War the UK had hosted many exiled European governments, had prevailed over Fascism while retaining her democratic structures, and had preserved her economy in relatively good shape, she retained ample prestige and goodwill in Europe. The British political system—for geographical and structural reasons relatively untainted in the recent past by Quislings and fellow travellers—came near to acting as an exemplar for non-Communist Europeans. In her welfare state, too, the UK seemed to offer Europe a characteristic British compromise between the USSR's statist socialism and the USA's rampant individualism. For Labour's manifesto in 1950 the UK was a middle-way 'beacon of inspiration and encouragement'.[25]

European union also offered significant strategic advantages. Collaboration would prevent the USSR from picking off each democratic nation one by one; hence Winston Churchill's European enthusiasms when in opposition between 1945 and 1951. Yet no more for him than for many of his successors did this require a choice: Britain's interest lay in participating in three circles of influence—Commonwealth, Europe, and with the USA—but without total commitment to any. In favouring European union in 1949, Churchill did not at all envisage the Commonwealth's exclusion from it.[26] Through encouraging democratic collaboration in Europe, but without directly participating in it, the UK could promote the democratic and economic interests of all three. For the UK to embrace only one of these options would have seemed a quite unnecessary and even humiliating concession, given her current economic and political prestige, and would have been decidedly unwelcome at home. So in 1950, when Britain had to decide whether to join the six European nations in preliminary discussion of the Schuman plan for pooling French and German coal and steel, Morrison as Foreign Secretary would have none of it: 'it is no good. We can't do it, the Durham miners won't wear it'.[27] In its manifesto of 1950 the Conservative Party sought to have it both ways, claiming to favour 'ever closer association with Western Europe and the United States', while at the same time placing 'in the fore-front of British statesmanship . . . the vital task of extending the unity, strength and progress of the British Empire and Commonwealth'. Not until several years later could such a claim seem to combine incompatibles,

[25] I. Dale (ed.), *Labour Party General Election Manifestos 1900–1997* (2000), 72.
[26] M. Gilbert, *'Never Despair': Winston S. Churchill 1945–1965* (1988), 496.
[27] Horne, *Macmillan 1894–1956*, 319.

and when choices had to be made, it was the 'special relationship' with the USA that UK governments cultivated. Churchill once said that, with a choice between Europe and the open seas, Britain would always choose the open seas.[28]

So in the circumstances of 1945–51, cultivating the 'special relationship' with the USA seemed the only option, if only because it was becoming clear that in the new 'cold war' situation this would not kill off the empire. Churchill in his 'iron curtain' address at Fulton, Missouri, in March 1946 had called for 'a special relationship between the British Commonwealth and Empire and the United States', recommended shared defence procedures, and even predicted 'the principle of common citizenship'.[29] This was a new development: the Victorian UK governing elite had taken a patronizing view of the Americans, and despite their sudden and striking importance to the UK in 1917–18, a somewhat aloof view of interwar American culture remained widespread up to 1939. Americans, in their turn—rejecting British imperialism from the start, and demographically diminishingly Anglo-Saxon—disliked any close UK entanglement, and between the wars had retreated into isolationism. Late-Victorian British aristocratic marriages to American heiresses had already begun to break down the barriers, however, and from 1900 to 1939 a tight Anglo-American network of elite cultural and educational contacts between the two countries strengthened the relationship (as yet without a name). This the two world wars infused with a new fervour: then and later the two countries' centuries of shared language and political traditions acquired a sudden importance, and the friction which had generated the American revolution came to seem relatively ephemeral. The Second World War's network of service contacts and friendships generated shared instincts, constraints, and responses, and during the late 1940s while jointly containing Communist ambitions in Europe, these affinities matured.

Because the Third World War has not yet occurred, it is easy to forget how close it seemed for decades after 1945. Pondering in 1948 what livelihood his adopted son might pursue, Orwell favoured farming as an occupation likely to survive an atomic war. Even if the bombs were not dropped, there was concern at nuclear weapons' likely impact on democracy. In the previous year Orwell had feared 'the worst possibility of all': division of the world between two or three super-states with nuclear weapons whose prolonged rivalry destroys democracy within each. 'Civilizations of this type', he added, 'might remain static for thousands of years'.[30] The Attlee government in 1948 secretly drew up a register of tunnels, mines, and caves in 150 locations to see how many

[28] I. Dale (ed.), *Conservative Party General Election Manifestos 1900–1997* (2000), 87. Churchill quoted by Robin Turton in *HC Deb.* 21 Oct. 1971, c. 944.

[29] W. S. Churchill, *The Sinews of Peace: Post-War Speeches*, ed. R. S. Churchill (1948), 98.

[30] G. Orwell, 'Towards European Unity' (1947), in his *Complete Works*, xix (1998), 163.

lives could be preserved during a nuclear war.[31] President Truman's handling of the press conference on 30 November 1950 during the Korean war alarmed the UK when he was trapped into admitting that there was always 'active consideration' of using nuclear weapons to halt the Chinese advance across the Yalu river.[32] From the first flight on 25 June 1948 in the airlift to sustain the Berlin enclave that the USSR had cut off from the West, the British and Americans resumed their close wartime collaboration. No formal treaty was required to establish USA bases on British soil: these were Britain's safeguard against Communist domination in Europe and the USA's first line of national self-defence. By the early 1950s, with 40,000–50,000 American servicemen in Britain, marriages with British women were running at the rate of 200 a month.[33] Such networks and attitudes help to explain how the Anglo-American connection survived two hazards: on the British side, snobbery, jealousies, and resentments, especially over American anti-imperialism and great-power status; and on the American side, the perennial temptations of isolationism, and the growing proportion of its population drawn from non-British or even anti-British traditions.

So in 1951 the 'special relationship' was uncontroversial between the political parties. Anthony Eden (shadow spokesman on foreign policy at the time) famously acknowledged this when saying of Bevin that 'I would publicly have agreed with him more, if I had not been anxious to embarrass him less'.[34] For although a decidedly un-American socialist critique of capitalism had been integral to the Labour Party's earliest traditions, so also had been a free-trading and classless libertarianism. The latter, together with close wartime collaboration and substantial wartime debts to the USA, made the American connection almost inevitable from the start. Widespread too in Britain was a notion of complementarity: the UK might no longer match the USA's economic might, but her long parliamentary and diplomatic experience could perhaps equip her to play Greece to America's Rome. The USA might either itself assume the imperial commitments which the British economy could no longer afford, or subsidize their continuance. With Stalin's help, painful choices between Commonwealth and the 'special relationship' could thereby at least be postponed. None the less, Sir Henry Tizard's minute of 1949 was telling: as chief scientific adviser at the Ministry of Defence he felt bound to say that 'we are not a Great Power and never will be again. We are a great nation, but if we continue to behave like a Great Power we shall soon cease to be a great nation.'[35]

[31] *G* (3 Jan. 2001), 4.
[32] A. Farrar-Hockley, *The British Part in the Korean War*, i (1990), 353.
[33] *HL Deb.* 8 July 1953, cc. 357, 374.
[34] *The Memoirs of Rt. Hon. Sir Anthony Eden: Full Circle* (1960), 5.
[35] Quoted in H. Young, *This Blessed Plot: Britain and Europe from Churchill to Blair* (London and Basingstoke, 1998), 24.

2. THE FACE OF THE COUNTRY

For the UK in 1951 ignorance about the environment was bliss: the UK's view of its continually shifting size and shape was relatively unconcerned. This was partly because until the 1970s accretion and artificial reclamation (mostly in tidal estuaries, seaports, and seaside resorts) more than compensated for coastal erosion elsewhere. Accretion in the Humber, Thames, and Solent estuaries counterbalanced serious cliff erosion in Holderness, East Anglia, and southern England. Accretion in the Wash had been proceeding at least since Anglo-Saxon times, and persisted after 1951.[36] Over the very long term, however, the entire UK land mass was slowly tilting upwards in the north and east, and downwards in the south and west, with the added threat stemming from melting polar ice, which caused sea levels slowly to rise. In 1951 this long-term trend evoked only a pragmatic and piecemeal response: erecting barriers against the sea where urgently needed—though this had not prevented serious floods in London during January 1928 and in Horsey in February 1938. In other respects the weather, then much more difficult to predict, was more salient in people's lives: 3 per cent of the UK workforce in 1951 still worked in agriculture and forestry,[37] and car ownership then provided only a small minority with a mobile umbrella.

The area in cultivation had long been shrinking from its mid-Victorian peak, but the need for wartime national self-sufficiency had sharply driven up the proportion of cultivated land devoted to crops; between 1939 and 1944 the arable area in England and Wales grew by 63 per cent, an increase unique in English agricultural history.[38] These priorities were not reversed in 1945, but were reinforced by the wartime prestige and subsequent persistence of the farming lobby, by fear that the countryside might revert to its run-down prewar state, by the need from the 1940s to the 1960s to conserve scarce currency, by a powerful combination of planning and advance in agricultural chemicals, and by the political parties' desire to win rural marginal seats. The peacetime regime was launched by the Agriculture Act (1947), which stabilized and subsidized farm incomes and made the countryside something of a tax haven. This was in effect a third agricultural revolution to succeed the first two: neolithic crop rotation and eighteenth-century enclosure. It carried to their logical conclusion earlier experiments in industrializing the countryside, with arable farmers leading the way. Despite a growing population that was eating more, UK self-sufficiency after 1945 continued in milk, potatoes, and oats; it grew in sugar, wheat, cheese, barley, and eggs; and from the 1960s it also grew

[36] See E. C. F. Bird, *Coastline Changes: A Global Review* (Chichester, 1985), 59–60; the map in P. Doody and B. Barnett (eds.), *The Wash and its Environment* (Peterborough, 1987), 321—references I owe to generous help from Professor A. S. Goudie of Oxford University.

[37] *BHS* 115–16.

[38] D. Grigg, *English Agriculture: An Historical Perspective* (Oxford, 1989), 40.

in butter and meat.[39] And if there were fewer animals in the countryside of England and Wales in 1949 than in 1938,[40] antibiotics benefited animals as well as human beings, and animals were healthier. For example, tuberculosis, long under attack, had by 1960 been eliminated from UK cattle.

Rural planning extended beyond farming. The Town and Country Planning Act (1947) procedures lasted for three decades: there were controls on the use of land, local authorities were required to prepare development plans looking twenty years ahead, and a tight curb on ribbon development separated town from country by surrounding cities with 'green belts'. It was the Attlee government which curbed the frontier-style popular individualism of 'plotlands': the inter-war sprawl of holiday and retirement bungalows over large parts of the British coastline.[41] Two years later the government set up the Nature Conservancy Board, which among other things established nature reserves, with power to own land. Also in 1949 it set up the purely advisory National Parks Commission, with the power to establish national parks and to designate separately administered and smaller 'areas of outstanding natural beauty'. On the other hand, the war left a large mark on the countryside: service requirements at their peak had reached a fifth of Britain's land mass, and in 1947 remained at four times the prewar level;[42] nor did the Ministry of Defence feel any pressing need to clear away wartime temporary structures. Reminders of the war survived in many British towns, too: air-raid shelters, pill-boxes, nissen huts, gaps in the iron railings. The many bomb-sites were only slowly acquiring new life as car parks; shreds of wallpaper hung from adjacent walls, traces of the one-time occupants, together with the zigzag lines marking where vanished staircases had once linked floors, now collapsed, each with its oblong cavity denoting long-lost fireplaces.

The austerity of compulsory community was another wartime legacy, one ingredient in the prevailing socialism of scarcity. Public transport in the 1940s was ubiquitous; there were no motorways to compete with the trains, and few cars to compete with the buses. Three-fifths of holiday-makers in 1948 got to their resorts by rail and/or sea, one-fifth by motor coach and less than one-fifth by private or hired car.[43] Nationalization in 1947 of a third of the canals in parallel with the railways (with which on the narrowly economic front they competed) threatened the canals' very survival at a time when their recreational potential was only beginning to emerge, and entrusted them to the unsympathetic Transport Commission. Inspired by L. T. C. Rolt's *Narrow Boat* (1944), the Inland Waterways Association was formed in 1946 to protect them, and from the

[39] Ibid. 14; T. Beresford, *We Plough the Fields: Agriculture in Britain* (Harmondsworth, 1975), 75–80.

[40] For figures, see Grigg, *English Agriculture*, 82.

[41] For an illuminating study of plotlands culture, see D. Hardy and C. Ward, *Arcadia for All: The Legacy of a Makeshift Landscape* (1984).

[42] Ministry of Defence, *Report of the Defence Lands Committee 1971–73* (1973), 9.

[43] Hulton Press, *Patterns of British Life*, 112, cf. 117 for analysis by age and social class.

outset attracted the conservationist poet John Betjeman as a member. In 1950 its much-publicized festival and rally at Market Harborough attracted more than 100 craft; the transport system's sleeping princess was beginning to wake up.

Wartime urban austerities—queues, prefabs, drab colours, rationing—accompanied smoke-blackened buildings, second-hand clothes, slag-heaps, pawnshops, cheerless pubs, fog, neon lights unused, slot machines decayed and empty. Light and heat were luxuries vulnerable to power cuts, especially in the particularly cold winter of 1947. James Lees-Milne—diarist, conservationist, and architectural historian—kept warm after office hours by sitting in the National Gallery or by reading in bed wearing a Balaclava helmet and mittens.[44] East European towns exposed to Western eyes after the USSR's collapse from 1990 jolted memories of what British towns had once been like. The drabness should not be exaggerated. British urban public life grew out of a host of local communities, and was often reinforced by a rather desperate residual municipal pride. Scarcity rendered social life more communal, shops had known proprietors and regular customers, and because there were relatively few married women in the full-time labour force, residential areas were still face-to-face daytime and weekday communities. Towns in 1951 were more united than divided by their streets, which could still accommodate markets, recreation, and sociability. Work and residence had been moving apart for some decades, and local authorities by 1951 aimed to carry that further, but many small workshops survived in inner-city residential areas, and many housing estates were appendages of big factories. In 1950 the socialist intellectual G. D. H. Cole saw the neighbourhood group as central to fostering civic consciousness and local democracy.[45]

In 1950 nearly a quarter of York's working-class families were sharing their house with another family; in 1951 more than a third of Great Britain's households lacked a shower or bath, and a twelfth lacked either an internal or external flush lavatory.[46] True, birth control and diminished domestic service had meant fewer people per house between 1931 and 1951,[47] but the wartime bomb damage and the slowdown in new building combined in the late 1940s with a newly growing population's rising expectations to generate an acute housing shortage. Of the UK's gross stock of private dwellings in 1961 46 per cent dated from before 1920, 33 per cent from 1920–38, 18 per cent from after 1947, but only 3 per cent from 1939–47.[48] More relatives were living in the postwar household than at any time in recorded British family history. Over

[44] J. Lees-Milne, 'Introduction' to his *Diaries 1946–1949* (1st publ. 1983–5, amalgamated edn. 1996), p. vii.

[45] M. Cole, *The Life of G. D. H. Cole* (1971), 257.

[46] B. S. Rowntree and G. R. Lavers, *Poverty and the Welfare State* (1951), 89; *Social Trends* (1995), 178.

[47] *BST* 366.

[48] G. Dean, 'The Stock of Fixed Capital in the United Kingdom in 1961', *Journal of the Royal Statistical Society*, series A, 127/3 (1964), 343.

half the couples marrying between 1947 and 1955 began married life in shared accommodation, mostly with relatives.[49] At the general elections of 1950–1 the political parties competed on which could build most new homes fastest. Of the total housing stock in England and Wales in 1951, half was rented from private landlords, a third was owner-occupied, and a fifth rented from the council.[50] Local-authority building for rent seemed the way forward, and a massive programme of council-house building began concurrently with the fashion for 'slum clearance' of people from the town-centre terrace house into the council flat and the suburban council estate. For the planners, council flats seemed to bring at least two advantages: they would conserve agricultural land by substituting high-density council flats for low-density interwar council-house suburbs, and higher buildings offered every tenant fresh air and a parkland setting. To this the planners added a controlled variant of the suburb in the twelve new towns (eight of them aiming to relieve the pressure on London) designated between 1946 and 1950, together with 160,000 temporary 'prefabs' erected between 1945 and 1948. The new towns at first embodied a high-minded, somewhat austere socialist ideal of living, centrally managed by the Ministry of Housing, but their abundant public spaces gave landscape architects their first big chance in Britain. Such locations might even tempt as residents urban middle-class equivalents of the rural aristocrat who deplored suburban sprawl: the scholar architect, the radical lawyer, the improving schoolteacher, the pollution-conscious doctor, and the well-to-do resident keen to uphold his property's value.

By later standards the UK was in 1951 still regionally very diverse. 'If you have a chance to travel about', the United States War Department told American servicemen stationed in Britain in 1942, 'you will agree that no area of the same size in the United States has such a variety of scenery'.[51] Apart from the universities of Oxford and Cambridge, national in their recruitment and aspirations, higher education remained predominantly local in its catchment areas and loyalties, nor were general elections yet centralized on London-based mass-media events. The railways offered a fast nationwide network, far more comprehensive than existed after the 1960s, though they could not rival the motorways' later achievement in knitting the nation together. However, in the late 1940s local government was rapidly giving ground, given the centralizing impact of nationalization and public welfare. Regional and local loyalties diminishingly diluted the social-class loyalties next to be discussed.

[49] R. Wall, 'The Household: Demographic and Economic Change in England 1650–1970', in R. Wall (ed.), *Family Forms in Historic Europe* (Cambridge, 1983), 506. F. M. L. Thompson (ed.), *Cambridge Social History of Britain 1750–1950*, ii. *People and their Environment* (1990), 60. [50] *TCBST* 487.

[51] United States War Department, *Instructions for American Servicemen in Britain* (1942, repr. Oxford, 1994), [7].

3. THE SOCIAL STRUCTURE

Philistine, unimaginative, hating public ceremonial, sometimes politically naive, and ever shackled by his disabling stammer, King George VI was a born worrier who had never wanted the throne. He inherited it in 1936 after the abdication of Edward VIII, the brilliant elder brother in whose shadow he spent a lifetime. The King was painfully shy, but servants were warned that he was well able to shout when annoyed, and his fits of temper were known within the family as 'gnashes'.[52] 'How I hate being a King!', he was reported as saying in 1946; 'sometimes at ceremonies I want to stand up and scream and scream and scream'.[53] No outsider would have guessed it, for his achievement was considerable: dignified yet unpretentious in public, he had in his wartime role usefully complemented Churchill's while at the same time bringing the monarchy through unscathed as though the abdication had never occurred. This thoroughly decent family man, fond of country sports, conservative in outlook, and in some ways out of sympathy with his times, was loyal to his ministers regardless of party, and was powerfully driven forward by a sense of duty. It was no accident that he shared his father's deep interest in uniforms, clothes, medals, and orders, for symbolism had now become central to the monarchy's function, though perhaps incongruously the King was privately fond of practical jokes. The fact that the British monarchy had survived when so many European monarchies had not, made the postwar throne seem an even more prized British attribute. The King's guild-loyalty to other monarchs made him hospitable to them, and assiduous in trouble-shooting, thereby helping to uphold the concept of monarchy through unsympathetic times.

There was much about postwar Britain to fuel the King's pessimism. Lees-Milne, sympathetically discussing Harewood House's future with the Princess Royal in 1947, recorded her request for privacy in a small strip of the terrace for herself and dog on opening days: '"One can get used to anything", she observed rather pathetically', adding later that whatever happened, her family must not emigrate or desert the UK, however tempted to do so. 'I thought to myself', Lees-Milne continues, 'royalty never emigrates. It either stays put or is pushed out.' 'Everything is going nowadays', the King told Vita Sackville-West in 1948, raising his hands in despair when she said that the National Trust was taking over the family seat at Knole: 'before long, I shall also have to go'.[54] He was wrong: several European countries in the late twentieth century demonstrated that monarchy can well survive without

[52] R. Lacey, *Majesty: Elizabeth II and the House of Windsor* (1st publ. 1977, rev. edn., paperback, 1979), 153; Bradford, *George VI* (1989, paperback edn. 1991), 530.

[53] H. Nicolson quoted in Bradford, *George VI*, 528.

[54] J. Lees-Milne, *Caves of Ice* (1st publ. 1983), republished in his *Diaries 1946–1949* (1996), 208–9 (26 Nov. 1947). H. Nicolson, *Diaries and Letters, 1945–1962*, ed. N. Nicolson (1968), 124. The remark seems to have been made on 12 Feb. 1948.

aristocracy. George VI restored the royal family as embodiment of political continuity and national values, and owed much to Labour's postwar leaders. Eager as Attlee's Labour government was for economy, its zeal stopped short here: 'it is a great mistake', said Attlee, 'to make government too dull'.[55] The King was not unsupported in his achievement: he would have been the first to acknowledge his wife's unusual combination of outward charm and inward steely determination. With the curiously twirling hand movement and tilt of the head with which she smilingly acknowledged the many expressions of popular affection she received, Queen Elizabeth was a consummate actress, presenting a friendly front even to the media, thereby softening the impact made by the stiff dignity and shyness of her husband and mother-in-law. She was the key figure in the British monarchy's twentieth-century history for three reasons: for her longevity, for loyally backing her husband (who sorely needed it) and later her daughter when Queen, and above all for instinctively making the appropriate gesture.

Yet the King rightly saw that the landed classes were under threat. Twentieth-century wars struck them a double blow: their military salience raised their casualty rate, and high taxation and the requisitioning of their property threatened their wealth. The proportion of personal net capital held by the top 1, 5, and 10 per cent of wealth-holders in the population of England and Wales fell consistently in four selected periods from 1911/13 to 1951/6, the share of rents in the national income had been falling since 1900, and the destruction of country houses, continuous from the late-Victorian period onwards, reached a new height between the wars, and accelerated after 1945 to its peak in 1950–4.[56] The war's redistribution of wealth from the top downwards had been substantial: between 1938/9 and 1949/50 the share of UK income held by the top 1 per cent, even before tax, fell from a sixth to a tenth, and that of the top 10 per cent from two-fifths to a third. Taxation policy accentuated the trend, so that in the same period after tax, the income share of the top 1 per cent slipped from an eighth to a twentieth, and that of the top 10 per cent from an eighth to a tenth.[57] The war's tight labour market made domestic servants even scarcer, and Lees-Milne described country-house occupants as enduring even in 1965 'discomforts which few council house dwellers would tolerate for a fortnight. They emerge from large, dusty, chilling apartments into Arctic corridors leading to cavernous kitchens, where on hard stone floors they struggle with antiquated ranges and boilers.'[58]

[55] *HC Deb.* 9 July 1952, c. 1328.

[56] *TBS* 96. P. Deane and W. A. Cole, *British Economic Growth 1688–1959: Trends and Structure* (2nd edn. Cambridge, 1969), 247, 301. M. Girouard, 'Country House Crisis?', *Architectural Review* (Oct. 1974), 243.

[57] Royal Commission on the Distribution of Income and Wealth, *Report No. 1* (Cmnd. 6171, 1975), 36–8.

[58] *Burke's Landed Gentry* (18th edn. 1965), p. xx.

By 1945 the armed services, government departments, and local authorities had encrusted country-house parkland with their nissen huts and had filled the great house with their cardboard partitions, iron bedsteads, and filing cabinets. Historic art collections, often central to the house's design, were dispersed,[59] surface coalmining sometimes came up to its very doors, and the nostalgia of Evelyn Waugh's *Brideshead Revisited* (1945) implied that the aristocratic world had gone for good. In his country-house travels Lees-Milne found determined and sometimes eccentric country-house owners pushed into corners of their homes in a quest for manageable living space, grumbling about high taxation and resigned to rearguard self-defence. With their paintings and furniture under dustsheets, fending off dry rot and struggling to remedy wartime neglect and damage, they could rely upon only a handful of loyal and underpaid servants, and sometimes themselves cleaned the floors and sewed up the tattered curtains [Plate 2]. 'This evening the whole tragedy of England impressed itself upon me', wrote Lees-Milne, struck in June 1947 with Lower Brockhampton's lack of a squire. 'A whole social system has broken down. What will replace it beyond government by the masses, uncultivated, rancorous, savage, philistine, the enemies of all things beautiful?'[60]

The landed classes were being undermined through overt criticism from newly empowered Liberal and Labour opponents of privilege at every social level: from socialists who believed, with Marx, that there was no place for aristocracy within the incipient two-class model that aligned bourgeoisie against proletariat—but also from rationalistic and self-consciously progressive professionals and meritocrats. The latter viewed the hierarchical virtues associated with empire as obsolescent: in an increasingly competitive world, Britain must live off its wits. After Germany's second and supposedly conclusive defeat, hopes revived that the United Nations might at last enable the world to resume and propagate peaceable middle-class values. A sense of obligation, too, was widely felt to the slum populations who had bravely endured wartime bombing raids without mounting a Marxian revolution from the backstreets, as well as to the trade union and Labour leaders so staunch in their anti-Fascism. The Second World War, like the First World War and later the Falklands War, had suddenly alerted those in authority to the fact that their values were more widely diffused than they had realized; in the first two cases this accentuated the pressures for downwardly redistributive public welfare. To generate the necessary funds, an attack on the well-to-do seemed necessary. This involved rejecting the country landowner's relatively long-term environmental and aesthetic outlook, and fostering instead a utilitarian preoccupation with the short term, a meritocratic dismissal of tradition and hierarchy. Unemployment was

[59] For examples see J. Cornforth, *The Country Houses of England 1948–1998* (1998), 5.
[60] Lees-Milne, *Caves of Ice*, 143 (16 June 1947).

repudiated at both social extremes, and the long-predicted egalitarian consequences of mass enfranchisement now loomed, together with endorsement for the economist Alfred Marshall's hope that 'gradually . . . public opinion may be worked up to the point at which a rich man who lives idly will be despised'.[61] The tight cohesion among the leading people in every dimension of British public life—political, social, economic, cultural, religious, intellectual, recreational—could not survive two world wars.

Yet all was not lost, for the war had in some ways strengthened aristocracy: in the short term, at least, it revalidated the combative values and aptitudes that lay near its heart, and war had simultaneously challenged the peaceable optimism associated with the trading classes. 1940 was a triumph for the aristocratic Winston Churchill over the Brummagem Neville Chamberlain, however prudent it seemed at the time to downplay that triumph. It was an apparent triumph too for Churchill's powerful combination of historically informed realism over the rationalistic middle-class and nonconformist progressivism pejoratively labelled as 'appeasement'. The drift in the Conservative leadership towards the middle class since 1911 was sent into reverse with Churchill's advent in 1940, and it was not till Edward Heath's advent as Conservative leader in 1965 that the party leadership's earlier middle-class trend resumed. There were even some postwar signs that the integrating structures and social functions of the upper classes would revive. A social elite which in the nineteenth century had cohered through such institutions as the London 'season', the public schools, the race meeting, the parliamentary session, and the county ball found in 1947 that presentations at court were being resumed. Proceedings became less formal, but only because the ceremony's wartime abeyance had increased the pressure of numbers; presentations persisted till 1958. Women were central to the postwar monarchy's newly enhanced social roles. Princess Elizabeth's marriage to the Duke of Edinburgh in 1947 carried further the ceremonial royal marriage as a recently invented tradition, and lent colour to an unusually grey period in British life. The *Tatler* in 1950 recorded the ongoing social round of the Anglo-Irish social elite, painstakingly collecting the obscurest names into its quarterly indexes. Photographed at hunts, dances, country-house parties, and rites of passage, its members merged with the worlds of Oxbridge, diplomacy, sport, charity, the arts, and the armed services—still retaining something of their interwar self-confidence and poise amidst the adverts for fashions, the London stores, wines, jewellery, and perfumes.

Furthermore, new sources of country-house income were being discovered. High taxation sent into tax exile Lawrence Johnston, creator of a garden at Hidcote Manor in Gloucestershire that Lees-Milne described in June 1948

[61] In 'Social Possibilities of Economic Chivalry', repr. in A. C. Pigou (ed.), *Memorials of Alfred Marshall* (1925), 344.

as 'a dream of beauty'; two months later Johnston, a naturalized American, signed the deed of gift to the National Trust. It had been 'a struggle' to bring about, wrote Lees-Milne, and was not at first lucrative; yet in the longer term he, Johnston, and the political hostess Sybil Colefax (an influential intermediary), had endowed the nation with a priceless asset. The Trust had hitherto been primarily preoccupied with land-owning, and then owned only six country houses: it was now launched in a new role as curator of great gardens.[62] More profitable in the short term was Longleat. Death duties ensured that the Marquess of Bath opened the house to the general public in 1949. It was the first stately home to go fully commercial, attracting 138,000 visitors in its first year; and in 1966 in collaboration with circus proprietor Jimmy Chipperfield he opened the first British safari park.[63] The Marquess's unashamed entrepreneurial flair had uncovered a recreational need which country houses were well able to supply, and in later years he found many resourceful imitators. Under the Attlee governments, major social transitions were still being masked through the retention of earlier outward forms: titles, honours, and the House of Lords all survived. The Fleming Committee of 1944 on the public (or, in later parlance, 'independent') schools had been radical, advocating their thorough integration into the state system on a basis of meritocratic admission, with new state boarding schools created to fill regional gaps in provision. The Attlee governments would have none of this: repairing wartime under-investment in the state schools was their first priority. Any assault on educational privilege could wait, or privilege might even slowly succumb to steeply graduated taxation and the advance of egalitarian values. 480,000 children attended independent schools in 1951, a far higher proportion of the school population than twenty years later.[64] As for the private preparatory schools which supplied these schools with recruits, their entrepreneurial flair ensured that no fewer than fifty-eight of those marshalled within the Incorporated Association of Preparatory Schools (IAPS) in 1963/4 had been founded in 1940–50, more than at any time in the twentieth century since 1900–14.[65]

While the upper classes were precariously surviving, the postwar middle classes went from strength to strength. Solidarity might be the hallmark of other social classes, but integral to middle-class growth was fragmentation, at several levels. There was first the informal divide between those who wished to

[62] Lees-Milne, *Midway on the Waves* (1st publ. 1985), republished in his *Diaries 1946–1949* (1996), 269 (26 June 1949); 293–4 (27 Aug. 1948). See also A. Pavord, *Hidcote Manor Garden: Gloucestershire* (1st publ. 1993, rev. edn. 2004), 21.

[63] Lord Montagu of Beaulieu, *The Gilt and the Gingerbread: Or, How to Live in a Stately Home and Make Money* (1967), 104. Obituary of Marquess of Bath in *T* (1 July 1992), 17.

[64] G. Walford (ed.), *British Public Schools: Policy and Practice* (1984), 10.

[65] P. L. Masters, *Preparatory Schools Today: Some Facts and Inferences* (1966), 108—a book which usefully discusses this neglected area.

assimilate with their betters and those who believed in standing alone or even in seeking allies lower down. The middle-class tendency to admire and even engineer admission to the upper classes did not cease in 1945: indeed, once the nineteenth-century middle-class battle for religious equality and political participation had been won, the middle classes had less reason to fear, let alone dislike, their betters. There were incentives, too, in the late 1940s for the middle classes to seek allies further up against seemingly over-assertive forces lower down. The distinctive benefits of middle-class status were slowly being eroded: holiday entitlement by the Holidays Pay Act of 1939, security of employment by postwar full employment, and high wage-differentials by well-organized trade unionism. Wages were rising markedly in their share of the national income[66] at the same time as inflation was undermining those in the middle class on fixed incomes. Wartime evacuation, with its many crossings of the class divide exposed to each side the unattractive features of the other. So the late 1940s witnessed the second among the twentieth century's three periods of middle-class assertiveness against those lower down—the other two being in the aftermath of the First World War and in the 1970s, both periods of rapid inflation. John Beavan, analysing middle-class militancy in a broadcast of 1952, accepted Bernard Shaw's distinction between 'upstarts' moving into the middle class from below, and 'downstarts' moving out of it from misfortune or improvidence: the militant mood, he thought, reflected the relative articulateness of 'downstart' writers and disgruntled housewives.[67] The future Labour politician William Rodgers wrote in with the brisk and somewhat optimistic suggestion that 'in the long run the healthy solution to the problem is to encourage social readjustment on the part of the middle classes and not morbid self-pity',[68] but the more predictable middle-class response was energetically to seek ways of marking themselves out from working-class 'upstarts'. Upper-class affinities and connections were thus reinforced.

An upper-class alliance could rest on a secure middle-class basis. There were many country-house echoes in the suburban detached or even semi-detached middle-class home and garden, and in the 1940s the clear distinction between its front door and 'tradesman's entrance' had not yet disappeared. British landed families had never been so exclusive as to spurn the lucrative marriage or to resist wealth's delayed and discreet upward move. Social ascent was easier for the commercial than for the manufacturing segments of the middle class, for commerce was closer to the professions, London-centred and untainted by provincial smokestacks; gentlemanly conventions lent polish to such entrepreneurship as survived in the City. Indeed, the professions were the major middle-class redoubt, a source of status whose certificated admission

[66] On this see Deane and Cole, *British Economic Growth*, 257, 302–3.

[67] 'Plight of the Middle Classes', *Listener* (17 Apr. 1952), 631.

[68] *Listener* (24 Apr. 1952), 675.

qualifications and certificated training simultaneously excluded and evangelized. To police them, 'qualifying associations' had been forming between 1910 and 1950 at the rate of two dozen per decade, so that by mid-century a quarter of their total went to engineering, a tenth to management and administration, and a twelfth to accountancy.[69] Repeatedly dividing and recombining in response to a ceaseless quest for enhanced professional status, professional people assumed that their and the community's self-interest coincided. They deployed their expertise to discredit amateurism higher up, while their meritocratic examinations extended an escalator to the self-improving lower down. Middle-class sails were trimmed to catch the growing prestige of science; engineers, surveyors, draughtsmen, architects, designers, technicians, and laboratory workers more than compensated for the professional numbers that were being eroded by the loss of faith.

The professions, commerce, and manufacture—customarily trained outside the universities—slowly began enhancing their status by recruiting from them, thereby entrusting the state with funding the in-house training for which employer and employee had earlier paid. William Baxter was the UK's sole full-time professor of accounting on reaching the London School of Economics (LSE) in 1947, whereas by 1971 there were twenty.[70] Once qualified, professional people wielded considerable authority not only over clients—schoolteachers over parents, doctors over patients—but also within communities, political parties, pressure groups, local and central government. Cane and stethoscope, slide-rule and reference manual, kept social inferiors firmly in their place. Manufacture and entrepreneurship had never acquired professional status, and complaints about this go back at least to Lyon Playfair in 1852. Interwar Fabians saw meritocratic and expert management as the answer. 'We must make an end of chance and nepotism in business enterprise', wrote Laski in 1934, 'if it is to attain the dignity of a profession.'[71] By the 1940s entrepreneurs had been in slow numerical decline for some decades as firms grew larger, with far fewer employers and proprietors in 1951 than in 1931, but far more managers and administrators; self-employment's share of national income, reasonably stable between the wars, went into steady postwar decline.[72]

One role of elite university and public school was to divert manufacturers' offspring towards commerce and the professions. A leading role of the IAPS schools, founded in 1892, was to maintain close contact with the public schools,

[69] G. Millerson, *The Qualifying Associations: A Study in Professionalization* (1964), 183.

[70] Obituary, *T* (7 Aug. 2006), 44.

[71] L. Playfair, 'The Chemical Principles Involved in the Manufactures of the Exhibition', in *Lectures on the Results of the Great Exhibition of 1851* (1852), 204. H. Laski, *A Grammar of Politics* (1st publ. 1925, 3rd edn. 1934), 204, cf. 202.

[72] Useful table in W. D. Rubinstein, *Capitalism, Culture, and Decline in Britain 1750–1990* (1993), 34. *TBS* 78, 83.

and to ease its pupils' passage into them through coaching for the 'common entrance' examination at age 13, and often also by inducting them early into boarding away from home. Bursarial instructions on buying the regulation school cap or hat, blazer or tunic were for middle-class offspring a rite of passage at least as important as later acquiring a bank account. In three-quarters of the public schools in 1946 the child was required to board,[73] often in isolated rural places in the south of England, sealed off by school rules as well as by location from home and family, and even from nearby communities. Middle-class educational fragmentation went further. Some public schools and universities carried more social cachet than others, and much depended on whether the child was on the right side of the great divide between public and grammar school. The careers of such middle-class Labour Party champions as Harold Wilson, Barbara Castle, and Hugh Gaitskell show how much the British left owed to the meritocratic grammar-school pupil's resentment at privilege or to the public-school pupil's repudiation of it. All this lent the middle class powerful influence within both major political parties. Labour's middle-class recruits included those who were simply bored with the Conservatives and wanted a change, together with the religious and secular idealists whose compassion subordinated their self-interest, the rationalistic enthusiasts for planning and for eliminating waste, and the professional people and state employees who felt they had nothing to lose from what then seemed the statist winning side.

Far from being hurled down into an expanding proletariat amidst polarized industrial conflict, the middle classes prospered at the expense of both social extremes. As early as 1940 the socialist theorist Evan Durbin had noted that British society was becoming 'more bourgeois in the literal sense', given the growing proportion of the population thus categorized; 'even more important, perhaps' was the fact that the trend was 'rapidly *adding bourgeois characteristics to the proletariat* itself'.[74] This was partly because working people, with help from increasingly meritocratic educational structures, were collectively moving into the fast-growing clerical and white-collar occupations. The grammar schools had for decades been syphoning talent upwards through rewarding the scholarship child, and in 1944 the Fleming Committee even recommended building on that pattern by extending local-authority awards throughout the public-school system, whether boarding or not. In the late 1940s the comprehensive-school idea was only beginning to advance over the Labour Party's long-standing respect for the grammar school. Whereas in 1911 only a fifth of Great Britain's occupied population had been white-collar workers (managers, professional

[73] R. Lambert, *The Chance of a Lifetime? A Study of Boys' and Coeducational Boarding Schools in England and Wales* (1975), 288.

[74] E. F. M. Durbin, *The Politics of Democratic Socialism: An Essay on Social Policy* (1940), 112; Durbin's italics.

people, technicians, foremen, clerks, and retail workers), by 1951 this had risen to almost a third, whereas manual workers had moved in the opposite direction from three-quarters to less than two-thirds. Between 1911 and 1951 the number of clerical workers had alone grown almost threefold, doubling their proportion of Great Britain's occupied workforce to more than a tenth.[75] This did not in itself remove them from the working class, but it fragmented the workforce into units smaller than was customary with manual labour, enhanced the proportion of women,[76] and closeted clerical workers more closely with their employers, whose lifestyle contrasted less forcibly with their own; thus was the ground prepared for the clerical worker's subsequent upward cultural shift.

The route out of the working class could be individual as well as collective. Well into the twentieth century the ideal of gentlemanly and ladylike conduct continued to percolate from top to bottom of British society. In 1952 Waugh lamented the decline of that socially important distinction between ladies or gentlemen and the rest. At one time, he said, 'everyone was convinced that there was a great impassable line between "gentlemen" and "the lower classes" and everyone drew that line immediately below his own feet. "You're no lady" was the traditional battle cry between two drunken charwomen scratching out each others [*sic*] eyes in a pub.'[77] The prevalence of domestic service ensured a broad following for such attitudes among working people. Like the clerical workers, the domestic servants' lifestyle was much influenced by associating closely with people socially much higher up. Acceptance rather than assertiveness, admiration rather than envy, was their mood, attracted as they often were by the glamour and charm of those they served. In pursuing security, they engaged not in collective self-defence but in an individualist search for a protector. Self-subordination may have been involved, but in a mood of mutual commitment, with the possibility that class loyalty might be transcended by a friendship tangibly acknowledged in the employer's will. In 1948 about one in seven families in the middle class and above had a live-in servant, rising to three in five if all types of paid domestic help are included; there was paid help even in a fifth of lower-middle-class homes.[78] Domestic service had long been in marked decline, but it left long memories behind. The outlook of many well-to-do people alive in the 1950s had been profoundly influenced by a close childhood relationship with a servant. They included the King and two prime ministers. George V's children had all suffered under a sadistic nurse, whereas Churchill's nurse, Mrs Everest, had in his early life been 'my dearest and most intimate

[75] See the valuable table in R. Price and G. Bain, 'Union Growth Revisited: 1948–1974', *British Journal of Industrial Relations* (1976), 346.

[76] For a breakdown by sex see J. H. Goldthorpe *et al.*, *Social Mobility and Class Structure in Modern Britain* (Oxford, 1980), 60.

[77] E. Waugh to Nancy Mitford, 8 Jan. 1952, in Waugh, *Letters*, ed. M. Amory (1st publ. 1980, paperback edn. Harmondsworth, 1982), 364.

[78] Hulton Press, *Patterns of British Life*, 29, 102–3.

friend', just as Harold Macmillan retained affectionate memories of 'Nanny' Last.[79] The ideal of personal service extended beyond the home, shaping relations between shopkeeper and customer, professional person and client, landlord and tenant, politician and elector. What was called the 'deference vote' still featured among the Conservative Party's assets when warding off Labour's bid for the entire working-class vote. Deference voters—older and possibly poorer than electors with more up-to-date and more directly utilitarian reasons for voting Conservative[80]—were a waning political asset, but their cultural impact was by no means dead.

A second individualist route out of the working class consisted in passing through one or both of two 'horizontal' layerings within the working class: through joining the occupational category of skilled or semi-skilled status rather than remaining a labourer, and/or through joining the moral category of the 'respectable' rather than remaining among the 'rough'. 'Some of them seem to be very slummy on this estate', a bricklayer's wife and council tenant told a social investigator in Woodford in the late 1950s; 'some of the people in this road are a bit rough', said a fitter's wife.[81] Investigating London working men in 1946–7, the sociologist Ferdynand Zweig saw the craftsmen—apprenticed, examined, and well unionized—as 'the aristocracy of the working class'. Though mixing freely with the labourers, 'the largest part of the working class', craftsmen would 'often go to the saloon bar, whilst a labourer goes to the public bar'.[82] The passport to respectability was no less well known for being informal. Instead of living for the day, respectable working people aimed to be relatively self-disciplined, sober, domesticated, and thrifty, their main concern being not to sink socially. With help from churches, schools, building societies, and workplace hierarchies, some respectables or their children even moved up—first moving to the better side of the street, thence to a better street, and thence to a better area, until at last the family felt that its past had been safely distanced. The large network of mail-order firms' agents, well-briefed on the working-class community's social relations, monitored credit-worthiness; they were drawn from people with good handwriting who had moved away from the blacklisted streets.[83] Self-improvement was not necessarily linked to social ambition: in 1951 the British labour movement still thrived on an intelligence that was willingly retained or arbitrarily trapped within the working class, and many working people were content to function within the network of

[79] J. W. Wheeler-Bennett, *King George VI: His Life and Reign* (1958), 17; Lady V. Bonham-Carter, *Winston Churchill as I Knew Him* (1965), 26–7; H. Macmillan, *Winds of Change 1914–1939* (1966), 181.

[80] R. McKenzie and A. Silver, *Angels in Marble: Working Class Conservatives in Urban England* (1968), 85, 257.

[81] P. Willmott and M. Young, *Family and Class in a London Suburb* (1960), 114.

[82] F. Zweig, *Labour, Life and Poverty* (1948), 84–5.

[83] R. Coopey, S. O'Connell, and D. Porter, *Mail Order Retailing in Britain: A Business and Social History* (Oxford, 2005), 115, 118.

educational and cultural institutions that grew out of Labour Party branches, co-ops, and trade unions.

These institutions flourished, together with Labour voting, in the class-segregated communities located well away from London: in the mining areas of South Wales, the Midlands, the north of England, and the Scottish lowlands; in the shipbuilding yards of Newcastle and the Clyde; and adjacent to the huge textile factories of Lancashire and Yorkshire. The war had if anything revived such communities, reinforcing employment in the north-west with a flight from the south-east of refugees and of activities forced for security reasons to move. From homes located close to the workplace and rented from the local authority, strenuous and often dangerous trades were pursued in these single-occupation townships, shaping Labour's trade union priorities, its class rhetoric, and its neighbourly ideals. It was a masculine, cloth-capped world where working men were readily identified: their weekday clothes differed sharply from those worn on Sundays—a contrast far less marked at other social levels.[84] 'The average worker has only to look at a man to see whether he is one of them or not', wrote Zweig in 1952; 'he looks first at his hands' to see whether they are soft.[85] The physical strength demanded by heavy industry was prized. Manual workers' sons left school as soon as possible, and displayed their manhood by following fathers into a heavy labour that was episodically relieved through rough recreation; the schoolteacher's language had not been theirs, whereas prowess in a trade was prized. Electricity-based light industry had been spreading between the wars, but full-time paid employment for married women was still widespread only in the textile areas. Where women did work, they were far less likely than the men to unionize. The concept of the male breadwinner earning a 'living wage' sufficient to support wife and children was still powerful, and a class-based mutual support between men and women was assumed. Respectable wives and mothers stayed at home, their rigid housekeeping timetables warding off the ever-threatening grime generated by communities without smoke-free zones, their frequent shopping minimizing the ever-present risk of food poisoning in a society without refrigerators, and their constant vigilance protecting offspring within homes heated by open fires and lighted by gas; in working-class communities there was every reason for male and female roles to remain firmly distinct. Socialism, a mere theory for some intellectuals in the 1940s, was a day-to-day experience within communities where life was lived almost entirely in company, and whose scarcities demanded mutual help and communal provision. This was as true in London as in working-class communities further north: 'the worker has a strong sense of . . . living for the community and by the community', wrote

[84] F. Zweig, *The British Worker: A Social and Psychological Study* (Harmondsworth, 1952), 205.
[85] Ibid. 202–3; cf. *Labour, Life and Poverty*, 60.

Zweig. 'He . . . has a sense of individual helplessness', and so 'counts first of all on the collective efforts of his group or class. He has a strong sense of solidarity. "All for one and one for all", is his motto.'[86]

For Zweig, 'the middle-class man achieves everything by competition: a working-class man everything by co-operation'. Within the less-skilled manual occupations, physical strength and endurance were essential, but these waned with advancing age, damaging both earnings and status. This precluded much sense of an evolving 'career', still less of jockeying for promotion: the emphasis lay rather towards staving off ill-health, accidents, and social slippage. 'Security', wrote Zweig, 'is one of the basic differences between the working class and the middle class.'[87] Workers' wages were unpredictable because subject to all the uncertainties of overtime, shift-work, piecework, and working conditions. Two interacting mechanisms made it possible to cope: public welfare and trade unionism. The larger the firm (and in 1951 factories were still getting larger), the more strongly unionized the workforce; the more concentrated the manual labourers by place of residence, the more likely they were to vote Labour. By 1951 more than nine million people were organized into trade unions, of whom nearly eight million were affiliated to the Trades Union Congress (TUC).[88] Total trade union membership had almost doubled in each decade since the early 1930s and was still rising. Their focus had by 1951 shifted from insuring only their own members towards the collectivist concept of national insurance through the Labour Party's welfare reforms. Mutual help, trade union protection, and public welfare seemed essential: hazards had to be minimized by what Churchill had once called 'the miracle of averages'.[89] This was the trade unions' collectivist and class-conscious face, and interwar socialists assumed that adult education would soon clarify the minds of working-class Conservatism's last remaining props—agricultural labourers and domestic servants—and that the class-consciousness of the workers, the largest and most fertile class, would make them politically supreme. Even in 1951 many thought it only a matter of time before the Labour Party secured a permanent electoral majority. Two predictions of 1935 about the trade unions were not borne out: Hugh Dalton's, that they would come to resemble the professions, raising standards, promoting research, and becoming less defensive; and William Beveridge's, that socialist planning would supersede free collective bargaining.[90] It was more the restrictive practices of the professions that the trade unions imitated, policing as they did

[86] Zweig, *Labour, Life and Poverty*, 59.

[87] Quotations from Zweig, *Labour, Life and Poverty*, 60; *British Worker*, 203; see also ibid. 205.

[88] *BPF* (8th edn.), 400.

[89] R. S. Churchill, *Winston S. Churchill*, ii. *Young Statesman 1901–1914* (1967), 305.

[90] H. Dalton, *Practical Socialism for Britain* (1935), 165. W. H. Beveridge, *Planning under Socialism and Other Addresses* (1936), 21 (Herbert Spencer lecture, 1935).

the gateways to advancement; and for all its rhetoric about socialism and class solidarity, the trade union's daily reality entailed upholding differentials and pursuing occupational rivalries. This was the trade unions' individualist and class-fragmenting face.

Social-class relationships in their rich complexity were central to the British social system in 1951, but their salience had long been declining. Middle-class scrutiny, allied with working-class respectability, had been curbing aristocratic arrogance and ostentatious idleness for a century and more, at the same time as the middle-class social conscience had been restraining class jealousies lower down. With the slow Victorian advance of the opportunity society, the uniforms that had once identified ranks and occupations became redundant. To this process the twentieth century added three relevant developments: the meritocratic recruitment of new science-based occupations whose social location was difficult to identify by accent; a growing affluence which, reinforced by public welfare and full employment, was by the 1940s chasing away the more visible marks of poverty; and the advent of a mass cheap clothing industry. Orwell noticed the latter's levelling impact as early as 1941,[91] though six years later he could point out that 'the great majority of the people can still be "placed" in an instant by their manners, clothes, and general appearance'; this was why interwar middle-class socialists had often worn working-class clothes at the same time as affecting working-class accents and avoiding the best restaurants.[92] Mass consumerism, however, worked with the class-levelling grain. Hitchcock, Disney, Charlie Chaplin, and the *Daily Express* attracted an interwar following at all social levels. 'To an increasing extent', wrote Orwell in 1941, 'the rich and the poor read the same books, and they also see the same films and listen to the same radio programmes.'[93] By then the war was reviving a sense of national community, and a consensus was accumulating behind attempts to prevent any recurrence of the interwar depression. One later solvent of class consciousness, however, was as yet hardly present in 1951: the ethnic loyalties fostered by large-scale immigration—all the more so, given that Huguenots, Jews, and European political refugees aimed at assimilation. This soon changed.

4. FAMILY AND WELFARE

The past is our sole guide through the present, and nowhere more than in population trends. Individuals' decisions on family size taken long before

[91] Orwell, 'The Lion and the Unicorn', 407–8.

[92] Orwell, 'The English People', 202. See also C. Mayhew, *Party Games* (1969), 26.

[93] Orwell, 'The Lion and the Unicorn', 407; cf. 'The Proletarian Writer' (1940), *Complete Works* (1998), 296.

1951 determined Britain's current educational and welfare needs, the shape of its workforce, and even its ethnic make-up. Such determinants are by no means always perceived at the time. Not till the 1970s, for instance, did the analysis of blood-groups seem to confirm the ongoing impact of pre-Conquest migrations,[94] and DNA profiling later exposed numerous hitherto unsuspected family relationships. Patterns of nutrition for babies born at the time of the Boer War were revealed ninety years later as having shaped their patterns of illness much later in life,[95] and in 1930 A. L. Bowley pointed out that First-World-War casualties would for half a century make men scarce in their generation.[96] Truby King, pioneer of books on child rearing, directly or indirectly influenced interwar babies as powerfully as Benjamin Spock moulded postwar generations; Spock, when faced with the outcome, thought some of his earlier theories had unduly discouraged firm parenting.[97]

Among the conscious inheritances from the past in 1951 was an official view of the family which assumed a lifelong partnership between husband and wife, each normally pursuing separate roles. On marriage the wife embarked upon childbearing, child rearing, and housekeeping—roles then relatively demanding. The family was supposed to be 'fertile', with its children born in wedlock. Exemplified in the royal family, endorsed by political and religious leaders, and built into the welfare structure, this ideal of the nuclear family might sometimes through death, infertility, and divorce prove impracticable, but such anomalies were usually thought regrettable, if only because the nuclear family reflected day-to-day necessity at many levels. The family was a moral unit, a source of social discipline. The individual's reputation flowed from his family's past; it could be helped or hindered by the conduct of its present members—respectable or otherwise, public-spirited or otherwise; and in a relatively slow-moving world it stretched more saliently into the future. Landowners were alert to family traditions and to their successors' environmental needs, professional and business people husbanded a reputation for integrity and solvency, and working people thrived on the parent's transmission of skills, aptitudes, and job opportunities. For the family was also an economic unit, at a time when parents frequently employed their children in a family enterprise or guided them towards employment with friends and relatives. It was a welfare unit, at a time when the state had only recently assumed substantial responsibility for education, health, and social security; personal achievement was seen as collective to the extent that it grew out of the educational and welfare roles the family still performed. And the family was a recreational and

[94] A. C. Kopec, 'Blood Group Distributions in Britain', in D. F. Roberts and E. Sunderland (eds.), *Genetic Variation in Britain* (Symposia of the Society for the Study of Human Biology), 12 (1973), 129–39.

[95] *O* (24 May 1992), 6.

[96] A. L. Bowley, *Some Economic Consequences of the Great War* (1930), 57.

[97] *T* (23 Jan. 1974), 1.

cultural unit, at a time when many families were sufficiently large and extended to be recreationally self-sufficient, in a society whose recreations were largely self-made.

The housewife who kept a clean and tidy house had long enjoyed prestige. In interwar Britain, as later in continental Europe,[98] abundant consumer goods enhanced domesticity's attractions for women at the same time as birth control released resources to spend on the home. Consumer goods and services—reinforced in their influence by interwar psychologists, doctors, and women's magazines—at first raised standards of housekeeping and in a sense professionalized it, though without the professional's pay. Housekeeping technology rarely cut the time spent on housekeeping, and more often simply made it possible to wash clothes and polish floors more thoroughly and more often, without undermining the separation of spheres.[99] The damage done by the wartime separation of parents from their evacuee children seemed so serious that keeping the family together was central to public policy thereafter, most notably in the Children Act (1948), which entrusted major responsibilities to the parent and sought a substitute family for orphans. The annual number of divorces had risen almost continuously since 1900, and by 1946–50 had reached 39,000 in England and Wales. Forty years later divorce had risen fourfold, whereas in 1951 divorce was still rare enough to bring moral discredit and social disapproval, and could seriously damage a career. Mothers' Union hostility to divorce was fierce and influential, and though by 1950 its members were declining, there were still half a million in the UK and Ireland.[100] The Marriage Guidance Council, founded in 1938, set up a state-subsidized national network of marriage-counselling centres ten years later with Home Office encouragement; it aimed to conserve and even crusade for the family's integrity, not (as later) to palliate the consequences of breakdown.[101]

Yet by 1951 the assumptions behind this ideal of the family, always somewhat unreal,[102] were already being publicly undermined from several directions. Feminism was not prominent among them. The first (Victorian) phase of British feminism pioneered votes for women, but focused on education and careers for the single woman, thus preparing opinion for women's venturing beyond the private sphere. Partly for tactical reasons, Edwardian second-phase feminism narrowed the focus to the vote, but women's enfranchisement in

[98] e.g. in Italy in the 1960s—see P. Ginsborg, *A History of Contemporary Italy: Society and Politics 1943–1988* (1990), 244.

[99] See the interesting discussion in S. Bowden and A. Offer, 'Household Appliances and the Use of Time: The United States and Britain since the 1920s', *Economic History Review*, 47 (1994), 734.

[100] Statistics from *TCBST* 62 (divorce), 597 (Mothers' Union).

[101] D. R. Mace, *Marriage Counselling* (1948), 147, 150. The Council's five principles, drafted in 1938, still applied with a few small modifications in J. H. Wallis and H. S. Booker, *Marriage Counselling* (1958), 100.

[102] See below, pp. 237–8, 297–9, 481–2.

1918 and 1928 enhanced the political parties' interest in catering for women's perceived wishes. In British feminism's third phase from the 1920s to the mid-1960s a feminist legislative agenda evolved: for equal pay, family allowances, and equal opportunities. Distractions from social class, foreign policy, and war, however, reinforced by the two-party system, slowed down feminist progress. Feminists could attract married women only through building upon their domestic role, which as yet they hardly challenged, and after 1945 the interwar success of the Women's Institutes and Townswomen's Guilds persisted. The Six Point Group (indirect descendant of Mrs Pankhurst's militant suffragettes) and what became the Fawcett Society (direct descendant of Mrs Fawcett's non-militant suffragists) lived unobtrusively on, but with diminishing impact after the 1920s. The conventional family in 1951 still assumed that men and women were clearly distinct psychologically, socially, and culturally as well as physiologically, and there was little support in 1947 for requiring 'national service' from women. The stereotypes of men and women were perpetuated in such popular literature as Mills and Boon novels; their heroes, said Alan Boon, were 'always what we call Alpha men—strong, mentally and physically tough, intelligent, tall and dark'.[103] It took much subterfuge and even hypocrisy to perpetuate this simplistic view of the family; in some interwar progressive circles even the subterfuge had been abandoned.

The first threat to the stereotypes came not from feminists, but from birth control's continuing advance. The Commonwealth's less crowded parts had hitherto expected to draw upon a surplus British white population, and at a time when a correlation between birth rate, national virility, and national morality was widely assumed, a falling birth rate seemed ominous for Britain's world influence. In national self-defence the balance between manpower and technology was only beginning to slant towards technology: anything which threatened the birth rate—birth control, careers for married women, homosexuality, abortion, prostitution—seemed not only morally reprehensible but a threat to national security. Given prevailing attitudes, the relative prevalence of birth control at higher social levels seemed also to threaten the stock of national intelligence. None the less, birth control had been promoted by late-Victorian Malthusians, not all of whom were feminists, and was popularized between the wars by Marie Stopes. With help from twentieth-century humanitarian rationalist and feminist reformers—groups occasionally aligned, but by no means identical—birth control's advance helps to explain why the total fertility rate in England and Wales halved between 1901/5 and 1931/5; it rose slowly from the 1940s to the 1960s, but resumed its fall in the 1970s to levels below those of the 1930s.[104]

[103] Obituary, *T* (9 Aug. 2000), 19. For national service, see also Broad, *Conscription in Britain*, 140.
[104] *TCBST* 35.

Birth control subverted the physiological justification for women's continued domestication, for if pregnancies were planned and less frequent, even married women could emulate the male lifelong paid career. Like all sexual matters in 1951, birth control was rarely discussed in public; nobody knew how much it owed to illegal abortion, which by the 1930s most doctors tolerated when they thought it medically justified. After 1945, however, diminished pregnancy, reduced emphasis on the disabling impact of menstruation and the menopause, and the recent memory of women's war work, made postwar women seem more employable. Already in 1943 an MP who deployed the menopause in a parliamentary debate as an argument against registering women for war work earned a rebuke from Eleanor Rathbone, the leading feminist of the day.[105] Women in the 1940s were also coming to seem more healthy. Feminists had long promoted women's sport as an aid to women's advance, and women increasingly saw themselves as competing on merit with men, with co-education as the natural long-term consequence. So with the incentives provided by wartime necessity, peacetime labour scarcity, the advance of light industry, and the beginnings of consumerism, married women by 1951 had begun to move into paid work: more than a quarter of them, by comparison with only a tenth twenty years earlier.[106] At least as significant was the change in the type of work they undertook: diminishingly in domestic service, textiles, and clothing and increasingly in commercial and clerical occupations.[107]

Birth control blurred the distinction between the sexes from another direction: by separating procreation from sexuality. By later standards, British society in 1951 was profoundly reticent on every aspect of sexuality—as evidenced by the ongoing elimination of suggestive surnames, for example. Whereas in 1881 there had been 3,211 Cocks, 320 Willys, and 781 Bottoms, the much larger population of 1996 could boast only 826, 185 and 511, respectively.[108] Birth control was therefore advanced unobtrusively in relatively progressive circles. Sexuality's separation from procreation was already being predicted in H. G. Wells's *Anticipations* (1901), and Bertrand Russell drew out its implications more boldly in his *Marriage and Morals* (1929). In 1951 these ideas were as yet moulding opinion only on the fringes of public debate, though they increasingly shaped private conduct. Likewise with homosexuality. *Sexual Behaviour in the Human Male*, published by Alfred Kinsey and his associates in America in 1948, illuminated the whole subject. A fat book, stuffed with statistics, and severely scientific and empirical in tone, it could reach the masses only through intermediaries. It did much to demystify, and in the early 1950s

[105] *HC Deb.* 24 Sept. 1943, cc. 605–6 (Dr Russell Thomas), cc. 608–9 (Rathbone).

[106] R. M. Moroney, *The Family and the State: Considerations for Social Policy* (1976), 19.

[107] There are useful statistics in E. James, 'Women at Work in Twentieth Century Britain: The Changing Structure of Female Employment', *Manchester School*, 30 (Sept. 1962), 291.

[108] *DT* (31 Aug. 2006), 4.

several British writers built upon it by arguing for a better understanding of same-sex relationships. There was no public debate in 1951 about significant pioneering ventures in the medical aspects of sex research. The London surgeon Sir Harold Gillies pioneered sex-change operations between the wars, yet when Michael Dillon published *Self: A Study in Ethics and Endocrinology* (1946), a pathbreaking document in the history of sex change, the word 'transsexual' was not available to describe people like its author. 'It is fast becoming evident', he wrote, 'that there are not only two sexes but several grades', and that 'intersexes' might have the physique of one sex but the temperament of the other; in such situations mind must be made to fit body, or body fit mind. 'The wonder is', he pointed out, when discussing hermaphroditism, 'not that there are people who might be said to be of the neuter gender, but that there is so high a percentage of normals as there appear to be.'[109] In his own case, reconciliation of mind and body had occurred, after extensive medical treatment, in 1944—the year when his birth certificate was changed to reflect his newly acquired male status. Dillon was a pioneer, too, in highlighting the many gradations in the spectrum between heterosexuality and homosexuality, and in making a quiet plea for tolerance.

Changed family attitudes, not yet obtrusive, had profound long-term implications for childhood. At whatever cost to the mother's self-realization, motherhood's semi-professionalization had ensured that by 1951 children's health in the first year and in all subsequent age-categories had improved continuously and massively since 1901.[110] A beginning had also been made in seeking from the earliest age to understand rather than condemn childish conduct. To take only one example, the influential, practical, closely observed and unpretentious manual *Understand your Baby* (first published in America by Anderson and Mary Aldrich in 1938) made a powerful plea for patience and empathy with the apparently selfish traits that the parents had themselves displayed in babyhood: 'a baby is not inferior', they wrote, 'he is merely younger'.[111] By 1951 the psychiatrist John Bowlby was complementing the interwar insights of the paediatrician Sir James Spencer with his campaign against the doctors' authoritarian practice of separating mothers from their sick children in hospital.

Childhood in 1951, as yet relatively uncommercialized, was an accepted status not to be regretted. The BBC programme *Listen with Mother*, for mothers with very young children, was launched in 1950, but given that the postwar priority lay in remedying wartime damage to the education of all children, central government cut its subsidy for new day-nurseries, and the

[109] M. Dillon, *Self: A Study in Ethics and Endocrinology* (1946), 39, 73–4.
[110] Statistics in *TCBST* 92.
[111] C. A. and M. M. Aldrich, *Understand your Baby: An Interpretation of Growth* (1939), 60.

percentage of children aged between 2 and 5 in maintained and grant-aided schools was lower in 1950 (12%) than in 1938 (16%).[112] Yet the BBC's regular programme *Children's Hour* was then in its heyday with a title that did not yet drive its audience away, and BBC television launched its *Children's Newsreel* in 1950. The pattern was by then well established for the 'schoolchild' to be in school between the ages of 5 and 14 or beyond. 'Boys' and 'girls' still flocked into organizations so designated: the Boys' Brigade and Boy Scouts in 1950 had yet to reach their peak membership, and the Girl Guides and Brownies were still recruiting fast.[113] In 1951 a distinct teenage culture had not yet emerged. Parents decided what their children should wear, and for teenagers this often meant adapted or even reach-me-down versions of adult clothes.

None the less, by the late 1940s parental authority was for three reasons being eroded by an emerging distinct culture of adolescence and even of childhood. There was first the growth of legal autonomy for the child. Early legislation against child cruelty, while conceding that parents were not always benevolent, did not go so far as to curb the parental (or, by extension, the teacher's) disciplinary powers, nor did it extend rights to the child. By 1951, however, the tension between respect for parental wishes and promotion of the child's interests was beginning to tighten. The Children Act (1948) owed much to the widely publicized manslaughter in 1945 of 12-year-old Dennis O'Neill from under-nourishment after the local authority had placed him with foster parents. There was, secondly, a new, widening and more widespread source of tension: the gap between the child's ever-earlier physical maturity and the ever-lengthening education which prolonged its dependence on parents. At this time childhood did not officially end until the age of maturity at 21, though in 1948 Lord Llewellin felt embarrassed to apply in legislation the word 'child' to an 18-year-old: instead he advocated the phrase 'young person'.[114] From the mid-nineteenth century the age of menarche had been falling by three to four months per decade, and by 1964 11-year-olds even in Glasgow were nearly four inches taller than in 1906.[115] Battles between parents and children over sexual conduct were in prospect. Finally there were significant developments in the media: the advent of television in 1936 and the growing postwar boom in an increasingly Americanized recording industry. The pursuit of literacy so central to communication and childhood discipline before 1951—with adults controlling access to knowledge and dispensing it sequentially—soon encountered formidable challenge from oral and visual culture within the home itself.

112 N. Whitbread, *The Evolution of the Nursery–Infant School: A History of Infant and Nursery Education in Britain, 1800–1970* (1972), 112.

113 For statistics see *TCBST* 612–13.

114 *HL Deb.* 10 Feb. 1948, c. 933.

115 J. M. Tanner, 'The Trend Towards Earlier Physical Maturation', in J. E. Meade and A. S. Parkes (eds.), *Biological Aspects of Social Problems: A Symposium Held by the Eugenics Society in October 1964* (Edinburgh and London, 1965), 42, 51.

Attitudes in 1951 to other age-groups were also changing. 'Middle age' is a concept at least as imprecise, time-bound, and shifting as 'childhood'. The term 'middle-aged' dates from the seventeenth century, 'middle-aged spread' from the 1930s. Middle age overlaps with adulthood, but is by no means synonymous with it, and its boundaries shift with growing longevity. In the second half of the nineteenth century, when lives were shorter, those who compiled the census defined it as located between 30 and 50, but early in the twentieth century its lower boundary moved up to 35 and later to 40, with eligibility for old-age pension as its frontier with old age. If middle age is defined as between 40 and 59, the number of middle-aged people in England and Wales was rising fast, and its proportion of the total population was rising too (18% in 1901, 27% in 1951), with women slightly outnumbering men within the age-group.[116] But there were contrasts between the sexes: by 1951 the spread of birth control and changing attitudes to the menopause made it less likely that women would display signs of ageing earlier than men, though the notion of a 'male menopause' was not yet in sight.

Both absolutely and proportionately, twentieth-century pensioner numbers in Great Britain rose steadily: 3.3 million (8% of the total population) in 1921, 6.7 million (14%) in 1951, 8.7 million (16%) in 1971. There were continuous increases also, from 1931, in the number and proportion of people living to the ages of 60, 70, and 80.[117] Longer life and growing resources had encouraged the late-Victorian idea of instituting a fixed age for retirement with a pension, and in the late 1940s concern about the balance between workers and dependants ensured that pensioners' needs were much discussed in the debate on social insurance prompted by Beveridge's report of 1942. While birth control had since 1900 been reducing the number of dependants under 14, longer life increased the number of dependants over 65. The advance before 1951 of statutory pensions in Britain and other industrial societies encouraged a growing proportion of men over 65 to retire.[118] Although in 1951 nearly half the men between 65 and 69 and a fifth of those aged 70 and above remained in paid employment,[119] already by then the gap (now familiar) between old age as biologically and socially defined had begun to widen. The brief wartime incursion of men over 65 into the workforce[120] was a reminder of the pensioner's continuing potential for work, which had earlier kept them in the workforce as long as health permitted. Some in the 1940s regarded pensioners as mere

[116] Calculated from *BHS* 15. For one of the few serious discussions of this important topic see J. Benson, *Prime Time: A History of the Middle-Aged in Twentieth Century Britain* (1997), 9, 11, 31.

[117] A. M. Warnes and R. Ford, *The Changing Distribution of Elderly People: Great Britain, 1981–91* (King's College, London, Department of Geography and Age Concern Institute of Gerontology, Occasional Paper, 37, 1993), 4.

[118] See the interesting cross-cultural graph in P. Townsend, *Poverty in the United Kingdom: A Survey of Household Resources and Standards of Living* (1979), 654.

[119] Ibid. 659.

[120] For statistics on this see Royal Commission on Population, *Report* (Cmd.7695, 1949), 115 n. 1.

passengers, others felt that they should now be joining the crew, but the Attlee governments responded by paying pensions at a lower level and enabling more people to qualify for them than Beveridge had recommended. Nearly a quarter of state pensioners in 1951 were therefore also receiving national assistance: Beveridge's aim of removing the aged from dependency had not been delivered.[121]

Unsurprisingly, many supplemented the state pension with an occupational pension. Paid as of right on the insurance principle, pensions of this type originated with thrift schemes in individual firms, but between the wars were promoted by the big insurance companies; eligible for them were an eighth of employees in Great Britain in 1936, rising twenty years later to more than a third.[122] Partly because women were much more likely to work part-time, men's direct benefit from occupational pensions was more than twice as high as women's.[123] Several factors, however, led women to accumulate a rising share of total personal wealth (33% of wealth in England and Wales in 1927, 42% in Britain in 1960[124]). There was a growing tendency for spouses to own their property jointly, there were tax advantages in dividing up wealth within families, and women were living longer. Whether widowed or divorced, women were relatively likely to be the householders in the one-person household which spread continuously in twentieth-century Great Britain.[125] Throughout the twentieth century, about a quarter of the rising numbers in England and Wales over 65 were over 75, and between 1931 and 1971 those over 85 as a proportion of those over 65 doubled from 3 to 6 per cent.[126] Women were still more prominent among the growing number of the very old. The number of people in England and Wales over 80 grew at the rate of 2–3 per cent a year from 1911, and of those alive in 1951, two-thirds were women; of the 300 centenarians in that year, only 46 were men.[127] The conservative political implications of an ageing population might have been serious but for the countervailing influence of old people's dependence on public welfare, central to the Labour Party's electoral appeal.

British demographers in the 1930s were less preoccupied than their successors with the ageing of the population, more preoccupied with the sharply falling birth rate, which they assumed would persist. From the end of the decade, however, two factors changed demographers' subsequent priorities. First, the birth rate began to stabilize; but, second, the advent of public welfare made

[121] See M. R. Miller's valuable Kent Ph.D. thesis: 'The Development of Retirement Pensions Policy in Britain from 1945 to 1986: A Case of State and Occupational Welfare' (1987), 34.

[122] Ibid. 266.

[123] For statistics, see *TCBST* 567.

[124] J. Revell, 'Changes in the Social Distribution of Property in Britain during the Twentieth Century', *Third International Conference of Economic History: Munich 1965* (Paris, 1968), i. 382.

[125] For statistics, see *TCBST* 77.

[126] Moroney, *Family and State*, 36.

[127] Calculated from table in A. R. Thatcher, 'Trends in Numbers and Mortality at High Ages in England and Wales', *Population Studies*, 40 (1992), 415.

it an urgent question whether there would be enough people of working age to support the growing number of pensioners.[128] This was partly because morbidity did not retreat as longevity advanced, so there was growing scope by 1951 for a specialism in the medicine of old age. Its advance was hindered by the overall scarcity of medical resources; 'it is dangerous to be in any way lavish to old age', wrote Beveridge in his report of 1942, 'until adequate provision has been assured for all other vital needs, such as the prevention of disease and the adequate nutrition of the young'.[129] For the increasing numbers of old people, especially those distanced from their children in wartime or with no children at all, defence needed to be organized, and from 1940 what later became Age Concern originated. Marjory Warren's experience at West Middlesex County Hospital prompted her campaign in the 1940s for the old to benefit from the same age-related specialization that (in paediatrics) had recently benefited the young; she also wanted medico-social workers to integrate the chronically sick into the community.[130] Some influential doctors denied that there was anything medically distinctive about the ailments of the old, and argued that specialization should focus on the illness, not on the age group, but Warren was among those who collaborated in 1947 to form what became the British Geriatrics Society; it aimed to improve medical services for old people and promote medical specialization in the area. J. H. Sheldon, himself a pioneer in this sphere, pointed out in the following year that the terms 'geriatrics' or 'gerontology' were premature: unlike 'paediatrics' they outlined more an agenda than a body of clinical achievement, and were 'little more at the moment than the staking out of a claim for a field that is almost untilled'.[131] The first professor of geriatrics in Britain, W. Ferguson Anderson, was not appointed till 1964.

The twentieth-century trend in attitudes to death, well under way by 1951, was to secularize, medicalize, and bureaucratize. People were increasingly likely to die in hospital rather than at home, and funeral directors developed expertise at guiding the body through the system. Cremation was slowly gaining ground, and when Churchill told the Cremation Society in 1943 that he wanted to be cremated, only 6 per cent of the population preferred it to burial. His letter was framed and mounted in the Society's council chamber, though when the Society asked in 1964 whether it could publicize his choice in a leaflet it was told that arrangements had changed and that the letter should not be advertised.[132]

[128] I owe this point to Professor David Coleman of Oxford, who provided most generous help at numerous points in this book.

[129] *Social Insurance and Allied Services: Report by Sir William Beveridge* (Cmd. 6404, 1942), 92.

[130] See her two articles, 'Care of Chronic Sick: A Case for Treating Chronic Sick in Blocks in a General Hospital', *British Medical Journal* (25 Dec. 1943), 822–3; 'Care of the Chronic Aged Sick', *Lancet* (8 June 1946), 841–3.

[131] J. H. Sheldon, *The Social Medicine of Old Age: Report of an Inquiry in Wolverhampton* (1948), 187.

[132] *T* (7 Apr. 1978), 1.

Traditional mourning patterns persisted longest lower down in society and in the Celtic fringe because associated with respectability and reinforced by a deep fear of the pauper burial. In 1926 Beatrice Webb predicted as 'one of the refinements of the future hedonistic society' that unwanted life would at the outset be prevented by birth control and at the conclusion by euthanasia.[133] We have already seen how that society was slowly coming into being at the start of life; doctors, increasingly skilled at preventing pain, were also slowly creating Webb's hedonistic society at the end of life too. By unobtrusively upholding quality of life rather than prolonging it for its own sake, they were in practice weakening the case for legalizing euthanasia: if euthanasia already in some sense occurred in practice, legislation would merely complicate matters. There was an affinity between such a stance and opposing the ban on suicide, which merely prompted evasive verdicts of 'temporary insanity' in courtrooms less censorious than parliament. There was an affinity, too, with the growing hostility to capital punishment; a respect for the dignity of the individual inspired all these stances. Legalized hanging with its associated melodrama, far from elevating the dignity of the law, corrupted public manners: 'what the hangman does with his hands', said the abolitionist Sidney Silverman, 'we each do in our hearts'.[134]

In 1951 there was widespread faith in the welfare state as another route towards enhancing human life and dignity. This was seen as a characteristic British middle way—between Communist centralized bureaucracy and the USA's free-market anarchy. London cockneys also saw it as a reward for their wartime sufferings, and when the Bangladeshi immigrants arrived in later years the cockneys staked out their territory with little street memorials to their war dead: they thought the newcomers had not paid the wartime price which would justify their benefits.[135] Public expenditure rose threefold and social welfare sevenfold in its share of gross national product between 1900 and 1950,[136] and a virtuous cycle seemed to be procuring humanitarian progress by linking public welfare, social engineering, and medical research. The overall death rate for both sexes had been falling at least since the early eighteenth century. Mortality in children had been declining steadily from the 1870s in England and Wales, and in young adults from soon after that. Maternal mortality plunged in the 1930s and 1940s,[137] and death rates of those over 45 in England and Wales, static throughout the nineteenth century, improved during the twentieth century, beginning with the age-band from 45 to 54 at the start of the century, moving

[133] B.Webb, *Diary*, iv. *1924–1943* (1985), 100 (18 Sept. 1926).

[134] E. Hughes, *Sydney Silverman: Rebel in Parliament* (1969), 156.

[135] G. Dench, K. Gavron, and M. Young, *The New East End: Kinship, Race and Conflict* (2006), 4, 215.

[136] Moroney, *Family and State*, 98.

[137] M. Anderson in Thompson (ed.), *Cambridge Social History of Britain 1750–1950*, ii (1990), 17, 25–6. I. Loudon, J. Horder, and C. Webster (eds.), *General Practice under the National Health Service 1948–1997: The First Fifty Years* (Oxford, 1998), 299.

on in the 1920s to those between 55 and 74, and reaching those over 74 after the Second World War.[138]

In 1950 some diseases were still far more prevalent lower down in society than higher up—tuberculosis, cancer of the stomach, heart disease, and bronchitis[139]—though by the late 1940s calorie and protein intake did not differ significantly between the social classes. Social-class contrasts in diet did not necessarily advance middle-class health: a modern nutritionist might welcome the middle-class taste for fruit and fish, but would be less keen on their eggs, butter, and milk.[140] Wartime government education had alerted the public to health issues, most notably on nutrition, but also on such issues as restraining the habit (once widespread) of spitting in public, in the hope of curbing tuberculosis; the injunction 'do not spit' on London buses in the late 1940s was by then preaching to the converted, and did not long survive.[141] In 1950 it was shown that the decline in poverty since 1936, with all its implications for health, owed much to the subsequent growth in full employment, though the decline had been accelerated by the welfare expenditure of the 1940s, especially through food subsidies.[142] Mortality ratios were improving at all social levels in the twentieth century, and the number of deaths in UK industrial accidents halved between the twentieth century's first and fourth decades. None the less, society's overall improvement did not preclude growing inequality in some respects: from the period 1949–53 onwards, mortality rates higher up in society were improving faster than lower down, widening the social-class health-gap.[143] Democracy had hardly yet entered the world of the hospital. Centralized hospital-dominated health care had long been doctor-dominated, doctors were authoritarian in manner, and big hospitals with their complex equipment were temples celebrating their status. An air of mystery had long accompanied diagnosis; patients were kept in the dark, and doctors were reluctant to say 'cancer' even when discussing George VI's final illness. 'I want to get a clear idea of *how long* I am likely to last', wrote Orwell, dying from tuberculosis in 1948, 'and not just be jollied along the way doctors usually do.'[144]

5. INDUSTRY AND COMMERCE

The late 1940s combined marked austerity with remarkable economic self-confidence, despite serious problems in the short term. Interwar Britain's

[138] *TCBST* 99.

[139] A. M. Carr-Saunders, D. Caradog Jones, and C. A. Moser, *A Survey of Social Conditions in England and Wales* (Oxford, 1958), 226–7.

[140] I. Zweiniger-Bargielowska, *Austerity in Britain: Rationing, Controls, and Consumption, 1939–1955* (Oxford, 2000), 43, 45.

[141] *HC Deb.* 2 Aug. 1956, c. 1760.

[142] Rowntree and Lavers, *Poverty and Welfare State*, 34–5, 40.

[143] *TCBST* 303 (accidents), 110–11 (mortality).

[144] Quoted in B. Crick, *George Orwell: A Life* (1981), 385. See also Bradford, *George VI*, 601.

overseas investments had produced a healthy prewar balance in invisible trade, which made it much easier to fund the food, fuel, and raw materials that a small and highly urbanized country required. The urgent need for war materials in 1939–45, however, had compelled the sale of overseas investments, and after 1945 a substantial growth in British manufactures was desperately needed, together with a powerful push for exports. The postwar economic settlement left the dollar supreme at a time when the Americans were pressing to expand international trade by reducing tariffs and by using fixed exchange rates between currencies to stabilize prices. Postwar British governments worried almost continuously about the balance of payments. Exchange control, originally imposed in 1939, was retained after the war almost unamended as, in the Labour Chancellor Hugh Dalton's words, 'an indispensable weapon for safeguarding our balance of payments'. While the Conservatives did not oppose it as a short-term expedient, they wanted it made only temporary, and when in 1946 the government intended to make it permanent, they had much to say about loss of freedom and challenges to parliament's authority. Dalton gave no ground: when asked for suggestions on a time limit which could be inserted into the Bill, his response was: 'I have suggested eternity'. In the following year Oliver Lyttelton told Churchill he favoured an overall 'decontrol policy', which would entail unpegging the pound in relation to the dollar, and 'at one sweep of the pen' abolishing 'most of the controls and allow price rises to take place'.[145] Britain's wartime dollar shortage was temporarily remedied through the UK's control over the Overseas Sterling Area: held in London in a shared pool, its reserves were deployed to smooth out temporary currency fluctuations within the Area. The sterling countries included several states (Iceland, Burma, and Libya, for example) no longer or never under British political control, and in her postwar economic weakness the UK (especially the City in its role as a world financial centre) benefited greatly from the Area's continuance. In the longer term, Keynes's vision, in his famous essay of 1930, retained its force. Extrapolating from existing growth patterns he had envisaged anything between a fourfold and eightfold improvement in the standard of life 'in progressive countries', given peace, population control, and the encouragement of science. While there were serious postwar worries about the first, there was every hope of delivery on the second and third.[146] By 1951 the UK's export surplus in manufactures had risen to 11 per cent of gross domestic product, more than three times its prewar level, and the rapid growth rate of the 1930s in electricity sales had resumed.[147]

[145] Dalton, *HC Deb.* 26 Nov. 1946, cc. 1425, 1448. Lyttelton in P. Addison, *Churchill on the Home Front 1900–1955* (1992), 397.

[146] 'Economic Possibilities for our Grandchildren' [1930] in his *Essays in Persuasion* (1931), 364, 373, and see below, pp. 48, 55, 487, 513.

[147] R. E. Rowthorn and J. R. Wells, *De-Industrialization and Foreign Trade* (Cambridge, 1987), 97. *BHS* 264.

With hindsight we can see that Britain's early start in industrialization hindered re-equipping and restructuring in the face of changing technologies and markets, but for several reasons the scale of the problem was not perceived at the time. First, the wartime swing to the left was associated with the belief that interwar unemployment had stemmed from ignorant or callous Conservative-dominated governments reluctant to regulate the free market—a problem that now seemed to have gone away. 'We were haunted by the fear of long-term mass unemployment,' Keith Joseph later recalled, 'the grim, hopeless dole queues and towns which died. So we talked ourselves into believing that these gaunt, tight-lipped men in caps and mufflers were round the corner, and tailored our policy to match these imaginary conditions.'[148] Second, between 1945 and the mid-1950s, Britain retained an illusory economic supremacy within Europe, whose shattered economies needed repair and restructuring;[149] the British economic growth rate was not yet thought inferior to any but the USA's.[150] Third, Britain by comparison with Europe, especially given the strength of the Anglo-American alliance, was a good home for American investment; this had been slowly cumulating since the mid-nineteenth century, and by 1955 the UK attracted 58 per cent of American manufacturing investments in Europe as a whole.[151] Fourth, the permanence of the decline in Britain's traditional staple industries—coal, textiles, shipbuilding—was not yet apparent; later it became clear that the war had only temporarily interrupted that decline, with its associated population drift southwards into the areas of new prosperity. Neither world war did more than interrupt the steady shift in population between 1871 and 1991 from Northern Ireland, Scotland, and northern England to Wales and still more to the south of England. Whereas during the nineteenth century northern England, Wales and Scotland had increased their overall share of the UK population (to 48% by 1901), that share fell between 1921 and 1951 to 45 per cent, while the Midlands and south of England increased theirs from 52 to 55 per cent.[152]

In so far as Britain's economic problems were perceived, the state seemed to hold the remedy. The corporatist tripartite alliance between government, employers' organizations, and trade unions had so enhanced the war effort and had so improved industrial relations that its peacetime utility seemed obvious.

[148] K. Joseph, Preston speech, 22 June 1974, in his *Reversing the Trend: A Critical Re-appraisal of Conservative Economic and Social Policies. Seven Speeches* (Chichester and London, 1975), 21.

[149] For a well-stated argument to this effect, see C. H. Feinstein, 'Success and Failure: British Economic Growth since 1948', in R. Floud and D. McCloskey (eds.), *Economic History of Britain since 1700* (2nd edn. 1994), iii. 117–19.

[150] See the table in S. N. Broadberry, 'The Impact of the World Wars on the Long Run Performance of the British Economy', *Oxford Review of Economic Policy*, 4/1 (1988), 26; the nations defeated in the Second World War showed the highest growth rates in 1950–73.

[151] J. H. Dunning, *American Investment in British Manufacturing Industry* (1958), 51.

[152] Warnes and Ford, *Changing Distribution of Elderly People*, 5.

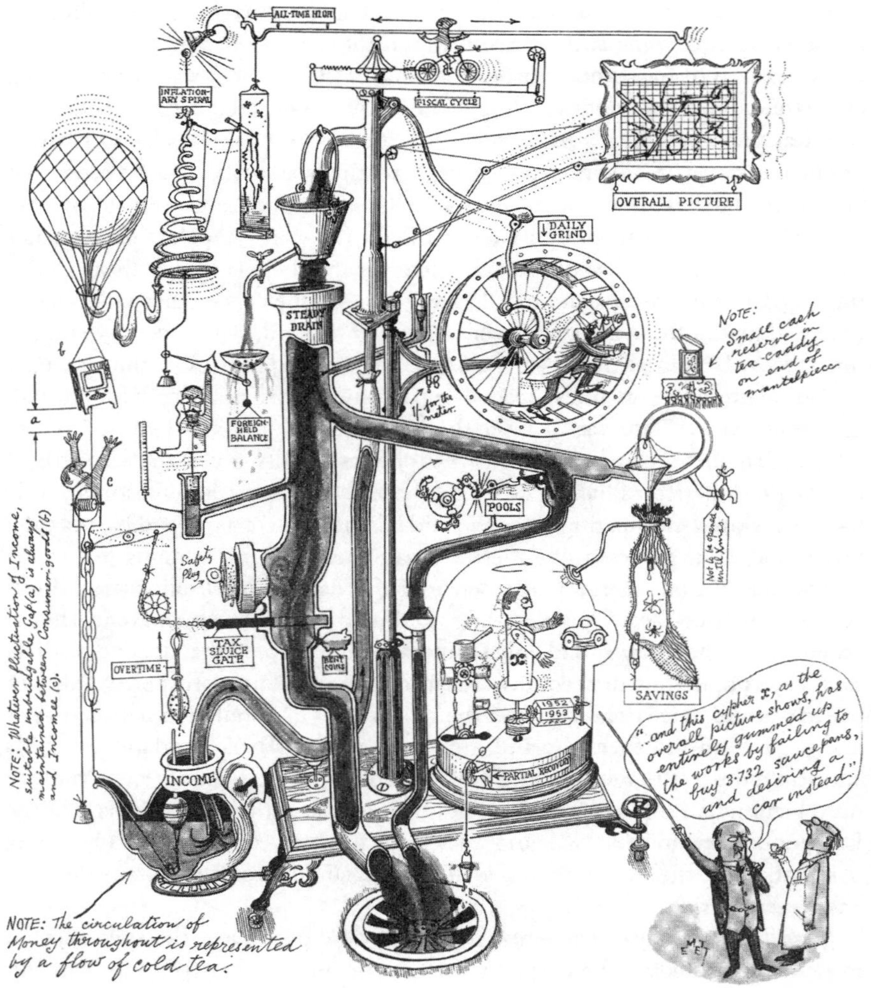

MACHINE DESIGNED TO SHOW THE WORKING OF THE ECONOMIC SYSTEM

Fig. 1. Emett cartoon showing the Phillips model: *Punch* (15 Apr. 1953), 457.

The voluntary collaboration that corporatism entailed was eminently compatible with the ideals of democratic participation, while simultaneously mobilizing a sense of national unity. It seemed an attractively pluralist compromise between state direction and the free market which could ensure continuity across governments of whatever party, though it carried the danger of entrenching vested interests within uncompetitive structures. Corporatist strategies were linked to the 'Keynesian' belief that fiscal policy could and should be used counter-cyclically: in times of falling demand the state would smooth out fluctuations in employment by running a temporary deficit until the economy recovered. All the postwar running, practically and intellectually, was made by planning, public welfare, and the management of demand by politicians, administrators, and experts. The new profession of planner, the allocator of scarce resources, spread through government departments and local authorities. Morrison, that able enthusiast for postwar nationalization, mobilized the public relations expert, the industrial psychologist, and the social investigator as guides to opinion—substitutes for the guidance to demand that the free market provides through the price mechanism, the advertiser, and the consumer's unfettered choice. The beginnings of an integrated government system for collecting economic statistics were by 1951 for the first time in place, with professional statisticians and economists advising the civil servants on how to use them. Already by 1950 the red liquid was flowing through the tanks, pipes, and valves of the model built at the LSE by the economist A. W. H. Phillips to demonstrate the flow of national income. On getting to hear about it, *Punch* christened it the 'financephalograph', got Emett to portray it in a cartoon [Fig. 1], and argued in a rather heavily facetious article that 'one financephalograph per nation is not enough'.[153]

The war also seemed, through its utility scheme, to have revealed central government's power to foster good design. Between the wars there had been all too little interaction between the art school and the technical school, and the Cotswold furniture maker Gordon Russell was unusual in perceiving the need to integrate design with the machine. Carrying forward William Morris's vision, yet without repudiating commercial values or technology, he built up an influential network of connections. His opportunity came with the plain and functional utility styles required during the war, and the Council of Industrial Design was set up in 1944 to promote the idea that good design is good business. It first made an impact in 1946 with the 'Britain Can Make It' exhibition at the Victoria and Albert Museum, attracting 1.5 million visitors. There was still in 1951 the hope that mass production and mass consumption could unite behind fine design, and Russell placed high hopes in the Council's involvement with the Festival of Britain.

The tight labour market after 1945, so very different from the situation after 1918, owed much to an unexpected conjuncture: armed services twice as numerous in peacetime as prewar, continuing British emigration to the Commonwealth, and a school-leaving age raised to 15 in 1947. Employment was so full that many women wartime workers remained in the workforce, and the government somewhat controversially encouraged immigrants from Europe. A quarter of all those from Europe who emigrated abroad in 1946–50 came to the

[153] R. Dahrendorf, *LSE: A History of the London School of Economics and Political Science 1895–1995* (Oxford, 1995), 386. *Punch* (15 Apr. 1953), 456–7.

UK, whose aliens aged 16 and above rose from 240,000 in 1939 to 430,000 in December 1950.[154] The workforce was changing in character. The long-term decline since 1901 in the number of miners and domestic servants persisted, agriculture's even longer-term decline continued, while manufacturing employment was still growing. Half the labour force in 1951 was in manufacturing and mining, a fifth in trade and transport, another fifth in service occupations.[155] These occupational changes carried implications for social-class attitudes. 'The old-style "proletarian"—collarless, unshaven and with muscles warped by heavy labour—still exists', wrote Orwell in 1941, 'but he is constantly decreasing in numbers; he only predominates in the heavy-industry areas of the north of England.'[156] Growing fast throughout the century were the many types of white-collar worker, and their relationship with the employer was, as we have seen, much closer. The retreat of heavy labour was also linked to a third change: women's advance within the workforce. While their proportion of employers and manual workers was not changing much, their proportion of white-collar workers was rising quite fast;[157] the proportion of married women who were in paid work was rising fast too, reaching by 1951 more than a quarter of all married women. Not only did the paid married woman worker shield the family against poverty: she brought access to goods 'which would formerly have been rejected without consideration as being entirely beyond their means'.[158]

Working hours within the day, the week, and the year reflect convention and convenience. The nineteenth century had seen increasingly precise attitudes to time: to get maximum return from expensive machinery, good timekeeping was required from its operators, nor could a railway timetable function nationwide without removing the local time variations which reflected local daylight patterns: Greenwich Mean Time became the national convention. The process was carried further forward by radio: it had introduced the six-pip Greenwich Time Signal by 1924, and by the 1940s required programmes to be precisely timed. In 1951 the timing of the working day was a matter for public debate. The twentieth century introduced the concept of 'daylight saving', and throughout the year from 1940 energy was conserved and productivity enhanced by prolonging 'summer time'—moving the clock forward by one hour in spring and moving it back in the autumn. In 1941 'double summer time' was introduced: two hours in advance of Greenwich Mean Time from spring to autumn, with 'summer time' prolonged throughout the year. Although these arrangements ended in 1945, the government retained and exercised thereafter the power to vary the length

[154] J. A. Tannahill, *European Volunteer Workers in Britain* (Manchester, 1958), 3, 5.

[155] Deane and Cole, *British Economic Growth 1688–1959*, 142–5.

[156] Orwell, 'Lion and Unicorn', in *Works*, xii. 408.

[157] See the useful table in G. S. Bain, *Trade Union Growth and Recognition* (Royal Commission on Trade Unions and Employers' Associations, Research Papers, 6, 1967), 6.

[158] Rowntree and Lavers, *Poverty and the Welfare State*, 54. See also Moroney, *Family and State*, 19.

of 'summer time' from year to year, and even briefly in 1947 to reintroduce 'double summer time', balancing rural against urban interests, Scottish against English, recreational against commercial. Such manipulation could not in itself change what people did, but by extending access to natural rather than artificial light, it could conserve energy by influencing when they did it.

The length of the working week for male manual workers had been declining for decades before 1951, and the trade-union-negotiated interwar norm of 47–8 hours fell to 44–5 soon after 1945, a change which affected about nine million manual workers, and often meant introducing a five-day working week. Lowering the norm did not necessarily affect actual hours worked: the reform was in effect a disguised pay increase, since overtime pay rates flourished in the widening gap between norm and actuality. Hours worked reached their postwar peak in 1955 at 49, higher than in 1938.[159] Paid annual holidays had taken a leap forward in the late 1930s, and by 1952 more than two-thirds of all wage-earners had three weeks' annual paid holiday. Already by 1948 three-fifths of the British adult population were holidaying away from home,[160] though the recreation industry had not yet fully geared up. It took a long time for British hotels to recover from wartime requisitioning, refurbish their buildings, and cope with power cuts. Besides, rationing did not end till 1954, nor had the hotel trade's consolidation into larger groupings yet proceeded very far. Government lent the trade little support, and there was much inertia: the only notable new hotels built between 1945 and 1960 were the Leofric in Coventry and the Westbury in Mayfair.[161]

The planned economy posed problems more readily perceived in retrospect than at the time. If the market was not to be freed, government needed to work closely with employers and employees—which in practice meant employers' organizations and trade unions guided by the TUC—to organize the supply of labour and foster productivity. This tended to privilege the large firm over the small, the established firm over the newcomer, the unionized employee over the non-unionized. The government in 1947 set about tackling the degradation involved in the dockers' casual labour by introducing the National Dock Labour Scheme, which gave registered dockers the legal right to minimum work and decent conditions. Through the National Dock Labour Board, on which employers and trade unions were equally represented, the unions gained control over recruitment and dismissal. Registered dockers laid off by employers within the Scheme had the right either to be taken on by another, or to generous compensation, though the Scheme's constraints on

159 National Board for Prices and Incomes, *Report No. 161: Hours of Work, Overtime and Shiftworking*, *PP* 1970–1 (Cmnd. 4554), xlv. 11–12. H. Ichihashi, 'Working-Class Leisure in English Towns 1945 to 1960, with Special Reference to Coventry and Bolton' (Warwick Ph.D. thesis, 1994), 4.

160 Ichihashi, 'Working-Class Leisure', 6. Hulton Press, *Patterns of British Life*, 112.

161 D. A. Stewart, *Hoteliers and Hotels: Case Studies in the Growth and Development of U.K. Hotel Companies 1945–1989* (Glasgow, 1996), 3–4.

employers had many unintended effects. Even the trade unions opposed any generalized direct government control over labour supply: their preference for free collective bargaining meant that between 1947 and 1950 the Attlee governments in steering the economy had to substitute fiscal for manpower budgeting. The government's laboriously engineered pact with the trade unions in 1948 to restrain wages could not long survive.

Government could not retreat from managing the economy, even had it wished, until the revived price mechanism was complemented by a revived banking and share-trading mechanism, yet in the late 1940s London's capital markets recovered only slowly. In 1946 the Attlee government reopened London's private dealings in rubber, furs, wool, coffee, tin, cocoa, and tea, but other prewar commodity markets remained for the time being inactive. As at 1951 the City's financial role had yet to revive. There was trouble, too, from the employers, some of whom opposed the government's aims. This was a major hindrance, given that the government lacked access to adequate planning mechanisms or expertise of its own. The British Iron and Steel Federation, the steel industry's trade association, boycotted the public corporation that had been established to control the industry after nationalization in 1948, and refused to accept the corporation's representatives on its council. A Labour government's periodic curbs on advertising during elections could not counteract the pressure of business publicity, employed most dramatically in Tate & Lyle's deployment of 'Mr Cube' against nationalizing the sugar industry.

To opposition from the producers were added problems from the consumer. Morrison believed that a nationalized or public-welfare structure would or should be more consumer-conscious than a private concern; yet within such a structure, production had to be guided by assumed needs rather than articulated wants. Whereas the experts might sometimes guess right, they had less control over consumers' overall expenditure, which often took unintended directions. Given that the war had liquidated the overseas portfolio investments of UK citizens (more than a quarter of national wealth in 1937[162]), the government aimed to channel national resources into exports through labour planning and rationing at home. This created shortages in the consumer goods required to motivate the workforce, whose resources often went on the only alternatives: drinking, gambling, smoking, and sport. 'Our lower classes', said Harold Nicolson snootily in 1946, 'are for some curious reason congenitally indolent . . . only the pressure of gain or destitution makes them work. When their profits are taken for income tax and they are insured against destitution, their natural indolence comes to the surface.'[163] The advertising industry, which had grown fast in the 1920s, was in decline. In the late 1940s

[162] Revell, 'Changes in Distribution of Property', 369.
[163] Nicolson, *Diaries and Letters, 1945–62*, 55 (11 Mar. 1946).

the powerfully motivating alliance of advertisers with goods to promote was in temporary abeyance, and this was accentuated by government policy and lack of newsprint. Only government exhortation remained to inspire productivity. This in itself entailed difficulty: if socialists regarded private advertising as a wasteful and Americanized affront to British reticence and self-denial, government advertising in the late 1940s risked allegations of totalitarian thought control.

By 1950 significant intellectual challenges had already been mounted to the corporatist consensus of the late 1940s. The philosopher and economist Friedrich Hayek's *The Road to Serfdom* (1944) stressed that once the state embarked, however benevolently, on trying to manage the economy, it would be ineluctably drawn in further, ultimately threatening liberty. His call for a revived Gladstonian Liberalism went for the moment unheard, but in 1947 the Mont Pelerin Society, a free-market pressure group influential in the longer term, was uncompromising when drafting its statement of aims: 'the freedom of the consumer in choosing what he shall buy, the freedom of the producer in choosing what he shall make, and the freedom of the worker in choosing his occupation and his place of employment, are essential not merely for the sake of freedom itself, but for efficiency in production'.[164] In the following year the economist John Jewkes, whose wartime experience had (unusually) led him to oppose state interference, knew he was consigning himself intellectually to the wilderness by publishing his *Ordeal by Planning*. 'Everything I have to say here, and indeed much more' had appeared in Hayek's 'masterly' *Road to Serfdom*, he wrote, and he knew that the critics of planning 'are in these days regarded almost as engines of evil. Their motives are impugned, their feeling for humanity doubted.'[165] He argued that the consumer, however inconveniently to the planner, knows his own wants best, nor should those wants be pre-empted by the alleged needs of some future generation. Resentment at the postwar persistence of rationing by queue gave the Conservatives a practical grievance to exploit. In 1949 a third of housewives queued regularly, and a survey in the previous year claimed that the queue was 'clearly to many . . . the symbol of all the frustrations of this post war era', with no other current topic prompting 'such immediate and fierce reaction'.[166] Conservatives were slow to go further by framing a more generalized and ideological assault on the Attlee government's outlook. Given the more immediate appeal of directly consensual policies, the recent memory and apparent success of the war's collaborative structures, and the party's eagerness in the late 1940s to capture what it saw as the middle ground, only a few backbenchers fully espoused the free market. Such notions could not yet be entertained by practical politicians.

164 R. M. Hartwell, *A History of the Mont Pelerin Society* (Indianapolis, 1995), 49.
165 J. Jewkes, *Ordeal by Planning* (1948), pp. ix (preface), 3.
166 Zweiniger-Bargielowska, *Austerity in Britain*, 118–19.

6. INTELLECT AND CULTURE

For decades after Darwin's *Origin of Species*, educated commentators worried about whether diminished religious sanctions would erode social discipline. Positivism, secularism, socialism, and the other non-religious ethical systems seeking to fill the void had little impact: their non-religious sanctions lacked force. The civic ethic seemed vulnerable to hedonistic and secular forms of unreason. For C. F. G. Masterman in 1909, conduct would not immediately be affected: custom and convention would prolong the behaviour that a Christian society had shaped 'long after the driving power of definite conviction has vanished, like a machine still running down after the motive power has ceased'.[167] This was no long-term solution, but Keynes from an entirely secular perspective in 1930 was famously optimistic: with the economic problem solved, he wrote, 'the arena of the heart and head will be occupied, or re-occupied, by our real problems—the problems of life and of human relations, of creation and behaviour and religion'. The coming problem for mankind was 'how to use his freedom from pressing economic cares, how to occupy the leisure, which science and compound interest will have won for him, to live wisely and agreeably and well'.[168] The supreme self-denial required in two world wars seemed at least temporarily to demonstrate the tenacity of social discipline, and amidst the gloom of blackouts, bombing, and rationing, Keynes's somewhat nervous hopes for the future precariously survived.

The postwar Church of England was in some ways stronger than in the Victorian heyday of organized religion, for the nonconformist challenge was fading fast. The massive decline in nonconformist Sunday-school attendance from the 1940s[169] was ominous. In a historically less literate society, the seventeenth- and eighteenth-century traditions so central to nonconformist vigour were fading, the strongest-felt nonconformist grievances had long disappeared, and a geographically mobile society threatened the localism integral to chapel life. The Roman Catholic Church, by contrast, was still growing,[170] fuelled by Irish and European immigrants, but its mood was not aggressive. Asian immigrants did not yet reinforce the non-Christian religious challenge to the established church. On no fewer than eleven occasions during the Second World War the Church of England had coordinated the Christian churches behind national days of prayer, and on Sunday 6 July 1947 'a national day of prayer and dedication' was mounted to unite and motivate the nation

[167] C. F. G. Masterman, *The Condition of England* (1909), 88.

[168] 'Economic Possibilities for our Grandchildren', pp. vii (preface), 367.

[169] See e.g. the statistics in J. Williams, *Digest of Welsh Historical Statistics* (Aberystwyth, 1985), ii. 272.

[170] See baptismal statistics in *TCBST* 652–3.

in grappling with the serious economic situation then prevailing.[171] Never did the Church of England dominate the public stage more magisterially than in the Queen's coronation of 1953 [Plate 6], when the soaring notes of Parry's 'I was glad' seemed to confirm its integrating power.

Yet its foundations were insecure. Already in 1949 the merging of declining rural parishes so as to conserve resources had begun, with the creation of a single pastoral unit around South Ormsby in Lincolnshire. The prevailing mood of tolerant pluralism that had removed the sting from nonconformity and ensured the advance of Roman Catholicism was not distinct from indifference to organized religion of any kind. Amidst the hurrying life of great cities, people were seldom without light, never silent, never undistracted, always beset by diverse beliefs and priorities. The stars were never seen, the weather's impact dwindled, insurance moderated the hazards of fire and flood, medicine and the natural sciences advanced inexorably, and religion's concerns and even its language were becoming unfamiliar. Urbanization and secularization are mutually reinforcing, and by concentrating attention on the (supposedly removable) fears stemming from human action, urban life left little room for the (irremovable) fears of what the Almighty might do. In the urban environment, scepticism and relativism flourished where indifference did not, and even reflective irreligion seemed redundant. By 1950 the social investigators Rowntree and Lavers feared the impact of religious decline on social reform: 'we are living nationally on what might be called "moral capital accumulated in the past" '.[172] Dwindling simultaneously with organized religion was the associated belief in ghosts. The ghost story and psychical research had flourished at the end of the nineteenth century on the cusp between an organized religion only half abandoned and an intelligent scepticism as yet only half embraced, but after the 1930s the ghost story had passed its apogee. While a sixth of the population sampled by Geoffrey Gorer in 1955 said they believed in ghosts, only 7 per cent claimed to have heard or seen one.[173]

Religion, retreating from the schools for decades, remained educationally important in 1951. Denominational schools broadly reflected the national pattern of religious allegiance, with Anglican schools dominating the sector at both the 'primary' (up to age 11) and 'secondary' (from age 11) stages, but with Roman Catholic schools on the advance.[174] The Education Act (1944) had established a three-way division of secondary schooling in England and Wales: for those qualified there were grammar schools at age 11, and for the rest there were technical schools and 'secondary modern' schools. 'To put this Act as a whole into effect',

[171] P. Williamson, 'The Modern British State and Public Worship: National Days of Prayer, 1900–56' (unpublished paper), n.p. I am most grateful to Professor Williamson for generous help here.

[172] B. S. Rowntree and G. R. Lavers, *English Life and Leisure: A Social Study* (1951), 226; see also 356.

[173] J. Briggs, *Night Visitors: The Rise and Fall of the English Ghost Story* (1977), 16, 19. G. Gorer, *Exploring English Character* (1955), 263–4.

[174] *TCBST* 196–7.

Ellen Wilkinson (Labour's Minister of Education) told parliament in 1946, 'is really a job for a generation'.[175] Repairing wartime damage and backlog and getting this new system into place was a huge task, and schools, like so much else in the late 1940s, competed for desperately scarce resources. All other considerations—diversified curriculum, broadened opportunity, refined approaches to discipline—took second place. By 1951 the 'modern' schools catered for 65 per cent of the secondary-school pupils in England and Wales, 'grammar' schools for 29 per cent, and 'technical' for only 4 per cent; in neglecting the technical school, the Attlee governments had lost the opportunity presented by the school-building programme to harmonize education and the economy more closely.[176] 21,000 primary and secondary state schools in England with 200,000 teachers educated 3,700,000 children in 1951. There were 31 pupils per teacher in primary schools, 21 per teacher in secondary schools, and the pupil–teacher ratio did not improve till the 1960s. The school-leaving pattern in England and Wales was the same for both sexes: in 1950–1 a seventh left at 14, two-thirds at 15, a seventh at 16, leaving only 37,000 pupils still in the system.[177] This was a huge enough state enterprise in itself, all the more impressive for its growing success since the late nineteenth century in combating parental opposition, truancy, and absenteeism—though even in 1951, setting illness aside, holidays with parents accounted for half the absenteeism among younger children in Britain, and 60 per cent of secondary-school girl absentees were helping out at home.[178]

State schooling, provided jointly by local and central government, was seen as offering self-fulfilment in a democratic society, and left only a small role for private provision or direct parental control. Far from making intellect less prominent in public life, Labour's interwar succession to the Liberals involved searching more thoroughly for it, and then lending it more scope through planning. It was on a train in December 1945 that Lancelot Ware met the rich Australian Roland Berrill for a chance conversation which sparked the idea of setting up a society, MENSA, for people of high measured intelligence. The society did not evolve in the directions Ware had envisaged, and the criteria for finding and usefully exploiting disembodied 'intelligence' are controversial, but MENSA's birth reflects the meritocratic mood of the time. There was little political controversy about educational policy: its meritocratic and democratic purposes were consensual. Labour leaders—deeply influenced by Ruskin, Morris, and Tawney—had great respect for education, which had often been their sole route to social opportunity. 'Coming from my kind of background',

[175] *HC Deb.* 1 July 1946, c. 1806.

[176] *BHS* 806–7. B. Alford, '1945–51: Years of Recovery or a Stage in Economic Decline?', in P. Clarke and C. Trebilcock (eds.), *Understanding Decline: Perceptions and Realities of British Economic Performance. Essays Presented to Barry Supple* (Cambridge, 1997), 207.

[177] Dept of Education and Science, *Statistics of Education: Schools in England 1996*, 14; *Statistics of Education 1971*, i. 2–3.

[178] M. J. Tyerman, *Truancy* (1968), 20.

said Harold Wilson, 'teachers were the most important adults in your life.' From Labour's ladder concept of the schools system stemmed the party's loyalty to the grammar school, which it saw as purveying education of the finest type to all who strove for and could benefit from it. Labour's ideal was the grammar school as gateway to opportunity for all, and here the party's aspirations fused with the hopes of those working-class parents who sought for their children the status and security of white-collar employment.[179] With such all-party backing, the grammar schools with their long traditions had little to fear. Any narrowly vocational agenda for schools Labour rejected: working-class status would not improve if working-class children were denied a fully rounded education. Besides, the trade unions feared that a more vocational emphasis would overproduce skilled technicians.

Examinations were seen, not as burdens or barriers, but as merit's opportunity for revealing itself. The schools' examination structure, originating in the university selection process, had been formalized by the universities in 1917 with the aim of producing a broad and balanced curriculum in a two-stage sequence: the school certificate taken at 16, and the higher school certificate taken at 18. By 1951 the system was coming to seem unduly rigid, and school textbooks and examination questions had changed only slowly during the preceding thirty years. Because the examinations targeted candidates aged 16 and above, and because the school-leaving age had risen to 15 so recently, the examinees came overwhelmingly from the independent and grammar schools. With the universities and grammar schools shaping the schools' examination system, the half-articulated resentments felt by its less academic but captive adolescents presented a challenge. They and their working-class parents, with their down-to-earth concern for their children's welfare, doubted whether they were getting the skills the labour market required. The schools' academic priorities may even have helped to devalue such skills: serious disciplinary problems among bored but restless teenagers were bound to result. In his evocative and reflective account of life in a secondary modern 'Middle School' in the early 1960s, John Partridge described how the headmaster kept a cane on top of a tall cupboard in his office: it was 'feared throughout the school . . . short rather like a riding crop being about 18 inches long and about half an inch in diameter', and was applied somewhat randomly to the hand,[180] as were the pieces of wood about two feet long wielded by other teachers.

None the less, in so far as resources allowed, the late 1940s instituted a liberal phase within the British education system's continuously syncopating liberal and reactionary sequence. At least since the 1930s voices had been raised against

[179] B. Pimlott, *Harold Wilson* (1992), 27. M. Sanderson, 'Social Equity and Industrial Need: A Dilemma of English Education since 1945', in T. Gourvish and A. O'Day (eds.), *Britain since 1945* (1991), 163–5, 168–9.

[180] J. Partridge, *Middle School* (1966), 98.

the discipline-and-memorize regime. There were, for instance, anticipations of the 1960s in the report of 1931 from the Board of Education's consultative committee on the primary school: 'the curriculum is to be thought of in terms of activity and experience rather than of knowledge to be acquired and facts to be stored'.[181] By 1947 two-fifths of schools in England and Wales were registered for listening to BBC schools broadcasts.[182] There were even moves to ease the road to literacy through spelling reform, which promised to end the divergence between spoken and written word that had been opening out since the seventeenth century. Promoted from the nineteenth century by Isaac Pitman and reinforced later by Bernard Shaw, the cause was pushed in parliament by the Labour MP Dr Mont Follick, with parliamentary debates on 11 March 1949 and 27 February 1953. Other countries had reformed their spelling systems, he said: why not Britain? He did not prevail for several reasons: vested interests and prejudice, failure of the reformers to agree on a single scheme, and ministers' instinct that the reform was neither important nor popular. For Churchill it was 'one of the stupidest things the House of Commons has ever had before it'.[183]

Despite the state schools' steadily growing numerical dominance, the private schools had long been fertile in new ideas, if only because their very survival required an alert response to changing parental demand. Until 1870 all schools in England and Wales had been private. Even after that, anybody could found a school, and not until 1944 did the state set about counting, inspecting, and (when necessary) closing private schools. The years after 1951 were not a time for educational entrepreneurship, nor a time when the private sector was at its most inventive: the state schools now set the educational fashions. Yet educational entrepreneurs had not died out: in 1951 more of the elite schools in the IAPS had been founded in the 1940s than in any decade since 1900.[184] The Association dated from 1892, when seven prep-school headmasters met in a Marylebone station waiting room to agree on the best size of cricket ball for their pupils. It was at the private prep school that ambitious or assiduous fee-paying parents began buying educational privilege for their children, thereby launching them into a private educational structure that ran in parallel with the state system. Where the state advanced markedly after 1870 was first in primary and then in secondary schools, but private education remained decidedly lively, and throughout the second half of the twentieth century accounted for half a million pupils.[185]

There was a spontaneous twentieth-century dynamic within the British educational system whereby expanded primary education gradually caused

[181] Board of Education, *Report of the Consultative Committee on the Primary School* (1931, rev. edn. 1948), 75.

[182] A. Briggs, *The History of Broadcasting in the United Kingdom*, iv. *Sound and Vision* (Oxford, 1979), 823.

[183] *T* (3 Jan. 1984), 2.

[184] Masters, *Preparatory Schools Today*, 108.

[185] Table 2 in G. Walford, *Privatization and Privilege in Education* (1990), 17.

secondary education also to expand, and this in turn pushed up university numbers. The percentage of the age group entering full-time higher education rose throughout the century, and by the early 1950s had reached 3 per cent, less than a quarter of whom were women. Of university students in Great Britain in 1949–50, 44 per cent studied arts and social sciences, 16 per cent pure science, 16 per cent applied science and technology, and 21 per cent medical sciences, with the women heavily slanted towards arts and social studies courses.[186] At 24 per cent in 1950/1, the proportion of university students living in colleges or halls of residence was small by later standards, whereas the proportion in lodgings (39%) and at home (37%) was relatively large. However, the genuinely local university, with all its advantages of cheapness and local loyalty, was on the point of decline. Universities were increasingly funded by central government, with a shrinking share of their income drawn from local authorities, fees, endowments and donations.[187] With universities expanding fast, with state scholarships opening them up to new talent, with full employment, and with British political institutions validated by wartime victory, British university student politics fed readily into the two-party system. Rejection of the established political structure was far less modish in 1951 than in the 1930s and the 1960s.

Reinforcing growth was the inexorable advance of natural science, whose prestige the war had boosted. The discovery of penicillin, radar, atomic power, and the jet engine symbolized national scientific achievement and potential. Already by 1938/9 the arts and social sciences had become a minority among the staff of British universities, and their proportion continued to fall thereafter, whereas the proportion in pure and applied science had been rising for decades.[188] J. D. Bernal had trenchantly asserted the claims of natural science in 1939 through his widely read *The Social Function of Science*: scientific research simultaneously benefited mankind, he said, by solving the problem of scarcity, and was 'profoundly satisfying' to the researcher. He wanted research placed at the heart of science teaching, with a career ladder enabling the lab assistant to join the new profession of research scientist. There was a tenfold real increase in government expenditure on civil science between 1945/6 and 1962/3,[189] with rapid growth in both university-based science and government-sponsored civil and defence research. The impact of so huge an influx on the universities' priorities, style, vocabulary, and overall culture was profound; research, often collaborative and costly, became ever more central to their role.

The internationalism of twentieth-century research, integral to natural science, further boosted growth, and was reinforced during the 1940s by

[186] *TCBST* 226, 237. *TBS* 216. [187] *TCBST* 239, 246–7. [188] *TBS* 216.

[189] J. D. Bernal, *The Social Function of Science* (1st publ. 1939, 2nd edn. 1940), 94. T. Wilkie, *British Science and Politics since 1945* (Oxford, 1991), 49.

European immigrants. Under capitalism, wrote Karl Marx, 'national one-sidedness and narrow-mindedness become more and more impossible, and from the numerous national and local literatures there arises a world literature'.[190] However worldwide her seaborne trading connections, Britain's interwar cultural connections had been relatively narrow, and Jewish immigrants of the 1930s eventually endowed Britain with thirteen Nobel prizewinners, sixty-three Fellows of the Royal Society, and thirty-one Fellows of the British Academy.[191] Without the conductor Fritz Busch and the producer Carl Ebert, the Glyndebourne Festival Theatre could hardly have rejuvenated British opera in the 1930s; and without its first artistic director Rudolf Bing, the Edinburgh Festival might never have got off the ground. Refugees infused British cultural life with European perspectives, pushing further forward the attack that Albert Prince Consort had conducted a century earlier on British cultural insularity.

So heady an intellectual climate drowned out anxieties about the trend, but already in 1930 the Cambridge critic F. R. Leavis had found the pejorative term 'high-brow', American in origin, 'an ominous addition to the language'; he and his wife put their faith in a missionary intellectual elite which would counteract the cultural drawbacks of aristocratic decline. By the late 1940s the mutually supportive alliance between aristocracy, established church, and high culture was breaking up, and standards seemed to need new safeguards. T. S. Eliot was among the sceptics: in 1948 he noted how an increasingly complex society fragmented the elite. The intellectual elite's internal diversification (philosophical, artistic, scientific) seemed 'a growing weakness of our culture'. The mutual isolation was damaging enough in itself, but 'perhaps even more important' was 'the lack of those contacts and mutual influences at a less conscious level'.[192] The 'learned journal' had almost completely ousted the great Victorian monthly and quarterly reviews, and unlike them attracted only specialists. The diminished influence of the classical languages and the Bible placed many English literary classics out of reach. Doubts were reinforced by fears of Americanization, which at a more popular level was the major postwar cultural influence on Britain. American usages, slang, fashions, and popular music carried great postwar prestige. American affluence and glamour pervaded British postwar youth culture in a non-political way, and Britain lacked the insulating language barrier which protected the French against them, for all the BBC efforts to clarify the proprieties in its 'Green Book'. In 1948 Wilson as President of the Board of Trade felt the need to attack 'the gangster, sadistic and psychological films' that the Americans were exporting, urging screen writers

[190] K. Marx, *The Communist Manifesto* (1st publ. 1848; ed. H. J. Laski, 1948 edn.), 125.

[191] P. Pulzer, 'Foreigners: The Immigrant in Britain', in W. E. Mosse, *Second Chance: Two Centuries of German-Speaking Jews in the United Kingdom* (Tübingen, 1991), 8 n. 4.

[192] F. R. Leavis, *Mass Civilisation and Minority Culture* (Cambridge, 1930), 25. T. S. Eliot, *Notes towards the Definition of Culture* (1st publ. 1948, paperback edn. 1962), 38.

instead 'to go up to the north of England, Scotland, Wales and the rest of the country, and to all the parts of London which are not so frequently portrayed in our films'.[193]

The Liberal and Labour critics of aristocratic culture in the late 1940s had not yet lost hope or sold out. The wartime Army Bureau of Current Affairs and the energy of Penguin Books ensured that postwar adult education was very much alive, and meshed in well with the Leavises' programme, promoted through their periodical *Scrutiny* until its demise in 1953. The private circulating libraries had been declining since the 1930s, and the second-hand bookshop, once so central to popular self-education, was already heading for its late-twentieth-century downturn. Nostalgia pervaded Harold Laski's account in 1943 of the 'magic shop' in Sheffield's Glossop Road which had supplied all his wants: 'a town without a good bookseller', he wrote, 'is like a body without a soul'. On the other hand, public library books in stock and book issues mounted continuously in twentieth-century Britain, and grew by leaps and bounds after 1945,[194] and British publishing was vibrant: by 1951 the total number of book titles issued by British publishers had recovered from its wartime trough and surpassed its prewar level.[195] Although in the number of books (as distinct from book titles) produced in 1952 the UK could not even approach the USSR, it easily surpassed the rest, including the USA. Of the titles published in the UK and Ireland in 1953, 'literature' took up by far the largest proportion with 38 per cent, followed by useful arts/applied sciences (14%), social sciences (13%), history/geography (11%), and pure science, religion, and fine arts/recreation (each with 6%).[196]

Hopes were still high in 1951 of what the state could achieve through funding the fine arts. Outlining in 1945 the role of the new Arts Council, Keynes looked forward 'to the time when the theatre and the concert-hall and the gallery will be a living element in everyone's upbringing, and regular attendance at the theatre and at concerts a part of organised education'; the Council would, he claimed, be keen to encourage artistic enterprise outside London. Arts patronage from this new source—supplementing what government already spent on historic buildings, museums, and galleries—grew fast, and almost doubled in real terms between 1946 and 1951.[197] The outcome did not necessarily gear in with

[193] *HC Deb.* 17 June 1948, c. 775.

[194] *NS* (31 July 1943), repr. in K. Martin, *Harold Laski (1893–1950): A Biographical Memoir* (1953), 278. *BPF* (8th edn.), 367.

[195] See figures in *Bookseller* (31 Dec. 1936), 736; (5 Jan. 1957), 11; *Mumby's Publishing and Bookselling in the Twentieth Century* (6th edn., 1st publ. 1982, paperback edn. 1984), 220 (app. 1).

[196] R. E. Barker, *Books for All: A Study of International Book Trade* (Paris, 1956), 23, 20.

[197] Keynes, 'The Arts Council: Its Policy and Hopes', *Listener* (12 July 1945), repr. in his *Collected Writings*, ed. D. Moggridge, xxviii (1982), 371. For a good run of statistics see House of Commons Education, Science and Arts Committee, *8th Report, Session 1981–2: Public and Private Funding of the Arts* (1982), ii. 308.

popular taste. In order to decide what should be funded, public bodies (unlike the private collector) were not required to back their hunches with their own money, nor did they have to live with the consequences of their decisions, which were reached in committees of alleged experts. This made for compromise or 'safe' choices acceptable to those in the know, if not to the general public. By mid-century many artists and writers were lifting up their skirts to avoid being soiled by any search for popularity. At a time when rising real incomes and reduced working hours presented British cultural life with major new opportunities, the gulf between high and low culture remained wide.

Few in 1951 thought of using the term 'media' as a collective noun to describe printed and electronic means of communication, though the career of Lew Grade (theatre impresario, film producer, and television guru) was by no means unique in moving freely between them.[198] In the 1950s and 1960s newspapers were still the major organs for public discussion. The Royal Commission on the Press in 1949 thought it 'generally agreed that the British press is inferior to none in the world' in being so free from corruption and the direct influence of advertisers on policy. If the process had not been so familiar, the newspapers' daily production process, gathering and distributing material from all over the world 'for less than the price of a box of matches . . . would be recognized as an astonishing achievement'.[199] The process itself generated built-in organizational conservatism: no product then depended so heavily for its production on collaboration between workers by hand and brain. The trade unions were entrenched against change, and proprietors beset by intense competition appeased rather than risk a stoppage. So while national papers occasionally died, relocated, or changed their name, few new ones appeared, and the overall slow trend favoured amalgamation.

Of both the daily and the weekly (including Sunday) British papers on sale in 1947, the national dailies accounted for two-thirds of the circulation, the provincials for the rest. The so-called 'quality' daily national papers had by then captured less than a tenth of the total daily nationals' circulation, and only 4 per cent of the Sunday nationals' circulation—a situation almost identical with that prevailing ten years before. In all categories of newspaper, however, circulation was much higher in 1947 than ten years earlier,[200] and the circulation of weekly and monthly periodicals was much healthier in 1951 than later. Of the five 'class' weeklies, *Punch* and the *Listener* each sold about 14,000, the *New Statesman* about 70,000, *The Economist* about 50,000, and the

198 Briggs, *Sound and Vision*, 17. *T* (14 Dec. 1998), 21 (Grade).

199 Quotations from Royal Commission on the Press, *Report*, PP 1948–9 (Cmnd. 7700), xx. 149, 37.

200 C.-J. Bertrand (ed.), *The British Press: An Historical Survey* (Paris, 1969), 202. The 'qualities' then conventionally comprised the daily *Times, Daily Telegraph,* and *Manchester Guardian*, later joined by the *Independent* and (as it became less specialized) the *Financial Times*. On Sundays they comprised *The Sunday Times* and the *Observer*, later joined by the *Sunday Telegraph* and *Independent on Sunday*.

Spectator about 30,000. There was also a lively trade in popular weeklies. The leaders were *Reveille*, with a spectacular recent rise to about 3,600,000; *Woman* (3 million), also sharply rising; and *Woman's Own* (2,200,000). All round about the million mark were *Picture Post*, with a distinguished wartime history but now on a declining trend together with *Everybody's* and *Illustrated*, though *John Bull* had arrested its earlier decline;[201] all four died between 1957 and 1960. Circulation figures in themselves say little: at least as important are readership and content. By American standards British national newspapers in 1951 were small, reaching an average of eight pages by 1952,[202] and newsprint controls were not finally lifted till the end of 1958. Newspapers in 1951 had not yet succumbed to the curtailed attention span and visual emphasis later imported from television; *The Times* had not even succumbed to headlines. Political and high-cultural influence rested with the quality dailies and Sundays, but the *Daily Mirror*'s irreverent populism illustrates how a tabloid, too, could make a distinctive impact.

The 1940s were the heyday of the film, with cinema and admissions numbers only beginning to decline towards the end of the decade. Representative of the nation as a whole by sex and social status, though slanted towards youth, these audiences went on average fortnightly to one of the 4,597 cinemas open in 1951.[203] They took their accent, behaviour, and expectations from what they saw on the screen: in 1951 Miss D, an 18-year-old bank clerk, was quoted as saying that 'after seeing the polished lover on the screen it is rather disillusioning to be kissed by a clumsy inexperienced boy'.[204] Going to the cinema was an event, with large and often rather grand auditoria, with a documentary newsreel in addition to main and supporting films, and with the national anthem as a grand finale. Radio, unlike television, complemented the cinema and posed little threat to it. 11.5 million sound licences had been taken out by 1951, but only 760,000 combined sound and vision licences.[205] Monopoly until 1955 made the BBC an integrating national institution, a position consolidated by popular national serial programmes such as *Have a Go* (launched in 1946), *Dick Barton, Special Agent* (1946), *Gardeners' Question Time* (1947), *Take It From Here* (1947), *Mrs Dale's Diary* (1948), and *Any Questions* (1948). In 1951 few people owned a television set (only 4% of the UK's adult population in 1950). Launched in 1936, television had been shut down during the war, and did not revive till 1946. By 1951 some programmes were already making a national impact: for example, Philip Harben's cookery programmes from 1947, the first

[201] A. P. Wadsworth, 'Newspaper Circulations 1800–1954', *Transactions of the Manchester Statistical Society* (session 1954–5), 39–40.

[202] D. C. West, 'The Growth and Development of the Advertising Industry within the United Kingdom, 1920–1970' (Leeds, Ph.D. thesis, 1984), 60.

[203] Rowntree and Lavers, *English Life and Leisure*, 229–31. *TBS* (1972), 558–9.

[204] Rowntree and Lavers, *English Life and Leisure*, 250.

[205] Briggs, *Sound and Vision*, 240.

televised report of general election results in 1950, and *What's My Line?* in 1951. Although the high cost of a set excluded the poor, and a higher proportion of the rich owned one, by no means all the well-to-do wanted one: indeed, there was for many years a certain snob value in not having one. Demand was increasingly driven from below: whereas 16 per cent of those owning a television in 1954 came from the most affluent eighth of the population, 59 per cent came from the least affluent two-thirds.[206] Television was now beginning to compete with the cinema; it also competed with the press for providing the latest news, specially hitting the evening papers, which had hitherto often been bought for their sports results.

Postwar Britain saw recreational opportunity richly diversified in other areas too, so that leisure was already becoming a distinct area of life with its own entrepreneurs, locations, and even values. Footballing professionalism had begun in the north of England, but from the 1920s began to spread southwards; with the subsequent long-term decline in Britain's staple industries, the proportion of northern clubs in the First Division fell from two-thirds in 1930 to only a quarter in 1990. Working-class sporting skill was amply displayed on the postwar football field, and in the first quarter of 1949 football pools attracted more than 11 million people over 21, at every social level, though more commonly lower down than higher up, and with a marked male slant.[207] It did not yet seem that Britain had much to learn from other countries on the sporting front: British superiority in the national sports—football and cricket—was taken for granted, as were the associated traditions of fair play. Gambling was particularly widespread in sports involving animals: in a sample of 1949 only a quarter of British adults over 16 refrained from all betting, and about half the men and a third of the women laid a bet in the Derby. In the following year attendance at the large greyhound racing tracks, though falling fast, still totalled almost four million.[208] Sport's long-standing links with country life, the landed classes, and war were now weakening, but in 1951 the universities remained centres of sporting excellence, and the amateur prowess of the better nourished classes had not yet succumbed to sporting professionalism.

Orwell's private people of flower-lovers, pigeon-fanciers, and crossword-puzzle fans remained active in their gardens, pubs, and clubs. Mrs Cruft had sold the family's dog show to the Kennel Club during the war, and the first show held under the Club's auspices was at Olympia in 1948. Diet was diversifying as refrigeration enabled new foods from overseas to tempt the

[206] *TBS* 552. Briggs, *Sound and Vision*, 12; see also 250–1.

[207] J. Bale, *Sport, Space and the City* (1993), 136. Rowntree and Lavers, *English Life and Leisure*, 126, 135–6. Hulton Press, *Patterns of British Life*, 142.

[208] Carr-Saunders *et al.*, *Survey of Social Conditions*, 249–50; M. Clapson, *A Bit of a Flutter: Popular Gambling and English Society, c.1823–1961* (Manchester, 1992), 154, cf. 158.

British palate, and new dietary choices were being consolidated. Teetotalism and vegetarianism had advanced dietary freedom in the nineteenth century, and in 1944 the conscientious objector Donald Watson launched the vegan offshoot from vegetarianism with his *Vegan News*.[209] As for improved home cooking, the ground had been laid before the war. Rosemary Hume's interwar cookery school for the well-to-do was relaunched in collaboration with Constance Spry in 1945, eventually settling with its associated restaurant in Marylebone; 'coronation chicken' was a dish allegedly invented by Spry when asked to help with catering at the coronation of 1953. Orwell's list in 1945 of foods unique to Britain included kippers, Yorkshire pudding, treacle tart, roast potatoes, and Cox's apples, but because most pubs then served only drink, good English food was usually available only at home. The trend towards eating out had, however, begun, and Chinese, Greek, and Italian restaurateurs set the pace. It was a much-needed improvement: Doris Lessing vividly recalled the postwar scene where the municipally subsidized dining rooms 'were often the only places to eat in a whole area of streets. They served good meat, terrible vegetables, nursery puddings. Lyons restaurants were the high point of eating for ordinary people—I remember fish and chips and poached eggs on toast . . . You could not get a decent cup of coffee anywhere in the British Isles.'[210]

7. POLITICS AND GOVERNMENT

Victory in 1945 encouraged complacency about the British political system. Criticized on all sides—by Liberals, Fascists, and Communists—between the wars, its prestige had now revived: European democracies might succumb to authoritarian regimes, but British democracy seemed to possess some magic ingredient. For these reasons, and because economic and international issues were more pressing, the Attlee governments were more conservative on constitutional matters than any subsequent Labour government. Complacency was perhaps not harmful in the short term, for when victory in war is followed by long-term decline, constitutional continuity brings stability and reassurance. Given the politicians' skill in managing Britain's decline, the virtues of such novelties as proportional representation, federal structures, and judicial review did not seem obvious. The BBC's postwar ban on jokes about the political system in comedy programmes reflected respect for the system, not fears for its future.

The monarchy's role had by 1951 become more social than political: Earl Attlee could not recall a single instance during his premiership when the King's

[209] Obituary, *T* (8 Dec. 2005), 67.

[210] D. Lessing, *Walking in the Shade* (1997), 4. See also Orwell's 'In Defence of English Cooking' (1945), in his *Complete Works*, xvii (1998), 446–7.

views influenced appointments or policy.[211] Attlee's aim as prime minister was efficiently to coordinate powerful colleagues. In 1949 at a dinner for socialist journalists, after patiently hearing suggestions for lending government personalities more impact, he declared that 'Public Relations Officers do not exist in order to build up the personalities of Ministers. They exist in order to explain Government policy', adding disarmingly, 'I should be a sad subject for any publicity expert. I have none of the qualities which create publicity.'[212] In 1951 it was neither monarch nor prime minister, but parliament and party that were central to the system. Their influence was coordinated through a rather earnest and high-minded cabinet scrupulous about keeping election pledges, keen to keep the state machine uncorrupt, and constitutionally correct. Even on the crucial decision for an independent nuclear deterrent, where a secretive Attlee allegedly impaired democratic control, a delicate balance had to be struck: democracy's practice required wide consultation, but its defence against the USSR required reticence.[213] An elaborate hierarchy of cabinet subcommittees inherited from Churchill's war cabinet was continued in peacetime to ensure the cabinet's overall grasp of what became an ambitious legislative programme. This was coordinated through Morrison, who as Leader of the Commons skilfully managed parliamentary pressures. He loved the House of Commons, had a good feel for its moods, and defused potential trouble through being accessible to MPs and mobilizing them into policy groups and committee work. 'The Parliament of 1945–50 achieved great things', he wrote later; 'it demonstrated that Parliament could be a workshop as well as discharging its necessary functions as a talk-shop. It was shown that legislative programmes could be planned in good time for the Session, and over the Parliament as a whole.'[214]

The Westminster-based political system, monarchical in origin, was highly centralized, and the Victorians had given it an uncorrupt civil service, reinforced after the 1860s by nationwide party structures which marshalled opinion behind it. Underpinning the system were a class structure that centred on the London 'season', on parliament, and on the City of London; a system of independent boarding schools for the elite; and a pair of 'national' universities, powerful within the entire educational structure, ready to help government when in trouble, and adept at preparing pupils selected on merit to join it. Margaret Thatcher, plucked by Oxford from Grantham in the 1940s, had no intention of going back there.[215] The Attlee governments' programme of nationalization and public

211 J. P. Mackintosh, *The British Cabinet* (1st publ. 1962, 3rd edn. 1977), 7.

212 Nicolson, *Diaries and Letters, 1945–1962*, 163.

213 R. Blake, *The Office of Prime Minister* (1975), 52; comments of George Strauss in 'Everybody's Politician' (Radio 4 broadcast, 2 Jan. 1983).

214 H. Morrison, *Government and Parliament: A Survey from the Inside* (3rd edn. 1964), 254.

215 H. Young, *One of Us* (1st publ. 1989, final edn. 1993), 28–9.

welfare extended central government's size and reach still further. Less wary of civil servants than any later Labour governments, the Attlee governments felt no need for numerous political advisers to enforce the politician's will. Later commentators were surprised that these governments left the civil service largely as they found it. The commentators were hindsighted: the civil service was busy enough with serious economic and foreign-policy pressures, and needed no other distractions. Besides, restructuring was redundant, given the successful wartime operation of a machine which was adapting readily to peacetime working. The Labour Party did not seek to change the system: it wanted to show its supporters and others that it could run it as effectively as anybody else.

In two respects, centralizing pressures were more powerful in 1951 than later. The UK was seen politically and in other ways as an entity. Although southern Ireland in the late 1940s was in the last stages of disentangling itself constitutionally from Great Britain, the solidarity between England, Scotland, Wales, and Northern Ireland had been nourished by their shared contribution towards the growth of empire and towards victory in two world wars. The pressures for devolution, seemingly advancing until the 1920s, had fallen back thereafter and had yet to revive. The two-party system, at its apogee in 1945–66, worked in the same direction. The Labour Party in alliance with the trade unions had done much to integrate the first three of these four regions through highlighting social-class and welfare issues together with the need to resolve them through nationwide redistribution and planning. Aneurin Bevan in 1944 denounced from the Labour back benches the very idea of having a 'Welsh day' in parliament as a 'farce'; the Miners' Federation, he said, 'have no special Welsh solution for the Welsh coal industry which is not a solution for the whole of the mining industry of Great Britain. There is no Welsh coal problem.'[216] The Conservative Party upheld the union less subtly, through marshalling an explicit commitment to it, especially in the Scottish lowlands and Northern Ireland, where Unionists seemed as yet in full control. Ulster Unionism, unlike Welsh and Scottish nationalism, was a form of local nationalism whose essence was to uphold the union, whereas Welsh and Scottish nationalism undermined it. For the moment, though, Celtic nationalism seemed an impractical, backward-looking, minority, and even eccentric cause.

Centralization's second dimension in 1951 was the cultural concomitant of the UK's political integration: the idea that metropolitan ways of speech and even culture are superior to provincial. 'Provincial' accents within England had for long been discouraged among the socially ambitious in favour of the 'correct' English or 'received pronunciation' that had originated in the south-east of England, and an army of elocutionists and schoolteachers upheld

[216] *HC Deb.* 17 Oct. 1944, cc. 2312–13.

it. By the 1940s the dialect of southern England brought social status, and was spoken everywhere within the social elite. Partly because dominant in the media, this was still the basis on which foreigners were taught the English language half a century later, despite then being spoken by only 3 per cent of the English population. So for many children there were practical arguments for spontaneously forsaking their parents' traditional ways of speech, especially when industrialization and war generated large movements of population. Thatcher was born in 1925; as a Grantham teenager aiming high, she got her father to fund elocution lessons. According to her headmistress, 'she simply told her father, then a school governor: "Daddy, one has got to speak properly"'.[217]

Similar considerations applied between the UK nationalities. The Scottish tradition of seeking a fortune in England continued, and the English-born minority in Scotland simultaneously grew consistently throughout the twentieth century, except for the 1920s, especially when English servicemen moved north during the Second World War and later for national service.[218] Population movements accelerated the decline in minority languages. Between 1891 and 1961 the percentage of Gaelic speakers in Scotland fell continuously; by 1951 only 2 per cent spoke the language, of whom only 2,661 people were Gaelic monoglots.[219] After the seventeenth century even English in its lower-status Scottish variant came under sustained attack from elocutionists and others, and eventually ceased to be distinct. As for Wales, the share of Welsh-speaking monoglots in its population over 3 years of age had fallen continuously since 1891 to 1.7 per cent in 1951, when only 29 per cent could speak the language. In the Isle of Man there were no monoglot Manx language speakers at all in 1931, and by 1951 only 355 people at most could speak the language.[220] The Cornish language had long disappeared, and the county's identity seemed so much at risk as to prompt the foundation of Mebyon Kernow (Sons of Cornwall) in 1951, with self-government in the Channel Isles and the Isle of Man as the model, 'to maintain the character of Cornwall as a Celtic nation, to promote the interests of Cornwall and the Cornish people and to promote the constitutional advance of Cornwall and its right to self government in domestic affairs'.[221]

If its social-class preoccupations opposed the Labour Party to nationalism, its welfare and planning preoccupations in practice opposed it to local government. In such spheres, efficiency and fairness seemed to dictate uniformity and hence

217 Margaret Gillies in *Daily Mail* (5 May 1979), 6. See also A. Hughes and P. Trudgill, *English Accents and Dialects: An Introduction to Social and Regional Varieties of English in the British Isles* (1st publ. 1979, 3rd edn. 1996), 3.

218 For a good discussion see M. Watson, 'Using the Third Statistical Account of Scotland to Expose a Major Gap in Scottish Historiography', *Contemporary British History* (Spring 2004), 104–5.

219 C. W. J. Withers, *Gaelic in Scotland 1698–1981* (Edinburgh, 1984), 213, 238.

220 Williams, *Welsh Historical Statistics*, i. 86. G. Price, *The Languages of Britain* (1984), 81–2.

221 P. B. Ellis, *The Cornish Language and its Literature* (1974), 177.

the erosion of local discretion. Just as efficiency seemed to require nationalized concerns to be run from London, with management devolved to large administrative regions, so fairness seemed to require shifting control of welfare structures upwards from the local community to the county borough or county council, and often to central government. The introduction of the National Health Service (NHS) in 1946, for example, transferred control over hospitals from local authorities to regional boards; and in 1948 the National Assistance Act abolished the poor law and transferred local-authority responsibilities for the outdoor relief of poverty to the assistance board. This centralizing transfer of power was opposed on democratic grounds at the time. Churchill, for example, speaking in Edinburgh in 1950, stressed the threat to Scotland's status that socialist centralization and nationalization entailed.[222] Later critics who say that the Attlee governments' socialist interventionism should have been more energetic neglect what was then the libertarian mood of the country and even of the labour movement itself. A worldwide battle had, after all, been recently fought to defend freedom. When the Minister of Town and Country Planning described the New Towns Bill as 'a daring exercise in town planning', his Stevenage audience jeered, and there were cries of 'dictator' and 'Gestapo'.[223] Wilson, then the young President of the Board of Trade, shrewdly realized in 1948–9 that popularity could accrue from a 'bonfire of controls'.

Behind all this lay a two-party system now well entrenched. By 1945 the Labour and Conservative parties had squeezed the Liberals into a very poor third place. The twentieth century had seen a continuously rising share of the adult population registered as voters—as many as 98 per cent by 1949. So automatic had the equation between voting and adulthood come to seem that when the age of majority fell in 1969, the qualifying age for voting fell with it.[224] Election turnouts, 84 per cent in 1950 and 83 per cent in 1951, were not yet declining. Both parties espoused notions of community. Labour's socialism had never been a dry or doctrinaire theoretical commitment: it was the political embodiment of neighbourliness, the working out at the national level of community values developed within nonconformist chapel, trade union branch, co-op, and close-knit working-class residential area. Long before assuming power, Labour had prefigured in its own structure—with its own classless institutions for mutual help and education—the type of society it envisaged for the UK as a whole. Many Labour cabinet ministers up to 1950 were drawn from middle- or working-class families with a strong tradition of public service, whether in local government, on the magistrates'

[222] W. L. Miller (ed.), *Anglo-Scottish Relations from 1900 to Devolution and Beyond* (Oxford, 2005), 28.

[223] G. Wilson, *Cases and Materials on Constitutional and Administrative Law* (2nd edn. Cambridge, 1976), 611–12.

[224] *BPF* (8th edn. 2000), 258. See also below, pp. 263, 505–6.

bench, in nonconformist chapels, humanitarian structures, or trade unions.[225] Labour was allied with a trade union movement whose strategy had never since the eighteenth century been conspiratorial, and which was now accepted as an estate of the realm. Likewise Conservatives still thought in terms of a national family whose inevitable hierarchies reflected the need to combine in self-defence against a hostile nature and against potentially hostile foreigners. The party's rural, traditionalist, and largely deferential notion of community differed more in rhetoric than in reality from Labour's ideal. Whatever Labour's formal constitutional structure and extra-parliamentary traditions might be, the powers of its leader and MPs were in practice by the 1940s as well adjusted as their Conservative equivalents to the need for a direct relationship between the MP and his constituent.[226] Established in power with a majority for the first time in 1945 after an electoral landslide, Labour was fully integrated into the British parliamentary system.

More than this, Labour in the 1940s saw itself as moving towards electoral supremacy. For several reasons the voters' conversion seemed only a matter of time and education: capitalism's defects had been exposed in the 1930s, the two world wars had advertised how the state could mobilize the economy and enhance welfare, the party's close link with fast-growing trade unions seemed a mounting asset, and important intellectual and middle-class interests lent Labour (despite its name) a classless appeal. After the party had substituted opting out for opting into the trade union political levy in 1946, the levy's real value leapt forward.[227] When Sir Hartley Shawcross declared in 1946 that 'we are the masters at the moment, and not only at the moment, but for a very long time to come'[228] (abbreviated by the press to 'we are the masters now'), his remark then seemed so obvious as to make little impact. In by-elections between 1945 and 1951 Labour did not lose a single seat, though the Independent Labour Party lost one Scottish seat to the Conservatives in 1948. At the dissolution of 1950 Labour had an overall parliamentary majority of 140, and at the general elections of 1950 and 1951 Labour's voters reached the highest levels to date. In 1965 R. H. S. Crossman, by then himself a Labour cabinet minister, even argued that if only Attlee had not called a general election in 1951, the short-term political and economic crisis would have passed and a third consecutive general election might have been won.[229]

In 1951 Labour was as important for its stabilizing role as for its radicalism. Its capacity for practical achievement and for working-class self-realization ensured that parliament was the beneficiary of radical forces in the country

[225] J. Bonnor, 'The Four Labour Cabinets', *Sociological Review* (1958), 45–7.

[226] See the argument in R. T. McKenzie, *British Political Parties* (2nd edn. 1963), 334, 639.

[227] M. Pinto-Duschinsky, *British Political Finance 1830–1980* (Washington, DC, and London, 1981), 213–14.

[228] *HC Deb.* 2 Apr. 1946, c. 1213.

[229] R. H. S. Crossman, *Planning for Freedom* (1965), 127.

which might otherwise have taken less democratic directions. Its welfare state took the edge off any working-class sense of grievance, and the wartime taxation structure brought the working class permanently within the reach of income tax, paradoxically exposing Labour's traditional voters to other suitors. Labour's instinctive corporatism also had the effect of drawing the trade unions (together with the Federation of British Industries) towards governmental responsibilities and away from voluntarism; the long-term collective welfare seemed thereby likely to prevail over the short-term self-interest of self-organized groups. The Attlee governments, when necessary, could be at least as robust as their Conservative successors in handling trade unions; secure in the backing of Bevin the interwar trade union grandee, Labour felt able to send troops into the docks during dock strikes on many occasions, and to brave opposition from the Transport and General Workers' Union (TGWU) leadership.[230]

Some socialists had been drawn towards Communism by the interwar Fascist danger, by doubts about whether capitalism could end the depression, and in the 1940s by respect for the USSR's wartime sufferings and determination. Once the Molotov-Ribbentrop pact between the two totalitarian powers Nazi Germany and the USSR (1939) had ended in 1941, Communists became the fiercest foes of Fascism. The true nature of Stalin's oppressive regime was not yet widely known, and within the British labour movement Communists won the status which flows from intelligence, self-denial, and commitment. Their opponents within the labour movement were forced to mobilize and elaborate a counter-case: 'right or wrong in their opinions, the Communist Party members had opinions', an anti-Communist secretary of Hackney Trades Council somewhat nostalgically recalled after the USSR's collapse. 'They had texts. They had an interpretation and we had to argue with it. And argue we did, meeting after meeting.' He might have added that the Communists' strange amalgam of idealism and cynicism offered a moral challenge. Mainstream Labour politicians like Wilson admired Soviet planning and yearned to reconcile it through the Labour Party with democracy and liberty;[231] Conservative centrists fed off the desire to render capitalist society defensible; and Conservatives further right were forced to uphold capitalism practically and sometimes even theoretically. Thus did the Communists edge the entire British political system leftwards.

This helps to explain why the Conservative Party, some of whose traditions were wary of the state and inclined towards the free market, challenged socialism so cautiously. The Conservatives' rhetorical challenge was vigorous enough, and they saw propagandist value in officially describing opponents as 'Socialist'

[230] J. Phillips, 'The Postwar Political Consensus and Industrial Unrest in the Docks, 1945–55', *TCBH* 6/3 (1995), 316–17.

[231] Michael Knowles in *G* (31 Aug. 1991), 23. P. Foot, *The Politics of Harold Wilson* (Harmondsworth, 1968), 111.

rather than 'Labour'. The Conservative manifesto of 1951 claimed that 'the attempt to impose a doctrinaire Socialism upon an Island which has grown great and famous by free enterprise has inflicted serious injury upon our strength and prosperity'.[232] We have seen how Hayek's *The Road to Serfdom* had already presented the free-market case against the Attlee governments' approach before Attlee had even won power. 'Today it is almost heresy to suggest that scientific knowledge is not the sum of all knowledge', wrote Hayek in 1945, yet only the spontaneous operation of the free market could make publicly available information known to individuals which governments could not acquire.[233] None the less, such ideas, however welcome they might seem to some Conservatives, could not be overtly espoused in the late 1940s. Some prominent Conservative centrists even thought their party's name embarrassing, Woolton preferring 'Union Party' and Macmillan 'New Democratic Party'.[234] In 1976, recalling how his *Road to Serfdom* was received, Hayek said he 'was made to feel by most of my fellow social scientists that I had used my abilities on the wrong side'.[235] Conservatives in the late 1940s were bidding for Liberal voters moulded not only by the Liberal Party's individualist traditions, but by its collectivist traditions as well. Besides, Conservatives had worked so closely with Labour leaders in the wartime coalition as to render implausible the claim of the philosophers Hayek and Karl Popper that socialism was inextricably linked to Fascist and/or Communist authoritarianism. A Conservative consensual and pragmatic appeal, capitalizing on the Attlee governments' mistakes but accepting some of their most popular reforms, chimed in with electoral prudence, but also with the instincts and traditions of the party and its leader.

Political participation could be less widely diffused in the more deferential society of the 1940s, where information was less public and less abundant than later. The American term 'pressure group' was rarely used in Britain till the 1960s, though the British pedigree for its reality was long indeed. Such pressures on government as then existed often came from within the establishment, aiming to help it. There was a long tradition whereby British governments interacted with the public through semi-autonomous intermediaries: the University Grants Committee (UGC) and the BBC, for example.[236] Other such groups—smaller and London-based, some of them later labelled 'think tanks'—specialized in applying academic disciplines to governments' practical problems. Several shadowed Whitehall departments: for the Ministry of Education, the Institute of Education (founded in 1902); for the Foreign Office, the Royal Institute of International Affairs (founded in 1920); for the

232 Dale (ed.), *Conservative Manifestos*, 95.
233 F. A. Hayek, 'The Use of Knowledge in Society', *American Economic Review* (Sept. 1945), 521.
234 Horne, *Macmillan*, 298.
235 F. A. Hayek, *The Road to Serfdom* (1944), p. vii (preface to 1976 edn.).
236 *T* (13 Sept. 1978), 2.

Treasury, the Institute of Economic and Social Research (founded in 1938).[237] The British Legion (founded in 1921) and Political and Economic Planning (founded in 1931) exemplify influential pressure groups not tied to any one department or political party. Much external pressure was channelled through political parties, and some pressure groups were associated, not always overtly, with them: for Labour, the Fabian Society and many trade unions for example, and for the Conservatives, such bodies as Aims of Industry (founded in 1942) and the British Housewives' League (founded in 1945). But in the 1940s many pressures emerged from informal gatherings at Westminster, at the elite universities, and within the churches: from dining clubs, networks of friends, self-consciously altruistic professional associations, and commercial groups which saw no conflict between self-interest and the public interest. For all its overtly socialist and democratic self-image in 1951, Britain by later standards could offer only a diluted variant of political participation.

8. A BACKWARD AND FORWARD LOOK

The sevenfold discussion above has shown that Britain in 1951 was by later standards relatively integrated. It was self-confident enough to engage in mild forms of national self-mockery, and national pride did not prompt self-glorification. The national memory for military defeats and setbacks was lively, and little need was felt until the 1960s for national self-advertisement through commemorative stamp issues. The UK's wartime role in defending democracy had been distinctive and important, and its political institutions had stood the strain. Although several immigrant groups arrived in the 1940s, they did not disturb what later seemed the somewhat hermetic flavour of British society. In so far as the UK had overseas links, the strongest still lay with the empire/Commonwealth, which did not yet seem doomed to rapid decline; indeed, it seemed all the stronger for the fact that Britain and her allies had prevailed in a just war. British great-power pretensions were exercised in three spheres of influence—Europe, Commonwealth, and Atlantic alliance—though without exclusive commitment to any. In town and country the UK combined the warmth of a face-to-face society with the austere communalism required by a postwar scarcity whose impact was shaped by socialist rhetoric. Environmental concern was advancing, but had yet to transcend a defensive conservation, and neither housing nor transport had been predominantly privatized. The royal family's shared wartime experience had confirmed it in the national affections: people stood up for a national anthem that was frequently played, and British postage stamps seemed to need no further identifier than the monarch's profile. The landed classes

[237] A. Sampson, *Anatomy of Britain* (1962), 242–4.

were fading from the public scene, with their economic resilience as yet concealed. The middle classes, too, felt on the defensive, but their underlying strength lay in multi-dimensional fragmentation: social alliances above or below, service versus manufacturing occupations, grammar versus public school, state versus private employment, professions versus entrepreneurs, profession versus profession. For the moment, organized labour seemed politically and organizationally dominant, with salience for war-nourished, male-dominated, heavy-industry, heavily unionized communities. Yet there were already signs that its prewar decline would resume, eroded as it was from several directions: from collective shifts such as the gradual move out of manufacture and into services and the growth of educational meritocracy, but also from individual aspiration—whether for social status, occupational advancement, or respectability.

With the family, too, significant change was only gestating in 1951: still enthroned was the nuclear family, resting upon an ongoing separation of spheres between the sexes. Yet it was already under unobtrusive challenge, most notably through growing understanding of sexuality's complexities, through the spread of birth control, and (as part-consequence) through the growth in married women's paid employment. The conditions were set, too, for subdividing childhood as a category, and for friction with parents. Old age was another age category stirring increased interest—one of many impulses to the ongoing advance of public welfare. In the late 1940s high hopes rested on its assumed affinity with improving health. Interventionism also prevailed on economic matters, and the free-market challenge, though already mounted, was muted. None the less, many of the difficulties involved in combining a planned economy with a free society were already evident: problems in motivating the workforce, non-socialist employers' refusal to cooperate, and the special difficulties presented to the politicians who had to yoke voluntarism to statism. Many serious people hoped that Britain could solve such problems by mobilizing for public purposes a powerful combination of evangelical inheritance with civic ethic. Yet the planned economy, like the state-controlled and meritocratic school and university, was one dimension of a secularization whose other powerful dimension, as yet suppressed, was growing recreational diversity. The war might have converted St Paul's and Coventry cathedrals into symbols of national determination, rendering the Church of England an integrating and inclusive structure, but even in 1951 its foundations were insecure. Again, Reith's BBC might in the war have acquired the national status and image for impartiality that he had always sought, but its monopoly could not long survive the age of television, and in so far as it had become a substitute for the national church it too was under threat. The values associated with growing recreational abundance soon showed signs of undermining both Church and BBC, not to mention the exaggerated hopes earlier held out for a democratized high culture. It was not clear in 1951 that any such culture would flourish within the enlarged and secularized schools and university system, increasingly state controlled, that was already building up, together with the ongoing specialization which fragmented intellectual life.

There were serious uncertainties and anxieties during these years: the Berlin airlift, nuclear fears, the scuttle from India, the industrial disputes, and the persistence of rationing into peacetime. Within the political elite it had long been widely recognized how precarious was Britain's hold over so large a world empire, though no such recognition yet pervaded the population as a whole. During the six most difficult years of twentieth-century British peacetime history the Attlee governments grappled with problems and dilemmas that were numerous, complex, and simultaneous. Yet to the British people in 1951 their country's past seemed a proud inheritance. The political system, still bearing many traces of its medieval origins, had been refined in the seventeenth century during the civil war and revolution of 1688, and had subsequently evolved without serious discontinuity. Victory in the Second World War had apparently endorsed British political institutions, which seemed to exemplify how common sense and compromise could integrate a multi-nation state under stable government amidst remarkable socio-economic transformation. The union between England, Scotland, Wales, and Northern Ireland was not yet seriously challenged, and social cohesion had gained from public welfare's advance and from co-opting organized labour.

Complacency, philistinism, insularity, and even anti-intellectualism might be the downside of these national qualities, but the two-party system was in secure and sustained operation, with what seemed attractive cultural consequences. The polarized government and opposition that keep well within the rules, the civil servant who knows his place, the uncorrupt and unarmed policeman, the sportsman who obeys the referee—all these seemed built into British life and even into the British character. The constitutional monarchy, Big Ben, and Mr Speaker's impartiality all seemed to provide a stable and secure framework within which the decent life could be lived.

CHAPTER 2

The United Kingdom and the World

If the UK is to be set into its world context, diplomats cannot be centre stage because technological, recreational, economic, and intellectual changes were increasingly crossing national boundaries. International contact on a day-to-day level was tightening, so discussion will first centre upon internationalism in its several dimensions, beginning with international structures and moving on to population movements. The chapter's last three sections focus on the management of relations between states, and consider first the predominant international feature of the period, the 'cold war'. This had implications for the topics covered in the last two sections, which successively discuss the gradual shift from empire to Commonwealth, and the UK's gradual approach to the EEC, culminating in its first two (failed) attempts in 1961–3 and 1967 to join it.

1. DIMENSIONS OF INTERNATIONALISM

By 1951 air travel and an escalating electronic revolution were already diminishing the UK's physical and psychological isolation. Because planes could carry bombs, there had for some time been no moat around Fortress Britain. From the 1920s to the 1950s progress in astronomy and the needs of national self-defence marched in step: planes gave way to rockets, and rockets moved towards carrying satellites instead of bombs. Popularizers like the prolific author and broadcaster Patrick Moore helped to stimulate an unprecedented interest in astronomy with his television programme *The Sky at Night*, launched in 1957 and still running half a century later. The huge telescope rising above the trees at Jodrell Bank lent a surreal air to modern science, and its impact shaped daily conversation; the phrase 'big bang', for example, employed to describe the origins of the universe, was also applied in 1986 to a major reform of the stock exchange. Bishop Robinson in 1963 felt the need to get away from the idea of God as an old man in the sky; the 'Copernican revolution' prompted by radio telescopes, he said, made it impossible to locate God in some unknown area: 'now it seems there is no room for him, not merely in the inn, but in the entire universe: for there are no vacant places left'.[1] On 20 July 1969 the fifth of the earth's population who watched the moon-landing on television included nearly half the British population. So widely was it discussed that the actor Kenneth Williams privately expressed himself 'utterly sick of the moon', complaining that the papers 'never stop giving it headlines'.[2]

The marked public interest in outer space in the 1950s was reflected in science fiction's popularity. Its pedigree reaches at least as far back as the Gothic horror tale, but Aldous Huxley and H. G. Wells nourished the transfer of concern about the future from the afterlife to mankind's earthly destiny, and to the place of science within it. The radio adaptation in 1950 of Wells's *The War of the Worlds* (1898), adorned by Holst's 'Planets' suite, made considerable impact. C. S. Lewis carried the genre further, as did the television series *Quatermass* (from 1953) and *Dr Who* (from 1963). Schoolboys in the 1950s became familiar with space exploration through the *Eagle*, the high-minded middle-class comic whose hero Dan Dare battled against the intelligent green-skinned Treens led by the Mekon,[3] and Hammer Films carried the teenage science-fiction cult-following into the cinema. Interest extended to preoccupation with 'flying saucers', a term used from 1947 and replaced ten years later by the less mystical 'unidentified flying object' or UFO. This craze began in the USA, reached its first peak in 1952, and then a minor peak after the USSR's Sputnik satellite went up in October 1957. From 1953 groups of UFO enthusiasts were mobilizing in Britain, inspired mainly by a lower-middle-class and somewhat unsystematic enthusiasm for self-education, and for harmonizing science with religion. Often unmarried, they were ambivalent towards official science, and were increasingly (in the 1960s) moving on from science to the occult, and prone to suspect government conspiracy—though interest in 'flying saucers' rose as high as Earl Mountbatten and the Duke of Edinburgh.[4] In this pursuit of undiscovered worlds, as in the contemporary Campaign for Nuclear Disarmament (CND), two types of fear were combined: of authority, but also of trends in natural science.[5]

Internationalism advanced after 1951 at different levels of intensity in several spheres: political, economic, cultural, humanitarian, environmental, recreational, demographic. Defeat for Nazism's narrow nationalism boosted

[1] J. A. T. Robinson, *Honest to God* (1963), 14.

[2] K. C. Williams, *The Kenneth Williams Diaries*, ed. Russell Davies (1st publ. 1993, paperback edn. 1994), 355 (18 July 1969). See also J. Potter, *Independent Television in Britain*, iv. *Companies and Programmes 1968–80* (Basingstoke and London, 1990), 113.

[3] For an obituary of its founder-editor Marcus Morris, see *T* (17 Mar. 1989), 20.

[4] H. T. Buckner, 'The Flying Saucerians: A Lingering Cult', *New Society* (9 Sept. 1965), 14; S. McIver, 'Ufology in Britain: A Sociological Study of Unidentified Flying Object Groups' (York D.Phil. thesis, 1983), 4, 12, 200. P. Ziegler, *Mountbatten: The Official Biography* (1985), 493–4.

[5] McIver, 'Ufology', 52–64, 131–2, 151; Buckner, 'Flying Saucerians', 16.

political internationalism, together with independence for hitherto subordinate nations. Political internationalism through the United Nations after 1945 rapidly succumbed to the cold war, but commercial, humanitarian, and electronic changes buttressed internationalism in its less obtrusive yet more tenacious variants. Macmillan as Conservative prime minister acquired his informal media manner largely through addressing the cameras in airport VIP lounges when conducting international diplomacy. Whitehall departments outside the Foreign Office had been establishing their own international networks at least since the Edwardian period, beginning with the defence ministries and working outwards[6]—networks which gradually denied the Foreign Office its distinctive role. Defence relationships, trade agreements, and contact with proliferating international bodies all required government departments to undertake for themselves what were in effect international relations. There were also new international political structures, most notably those growing out of the United Nations in New York and Geneva—their growth symbolized by the spread of acronyms such as NATO, UNESCO, EEC, and NGO. The political parties, too, were developing international linkages. The Conservative Party as the self-consciously patriotic party almost by definition lacked formal international connections, but it was growing closer to Europe. Tariff union within the empire, rendered impracticable by (among other things) the British economy's weakness and by American hostility, was already by 1951 waning as a Conservative cause. Internationalism had always been integral to Liberalism; and in reinforcing that tradition the Labour Party fused it with an internationalism which viewed national loyalties as a falsely conscious diversion from class loyalties. Internationalism had a special appeal for rationalistic intellectuals: J. D. Bernal, for example, argued that scientists, by promoting their research through pooling discoveries, applied communism in their daily lives.[7] Such sentiments led the nuclear physicist Klaus Fuchs, who had arrived penniless in Britain from Germany in 1933, to offer the USSR secrets so important as to advance the USSR's first nuclear test (on 29 August 1949) by eighteen months, seriously endangering Anglo-American nuclear collaboration.[8]

Nowhere more than in the economic sphere were institutions interlocking internationally after 1945. National markets by mid-century were merging into a world market, generating the need from the 1960s for the new term, 'globalization'. With closer contact came the need for standard procedures

[6] A. Horne, *Macmillan 1957–1986* (1989), 74. F. M. G. Willson, *The Organization of British Central Government 1914–1964* (1st publ. 1957, 2nd edn. 1964), 200–5.

[7] G. Werskey, *The Visible College: A Collective Biography of British Scientists and Socialists of the 1930s* (1978), 189.

[8] P. Hennessy (ed.), *Cabinets and the Bomb* (2007), 77. Brian Cathcart's obituary, *Ind.* (30 Jan. 1988), 32.

and accumulated international law. The nineteenth century had found it convenient to establish international conventions on such matters as the Morse code, typewriter keyboards, and cataloguing of library books. To these the twentieth century added an interwar enthusiasm for international languages, and subsequent pressures to standardize procedures for traffic flow and scientific communication. By mid-century, international conferences and exhibition centres were proliferating. Also extending was international concern about the seabed and the environment. The growing postwar bulk transit of oil in tankers made previous voluntary agreements ineffectual, and in 1955 parliament legislated against the discharge of oil in UK territorial waters. The continuing problem led British governments to convene international conferences on the subject, but international compliance was very limited. The postwar lowering of trade barriers fostered international flows of capital reminiscent of the world before 1914. By the 1950s Britain was second only to Canada in its share of total American foreign direct investment; American-owned manufacturing firms were by 1954 employing 300,000 people in Britain, and 550,000 by 1966.[9] American factories—especially prominent in the 1950s in engineering and in making ships and vehicles—tended to cluster in London and the south-east; in mid-decade they accounted for an eighth of total British manufacturing exports.[10] The workforces of American firms in Britain were in 1968 almost ten times the size of their British counterparts, and by injecting more capital per worker, they obtained higher productivity. Between 1950 and 1970 the value of American direct investment in the UK grew annually at 12 per cent, about twice as fast as Britain's gross national product.[11] By the mid-1960s Britain attracted 7.5 per cent of multinational companies' total world investment, and such companies were more prone than indigenous companies to export and import; their inward investment generated 7.2 per cent of the British gross domestic product, a far higher proportion than in other large economies, and brought dominance within some areas of British production such as colour film, sewing machines, and typewriters.[12]

The slow retreat from fixed exchange rates was a worldwide trend from the 1960s, but an interventionist instinct and a concern for national status deterred the UK from participating. The dollar was strong enough for the USA to abolish exchange control almost immediately after the war, and in 1969 the strong deutschmark forced West Germany reluctantly to follow suit,

[9] P. Dicken and P. E. Lloyd, 'Geographical Perspectives on United States Investment in the United Kingdom', *Environment and Planning*, 8 (1976), 686.

[10] J. H. Dunning, *American Investment in British Manufacturing Industry* (1958), 58, 84–5. F. Bostock and G. Jones, 'Foreign Multinationals in British Manufacturing', *Business History* (Jan. 1994), 118.

[11] Dicken and Lloyd, 'Geographical Perspectives', 688.

[12] Bostock and Jones, 'Foreign Multinationals', 117–18, 120.

but not till the late 1970s was sterling strong enough for the UK to do likewise. From the 1940s to the 1970s this was unfinished business at the back of Conservative minds. The Sterling Area's demands seem in retrospect to have added yet another 'imperial' burden to defence expenditure's diversion of scientific expertise, personnel, and raw materials from Britain's domestic economy,[13] but for a moment in 1952 a remedy seemed at hand. R. A. Butler as Conservative Chancellor of the Exchequer proposed to make a virtue out of the apparent short-term need to devalue the pound after a run on sterling in winter 1951–2. Why not float it, thereby freeing the British economy for the foreseeable future from 'stop–go' constraints—whereby the economy expanded only to be arrested by the need to curb inflation or protect the dollar reserves, or both, and then the cycle would resume—by henceforth running it with only two regulators: the exchange rate and bank rate? Under this so-called ROBOT scheme, an acronym made up from the names of its three authors,[14] the pound would have been freed from the exchange rate Cripps had fixed in 1949 and would have floated presumably downwards. At the same time the scheme envisaged continuing to prevent other countries within the Sterling Area from converting their sterling balances into dollars, but it would have freed countries outside the Area to convert them into dollars at the foreign-exchange market price. The Treasury would thereby have escaped the consequences of huge accumulated sterling balances within the Area, and would no longer have to defend a vulnerable exchange rate for the pound.

Supported by the Treasury and the Governor of the Bank of England, ROBOT was none the less ultimately backed by only one cabinet minister (Butler), and was rejected. Eden opposed the scheme as likely to frustrate hopes for a European Defence Community, associated as it was with a European Payments Union which assumed fixed exchange rates. Fear of disrupting world trade relations and of upsetting the trade unions by producing short-term unemployment scotched the scheme: 'if the people are both unemployed and hungry under a Tory government, they will be very angry', was Macmillan's off-the-cuff comment. Churchill and his government were keen to retain the centre ground, an aim which ROBOT would have frustrated: when told about the scheme in November 1954, the future Labour leader Gaitskell thought that had it been implemented 'we might now be back in power, or at least have a much better prospect of getting there'.[15] Devaluation did not prove necessary in the short term, given that ending the Korean war improved the terms of trade.

[13] See below, pp. 93, 305–6, 535.

[14] Sir Leslie *RO*wan, Second Secretary, HM Treasury; Sir George *BO*lton, Executive Director of the Bank of England; and Sir Richard (O*T*to) Clarke, Under-Secretary, HM Treasury. For a full discussion of the scheme see P. Hennessy, *Having It So Good: Britain in the Fifties* (2006), 199–213.

[15] *The Macmillan Diaries: The Cabinet Years, 1950–1957*, ed. P. Catterall (2003), 148 (29 Feb. 1952). H. Gaitskell, *Diary*, ed. P. M. Williams (1983), 316 (9 Nov. 1954).

Thereafter, exchange control became so much part of the furniture that when its initial justifications disappeared, new ones were discovered. Britain's world status seemed to require a system of fixed exchange rates to prevent sterling from depreciating, and yet so-called 'stop–go' movements in the economy were the consequence. ROBOT later came to seem especially interesting as one of several 'Thatcherite' options rejected by Conservative governments of the 1950s.[16]

Later in the 1950s opportunities for relatively painless devaluation were lost, rendering devaluation when it eventually came in 1967 much more disrupting. Even the small-scale liberalization of 1958, whereby sterling was freed for conversion into other currencies during trade transactions, exposed the pound to speculative short-term capital movements. This was because firms tweaked their patterns of international payment and receipt so as to exploit currency fluctuations. Callaghan as Labour's Chancellor of the Exchequer seriously considered floating the pound early in 1967 but feared that what would then have seemed a bold and unexpected move might lead markets to exaggerate sterling's plight, which might prompt a general flight. On top of that, a lower pound would generate higher prices, which would endanger the incomes policy then operating. So he decided against, and a fixed exchange rate was still in place when devaluation became inevitable in November. There followed a general move of long-term funds out of sterling, effectively ending the Sterling Area before its formal abolition in the Basle agreements of September 1968.[17] In this volatile situation, devaluation had to be accompanied by a secret package, 'Brutus', to be implemented if a further run on the pound occurred before the reserves had built up. 'Brutus' aimed to avoid a second devaluation by including import quotas, drastic cuts in defence and overseas expenditure, a ban on foreign holidays, and a float for the pound.[18]

The package was never needed, but it later emerged that in the longer term fixed exchange rates were doomed. The relaxing of tariff barriers after 1945 helped to ensure that the Overseas Sterling Area's share of world trade and the proportion of each component country's trade conducted with other Area countries fell steadily. The gradual mid-century worldwide freeing up of capital markets, together with the rapid growth in exports from Japan and in oil exports from the Middle East demanded more flexibility in the system. Yet we have seen how the introduction in 1958 of the pound's convertibility on current account accentuated short-term speculation; this rendered UK reserves of gold and foreign currency even more vulnerable, so that the Bank of England often had to intervene. When in September 1969 West Germany reluctantly

[16] e.g. N. Lawson, 'Robot and the Fork in the Road', *TLS* (21 Jan. 2005), 11–13.

[17] J. Callaghan, *Time and Chance* (1987), 210–11. For a good discussion see D. Sanders, *Losing an Empire, Finding a Role: British Foreign Policy since 1945* (London and Basingstoke, 1990), 203–4.

[18] *T* (1 Jan. 1999), 1. B. Castle, *The Castle Diaries 1964–70* (1984), 462 (13 June 1968).

floated the mark, then strong, the Conservative backbencher Enoch Powell welcomed the decision, and wanted Britain to follow: it is politicians who create balance-of-payments problems, he said, 'by the perfectly simple method of fixing the prices of their respective currencies in terms of other currencies, and then swearing that the Almighty meant it to be so. The price being fixed, there was automatically a glut or a dearth. Then, the politicians said, we had to put this right for this was a "financial crisis"'.[19] By this time long-term Sterling Area funds were being increasingly channelled to currencies other than sterling, which ceased to be a reserve currency, and in 1972 the pound was allowed to float.

Economic, cultural, and humanitarian internationalism intertwined. Bernal in 1939 had yearned for a modern equivalent of Latin as a single means of communication between scholars, and held out the hope that this might be 'Basic English', an idea which four years later attracted even Churchill.[20] Help was at hand, for Hitler's expulsion of Jewish scientists and his failed bid for world domination ensured that English became the postwar international medium for natural science without even needing to become 'basic'. Whereas in the 1920s a scientist needed to know German, fifty years later English had become the language of international scientific conferences. And whereas Bernal had seen prewar nationalism as ominously fracturing the internationalism of natural science, the postwar generation witnessed an Anglo-American free trade in ideas and products. Britain was well placed to combine her defence-related American and Commonwealth scientific links with her slowly recovering scientific contacts in Europe, and English had become a world language. None the less, Britain was slipping in the world's wealth ranking, and wage differentials within Britain had long been flattening. If really able managers, scientists, technologists, and entrepreneurs were required—the rare oil-capping talents of a Red Adair from Texas,[21] for example—they would move only if paid at the worldwide going rate. Talk about the 'brain drain' from Britain had begun by 1963, the year of the *Oxford English Dictionary*'s first citation, in the context of young British scientists and technologists lost to the USA. International academic exchange had become common enough by 1975 to be satirized in David Lodge's novel *Changing Places*, and cross-cultural comparisons were becoming integral to research. The internationalism of natural and social science was increasingly exploiting opportunities for international collaboration—for example, the sort of cross-country social and medical research that involved eliminating cultural variables: demographic research into the influences on family size, criminological research on the impact of penal systems, or medical research

[19] *DT* (17 Sept. 1969), 29 (speech at Maidstone). *T* (1 Oct. 1969), 7 (National Liberal Club dinner).

[20] J. D. Bernal, *The Social Function of Science* (1940), 302. For Churchill see *The Diaries of Sir Alexander Cadogan O.M. 1938–1945*, ed. D. Dilks (1971), 543 (12 July 1943).

[21] Obituary, *T* (9 Aug. 2004), 25.

on the impact of smoking and diet. One distinguished career exemplifies the growing international links between medical research and humanitarian impulse: that of the Liverpool-based bacteriologist Allan Downie, who pressed the World Health Organization into campaigning against smallpox, a disease that in the 1960s was killing ten million people a year, yet which has produced no case since 1978.[22]

Several of the English language's features were specially suited to an international role. First, although between the wars English and French had been the two official languages in the League of Nations, the earlier powerful interaction of natural science with industrialization—first in Britain, and then in the USA—helped to make English the scientists' language. Second, the nineteenth-century breadth of British trade and imperial connections ensured that its speakers were geographically dispersed; indeed, the English language even helped to unite some multilingual postcolonial developing countries (India, for example). Third, English is relatively easily pronounced, there are many short words, and its syntax has simplified while evolving. True, its spelling often does not reflect its pronunciation, as spelling reformers of the 1940s consistently emphasized when pressing for it to become a world language. Yet this drawback did not prevent UK publishers in 1952 from producing 375 book titles per million of population. And although in number of books produced per head of population several European countries surpassed the UK, on this criterion the UK far surpassed both USA and USSR. It was a reflection of the English language's world role that a higher proportion of the books produced in Britain in 1952 (more than a third) was exported, mostly to Commonwealth countries, than in any other among the seven countries (including the USA) surveyed.[23] For similar reasons, Britain came very low when rated against other countries for the proportion of translations among the books it produced: the more books a country produced, the fewer it needed from elsewhere. On the basis of gross figures for the number of titles published, however, Britain by 1962 had fallen from second to third position (behind Russia and China): the number of its titles published had grown by a third, but more slowly than in the world as a whole, and both Japan and Germany were catching up fast.[24]

The twentieth century reinforced the empire's earlier contribution towards the English language's impact: Germany's defeat in two world wars ensured that English diffused far beyond the empire's boundaries even at their largest extent. But the UK rapidly ran down its wartime propaganda machine after 1945, and in the 1950s a strange amalgam of self-effacing arrogance deterred Britain from

[22] C. S. Nicholls (ed.), *Dictionary of National Biography 1986–90* (Oxford, 1996), 109.

[23] R. E. Barker, *Books for All* (1956), 21, 24.

[24] R. Escarpit, *The Book Revolution* (London and Paris, 1966), 99, 56–9.

advertising its culture overseas; indeed, to the British people 'culture' was then itself somewhat suspect, even sinister—particularly for the *Daily Express*, then embattled against the British Council. The Post Office in the 1950s was reluctant to advertise the UK through its stamps: 'the days when it was sufficient for this country to stand upon its ancient tradition and reputation are, I think, past', said the Bishop of Exeter in 1956, unsuccessfully promoting national postal self-advertisement in the House of Lords.[25] In the highly competitive world of the 1950s, the UK's false modesty was damaging. Here the UK diverged from France, which generously subsidized the promotion of French cultural values abroad while their language protected them (most notably with French films) against Americanization at home; by contrast, British governments' zeal for short-term economies discouraged the cultural route to long-term international influence. Battling with the Treasury in July 1968 to complement diminished defence expenditure with more overseas aid and publicity, Crossman was surprised to find no cabinet committee concerned with overseas publicity. In 1950 the BBC comfortably exceeded other countries (including the USA) and USSR in overseas radio broadcast hours, but from then till 1975 these rose only marginally, whereas elsewhere they rose markedly—so by 1975 the BBC's hours were only a third of the USA's and USSR's, and not far above Egypt's.[26]

In other respects the British media between 1951 and 1970 were decidedly internationalist in tendency. Television enhanced the domestic impact of overseas correspondents, instantly reporting those memorable events of the 1960s: student radicalism in California, the Vietnam war, and Russian tanks in Prague.[27] What sociologists call 'fugitive terminology'—novel but ephemeral words and phrases flitting round the world—flourished within the teenage underground of the 1960s.[28] So-called 'media moguls' had begun to appear: the Canadian Roy Thomson bought *The Sunday Times* in 1959, for example, and *The Times* seven years later. In 1969 the Australian Rupert Murdoch bought the *News of the World* and then the *Sun*, which he converted into a successful tabloid; in 1981 he bought *The Times* and *The Sunday Times*. The really powerful cultural influence at this time came from America. The USA's direct impact on the interwar BBC had been small,[29] but British politicians did little to protect the postwar British cinema against it. The cheapness of American films was their great strength; Harman Grisewood told Harold

[25] Robert Cecil Mortimer, *HL Deb.* 17 May 1956, c. 514.

[26] *The Diaries of a Cabinet Minister*, iii. *Secretary of State for Social Services 1968–70* (1977), 130 (11 July 1968). See also Central Policy Review Staff, *Review of Overseas Representation* (1977), 227.

[27] See Crossman's comments on this in his *Diaries of a Cabinet Minister*, iii. 172 (4 Aug. 1968).

[28] Wilfred De'Ath, 'Notes from the English Underground', *Listener* (20 Aug. 1970), 245.

[29] A. Briggs, *The History of Broadcasting in the United Kingdom*, ii. *The Golden Age of Wireless* (1965), 109.

Nicolson in 1961 that 'there is a vast T.V. audience in America, and when the films have gone the rounds of the United States, they are sent over here and sold cheaply to the B.B.C.'[30] In sport, however, internationalism (in cricket) took Commonwealth and (in football) European directions; baseball never prevailed in the UK. The Olympic Games helped to ensure that by the 1960s there were international as well as national governing bodies for the major sports to establish rules and procedures. As the Marquess of Exeter pointed out in 1963, 'although World Government is, in politics, at this stage of history, a pipedream, it is an accomplished fact in the world of amateur sport'. Faster and cheaper travel encouraged international competitions, and access to them became a pawn in the diplomatic game: for example, sportsmen from East Germany were banned for political reasons from visiting Britain in 1963. The spread of communication satellites made it possible in 1964 to broadcast the Tokyo Olympics live to thirty-nine countries.[31]

Internationalism through easier travel was not all benefit: with the mid-twentieth-century growth in fast air travel across vast distances there arrived infections whose incubation period lay well within the travel time, so that doctors needed increasingly to know the patient's travel history.[32] Nineteenth-century British trade and travel imported environmental problems that many years later became manifest: plants without indigenous predators such as the Japanese knotweed or rampant rhododendrons, for example.[33] And although improved understanding of bird migration made it easier to see the need for international regulation to protect endangered species,[34] the scale and cruelty of the international bird trade soon made regulation urgent. Each year by the early 1970s Heathrow Airport alone received, mainly from Africa and Asia, 600,000 birds for import, together with another 450,000 destined for other countries; given the high death rate in transit, the trade massively threatened endangered species.[35]

2. WORLDWIDE MIGRATIONS

The most eloquent symbol of growing internationalism was the growing willingness permanently or temporarily to cross national frontiers. Although the UK's population was slowly rising in the first half of the twentieth century, Europe's, excluding the USSR, was rising faster, so whereas in 1950

[30] Nicolson, *Diaries and Letters, 1945–1962*, 397 (24 Aug. 1961).

[31] *HL Deb.* 22 May 1963, c. 303. G. Whannel, *Fields in Vision: Television Sport and Cultural Transformation* (1992),71.

[32] As classically expounded by B. Maegraith, 'Unde Venis?', *Lancet* (23 Feb. 1963), 401.

[33] *FT* (21 Aug. 2001), 5.

[34] See e.g. speech of Viscount Templewood, *HL Deb.* 3 Dec. 1952, c. 707.

[35] T. P. Inskipp, *All Heaven in a Rage: A Study into the Importation of Birds into the United Kingdom* (Sandy, 1975), 34–5, 39.

the UK (with 50.6 million) had the largest population in Europe outside the USSR, the Federal Republic of Germany (with 55.7 million in 1970) overtook it, and Italy was fast catching up.[36] The relative decline in Britain's population, which reflected a declining birth rate, would have fallen still faster if (as in the nineteenth century) emigrants had exceeded immigrants. Between 1931 and 1966, however, the reverse applied—though the nineteenth-century pattern resumed thereafter with somewhat less force. The UK's net loss from population movements between 1951 and 1984 was 443,000, but it was now common for whole families rather than single men to emigrate from Britain, so the UK balance between the sexes was less disrupted.[37] Governments before 1945 had encouraged emigration for a double reason: to relieve poverty at home and to strengthen white settlement in the old white dominions. After 1945, however, a threefold decline—in empire, UK poverty, and the UK birth rate—changed everything. Not only was there return migration from many former colonies of white settlers or employees, who soon merged with the domestic population, there was also controversy about the merits of continued emigration. Whereas some worried more about emigration's impact on the UK population's age balance and calibre, for others[38] the concern was with the dilution of the British-born within the UK—more important to them than ethnic dilution in remoter and racially more vulnerable white territories.

Youth and talent gravitate from poor countries to rich, and in 1945 many European countries were poorer than Britain. The huge late-Victorian influxes from Eastern Europe of poverty-stricken Jewish refugees had by then ended, but Jewish immigration had been reinforced after 1933 when Britain offered both relative prosperity and liberty—first from Nazism, then from Soviet Communism. By the 1950s the relatively few middle-class interwar Jewish German immigrants were being steadily assimilated: overall Jewish numbers in Britain reached a peak in the 1950s and then began to decline as their distinct identity faded. The advent of refugees from Communism—the Russian pianist Vladimir Ashkenazy in 1963, for example—was insufficient to prevent the self-consciously Jewish hard core by the 1970s from ageing and waning in number; by then there were probably not more than about 250,000.[39] The largest postwar immigration from Europe involved manual workers attracted into Britain's tight postwar labour market. In the 1950s and 1960s only France (among six other European countries investigated) was taking foreign-born

[36] M. Macura, 'Population in Europe 1920–1970', in C. M. Cipolla (ed.), *The Fontana Economic History of Europe*, v/1 (1977), 22 (table 4).

[37] *BST* 562, cf. 101.

[38] e.g. R. C. K. Ensor, 'The Problems of Quantity and Quality in the British Population', *Eugenics Review* (1950), 132.

[39] *BST* 602. D. A. Coleman and J. Salt, *The British Population: Patterns, Trends, and Processes* (Oxford, 1992), 494–5.

residents in numbers comparable to Britain's, though West Germany was fast catching up. The three-phase process of migration was, by no means unique to Britain's immigrants. In the first phase young and predominantly male single people arrive; in the second, the family regroups and consolidates; and in the third, a settled, balanced, and identifiable minority evolves.[40] The newcomers arrived from the Irish Republic, Mediterranean countries, the Baltic States, and especially from Poland, which by December 1950 had contributed 130,000, including dependants.[41] The number of Italian-born British citizens grew threefold between 1951 and 1971; a marked influx of labourers from southern Italy produced clusters in Bedfordshire brickfields, South Wales steel towns, and Lea Valley horticulture—quadrupling the British Italian community in twenty years.[42]

As the gap in prosperity between Britain and European countries narrowed, Britain drew its 'economic' migrants from further afield. Between 1945 and 1985 Western Europe and the USA each admitted about 15 million people from Latin America, South Asia, and Africa, a million of whom came to Britain.[43] Turkish, Hispanic-American, and Filipino long-distance economic migrants flocked into the USA and Western Europe for tasks shunned by the locals. Friction with the British authorities within Cyprus did not deter Cypriots in the 1950s from becoming economic migrants to the UK, where Cyprus's Greek/Turkish population balance was replicated; 3,500 Cypriots reached the UK annually, and by 1966 there was one in Britain for every six in Cyprus.[44] The Soviet sphere of influence also generated migrants to Britain after 1951, most notably 21,000 of the quarter-million Hungarians who fled in 1956, and the 2,000 Czech refugees who arrived in 1968.[45] The Hungarian refugees included scientists and miners, one of whom was the heavyweight boxer Joe Bugner; many of their compatriots, some distinguished, had arrived earlier, including 'Vicky' the cartoonist, and the economists Nicholas Kaldor and Thomas Balogh. Fifty years later, forty-nine of the refugee students, in a joint letter to *The Times*, expressed gratitude to the British people and their institutions of higher education 'for so wholeheartedly helping us'.[46]

Between the European and the so-called 'New Commonwealth' immigrants to Britain, there were significant contrasts: first, there was often a colonial

[40] S. Castles, *Here for Good: Western Europe's New Ethnic Minorities* (1984), 88, 86.

[41] J. A. Tannahill, *European Volunteer Workers in Britain* (Manchester, 1958), 5.

[42] *BST* 599. T. Colpi, *The Italian Factor: The Italian Community in Great Britain* (Edinburgh, 1991), 135.

[43] *BST* 563.

[44] R. Oakley, 'Cypriot Migration and Settlement in Britain' (Oxford D.Phil. thesis, 1971), 7, 27, 32.

[45] S. E. Hale, 'The Geography of Vietnamese Secondary Migration in Britain' (Swansea Ph.D. thesis, 1991), 88–9.

[46] *T* (2 Oct. 2006), 18. I gratefully acknowledge Professor Colin Holmes's helpful guidance in his letter of 27 Jan. 2004 (author's collection).

connection—as with Indonesians arriving during these years in Holland, or North Africans arriving in France. Conservative governments after 1951 encouraged Commonwealth immigrants partly from imperial sentiment, but also because Conservatives baulked at the alternative to immigration: cutting the cost of British employees through reforming management and trade union practices. Second, there had been relatively few predecessors: West-Indian-born British immigrants, for instance, had hitherto centred largely upon seaports, though more arrived in the early 1940s as servicemen, or as war workers filling gaps in the British labour market. So unfamiliar in 1948 was the idea of non-white immigration from the Commonwealth that the British Nationality Act of that year was concerned mainly with what was seen as a welcome free movement between Britain and the old white dominions.[47] Third, the 'New Commonwealth' immigrant was often identifiable by colour or facial appearance—so much so, that by the 1970s the terms 'immigrant' and 'coloured person' were being used almost synonymously, even though by then only one in three of all immigrants entering and remaining in Britain came from these regions.[48] Rather more than half the immigrants from India and Pakistan in 1961 were white, and mounting numbers living in Britain had been born in the Old Commonwealth—137,000 of them in 1981.[49] But the darker skinned, more visibly 'New Commonwealth' immigrants inevitably made more immediate impact [Plate 8]. Between the 1940s and the 1970s the term 'negro' became unacceptable, at least in the mouths of white people, and gave way to 'coloured' until changing fashion ousted that too.[50]

The 'New Commonwealth' group was also distinctive for its sheer size, and its culmination in the 1960s, in contrast to the 1950s, coincided with rising unemployment in Britain. Comparing the numbers living in the UK but born elsewhere in 1951 and 1971, Old Commonwealth numbers rose by 44 per cent, the Irish Republic by 33 per cent, elsewhere by 35 per cent, but the New Commonwealth by 428 per cent.[51] This meant a marked change in the distribution of the overseas-born in Great Britain: whereas in 1951–71 the Irish Republic's contribution fell from a third of them to a quarter, Europe's from a third to a fifth, and the Old Commonwealth's from a twelfth to a sixteenth—the New Commonwealth's contribution rose from a seventh to two-fifths.[52] Viewed until

[47] R. Hansen, 'The Politics of Citizenship in 1940s Britain: The British Nationality Act', *TCBH* 10/1 (1999), 89.

[48] A. H. Richmond, *Migration and Race Relations in an English City: A Study in Bristol* (1973), 263.

[49] *TBS* 454. Coleman and Salt, *British Population*, 482.

[50] See K. Hudson, *A Dictionary of the Teenage Revolution and its Aftermath* (London and Basingstoke, 1983), 16–17. K. Little, *Negroes in Britain: A Study of Racial Relations in English Society* (rev. edn. 1972), p. xi (preface).

[51] Calculated from table in Castles, *Here for Good*, 43.

[52] See the valuable table in J. Haskey, 'Population Review: 8: The Ethnic Minority and Overseas-Born Populations of Great Britain', *Population Trends* (Summer 1997), 88, 16.

the late 1950s primarily as a Commonwealth issue, immigration from outside Europe did not prompt soul-searching about Britain's ethnic composition. Improved air travel, however, was cutting the cost of migrating from overseas at the same time as decolonization broadened the Commonwealth's ethnic composition: it could no longer be assumed that Commonwealth citizens claiming rights of settlement would be relatively affluent and white, yet any overt restriction on non-white entry would antagonize newly independent non-white Commonwealth governments. Here the politicians, cross-pressured by mass migration and the resentments it evoked, struggled for control. Unsurprisingly, there was no single governmental mind on the issue. The Colonial Office pulled one way and the Home Office another, and both political parties were split: Labour's divide between trade unionists worried about labour dilution and idealistic middle-class internationalists was complemented by the Conservatives' divide between populists worried about ethnic dilution and idealistic enthusiasts for the Commonwealth. The obvious way out was to find administrative devices (such as passport controls and deterrent publicity) for preferring Old Commonwealth white immigrants without accelerating any influx from the New. As Churchill's Private Secretary put it, 'the minute we said we've got to keep these black chaps out, the whole Commonwealth lark would have blown up'.[53]

The success in 1953 of the Everest expedition, announced on the morning of the Queen's coronation, illuminated contemporary ambiguities in British attitudes to race. Led by John Hunt—born in Simla, educated at Marlborough and Sandhurst with a distinguished war record—and executed by the white New-Zealand-born Edmund Hillary, the expedition seemed a Commonwealth achievement to be proud of. The British had in some sense got there first, and both Hillary and Hunt were knighted. Celebration was slightly dampened, however—except in Nepal—by the fact that Sherpa Tenzing was at the summit with Hillary, became a mountaineering celebrity in his own right, and found the French and the Swiss less patronizing than the British towards him;[54] for him there was no knighthood, only a George Medal.

As long as their Commonwealth loyalties survived, Conservative governments would have found it difficult to curb immigration even had they wished. The Churchill government in 1955 contemplated restricting non-white immigrants to a five-year right of settlement, but eventually rejected the idea.[55] The Notting Hill riots of 1958, however, helped to build up the case for the first legislative restraint on entry. By the late 1950s the overseas pressures for and the domestic pressures against admitting immigrants, at a time when

[53] Quoted in A. Roberts, *Eminent Churchillians* (1994), 225.

[54] G. T. Stewart, 'Tenzing's Two Wrist-Watches: The Conquest of Everest and Late Imperial Culture in Britain 1921–1953', *Past and Present*, 149 (Nov. 1995), 189, 193, 194.

[55] *T* (3 Jan. 1986), 3.

British enthusiasm for the Commonwealth had begun to wane, made curbs inevitable. Hence the Commonwealth Immigrants Act (1962), which used occupational skills and shortages as a way to control entry. It confined entry to those with work permits, and to the close relatives of residents and permit holders—paradoxically escalating annual New Commonwealth immigration to a peak of 75,000 in 1961 as people tried to beat the restriction.[56] Asians from the subcontinent and from East Africa now overtook the West Indies as a source of immigrants, culminating in the late 1960s and early 1970s. Restrictions were further tightened by new rules introduced in 1965, and the Commonwealth Immigrants Act (1968) removed the right of entry for British passport holders without a parent or grandparent born in the UK. The Immigration Act of 1971, in distinguishing between 'patrials' (with a parent or grandparent born in the UK) and 'non-patrials', in effect put the Commonwealth immigrant on the same footing as the alien, and restricted New Commonwealth immigrants largely to dependants, almost all Asians.

The number of people who moved temporarily rather than permanently between nations was also growing fast. Within every nation, tourism built up powerful groups with an interest in upholding domestic order and international harmony. Currency restrictions on British people travelling abroad ensured that the tourist impact was first felt through incomers. Already in the 1920s an annual average of 94,000 American visitors were visiting the UK, and by the early 1950s almost twice as many, with matching numbers from the Commonwealth.[57] Mass tourism from abroad in the long term made places less worth visiting, spoiling and standardizing the locations, given that many tourists sought overseas only what they could get at home. To well-to-do British people who had travelled abroad between the wars, the outcome seemed disastrous. Already by 1953 the distinguished actor and playwright Noel Coward, then visiting Venice, was deploring the impact of tourists 'in vast hordes buying postcards, photographing each other, jostling, shouting, squealing'; and in 1962 from Honolulu he grumbled at what 'American progress . . . is doing to the world. It is not only that they have loud, ugly voices and too much money, it is that their basic sense of values is dead wrong.'[58]

More important than immigration for its longer-term impact on British society was the fact that after 1951 a relatively insular people embarked on a worldwide recreational voyage of discovery, slowly forsaking their domestic holiday resorts for flights to nearby Europe. Not till the mid-1970s did overseas package-tour holidays become cheap enough for all, free from currency restrictions and within the same price range as holidays in Britain. So the British

[56] Statistics usefully tabulated in Coleman and Salt, *British Population*, 449.

[57] L. J. Lickorish and A. G. Kershaw, *The Travel Trade* (1958), 339.

[58] *The Noel Coward Diaries*, ed. G. Payn and S. Morley (1982), 281 (22 Aug. 1953), 498 (Feb. 1962).

seaside resort declined only slowly, at first shedding only the market's classier end. Indeed, the 1950s were its golden decade. Its mass market could then travel only by train; not till they bought cars could home tourists holiday outside specialized leisure towns and range more widely within the UK.[59] This made railway lines to holiday resorts, especially in the west of England, vulnerable to closure.[60] Also in the 1950s the package holiday married up the airline and hotel trades, offering many the additional bonus of chasing the sun or snow without too much contact with the foreigner. The pioneer was Vladimir Raitz, and Horizon Holidays first applied his concept of the charter flight in 1950 with its trips to Corsica. Henceforth the masses followed in the wake of the well-to-do, who between the wars had set out to pursue a Mediterranean tan. Between 1951 and 1970 the proportion of the British people's holidays taken abroad rose steadily,[61] and passengers carried on international flights from the UK grew from 887,000 in 1951 to 14,964,000 in 1980, increasing during the period in all but three years. By 1968 a tenth of British adults were taking holidays abroad, and of these nearly a third went to Spain, a tenth each to France, Ireland, and Italy; the numbers travelling by air to winter holidays trebled between 1967 and 1971.[62]

For many tourists, travel meant liberation from badly cooked, badly served British food. Here was one of many areas where King George V shared his people's tastes: for him, anyone who declined the offer of roast beef on Sunday could not be an Englishman.[63] On his definition there were far fewer Englishmen after the 1950s, when food's ingredients and preparation began to improve. 'I despair of English cooking', wrote Nicolson in 1953 after suffering at a Newbury inn: 'it is no good training the producer; it is the consumer who must be taught to notice when food is lazily cooked'. He noted that 'they gave us what they call *Tartelettes de Fruit*—a crumbly piece of shortbread with two cherries and artificial cream'.[64] The initiative came from the middle classes in the south-east of England. Penguin cookery books originated when the Ministry of Food was approached in 1948, with the *Penguin Cookery Book* (1952) as the outcome. Compiled by the Ministry's wartime employee, the New Zealand-born journalist and broadcaster Bee Nilson, it was an instant and lasting success. Her husband gathered many of its recipes through European business travel. American cereals had already

[59] J. C. Demetriadi, 'English and Welsh Seaside Resorts 1950–1974 with Special Reference to Blackpool and Margate' (Lancaster Ph.D. thesis, 1994), 5–6, 42, 145, 176.

[60] See C. Loft's excellent *Government, the Railways and the Modernization of Britain: Beeching's Last Trains* (2006), 96.

[61] There are figures in P. Lyth and M. L. J. Dierikx, 'From Privilege to Popularity: The Growth of Leisure Air Travel since 1945', *Journal of Transport History* (Sept. 1994), 106.

[62] *BHS* 561. *T* (29 Aug. 1970), 10. *O* (6 Sept. 1970), 11.

[63] J. Gore, *King George V: A Personal Memoir* (1941), 360.

[64] Nicolson, *Diaries and Letters, 1945–62*, 245 (28 Aug. 1953).

conquered the interwar British breakfast table, and their continuously rising consumption in the 1950s and 1960s undermined porridge; muesli's launch in 1972 brought further diversity.

The real postwar innovation, however, lay in the Mediterranean impact on lunch and dinner, partly because of European travel, partly because of home-grown missionary zeal. The Hungarian-born Egon Ronay fled from the Russians and arrived penniless in England in 1946. Appalled at the low level of British cooking, he opened a successful restaurant in 1952, and from 1957 single-handedly wrote and published his restaurant guide. Meanwhile Elizabeth David was lending vegetables a new glamour while sprucing up middle-class soups and stews with herbs, garlic, and spices. She brought a new seriousness to cookery writing, publishing her *Book of Mediterranean Food* in 1950, *French Country Cooking* in 1951, *Italian Food* in 1954, and *French Provincial Cooking* (her masterpiece) in 1960.[65] Sophisticated restaurants and kitchen shops (most notably Terence Conran's Habitat) sprang up in the wake of the new-style cookery books. So powerful was this movement that in 1970 David felt able to go into reverse with her *English Cookery*, thereby helping to revive indigenous cookery skills lost during the industrial revolution. Practical reinforcement came from her disciple George Perry-Smith, based on the 'Hole in the Wall' in Bath from 1952, and rivalled only by Francis Coulson at the Sharrow Bay Hotel on Lake Ullswater.

Dietary diversity was enhanced by the many postwar European immigrants to Britain, especially from Italy, Spain, Greece, and Cyprus. Their coffee bars and restaurants looked out on British streets that hummed increasingly with Italian Lambretta and Vespa mopeds, and drew their custom from middle-class Scandinavian-furnished homes. Such places extended to young people the emancipating unsupervised meeting places that teashops had brought to earlier generations of women. To the scampi and pizza of the 1950s were added the prawn cocktails, avocados, chicken Maryland, coq au vin, and Black Forest gateaux of the 1960s, with Swiss fondue to follow in the 1970s. The first Pizza Express restaurant opened in London in 1965, the second in 1967, and by 2004 the UK had more than 300. Chinese restaurants diversified British diet still further. They began to prosper in London's West End during the Second World War, when many servicemen were on leave. A combination of demand and supply caused their number to grow thereafter, so that whereas there were only fifty Chinese restaurants in the whole of Britain in 1957, there were more than 1,400 in England alone by 1963.[66] Demand had by 1970 given almost every British town and suburb its Chinese restaurant, later diversifying (backed by associated wholesale suppliers) into take-away firms which one family could run because waiters were not needed. As for the supply, it owed much to

[65] Portrait in *O* (5 Jan. 1986), 7; obituary in *DT* (23 May 1992), 21.

[66] *BST* 595.

population pressures in Hong Kong and the growing ease of air travel. By 1974 £9 of every £100 spent on eating out by the UK population went on Chinese meals; Chinese restaurants sold two million meals, ten times that of all Indian and Pakistani meals put together, and almost three times that of meals from Italy, which ranked next.[67] In these respects, at least, British life after 1951 was richly diversifying.

3. THE 'COLD WAR'

Central to Britain's international relations between 1951 and 1990 was the cold war. The Berlin wall's disappearance in 1989 and the USSR's sudden and unexpected breakup in 1991 so transformed the international scene that imagination is now required to recapture the climate during the previous four decades. On 25 June 1950 the cold war suddenly and unexpectedly became hot in a far away place of which we knew nothing: North Korean forces broke out of the Communist zone and aimed to subjugate the entire American zone in the south. Several British cabinet ministers two days later did not know where Korea was; when the service chiefs were asked what the UK could do to help, the First Sea Lord's immediate and informal jocular response was to say 'not much'; Churchill complained that he had 'never heard of the bloody place' until he was 74, and Britain had no direct economic or strategic interest there.[68] Furthermore, British forces were already overstretched with more pressing commitments: in Germany, Malaya, and Hong Kong.

It was not concern for Korea, but national self-defence—viewed on a worldwide scale, together with the need to consolidate the Anglo-American alliance—that got the UK involved. Here the appeasement analogy which influenced Bevin and Attlee was for once appropriate: if the Communists were not resisted there, they might be emboldened much closer to home, where American backing was vital. To quote Attlee's broadcast on 31 July: 'the fire that has been started in distant Korea may burn down your house'.[69] If Britain backed America in Korea, America might back Britain in Europe; and if Britain aligned with America, now zealously anti-Communist, she had a better chance of seasoning American zeal with caution. So in September 1950 the national-service term was extended from eighteen months to two years, and in the war's first winter the defence proportion of the UK budget rose to 10 per cent, an

[67] C. H. W. Cheung, 'The Chinese Way: A Social Study of the Hong Kong Chinese Community in a Yorkshire City [York]' (York University M.Phil. thesis, 1975), 78–9, 81. D. Jones, 'The Chinese in Britain: Origins and Development of a Community', *New Community*, 7/3 (Winter 1979), 400–1.

[68] A. Farrar-Hockley, *The British Part in the Korean War* (1990), i. 1, 47. Lord Moran, *Winston Churchill: The Struggle for Survival, 1940–1965* (1st publ. 1966, paperback edn. 1968), 446 (5 July 1953).

[69] Farrar-Hockley, *Korean War*, i. 113, cf. i. 203.

expenditure per head of population higher than the USA's.[70] Britain became the second largest among the sixteen United Nations members participating in a war which killed 1,078 British service personnel and wounded 2,674; four of those serving won the Victoria Cross. Yet of the combined UK/USA peak strength in Korea, the UK contributed only 9 per cent, of those wounded only 4 per cent, and of those killed only 3 per cent.[71] Given such figures, the UK's military influence over American conduct of the war could never be more than marginal. UK diplomats and politicians precariously managed during the war to play down divergence between British and American interests in relation to Communist China, which the UK, but not the USA, had recognized in January 1950. British pressure made it easier for Truman in April 1951 to dismiss General MacArthur, but the dismissal would have occurred anyway, since he threatened the President's authority and seemed bent on converting the Korean war into an all-out war between Communist China and the USA.[72] UK and Commonwealth pressures helped to secure the terms of the ceasefire in January 1953,[73] but the war advertised the UK's growing dependence on the USA.

The cold war influenced far more than foreign policy: it shaped many aspects of British society. Powerful enemies had moulded national attitudes in earlier centuries—most notably Spain, France, Russia, and Germany. But what produced in Britain after 1945 a special combination of fear and fascination—even, on occasion, melodrama—was the coincidence between ideological conflict and access to weapons of unprecedented destructive power. For some, the relevant analogy was Islam's threat to Christianity in the late Middle Ages; for Churchill, it was the Catholic threat to British Protestantism from the seventeenth century to the nineteenth; yet in neither case had such terrible weapons been available. Soviet Communism seemed the more formidable to the UK because the Marxist-Leninist linkage between social-class and colonial exploitation led the USSR to reinforce its huge land mass with outposts throughout the colonial or ex-colonial world. This forced diplomats to interest themselves in countries hitherto ignored, many now influential in the United Nations. Churchill as prime minister after 1951 was often cross about having to take account of such places as Cambodia and Laos. 'I'd never heard of this bloody place Guatemala', he exploded to Lord Moran on 28 June 1954, 'until I was in my seventy-ninth year'.[74]

[70] C. MacDonald, *Britain and the Korean War* (Oxford, 1990), 1. K. O. Morgan, *Labour in Power* (Oxford, 1984), 279.

[71] Farrar-Hockley, *Korean War*, ii (1995), 491. For US dead and wounded see <www.aiipowmia.com/koreacw/kwkia_menu.html> consulted 14 Jan. 2008.

[72] Farrar-Hockley, *Korean War*, i. 301, 351, 369; ii. 28.

[73] Ibid. ii. 342–51, 387.

[74] Moran, *Struggle for Survival*, 596 (28 June 1954); cf. 428 (28 Apr. 1953, Cambodia), 446 (5 July 1953, Korea) and M. Gilbert, *'Never Despair'* (1988), 825.

Complementing these overseas Communist outposts were cells of influence within non-Communist industrial societies among key groups of workers. Orwell claimed in 1947 that 'nothing has contributed so much to the corruption of the original idea of Socialism as the belief that Russia is a Socialist country and that every act of its rulers must be excused, if not imitated'.[75] The Soviet combination of austerity with progressivism held a certain appeal on the left: for the young Labour politician Tony Benn, for example, impatient at the relatively elegant but apolitical hospitality offered in 1959 at an American ambassadorial dinner. 'I cannot but feel Western civilization has reached its peak', he wrote in his diary, 'and is now slowly declining before the upsurge of pressure from the more serious societies.' In his last Labour Party conference speech Bevan, by then a seasoned ex-minister, expressed the fear that through state planning the USSR would eventually overtake the West;[76] it was a fear widely held among idealists and tidy-minded progressives, whether on right or left.[77] Soviet Communism, with so many of its defects as yet unknown or not believed, seemed both to pose a moral challenge to the right and to energize the left, not only through its links with the trade union movement, but through its uncompromising rejection of capitalism. Hence the capacity of the British left, even when in opposition, to prescribe so much of the British political agenda from the 1920s to the 1980s: had the USSR not existed, the planners and the collectivists would have needed to invent it. Indeed, in a many-layered paradox, British Communists, with their political activism and their principled and often self-denying intellectual dissent, continuously tested and even unintentionally nourished British libertarian traditions.

With all the self-confidence and drive of a secretive and monopolistic secular cult, an unyielding Soviet Communism seemed continuously to exploit the pluralism, scepticism, and free discussion pervading liberal democratic societies. Seemingly indecisive and fragmented, such societies were thought by some to require a rival ideology. Given the West's religious diversity, this could hardly be Christianity, though Moral Rearmament made an attempt at it. Brooding over the problem as chief of defence staff, Earl Mountbatten surveyed other candidates for the role and eventually alighted upon the democratic way of life (embracing the welfare state, free speech, equal opportunity, world disarmament, and a world authority), but he admitted that this would be 'difficult to put over', and nothing was done.[78] No secular and utilitarian ethic

[75] Orwell, preface to the Ukrainian edn. of *Animal Farm* in Orwell's *Complete Works*, viii (1997), 112–13.

[76] T. Benn, *Years of Hope: Diaries, Letters and Papers 1940–1962*, ed. R. Winstone (1994), 322 (8 Dec. 1959). For Bevan see Pimlott, *Wilson*, 230.

[77] See (e.g. for Wilson) Foot, *Politics of Harold Wilson*, 111; for Balogh see Pimlott, *Wilson*, 276.

[78] Ziegler, *Mountbatten*, 592–3.

in the West could in the short term hope to rival the powerful Communist combination of popular appeal and substitute religion. Such considerations help to explain how highly intelligent and civilized individuals like Anthony Blunt and John Cairncross could so readily betray their country. A sensation was created when the well placed and well connected bisexual diplomat Donald Maclean fled behind the Iron Curtain on 25 May 1951 with the homosexual Guy Burgess, another of Cambridge's Communist spy ring of five, days before MI5 was due to interrogate him. This seriously damaged not only British and American nuclear secrets, the reputation at home and abroad of the British social elite, and the case for homosexual law reform, but also the 'special relationship' with the USA.

Within this overall context, British governments had access to three non-Soviet alignments: with the Commonwealth, Europe, and the USA. Because between 1951 and 1990 these options were seldom mutually exclusive, politicians could postpone making any clear choice between them. The Attlee governments' anti-Communist stance could readily reconcile USA and Commonwealth alignments, given that the USA was more anti-Communist than anti-empire. Although there was no British equivalent of McCarthyism, the Conservative Party and dominant groups within the Labour Party were by the early 1950s fully enlisted behind the cold war, and the hostile tone of British films—tweaked for costume and accent—could readily shift the enemy from Nazis to Russians. For a brief moment in 1953 it seemed that the clouds might lift: 'Stalin is dead. Thank God!', exclaimed Lees-Milne in his diary.[79] The gloom soon returned, and from then up to 1970 defence expenditure continued to rise in nominal terms, and remained static in real terms. The long decline in the defence share of gross national product and in total government expenditure did not begin until the late 1950s. Of NATO's fifteen members, Britain in 1962 was third highest (behind only the USA and Portugal) in the share of its gross national product spent on defence.[80]

There were severe costs to the labour force, too, given that British governments at first competed militarily with the USSR in both manpower and weapons. Manpower rivalry entailed peacetime conscription (or 'national service') between 1945 and 1960 for the first sustained period in British history. Conscripts in the early 1950s became central to the British defence effort. As a proportion of the total in the armed services they accounted for 41 per cent in 1950, and the army's conscripts peaked in 1953 at 228,000. National servicemen's impact on the professionals was greatest in the army, which took

[79] J. Lees-Milne, *A Mingled Measure: Diaries 1953–1972* (1994), 13 (6 Mar. 1953).

[80] Statistics in A. J. Pierre, *Nuclear Politics: The British Experience with an Independent Strategic Force 1939–1970* (1972), 343–4; see also 197.

two-thirds of the 2,300,000 conscripts.[81] They accounted for almost half the army's numbers throughout the 1950s, and specially boosted the number of its lower ranking officers, as well as the technically better qualified among its other ranks, not to mention the reserves. National servicemen also eased the pressure on regular soldiers to serve long terms overseas, and 395 were killed in action.[82] Conscripts supplied less than a third of the RAF's manpower in the 1950s and only 6 per cent of the Navy's;[83] the latter's needs were less pressing and its training period relatively long. The collective exposure of so many in their age group throughout the 1950s to an unforgettable two-year experience in the armed services was a major event in British social history. The memory transferred into 'civvy street', affecting a lifetime's behaviour and attitudes—from discipline to sport, from humour to social hierarchy and dress, from sex roles to health, working practices, posture, and manners. Conscription, with its creation of a strongly disciplined all-male world, cut across central features of the otherwise growing teenage culture. These young conscripts were, after all, experiencing in a mild form what their fathers and grandfathers had all too recently endured in two world wars.

Prominent in the national serviceman's memory was the initial medical inspection, with its introduction to compulsory nakedness; then the warrant for a train journey to bleak and unfamiliar locations; the uncompromising military haircut and the non-commissioned officers' elaborately bad language; the early rising on bitterly cold mornings and the excruciating physical exercises; the terrible food; the two-day knockout blow delivered by the TABT injections against tetanus, typhoid, and smallpox; the separation from home in an all-male environment. There were also the unfamiliar, often mindless domestic and other duties, a fine training for the art of 'skiving'—that is, for quietly disappearing when unpleasant jobs loomed. There was safety in numbers, and it seemed important never to complain, never to volunteer, always to conform. Above all, there was the loss of individuality. To quote one conscript, 'you were transported into another world and you were in complete limbo, that's how I felt. You suddenly didn't belong to yourself any more at all.'[84] National service prompted a class mixing that was for many conscripts a revelation, for some even traumatic. 'What shocked me . . .', Richard Ingrams recalled, 'was being put in a barracks with a whole lot of mainly working class people, and all sorts of effing and blinding all day long.' Led by Shrewsbury School to expect a commission, Ingrams found himself permanently consigned to the

[81] R. Broad, *Conscription in Britain* (2006), 71. B. S. Johnson (ed.), *All Bull: The National Servicemen* (1973), 290–1. R. L. Raitt, *National Service 1945–61* (George Knight Clowes Memorial Prize Essay, 1961), 36.

[82] Johnson (ed.), *All Bull*, 15.

[83] T. Hickman, *The Call-Up: A History of National Service* (2004), 333.

[84] S. Martin, 'Did Your Country Need You? An Oral History of the National Service Experience in Britain, 1945–1963' (University of Wales, Lampeter, D.Phil. thesis, 1997), 93.

other ranks: 'they seemed to be like people from another planet . . . They were obsessed by sex, and spent the whole time smoking', with drinking as almost their sole off-duty recreation; yet they gave him the unexpected perspective on British society that shaped his entire career in *Private Eye*.[85] National service, like all wartime experience, deeply influenced British comedy. It helped to shape the surreal humour of the Goons, honed on the absurdities of military hierarchy, the unrealities of wartime propaganda, and the subsequent fear of nuclear weapons; Spike Milligan was a founder member of the Direct Action Committee Against the Bomb.[86] The small elite of 5,000 who spent their two years in secret classrooms and university enclaves learning Russian, mostly national servicemen, constituted a latter-day mini-Bletchley in their concentration of talent; their distinguished alumni included Alan Bennett and Michael Frayn.[87]

The national service experience was inevitably written up by the articulate, many of whom counted the days until they could be 'demob happy'. Against this should be weighed what later seemed the conscripts' surprising acquiescence at its disruption of their lives. This was partly a matter of male self-respect, of accepted sex-roles endorsed: the 16 per cent rejected as unfit for service were not always envied.[88] But it was more than that: many national servicemen voluntarily extended their period of service. Between 1949 and 1960 about a third of those in the RAF signed on (though admittedly with the encouragement provided by a three-year engagement that doubled their pay); and in the early 1960s national servicemen contributed a quarter of all those on three-year engagements in the army and nearly a third of those in the RAF.[89] The memories were not always painful: out of deprivation came forth the brief ecstasy of leave-periods, the close friendships nourished by isolation, the moments of intense hilarity when the hierarchies broke down. But the attractions were more than merely negative; there were the excitements of going abroad for the first time, as well as the security of a closed community within which responsibility could be shared or shed, difficult decisions postponed, and fulfilment of a kind secured.

During the early 1950s Labour MPs, reacting against the Attlee governments, began to question the continued need for national service, if only because the UK's was less selective than the USA's, and because its two-year span was longer than in most other countries. By the mid-1950s the successors to the conscripts who in the late 1940s had been called up to deal with a pressing European threat were being diverted into holding the imperial line in Egypt,

85 Interview with D. Danziger, *Ind.* (26 Mar. 1990), 16.
86 Whiteley, *Pop Design*, 17.
87 G. Elliott and H. Shukman, *Secret Classrooms: A Memoir of the Cold War* (2003), 11.
88 Martin, 'Did Your Country Need You?', 75.
89 Johnson (ed.), *All Bull*, 9. Hickman, *Call-Up*, 233.

Kenya, and Malaya. By then Labour was becoming more accessible to anti-colonial African and Asian nationalists, the Russian threat seemed with Stalin's death to be fading, and nuclear weapons made it seem less necessary for the UK to compete on the manpower front. The idea was gaining ground 'that universal military service, which came in with the French Revolution, will go out with the Nuclear Revolution, and be succeeded by small, long-term, highly trained armies in charge of very expensive and highly complicated weapons'.[90] Such arguments gained all the more force from claims that trade rivals like Germany and Japan, with their relatively low defence budgets, were stealing an unfair economic advantage.

By American standards, British defence debate did not open out widely: it involved only the informed members of a rather small group: the armed services, pressure groups concerned with defence matters, and a few media people and academics. With American encouragement, West Germany was now rearming to play its part in NATO's collective defence of Western Europe. So greatly had the world changed since 1945 that the need to resist Russian ambitions overrode Labour Party and French fears of revived German militarism. The subsequent rethink focused on the implications of nuclear weapons. Should the RAF now replace the Navy as the decisive component in national defence? Should nuclear weapons free the army from competing with the USSR on the manpower front, thereby rendering conscription redundant? The debate acquired pace from the public-expenditure cuts demanded by the perceived weakness in the British economy; indeed, in the 1950s and 1960s reduced commitments tended hastily to follow cuts rather than precede them in a carefully planned way. The Suez crisis (1956) added geopolitical motives for cuts, which by this time were complicated by the temptation to defer developing any one generation of weapons for fear of precluding later options: 'the vice of preparing for the last war was joined by that of getting ready for the next but one'.[91]

British defence policy had hitherto emerged from compromise settlements after fierce inter-service competition for waning resources, but from 1957 Macmillan as prime minister ensured primacy for the politicians by backing Duncan Sandys, his abrasive Defence Minister, in imposing a considered settlement. Sandys argued that Britain's share of Western defence responsibilities was too large, and was starving her economy of much-needed manpower, scientific skill, and raw materials. 'It must be frankly recognised', said his forthright white paper, 'that there is at present no means of providing adequate protection for the people of this country against the consequences of an attack with

[90] R. H. S. Crossman, 'The New Case against Conscription', *NS* (13 Aug. 1955), 176.

[91] L. W. Martin, 'The Market for Strategic Ideas in Britain: The "Sandys Era"', *American Political Science Review*, 56 (1962), 24.

nuclear weapons',[92] some of which would get through, so deterrence must now take priority. This led him to recommend abolishing conscription and almost halving the combined strength of the three armed services in five years. The armed services, competing freely within the labour market, must henceforth offer better conditions to a volunteer national defence force that would be smaller, better integrated, and more professional. Smaller but relatively mobile ground forces would be deployed in conjunction with missiles on shorter term operations, with the implication that longer-term and more ambitious schemes for imperial defence would cease. Numbers in the British armed forces fell fast: from 838,000 in 1951 to 469,000 in 1961 to 368,000 in 1971. British defence spending fell by a quarter in real terms during the seven years after its peak in 1953, and fell still further in its share of gross national product; between 1951/5 and 1975/6 UK expenditure on defence fell in its share of total public expenditure from 23 to 9 per cent.[93]

Royal Navy battleships lingered on until 1960, when HMS *Vanguard*, pride of the postwar fleet, was scrapped, and 'with it went a way of life'. By 1961 the British navy's total strength had fallen to 96,330—larger by a third than the French navy, but only a sixth as large as the American navy, and only a fifth as large as the USSR's. The British navy had first been built up to protect British interests abroad, and had then helped to establish great imperial bases. It was now returning to its origins: by 1962 the distinguished journalist Anthony Sampson saw it as 'retreating from the shore bases, back to the safety of the sea'.[94] Hence the UK's relatively tenacious resistance to decolonization in Cyprus, Aden, Singapore, and Borneo:[95] through a string of naval bases it was hoped to perpetuate British world influence long after the large land masses had gone. The navy could still dream of operating as a sort of free-floating base without overseas land attachments, on the precedent set by the American Sixth Fleet, complete with its own air force, missiles, and tankers. But the UK was powerless to scotch Southern Rhodesia's bid for continued white-settler dominance in the 1960s,[96] and its international standing suffered accordingly. There could be no question of giving active or overt help to friends behind the iron curtain, whether Hungarian in 1956 or Czech in 1968. The cuts were depressing enough for servicemen, but in shedding their conscripts in the early 1960s, the armed services were at least freed to become less traditionalist and hierarchical, technically more sophisticated,

[92] *Defence: Outline of Future Policy. Presented by the Minister of Defence to Parliament . . . April 1957* (PP 1956–7, xxiii, Cmnd. 124), 2.

[93] *BHS* 121. S. Brittan, *Steering the Economy: The Role of the Treasury* (1969), 245. CPRS, *Review of Overseas Representation*, 29.

[94] A. Sampson, *Anatomy of Britain* (1962), 256; see 253 for a good table specifying types of ship.

[95] J. Darwin, *Britain and Decolonization* (1988), 285.

[96] Castle, *Diaries 1964–70*, 191 (28 Nov. 1966), 197 (4 Dec. 1966).

more meritocratic, more professional. From the mid-1950s new occupational categories were exempted from conscription, and medical tests for selection were tightened. By 1955 the army's conscript numbers had fallen to 205,000, and by 1957 to 174,000. The decline thereafter was rapid: of men born in 1930, national service drew in 68 per cent; in 1936, 51 per cent; in 1939 only 25 per cent. By the late 1950s nearly half the eligible age group were not being required to serve, in 1960 conscripts as a proportion of the total in the armed services accounted for only 22 per cent, and in May 1963 the last national serviceman was released.[97]

Churchill's continuous private and almost pleading struggle when prime minister to involve the American President in direct conversation with the Soviet leaders did not represent an old man in a hurry with inflated views of Britain's world status. On the contrary, Churchill was acutely aware of, and saddened by, Britain's decline. What motivated him was an acute awareness of what was at stake. 'Human minds recoil from the realization of such facts', he told Eisenhower in March 1954, after reading recent American expert comment about nuclear weapons' destructive potential. 'The people . . . can only gape and console themselves with the reflection that death comes to all anyhow, some time. This merciful numbness cannot be enjoyed by the few men upon whom the supreme responsibility falls. They have to drive their minds forward into these hideous and deadly spheres of thought . . . I consider that you and . . . I cannot flinch from the mental exertion involved.'[98] So preoccupied was he with these horrors that he made them central to his last major speech in the House of Commons. After devoting long hours to composing the speech himself, he was still capable at 80 of reflective oratory and powerful phrase-making on a major subject: for forty-five minutes the House was compelled to almost complete silence, his voice remaining strong throughout. He saw 'an immense gulf' in the transition from atomic to hydrogen bomb : 'the entire foundation of human affairs was revolutionised, and mankind placed in a situation both measureless and laden with doom', for global war would now produce 'mutual annihilation'. Reluctantly but staunchly championing the strategy of mutual deterrence, he said it would be 'a sublime irony' if mankind had reached a stage 'where safety will be the sturdy child of terror, and survival the twin brother of annihilation'.[99]

The British were beset by twin fears: that America might withdraw its nuclear shield, yet also that it might use the weapons, with Britain's destruction as the indirect outcome.[100] Some thought that the government's decision in 1957 to

[97] Broad, *Conscription in Britain*, 71. Johnson (ed.), *All Bull*, 290–1. Hickman, *Call-Up*, 340.

[98] Quoted in M. Gilbert, *'Never Despair'*, 959, after reading Sterling Cole's comments at Chicago on 17 Feb.

[99] *HC Deb.* 1 Mar. 1955, cc. 1894–5, 1902, 1899.

[100] Pierre, *Nuclear Politics*, 171.

authorize American missile bases in Britain made matters worse, if only because the UK might now be at the eye of the nuclear storm. From the late 1940s Britain had acquiesced in the establishment of 'little Americas' on British soil, initially in eastern England but later in more central counties. These provided runways for long-range bombers, serviced by United States Air Force bases constructed with American know-how and components. They became self-contained communities with American accents, cars, street names, sports and shops, and dollars for currency.[101] Fear was accentuated by much-publicized photographs of Soviet rockets allegedly targeted on Western cities; for a time the rockets were located on mobile launchers near East Berlin, were directed at military bases in Norfolk and Lincolnshire, and carried warheads with a payload twenty times that of the Hiroshima bomb.[102] The chief of defence staff, Earl Mountbatten, was alarmed even by American nuclear storage facilities: on first seeing a huge underground silo for a Titan nuclear missile at Vandenberg in 1959 he wrote in his diary that 'the whole thing has a gruesome and horrific effect which makes one really fear for the sanity of mankind'. A country as urbanized as Britain had much to fear, and a Gallup poll in 1958 showed that 80 per cent of the British public expected fewer than half the British population to survive a nuclear war.[103] Yet in his speech of 1 March 1955 Churchill had plucked hope from despair, for the more horrible the weapon, the less the incentive for any side to use it, and by spreading the destruction so widely, the hydrogen bomb might actually enhance mutual deterrence by bringing to larger and more scattered populations destruction on a scale that had hitherto been confined to smaller and more crowded states like the UK. A bystander recalled that Macmillan, when the American ambassador showed him photographs of Russian missiles in Cuba on 22 October 1962, 'looked at them for a little while and then said, more to himself than to us, pointing at the missile sites, "Now the Americans will realize what we in England have lived through for these past many years" '.[104]

Britain's diminished military power did not curb her taste for wielding worldwide influence. 'I do not take the view that Great Britain is a second-class Power', said Bevan late in 1956: 'on the contrary . . . this country is a depository of probably more concentrated experience and skill than any other country in the world'. CND, in recommending the UK unilaterally to abandon nuclear weapons, ensured that morality stepped in where the military now feared to tread. 'Alone, we defied Hitler', wrote the novelist J. B. Priestley in an influential

[101] W. D. Cocroft and R. J. C. Thomas, *Cold War: Building for Nuclear Confrontation 1946–1989*, ed. P. S. Barnwell (Swindon, 2003), 70.

[102] *T* (18 Jan. 2000), 1–2.

[103] Ziegler, *Mountbatten*, 590. T. Shaw, *British Cinema and the Cold War: The State, Propaganda and Consensus* (2001), 135.

[104] Churchill, *HC Deb.* 1 Mar. 1955, c. 1899. Chester Cooper, quoted in A. Horne, *Macmillan, 1957–86* (1989), 365.

article, 'and alone we can defy this nuclear madness into which the spirit of Hitler seems to have passed, to poison the world.'[105] Revd Michael Scott was one among many who combined their unilateralism with progressive views on empire, another potential British arena for moral self-display. A determined opponent of CND claimed that 'unilateralism is not internationalism. It is nationalist egoism gone mad.'[106] Riddled with puzzles and paradoxes, this strange movement opposed the very weapons that eased Britain's defence cuts and terminated conscription. CND's timing, too, was surprising—failing to appear in 1945 at the only time when nuclear weapons had been used on civilian targets, it was past its peak during the one episode when the cold war almost became hot: the Cuba crisis of 1962.

CND reinforced its moralistic impulse with intense suspicion of government, a sentiment nourished by the secret and surreal defensive devices erected from the 1950s onwards: severely functional buildings, mainly constructed from concrete, steel, and earth, frequently partially or totally underground, and often novel in structure, materials, and design.[107] Surveillance equipment, hangars, bunkers, radar stations, storage depots, airfields, control towers, missile emplacements and silos sprang up in remote places or on seasoned secret sites. Weird structures surfaced: pagodas on Orford Ness in the 1950s [Plate 9], spherical 'radomes' at Fylingdales in 1963. Backed up by large and costly research programmes, their roles and mutual relationship were obscure enough to need explanation half a century later. It was to the atomic weapons research establishment at Aldermaston that the first protest march of what became CND was directed on Good Friday 1957. The weapons' creators and controllers, wrote Priestley, 'live in an unhealthy mental climate, an atmosphere dangerous to sanity', responsible neither to the taxpayer nor to public opinion. 'The whole proceedings take place in the stifling secrecy of an expensive lunatic asylum. And as one ultimate weapon after another is added to the pile, the mental climate deteriorates, the atmosphere thickens, and the tension is such that soon something may snap.'[108]

Bible readers thought apocalyptic images apposite, with the bomb symbolizing a revived conviction of human sinfulness. Noel Coward was not alone in 'being a little haunted' by Nevil Shute's *On the Beach* (1957), a novel about nuclear war and its aftermath which became a film in 1959,[109] though self-censorship deterred most film-makers from discussing the subject.[110] The very

[105] Bevan, *HC Deb.* 19 Dec. 1956, c. 1404. Priestley, 'Britain and the Nuclear Bombs', *NS* (2 Nov. 1957), 556.

[106] Dalton in *DT* (25 Oct. 1960), quoted in B. Pimlott, *Hugh Dalton* (1st publ. 1985, paperback edn. 1986), 636.

[107] Cocroft and Thomas, *Cold War*, 2–3.

[108] 'Britain and the Nuclear Bombs', *NS* (2 Nov. 1957), 554.

[109] Coward, *Diaries*, 378 (1 May 1958); cf. R. Hoggart, *A Sort of Clowning* (1990), 197.

[110] Shaw, *British Cinema and the Cold War*, 132.

idea of 'civil defence' in such circumstances could not carry conviction, and the House of Lords debate on the subject on 2 November 1955 makes chilling reading. From 1955 to the 1960s the BBC was banned from broadcasting any programme suggesting that there was no effective civil defence against a hydrogen bomb attack's effects.[111] Governments were in a dilemma: the threat to national safety was huge, but so was the cost of effective civil defence; sufficient civil-defence volunteers could be mobilized only through highlighting the danger, yet the public must not be panicked. Diplomatic methods and (on the left) unilateral disarmament seemed preferable. Meanwhile, the government's responsibility for organizing national self-defence was absolute, and given the Soviet capacity to explode a hydrogen bomb, eleven regional seats of government were planned in 1963 so as to render flexible such authority as survived any disaster. By no means all were in well-known governmental locations: Cambridge, York, and Preston, perhaps, but also Drakelow, Bolt Head, and Warren Row.[112]

In at least one respect amidst all the gloom, CND struck an optimistic note, for beneath its emotionalism it combined Enlightenment rationality with the nineteenth-century Liberal's faith in the active citizen. Individuals, if only they organized themselves, could make a difference. Middle-class people young and old joined intellectuals, a handful of distinguished scientists, and veterans from the interwar peace movement for one of the last and most notable British popular protest movements in the long tradition running from anti-slavery to the suffragettes. Uniting Quaker, humanitarian, and near-Communist sympathies with concern for the environment, a small group of sympathetic British scientists built bridges with scientists in Eastern Europe, thereby helping to effect the Test Ban Treaty of 1963.[113] The philosopher Bertrand Russell was CND's figurehead and Gerald Holtom's white missile-shaped design on a black circle was its symbol. It seemed so obvious that national wealth would be better spent on such things as welfare and education rather than on these terrible weapons; CND was in part a protest at the apparent timidity and even alleged cynicism of religious and political leaders, especially Labour leaders. Claims on the right that CND was allied with Communism were not justified, but defeatism was certainly widespread on the left. Crossman neatly articulated in his diary in November 1957 what was later seen as an inversion of the truth: it was 'futile to believe that the Western world, with its present type of capitalist organization, could discipline itself to a twenty-year arms race. So back we come to the idea that it might be better to opt out of that race, reckoning that the Russians have nothing much to gain

[111] *G* (20 Aug. 1999), 6. [112] Cocroft and Thomas, *Cold War*, 204–5.

[113] For a useful discussion see G. Jones, 'The Mushroom-Shaped Cloud: British Scientists' Opposition to Nuclear Weapons Policy, 1945–57', *Annals of Science*, 43/1 (Jan. 1986), 1–26.

by mopping us up.'[114] At CND's peak, its anti-war demonstrations became impressive.

The Cuba crisis reached its denouement in October 1962 when the Americans forced the USSR to retreat from planting nuclear missiles in Cuba. Macmillan was alarmed at intelligence information on the Americans' likely response if the USSR retaliated against Berlin: they would have unilaterally declared a nuclear war without consulting allies.[115] The crisis was among a handful of twentieth-century world events that at the time seemed so alarming as to root in people's memories what they had been doing at its climacteric. The palaeontologist Professor Ian Simmons was then spending much of his time at a microscope counting pollen grains, but recalled thinking that 'if we were all soon to disappear in a column of radioactive smoke then there were more enjoyable things to be done. Being young, I went and did them!'[116] Two members of CND's 'Committee of 100' fled to Ireland, and the theatre critic Kenneth Tynan decamped to Australia; Noel Coward in January 1963 found him 'deeply scared of the atomic bomb. I mean genuinely, gibberingly scared!' To Coward, such a reaction seemed surprising because this was 'far too vast a nightmare to be frightened of'. 'During this nightmare week', wrote Bertrand Russell, 'every moment seemed likely to be the point of obliteration for humanity.'[117]

Why, at such a juncture, did CND not advance further? CND's decline in the early 1960s owes something to the controversy its direct-action tactics evoked, for the split between constitutionalists and direct-action militants, latent in any protest movement, had surfaced with the formation in September 1960 of the 'Committee of 100' to promote mass civil disobedience. Also relevant for CND's decline was the way the French and Chinese nuclear tests (in February 1960 and October 1964, respectively) weakened the likely moral impact of British unilateral disarmament—though this further nuclear proliferation exemplified precisely the danger against which CND had earlier warned. What ultimately consolidated CND's decline had been the Labour Party's slow build-up in the early 1960s towards an electoral victory, which then came to seem a more effective route towards attacking Conservative defence policy. And although CND soon found itself outmanœuvred, and realized that even a Labour government would cling to the independent nuclear deterrent, its hopes of the new regime were not completely disappointed. With an independence whose sheer difficulty of attainment could perhaps be fully appreciated only after the Iraq war of 2003, the Labour prime minister Wilson (probably against his private inclinations in 1965) kept Britain out of overt

[114] *The Backbench Diaries of Richard Crossman*, ed. J. Morgan (1981), 624 (6 Nov. 1957).

[115] *DT* (3 Apr. 2006), 8.

[116] Author's collection: letter to the author, 23 Jan. 1997.

[117] Coward, *Diaries*, 525 (12 Jan. 1963). Russell to Max Born, 30 Oct. 1962, in N. Griffin (ed.), *The Selected Letters of Bertrand Russell: The Public Years, 1914–1970* (2001), 556.

commitment to the Americans in the Vietnam war which CND supporters and many of his backbenchers so strongly opposed. In this Wilson was in tune with British public opinion: in 1965–6 a consistent and growing majority of those polled by Gallup opposed recent American armed action, and when asked in 1966–7 whether they would favour sending British troops to Vietnam, an overwhelming majority disapproved.[118] Heath, the Conservative leader, would have given full backing to the USA, but as prime minister (1970–4) he distanced himself rather ostentatiously from the USA, and it was not long before he decided that both Commonwealth and USA should sink below the EEC among the UK's overseas priorities.

British nuclear policy in the 1950s and 1960s sheds light on the changing nature of the so-called 'special relationship' between Britain and the USA. We have already seen how it emerged in the 1940s; but for all the sentiment, the rhetoric, the memories of wartime collaboration and the warm high-level personal connections, that relationship never transcended shared interest. During the 1960s the 'special relationship' weakened further, concurrently with the British economy. Asked why he did not condemn USA action in Vietnam more strongly, Harold Wilson replied: 'because we can't kick our creditors in the balls'.[119] Decolonization was accelerating, Britain offered only symbolic help in the Vietnam conflict, and a Labour government was reluctant to do even that. In the second half of the twentieth century the British were keener than the Americans to refer to the 'special relationship' because in two respects it was a shield: in the short term against the Communist danger at home and abroad, and in the longer term against the UK's acknowledging its diminished world influence. For the USA the British connection was useful as a conduit for American influence in large parts of the world: in Europe, in the Commonwealth, and in the United Nations. British influence on American policy during the Cuba crisis was negligible, but the British government's support, especially within the United Nations, was crucial for protecting the USA from the isolation that Britain had experienced during the Suez crisis.[120] Once the USA had enlisted in the worldwide crusade against Soviet Communism, the British empire's remnants had their uses, and there seemed no urgent need for a total dismantling. The UK developed its nuclear weapons with the Americans as well as the Russians in mind. The bomb not only preserved some British freedom of manœuvre: it also enhanced the British component in the Anglo-American balance of power. As Eden pointed out,

[118] *T* (1 Jan. 1996), 6 (Wilson). G. H. Gallup (ed.), *The Gallup International Public Opinion Polls: Great Britain 1937–1975* (New York, n.d.), ii. 816, 819, 824, 850, 853, 871, 876, 882, 883, 904, 955.

[119] W. R. Louis, 'The Dissolution of the Empire in the Era of Vietnam' (2002), in his *Ends of British Imperialism . . . Collected Essays* (2006), 559.

[120] P. G. Boyle, 'The British Government's View of the Cuban Missile Crisis', *Contemporary British History* (Autumn 1996), 34.

'one consequence of the evolution from the atomic to the hydrogen bomb was to diminish the advantage of physically large countries': all countries, large and small, were now vulnerable.[121]

4. EMPIRE TO COMMONWEALTH

In 1951 it was not at all obvious that Britain had lost her long-treasured freedom to choose between Europe and the open seas. Her offshore European location and long-standing worldwide trading and cultural links made it seem natural to keep all options open, and to reap the cultural and economic benefits of acting as entrepot between Europe and a wider world. The Commonwealth in the 1950s and 1960s was an international association much more ambitious in area and potential than any hypothetical European union. It could mobilize deep-rooted family affections, historical associations, wartime loyalties, and long-established tariff-protected economic links; a war-torn Europe was, by contrast, far from being an economic, let alone a political, unit. Cultural links with the Commonwealth were drawn still closer in the 1950s and 1960s when British universities helped to establish new universities in former colonial territories. Not till the late 1950s did Empire Day and the Empire Games substitute the new-fangled word 'Commonwealth' for 'Empire'. School text-books and schoolboy fiction still echoed the sentiments of Haggard, Henty, and Kipling. W. E. Johns's Biggles adventure stories for boys—robustly patriotic, masculine and anti-Communist in tone—were at their height of popularity in the 1950s, and several were dramatized on BBC radio; Johns published ninety-six Biggles books, and was working on yet another when he died in 1968. Not till the 1970s did his alleged racism help to send him out of fashion.

Far from acquiescing in imperial decline, British governments in the early 1950s had ambitious plans worldwide through federation. A double advantage was anticipated from this: the Commonwealth's components would become politically and economically more viable, and there would be less risk of the Commonwealth becoming a United Nations in miniature, inconveniently dominated by small non-white states. British governments in their reforming zeal were prepared to break with older indigenous power structures where necessary—hence the tenacious UK positions taken up in Malaya and Kenya, and the protracted struggle for succession in Rhodesia/Zimbabwe.[122] There was much talk after 1952 of a 'New Elizabethan age', and in November 1953 the Queen and Prince Philip resumed their extended tour of the Commonwealth.

[121] *Memoirs of Eden: Full Circle* (1960), 368.

[122] See the excellent discussion in R. Holland, 'The Imperial Factor in British Strategies from Attlee to Macmillan, 1945–63', *Journal of Imperial and Commonwealth History* (Apr. 1984), 174–5.

In her broadcast on Christmas Day 1953 the Queen saw the Commonwealth as 'an entirely new conception—built on the highest qualities of the spirit of man: friendship, loyalty and the desire for freedom and peace'.[123] The heights of Commonwealth achievement seemed scaled in 1953 with the conquest of Mount Everest, in 1954 with Roger Bannister's four-minute mile, and in 1966–7 when the 65-year-old Francis Chichester sailed solo round the world with astonishing courage and self-discipline. As late as 1955 Dom Mintoff still thought it worth negotiating with the British government on Maltese union with the UK. 'It is difficult to define just what the Commonwealth is', said the Commonwealth Secretary in 1961, 'but it is easy to explain some of the things which it is not.'[124] It was, he said, an association with a shared belief in liberty and parliamentary government. If these ideals were not always later realized, the Commonwealth could at least exert pressure in their favour, wielding its sanction of expulsion when needed. Its practical advantages were important too. For its members it was a club united by sentimental connection and to some extent by economic self-interest; and for the UK, an electorally convenient face-saving device during the early years of diminished British world influence. Its effect, if not its intention, was to conceal from the world, as from the British people, the scale of the British retreat. 'To lose 400 million citizens as if it were some tremendous acquisition', wrote Harold Nicolson in August 1947, commenting on the loss of India, 'will be regarded by foreigners as a proof of our outrageous hypocrisy. It is not that. We do not desire to deceive others; we wish only to comfort ourselves.'[125]

American postwar backing revived in a new form the Victorian British imperial mission to contain Russian expansionism in the Near and Middle East and in the Himalayas. Even in the 1960s there was still an implied Anglo-American bargain: the British fought Communists in Malaysia, supervised much of Africa, and maintained a naval presence in the Indian Ocean, while America reciprocated by sharing her nuclear secrets and baling out the British economy when required.[126] In 1963 the Americans even sought to stave off independence for Guyana until its electoral system could be tweaked so as to keep the Communists in a minority.[127] Colonial wars provided training, later applied in Northern Ireland, in what were later called 'low-intensity operations': coordinating liaison with the civil power, intelligence gathering, and small-scale decentralized military operations using minimum force. 'In practice,

[123] Quoted approvingly by the Nigerian Minister of Transport and Aviation at the 7th Commonwealth Parliamentary Conference, London, Sept. 1961, in his speech printed in N. Mansergh (ed.), *Documents and Speeches on British Commonwealth Affairs, 1931–1952* (1963), 768.

[124] Sandys, speech at the 7th Commonwealth Parliamentary Conference in London, Sept. 1961, quoted in Mansergh, *Documents and Speeches 1931–1952*, 766.

[125] Quoted in Bradford, *George VI* (1991), 526.

[126] Pimlott, *Wilson*, 383.

[127] R. Lamb, *The Macmillan Years 1957–1963: The Emerging Truth* (1995), 364–7.

the Americans gave priority to anti-communism over anti-colonialism', yet neither the Americans nor the British could publicly acknowledge the fact: the Americans wished to preserve their anti-colonial image, while the British had no wish to publicize their dependence.[128] American backing for empire could not last, however, if only because the resultant scale of British defence commitments worsened the British balance of payments.[129] Besides, the USA could never openly align itself with colonialism: while the USSR was anti-imperialist in theory but imperialist in practice, the USA was anti-imperialist (in the sense of formal annexation) in both theory and practice. And while the USA showed not the slightest sympathy with the notion of the Commonwealth as an economic (let alone political) entity, the British resented being supplanted in world naval influence. The Americans, wrote Nicolson in 1953, 'are decent folk in every way, but they tread on traditions in a way that hurts'. A defensive mood had grown up within the Foreign Office by the early 1950s: 'people were trying to take things away from us or to hit us, or to change things in a way which we thought unreasonable, and we were resisting that. So our daily activity was about managing that decline.'[130]

None the less, the American connection did much to destroy Joseph Chamberlain's early twentieth-century vision: the hope that Britain's world empire could strengthen through combining imperial preference with social reform. From being cosmopolitan up to 1914, British overseas investment and exports had thereafter until the 1960s homed down on the empire/Commonwealth,[131] with Joseph Chamberlain's vision still seducing some Conservatives in the early 1950s. Yet British postwar governments, dependent on American loans to stay solvent, had to go along with the USA's postwar General Agreement on Tariffs and Trade, and cut tariffs. Furthermore, plans for an integrated Commonwealth defence system based on the UK had come to nothing as early as 1946. The ANZUS treaty of 1951 between Australia, New Zealand, and the USA (without Britain) indicated that Commonwealth countries would pursue their separate interests when allying with foreign powers. Besides, Conservatives had long been recruiting one-time internationalist and free-trading refugees from the British left, and in a vote at the party conference of 1954, L. S. Amery and his tariff reformers were beaten for the first time.

[128] R. Louis and R. Robinson, 'The Imperialism of Decolonization', in R. Louis, *Ends of British Imperialism: The Scramble for Empire, Suez and Decolonization. Collected Essays* (2006), 467; see also 461.

[129] Pimlott, *Wilson*, 388.

[130] Nicolson, *Diaries and Letters, 1945–62*, 245 (28 Sept. 1953). D. Hurd, 'Letters from a Diplomat: 1. A Bowler Hat and a Tightly Furled Umbrella' (Radio 4 broadcast, 3 June 1996).

[131] J. Stopford and L. Turner, *Britain and the Multinationals* (Chichester, 1985), 9–10. A. McKinlay *et al.*, 'Reluctant Europeans? The Federation of British Industries and European Integration, 1945–63', *Business History* (Oct. 2000), 94, 98.

Macmillan liked to see the Victorian age as an aberration in British history: before and after it, he mused, Britain's international standing had been precarious.[132] Even the Victorians had worried continuously about over-extended British lines of defence, especially in the face of potential European enemies, and with Ireland not securely under control. They had known well enough how necessary was self-confidence, even bluff, in preserving empire: as Winston Churchill's father Lord Randolph, shortly to be Secretary of State for India, told a public meeting in 1885, 'our rule in India is, as it were, a sheet of oil spread over a surface of, and keeping calm and quiet and unruffled by storms, an immense and profound ocean of humanity'. Morale and prestige alone enabled so few to govern so many, and during the 1950s both were waning fast.[133] By 1951 they had for decades been undermined from within: by the writings of E. M. Forster, Leonard Woolf, George Orwell; by the political actions of the empire's critics on the left; and by humour. David Low's Colonel Blimp in the 1930s, ITMA's Colonel Chinstrap in the 1940s and the Goon Show's Major Bloodnok in the 1950s all caricatured and subverted the unthinkingly decisive and hierarchical imperial outlook. '"Native" is a good word that may not now be employed without giving deep offence', Ivor Thomas announced as early as 1948.[134] Thereafter, civil servants within the Colonial Office such as Sir Andrew Cohen edged the entire decolonization process forward.[135]

A British empire acquired in a fit of absence of mind, and without structures or ideology to fend off concession, could with skilful presentation and timing be unobtrusively spirited away. German and Japanese wartime conquests had alerted colonial peoples to the weakness of the allied empires, and Fascism discredited authoritarianism as such. The Atlantic Charter undermined the moral justification for empires and prepared the ground for their peaceful overthrow. Though self-government for the colonies of white settlement had come peacefully and uncontroversially enough, its equivalent in South Asia—at first slow, controversial, and reluctant—had in its final phase during 1947–8 come in an ugly rush. Thereafter, with Irish and Indian independence conceded, the anti-imperialist genie was out of the bottle. It took only the Suez crisis of 1956 to accelerate decolonization. In what Churchill viewed as a policy of 'scuttle',[136] Eden had persuaded the Conservative government in 1954 to transfer its Middle East base from the Suez canal zone to Cyprus, and the last British officer left the zone in June 1956. When President Nasser

[132] A. Sampson, *Macmillan: A Study in Ambiguity* (1st publ. 1967, paperback edn. 1968), 170.

[133] To a Primrose League banquet on 19 Apr. 1885, on returning from India: R. R. James, *Lord Randolph Churchill* (1959), 162. See also W. S. Churchill, *Lord Randolph Churchill* (1st publ. 1906, 2nd edn. 1907), 720.

[134] *TLS* (9 Oct. 1948), 569.

[135] See R. E. Robinson's memoir of him in *Dictionary of National Biography 1961–70*, 227–9.

[136] Moran, *Struggle for Survival*, 509 (11 Oct. 1953).

of Egypt in the following month unilaterally nationalized the canal, decent standards of international conduct seemed threatened, yet Eden two years earlier had weakened Britain's hand. The situation was worsened by the lack of any comprehensive anti-Soviet defensive alliance located between NATO and SEATO to protect Africa and West Asia from Communist penetration. It seemed essential to prevent an anti-colonial nationalist from unilaterally threatening the Middle East oil supplies then essential to West European economies. When President Nasser of Egypt played off USA against USSR and placed himself at the head of Arab nationalism, parallels with Hitler were rapidly drawn by Gaitskell as well as by Eden, and even Bevan from Labour's left shared Eden's desire to topple Nasser. Theirs was the anti-appeasement generation, and it seemed essential to avoid repeating the mistake with Nasser. As Macmillan told the American Secretary of State Foster Dulles: 'we just could not afford to lose this game. It was a question not of honour only but of survival.'[137]

Given that the United Nations had never acquired its projected military strength to enforce international law, even a Liberal intellectual like Gilbert Murray saw French and British forces as a substitute. What was not publicly revealed was that both nations had colluded with Israel to separate the combatants once Israel had invaded, and in the process to seize the canal. Such resolute tactics eventually alienated much of the liberal-minded British opinion that had initially favoured resisting Nasser. Many more would have been alienated if the collusion's full extent had then been public, and if it had got out that the Lord Chancellor's endorsement of the invasion had been furiously contested by the government's legal advisers.[138] Eden, a lifelong civilized and self-consciously progressive Conservative, had never backed the atavistic style of Conservatism which hated American dominance and resented British imperial decline, yet now his allies were traditionalists on both sides of the political divide, for on the Labour side liberal intellectuals found themselves undermined by widespread working-class endorsement of force. The plan secretly concerted during October between the British, the French, and the Israelis was at first almost too successful: the Israeli attack on 29 October produced a victory so quick that the Franco-British presence to separate the combatants (with airborne assault on 5 November and seaborne landings on 6 November) was hardly required, and after the successful Anglo-French operation had incurred only light casualties Eden terminated it with only a third of the canal in Anglo-French hands. This was because the Treasury could no longer support sterling at the current rate of exchange without an immediate loan, and the lenders (largely under USA control) refused. The

[137] Macmillan, *Diaries*, ed. Catterall, 580 (1 Aug. 1956).

[138] *T* (1 Dec. 2006), 31 (newly released secret papers).

crisis had advertised the devastating consequences for the UK of not being frank with the Americans. The bad personal relations between Eden as Foreign Secretary and Secretary of State John Foster Dulles were the least of it: the British had underestimated President Eisenhower's control over foreign policy and the intensity of his anti-colonialism. The consequences for British armed intervention in Egypt were immediate. The message thus delivered was painful, and feeling ran so high that blows were exchanged in the House of Commons.[139]

The Suez venture's longer-term implications for British domestic and overseas policy were considerable. Reflecting on its lessons soon afterwards, Eden thought that it had 'not so much changed our fortunes as revealed realities'. Two of his deductions from this shaped policy under Macmillan thereafter: the realization that international influence must rest upon economic and therefore scientific strength; and, flowing from that, the recognition that the armed forces needed to be smaller, more modern, and more flexible.[140] While publicly playing down the scale of the Suez setback, Macmillan took care behind the scenes to promote penetrating and wide-ranging inquiries as a basis for new directions in British overseas policy. These included what he called 'a profit and loss account for each of our Colonial possessions' as a basis for deciding which should be retained, the first such report in the empire's history;[141] and analyses of defence and foreign policy which led eventually to the UK's first bid for entry to the EEC. Lord Franks described in 1990 how the Suez crisis had been 'like a flash of lightning on a dark night', throwing into relief the UK's loss of superpower status. Rapid repair work had to be undertaken, for henceforth 'virtually none of the Third World countries took the British at their word. Suez had shattered Britain's ethical position',[142] freeing Nasser henceforth to exemplify anti-Western nationalism. In his diary for January 1957, Britain's permanent representative to the United Nations Sir Pierson Dixon described himself and colleagues wandering about UN halls 'like lost spirits. Our best friends averted their gaze or burst into tears as we passed.'[143]

The consequences for decolonization were soon apparent. The fiasco caused the French to lose their colonial self-confidence, and by 1960 they had lost most of their empire. This had serious implications for other empires. African decolonization was neither sudden nor deliberate, nor did it reflect any worldwide nationalist movement uniting colonial peoples: within underdeveloped societies, cultures were too diverse, ethnic loyalties too intense,

[139] Benn, *Years of Hope*, 200 (3 Nov. 1956), 205 (5 Nov. 1956).

[140] Eden quoted in Hennessy, *Having It So Good*, 462; see also 460.

[141] Ibid. 472, 475.

[142] Quotations ibid. 458. Louis and Robinson, 'Imperialism of Decolonization', 466.

[143] Quoted in R. Louis, 'The United Nations and the Suez Crisis: British Ambivalence towards the Pope on the East River', in Louis (ed.), *Ends of British Imperialism*, 683.

and local circumstances too varied for that. The decolonizing impulse came from elsewhere: partly from a complex interaction between different empires, partly from interaction between different sections of the same empire. Empires form interlocking systems whose cumulative construction is mirrored by their cumulative decline. With no French empire there was less reason for a British one; with India lost, there was less reason to hold Suez; and with Suez lost, a British presence east of Suez was less feasible, and perhaps less desirable. Decolonization was a house of cards in slow-motion collapse. The Suez venture had not been Eden's personal aberration: it was a planned consequence of Britain's determination to retain freedom of manœuvre from the USA on the world's stage:[144] the limits to that freedom had now been cruelly exposed.

Decolonization also flowed from liberal attitudes and pluralistic structures at the centre; their absence in Portugal and the USSR helps to explain why imperialism in Lisbon and Moscow lasted longer. Britain had learnt lessons in handling colonial opinion very early from the loss of the American colonies, and later from India and Ireland. In southern Ireland the British liberal elite had shown after 1918 that it would not back last-ditch resistance to anti-British nationalism. When in 1956 Sir John Harding, Governor of Cyprus, told the Cyprus conciliation committee meeting in the House of Commons that EOKA consisted of fifty wild men who terrorized the rest, Attlee replied that he remembered being told something similar where Indian and Irish nationalists were involved.[145] By seldom getting itself entrenched against concession, Britain's political elite averted traumatic moments. Bloodshed, discontinuity, and inefficiency inevitably accompanied the handover at some points, but by the standards set in other imperial breakdowns, particularly those in more authoritarian regimes, Britain's decolonization was handled skilfully. Macmillan as prime minister was remarkably successful from 1957 at blurring the setback that the Suez crisis represented. The impact made by the scale and persistence of decline was muted because so often revealed only incidentally in other contexts. British defence spending declined fairly steadily after 1953 in its percentage of gross national product from 9.8 to 4.6 in 1978,[146] yet at no stage did the politicians confront the British public with this situation or initiate a public debate.

Resistance to independence movements would not have been feasible within the UK's two-party system. With British colonies in the 1950s, as with Ireland up to 1922, the system prevented British governments from holding

[144] Holland, 'Imperial Factor', 178. Those who have read D. Fieldhouse, *The Colonial Empires: A Comparative Survey from the Eighteenth Century* (1966), 402–7, and Darwin, *Britain and Decolonization*, 17–19, 128, 171, 174, 252, 288, will recognize how much this discussion owes to them.

[145] Nicolson, *Diaries and Letters, 1945–62*, 303 (12 June 1956).

[146] T. Gourvish and A. O'Day (eds.), *Britain since 1945* (1991), 157.

to any consistent imperial line. Unionist governments might at any one time seem stable, but everyone knew that Liberal or Labour governments would eventually ensue. Many African and Asian nationalist leaders had learnt their libertarian ideas and legal aptitudes from British guides: Harold Laski in the interwar LSE, reinforced by the British theorists of anti-imperialism from J. A. Hobson to John Strachey. Callaghan recalled that Labour's conference of Commonwealth socialist and allied organizations in Dorking in 1957 'was almost a forerunner of later Commonwealth Heads of Government meetings, with many of the same personalities attending'.[147] British Labour and colonial nationalist leaders thought poverty would vanish only through state planning and socialism, and agreed that the redistribution of wealth so central to socialism applied internationally as well as within nations. Labour also thought the Communist threat best warded off by this route: Third World skills should be enhanced through help with educational and technical improvement. With Attlee's help, Wilson founded War on Want, and published *The War on World Poverty* in 1953. In his first year as leader ten years later he made a rejuvenated Commonwealth one of Labour's central themes.[148] There were close links between anti-colonialism, hostility to nuclear warfare, and opposition to apartheid in South Africa. The latter from the late 1950s, a time of escalating concern about immigration levels at home, conveniently united domestic and overseas causes. Opposing apartheid was a cause particularly convenient for a Labour leader like Wilson, who wanted to seem more radical than party unity and his government's cautious domestic economic policy allowed. Labour politicians' Commonwealth enthusiasms chimed in with widespread British optimism about overseas aid. A powerful combination of guilt and idealism, voluntary action and state intervention, had sent late-Victorian university graduates on semi-religious missions into the London slums. Voluntary Service Overseas, launched by Alec Dickson and Launcelot Fleming (then Bishop of Portsmouth) in 1958, provided their grandchildren and great-grandchildren with a similar impulse, but for secular missions abroad. By 1967/8 there had been more than 4,000 of them—initially sixth-formers, but from the early 1960s predominantly graduates and experts.[149]

Hitherto governed on colonialism by a Fabian paternalism, Labour moved during the 1950s towards backing decolonization—thus extending the prevailing leftward ratchet effect on domestic policy across the entire political system, and edging the Conservatives by the early 1960s on to the conciliatory ground that had been Labour's territory in the early 1950s. The Conservative

[147] Callaghan, *Time and Chance*, 130.

[148] H. Wilson, *Memoirs: The Making of a Prime Minister 1916–64* (1986), 146. Foot, *Politics of Harold Wilson*, 238, 247, 292.

[149] See Dickson's obituaries, *T* (26 Sept. 1994), 21; *DT* (17 Sept. 1994), 23. For statistics, M. Adams, *Voluntary Service Overseas: The Story of the First Ten Years* (1968), 223.

governments of the 1950s were also constrained by needing allies overseas. Instead of immediately abandoning the American connection for a European destiny, British diplomacy after 1956 sought to restore the 'special relationship', whereas Suez taught the French never to trust the Americans and probably not the British either.[150] Clinging tightly to the American connection, Macmillan as prime minister was as active in high-level diplomacy after 1957 as Churchill between 1951 and 1955. With languid arrogance, especially given the prominence of intellectuals in formulating American policy,[151] he saw Britain as playing Greece to the USA's Rome. During the general election of 1959 he exploited television to extract maximum capital from entertaining President Eisenhower to dinner at 10 Downing Street on 31 August.[152] British cultivation of such an ally made firm resistance to decolonization inconceivable for the UK as soon as the USA required it: the so-called 'wind of change' blew more forcibly from Washington than from Westminster.

From the late 1950s decolonization's timing largely reflected whether the region possessed a non-British elite 'responsible' enough to receive sovereignty.[153] The Mau Mau tragedy in Kenya illustrates the horrors stemming from the lack of any such elite during a colonial transition, not to mention the complexities of the decolonization process as such. Superimposed on the long-standing Kikuyu land grievances, the disappointed expectations of Kikuyu who had served in the Second World War accentuated nationalist feeling. Kenya's white settlers (0.6% of its population in 1963) and Asians (2.0%) provided too narrow a base for a successor elite, but the African population (97.4%) was too sharply divided for the purpose, not only tribally but generationally: between traditionalist chiefs and progressive nationalists, though the latter included Jomo Kenyatta, Kenya's first president from 1963.[154] British government in the early 1950s, however, did not envisage for Kenya any swift independence, especially while Mau Mau was being contained between 1952 and 1959. Its barbarous and seemingly random slaughter, together with its superstitious oath-takings, accentuated white-settler racist attitudes, and fomented civil war among the Africans. Mau Mau's subsequent ruthless repression evokes the timeless brutalities of the gulag and the concentration camp, but also the evasions and hypocrisies of supposedly democratic regimes, whether in the Maze

[150] R. Jenkins, 'British Foreign Policy since 1945', *Proceedings of the British Academy* (1972), 158.

[151] As noted in Alastair's Buchan's 'Mothers and Daughters (or Greeks and Romans)', *Foreign Affairs* (July 1976), 665. See also Horne, *Macmillan 1894–1956*, 160.

[152] M. Cockerell, *Live from Number 10: The Inside Story of Prime Ministers and Television* (1st publ. 1988, paperback edn. 1989), 66–7. This book is very informative on politicians' relations with the media.

[153] D. Goldsworthy, *Colonial Issues in British Politics* (1971), 361–4.

[154] The discussion which follows owes much to David Anderson's *Histories of the Hanged: Britain's Dirty War in Kenya and the End of the Empire* (2005). Caroline Elkins's *Britain's Gulag: The Brutal End of Empire in Kenya* (2005) is less nuanced but also valuable. Figures calculated from Anderson, *Histories of the Hanged*, 345.

prison or Guantanamo Bay. It involved tightened direction of a war that for tactical reasons was not a war, clumsy attempts at brainwashing, ruthless intelligence, and forcibly resettling more than a million Kikuyu in fortified villages during fifteen months in 1954–5. Governmental coverings-up and deception were endemic, together with numerous perversions of justice; 1,090 Kikuyu were hanged for Mau Mau crimes, and Kenyatta was imprisoned and demonized as an oath-taking revolutionary.

It is the fragility of Kenya's white authority that paradoxically explains the scale of the brutality in British-run camps and fortified villages. Although the Colonial Office devolved much discretion to the Governor, he controlled the white settlers only precariously; with powerful connections in London, they readily took the law into their own hands, blind to the need for cultivating loyalist black opinion. A Governor without insight into African opinion and institutions could scarcely expect his writ to run within detention camps run by white-settler sympathizers through black collaborators, even had he desired it. Besides, he was being pressed by simultaneous contrary pressures from Conservative prime ministers: seeking all-party consensus at home, they wanted a negotiated settlement, especially given growing Labour disquiet about atrocities in the camps. London was also pursuing consensus within the Commonwealth: on the anniversary in 1953 of the Amritsar massacre (1919), Nehru pledged India's moral support for the Mau Mau freedom fighters, and at the Commonwealth prime ministers' meeting on the day after the coronation Churchill doubted whether the Commonwealth could unite on the issue.[155] By 1959 disquiet at the double standards of justice operating in Kenya was spreading beyond the Labour Party. On 27 July Enoch Powell made the speech of his life when attacking the authorities' cover-up of atrocities at the Hola camp. Rebutting in his peroration the claim that things are different in Africa, he emphasized that 'we cannot say, "We will have African standards in Africa, Asian standards in Asia and perhaps British standards here at home"... We must be consistent with ourselves everywhere.'[156] The way was now clear for Iain Macleod, as Colonial Secretary from 1959 to 1961, to accelerate African decolonization. Thereafter Kenyatta was released and reinvented as the moderate and somewhat traditionalist reconciler that he had always been. The scale of Kenya's governmental abuses in the 1950s was not only hushed up at the time but was prudently forgotten under Kenyatta's multi-racial successor regime. Whereas the sufferings of confinement were burnt into the consciousness of other ex-colonial nations through their leaders' experience, in Kenya the suffering was the experience of an entire people.[157]

155 Anderson, *Histories of the Hanged*, 105.
156 *HC Deb.* 27 July 1959, c. 237.
157 Anderson, *Histories of the Hanged*, 314.

There were all-party international and domestic reasons for the concessionary approach British governments so often adopted elsewhere. For Labour and Conservatives, the conciliation of friendly local elites offered some hope of retaining a Commonwealth link for countries otherwise vulnerable to Communist penetration. Such a strategy applied overseas the anti-Communist stance that Labour was adopting at home. Here was a new arena where the British political elite could practise its well-honed skills in timely concession, though the implications for the Commonwealth's tone were considerable. Should the newly independent small states—smaller, without federation, than had been intended—receive full status within the Commonwealth? Was the Commonwealth to be, as Macmillan (in a reference to London clubs) confidentially put it, 'the R.A.C. or Boodles?' Archbishop Makarios dismissed any notion that the Greek portion of Cyprus should be consigned to the Royal Automobile Club (RAC) category, and so in 1961 Cyprus joined what was becoming a Commonwealth of small states. Attendance at the Commonwealth prime ministers' meetings was growing, with Ghana the first African member there in 1957, and with 1960 as the last year when the cabinet room at 10 Downing Street could accommodate those present. In 1962 Macmillan privately confessed to the Australian premier Robert Menzies that he now shrank from any Commonwealth meeting 'because I know how troublesome it will be'.[158]

If the Labour Party increasingly turned against colonialism in the 1950s, this is not because it disliked the Commonwealth, nor did it yet acquiesce readily in Britain's diminished world influence. Labour's Commonwealth sympathies were deep-rooted, and resurfaced in the 1960s and 1970s whenever they seemed to conflict with Europe's demands. Such sympathies reflected the ongoing personal links of many working-class families with the colonies of white settlement. They also owed something to the Anglo-Australasian labour movements' affinities on welfare and democracy. The anti-aristocratic repudiation of class privilege persisted as a theme within the British left for long after the Liberal Party's interwar demise, and evoked a strong Australasian resonance. Besides, Labour was with ex-colonial peoples as optimistic as it had earlier been with the British working class: overseas, as at home, it anticipated instinctive allies among the underprivileged. Here, as so often elsewhere, Labour inherited the libertarian and liberationist instincts of its Liberal precursors, and bid energetically for the continuing liberal constituency among British voters. The larger the Commonwealth—'this remarkable multi-racial association, of independent nations, stretching across five continents, covering every race', as Gaitskell described it in his party conference speech repudiating entry to the

[158] Quotations from J. M. Brown and W. R. Louis (eds.), *The Oxford History of the British Empire*, iv. *The Twentieth Century* (Oxford, 1999), 698–9.

EEC in 1962[159]—the more friends Labour could anticipate overseas. Failures in the UK's decolonization process even had the effect of enlarging the United Nations faster than planned. Of the Commonwealth's federated successor states, three (Nigeria, the United Arab Emirates, and Malaysia except for Singapore) proved viable, but three others (the West Indies, Central Africa, and Aden) broke up: hence more United Nations seats.[160] Hope had not yet died on the left that the United Nations might one day rectify the world's injustices.

Labour's enthusiasm for scaling down Britain's worldwide commitments had always been constrained by the limited domestic appeal of progressive humanitarian internationalism. This offered little to Labour's potential supporters among down-to-earth and sometimes authoritarian working-class electors. In 1953 the secretary of the Labour Party branch in the Yorkshire mining village of Ashton offered to regale its meeting with a letter about problems in British Guiana: '"Don't bother", one of the ladies cried out. "We've enough trouble in Ashton".'[161] The Suez episode had exposed chauvinism in both parties: 'there are many more Labour people than we sometimes like to think who feel they would like to have a go at Nasser', wrote Crossman.[162] Overseas obligations could not be easily shed when Labour's Commonwealth friends like Lee Kuan Yew wanted Britain to honour commitments east of Suez.[163] So on Commonwealth matters Labour governments after 1964 were almost as reluctant as their precursors to move on or out. Add to these factors inertia, tradition, and British politicians' zest for world-class status, and the all-party persistence well into the 1960s of British worldwide pretensions becomes explicable. And as Crossman pointed out in 1967, parliament too lived 'in a world of wish-fulfilment and illusion, discussing how Great Britain should shape the future of the Middle East' at a time when Israeli victory had exposed British impotence.[164]

Developments within the former colonies moderated Labour's initial enthusiasm for the Commonwealth ideal, at least as an instrument of British policy. South Africa's departure in 1961 might be seen as confirming the Commonwealth's new multi-racial flavour, but enthusiastic decolonizers assumed rather too readily that colonial nationalists genuinely represented local opinion, and were too ready to equate independence with freedom and democracy. This was not always realistic in regions without pluralist traditions or democratic

[159] Quoted in P. M. Williams, *Hugh Gaitskell: A Political Biography* (1979), 735.

[160] W. R. Louis in *TLS* (9 Nov. 2007), 8

[161] N. Dennis, F. Henriques, and C. Slaughter, *Coal is Our Life: An Analysis of a Yorkshire Mining Community* (1956), 165–6.

[162] *Backbench Diaries*, 517 (28 Sept. 1956), cf. 549 (21 Nov. 1956).

[163] R. Jenkins, *A Life at the Centre* (1991), 228.

[164] R. H. S. Crossman, *The Diaries of a Cabinet Minister*, ii. *Lord President of the Council and Leader of the House of Commons 1966–68* (1976), 381–2 (13 June 1967).

structures and beset by rival ethnic, linguistic or religious groups. A special problem presented itself in Rhodesia, where the white minority's declaration of independence in 1965 under its first prime minister Ian Smith cited the crumbling in other former colonies of 'those very precepts upon which civilization in a primitive country has been built . . . the principles of western democracy and responsible government and moral standards'.[165] In Rhodesia as earlier in Kenya, nationalism of the white-settler variety caused British governments far more trouble than the African variant.[166] In seeking to get a multi-racial successor regime there, Wilson in September 1966 found himself in the midst of 'a nightmare [Commonwealth] conference, by common consent the worst ever held up to that time', where he was accused of racism, and where press leaks precluded confidential discussion.[167] Britain's failure to topple the Smith regime in Rhodesia reaped contempt in Africa, and the Commonwealth's standing slipped still further in 1965 when the USSR, and not the Commonwealth, mediated in the war between two Commonwealth countries, India and Pakistan.

Add to all this the economic mismatch between UK and Commonwealth which had emerged by the 1960s. Whereas the UK now wanted manufactured goods rather than the Commonwealth's raw materials, the Commonwealth wanted more (and better) manufactured goods than the UK, by then perceived as being in relative economic decline, could supply.[168] The 1950s and 1960s saw a massive shift in British exports towards the most developed countries: the share of Western Europe and the USA in UK exports grew steadily from 32 per cent in 1950/4 to 55 per cent in 1970/3, whereas in those years the share of former dominions fell from 30 to 17 per cent, and of former colonies from 23 to 10 per cent, with little change in the share going to the 'informal empire'. In thirty ex-colonial Third World states, imports from Britain as a share of their collective imports fell from 36 per cent in 1955 to 9 per cent in 1984, and in the same period exports to Britain fell in its share of collective exports from 29 to 7 per cent.[169] So the end of empire did not significantly raise the cost of imports, shrink the market for exports, or cut the income available from overseas assets. The world trade boom in these years reflected stability in the international monetary system, freer trade, and technological advance.[170] Powell was now even beginning to peddle the idea that the Commonwealth

[165] A. F. Madden (ed.), *Imperial Constitutional Documents, 1765–1965: A Supplement* (1st publ. 1953, 2nd edn. Oxford, 1966), 113.
[166] As noted in Darwin, *Britain and Decolonization*, 194.
[167] H. Wilson, *The Labour Government 1964–1970: A Personal Record* (1971), 277.
[168] For a valuable discussion of these points see J. Tomlinson, 'The Decline of the Empire and the Economic "Decline" of Britain', *TCBH* 14/3 (2003), 213–21.
[169] Sanders, *Losing an Empire*, 130.
[170] C. H. Feinstein, 'The End of Empire and the Golden Age', in P. Clarke and C. Trebilcock (eds.), *Understanding Decline* (1997), 228–9, 232.

weakened the British economy.[171] By June 1966 Crossman thought that the government's commitments east of Suez were 'all a fantastic illusion', and in January 1967 that the British electors would 'be perfectly content to accept the end of our imperial pretensions and to cut-back the mumbo-jumbo and humbug' in favour of a more realistic foreign policy.[172] Cuts in government expenditure soon effected this, and by 1968 Wilson could say that Britain had herself achieved independence within the Commonwealth.[173] Both British and Soviet empires collapsed primarily through a loss of nerve at the centre, but whereas the sudden collapse at the authoritarian Soviet centre in the early 1990s preceded anti-colonial feeling at the periphery, the British colonial collapse in the 1950s was more gradual, and stemmed from an institutionalized debate at the centre which interacted with an already growing dissidence at the periphery.

5. AN EMPIRE IN EUROPE?

The improved air travel that drew Britain closer to her colonies drew her (and the growing mass tourist market) even closer to Europe. Nostalgic for empire in 1969, the right-wing Conservative Julian Amery thought it 'perhaps, a tragedy for the development of the British Commonwealth that the aeroplane was not invented and developed fifty years earlier'—when European union had not yet even been envisaged. Yet imperial instincts were not absent from Britain's application to join the EEC, which potentially called into existence a new sphere of influence to redress the waning of the old,[174] for Britain's first application in 1961 was conducted in no humble spirit. Wounded British pride at the decline of empire could be assuaged not only by setting an example to the world in abandoning nuclear weapons or voluntarily abandoning colonial exploitation, but also by exporting to the EEC Britain's well-honed experience of operating democratic institutions. The EEC had after all originated partly to reinforce precariously democratic political structures and shattered free-market economies in the face of an authoritarian USSR that might at any moment break loose.

As we have seen, the Attlee governments never took the European movement seriously, though collaboration at this point would have enabled Britain to

[171] See e.g. Powell's speech at Trinity College Dublin (13 Nov. 1964), cited in K. Middlemas, *Power, Competition and the State*, ii. *Threats to the Postwar Settlement: Britain, 1961–74* (1990), 436.

[172] R. H. S. Crossman, *The Diaries of a Cabinet Minister*, i. *Minister of Housing 1964–6* (1975), 540 (15 Jun. 1966); *Cabinet Diaries*, ii. 182 (1 Jan. 1967).

[173] Wilson, *Labour Government 1964–70*, 582.

[174] J. Amery, *Joseph Chamberlain and the Tariff Reform Campaign* (1969), 528. For useful chronologies of 'European' events, see R. J. Lieber, *British Politics and European Unity: Parties, Elites and Pressure Groups* (Berkeley, Calif., 1970), 154 and ff.; D. E. Butler and U. Kitzinger, *The 1975 Referendum* (1976), pp. ix–xi.

mould European institutions from the start, especially as Churchill had already prepared British and European public opinion for British involvement. If embarked upon at any time up to 1951 or even in 1955–6 rather than in 1961, UK entry would have been much more acceptable to its six founder members, would have enhanced rather than eroded European goodwill towards Britain, and would have promoted British interests more comprehensively. As it was, Britain's three applications seemed merely unconstructive, and came too late to avoid a humiliating risk of rejection. Yet the many later commentators who regretted these missed opportunities were hindsighted. The EEC in the early 1950s seemed a harmless enough idea, if practicable, but joining it would have been very risky for Britain. The great geographer Sir Halford Mackinder noted that Britain had been for 2,000 years 'at the margin, not in the centre, of the theatre of politics', but the major fifteenth- and sixteenth-century discoveries had repositioned her at the hub of a known land hemisphere which included the Americas, Africa, and Eurasia.[175] To join the Six would once more have restored the UK to the margin, for by comparison with Britain's wider world, the EEC then seemed a relatively small and introverted sphere; nor could Conservatives, then battling for the centre ground, have risked moving far ahead of a public opinion not yet known to support entry: a revived Elizabethan England seemed the better bet. All the ties of sentiment and personal connection, reinforced by wartime memories, lay with the American and Commonwealth connection, whereas Europe provided only Italian waiters, French onion-sellers, and German au pair girls. Besides, the EEC, however attractive as an idea, seemed impractical after so recent a war between its proposed members; even French ratification was at times in doubt. So the British played down the importance of the Messina conference creating the EEC in 1955: Macmillan, Foreign Secretary at the time, had himself been a postwar enthusiast for European integration, but told his diary in 1955 that 'the French will never go into the "common market" ', and that 'the German industrialists and economists equally dislike it'. Even Gladwyn Jebb, later an enthusiast for the EEC, could write 'embrace destructively' on a Foreign Office brief about plans for the EEC in 1955, and Macmillan later regretted his own lack of vision at this point.[176] Thus was established the recurring pattern whereby at each stage in the EEC's journey the UK seemed about to miss the bus, then scrambled belatedly on board with much loss of goodwill and influence, then got off at the next stage, only to scramble crossly on again later with still more credit lost, and always leaving the other passengers to determine the vehicle's pace and direction.

[175] H. J. Mackinder, *Britain and the British Seas* (1st publ. 1902, 2nd edn. 1907), 1.
[176] Horne, *Macmillan 1894–1956*, 362–4.

Once created, the EEC at first aroused very little interest in Britain. Then Macmillan's bold bid in July 1961 to join it placed the EEC at the heart of British political debate. The French statesman Paul Reynaud once said that 'in England statesmen are pro-European when they belong to the opposition and anti-European when they are in power', yet here was a prime minister committing himself to an alignment he had only recently dismissed. Even in 1956, however, that dismissal could only have been provisional, given his comment to Sir Edward Bridges in that year: 'I do not like the prospect of a world divided into the Russian sphere, the American sphere and a united Europe of which we are not a member.' British ties with the Benelux countries had always been strong, and had been consolidated by the Second World War, but it took much sacrifice of national pride to seek entry from two recently defeated enemies (Germany and Italy) and from a long-standing rival (France). Beaverbrook told Macmillan privately in 1962 that 'as our power was broken and lost by two German wars, it is very hard on us now to be asked to align ourselves with those villains'.[177] No Conservative was at this stage publicly urging membership: Macmillan, as leader of a party with strong imperial traditions, was pushing its pragmatic instincts to the limit.

Yet several recent developments helped him. In failing to unite behind Britain during the Suez crisis, the Commonwealth revealed itself as a shrunken asset for the UK, and it was now defined vaguely enough to stave off for even longer any clear choice between Commonwealth and Europe; indeed, the UK's bid to join the EEC seemed in itself a declaration of UK independence within the Commonwealth. British trade connections were moving towards Europe: by 1954 the prewar share of Britain's trade accounted for by the six countries which later formed the EEC (about a fifth) had been regained, and from the mid-1950s British trade with the whole of Western Europe (not just with the Six) and the USA grew much faster than with the Commonwealth.[178] At the same time there was in Britain a growing combination of apprehension and envy at the faster growth rates in West Germany and later in France and Italy.[179] An enthusiasm for French planification pervaded the leading businessmen, senior civil servants, and economists who met at a conference sponsored by the FBI at Brighton in 1960—a conference followed by several less formal discussions and by a London conference addressed by Pierre Massé, head of the French planning commission.[180] There was also a surprised discovery on holidays abroad that the UK, which had long prided itself on being better organized and richer than continental European countries, was being outclassed. Businessmen travelling abroad were increasingly struck by the contrast between Britain's

[177] Reynaud quoted in Sampson, *Macmillan*, 94. Macmillan quoted in Young, *Blessed Plot*, 115–16. For Beaverbrook, Horne, *Macmillan 1957–86*, 262.

[178] Sanders, *Losing an Empire*, 150–4.

[179] For figures, see R. Coopey *et al.* (eds.), *The Wilson Governments 1964–1970* (1993), 20.

[180] T. Smith, *The Politics of the Corporate Economy* (Oxford, 1979), 146.

self-image and her reputation overseas. There were frequent references to 'the British disease': a poisonous cocktail of poor labour relations, poor-quality goods, and poor delivery times. Michael Young deplored the contrast between public facilities and services available on the continent and their shoddy British equivalents—all too evident to the traveller returning home.[181] People were beginning to think that if British workers would not help British governments to improve matters, perhaps the EEC's bracing impact would shift them. In the late 1950s the idea of joining the EEC was gaining ground with younger civil servants, and the Foreign Office was beginning to change its stance.[182] For a lacklustre government keen to win the next election, a successful bid to enter the EEC promised rejuvenation simultaneously for party and country.

Having rejected the chance of joining the EEC at the start, the UK set about creating the European Free Trade Association (EFTA) with Austria, Denmark, Sweden, Switzerland, and Portugal. In January 1960 the group's Stockholm agreement aimed to establish a free-trade area within a decade, but EFTA was little more than a card to play in negotiating with the EEC. Macmillan's campaign for entry skilfully minimized opposition at home. The impulse to apply for entry came entirely from above. He ordered a secret review of British economic and military strength from civil servants in 1959–60, and this prompted a review of relations with the EEC which in July 1960 recommended applying for membership.[183] The cabinet reached the same view in the following year, and British business warily followed Macmillan's lead. At this stage neither pressure groups nor the general public were involved. Macmillan aimed to avoid confronting the country with any need for sudden choice, and to move slowly towards acclimatizing cabinet and party to the idea of membership through first discussing whether negotiations should begin, then discovering the terms, then negotiating to improve the terms, and only then requiring decision about a package that could be sold to the country as the best deal on offer. He did not publicly voice his private enthusiasm for joining, or the reason for it: his desire to recoup Britain's declining world influence. Conservative support needed to be coolly pragmatic: it must play down the new alignment's likely impact, and must avoid overtly repudiating the 'special relationship' or the UK's imperial past. Besides, too much UK public enthusiasm for joining would weaken Macmillan's hand in a poker game played with the EEC. It was difficult even for sceptics to oppose the proposal merely to seek entry, and in the parliamentary vote on 2 August 1961 only thirty Conservative MPs abstained and only one opposed.

[181] M. Young, *The Chipped White Cups of Dover: Discussion of the Possibility of a New Progressive Party* (1960), 3–5.

[182] Young, *Blessed Plot*, 100–1, 103, 175–80, 210, 213.

[183] *Ind.* (2 Jan. 1991), 1.

Not until September 1962 did Macmillan try to mobilize public opinion behind entry.

Hitherto the EEC had not been controversial between the parties, and with his governmental instincts and personal connections Gaitskell (Labour's leader from 1955 till he died in 1963) might also have been expected to follow Macmillan's lead. His revisionist ally Roy Jenkins had, after all, been attending European conferences for some years, and argued in January 1962 that 'the Commonwealth is inevitably a declining interest. And the Labour Party already has enough declining causes to support without gratuitously adding another one to the list.'[184] But there was an anti-establishment Englishness about Gaitskell that aligned him with Labour's rank and file, as well as with its persisting enthusiasm for the Commonwealth. The government's negotiations with Australia and New Zealand had been difficult. Their privileged access to UK markets had somehow to be reconciled with a European alignment; R. A. Butler recalled accusations of betrayal flying, and 'terrible talks with Bob Menzies'.[185] Gaitskell disliked and distrusted Macmillan and the media pressure that was now building up, and to the academic in him the oversimplified arguments on each side seemed crude. He and his party's unity also had something to gain from its internal alignments cross-cutting rather than cumulating: he had dissented from many supporters over nuclear disarmament and nationalization, and by opposing EEC entry he might conciliate newly acquired enemies. His natural allies, the revisionist Labour MPs, were three to one in favour of entry[186] and, as his wife pointed out, immediately after his major speech at the party conference on 3 October 1962 had deployed 'a thousand years of history' against Macmillan's proposal, 'all the wrong people are cheering'.[187]

Yet it was not Gaitskell who unhorsed Macmillan, but General de Gaulle. 'All our policies at home and abroad are in ruins', Macmillan told his diary on 28 January 1963, the day before France issued its veto on British entry to the EEC, for the alternative was not as yet clear.[188] If Macmillan had made his first move sooner after winning the election in 1959, de Gaulle's position in France would have been weaker: hence no 'non'. As it was, Macmillan's cautiously calculating management of the issue gave more attention to potentially hostile British opinion than to the need for convincing de Gaulle that the British were now fully committed to their new alignment: Macmillan's success in the smaller arena entailed failure in the larger. De Gaulle's vetoes of 1963 and 1967 were entirely comprehensible at the time as holding operations, and in the light of Britain's behaviour within the EEC after 1973, they even seem far-sighted.

184 Quoted in J. Campbell, *Roy Jenkins: A Biography* (1983), 70; cf. 49.

185 Quoted in M. Charlton, *The Price of Victory* (1983), 278.

186 S. Haseler, *The Gaitskellites: Revisionism in the British Labour Party 1951–64* (1969), 228–9.

187 Williams, *Gaitskell*, 736, cf. 739.

188 Horne, *Macmillan 1957–86*, 447.

Painfully slow moves were now made towards aligning British with European practice in day-to-day matters. In 1963 a Ministry of Transport committee successfully recommended Europeanization of British roadsigns, but there was no switch to driving on the right-hand side of the road; 29 per cent of those polled in January 1967 supported this adjustment but 64 per cent opposed it. And while a sizeable majority favoured decimal coinage between 1961 and 1971, there was no majority from the mid-1960s for going further and decimalizing measures of length and volume.[189] Commercial pressures favoured decimalized coinage, given that decimalization had been advancing worldwide in former British territories from the early 1950s; by 1970 about three-quarters of British exports went to metric countries.[190] Progress was slow because of controversy about how the coinage was best decimalized, and because politicians feared public hostility; even the gradual introduction of the new coinage in 1968–71 was delayed in 1970 by a sentimental campaign to preserve the sixpence.[191]

Given this climate of opinion, why did Labour warm to the EEC after 1962? Partly because Gaitskell and Macmillan soon left the political scene, but also because British opinion was becoming acclimatized to the idea of entry. The Foreign Office now favoured entry; and the gatekeeper's every 'non' enhanced the forbidden garden's charms, for the UK must surely benefit from something the French were so keen to prevent. Furthermore the UK was becoming ever more aware of its economic decline by comparison with the EEC. On all the key statistics—gross domestic product, gross fixed capital formation, exports, imports, labour productivity, and wages—Britain between 1961 and 1974 was falling behind the Six.[192] The European elixir would, it seemed, rejuvenate the British economy. From 1961 to 1967 Gallup polls showed support for EEC entry consistently and substantially outweighing hostility.[193] Labour's corporatism at this time was not so very distant from European statism, whether (in France) inside the EEC or (in Sweden) as yet outside it. *The Future of Socialism* (1956) by the socialist intellectual C. A. R. Crosland drew upon Labour's long-standing Scandinavian affinity, claiming that Sweden with its welfarist and egalitarian outlook came near to realizing the socialist ideal of the good society.[194] Beveridge was among many for whom French planification was a model in the early 1960s for a UK which needed to refurbish its wartime domestic settlement—a UK now less complacent about British

[189] On transport see *Gallup Polls*, ii. 910. On decimalization, i. 613, 705; ii. 815, 872, 908, 1113, 1124, 1345, 1389.

[190] R. D. Connor, *The Weights and Measures of England* (1987), 302.

[191] Crossman, *Cabinet Diaries*, iii. 822 (17 Feb. 1970), 895 (21 Apr. 1970). Compare the outcry against phasing out the pound in 1984: Lawson, *The View from No. 11: Memoirs of a Tory Radical* (1992), 310.

[192] See the discussion in Butler and Kitzinger, *1975 Referendum*, 2–3.

[193] *Gallup Polls*, i. 599, 602, 609, 613, 626, 647, 654, 656, 660, 665; ii. 807, 813, 817, 824, 835, 840, 847, 850, 854, 863, 866, 872, 877, 884, 890, 895, 900, 908, 910, 917, 926.

[194] C. A. R. Crosland, *The Future of Socialism* (1956), 249.

political structures.[195] British negotiations to enter the EEC enhanced respect for European institutions, with France and Sweden strongly influencing British civil-service reform plans of the 1960s: British admiration greeted Swedish open government, ombudsmen, and agencies, together with the French civil service's professionalism and meritocratic structures.[196]

Conservative Europeans remained staunch, and Labour leaders who had supported Gaitskell's stance of 1962 began to shift towards them.[197] Wilson had then attacked the EEC as incompatible with national planning,[198] but Labour's move towards the EEC in the mid-1960s can be seen as an international extension of its zeal for economies of scale: a strong home market and a powerful research base would free the British economy from undue dependence on the American. Labour's National Plan of 1965 saw a Channel tunnel as 'of considerable long-term significance for our trade and traffic with Western Europe'.[199] By the late 1960s the proportion of British imports and exports from Western Europe was rising fast,[200] and Commonwealth economies were better able to fend for themselves. Arguably the flag must now follow the trade. By 1967 the Plan was being quietly dropped, but on 2 May Wilson persuaded his Cabinet to reapply for EEC entry, and the Conservatives backed the move. By shunning questions of principle and focusing on the terms of entry, Wilson (like Macmillan earlier) managed to avoid any clear moment of decision, and was proud of his cabinet's unity while the application was prepared and considered.[201] On 27 November he too encountered de Gaulle's 'non'. It came only days after sterling's devaluation on 18 November—yet another national humiliation to add to the Suez crisis of 1956, whether one supported the expedition or not, and to de Gaulle's first 'non' of 1963. For the prominent Labour backbencher Michael Foot in December, the government's letter of intent to international bankers in 1967 had been 'an ignominious letter which should never have been signed by a member of a British Cabinet'; he claimed to be working 'for a Government which can save us from these humiliations',[202] yet the European escape route now seemed blocked. How could the situation be improved?

In the UK's 'second try' at EEC entry, public opinion was even less involved than in 1961–3. Such pressure groups as did exist divided between

[195] K. Middlemas, *Power, Competition and the State*, i. *Britain in Search of Balance: 1940–61* (1986), 340.

[196] See e.g. J. Fulton (Chairman), *Committee on the Civil Service 1966–8*, i. *Report* (Cmnd. 3638, 1968), 12, 61, 92, 133–40.

[197] Williams, *Gaitskell*, 748.

[198] Foot, *Politics of Harold Wilson*, 224.

[199] *The National Plan* (Cmnd. 2764, 1965), 131.

[200] See the table in Floud and McCloskey (eds.), *The Economic History of Britain since 1700*, iii (2nd edn.), 259.

[201] Wilson, *Labour Government 1964–70*, 387. C. Ponting, *Breach of Promise: Labour in Power 1964–1970* (1st publ. 1989, paperback edn. Harmondsworth, 1990), 209–10, 213.

[202] *HC Deb.* 5 Dec. 1967, c. 1152. For the context, see above p. 75, and below p. 309.

Europhile elite-oriented groups and Europhobe mass-based groups. If Britain was securely to enter the EEC, the general public needed to be more fully involved. This presented Labour with special difficulties: broadly speaking, the greater the geographical distance from Europe and the lower down in society, the less the support for entry.[203] Labour's heartlands lay in Scotland, South Wales, and the industrial north, whereas the EEC's heartland within the UK lay in the more prosperous south-east. In failing to consult more widely, Labour's Europhiles were slowly preparing the ground for the later complaint that they were pushing the British people into joining the EEC without their 'full-hearted consent'. On the other hand, for three reasons Britain's second try was arguably a 'successful failure': it demonstrated, more forcibly than the first, a genuine commitment to the EEC; it showed that the British issue must be settled before EEC enlargement policy could advance; and by opening up wide divisons among 'the six' it left France more isolated.[204] To that extent, Britain's second application made the success of its third more likely.

In this chapter we have seen how the UK, like other countries, was opened up to globalizing trends, though in Britain's case the response was hesitant. What would earlier have seemed immigration on a grand scale was being precariously digested, and both the cold war and the Suez crisis had at least been survived. Decolonization had spontaneously advanced with surprisingly little public disquiet or economic disruption, and an approach to EEC membership became acceptable to UK opinion remarkably quickly—though de Gaulle was not impressed.

In this sequence all but two of the Introduction's eight motifs[205] have surfaced. So powerful was the war's legacy (the first motif) that it delayed the retreat from empire (with Nasser viewed as a revived Hitler) and the move towards the EEC. The tension between hermetic and receptive responses (the second motif) was reflected in the UK's equivocal responses to mass immigration and to the EEC's early evolution. What at first sight seemed time-saving advances in travel and communication (the fourth motif) enriched leisure in its diversity and locations, but simultaneously enhanced day-to-day pressures in two ways: first by the associated disruption in working practices, and second by the cost and complexity of escaping from work by organizing more recreations and holidays further afield. The politicians' relatively smooth handling of the immigration, decolonization, and EEC issues saw major changes occurring without disruption to UK political institutions (the sixth motif). All three issues, together with

[203] For opinion-poll information see *T* (30 June 1970), 6. For pressure groups see Lieber, *British Politics and European Unity*, 217–18.

[204] O. J. Daddow (ed.) *Harold Wilson and European Integration. Britain's Second Application to Join the EEC* (2003), 25, cf. 136, 139.

[205] See above, pp. xx–xxi.

the cold war, advertised the scale of the politician's responsibilities, and the skills required for handling them: voluntarist traditions might complicate the politician's domestic task (the seventh motif), but complexity was compounded by voluntarism at the international level, in the form of the autonomous nation state. The Chancellor of the Exchequer told parliament in January 1968 that 'we are no longer, and have not been for some time, a super Power. It does not make sense for us to go on trying to play a role beyond our economic strength.'[206] Overseas opinion could now increasingly constrain even UK domestic policy, and in foreign policy the approval of the USA and Commonwealth countries, and less often of Western Europe, was essential. On the other hand, new roles for the UK (the eighth motif) could present themselves in this changed international situation. In seeking world influence, the UK now saw itself as junior partner with the USA in championing democracy worldwide. This coincided with the UK's somewhat patronizing mood in approaching the EEC, and accelerated the changes in attitudes to race and political structures that the move from empire to Commonwealth entailed. Some even hoped that the UK would become worldwide exemplar of multi-racial harmony, as well as of democracy. This was not the first time that Britain had displayed worldwide moralistic pretensions, but CND carried these into new and controversial directions by envisaging UK leadership through renouncing rather than accumulating power.

[206] R. Jenkins, *HC Deb.* 17 Jan. 1968, c. 1797.

CHAPTER 3

The Face of the Country

Whether by day or by night, the United Kingdom's surface when viewed from the air changed markedly between 1951 and 1970. Superimposed on old patterns were the new field shapes and changed watercourses stemming from intensive farming. The new motorway system was taking shape; new towns and universities were springing up on greenfield sites; housing geography was in flux. Closer scrutiny would have exposed much that was changing inside even the old buildings, let alone the new: changed attitudes to the environment, to family geography, and to relations between the UK's component peoples. These are the themes of this chapter, whose focus moves successively from farming and the environment to transport change: and from urban problems and housing policy to the shifting relationship within the UK between town and country, London and provinces, nation and nation.

1. ENVIRONMENTALISM AROUSED

The face of the country was changing at least as fast between 1951 and 1970 as at any other time, but attitudes to the British landscape were changing even faster. Urbanization and industrialization involved viewing nature with less awe. With industrialization putting workers under cover, and the self-sufficient home (with the car as its mobile extension) shielding people from the elements, nature seemed under control. Important technical developments interacted with new economic interests to ensure that more was now known about the land, and especially about the seashore. With central heating insulating homes, bad weather became something more to be looked out at than experienced, except when its challenge was taken up as a recreation. Mid-century maps and atlases could now lay less stress on physical geography.[1] With ever brighter and more abundant street lighting and neon signs, with ever more efficient electronic and other guides to location, people less easily got lost. On 2 April 1949 the neon signs lit up the shops, and floodlights illuminated British cities for the first time after a ten-year wartime absence. Piccadilly Circus witnessed

[1] J. Black, *Maps and Politics* (1997), 60.

the biggest crowds since the war had ended, with traffic almost at a standstill. Buildings on one side of it 'were aglow with well-remembered signs', and 'the red, green, gold and white legends, staccato-flickering devices, and modest floodlights' were thrown into relief by the fact that lighting elsewhere remained by prewar standards muted.[2] For practical purposes the stars were for most people becoming redundant, and yet in these years they came to fascinate people all the more.

The weather's mysteries were beginning to unravel. There was as yet little sustained research into long-term weather patterns, but in the Meteorological Office the pioneer climatologist Hubert Lamb was already publishing important work on historical series, and was growing critical of the prevailing view that for the foreseeable future the climate would be static.[3] Weather forecasts were slowly ceasing to be a joke. The first televised weather forecast in Britain occurred on 29 July 1949, the first weatherman was televised on 11 January 1954, the London Weather Centre opened in 1959, the Americans launched the first weather satellite in 1960, and the Meteorological Office got its first computer in 1962.[4] In 1967 three-quarters of those surveyed by Gallup thought it worth consulting weather forecasts daily.[5] Concern about the rising sea level associated with 'global warming' had not yet prompted abandonment of defences against the sea, but the serious floods on the east coast from Spurn Head to Kent on 31 January 1953 showed that the elements must still be respected; the storm surge caused 307 deaths. Several factors interacted to accentuate the disaster. Too little was known about the dynamics of North Sea storms, so local authorities were caught unawares by a night-time combination of spring tide and high winds funnelling southwards as the North Sea narrowed towards the English Channel. The weathermen did predict the storm surge, but the wind brought down telephone lines in Lincolnshire and Norfolk, and there was little or no warning further south; the ten-foot-high surge breached sea defences in more than a thousand places. More were drowned than in earlier floods because houses had recently been built on reclaimed but vulnerable land. The countless minor tragedies included the immersion of Benjamin Britten's record collection, kept in his cellar at Aldeburgh: the labels floated off, and henceforth a supposedly Bartok record was found to contain Bach or Beethoven.[6] Reinforced by bulldozers and by wartime equipment that had

[2] *T* (4 Apr. 1949), 2.

[3] For Lamb's obituary see *G* (30 June 1997), 15. For annual rainfall in Edinburgh and London as compared with other European cities 1750–1969 see B. R. Mitchell, *European Historical Statistics 1750–1975* (1st publ. 1975, 2nd edn. 1981), 2–15.

[4] I am most grateful to Ms Helen Young and her colleagues at the BBC Weather Centre for generous help on this important subject.

[5] *Gallup International Public Opinion Polls*, ii. 935 (June 1967).

[6] B. Britten, *Letters from a Life*, iv. *1951–1957*, ed. D. Mitchell, P. Reed, and M. Cooke (Woodbridge, 2008), 124–5.

only recently become available, a massive labour force of 30,000 ensured that by mid-March all the sea-wall breaches had been sealed [Plate 5]. Still, the damage was immense, and many lessons were learnt, especially from Holland, whose engineering skills impressed Lord Waverley as president of the subsequent inquiry.[7]

The legal status of seashore and seabed prompted growing interest, given that the continuous changes in the shape, and still more in the perception, of the seashore affected property and amenity. Noting in 1968 that the UK's area varies with time and circumstance, a judge pointed out that 'the accreting shingle bank at Dungeness is no Alsatia in which a citizen enjoys immunity from the law of the land'.[8] Fossil fuels greatly enhanced worldwide interest in the continental shelf, and by 1947 offshore wells were already being drilled in the Gulf of Mexico. By the 1960s several factors concentrated oil and gas prospectors' interest on the North Sea. These included the discovery in 1959 of the giant Groningen onshore gasfield; the new theory of plate tectonics, with its implications for under-water fuel deposits; improved techniques for geophysical exploration; and the need to reduce UK dependence on imported oil and natural gas. Prolonged United Nations discussions about establishing a convention on the continental shelf came to a head, and in 1964, when the UK became one of the twenty-two signatories to the convention, coastal states gained sovereign rights over the shelf, as defined, 'for the purpose of exploring and exploiting its natural resources'.[9] The British government awarded the first licences to fifty-one companies in autumn 1964, and at the end of 1965 the first commercial find was reported.[10] Leman Bank was then one of the two largest known offshore gasfields in the world, and the first natural gas from West Sole arrived at Easington on 6 March 1967. British Gas soon felt able to take the bold decision to convert entirely from coal- or naphtha-derived gas to natural gas.

By the mid-1970s oil prospecting had progressively deepened the diver's range, and 500-foot commercial diving had become routine. The distinguished geographer J. A. Steers, urging the need for seabed research to extend beyond the low-water line, predicted in 1960 that the UK would soon witness the aqualung methods already widespread in California.[11] On their television screens the British public saw Jacques Cousteau discovering wrecks in overseas waters, and soon realized that Britain possessed 'a time capsule which we have only just

[7] Conference on the North Sea Floods of 31 Jan./1 Feb. 1953, *A Collection of Papers Presented at the Institution in December 1953* (Institution of Civil Engineers, 1954), 3.

[8] Diplock, LJ, in Court of Appeal, *PO* v *Estuary Radio*, in G. Wilson, *Cases and Materials on Constitutional and Administrative Law* (Cambridge, 1976), 229.

[9] K.Chapman, *North Sea Oil and Gas: A Geographical Perspective* (1976), 37.

[10] G. C. Band, 'Fifty Years of U.K. Offshore Oil and Gas', *Geographical Journal* (July 1991), 180.

[11] J. A. Steers, 'Defence against the Sea', *Advancement of Science* (May 1960), 13.

begun to know how to open, the past locked up underwater round our shores'.[12] Beneath were five million wrecks, said Roy Mason in 1973, and 'a ship sunk as a whole . . . is a complete piece of history, frozen in time from the moment it went down'.[13] Unlike land-based archaeological sites, sea wrecks preserved artefacts at the moment of use: the law had to protect them against plundering divers, especially given that high-pressure hoses and proton magnetometers seemed likely to expose so many. The seashore was also of increasing interest above the surface, given sailing's growth as a hobby in the 1960s: the 'marina', a word in widespread use by the early 1960s, not only altered the coastline, but raised difficult questions of ownership. As for the pirate radio stations, operating from ships near the mainland in the late 1960s, they raised similar issues: politicians had to tread delicately if they were to regain control by extending territorial limits without simultaneously infringing the freedom of the high seas.

The demand for fish was growing, yet stocks were shrinking. Deep-sea fish, including the herring, once a low-status fish, became more expensive. Mass-production methods seemed for the moment suited only to fresh-water fish, and developed only slowly. While annual landings of fish remained stable in the 1950s and 1960s at more than 800,000 tons, the number of fishermen fell steadily.[14] Iceland's economy, dependent on fish, prompted its citizens' vigorous response to the growing scarcity: its territorial limit was extended from three miles to four in 1950, to twelve in 1958, to fifty in 1972 and to 200 in 1975. The last three extensions led to what were called 'cod wars' between the UK and Iceland, though without loss of life. Whatever the legalities, this small nation deployed its seafaring skills with courage and resource, and skilfully turned the cold war to its advantage by playing off the Russians against the Americans, leaving the British stranded in between. British governments handled the situation clumsily and, in a little-publicized national humiliation, eventually had to back off.[15]

The UK's face was also being further exposed inland. Air transport brought new angles to bear. There had been airborne surveys since the First World War, and in 1920 the Ordnance Survey published the first civil map thus compiled. Hitherto unknown archaeological sites had been highlighted, and the archaeologist O. G. S. Crawford's interwar historical maps became valuable aids to scholarship. After 1945 aerial photography was carried much further by Kenneth St Joseph, whose wartime experience in RAF intelligence equipped him to transform Roman archaeology by tracking the Roman legions much further north of Hadrian's Wall than had earlier been suspected.[16] By the 1980s

[12] Cranley Onslow, *HC Deb.* 11 Mar. 1970, c. 1372.
[13] Roy Mason, *HC Deb.* 2 Mar. 1973, c. 1854.
[14] *BHS* 115–19, 213.
[15] Sir A. Gilchrist, *Cod Wars and How to Lose Them* (Edinburgh, 1978) recounts this sorry episode.
[16] See obituaries in *Ind.* (18 Mar. 1994), 30; *T* (26 Mar. 1994), 21.

the new technique had trebled the number of known Roman forts and camps in Wales by comparison with fifty years earlier, and the number of known marching camps in the north of England had risen fivefold.[17] In an eclectic combination of approaches—history, archaeology, aerial photography—Maurice Beresford's *Lost Villages of England* (1954), dedicated to 'my friends who walked and dug with me', won much publicity. He and others identified about 1,500 deserted medieval villages, hitherto seen as rare curiosities, and their known number doubled within the next thirty years. Reinforced by W. G. Hoskins's *Making of the English Landscape* (1955), 'landscape history' was now launched as a subject for study.[18]

Aerial photography helped to ensure that British archaeology flourished after 1950 as never before. The two university departments devoted to the subject in 1950 had become more than twenty by 1986. Archaeological technique improved too: radio carbon dating, dendrochronology, thermoluminescence.[19] Much light was shed on prehistory by relating man more closely to his natural environment. A powerful combination of bombing, redevelopment, deep ploughing, and motorway building raked over the UK's face, with all the deep probing facilitated in the 1960s by the new earth movers. Joseph Bamford, inventor of the JCB excavator, had by 1948 developed the first hydraulically operated two-wheeled tipping trailer, and five years later his JCB logo made its first appearance—on his hydraulic excavator loaders. The bulldozer and deep ploughing destroyed much, yet revealed much. 'Rescue archaeology' became essential, and imposed on the archaeologist in his smaller sphere the same need for synthesis amidst an abundance of data that the huge scannings of the universe imposed upon the astronomer. Bombing had destroyed more than a sixth of the area covered by Roman London, bringing major archaeological discovery in its wake.[20] Since 1939 the annual number of discoveries had doubled,[21] and the resulting strides in Romano-British studies were symbolized in 1970 by the launch of the annual journal *Britannia*.

Prehistoric and Roman Britain were now revealed as more populous than scholars had supposed: as much land had probably been farmed in Roman Britain as in the eighteenth century, and its population had exceeded that of the Middle Ages at any time.[22] Whereas archaeologists had tended hitherto to sacrifice all later surface layers to research at the Roman level, they now

[17] T. Potter, 'A Roman Province', in I. Longworth and J. Cherry (eds.), *Archaeology in Britain since 1945: New Directions* (1986), 80.

[18] J. Hurst, 'The Medieval Countryside', in Longworth and Cherry (eds.), *Archaeology in Britain*, 233. For an obituary of Beresford see *G* (22 Dec. 2005), 32.

[19] Longworth and Cherry (eds.), *Archaeology in Britain*, 7, 11.

[20] For a good discussion see Potter, 'Roman Province'.

[21] *Britannia*, 1 (1970), xvi.

[22] Hurst, 'Medieval Countryside', 202.

showed growing interest in the upper levels too, greatly advancing Anglo-Saxon archaeology, and founding the Society for Medieval Archaeology in 1956. They ventured still further: the term 'industrial archaeology' dates from the early 1950s, and a disparate group of enthusiasts, many of them volunteers, emerged just in time to preserve key aspects of a rapidly disappearing eighteenth-century environment. By the early 1970s this new discipline could mobilize about 1,500 front-line troops, working on their own or in groups.[23] The effect of research in each successive period was to emphasize continuity: to show how each of the UK's cultures had unobtrusively evolved from its precursor, and had in turn given relatively painless birth to its successor.

Britain's wartime emphasis on agricultural productivity persisted after 1945. It took in its stride a growing human population with a richer diet, and by the early 1970s had greatly reduced Britain's dependence on overseas-produced meat, sugar, eggs, wheat, and animal feed. Better feeding and management, antibiotics and vaccines, ensured higher productivity from cattle, pigs, and hens,[24] and the pressure for leaner meat and smaller joints interacted with improved breeding to ensure that animals bred for slaughter were on average much younger than a century earlier.[25] Hens were laying faster than ever: 176 eggs a year before the war and 270 a year half a century later.[26] The UK's population of pigs and poultry had doubled, and cereal production had gone up threefold since the late 1930s.[27] A combination of science, specialization, and mass production ensured a much better diet for a larger population despite cultivating less land. The overall acreage for arable crops was almost static: between 1945 and 1980 only barley's acreage showed any marked increase, and this was at the expense of oats, potatoes, and root crops; wheat, small fruit, and orchard acreages also declined somewhat.[28] By 1951 British farms had so few employees to lose that their output could rise only through developing mass-production techniques in factory-like premises. Nowhere in Britain were these techniques applied more effectively after 1951 than to pigs and poultry. British poultry production had exceeded prewar levels by 1949 and almost doubled between then and 1980;[29] chicken was declining from delicacy to dietary staple. The pattern with pig farming was very similar: prewar production levels were regained by 1951, and production rose threefold during the subsequent twenty years; from 1960 the UK became virtually self-sufficient in pork, and from 1982

[23] K. Hudson, *A Social History of Archaeology: The British Experience* (London and Basingstoke, 1981), 176.

[24] For statistics see D. Grigg, *English Agriculture* (Oxford, 1989), 95, 194.

[25] Ibid. 96.

[26] Ibid. 194. For a useful, statistically informed, and concise overview of agricultural policy until the 1970s see J. K. Bowers, 'British Agricultural Policy since the Second World War', *Agricultural History Review* (1985), 66–76.

[27] T. Beresford, *We Plough the Fields. Agriculture in Britain Today* (Harmondsworth, 1975), 75, 78, 80. Grigg, *English Agriculture*, 9.

[28] *BHS* 186–9.

[29] *BHS* 203–4.

a net exporter.[30] The ill-health of unwanted rabbits helped: the myxomatosis epidemic reached Kent from France in 1953 and spread rapidly with some human assistance throughout England and Wales and to parts of Scotland, greatly benefiting cereal farming and forestry. By winter 1955/6 99 per cent of Britain's rabbits were dead, and fewer survived than at any time since the medieval period, though during the 1960s their numbers stabilized.[31]

Behind this huge agricultural expansion lay major changes in technology and workforce. A quarter of farms were connected to the national grid in the early 1940s, 85 per cent twenty years later, and almost all of them twenty years after that.[32] With ready access to electricity, new farming practices became feasible. By 1965 over 300,000 milking machines were being used in the UK, and only 3 per cent of cows were being hand-milked.[33] Horses were disappearing from farms: from a peak of more than two million in the UK in 1904–10, they had vanished by 1974–6. By contrast, the number of tractors more than doubled between 1946 and 1956, with even larger increases in the number of combine harvesters and pick-up balers.[34] Agricultural chemicals, increasingly used from the 1930s, were not seriously suspected of polluting the environment till the late 1950s,[35] and productivity in many areas gained from enhanced specialization. Farms were growing larger, and mixed farming was declining in favour of specialization between areas: milk production concentrated in the west, sheep in the uplands, and arable in the east. Horticultural and vegetable production had become even more specialized by the late 1960s: three-quarters of the country's celery was produced within fifteen miles of Littleport in Isle of Ely, nearly half its brussels sprouts were grown near Biggleswade, and more than three-quarters of British raspberries came from Scotland.[36] The more perishable among these crops were grown in greenhouses and orchards near the urban consumer.

All this was achieved with fewer farm workers. Already by 1913 they made up a far smaller proportion of the total workforce in Britain than in other industrial societies, and their number (full- and part-time) halved between 1946 and 1967. But because the same trend advanced much faster elsewhere, Britain's agricultural sector was, by the end of the century, far less distinctively

[30] H. F. Marks, *A Hundred Years of British Food and Farming: A Statistical Survey*, ed. D. K. Britton, 1989), 77.

[31] J. Sheail, *Rabbits and their History* (Newton Abbot, 1971), 15, 201, 206. For a valuable overall discussion see P. W. J. Bartrip, 'Myxomatosis in 1950s Britain', *TCBH* 19/1 (2008), 83–105.

[32] Grigg, *English Agriculture*, 153.

[33] G. M. Robinson, *West Midlands Farming, 1840s to 1970s: Agricultural Change in the Period between the Corn Laws and the Common Market* (Cambridge, 1983), 116.

[34] V. H. Beynon, *Agriculture and Economics: An Inaugural Lecture* (Exeter, 1979), n.p.

[35] See e.g. Earl Waldegrave, *HL Deb.* 25 Apr. 1961, cc. 829–30.

[36] Grigg, *English Agriculture*, 211. J. G. S. and F. Donaldson with D. Barber, *Farming in Britain Today* (1969), 175.

small than at the beginning.[37] At the same time the British taste for growing food in gardens and allotments unobtrusively persisted. The food productivity of suburban gardens seemed substantial enough in 1956 to prompt a scholarly controversy about whether agriculture would really gain from building suburbs at higher density.[38] In the late 1960s the average allotment holder in England and Wales was spending ten hours a week on his allotment in the spring, thirteen in summer, eight in the autumn, and three in the winter.[39] The striking overall British growth in food production was in itself a major success story, and compared well with what was happening in many European countries.[40] By 1960 the British farming population's output per head exceeded that in any West European country except Holland, and during the 1960s British agricultural productivity rose twice as fast as in manufacturing.[41] 'If only the whole of industry had performed as well as British agriculture', said Thatcher in 1981, 'the economy of this country would have been transformed'. Good labour relations without restrictive practices had enabled British agriculture to produce 64 per cent more than twenty years earlier: 'that shows what we can do', she added, 'when we are free of these things'.[42]

Yet this did not lead her to deduce how constructively the state could promote economic growth, nor did she then focus on the associated environmental cost, though others were beginning to do so. Change in the rural environment during the 1950s and 1960s was rapid, with ever faster transport, ever more land cleared for cultivation through hedgerows being grubbed up, ponds filled in, and marshes drained. Probably typical of the rapidly expanding arable areas of eastern England at the time were Norfolk's farmland hedgerows, nearly half of which disappeared (often with government help) between 1946 and 1970,[43] together with the earthen bank from which they sprang. Surviving hedges were kept unprecedentedly tidy with the newly invented but ecologically clumsy mechanical hedge-trimmer, which endangered trees. Afforestation policy, too, paradoxically put trees at risk, for the authorities tended to view Britain's ancient woods as waste land which should be assigned to farmers or foresters; in the

[37] Donaldson, *Farming in Britain*, 304. See also the valuable table in R. Floud and D. McCloskey (eds.), *Economic History of Britain since 1700*, iii. *1939–1992* (2nd edn. 1994), 335.

[38] For a breakdown of propensity to garden or keep an allotment by social class, gender, age-group see the table in Hulton Press, *Patterns of British Life* (1950), 107–8. See also R. H. Best and J. T. Ward, *The Garden Controversy* (Ashford, 1956), 26.

[39] R.McKibbin, 'Work and Hobbies in Britain, 1880–1950', in J. Winter (ed.), *The Working Class in Modern British History* (Cambridge, 1983), 132.

[40] Sir Emrys Jones in Wooldridge Memorial Lecture, *T* (22 Sept. 1977), 4. For detailed comparative figures, see Mitchell, *European Historical Statistics*, 290.

[41] B. Burkitt and M. Baimbridge, 'The Performance of British Agriculture and the Impact of the Common Agricultural Policy: An Historical Review', *Rural History*, 1/2 (Oct. 1990), 268.

[42] *T* (7 July 1981), 2 (speech at Royal Show in Stoneleigh).

[43] W. W. Baird and J. R. Tarrant, *Hedgerow Destruction in Norfolk 1946–1970* (Norwich, 1973), 23. O. Rackham, *Trees and Woodland in the British Landscape* (1st publ. 1976, rev. edn. 1990), 191.

thirty years after the war, half of them were destroyed,[44] whereas afforestation entailed the mass planting of conifers on upland moors or to replace deciduous woods. By the mid-1960s the area under woodland was one-third larger than fifty years before, and covered 7 per cent of the country; by 1983 it was larger by one-seventh than in 1945. This was cultivated woodland, not wilderness, and owed much to the Forestry Commission's high-ground conifer plantations in Scotland and Wales, whereas private woodland area was in decline. The area of broadleaved woodland, concentrated in the south and east, did not decline, though its composition changed, with fewer oaks but more sycamore, ash, and birch.[45] None the less, a smaller proportion of land in England was afforested in the late 1960s than in any other European country, including countries more densely populated and ecologically less suited to trees.[46]

For very different reasons the industrial landscape began to change markedly in the 1960s. The postwar requirement that industry should reclaim after use set limits to environmental damage, but did not rectify the nineteenth-century backlog. In 1963 there were about 150,000 acres of derelict land in England and Wales, nearly a third of it heaps, nearly a third holes.[47] Hitherto people living nearby either had not noticed them or were resigned to their presence, whereas strangers did not know about them or kept away. Several factors generated change: in the 1960s a Labour government was alert (if only from constituency self-interest) to industrial dereliction, the industrial areas knew they needed an improved image to attract talent, new equipment made extracting and moving materials cheaper, the debris from heaps and holes could be used to build roads, and landscaping skills had recently advanced. The 'spoil heaps' resulting from mineral manufacture had for some time been saleable, but till the late 1960s the coal industry's 'slagheaps' were not; then at last it was found that they too could be used for road-fill. A sense of urgency was injected on 22 October 1966 by the disaster at Aberfan, where a slagheap's collapse killed 144 people, 116 of them children [Plate 14]. By 1975 Viscount Ridley in a House of Lords debate could see derelict land's reclamation as 'very much a non-political subject' and as 'very much a success story'; all his life he had lived within a mile of a pit heap, and now that it had gone 'I have the feeling that I shall miss it, at least from a distance'.[48] Landscaping was an interwar offshoot from the architect's profession: it favoured working with the grain of nature, and entailed a new valuation of trees and wild flowers in a natural

[44] Rackham, *Trees and Woodland*, 104–5. I gratefully acknowledge the generous help I received on forestry matters from Dr Peter Savill, of Oxford University's Dept of Plant Sciences.

[45] R. H. Best and J. T. Coppock, *The Changing Use of Land in Britain* (1962), 99, 107, 113, 229; G. M. L. Locke, *Census of Woodlands 1965–67: A Report on Britain's Forest Resources* (Forestry Commission, 1970), 80; *T* (11 Nov. 1983), 3.

[46] Donaldson, *Farming in Britain*, 83.

[47] Ministry of Housing and Local Government, *New Life for Dead Lands* (1963), 2.

[48] *HL Deb.* 29 Jan. 1975, cc. 483, 489.

setting. Owing much to Scandinavian inspiration, and with help from the Festival of Britain, Brenda Colvin (1897–1981) was the key influence. She summarized the aims of her long career in her *Land and Landscape* (1948), which sought harmony between man and the environment, town and country, science and the arts. With many public commissions during the 1950s and 1960s for power stations, universities, slagheaps, and even barracks, she exerted profound influence, together with colleagues who seized the opportunity the new towns presented in the 1950s. By 1965 Crossman, as Minister of Housing from 1964 to 1966, was urging the need for quarries to be landscaped into a lagooned 'blue belt'.[49]

It was also necessary to protect areas that were as yet unspoilt. The early nature reserves tended to be organized on wetland or coastland sites by volunteers, and in 1984 the RSPB acquired its hundredth reserve. The sportsman, war hero, and wildlife conservationist Peter Scott was the most outstanding of the early volunteer conservationists, and the wildfowl in his paintings and china reproductions adorned many a drawing-room wall in the 1950s. He did much to promote his ideas as a prolific and popular water-colourist from the 1930s and as an enthusiastic broadcaster in the 1950s. His work with the Severn Wildfowl Trust, established in 1946, led to his prominence in launching a grander enterprise, the World Wildlife Fund International, in 1961.[50] The birds' defenders increasingly defended eggs against collectors. Dutch conservation effort prompted the avocet's return to the Suffolk coast in the late 1940s, and the RSPB in 1949 made Havergate Island, near Orford, a first-class bird sanctuary. The Society stirred huge interest with its efforts in the late 1950s and early 1960s, ultimately successful, to reintroduce the osprey. So after many years when species of birds breeding regularly in Britain had been static, their number began to rise from 1950 by five species per decade; by 1974 more species were breeding regularly in Britain and Ireland than at any time since ornithological recording began.[51] The 1960s saw the environmentalist volunteer take off: after decades of slow growth the National Trust's membership, which had doubled in the 1950s, doubled again in the 1960s, the decade in which the RSPB's membership also doubled.[52]

As for state action, attempts were made in the 1950s to supplement London's plans by designating 'green belts' to prevent other cities from merging into conurbations; by 1960 nearly a tenth of England and Wales was thus protected,[53] and by 1988 the green belt was in aggregate larger than Wales.[54] The Attlee

[49] *Cabinet Diaries*, i. 412–13 (15 Dec. 1965).

[50] For fine obituaries see *T* (21 Aug. 1989), 12; *DT* (31 Aug. 1989), 4.

[51] J. T. R. Sharrock, 'The Changing Status of Breeding Birds in Britain and Ireland', in D. L. Hawksworth (ed.), *The Changing Flora and Fauna of Britain* (1974), 203, 205.

[52] *TCBST* 611.

[53] J. Blunden and N. Curry (eds.), *The Changing Countryside* (1985), 89. See also D. Thomas, 'London's Green Belt: The Evolution of an Idea', *Geographical Journal* (Mar. 1963), 20.

[54] *BST* 115.

governments' conservation structures bore fruit: by 1963 Nature Conservancy was responsible for forty-seven national nature reserves in England and Wales, and two years later it became part of the new Natural Environment Research Council (NERC). Between 1950 and 1956 the National Parks Commission (replaced in 1968 by the Countryside Commission) had designated ten national parks, centring on the remoter areas to the north and west. Three were in Wales, a fifth of whose land mass they occupied by 1974, though none were in Scotland;[55] their populations were substantial, and their protection demanded vigilance. The designated 'areas of outstanding natural beauty' were oriented more towards the south and east, and especially towards coastal areas.[56] These too were in danger, given the growing demands of heavy industry, oil, gas, and electricity. Of the coastline in England and Wales in 1966, a quarter was already built up, and a sixth of the rest was unprotected by planning policy.[57] In 1965 the National Trust, which already owned 287 miles of coastline, launched its 'Enterprise Neptune', a state-aided fund-raising venture, to add more: by 1969 it had added 100 miles—a total which by 1985 had reached 250, and 413 by 2005.[58]

The concept of 'global warming' grew out of an attempt to discern long-term worldwide patterns amidst the environment's many short-term, localized, small-scale, and disparate changes; in the 1950s and 1960s the phrase had yet to emerge. It was much easier, though still difficult, to tackle changes that were more clearly under human control. In the 1960s several distinct strands of largely defensive opinion flowed into one another on discovering their overlapping concerns. There were first the long-standing critics of indiscriminately pursuing industrial and agricultural productivity: they feared its longer-term environmental consequences. In promoting rural conservation there was an implicit alliance between on the one hand Liberal-Labour critics of industrialism with bucolic ideals, and on the other hand well-to-do Conservatives worried about the erosion of rural values, and operating through such bodies as the National Trust and the Council for the Preservation of Rural England. Both groups knew that institutions, whether an aristocratic family or a public authority, can take a longer-term view of the landscape than any individual. Large enough to house all generations, the aristocratic country house had been able to adapt to the fluctuating fortunes of any one family member or generation, whereas at lower social levels such fluctuations required the family to move house at each stage in the life sequence or property cycle. 'We are planting some more trees in the park', wrote Macmillan at

55 *HL Deb.* (2 July 1974), c. 154.

56 For a map see M. Shoard, *The Theft of the Countryside* (1980), 138–9.

57 Countryside Commission, *The Planning of the Coastline* (1970), 53, 60.

58 J. A. Steers, 'Saving the Coast: The British Experience', *Coastal Zone Management Journal*, 4/1–2 (1978), 17. Statistics from *G* (26 May 2005), 12.

Birch Grove in his diary for 6 December 1953: 'I shall not live to see them, but I hope Alexander will still be living here when they begin to make a show.'[59]

In the 1960s the more traditional environmentalists were joined by the opponents of factory farming. Already by 1953 half of those polled thought the battery farming of hens cruel, whereas only a quarter did not.[60] The animal welfare campaigner Ruth Harrison, from a Quaker background, soon began undermining the 'don't knows' after a leaflet on factory farming had been pushed through her door. Her influential *Animal Machines* (1964) had a preface by Rachel Carson, whose *Silent Spring* (first published in America in 1962 but not published in Britain till 1963), blisteringly attacked indiscriminate use of chemicals to control pests and diseases; it was the sort of book whose content and timing ensures readers. The early 'green' movement also had an anti-science dimension, in a loose alliance with vegetarians, anti-vivisectionists, and opponents of nuclear warfare. The breadth of natural science ensured that

"This is the dog that bit the cat that killed the rat that ate the malt that came from the grain that Jack sprayed."

Fig. 2. *Punch* (6 Mar. 1963).

[59] *Macmillan Diaries*, ed. Catterall, 277–8 (6 Dec. 1953). Alexander was eldest son of Macmillan's only son Maurice Victor Macmillan (1921–84).

[60] *Gallup Polls*, i. 303 (July/Aug. 1953).

it could reinforce both its friends and critics: environmentalists could draw upon its research in ornithology, zoology, and the new science of ecology. Environmental studies were in fashion by the 1960s, with Crossman promoting what in 1965 became a research council (the NERC) concerned with the subject.[61] With the environment more generally, as with slagheaps, a disaster focused opinion, and almost every aspect of its mitigation required scientific expertise of some kind. On 18 March 1967 the oil tanker *Torrey Canyon*, then among the largest ships in the world and aiming for Milford Haven, ran aground on Seven Stones off Cornwall, spreading unprecedented pollution from a huge slick of crude oil. Detergent was sprayed over the slick on the same day, and ten days later the tanker was bombed so as to burn off the remaining oil on board; troops and others were kept working for weeks tackling the oil pollution, which spread as far as Brittany. Countless sea birds and sea creatures died in consequence, as much from the detergent as from the oil, thus compounding from a new direction a newly perceived commercial threat to the bird population. The damage done to birds and even animals by agricultural chemicals had first been recognized in the late 1950s [Fig. 2] and was publicized by bird lovers and foxhunters; in 1960 the RSPB's inquiry into the peregrine, for example, showed that its numbers had halved since the 1930s.

Public interest in animals, too, was escalating. Zoos could now make money, and their number rose from about thirty in 1960 to about 100 in 1972. But the taste increasingly lay towards observing animals in their natural setting, retrospectively converting Whipsnade (established in 1931) into a trendsetter, and fuelling the UK growth of the safari park, of which by 1972 there were seven.[62] The same trend prompted the growing concern to conserve and reintroduce animals in the wild, especially in the inland waters whose pollution was at last being tackled directly and (through abandoning agricultural chemicals) indirectly. Hence the precarious mid-century survival of the otter and most species of bat. By no means all new flourishing mammals were introduced or preserved deliberately. To take only a few twentieth-century examples: the decline of game-preserving enabled the polecat spontaneously to emerge in mid-century from its remote fastnesses; nobody planned the ousting of the red squirrel by the grey; escapes from zoos and fur farms prompted the advent—by no means always welcome or deliberate—of muntjac, mink, and the South American coypu, the last of these so damaging to conifers that energetic extermination had succeeded by 1989. Tackling pollution and agricultural chemicals led naturally to concern for wild flowers, but bills in

[61] *Cabinet Diaries*, i. 228 (25 May 1965), 233 (27 May 1965), 237 (31 May 1965), 311–12 (22 Aug. 1965), 390 (25 Nov. 1965), 472 (7 Mar. 1966), 474 (8 Mar. 1966).

[62] *HL Deb.* 21 Mar. 1972, cc. 634, 649, 651.

the 1930s and 1967 to defend them got nowhere, if only because legislation would have been so difficult to enforce. None the less, by 1970 attitudes to the environment were changing fast, though these new insights had yet to influence the daily conduct of the British people, especially when travelling.

2. TRANSPORT REVOLUTIONS

No revolution in attitudes and conduct after 1951 surpasses that stemming from the private ownership of cars: their number in use rose fivefold in Great Britain between 1950 and 1970. As elsewhere in Western Europe, this growth rapidly outpaced the slowly rising number of commercial vehicles, whose number in Britain almost doubled.[63] By 1966 half the nation's households owned one or more cars.[64] More likely to be male and affluent than the population as a whole, motorists formed pressure groups that only a forceful transport minister dared challenge.[65] This major social change was important not only in itself, but for its associated minor revolutions. Streets filled with cars ineluctably lost many earlier roles, and gradually became barriers within rather than links between communities. Streets had once been places for trading, talking, playing, and entertaining, but rising noise levels together with sharper segregation of road from pavement drove away open-air commerce, entertainment, and sociability; many urban open spaces became inaccessible roundabouts, and pedestrians were pushed underground. The number of pedestrians who died rose by a third between 1950 and 1969, maintaining a fairly steady level of two-fifths of total road deaths in these years. And this despite Belisha beacons from 1934, zebra crossings from 1951, lollipop ladies from 1954, and panda crossings with their black-and-white road markings and push-button flashing lights for an unsuccessful experimental year in 1961. Far more important than palliatives in cutting accidents was to segregate pedestrians from vehicles; this explains the longer-term plunge in pedestrian deaths when related to traffic levels—from 41 per billion vehicle kilometres in 1938 to 21 in 1959 to 8 in 1979.[66] Yet walking in towns was becoming less pleasant. In their covered markets and arcades the Victorians had acknowledged the urban pedestrian's needs, and among the postwar new towns Harlow was the first with a pedestrianized town centre, 'an adventure in design', as its architect-planner recalled.[67] Transatlantic and European precedents prompted the country's first conversion of a street into a pedestrian precinct in 1967, the year when the Road Traffic Regulation Act permitted such developments. Shopkeepers, initially apprehensive at the advent of 'foot streets', were won

[63] *BHS* 558. [64] Mitchell, *European Historical Statistics*, 672. *TBS* 551.
[65] See Castle's interesting interview in *G* (3 July 1967), 4.
[66] Statistics calculated from Dept of Transport, *Transport Statistics: Great Britain 1996* (1996), 184.
[67] J. Morton, *Harlow: The Story of a New Town* (Stevenage, 1980), 140.

over by the results: the dramatic improvement in Norwich's London Street inspired imitation elsewhere.[68]

Faster and busier roads threatened cycling, both for recreation and for getting to work. More than a quarter of Great Britain's population over 16 used a bicycle in 1949, and of these two-thirds used it more than once a week.[69] Buying a bicycle and learning to ride it were a child's rite of passage in its slow journey towards independence, but after 1951 growing car ownership made cycling less necessary and more dangerous. Cycling went into marked decline, and for a time seemed likely to fade out altogether. Cyclists in 1952 accounted for more than a tenth of all passenger miles in Great Britain, but for only 1 per cent by 1970. For similar reasons motorcycle usage declined—from 3 per cent of passenger miles in 1952 to 1 per cent in 1970.[70] None the less, the moped and scooter came to symbolize the 1950s: there were more than 500,000 motor scooters in Britain by 1956, at least half of them Italian Lambrettas.[71] Communal road transport declined markedly: 42 per cent of passenger miles were travelled on buses and coaches in 1952, but only 15 per cent by 1970. Between these years trams and trolleybuses almost vanished, and taxis declined by half, though the number of buses and coaches (about 80,000) changed little; by contrast, the number of cars and commercial vehicles grew fast.[72] In 1955 the Nobel prizewinning physicist Sir George Thomson pronounced 'the most serious problem in modern transport' to be not obviously technological, but social: 'the problem of the rush-hour' was 'probably the greatest inefficiency of our civilization'.[73] Relatively inflexible working hours for an urban population meant that the transport system (whether by road or rail) was congested during the journey into and away from work, but was otherwise underused.

The Ministry of Transport's continuous efforts to keep road traffic moving drew upon its Road Research Laboratory and upon unsung heroes like the traffic-control expert Bill Hadfield, inventor of the yellow-line parking system, first introduced in 1956.[74] The dedication of Frank Blackmore as traffic engineer at the Laboratory (1960–81) was total: with a keen interest in junction design, he invented the mini-roundabout, first introduced at Peterborough in 1969, progressing to Swindon's famous multiple roundabout in 1972. 'His interest became an obsession', so that he often worked on schemes in his own time and 'family holidays were regularly punctuated with stops at intersections while he took photos from every possible vantage point'.[75]

[68] A. A. Wood, *Norwich: The Creation of a Foot Street* (Norwich, 1969), 24.

[69] Hulton Press, *Patterns of British Life*, 120–1; cf. graph for 1951–94 in *Social Trends* (1996), 203.

[70] *Transport Statistics 1996*, 178.

[71] F. Wilkins, *Transport and Travel from 1930 to the 1980s* (1985), 30.

[72] *BHS* 558.

[73] Sir G. Thomson, *The Foreseeable Future* (Cambridge, 1955), 53.

[74] For Hadfield's obituary see *T* (23 Aug. 1994), 19.

[75] Obituary, *G* (21 June 2008), 43.

The most dramatic among the Transport Ministry's traffic-moving innovations, the motorway, compounded the car's impact. Great Britain's road mileage increased far more slowly than vehicle ownership, from 185,000 miles in 1951 to 200,000 in 1970, but motorway mileage shot up from nothing in 1958 to 657 in 1970.[76] The word 'motorway' was first used in 1930 to denote 'a specially designated class of highway with two or more lanes in each direction, designed and regulated for use by fast motor traffic', and was in regular use by the 1950s. In December 1958, however, a new type of motorway appeared, defined as 'a limited access dual-carriageway road with grade separation, completely fenced in, normally with hard shoulders . . . for the exclusive use of prescribed classes of motor vehicles'.[77] In that month the first length of motorway in its new sense was opened by Macmillan as prime minister: the eight-mile-long Preston by-pass, later incorporated into the M6. Other countries—most notably the USA, Germany, and Italy—had begun earlier, and the British motorway system owed much to the civil engineer Tom Williams, whose observations on American motorways appeared in an influential paper of 1956.[78] Motorways came late to Britain for several reasons: British government was less dirigist, ministers of transport were transitory and weak, military priorities were less salient than in Nazi Germany or Fascist Italy, the Second World War postponed affluence in Britain on anything like the American scale, postwar full employment made employment-creating government schemes unnecessary, and land in a crowded island was expensive. Motorways appeared in the late 1950s in response to a consumer demand only recently aroused: from the private motorist, and from the manufacturer who needed more flexible access to components and customers in an increasingly integrated national market. To these motives were added the need to spread the nation's prosperity into areas of economic decline, and to protect the quality of urban life by syphoning off through-traffic.

Once launched, the twentieth-century motorways evolved continuously and almost organically, like the Victorian railways, and eventually joined up to form a nationwide system. The national motorway system was planned and built on a non-party basis, with the Conservative governments of the 1950s implementing trunk-road plans evolved by the Attlee governments. As for urban motorways, the Attlee governments discouraged plans for them, a task left for the late 1950s; Wilson's Labour governments were then primed for action. So heavy was motorway usage that within three years the M1, designed to last for twenty years without major repair, started to crumble.[79] By 1965 long stretches of the M6 and M5 were built or under construction: the M1 ran from Watford to Dunchurch and was extending northwards, the M4 was beginning to penetrate

[76] *BHS* 555–6.

[77] British Standards Institution definition, quoted in G. Charlesworth, *A History of British Motorways* (1984), 1.

[78] Obituary, *DT* (17 July 2001), 23.

[79] *T* (20 July 1998), 8.

London, and the M2 had been started. By 1971 the M5 and M6 were almost complete, and much progress was being made on the M3, M11, and M40, and in Scotland [Plate 16]. When 'Spaghetti Junction' opened in 1972 near Birmingham, it seemed a welcome sign that traffic was speeding up and was being syphoned out of or above the towns.

By comparison with nineteenth-century railway-building, and with the level of late twentieth-century anti-motorway feeling, the building of the system up to 1970 evoked surprisingly little protest. This may partly reflect the fact that decades earlier the railways had prepared the way for what became their arch-rival by undermining the political power of rural and aristocratic Britain. Any residual prejudice was moderated by the fact that the motorways were not built for profit: they were toll-free, and were seen as a public service. Greater care was taken, too, to situate and landscape the motorways sensitively; only in retrospect had railway bridges, embankments, and cuttings integrated themselves acceptably into the British countryside. The motorways' builders rapidly perceived the opportunity for engineering and architectural feats. For Castle as Labour minister of transport in 1966, such artefacts as the Almondsbury motorway interchange were 'the cathedrals of the modern world'.[80] Also noteworthy were the achievements of a firm such as Freeman Fox & Partners, which had built the Sydney Harbour Bridge in 1932, and had acted as consultant engineers for the Dome of Discovery. It went on to complete the Forth Road Bridge in 1964, the first of the two Severn road bridges (revolutionary in design) in 1966, and the Humber Bridge in 1981, as well as exporting its skills to bridge the Bosporus in 1973.[81] Given the cruising speeds that motorways and the motor designers now made possible, Great Britain shrank even more dramatically than with the railways' advent. There was at first no motorway speed limit, but in 1965 the 70 miles per hour limit was introduced experimentally, and became permanent two years later, with a brief reduction to 50 miles per hour during the oil crisis of 1973–4. By further segregating pedestrians from traffic, the motorways greatly reduced the road accident rate. Although the annual average killed in road accidents rose from 5,116 in 1951/5 to 7,396 in 1966/70, with injuries showing a similar pattern, motor traffic in the same period rose more than threefold.

The social life of the motorway could now burgeon. The interwar 'road house' succumbed to the motel, of which the first (the Dover Stage) was built in 1956–7; as for the motorway service area with food provided, Newport Pagnell on the M1 (opened in 1960) was the first. With long-distance travel so loosened up, people could, with self-catering, take holidays far beyond the seaside resorts; if the car was the family's mobile room, the caravan was its mobile

[80] Castle, *Diaries 1964–70*, 152 (22 July 1966).
[81] See obituary of Sir Ralph Freeman, *DT* (10 Sept. 1998), 27.

hotel. Whereas in 1955 a fifth of British holidaymakers took to their tents, caravans, holiday camps, and rented accommodation, more than a third were doing so in 1967. As for caravans, two million holidaymakers in Britain used them in 1955, 4.5 million in 1967. Nobody did more to popularize the caravan than Donald Chidson, the smartly dressed, publicity-conscious holder of the military cross who was the Caravan Club's secretary and director-general from 1951 to 1985.[82] By 1965 caravan sites in England and Wales accommodated up to half a million people, clustering especially on coastal sites in East Anglia and the west of England.[83] Long railway journeys had been expensive, and even then were not door-to-door, whereas self-driven journeys on toll-free motorways were cheaper, more convenient, and liberating. The rise of the second home was part of the same process: the combination of wealth, leisure, and mobility enabled more people to own what had earlier been called a 'holiday home', and to spend more time in it. The rapid growth in second-home ownership (simultaneously occurring in France and the USA) coincided with growing car ownership; second homes increased in the 1960s by 5,000 a year.[84]

Mass recreational travel was not all gain. The poet Philip Larkin in 1955 deplored its impact on Haworth parsonage: 'a good thing I'm not a Bronte worshipper or the sensation of being jammed in among 999 other trippers ("Old, ain't it"—"Here, luke here"—"Mam, I want the lav") would have driven me to unlawful wounding'.[85] The eagerness to defend the 'nonconformist Sunday' in North Wales did not stem simply from religious traditionalism: a whole way of life was threatened. In the 1960s Wales was deeply divided: the north favoured Sunday observance, the south sport on Sundays. In 1967 Crossman saw the combination among North Wales MPs to kill the Bill for opening up Sunday recreation as 'a good indication of what a very small group of M.P.s can achieve'.[86] In the 1970s tourism was among the influences reviving interest in the Cornish language, with signs even of a resentful Cornish Nationalist Party contesting elections.[87] Also vulnerable was the railway. From the 1950s freight carried by road increased much faster than the number of lorries because the lorries grew heavier, longer, and were allowed to travel faster: registered goods-vehicle numbers rose by 12 per cent between 1958 and 1986, but tonne-miles carried rose by 343 per cent. In the same period the permitted lorry size rose by half, and maximum length by 97 per cent;[88] articulated lorries became more common, and by the early 1970s the term 'juggernaut' had acquired a new application.

[82] Countryside Commission, *Planning Coastline*, 12, 25. For Chidson's obituary, see *T* (3 Nov. 2001), 25.

[83] Countryside Commission, *Planning Coastline*, 25–7.

[84] C. L. Bielckus *et al.*, *Second Homes in England and Wales* (Wye College Studies in Rural Land Use, Report 11, Dec. 1972), 61, 63.

[85] *The Selected Letters of Philip Larkin, 1940–1985*, ed. A. Thwaite (1992), 242.

[86] *Cabinet Diaries*, ii. 373 (9 June 1967), cf. 382 (13 June 1967).

[87] *T* (19 Apr. 1976), 2.

[88] M. Palin, 'Changing Transport', *Geography* (Oct. 1988), 309.

Much of the change reflected the growth from the 1960s of delivery by standardized container. The number of British Rail passenger journeys fell by a fifth between 1951 and 1970, passenger kilometres by nearly a tenth, tonne-miles of freight carried by more than a quarter, miles of British Rail track by two-fifths, and number of employees by a third.[89] When to this depressing picture were added the drawbacks of nationalization—discontinuities of management and policy, political interference, and centralized remoteness of control—the railways' plight seemed dire. British Rail's influential modernization plan of 1955 emphasized the railways' need to specialize in what they could do best: bulk carriage of passengers and goods. More investment, closure of uneconomic lines, abandonment of steam traction, and overall modernization were the route to solvency.[90] The strategy associated with Dr Richard Beeching, chairman of the British Transport Commission from 1961 to 1963 and of the British Railways Board from 1963 to 1965, was to pursue this course more systematically. Beeching was a physicist by training, and his avuncular exterior and reserved manner concealed a sharp analytic intellect. To harness it for the state, Macmillan was prepared to pay a salary more than twice the going rate for chairmen of nationalized industries.[91]

Of Beeching's two reports on the railway system, the first and best-known was diagnostic, influential, and yet in some ways backward-looking. He knew that to stem the railways' escalating losses, it was essential to move on from the piecemeal and pragmatic closure pattern of the 1950s, view the system as a whole, and speed up the closure process. Replete with maps, diagrams, and statistics, his first report adopted a purely commercial approach to railway profitability, leaving social and political considerations to others. His inquiry had itself to generate the requisite precise information, hitherto lacking, on the profitability of the system's various sectors. The art of cost-benefit analysis (pioneered in 1960 by the retrospective study of the M1) was only at the pioneering stage.[92] Beeching did the best he could within a tight timetable and with inadequate information. 'The railways should be used to meet that part of the total transport requirement of the country for which they offer the best available means', his report claimed: 'they should cease to do things for which they are ill suited.'[93] Beeching found that a third of the system's route mileage carried only 1 per cent of the total passenger miles, and a third carried only 1 per cent of freight tonne-miles; as for the stations, a third produced less than 1 per cent of total passenger receipts and half produced only 2 pre cent.[94] Unprofitable

[89] *Transport Statistics 1996*, 186. *BHS* 549. D. L. Munby, *Inland Transport Statistics: Great Britain 1900–1970*, ed. and completed by A. H. Watson (Oxford, 1978), 46–9.

[90] C. Loft, *British Government and the Railways, 1951–1964: Beeching's Last Trains* (2004), 36, 52.

[91] Lamb, *Macmillan Years*, 433–4.

[92] Loft, *Government, Railways and Modernization*, 84.

[93] British Railways Board, *The Reshaping of British Railways*, part 1. *Report* (1963), 57.

[94] Ibid. 10–11.

passenger stopping trains ('by far the worst loss maker'[95]) and their associated lines and stations were the report's main casualties; the faster and long-distance services seemed, however, to have a future. Macmillan's government was understandably nervous about how best to present the reforms, and eventually alighted upon courageous modernization as their theme.[96]

British Rail's staff fell by a quarter between 1948 and 1962,[97] and the first Beeching report (1963) caused a quarter of the remaining track and a third of the remaining stations to be abandoned.[98] His report did not fully tackle the need to rationalize the main-line system. The pruning of the 1950s which he systematized created problems because reserve routes for bypassing railway bottlenecks were sometimes removed, and unpredictable damage was done even to profitable lines by removing their access to what had hitherto been a national rail network. One of his critics likened Beeching to the efficiency expert for whom an orchestra would become more efficient if it eliminated one of its four oboe players because for long periods in a performance they had nothing to do, and some of its twelve violins because they were playing identical notes.[99] On the other hand, the inefficiencies stemming from the UK railway system's fragmented private-enterprise origins had to go, and modernization, already well under way before Beeching, now accelerated: in 1951 only 5 per cent of British Rail track was electrified, but 17 per cent by 1970. This was slower progress than in France, Germany, and Japan,[100] but it included the key section of main line between London and Crewe, halving travel time between London and Birmingham.[101] The construction of steam locomotives ended in 1960, and the last steam-hauled passenger train ceased operating in 1968; of total traction-miles run, diesel and electric power rose from 13 per cent in 1955 to 62 per cent in 1963.[102] Beeching could hardly have predicted subsequent population movements which revalidated some discarded suburban and rural lines; some of them could anyway be revived when needed. Political factors soon watered down his plans, and there was much subsequent indecision about management strategy, but by getting the plan of 1955 implemented more quickly, his reforms helped to ensure that by 1979 Britain had halved its rail workforce, and had probably acquired the most cost-effective railway system in Europe.[103]

Line closures and the decline of steam lent the railways a new and unexpected recreational role, with volunteers and enthusiasts to the fore. The civil servant Owen Prosser in 1951 founded the Railway Development Association, beginning with the Talyllyn project, whose first mile of track opened in 1955;

[95] British Railways Board, *The Reshaping of British Railways*, 7.
[96] Loft, *Government, Railways and Modernization*, 101–2, 111.
[97] *Reshaping of BR*, 50. [98] *TCBST* 448. [99] Lord Hughes, *HL Deb.* 1 May 1963, c. 255.
[100] *HL Deb.* 17 July 1969, c. 550. [101] *Transport Statistics 1996*, 186.
[102] M. Freeman and D. H. Aldcroft, *Atlas of British Railway History* (1st publ. 1985, paperback edn. 1988), 110. [103] Loft, *Government, Railways and Modernization*, 159.

he was the Association's secretary for more than twenty years. In 1960 part of the so-called 'Bluebell Railway' reopened in the Sussex Weald, and eight years later the Keighley and Worth Valley branch-line.[104] By 1970 the private railways accounted for 71 miles of narrow gauge track and 26.5 miles of standard gauge track on lines transferred from British Rail.[105] Prosser was also active in the Inland Waterways Association.[106] With canals and discontinued railways, the enthusiast's role was crucial not only in lobbying the authorities, but also in mobilizing volunteers for the delvings, refurbishings, and clearings of the undergrowth that now occurred throughout the country as old canals and railways once more came into use. With canal barges as with sailing ships, survival thrived on the link between enhanced leisure and a revived concern for the environment. And given that British canals so often penetrated hilly country, they donated some prize specimens to industrial archaeology.

Inland Waterways Association membership rose from over 800 in 1949 to 11,000 in 1973, and in 1958 the Association was registered as a charity which aimed to promote the canals' use, maintenance, and restoration.[107] An early priority was to broaden the authorities' perception of the canals' economic uses, and to prevent the Transport Commission from (literally) wiping off the map the waterways it aimed to close; early in 1959 only 380 of the inland waterways' 2,100 miles were navigable.[108] With the decline of the canals' freight-carrying role, urban canalside businesses had turned their backs on the water, precluding access to much canal shore; the longer-term aim was to reverse this process, while alerting the public to the fact that (as one MP put it in 1959) in the canals 'we have virtually 2,000 miles of glorious national park'.[109] These efforts bore fruit: by the mid-1960s restoration projects were enlisting volunteers in many parts of the country, the number of permits for pleasure craft on British inland waterways increased more than fourfold between 1951 and 1972, and over two million people used them in 1973.[110] With the marina's advent, two growing recreations (sailing and canal-cruising) could interfertilize in Britain, as earlier in America.

The continued prosperity of sea travel had hitherto owed much to the fact that only by sea could one cheaply get into and out of Great Britain, a country with more sea coast per square mile of land than any other in Europe. Coastal shipping had long been relatively dependent on carrying sea travellers rather than freight, there was as yet no Channel tunnel, and air traffic had not supplanted the continental ferry. Indeed, in 1955 Sir Christopher Cockerell

[104] See P. N. Grimshaw, 'Steam Railways: Growth Points for Leisure and Recreation', *Geography* (Apr. 1976) for a useful discussion.

[105] Mr Dennis Dunstone generously provided me with these figures.

[106] For Prosser's obituary see *T* (18 Feb. 2004), 26.

[107] P. J. G. Ransom, *Waterways Restored* (1974), 15.

[108] *HL Deb.* 17 Feb. 1959, c. 327. [109] *HC Deb.* 4 Dec. 1959, c. 1527.

[110] Ransom, *Waterways Restored*, 19. R. W. Squires, *Canals Revived: The Story of the Waterway Restoration Movement* (Bradford-on-Avon, 1979), 115.

filed a patent for his cross between the two: the blunt-nosed hovercraft. A prototype was built, but as yet evoked no commercial interest. The first commercial hovercraft service did not begin till 1968; travelling from Ramsgate to Calais, it took half a ship's time, and needed no special terminals.[111] Electronic developments were making travel safer by sea and air, and the number of lifeboat stations required had been diminishing steadily since the late nineteenth century.[112] Important new economic and technological developments rendered transit by sea still more attractive. The 1960s saw the early days of shipping cargo in standardized containers: these could be loaded and unloaded far more cheaply, securely, and quickly, and the containerized trade grew very fast thereafter. Britain's first container port opened at Tilbury in 1968, and London's older docks further west began closing. The deep-water terminal had arrived, reshaping British urban and transport geography.

Among the threats to long-distance railway travel was air transport. It extended to the masses travelling privileges once confined to the rich, though simultaneously but unobtrusively rendering long-distance travel less glamorous and exciting. By the early 1960s the shipping lines were shrewdly diversifying into independent air-travel companies. The number of passengers on domestic flights within the UK rose tenfold without a break between 1951 and 1970, though such flights as a proportion of total domestic passenger-miles travelled were still small, rising from 0.2 per cent in 1952 to 0.5 per cent in 1970.[113] It was a situation brimming with opportunities for entrepreneurs, as many postwar RAF pilots realized; they set up new and independent British carriers as both cause and consequence of diminished regulation, and their passengers increased much faster than those of the state-run BOAC and BEA.[114] Alternatives to the fixed-wing aircraft were also appearing. The helicopter proved its military value in Malaya during the early 1950s in crop spraying, patrolling, helping to contain disorder, and conducting search-and-rescue operations in difficult terrain. Its life-saving value was advertised during the floods of 1953 by its rescue function on both sides of the North Sea, its convenience for transporting important people was acknowledged when the Queen's Flight acquired two helicopters by 1959, and its role in difficult building operations was demonstrated when a helicopter topped out Coventry Cathedral with its spire in 1962.[115] During the 1950s Britain's helicopter industry advanced, with 1,022 British helicopters manufactured by 1960.[116]

[111] Wilkins, *Transport and Travel*, 48, 50.

[112] O. Warner, *The Life-Boat Service: A History of the Royal National Life-Boat Institution 1824–1974* (1974), 280 and ff. supplies useful statistics.

[113] *BHS* 561. *Transport Statistics 1996*, 178.

[114] For statistics 1953–61 see P. Lyth and M. L. J. Dierikx, 'From Privilege to Popularity: The Growth of Leisure Air Travel since 1945', *Journal of Transport History* (Sept. 1994), 103.

[115] J. Dowling, *RAF Helicopters: The First Twenty Years* (1992), 25–56, 203, 260, 365–7.

[116] M. R. H. Uttley, *Westland and the British Helicopter Industry 1945–1960* (2001), 2.

Important technical changes affected the Post Office, which then still ran both telephones and postal services. Between 1951 and 1970 for a population growing by a tenth, the quantity of postal items delivered in the UK rose by a third, whereas parcels delivered fell by a tenth[117]—the latter no doubt partly because car ownership brought self-delivery. Amidst rising labour costs, automation seemed essential, and in the 1960s attempts were made to improve postal deliveries, first by refining the system of postcodes. London's had been continuously improved since their introduction in 1857–8, and had spread to other cities. In 1963 the USA introduced zipcodes, invented by Robert Moon, but four years earlier the Post Office had already launched experiments at Norwich for a British variant, and on that basis between 1966 and 1974 all 22 million addresses in the UK were assigned codes containing a total of six letters and numbers.[118] The Post Office introduced a two-speed system of delivery (first and second class) in October 1968.[119] Telephoning, too, was changing. The number of phones connected, in the UK as in the USA, spread socially from the top downwards, and rose by 155 per cent between 1951 and 1970. In 1951–70 the number of calls rose by 189 per cent, and long-distance calls increased in the 1960s much faster than other types of call; there was a concomitant fall (by half) in the number of telegrams sent.[120] All-figure dialling was introduced in London in 1965–7. In 1955 Sir George Thomson envisaged eventual electronic improvements that might even moderate the rush-hour problem: 'It might be possible', he wrote, 'to arrange meetings of groups of people so that each could see and hear the speaker of the moment though each was seated in his own office.'[121] Decades elapsed before that came about.

All these shifts in communications seemed to shrink the UK. It became difficult to imagine a society where it had been normal to spend a lifetime in one place, when people had to rely on local resources for food and building materials, and when only the very rich travelled to London, let alone overseas. As late as 1939 Harold Wilson (born in 1916) visited London for only the third time in his life.[122] London's initial impact on Thatcher (born in 1925), visiting London for the first time when she was 12, 'was overwhelming . . . For the first time in my life I saw people from foreign countries . . . The sheer volume of traffic and of pedestrians was exhilarating.'[123] The proportion of the population born within their county of residence was already falling before the motorway's advent accelerated the trend.[124] The more mobile

[117] *BHS* 565.

[118] J. F. Raper *et al.*, *Postcodes: The New Geography* (Harlow, 1992), 48–9. For obituary of Moon see *G* (21 Apr. 2001), 18.

[119] Crossman, *Cabinet Diaries*, iii. 250 n. 1 (5 Nov. 1968) for a good discussion.

[120] *BHS* 567.

[121] Thomson, *Foreseeable Future*, 61.

[122] *Memoirs 1916–64*, 52.

[123] M. Thatcher, *The Path to Power* (1995), 10.

[124] D. C. Marsh, *The Changing Social Structure of England and Wales 1871–1961* (1st publ. 1958, rev. edn. 1965), 90–1.

the population, the more congested travel conditions became, for transport provision tends to lag behind demand. And because faster travel makes it easier to live further away, the average time spent in travelling does not fall proportionately. Furthermore, if faster transport's time gains for the traveller were unexpectedly small, the concomitant losses for others were considerable, especially for town dwellers.

3. URBAN UTOPIA POSTPONED

Transport changes after 1951 altered the location and internal geography of British towns: goods transported by road rather than by sea or rail created new communities near their major link points. Almondsbury and Spaghetti Junction—M4/M5 and M5/M6 crossing points, respectively—were the late twentieth century's Swindon and Crewe, except that warehouses and factories were more likely than homes to cluster round such noisy and fume-filled places. With motorways as with railways, the core of the system was the London/Birmingham/Manchester axis; but because the long-distance motorway traveller was free to turn off at will, the motorway fostered economic development (at a suitable distance) throughout its length, and service areas sprang up at intervals out of nowhere on greenfield sites. Cheap and rapid motorway transport helped to disperse the urban population, encouraging American-style commercial growth on the edge of towns. Earlier in the century inner-city populations had moved out from the centre (where they still worked) to live in the suburbs; after 1951 their jobs also moved out, especially from the City of London, and inner-city populations shrank.

The urban share of the population in England and Wales remained fairly steady after 1951, at about four-fifths of the total. Of the town dwellers, a rising proportion lived in medium-sized towns, fewer in conurbations[125]—a term which Patrick Geddes had applied to the city-region as early as 1915, and which had become fully accepted during the 1940s.[126] Conurbations' growth rate slowed down or even (as with Greater Manchester) declined, reflecting the falling birth rate, the creation of new towns, and the population's shift into the country. None the less, with 540 persons per square mile in 1951, rising to 606 in 1970, the UK had become more densely populated than anywhere else in the world except Taiwan, Belgium, Holland, and a few small island and city states. The crowding was all the greater given that the UK's population was so unevenly distributed, running all the way from 3.4 persons per acre in north-west England in 1968 to 0.5 in Wales and 0.3 in Scotland.[127]

[125] *BST* 326, 328, 330.

[126] T. W. Freeman, *The Conurbations of Great Britain* (1st publ. 1959, 2nd edn. Manchester, 1966), 1–2.

[127] *O* (4 Jan. 1970), 8. *TBS* 40.

Speeding up traffic between towns generates traffic within towns, and in London in the early 1960s the need to improve traffic flow became urgent, though for a time urban motorways were staved off by such palliatives as one-way systems, 'tidal flow' schemes, and urban clearways;[128] in 1958 London first acquired parking meters, hitherto viewed as an American fad. Birmingham's response was more drastic: its inner ring road was built between 1957 and 1971, its Bull Ring shopping complex completed in 1963. 'What a dreadful town!', exclaimed Kenneth Williams ten years later: 'even as you approach it, the heart sinks at the sight of such endless filth and appalling planning blight. Nothing but horrible buildings marooned inside networks of upraised roads and endless flyovers. One wrong turning and you start going round the whole mad set-up all over again.'[129] Faster traffic helps to explain why there were no decorative modern equivalents of Victorian street furniture. The wartime need to conserve iron and steel stocks had denied railings, often not replaced, to many hitherto-enclosed spaces. Larger shops, remoter and more centralized firms, and privatized travel eroded neighbourliness and a sense of place. Lighting became utilitarian, unsightly traffic signs proliferated, and fewer citizens felt the pride in community which had led their predecessors so generously to fund urban amenities. The religious motive and the sense of stewardship for wealth that had nourished the 'civic gospel' idea were waning, though as late as 1969 the Boundary Commission still 'considered it reasonable to assume that each existing constituency normally represents a community with its own distinct character, problems and traditions'.[130]

Transport pressures accentuated three urban problems: pollution of the ground, of the air, and of quietness. As goods were increasingly prepacked, the proportion of paper in dustbins rose sharply, and plastic appeared as a new item there.[131] The influential campaign with the slogan 'Keep Britain tidy' originated in 1955 in a Women's Institute resolution of the previous year, and was prompted by concern about rural litter,[132] much of it left behind by the increasing number of urban visitors driving there for pleasure. A recent visitor to Land's End described in 1957 how 'as soon as we rounded the last bend', arriving within half a mile of Land's End point, 'the whole of this beauty-spot—it was a bright sunlit day—looked as though it had been covered with snow. It was white and glistening—white with filthy paper, glistening with bottles and tins. We were so shocked that we turned round and went straight back.'[133] In towns the discardable packaging that reflected growing advertising and affluence could be cleared away only with difficulty, as the streets were now lined with parked cars. There was growing public interest in how to deal with

[128] D. Starkie, *The Motorway Age: Road and Traffic Policies in Post-War Britain* (1982), 23, 25, 30.
[129] K. Williams, *Letters*, ed. R. Davies (1st publ. 1994, paperback edn. 1995), 182.
[130] Wilson (ed.), *Cases and Materials*, 118, cf. 112, 114.
[131] *FT* (5 Aug. 1987), 6.
[132] *Ind.* (15 Jan. 2003), 18.
[133] Lt.Cdr. Maydon, *HC Deb.* 12 Apr. 1957, c. 1457.

litter,[134] and three successive bills were introduced on the subject, the third of which (enacted in 1958) built up national guidelines from best local byelaw practice.

As pollution of the air from coal fires declined in the 1950s, pollution from car fumes worsened. Permissive legislation launched from Manchester in 1935 had generated the smokeless zone concept, and in 1946 the council acquired the power to establish one. Other councils acquired similar powers, though by 1953 only Manchester and Coventry had used them. London's four-day smoke fog or 'smog' in 1952 powerfully influenced local opinion; in 1955 the entire city was designated a smokeless zone and enforcement gradually advanced thereafter. There was no major fog in London after 1962, London bird and wild-plant species began to diversify, and by 1973 smoke in central London had fallen to a fifth of the level considered normal twenty years earlier.[135] The legislation worked well partly because it ran with the grain of opinion, and did not alienate people by advancing too fast or too punitively. But its success also owed much to slum clearance; to British Rail's switch from coal to electric and diesel power; and to prior or concurrent autonomous changes in the use of energy, such as the substitution of gas, smokeless fuel, and electric heating for the open coal fire.[136] Between 1961 and 1971 daily average smoke concentration in urban areas fell by about 60 per cent and sulphur dioxide concentrations by 30 per cent. The overall discharge of sulphur dioxide, however, rose by a fifth between 1956 and 1964, much of it coming from the new power stations with their higher chimneys. So attention switched there, to pollution from traffic fumes,[137] and to cleaning up rivers and black-listed beaches.[138]

Growing road traffic accentuated a third kind of urban pollution: of quietness. Before the pollution of silence can be tackled, people need to be concerned about it. By no means all noise seems objectionable: birdsong and laughter, for example, are usually welcome. Noise is 'sound which is undesired by the recipient',[139] so its definition is inevitably subjective and changes with time and place. Pollution in this form receives less attention than pollution of

[134] For Enoch Powell's content analysis of press coverage on this see *HC Deb.* 2 Aug. 1956, c. 1760.

[135] B. W. Clapp, *An Environmental History of Britain since the Industrial Revolution* (1994), 48. H. A. Scarrow, 'The Impact of British Domestic Air Pollution Legislation', *British Journal of Political Science* (1972), 273–4.

[136] H. T. Bernstein, 'The Mysterious Disappearance of Edwardian London Fog', *London Journal*, 1/2 (Nov. 1975), 189–90. Scarrow, 'Air Pollution Legislation', 276–9.

[137] *T* (8 Aug. 1972), 2, quoting *National Survey of Air Pollution 1961–71*, i (1972). I. Low, 'Clearing the Air', *New Scientist* (22 Oct. 1964), 237–9.

[138] For Tony Wakefield's efforts see obituary, *T* (23 May 1998), 25.

[139] Sir A. Wilson (Chairman), Committee on the Problem of Noise, *Final Report* (Cmnd. 2056, 1963), 2. I gratefully acknowledge here the stimulating communications about noise that I received during 1995 from Dr R. R. A. Coles of Nottingham University, and in 1997 from David Symons (Noise Action Group) and Hillel Schwartz (Senior Fellow, Millennium Institute, Arlington).

other types partly because it tends to creep up on people only slowly, steadily advancing thresholds of tolerance. People balance their concern about noise against associated gains: affluence brings equipment in homes and gardens that is thought to earn its noisy passage: electric mowers, do-it-yourself electric drills, hedge-cutters, and the like. And because much noise is on the move, changes its nature and source, and evokes changing reactions, silence pollution is difficult to curb. Playing radios continuously as background for other activities, and often not heard at all, must go at least as far back as *Music While You Work*, first broadcast in 1940; it remained widespread in the late 1940s,[140] and spread much further in the 1960s when the transistor radio became popular. Concern about noise is also accentuated by crowded living, and worries about privacy grow in parallel.

Aircraft noise, increasingly frequent and intense, provided the first stimulus to public debate about noise, with a lively correspondence in *The Times* during September 1955 and a debate in the House of Lords on 3 November. Active in this cause was Lord Lucas of Chilworth, who lived near a military aerodrome outside Abingdon. He likened the need to curb aircraft noise to the pioneering curbs on noise from early motor vehicles: standards needed to be specified.[141] International jet flights made things worse: the first transatlantic jet service was launched in 1958 with Comet 4s and soon afterwards with Boeing 707–120s. Commercial self-interest, harnessing scientific ingenuity, demanded a solution because international airlines wanted to get passengers close to their destinations. MPs in the 1950s began to speak up for constituents in the flight-lines of major airports, and helicopter noise sometimes hindered politicians from hearing committee speeches.[142] Palliatives such as acoustic screens, strategic tree planting, and grants for insulating homes were by then widely discussed, together with scientific work on making planes quieter. Alleged and proved offences concerned with vehicle noise took a sharp upward turn in the late 1950s,[143] and it was time for a pressure group: in 1959 the Noise Abatement Society obliged. 'God is worshipped in silence but the devil is worshipped with noise', John Betjeman (an early supporter) declared.[144] The Society aimed from the first to bring commercial interests and intellectuals together, and initially thought in terms of appointing volunteer 'noise wardens', but soon gravitated towards legislation. There was so little opposition to the Noise Abatement Bill (1960) in the Commons that Sir Keith Joseph felt the need to remind MPs of the need to balance conflicting objectives: 'work can often be silenced at a cost in money; leisure can often be silenced at a cost in freedom . . . there has

140 B. S. Rowntree and G. R. Lavers, *English Life and Leisure* (1951), 275.
141 *T* (16 Sept. 1955), 11.
142 See Sir John Eden's complaint in *HC Deb.* 4 Mar. 1960, c. 1593.
143 For useful statistics see the Wilson Committee's *Final Report*, 168.
144 'My view', in *QP: The Journal of the Noise Abatement Society*, 1/1 (June/July 1960), 13.

to be a compromise between cost, freedom and tranquillity'.[145] In the Lords, however, a sharp conflict between the defenders and opponents of ice-cream chimes preceded the Bill's approval. This, the first measure to make noise a statutory nuisance, enhanced local-authority powers to tackle it, but only when emanating from loudspeakers, and not from planes or road traffic.

Expertise was now required: supplying it was the distinguished physicist Sir Alan Wilson, who chaired an admirably path-breaking, clear, wide-ranging, and expert inquiry on noise in 1963. Pointing out that not a single chair in acoustics existed in the country, the Wilson Committee stressed the need for more research at the subject's applied end, and the need to educate the public: 'if quietness were more often sought after by the public in domestic and industrial machinery, we have little doubt that the demand would in time be met'.[146] Fully aware of the need to define the problem, the committee formed subcommittees on the different sources of noise. There was now a basis on which national restrictions could rest, and each type of noise could be separately pursued. By the end of the decade the government could define maximum noise levels for aircraft taking off and landing, limit the number of planes moving at any one point, and specify their times of flight. The Air Navigation Noise Certification Order (1970) required new aircraft operating in the UK to be about half as noisy as current jet aircraft of the same weight. Urban noise was less easily regulated because so disparate. The street rowdiness and barrel-organs that had so troubled respectable Victorians had almost disappeared, and the noise which most troubled those polled by Gallup in the late 1960s came from road traffic; it scored way above neighbours, aircraft, and railways.[147] Here, as with aircraft manufacture, design requirements could be specified, as the Wilson Committee recommended: in 1968 limits on the noise allowed from exhaust systems were imposed, with prosecutions running at the rate of 13,000–14,000 a year, and in 1970 noise limits were imposed for new vehicles.[148] Noise had become a recognized social problem.

Town planning to cope with these and other problems was inevitable, but the best intentions of the geographers and architects who were in the forefront often proved disastrous. The fault did not lie in planning as such, but in plans that were inflexible and ill-informed, as exemplified in housing policy. The Attlee governments' planning mechanism aimed to cope with a serious housing problem, but assumed that economic growth would be only modest and government-inspired, and that population would be static. Homelessness is difficult to define and is not readily captured in official statistics, but its changing incidence defied the planners. When the wartime backlog had

[145] *HC Deb.* 4 Mar. 1960, c. 1631. [146] Wilson Committee, *Final Report*, 5.
[147] *Gallup Polls*, ii. 931 (June 1967), 943 (Aug. 1967), 1063 (Aug. 1969).
[148] *HL Deb.* 14 Mar. 1973, cc. 361–3.

been tackled, new regional needs were created by the resumed population drift from north to south, by large-scale immigration, by an unexpected rise in the birth rate, by the boom in car purchase, by social changes which made for smaller households, and by affluence, which prompted the desire for more houses and better amenities. Even in the late 1960s a sixth of all households lacked sole access to an indoor water closet, fixed bath, or shower.[149]

Whereas by the 1990s cultivated land seemed if anything too abundant, in the 1950s it seemed scarce: it was disappearing too fast, eaten up by industrial and suburban development, roadbuilding, and military training requirements. Integral to the postwar planner's nightmare were interwar ribbon development and suburban sprawl. The non-party remedy was to build high, whether for businesses or for homes. The impulse came not from technological innovation but from perceived social need combined with environmental concern. In 1956 Crosland said he would be prepared to 'pay any subsidy necessary to encourage more high building in cities in the interests of preserving the countryside'.[150] The high-rise ideal attracted almost everyone from the 1930s to the 1960s who wanted a better world: overcrowded Victorian slums would give way to light and airy apartments set within democratized equivalents of the eighteenth-century aristocratic park. Here at last was the ideal combination: a rural spaciousness and an economy in urban land which by transcending the ancient divide between town and country captured the benefits of both. Hitler's bombs, by opening up city-centre space, created a prize opportunity for repudiating an ill-planned past: science and technology would harness the architects' modern style in a powerful progressive union. Shared facilities and better accommodation would civilize the individual while nourishing a sense of community. All would now enjoy the privacy that well-to-do owner-occupiers had hitherto bought only for themselves; domestic life would escape the noise and dangers of the street; health and amenity would gain, and accidents would decline through separating people from traffic, work from residence. The 'Radburn' multi-level layout, separating cars from housing, was imported from America into several British towns in the early 1950s, and represented a major break with traditional town planning.[151] Order seemed poised to spring from disorder, and even half a century later the high-rise estate's clutter of parked cars, graffiti, makeshift fencing, streaky concrete, and swirling litter could not entirely conceal this bewitching vision.

Architect devotees of the modern style readily catered for the new demand. In escaping from what they saw as a fussy and finicking, dishonest past, they did not see themselves as espousing a 'style' at all: they had alighted upon a clean,

[149] P. Townsend, *Poverty in the UK* (1979), 482. [150] *Future of Socialism*, 526 n. 2.
[151] J. Burnett, *A Social History of Housing 1815–1970* (1978), 286.

rational, and honest approach to building that they thought would henceforth be the norm because it had emerged from the modern way of life. With the Festival Hall as their icon, the young turks of British interwar architecture had at last come into their own, though for several more years they had to battle against rearguard play-safe conservatism in the City and at Oxford and Cambridge universities. In Queens' College, Cambridge, for instance, an epic battle was fought in 1957–8 between the advocates of the traditionalist Stephen Dykes Bower and the modernist Basil Spence. Conservative politicians had always been wary of the Festival of Britain, and their governments after 1951 terminated its role in transforming the South Bank. Alan Bennett, by 1952 a national serviceman stationed at Coulsdon, Surrey, 'came up one Sunday hoping to catch an echo of the pleasure I'd had . . . I was a fool . . . It was a bomb site again . . . a real lesson for the future: the world in which we were never going to have it so good was on its way'.[152] With only the Festival Hall preserved, the Festival's Skylon and Dome of Discovery were torn down, and the exhibition site was left semi-derelict for years. The contrast with what Australia's third city Brisbane achieved on its south bank after Expo 88 is striking.

Still, the modern style seemed eminently suited to public housing, especially of the high-rise variety. Conservative governments after 1951 leapt into action: 3 per cent of approvals for public housing in 1953 were for high-rise, 26 per cent by 1964.[153] High-rise residential building reached its peak in the 1960s, with local-authority-approved blocks of fifteen to nineteen storeys in England and Wales growing from 0.1 per cent of public housing in 1956 to 8.3 per cent in 1964, and with the tallest blocks of twenty and more storeys growing from 0.3 per cent in 1959 to 4.5 per cent in 1967. The prime high-rise locations were London (with nearly half the high-rise buildings approved in 1966–71), conurbations, and inner-city areas short of housing.[154] The young Keith Joseph made his name among Conservatives as the minister determined to clear the slums and promote system building, with its prefabricated components, its destruction of the street as social arena, and its insensitivity to urban context.[155] 'I want to see the guts torn out of our older industrial cities', said Heath in the general election campaign of 1964, 'and new civic centres and shopping areas built there, the older houses torn down and new ones in their place.'[156] In 1955–75 nearly 440,000 high-rise flats were built. Former slum dwellers made up many of their tenants, and nine-tenths of the flats were built in inner-city areas; nearly two-fifths of the high-rise local-authority stock in 1972 was in

[152] A. Bennett, 'The Festival of Britain 1951'. See also J. Twigg, *A History of Queens' College, Cambridge 1448–1986* (Woodbridge, 1987), 373–6.

[153] Ponting, *Breach of Promise*, 123–4.

[154] See the valuable tables in P. Dunleavy, *The Politics of Mass Housing in Britain, 1945–1975: A Study of Corporate Power and Professional Influence in the Welfare State* (Oxford, 1981), 41–2, 44, 49.

[155] M. Halcrow, *Keith Joseph: A Single Mind* (1989), 29.

[156] J. Campbell, *Edward Heath: A Biography* (1993), 162.

London boroughs, and almost all the rest in county boroughs or conurbations like Birmingham, Glasgow, Leeds, and Liverpool.[157] High-rise history was in its way a notable success story for central and local government; both showed a resolute all-party determination to meet what was seen as a pressing need. Tony Benn, viewing new fourteen-storey flats in Bristol in October 1958, was enthusiastic: 'to see the bright airy rooms with the superb view and to contrast them with the poky slum dwellings of Barton Hill below was to get all the reward one wants from politics. For this grand conception of planning is what it is all about.'[158] The number of new homes built in England and Wales rose steadily in each five-year period up to 1969, and the total housing stock rose by 55 per cent in the thirty years after 1951. Whereas in 1951 38 per cent of British households lacked a shower or bath, and 8 per cent an inside or outside loo, by 1971 these figures had fallen to 9 and 1 per cent, respectively.[159]

Yet in retrospect the case against high-rise is patent, and Jane Jacobs had already made it in the USA during 1961 before Britain had experienced its full drawbacks.[160] Planning, she argued, must take account of how people actually live and why, yet in Britain very little public discussion attended the decisions both to begin and to cease building high.[161] The postwar prefab's unexpected popularity should have alerted the authorities to the sort of housing people really wanted: this despised and temporary response of the Attlee governments to housing shortage survived for decades longer than planned. By contrast, in the new high-rise flats, children had nowhere to play and fell off the balconies, neighbourliness withered, the buildings weathered badly, and the conditions in any one block were prescribed by its least considerate resident. The privacy and convenience of garden and backyard were swapped for the privacy of loneliness and isolation. Amidst the resultant anonymity, 'problem families' moved in, and crime and intimidation flourished. Today's progressive cause was tomorrow's social problem, and high-rise urban utopias like Liverpool's Kirkby or Sheffield's Hyde Park complex rapidly became places from which to flee. The planners were not solely to blame: they had not sufficiently allowed for unsympathetic governments and local authorities, national pressures for tax cuts, contractors' unsanctioned corner cutting, poor maintenance, and shared welfare facilities planned but not provided. The sheer scale of these projects made matters worse even before building started, for they condemned entire urban areas to 'planning blight'. The phrase first came into use during the 1960s, and became prevalent from the 1970s to denote the plight of land scheduled

[157] Dunleavy, *Politics of Mass Housing*, 1, 47.
[158] Benn, *Diaries, 1940–62*, 289 (18 Oct. 1958); cf. 299 (20 Feb. 1959).
[159] *BST* 363, 384. *Social Trends* (1995), 178.
[160] See her *The Death and Life of American Great Cities* (1st publ. 1961, London, 1962), 3–4.
[161] Dunleavy, *Politics of Mass Housing*, 143, 145.

for development and hence virtually unsaleable. Piecemeal interwar suburban sprawl had at least generated only small disasters: high-rise disasters were big.

By 1965 Crossman, no enemy to planning, was already growing disillusioned. In January he looked into what 'must be the largest hole ever created in a big city in the history of modern conurbations', a slum-clearance scheme in Manchester, and 'found myself impressed by the clearance but depressed by the standard of the houses with which they are filling it'.[162] He was disappointed in October with the 'enormous cube of flats of very poor quality' that Wigan's local authority was erecting, and predicted that Wigan in 2000 'will look just as bad as the old 1880 Wigan looks in the eyes of the 1960s'.[163] In April 1968 he was as depressed with what the modern style had produced when, as Secretary of State for Social Services, he moved to his Department's custom-built 'collection of huge modern glass blocks' in Elephant and Castle; the Department, he wrote, 'stands isolated and terrible', nor had it delivered the predicted improvement to the locality.[164] 30,500 families were living in tower blocks by 1968, but the reaction against them had already begun in the previous year when subsidies were abolished for every additional storey above six. On 16 May 1968 Ivy Hodge's decision to put on the kettle in her kitchen settled the matter: the resultant gas explosion caused nineteen floors in Canning Town's twenty-two-storey Ronan Point to collapse, killing five people [Plate 15]. The damage was patched up, but the reputation of tower blocks never recovered, and in 1984, when cracks appeared in Ronan Point's load-bearing walls, the flats were evacuated. By 1990 the entire estate of nine blocks had been demolished.[165]

Almost as disappointing was the situation in the new towns. These were designated in three waves in England and Wales: twelve between 1946 and 1950, five between 1961 and 1964, and six between 1968 and 1970, and by 1981 they housed more than a million people. In addition, there was planned expansion in sixty-six existing small towns to house conurbations' overspill.[166] Private enterprise was not prominent in their early years, freeing the new towns' development corporations to prescribe standardized external features. Conceived during the postwar reaction against interwar ribbon development, and when renting from the local authority was in vogue, the new towns were shaped by anti-urban attitudes, yet favoured industrialized systems of building. With their industrial estates discreetly segregated, they were oriented round landscaped 'neighbourhood clusters' of cottage-style homes interspersed with open space. Frederick Gibberd, Harlow New Town's architect-planner from 1947 to 1980, favoured taking account of people's housing wants, but also

[162] *Cabinet Diaries*, i. 125 (8 Jan. 1965); see also i. 177 (3 Mar. 1965).

[163] Ibid. i. 341 (2 Oct. 1965).

[164] Ibid. iii. 17 (22 Apr. 1968). Sir Keith Joseph was equally damning about the building in *G* (12 Nov. 1973), 13.

[165] *G* (17 May 1986), 30; (7 May 1993), ii. 21.

[166] See B. Wood's valuable table and discussion in *TBS* 331–2.

thought that architects should pioneer shifts in fashion, claiming that 'the standard of architectural design is always some 15 to 20 years ahead of public taste'.[167]

The new towns rapidly encountered difficulties. Macmillan as housing minister in 1951–4 favoured the new town idea, but focused on getting more houses built; this lowered housing standards, accentuating the new towns' longer-term maintenance costs. The towns also grew larger than planned in the late 1940s, when the planners had assumed guided but slow economic growth, an almost stationary population, and close government control over housing. In the 1950s these three conditions diminishingly applied, while Conservative lack of sympathy with new town ideals influenced their management structure: Crossman as Labour's housing minister in 1964–6 found new town corporations filled with colonial governors, Women's Voluntary Service (WVS) women, and Conservative surveyors feuding with the Labour groups which often ran the nearby local authority.[168] Serious problems were also pushing up from below, reflecting social structure, demographic make-up, and changing lifestyles. Beveridge chaired new town corporations at Newton Aycliffe and Peterlee, but they never approached realizing the Hampstead Garden Suburbs of his dreams: in these one-class towns 'the people are nice and the troops of children are lovely, but there's no conversation'.[169] Sylvia Calvert, in Angus Wilson's novel *Late Call* (1964), was fully prepared to admire the modern statuary located in the public areas of the new town she was getting to know, but 'she wondered what sort of supervisor they could have that would let it silt up with chocolate wrappers and ice-cream cartons like that'; revisiting it later in the day she saw that 'someone had dropped a whole *Daily Express* and its soggy pages had separated and wreathed themselves clammily around the ice-cream cartons'.[170] Early hopes of a vibrant community life, with abundant volunteer residents gathering in tenants' common rooms foundered on lack of leisure among the numerous young families who came predominantly from the skilled working class. An early survey of Harlow revealed an age structure resembling that of an underdeveloped country, with 40 per cent of the population under 15 [Plate 3]. Macmillan noted complaints that there were no aunties and grannies to help mind the baby,[171] and there was indecision about the balance struck between houses and flats.

Such problems were less likely to hit communities that evolved piecemeal, where change occurred in response to unmediated demand, and whose flexibility could more readily adapt to changed patterns of living. The new towns with

[167] Morton (ed.), *Harlow*, 104; also ibid. 114.
[168] *Cabinet Diaries*, i. 182 (7 Mar. 1965), cf. 126–7 (12 Jan. 1965).
[169] J. Harris, *William Beveridge: A Biography* (1st publ. 1977, rev. edn. Oxford, 1997), 463.
[170] A. Wilson, *Late Call* (1st publ. 1964; Harmondsworth, 1968), 136, 139.
[171] Morton (ed.), *Harlow*, 122. H. Macmillan, *Tides of Fortune 1945–1955* (1969), 419.

their cycle paths, their industrial 'zoning', and their central shopping precincts had been conceived before the advent of mass car ownership, let alone out-of-town shopping malls, mothers seeking paid work near home, and industrial centres landscaped and relatively unpolluted. By the early 1950s architects and sociologists were mobilizing in defence of 'privacy, safety, and urbanity',[172] with an emphasis on the variety, intimacy, and warmth of traditional town life. 'My goodness, it was terrifying', wrote Betjeman, visiting Stevenage new town on a rainy afternoon in 1953, describing a treeless concrete wilderness.[173] When in response to complaints about 'prairie planning' the architects came up with the grim hilltop multi-level town centre at Cumbernauld, Glasgow's overflow town, they won contemporary plaudits from the experts for what turned out to be a long-term planned disaster. The new towns' churches, envisaged as focal points of social life, were diminishingly relevant to a society that was slowly secularizing, their locked premises fortified on weekdays against the vandal. And beginning with one garage allocated to every twelve homes, the planners were by the 1970s recognizing that every home needed at least one.[174] Gibberd had seen front gardens as giving way to 'open fronts', with the house marking the dividing line between the public space at the front and the tenants' enclosed private space at the back. Yet in the 1970s, with public expenditure increasingly targeted at refurbishing the inner cities, owner-occupation was bound even without Thatcher to spread within the new towns, whose planned civic uniformities slowly succumbed to suburban privet hedges.

Opinion in the 1960s began to turn away from the modern style in architecture. Some modernist architects repudiated the style's Festival of Britain variant, which they thought too spindly and whimsical. In designing his uncompromising (and notoriously impracticable) History Faculty Building in Cambridge, commissioned in 1963, James Stirling aimed 'to fuck Casson': that is, overtly to repudiate the faculty buildings nearby that Hugh Casson had designed in picturesque modern style. Casson had been the Festival's Director of Architecture from 1948 to 1951,[175] but many of the Festival Hall's monumental modernist successors, including its ugly sisters the Hayward Gallery and the Queen Elizabeth Hall, heavily and deliberately rejected 'taste'. The Festival cannot be blamed for high-rise local-authority housing because high-rise monsters did not feature in its associated exhibition at Lansbury, where an entire neighbourhood of 400 homes was laid out to advertise local-authority planning and residential design. Furthermore, ugliness was not deliberately pursued by all modern architects who moved on from the Festival style. Particularly imaginative, yet at the same time practical, were the functionalist architects of

[172] F. Schaffer, *The New Town Story* (1970), 88.

[173] J. Betjeman, *Letters,* ed. C. Lycett-Green, ii (1st publ. 1995, paperback edn. 1996), 42 (to Evelyn Waugh, 24 May 1953).

[174] Schaffer, *New Town Story*, 96.

[175] M. Girouard, *Big Jim: The Life and Work of James Stirling* (1998), 58.

the telecommunications revolution, symbolized by Eric Bedford's remarkable Post Office tower built in London's West End in 1961–4, and a notable feature of London's skyline thereafter. A chain of similar towers was built across the country, sometimes on dramatic sites. Pevsner enthused about the tower at Stokenchurch in Buckinghamshire, for instance: 'this slender concrete spindle makes an elegantly sculptural statement against the Bucks landscape and is visible for miles'.[176] Some successful British modernists bestrode the world: Basil Spence, for example, designed Coventry Cathedral, but also advised the New Zealand government on its new parliament building and the United Nations on its new offices in Geneva; Denys Lasdun designed the National Theatre, but also the Gulbenkian Foundation's Gallery of Modern Art in Lisbon.

The 1960s demonstrated that a combination of high-rise modernist construction with roads for more and faster traffic could devastate a town. In the original draft of his *Shell Guide to Worcestershire*, toned down for publication, Lees-Milne said that Worcester had been sacked on five occasions: by Romans, Danes, Saxons, Welsh, and Roundheads, but never so disastrously as by the present mayor and corporation. Severe damage was also done in Norwich, King's Lynn, Gloucester, and Newcastle.[177] Human scale was gradually lost within the British cities worst affected. 'Take a road you could have driven blindfold a year ago', wrote Anne Scott-James in 1973, 'and it has become a lunar landscape' with 'half the streets you knew torn down'.[178] Rich property developers like Bernard Sunley, Charles Clore, and Jack Cotton were helping to transform the skyline of the larger cities and line their streets with cliff-like glass-fronted concrete office buildings squeezing out or thrusting between old churches and Victorian shops. No doubt space was used more efficiently and decaying areas were revived; but these newcomers, unlike the aristocratic developers who had so often preceded them, were pursuing short-term profit at the expense of long-term improvement;[179] insurance companies put up the money and left the developers to plan the outcome. At the Dorchester Hotel, Jack Cotton marshalled employees, allies, and friends for his company's annual lunch.[180] Surrounded in his suite there by his Renoirs, he usually prevailed, though not with his plans for rebuilding half Piccadilly Circus, which ran into a storm in 1959.

Large, complex, and relatively anonymous, the new consortia of architects, engineers, and designers—combining and recombining in ever larger concerns—matched the large, expensive, and often publicly funded projects

[176] N. Pevsner and E. Williamson with G. K. Brandwood, *Buckinghamshire* (2nd edn. New Haven and London, 2003), 651.

[177] Betjeman, *Letters*, ii. 276. See also Duke of Grafton, *HL Deb.* 11 Apr. 1973, cc. 690–1.

[178] A. Scott-James, 'When a Change is as Good as a Nightmare', *T* (9 Jan. 1973), 12.

[179] A. Sampson, *Anatomy of Britain* (1962), 417. See also 422.

[180] Ibid. 419–22.

that they tackled. Within these firms the architect became a mere coordinator between diverse professions at least as ambitious as his own. Height controls, after twenty years of restrictions, were relaxed in 1958 and Richard Seifert's unneighbourly Centrepoint (completed in 1964, but empty till 1979) was allowed to dwarf surrounding buildings in the Tottenham Court Road. His huge firm designed more than 500 office blocks and many hospitals and hotels. Astute in exploiting planning law, he pleased his many clients by providing ample rentable space. His architecturally undistinguished and skyscraping Natwest tower dwarfed St Paul's in the City of London, and helped to ruin one of the finest skylines of any great world city.[181] In Oxford the idea of conserving a skyline had been strong enough in the early 1960s for its planning authority to designate a central area within which it was protected against ill-considered new buildings.[182] Not so London's skyline: 'the London that slowly evolved after the Great Fire took about 300 years to build', the Prince of Wales complained in 1988, and 'took about 15 years to destroy'; no such vandalism would have occurred, he said, in Paris or Venice.[183]

With town planning as with high-rise, the tide began to turn in the mid-1960s. The redevelopment decades from the 1930s to the 1960s were, when viewed over the longer term, a deviation from the norm in British housing policy. During what for them must have seemed an architectural dark age, traditionalist architects went underground, though Dykes Bower's high altar for St Paul's Cathedral was completed in 1958, and the partnership between Quinlan Terry and Raymond Erith from 1962 quietly kept the classical flame aglow. It was from rehabilitation and conservation that the reaction against modernism initially came. Already by March 1965 Harold Wilson was pertinently asking why old housing had to be expensively redeveloped rather than be (more cheaply) renovated. For Crossman as minister for housing, 'preservationism' was not (as Evelyn Sharp his permanent secretary thought) reactionary, sentimental, and necessarily opposed to modern planning, and he came to prefer the Leeds policy of restoring older city-centre housing to Manchester's massive slum clearance and rebuilding. It was for him 'really a pleasure to see how happy old people are when their old traditional slum houses are transformed by being given a bathroom and a skylight in the attic and proper dry roofing and modern kitchens'.[184] By 1960 nearly a quarter of England's housing stock had been built since 1945, a proportion steadily rising thereafter, but by 1991 it had reached

[181] M. Hutchinson, 'Back in the High Life Again', *Ind.* (23 Feb. 1994), 20. For Seifert's obituary, see *T* (27 Oct. 2001), 27.

[182] C. Gale, 'How High?', *Isis* (28 Nov. 1962), 21.

[183] *DT* (29 Oct. 1988), 11, reporting his television programme the night before; cf. *T* (2 Dec. 1987), 24, for his speech at the Mansion House the previous evening. For similar complaints in 1984 see J. Dimbleby, *The Prince of Wales: A Biography* (1994), 316–17.

[184] Crossman, *Cabinet Diaries*, i. 177 (3 Mar. 1965), 623 (11 Aug. 1966), 127 (13 Jan. 1965).

only 53 per cent because by then so much earlier housing had been retained and adapted.[185]

Efforts to conserve historic buildings advanced during the 1960s. Their pedigree goes back to William Morris's Society for the Protection of Ancient Buildings, founded in 1877. 'Listing' of buildings had begun in 1908 with the establishment of the Royal Commission on Historical Monuments. Underpinning the entire urban conservation movement after 1945 was the National Buildings Record's system launched in that year to list individual buildings for preservation—a response to wartime bombing. Listing to prevent demolition or alteration began in 1947, and by 1982 embraced about a quarter of a million buildings.[186] The Historic Buildings and Ancient Monuments Act (1953) first provided funds for their restoration, and the *Architectural Review* in the 1950s fostered lively debate on urban conservation. In June 1955 Ian Nairn's special number, 'Outrage', deplored the low-density clutter that was accumulating in 'subtopia', and offered a platform for that influential champion of 'townscape', Gordon Cullen, whose standard textbook thus titled appeared in 1961, and who wanted buildings viewed and preserved in groups rather than in isolation: 'one building is architecture', he claimed, 'but two buildings is townscape'. He thought the relationship between buildings was important, and against the planners he championed intimacy, human scale, urban vitality, and 'civic warmth'.[187] Here was one root of the 'conservation area' concept enshrined in Duncan Sandys's Civic Amenities Act (1967). Crossman was keen to move on from rejuvenating individual buildings to preserving them in groups. He showed little patience in 1967 with Basil Spence's grandiose plans for completely redeveloping the Victorian complex of shops and houses in front of the British Museum, or with Leslie Martin's plans for massive clearances to house more civil servants in the Whitehall area.[188] When observing York on a visit in 1970 Crossman was pleased to have included it three years earlier among four historic towns for special survey as a conservation area.[189]

Helpful in all this was the Civic Trust, launched in 1957; business concerns funded it independently of government to educate opinion about the urban environment, and to involve the public in planning decisions. It promoted such participation through helping to draft the Civic Amenities Act so as to ensure adequate warning of impending destruction. Practical in its aims, the Trust valued 'neighbourliness' in buildings, local craftspeople, vernacular materials, and better street signs and street furniture. The number of local

[185] Calculated from table in *TCBST* 476.

[186] R. Hewison, *The Heritage Industry: Britain in a Climate of Decline* (1987), 24–5.

[187] G. Cullen, *Townscape* (1961), 133, 135.

[188] *Cabinet Diaries*, ii. 496 (26 Sept. 1967), 517; see also i. 176 (3 Mar. 1965), 525 (20 May 1966).

[189] Ibid. iii. 858 (14 Mar. 1970); cf. i. 517 (13 May 1966); ii. 194 (11 Jan. 1967), where five towns are specified.

amenity organizations affiliated to it grew fast: from about 200 at the outset to 570 after ten years and 1,247 after twenty.[190] A cluster of interrelated legislation between 1967 and 1974 crystallized and safeguarded the urban conservation programme.[191] From the mid-1960s onwards the listing of historic buildings advanced fast, and during the Act's first year of operation, in conjunction with the planning legislation of 1968, the demolition rate for protected buildings was halved. Whereas the first Ancient Monuments Act (1882) had listed only 68 sites, there were 12,800 a century later.[192]

Valuable backing came from the Georgian Group (founded in 1937) and the Victorian Society (founded in 1958); the latter flourished under the powerful if somewhat improbable literary–scholarly alliance between John Betjeman and Nikolaus Pevsner. The Society's stated aim was 'to make sure that the best Victorian buildings and their contents do not disappear before their merits are more generally appreciated'.[193] Pevsner reconciled his Victorianism with his almost principled faith in the modern style through advancing his somewhat strange claim that the second grew out of the first. The Society arrived just too late to rescue the Imperial Institute, demolished except for its tower in 1957, and the Society's attempt to defend the Euston Arch in 1962 failed, but its membership grew fast. It helped to protect Gilbert Scott's Foreign Office and St Pancras station from what soon seemed the vandalism of their proposed destruction, and to conserve the historic garden suburb Bedford Park. Oxford's growing respect for its northern inner suburb exemplifies this shift in mood. Already in 1940 Betjeman was claiming that the Gothic revival had 'produced some of Oxford's best architecture', and that Keble College, then seen by the sophisticated as almost as much of a joke as Kensington's Albert memorial, 'will come into its own'.[194] In 1952 the distinguished architect and architectural historian H. S. Goodhart-Rendel declared of the University Museum that 'its day has now come', and by 1968 the University's Hebdomadal Council, pressed by the Victorian Society, thought that 'in the present resurgence of interest in Victoriana', planning permission to demolish the abbot's kitchen (part of the University Museum complex) would be elusive. Efforts to preserve North Oxford as a classic Victorian suburb soon succeeded.[195]

Most people now wanted to settle in a permanent home. From gypsies (as they were then called) to Bedouins, dissidents from such notions were retreating worldwide, and in Britain the migrant lifestyle prompted concern,

[190] K. A. Oliver, 'Places, Conservation and the Care of Streets in England, 1957–1981' (University College London Ph.D. thesis 1983), 128—a thesis to which this discussion owes much.

[191] Listed ibid. 249–50.

[192] *HL Deb.* 11 Apr. 1973, c. 683. Hewison, *Heritage Industry*, 24–5.

[193] Betjeman, *Letters*, ii. 128.

[194] J. Betjeman, 'Gothic Revival in Oxford in the Nineteenth Century', *Oxford*, 6/3 (Spring 1940), 57.

[195] Oxford University, *Hebdomadal Council Papers*, 213 (Sept.–Dec. 1952), 28 (Goodhart-Rendel), cf. 23. See also vol. 259 (Jan.–Mar.1968), p. lxxi; vol. 258 (Sept.–Dec. 1967), 586; P. Howell, 'North Oxford: A Threatened Paradise', *Oxford*, 23/1 (1969), 51.

distaste, or both. But the twentieth century did not enjoy the Victorians' wide choice of housing tenures or its broad span of housing quality. From 1945 to the late 1980s the interwar trend persisted whereby egalitarian and public-health trends narrowed the choice increasingly to two types of tenure: renting from the local authority, and buying through a mortgage. Both tenures gained ground over the third: renting from a private landlord. Rent control since the First World War had made Britain's rented sector unusually small by international standards. Whereas in England and Wales between 1951 and 1971 owner-occupied housing stock rose from nearly a third to more than a half of the total, and local-authority or new-town-corporation housing from a sixth to more than a quarter, other rented and miscellaneous tenures fell sharply from half to a fifth.[196] Renting from the local authority or new town corporation chimed in with Labour's ideal of community and welfare, whereas owner-occupation chimed in with what had become the Conservative ideal of self-help and respectability. Rented accommodation shrank further under the Attlee governments' continuance of wartime rent control, which the Conservatives after 1951 did not immediately reject. Macmillan, at housing from 1951 to 1954, demonstrated how much a resourceful, energetic and courageous minister could achieve despite Treasury hostility and an ineffective permanent secretary. Skilful with publicity [Plate 4] and forceful in cabinet, he was backed by his party and prime minister, with powerful help from his industrial adviser Sir Percy Mills and his parliamentary secretary Ernest Marples.

There was as yet no middle way: decontrol of private rented accommodation had yet to become a Conservative cry. In 1945–51 the party criticized the Attlee governments for not getting enough houses built, not for encouraging public-sector housing, and after 1951 the Conservatives did little to restore the free market in housing for fear of upsetting marginal voters, thus prolonging the long-term decline in the privately rented sector. Both parties were keen to build houses rented from the public authority, and by unintentionally shrinking the private rented sector, rent control failed to channel housing subsidy towards those most in need, and made the workforce geographically less mobile. Neither party wanted to be identified with that unpopular figure, the private landlord, and the Conservative move towards decontrolling rents, in the Rent Act of 1957, was cautious indeed. In the 1950s the ruthlessness of the Polish-born London landlord Peter Rachman added the unsavoury word 'Rachmanism' to the English language. By 1959 he controlled 144 homes through 23 companies,[197] and Conservatives, competing with Labour for working-class votes, distanced themselves from him.

On the other hand, by 1954 Macmillan was stepping up building for owner-occupation, and the balance in house building was beginning to tip from

[196] *TCBST* 487. [197] *Ind.* (27 Sept. 2002), 12.

council houses to owner-occupation. The British taste for owner-occupation began between the wars. Because the rent control introduced in 1915 survived the First World War, the privately rented sector began its long decline, whereas house purchase was encouraged by the fall in land prices and interest rates, by building societies eager to lend, and by governments sympathetic to the practice and willing to provide tax relief on mortgage interest paid.[198] Macmillan cautiously revived the interwar trend by authorizing local authorities to sell council houses, though up to the general election of 1955 only 3,000 had been sold.[199] Conservatives were often later accused of slanting their investment priorities between 1951 and 1964 too firmly towards housing, and of neglecting the infrastructure such as roads.[200] House building for local-authority rent or for purchase was one of several allegedly political reasons (the electoral cycle's fluctuations of policy, especially on nationalization, was another) for Britain's relatively poor economic performance. Conservatives later came to see privatization and rent decontrol not only as important housing reforms in themselves, but also as neglected remedies for regionalized unemployment; not till then did housing move to the centre of party conflict. Britain's future lay with the suburban sprawl of Australia and the United States, not with the huge high-rise concentrations on the fringes of Moscow and Leningrad. Crossman as Labour housing minister found it difficult in 1966 to convince builders and building societies that he really favoured owner-occupation, and was surprised at his Ministry's distance from private builders and building societies.[201] In Labour's heartland areas such as Scotland during the late 1960s, the public sector accounted for more of the new housing than in any other country in Western Europe, and for more even than in several Communist countries.[202]

Conservatism and suburbanization, with its privatized and semi-rural values, had long been allied. The owned suburban home, detached or semi-detached, had been despised for decades by an alliance of progressive urban and nostalgic rural critics. Standing in its own garden, however, it embodied the ideals of privacy and independence, though after 1951 it extended still further the suburban sprawl that had disfigured interwar Britain; in the late 1960s, 42 per cent of owner-occupiers lived in detached houses, but only 1 per cent of council tenants.[203] Suburban self-interest was by no means always anti-social, for the 'green belt' brought major collective benefits. The suburban home was very adaptable, backed by the owner-occupier's direct money power. Legislation set

[198] I appreciate generous help here from Professor Martin Daunton.

[199] Horne, *Macmillan 1894–1956*, 338–9.

[200] e.g. M. Pinto-Duschinsky, 'Bread and Circuses? The Conservatives in Office, 1951–1964', in V. Bogdanor and R. Skidelsky (eds.), *The Age of Affluence 1951–1964* (1970), 63.

[201] *Cabinet Diaries*, i. 507 (27 Apr. 1966), 626 (11 Aug. 1966).

[202] D. Niven, *The Development of Housing in Scotland* (1979), 34, cf. 88.

[203] Townsend, *Poverty in UK*, 496.

minimum housing standards, and local-authority house building acted upon them, but it was the private builder who slowly raised standards.[204] Kitchen ranges, coal fires, and solid-fuel stoves gradually succumbed to central heating and electric cookers, which chased away the housewife's old enemy: dust. Labour-saving devices, anodized metalware and readily cleaned surfaces each helped to free her for paid work outside the home. From the 1950s onwards, refrigerators, detergents, washing machines, and the family car reduced the number of necessary shopping expeditions and laundry visits. Indeed, for domestic purposes the laundry almost vanished. In 1949 the launderette, American in origin, first appeared in Britain; during the 1950s the term became widely used, and by 1970 there were 7,000.[205] Yet it was no more than a half-way house—convenient perhaps for the student or lodger, but downmarket and readily discarded when the home-based washing machine could be afforded.

However unsightly it might collectively be, the owner-occupied suburb has remained relentlessly popular since 1951, ceaselessly busying itself with individualized and unobtrusive improvement and renewal. 'This was the English passion, not for self-improvement or culture or wit, but for DIY . . . for bigger and better houses with more mod cons, the painstaking accumulation of comfort and, with it, status.'[206] New suburban houses were built, and old ones continuously adapted for new purposes, anticipating government policy in the 1960s for council housing. Most suburban improvement was myopic, focused on improving the individual home, and often blind to the locality's overall image. Nowhere more so than in gardening: the suburbs gave short shrift to the landscape planning movement's collectivism. The suburban owner-occupier's taste for do-it-yourself, fenced-in, and fragmented garden landscaping reigned supreme. Indoors, too, individual decisions thrust dormer windows through suburban roofs to accommodate larger families and growing children, conservatories and annexes stretched out into gardens and over garages to house indoor plants and grandparents. Much else went on inside the house. Open plan remained the fashion in interior design, so the interwar semi's small and specialized rooms were merged into multi-purpose living space; downstairs drawing and dining rooms were knocked into large living rooms, and refurbished kitchens now doubled up as dining areas.

By the 1960s the scene was set for owner-occupation to encroach further on council-rented accommodation. With birth control percolating downwards, the contrast between the amply spaced owner-occupied home and the cramped public-authority home was shrinking. 'The modern Council house', Orwell was already writing in 1940, 'with its bathroom and electric light, is smaller than

[204] Ibid. 477 for a discussion of how social perceptions of housing standards change.
[205] S. S. Bloom, *The Launderette: A History* (1988), 16, 66.
[206] H. Kureishi, *The Buddha of Suburbia* (1990), 75.

the stockbroker's villa, but it is recognizably the same kind of house, which the farm labourer's cottage is not.'[207] Accommodation after 1945 improved less because houses got bigger than because households got smaller. To many postwar birth-controlled servantless middle-class families, an interwar 'council house' seemed quite spacious, with a sell-off as the logical outcome. The late 1960s gave a brief foretaste of what was to come. Crossman as housing minister tried in 1965 to counter the feeling 'in most socialist minds . . . that as a Party we stand for council houses and that private-enterprise building is something foreign to us'.[208] Two years later a Gallup poll showed 74 per cent favouring the idea that occupiers should be free to buy their home from the local authority, and only 17 per cent against.[209] Also in 1967 Birmingham City Council came under some criticism from the left for selling off council houses to tenants keen to buy. Labour's attitudes were beginning to shift: Bob Mellish, briefly Labour's housing minister, and aiming in 1970 to build council houses for sale with 100 per cent mortgages, said he wanted 'to make Britain a great property-owning democracy where everyone has a chance of owning their own house'. He was echoing the Conservative Party manifesto of 1955.[210]

4. A KALEIDOSCOPE OF REGIONS

In Britain in the 1950s and 1960s three partially overlapping regional alignments were important socially, politically, and culturally: between town and country, between metropolis and provinces, and between England and the UK's three other national groupings. Within living memory the countryside had intimately penetrated the town. In 1966 Macmillan recalled the rural smells of late-Victorian London, whose horse-drawn carriages made it 'in a sense still a country town', with 'dung, straw, and sparrows . . . everywhere'.[211] The countryside lurked within every Londoner's allotment, window box, and bird bath, and 43 per cent of families, spread fairly evenly by social class, kept dogs, cats, or cage birds as pets in 1949.[212] None the less, many in 1951 could recall a contrast between town and country which had been as much cultural as regional or demographic. Well into the twentieth century, town and country had contrasted in their lifestyles, social relations, and values. Further back, the towns had been vulnerable in the face of overwhelming rural and aristocratic power, and even after 1945 land and agriculture exerted far more political and social influence than their wealth and numbers justified; their ongoing influence was reflected in the royal family's relatively rural connections.

[207] Orwell, 'Lion and Unicorn', *Works*, xii. 408.

[208] Crossman, *Cabinet Diaries*, i. 377 (11 Nov. 1965); cf. 383 (18 Nov. 1965).

[209] *Gallup Polls*, ii. 918 (Mar. 1967).

[210] *G* (1 Jun. 1970), 1; see also *NS* (18 Aug. 1967), 189, and below, p. 204.

[211] Macmillan, *Winds of Change*, 30.

[212] Hulton Press, *Patterns of British Life*, 100.

On some issues the long-standing friction between town and country persisted after 1945. The will of the urban majority was now beginning to push hard on the lifestyle of what had now become a small rural minority. When Liverpool's need for water prompted the flooding of Tryweryn Valley in Merioneth, submerging a Welsh-speaking community, Capel Celyn in 1965, Welsh indignation had already prompted sabotage attempts.[213] The urban trend for buying second homes was also resented, and reinforced nationalist feeling in the Scottish highlands and rural Wales;[214] rural communities overpopulated in the summer became ghost towns in the winter, yet local people were being priced out of the housing market. There was a decidedly urban flavour about the attack in the 1950s on hunting and other traditional rural sports, and the attacks of the 1960s on factory farming threatened the countryman's livelihood. So numerous were even short-term visitors that they threatened to destroy what they had come to see: already in the 1970s there was a perceived conflict between the national parks' preservational and recreational roles.[215]

Town and country competed for space, especially in the south of England, where the fastest urban growth threatened some of the country's most fertile land.[216] Central government's role was to coordinate the plans for land use initiated by the counties and county boroughs. Neighbouring rural counties struggled—fiercely, in the case of Cheshire against Liverpool and Manchester—to resist their urban neighbours' demands.[217] Industrial growth and an increasingly demanding and growing population ensured that of Great Britain's surface, urban requirements took up 5 per cent in 1931 and 8 per cent in 1971; and although woodland's share also rose (from 6 to 8 per cent), agriculture's share fell from 80 to 78 per cent.[218] The Ministry of Defence did not readily give ground: in 1970 it held at least twice its interwar acreage, and government departments took up as large a proportion of the coastline in England and Wales as industry and commerce, with special concentrations on the east coast and in South Wales.[219] Writing in 1965, Lees-Milne contemplated with alarm the land greed of a continually rising population. He thought England would soon resemble Holland, and become a sort of enlarged Middlesex interspersed with a few national parks: 'those who live in the country and love it are well advised to recognize its dire need of defence, and to unite in a hard fight to preserve what remains of its landscape beauties'.[220]

213 *DT* (24 May 2004), 23. 214 *T* (6 July 1970), 2; (16 May 1973), 19.

215 *G* (17 Jan. 1976), 10. 216 Best and Coppock, *Changing Use*, 22.

217 B. Cullingworth, 'Fifty Years of Post-War Planning', *Town Planning Review* (1994), 279.

218 R. H. Best, *Land Use and Living Space* (1981), 47.

219 Countryside Commission, *Planning Coastline*, 49. See also Ministry of Defence, *Report of the Defence Lands Committee* (1973), 9; *DT* (3 Jan. 1991), 4.

220 *Burke's Landed Gentry* (18th edn. 1965), p. xxiii.

The time had to come when dwindling rural numbers brought diminished influence unless backed by powerful urban interests. The industrial revolution had occurred too early in Britain for its countryside in 1951 to provide the reservoir of cheap labour that then powered the envied high growth rates of France, Italy, and Germany. Most British rural people tempted by town life had succumbed decades earlier, and agricultural workers were so few that they could no longer set the tone even in the countryside, let alone elsewhere. Agriculture, forestry, and fishing contributed 5 per cent of the UK's gross domestic product in the 1950s, and only 3 per cent by the 1970s, at a time when British agriculture was both prosperous and by European standards very efficient; the workforce in these categories fell from 4 per cent of the total in 1951 to 2 per cent in 1971.[221] Rural self-defence was the more difficult because the countryside was in effect ousted from the party of the left. Labour's rural outposts—always weaker than the Liberals' had been before 1914—died altogether after the 1950s, rendering the countryside especially vulnerable when Labour was in government. After the general election of 1970, for the first time since the war no Labour MP sat for an English seat that was mainly rural; the National Union of Agricultural Workers' long tradition of representation through Labour-held seats in East Anglia was broken.[222]

The countryside's ultimate surrender entailed its merger with the town. This was proceeding from both directions after 1951. On the one hand the towns were in some respects becoming more rural. We have seen how a rural ideal inspired even the high-rise housing estate, let alone suburban estates and the landscaping of former mines and quarries. By the 1960s towns were realizing that they could attract talent only by presenting an attractive image. Rural aspirations pervaded people's growing quantity of leisure time—catered for by craft markets, national parks, gentrified pubs, theme parks, historic sites, country houses, and garden centres. Victorian conservatories, long decayed, were revived and even replicated in response to the growing fashion for indoor plants, encouraged by the *Architectural Review* in its special issue of May 1952; Flanders and Swann hit home with their jest later in the decade that 'the garden's full of furniture and the house is full of plants'. Dating from 1965 is the phrase 'garden centre', an American-inspired horticultural supermarket which spread fast in the 1970s and was for gardeners what Sainsbury's was for the cook. Conversely, the countryside was becoming more urban. As the suburbs and motorways probed ever deeper into the countryside, town and country merged visually as well as culturally. And with modern farming methods came cheap purpose-built factory-style structures: workshops, silos, warehouses for bulk storage, and wide-span often temporary structures owing little to local building materials.

221 *BHS* 825. For the workforce, ibid. 115–16, 119–20.

222 D. E. Butler and M. Pinto-Duschinsky, *The British General Election of 1970* (1971), 400.

The towns were in some ways getting to know the countryside better, if only because cars made it more accessible. Of those who holidayed in Britain in 1969, a fifth went to the south-west and a sixth to the south coast—with Scotland, Wales, and the north-west as close runners up.[223] More permanent in their moves to the rural south were old people. England was now becoming older than the UK as a whole: in 1871 a fifth of those aged 65 and above in the UK lived in Scotland and Northern Ireland, but only a tenth in 1991.[224] Within England, people aged between 25 and 44 settled disproportionately in a broad swathe of counties to the north and west of London, whereas older people were moving out of urban areas, and especially out of London and north-west England.[225] Downsizing their homes or moving permanently into what had earlier been a second home, and capitalizing on regional house-price differentials, those who did not stay put or retire to hotter climates overseas gravitated to seaside resorts and small towns in the more attractive parts of England, especially to the south coast, and to rural areas such as Wales and the south-west. By the 1970s the entire non-industrial coastal area south of Yorkshire and Merseyside had an above-average proportion of the elderly—a modest British counterpart of the retired American's move to the deep South or the retired Frenchman's to Languedoc.[226]

The media helped the towns to understand the countryside better. Godfrey Baseley, creator in 1948 of the radio serial *The Archers*, which he edited for twenty-two years, based its 'Brookfield Farm' on his Worcestershire family home at Summerhill Farm in Hanbury.[227] Operating at a rather different level was Ludwig Koch, a Jewish refugee from Hitler in 1936; his German musical career led him to pioneer in the UK the recording of bird song. He collaborated closely with the BBC even after retiring in 1951, and did much to stimulate public interest in wild birds. Like Nikolaus Pevsner he became well known, even a national treasure, partly because of his distinctive accent. As for television, Eric Ashby's expertise with foxes and badgers made him one of the first film-makers to get close to animals without frightening them; his broadcast of 1961 on *The Unknown Forest* made a special impact because unstaged in its setting, filmed in the wild near his home in the New Forest.[228]

The countryside was the more attractive as an urban destination because it now enjoyed many facilities hitherto urban. Mains electricity and water, and access to telephones, were steadily becoming universal, and the Post Office was

[223] *T* (29 Aug. 1970), 10.

[224] A. M. Warnes and R. Ford, *The Changing Distribution of Elderly People* (1993), 5.

[225] See the map in D. A. Coleman and J. Salt, *The British Population* (Oxford, 1992), 92. Warnes and Ford, *Changing Distribution*, 10–11.

[226] C. M. Law and A. M. Warnes, 'The Changing Geography of the Elderly in England and Wales', *Town Planning Review* (1976), 456–7.

[227] Obituary, *DT* (3 Feb. 1997), 21.

[228] Obituary, *DT* (13 Feb. 2003), 27.

simultaneously reducing maintenance costs and enhancing the rural scene by burying telephone wires. The proportion of rural people in England and Wales without piped water fell from about a third in 1945 to only 3 per cent in 1970, with the national demand for water growing at the rate of 2–3 per cent a year in the 1950s and 1960s.[229] At the end of 1951 56 per cent of BBC television licences were held in the London region, 36 per cent in the Midlands, and 17 per cent in the north, but only 1 per cent outside England.[230] Thereafter BBC and (from 1955) Independent Television (ITV) chased one another across the landscape, with ITV spreading out from its initial London base in 1955 into the Midlands and the north during 1956, and penetrating the Scottish lowlands in 1957, Wales in 1958; by 1963 ITV's coverage of all but some mountainous areas was complete.[231] What country people gained in diversity of opportunity they lost in distinctiveness and smallness of scale; supermarkets, comprehensive schools, and the mass media meant no village shops, schools, or policeman, and fewer of the rural recreations that had once owed so much to silence and space.

Partly coinciding with the polarity between town and country was the long-standing polarity within England between metropolis and provinces, and especially between predominantly rural south and predominantly industrial north. While the north had its large tracts of countryside and the south its huge metropolis, the great and self-confident Victorian cities in the north and Midlands had tended to view the south, including London, as slow, traditionalist, and difficult to rouse. For them, London's mood reflected its rural (and especially aristocratic) surroundings, whereas the northern cities' relatively radical politics had usually been locally more salient. The subsequent decline in Britain's staple industries, together with fast-growing electricity-based industries in the south, undermined northern morale, with serious cultural consequences: 'culturally . . . the country is very much over-centralised', Orwell was already complaining by 1947. London was, he thought, too dominant, and the sense of locality had been undermined, 'nor is there any important literary or artistic movement that is truly independent of London and the university towns'.[232]

During the 1950s this began to change, and the new universities of the 1960s helped to nourish within England a broad-based revival in non-metropolitan culture. Nowhere more so than in changed attitudes to accent. We have seen how traditional dialects, and still more regional languages, had long been viewed as doomed, and from the early nineteenth century new and faster modes of communication rendered such views plausible. Together with mass education, these changes had destroyed or undermined regional languages. Just in time, the Manx Language Society discovered in the mid-1950s that

[229] J. Hassan, *A History of Water in Modern England and Wales* (Manchester, 1998), 89.

[230] A. Briggs, *Sound and Vision* (Oxford, 1979), 252–3.

[231] B. Sendall, *Independent Television in Britain*, i. *Origin and Foundation, 1946–62* (London and Basingstoke, 1982), 292.

[232] Orwell, 'The English People', in *Works*, xvi. 225.

only fourteen native speakers then survived, and set about preserving their speech forms systematically on an early tape recorder; Ned Maddrell, the last surviving Manx-speaker, died in 1974. The Manx language could thus be revived authentically, unlike the long-dead Cornish language—though Cornish consciousness had revived sufficiently by 1967 for a Cornish stamp to be suggested (in vain) to commemorate St Piran's day.[233]

By the 1950s the 'traditional' dialects, largely rural, had become subordinate speech forms used only in limited contexts. They were now curiosities for scholarly study, and for day-to-day purposes were merged into the blander regional city-based 'mainstream dialect' speech forms which ultimately hugged the coat-tails of an allegedly 'correct' English accent—otherwise known as 'received pronunciation', 'BBC' or 'standard' English. Most people, if they spoke standard English at all, did so only on special occasions, and for day-to-day purposes retained either their local 'mainstream' or their traditional-dialect ways of speaking.[234] In the mid-twentieth century, however, the idea that elocutionists should persist with rooting out non-standard English from polite society gradually fell out of favour, especially among university philologists—though in the 1970s safety considerations could still lead the Coal Board to standardize the dialect-speaking miners' rich variety of specialized mining terms.[235] The philologists noted that 'standard' English had once simply been the dialect of the south-east, and government's presence there had lent it status. So the mainstream regional speech forms gradually 'came out', and even acquired prestige, though it was too late for the traditional dialect forms to do the same. Lord Reith found himself on the defensive in 1967 for allegedly imposing an 'Oxford accent' on British radio. Claiming to have been keen to preserve dialects, and to be 'vehemently opposed to . . . the Oxford accent', he had to confess that his aim had been to identify the BBC through its announcers with a way of speaking that 'was the very best thing we could do, in that it didn't particularly irritate any one part of the country'.[236]

Non-metropolitan culture revived in other dimensions after 1951. Faster travel and the growing influence of the media, far from inculcating cultural uniformity, prompted eagerness for diversity. Labour politicians were particularly alert to what the *Times* political correspondent called 'socially adjusted accents'; he noted in 1981 that Castle and Wilson could 'subtly alter their way of speech as though they have clear rules about regional boundaries the moment

[233] For Manx, G. Price, *The Languages of Britain* (1984), 71. For Cornish, *HC Deb.* 6 Mar. 1967, written answers, c. 218, in response to Mr Nott's question.

[234] For a valuable discussion of this see P. Trudgill, *The Dialects of England: Studies in Grammatical Variation* (Oxford, 1990), 5, 9–10, 124. Professor Trudgill corresponded most helpfully with me on these matters; for my deductions he is not at all to be blamed.

[235] C. Storm-Clark, 'The Miners, 1870–1970: A Test-Case for Oral History', *Victorian Studies* (Sept. 1971), 62.

[236] *Listener* (7 Dec. 1967), 744–5.

the Euston train passes through Watford'.[237] Whereas the BBC had initially aimed to hold the UK together through standardizing and centralizing, it was by the late 1940s fostering regional programming initiatives, several of which later became important nationally: *Have a Go* from the north, *Any Questions* from the west, and *The Archers* from the Midlands. ITV's advent in 1955 supplemented this with the diversity prompted by competition, and the phone-in programme on local radio late in the 1960s demonstrated that radio could sometimes harness the prevailing participatory mood more effectively than television. In literature, university teachers outside Oxbridge and London were prominent in reviving a non-metropolitan and anti-elitist dissenting literary tradition, and henceforth those seeking to be in the van of fashion were careful not to apply the term 'provincial' pejoratively. William Cooper's *Scenes from Provincial Life* (1950), set in his home town of Leicester between the wars—ironic, detached, and preoccupied with the kaleidoscopic subtleties of personal relations—strongly influenced younger writers in the 1950s. Amis, Wain, and Larkin in their non-metropolitan heterosexual Englishness reacted somewhat austerely against Bloomsbury's modernist and cosmopolitan intellectualism, against the fashionable London critics, and against the Second World War's patriotic romanticizing of great events. There was some fuss in the 1950s about whether these authors could usefully be categorized as 'The Movement', and Larkin for one denied any close cohesion.[238] More important than mutual influence were the attitudes they shared. They traced their plain-speaking pedigree from Hardy through Housman and Kipling to Wilfred Owen and Betjeman,[239] and their down-to-earth and traditionalist appreciation of human decency in ordinary situations owed much to D. H. Lawrence and Orwell. Kingsley Amis's hilarious *Lucky Jim* (1954), dedicated to Larkin, was important for creating the archetypal anti-hero, the irresponsible and amoral 'redbrick' history lecturer James Dixon, as well as for injecting new life into the university novel as a genre.

Behind these cultural movements lay a revaluation of provincial England which extended far beyond literature. The renaissance of topographical writing in the 1950s owed much to the popular 'Shell guides' to UK counties, with John Betjeman and John Piper as successive general editors. Launched in 1933, but in wartime abeyance, the series revived with *Shropshire* in 1951. It emphasized landscape, buildings, and the 'spirit' of a place, and thirty-four counties had been covered when it came to an end in 1984.[240] In Malcolm Bradbury's *Stepping Westward* (1965), the Trent was for James Walker, crossing it from

[237] David Wood, 'Pygmalion Takes on the Politicians', *T* (24 Aug. 1981), 9.

[238] Larkin, *Letters*, 285.

[239] B. Bergonzi, *Wartime and Aftermath: English Literature and its Background 1939–60* (Oxford, 1993), 162–4.

[240] See the informative website, <www.shellguides.freeserve.co.uk/history.htm>, consulted 4 Dec. 2007.

Nottingham by train, 'the boundary between the north of England and the south. Behind him, now, lay decency, plain speaking, good feeling; ahead lay the southern counties, all suède shoes and Babycham'.[241] The north of England was a concept as well as a location.[242] It had lost much of its nineteenth-century self-confidence. Manchester no longer thought today what the world thought tomorrow, and the northerner's capacity to evoke laughter in twentieth-century theatres with relatively slow-moving dialogue reversed the nineteenth-century idea that northerners were smart and southerners slow. Longer lasting was the nineteenth-century image of the north, whose bleakness had been riveted into the national consciousness by the Brontes and the social novels of the 1840s—a stereotype confirmed by Lawrence and Priestley. In the 1950s the slagheaps and ugly buildings so integral to the stereotype had not yet been cleared, and significant novels and films of the time even temporarily reinforced the north's traditional image.[243] David Storey, son of a mineworker, was determined to get out of Wakefield, and in basing himself on London as an artist he straddled two seemingly irreconcilable worlds,[244] but reunited them with his novel *This Sporting Life* (1960). The home team were central to the identity of such cities, and indeed of the entire region: they were 'our lads', heavily built miners and steelworkers with a strong sense of local loyalty, and local small businessmen managed the teams. Storey skilfully captures the physicality of rugby football, and how its macho values moulded the lives of players who dragged wives and mothers in their wake. The bleak industrial environment and its associated power structure provide the context for the poignant story of misunderstanding between football hero Arthur Machin and his landlady Mrs Hammond. However culturally innovative such fiction might seem in the literary world, it was backward-looking in concealing how greatly such communities had already begun to change. John Braine, librarian in Bingley, perhaps wisely located his *Room at the Top* (1957, filmed in the following year) in the mid-1940s rather than later.

The theatre outside London, too, was newly assertive. The pattern of subsidy helped to ensure that eighty theatres between 1956 and 1968 ceased to focus on receiving London productions on tour, usually setting up repertory companies of their own; by the early 1970s there were only a quarter as many touring theatres as in the mid-1950s.[245] In 1959 Tynan welcomed the advent of provincial accents and dialect to the London stage during the past five years because 'suddenly . . . a group of plays has sprung up for which B.B.C. English

[241] M. Bradbury, *Stepping Westward* (1st publ. 1965, paperback edn. Harmondsworth, 1968), 41.

[242] D. C. D. Pocock, 'The Novelist's Image of the North', *Transactions of the Institute of British Geographers*, 4 (1979) is valuable on this.

[243] See below, pp. 396, 474–5.

[244] Interview with Storey in J. Haffenden (ed.), *Novelists in Interview* (1985), 266–8.

[245] R. Stevenson, *The Oxford English Literary History*, xii. *1960–2000: The Last of England?* (Oxford, 2004), 285. J. Elsom, *Post-War British Theatre* (1st publ. 1976, rev. edn. 1979), 132.

is utterly useless'.[246] The provincial careers of tough and virile actors like Alan Bates and Albert Finney could now culminate in the West End. This was not welcomed by that arch-professional Noel Coward, for his generation of actors had in their training 'banished from their speech, both on the stage and off it, the restricting accents of their early environments', thereby acquiring a versatility now absent.[247] The 'Mersey sound' was a provincial voice which brought popular appreciation of poetry as well as music. Deeply influenced by the American traders and seamen who regularly arrived there with the latest blues and rock records, Liverpool became a major centre of 'country and western' music. It was through imitating their American rock heroes, the Crickets, that the Beatles acquired their name. Exposed to a powerful mix of American, Irish, and Welsh influences, Liverpool's many pop groups in these years grew up in a family-based culture of music-making with a strong sense of loyalty to their city. After making their names in London, the Beatles were nervous at returning spruce and suited: 'we were worried that friends might think we'd sold out', John Lennon recalled, 'which we had, in a way'.[248]

No regional alignments in England compared with the polarity between north and south, and even that was an over-simplification: London was far too dominant for the south to have any clear identity or boundary. And did 'the north' include the border counties? Could it really hold together across the Pennines? In some other parts of Britain the east/west contrast was important, especially in Scotland with its long-standing rivalry between Edinburgh and Glasgow. Indeed, this polarity was if anything accentuated by the gradual mid-century industrial shift from the old staples and towards oil, and by the shift in trade from the Atlantic and Commonwealth towards Europe.[249] The Midlands, too, were contested territory: between Birmingham in the west and Nottingham in the east, and in no English region were regional identities strong enough to create significant distinct regional political and cultural institutions.

The situation in Scotland, Wales, and Northern Ireland was so different that the politics of all three demand separate consideration later.[250] But the same population movements that partially countervailed the revival of cultural provincialism in the 1950s and 1960s also diluted the distinctness of the UK's four nations, if such they can usefully be called. England's relative affluence encouraged talented Irishmen, Welshmen, and Scotsmen in the 1950s and 1960s to migrate south and east, and to see their careers in a UK rather than nationalist perspective—as had Bernard Shaw, Lloyd George, and Thomas

[246] K. Tynan, *A View of the English Stage* (1st publ. 1975, paperback edn. 1976), 253.

[247] 'The Scratch-and-Mumble School', *ST* (22 Jan. 1961), 23.

[248] Lennon quoted in H. Davies, *The Beatles* (1st publ. 1968, rev. edn. 1985), 247. See also L. E. and B. L. Cooper, 'The Pendulum of Cultural Imperialism: Popular Music Interchanges between the United States and Britain, 1943–1967', *Journal of Popular Culture*, 27/3 (Winter 1993), 62, 66.

[249] For more on this see below, p. 316. [250] See below, pp. 424–7.

Carlyle before them. The reverse flow has in most periods been small. So England had absorbed a rising share of the population of the British Isles (including the whole of Ireland) from at least as far back as 1801, and during the twentieth century up to the 1960s the share of Scotland, Wales, and Ireland north and south fell slowly; by 1966 England had 79 per cent of the total.[251] Mounting numbers of English-born people settled in Scotland after 1861, and between 1951 and 2001 their numbers grew by 84 per cent, making them the fastest-growing and by far the largest of Scotland's minorities born elsewhere. But although the English-born Scots were nearly twice as numerous as all Scotland's other migrant communities put together, they still in 2001 made up only 8 per cent of its population, and their impact was diluted by the fact that they dispersed throughout Scotland, took up a wide range of jobs, did not form ghettos, and did not arrive in bulk.[252]

When southern Ireland left the Commonwealth in 1949, the UK did not classify her citizens as foreigners, and if anything Anglo-Irish relations drew closer thereafter, not least in movements of population. In the 1970s travel between the Republic and the UK was as frequent as travel between Northern Ireland and Great Britain; telephone calls and freight movements convey a similar picture, and by the mid-1960s two-fifths of the Republic's television-owning homes could receive British programmes.[253] In the mid-1960s over 80 per cent of Irish trade was still with the UK, and the Republic could not negotiate entry to the EEC independently from Britain.[254] Except for a brief moment in the 1970s, the Republic's long-standing drain of population to Great Britain persisted after 1951. Inhabitants born in the Republic might constitute only about 2 per cent of the UK's total in the 1960s, but from the Republic's point of view the outflow was substantial; the 409,000 net emigrants to Great Britain between 1951 and 1961 amounted to one in seven of its entire population in 1961.[255] Many immigrants from the Republic saw their migration as temporary, or even as only seasonal, and their homeland was geographically close enough for them to keep their contacts warm. To that extent, integration with English culture was postponed, resentment against British attitudes longer lasting, and the Irish move out of their British urban ghetto delayed. As for Northern Ireland, its 'troubles' disrupted earlier demographic patterns, and by leading more Protestants than Catholics to leave for Great Britain contributed to the Catholics' slowly rising share of the province's population, with all the

[251] See the useful table in R. Rose, *Governing without Consensus: An Irish Perspective* (1971), 72.

[252] M. Watson, 'Using the Third Statistical Account of Scotland', *Contemporary British History* (Spring 2004), 101, 104. M. Watson, *Being English in Scotland* (Edinburgh, 2003), 27–30, 41–2.

[253] A. H. Birch, *Political Integration and Disintegration in the British Isles* (1977), 40, 47. F. S. L. Lyons, *Ireland since the Famine* (1971), 680.

[254] S. Strange, *Sterling and British Policy: A Political Study in an International Currency in Decline* (1971), 117–18.

[255] Coleman and Salt, *British Population*, 444. *BST* (1988), 571.

tensions flowing from that.[256] On the other hand, the presence in Great Britain of so many Irish-born settlers who wished to remain there probably helped to restrain militant nationalist tactics within Britain.

The pressures towards linguistic uniformity had gone so far by the early twentieth century as to require special efforts if the Irish language was to be kept alive. Speakers of Gaelic and Welsh dwindled markedly throughout the twentieth century, Gaelic much faster than Welsh. By 1961 Gaelic was spoken by fewer than 2 per cent of Scotland's inhabitants, mainly in the highlands and islands in the far north-west; it had never been integral to Scottish consciousness. Very different was the situation with Welsh, which in 1961 was spoken by 26 per cent of the Welsh population over 3, though only 1 per cent spoke it as their sole language.[257] None the less, the Welsh-language experts thought 'the analogy of a lake in a period of drought drying up into a series of pools' apt: the core Welsh-speaking area in the north and west of Wales was being eroded from the east as the English-speaking frontier moved westwards, and from the west as an English-speaking recreational community grew up within the Welsh-speaking western seaboard.[258] By the late 1950s schemes were under way to get Welsh taught in schools, and little heed was paid to Lord Raglan in 1958 when (with Irish precedents in mind) he expressed embarrassingly frank contempt for 'trying to keep a dying language alive by artificial respiration'.[259] The census of 1961 prompted in Saunders Lewis fears about the decline of Welsh speaking; these were integral to his famous nationalistic lecture of 1962, which deplored the language's betrayal by Welsh church and university leaders.[260]

By expressing his fears so strongly, Lewis probably helped to ward off the danger, especially as some of his admirers favoured direct action in the Welsh Language Society whose creation his lecture helped to inspire: educational and government circles took avoiding action during the 1960s. But if the language was to survive, it could not be on the old basis of hiding within a nonconformist enclave inside a sheltered Welsh community. No such community could hope to withstand modern society's secularizing pressures and geographical mobility: the steady contraction after 1961 of Sunday pub-closing, backed by referenda, testified to that. Secularization likewise undermined Protestant culture in Northern Ireland, whose anti-Catholicism had dwindling resonance in Great Britain. The shared experience recorded in the five chapters which follow all had implications, not always articulated, for nationalist vitality.

[256] Coleman and Salt, *British Population*, 499, 501.

[257] Withers, *Gaelic in Scotland*, 213. Williams, *Welsh Historical Statistics*, i. 86.

[258] H. Carter, 'Patterns of Language and Culture: Wales 1961–1990', *Transactions of the Honourable Society of Cymmrodorion* (1990), 265–71. For the plight of Welsh compared with that of other European minority languages, see G. Price, 'Minority Languages in Western Europe', in M. Stephens (ed.), *The Welsh Language Today* (Llandysul, 1973), 1–17.

[259] *HL Deb.* 26 Nov. 1958, c. 854.

[260] S. Lewis, 'The Fate of the Language', in A. R. Jones and G. Thomas (eds.), *Presenting Saunders Lewis* (Cardiff, 1973), 132–4.

This chapter has shown how, in the 1950s and 1960s, the UK's face was scrutinized and scoured as never before, enhancing understanding of its old features while developing new farming practices, new modes of communication, new patterns of urban settlement, new styles of living. New attitudes to the environment were simultaneously emerging: growing awareness of ecological fragility, and a painful and eventually humbling learning through experience of the limits to what self-conscious modernization could achieve. The equivocal impact on human relations of closer contact, already discussed at the international dimension, was experienced within the UK as well: nowhere were national boundaries less relevant than in environmental matters, and yet faster and easier travel did less to integrate the UK's regions and nations culturally and politically than had been expected.

All but two of the Introduction's eight motifs have once again surfaced in this chapter. Here wartime legacies which had at first seemed beneficial turned sour: the wartime strategy which made the UK a pacesetter worldwide in high farming generated unforeseen environmental problems and after 1970 had to be abandoned; and the scale of the urban renewal encouraged by Hitler's bombs failed to meet the needs of community. The juxtaposition of growing private affluence and public anxiety about it (the third motif) was inevitably accentuated by the unforeseen consequences of dramatic growth in housing and transport provision. The long time-perspectives of environmental change interacted with the speeded-up benefits of faster and more convenient transport and better housing, but the latter relieved the time pressures in daily living less than had earlier seemed likely (the fourth motif), and in the new towns there seemed all too little time for the citizen participation that had been planned, let alone for the civic consciousness there and elsewhere that had nurtured the great Victorian cities. A home- and car-based individual self-sufficiency fostered the secularized materialism that was in tension not only with Christian values (the fifth motif), but also with a simultaneously rising environmental consciousness. So far the existing political structure seemed able to accommodate these dramatic social changes (the sixth motif), though they were accumulating problems for the future. Changes in the face of the country advertised the voluntarist constraints on the politician (the seventh motif): conservationists, environmentalists, and local and regional activists were particularly active, and the pressures from international opinion (on oil spillages, smoke pollution, and aircraft noise, for example, not to mention hostility to nuclear tests) were mounting. There was no sign, though, that in this area the UK would assume any distinctive world role: the environmentalist pace was being set elsewhere.

CHAPTER 4

The Social Structure

Because social class was so central to British life in the 1950s and 1960s, a chapter on social structure must highlight hierarchy: monarchy, upper classes, middle classes, and working class. But already in the 1950s there were signs of what was for Britain a new and cross-cutting alignment: ethnic loyalty, discussed in the chapter's fifth and final section. The influx of ethnic minorities was discussed in the second section of Chapter 3; here the emphasis is on their patterns of settlement. Initial emphasis must in this chapter, however, go to the complexity and subtlety of class alignments and attitudes in these decades, and to these the sociologists were increasingly alerting a wider public, for between the 1940s and the 1970s the UK recovered the sociological awareness that Edwardian Britain had gained from Charles Booth and Seebohm Rowntree. During the interval, the First World War and the split between Liberals and Labour had weakened this reformist drive, and the British tradition of empirical sociology had become less salient. The Second World War, however—together with Mass Observation, the highly participatory prewar movement for social investigation, and the planning enthusiasms of a resurgent left—revived faith in social engineering and resourcefulness in consulting opinion. The rapidly expanding and increasingly meritocratic postwar universities were keen to influence public policy, and in his *The Future of Socialism* (1956) Crosland cited sociological writing just as Lloyd George in his speeches before 1914 had cited Booth and Rowntree. It was in sociology, wrote Crosland, not in economics and politics, that 'the significant issues for socialism and welfare will increasingly be found to lie'.[1]

The blue-jacketed postwar volumes in Routledge's International Library of Sociology and Social Reconstruction were numerous and influential, and some sociologists were popular enough to appear in Penguin paperback, particularly those connected with the Institute of Community Studies, founded in 1953. Strongly empirical, with an infusion from social anthropology, the Institute was unpretentiously well-intentioned, and was preoccupied with bridging

[1] Crosland, *Future of Socialism*, 12; cf. B. Crick, 'Labour Publicity', *Political Quarterly* (Sept. 1960), 362.

the class divide, though it lacked Booth's and Rowntree's strongly practical and governmental emphasis. Its somewhat romantic view of Bethnal Green's traditional working-class community led it simultaneously and rather unusually to oppose both unbridled capitalism and paternalistic planning. It grew up from outside the university world, and its sociology was largely self-taught. Its emphasis on communicating with its working-class informants lent its writings a popular appeal not subsequently attained by university-based sociology in its Americanized, more severely theoretical, and academic guise.[2] Preoccupation with social structure in Britain after 1951 was more than narrowly academic. Novelists were much interested in social relationships, and a sociological slant pervaded influential books like Richard Hoggart's *The Uses of Literacy* (1957) or Sampson's *Anatomy of Britain* (1962). Social anthropologists realized that they had something to contribute at home as well as overseas, and the secession of the 'New Left' from the Communist Party (CPGB) in 1956 added a new vigour to sociological debate. Film-makers, from Ealing Studios to Lindsay Anderson, showed a new and sometimes sentimentally idealized interest in the working class, with their appearance on screen pioneered in *It Always Rains on Sunday* (1947).

The British people were as vague in defining social-class frontiers as nationality, but common parlance assumed that there was an 'upper', a 'middle', and a 'working' (or, less commonly, a 'lower') class. There had initially been three classes of railway compartment to confirm the three-class model, but the third class disappeared in 1956, and the second class slowly lost its class label at a time when the middle class was growing, which showed the model's limited usefulness. Furthermore, there could hardly be middle and lower classes without an upper class, and yet the upper class was a Cheshire cat with contours unclear or even deliberately concealed—evoking much fascination and little resentment. The British sociologists of the 1950s were rather unhelpful here because primarily preoccupied with the deprived rather than the privileged. In so far as they thought the privileged interesting at all, sociologists were concerned less with how they lived and thought, more with how they were recruited and perpetuated. Wealth was a necessary but not sufficient condition for entering the upper classes, who by no means included the UK's wealthiest people. Wealth for full acceptance needed to be of a particular type: preferably landed,'old', and with the accoutrements of age: cultural self-confidence, sporting expertise, and a dignified and rural home. To describe a family as 'landed' was to indicate its high status within the upper classes. Wealth, aristocracy, and the upper class overlapped, but not exactly.

[2] For a penetrating and perhaps unduly critical view of the Institute's work see J. Platt, *Social Research in Bethnal Green: An Evaluation of the Work of the Institute of Community Studies* (1971). Willmott and Young's response is 'On the Green', *New Society* (26 Oct. 1971), 840–2.

Three other class models were widely discussed. The Marxian bipolar divide between bourgeoisie and proletariat seemed to fit people's tendency to see themselves as either 'middle' or 'working' class.[3] Yet in the 1950s the Marxian scenario was unrealized: the middle classes were not in difficulty, nor were they contracting, nor was the class war hotting up. The bipolar model left no room for an ongoing 'upper' class, and could not accommodate the growth and growing diversity within the 'middle' class. The social-democratic rival to the Marxian model suffered from none of these defects; like its Gladstonian Liberal precursor, it was also bipolar, but less confrontational, and differently composed, aiming to harness the progressive middle class to organized labour in a joint attack on 'privilege' in wealth, education, and lifestyle. This model had the double advantage of acknowledging the continuing importance of the upper class and the mounting importance of service-sector and white-collar employment. Some government employees and sociologists favoured yet another model, less conflict-ridden than the rest; it envisaged a multi-runged social staircase or ladder climbed continuously by people aiming at a destiny obscure. Its great merit was to acknowledge that all three classes were neither monolithic nor impermeable, that within each there were small-scale but significant gradations, and that between each there was continuous movement up or down. Its drawback was that it could not reflect the three-class terminology so widely used. Any social-class model employing the widely used phrase 'working class' implied the existence of a class that defined itself by not working. Hard work had long been a middle-class hallmark, and the British landed aristocracy had never been idle, if only because its estates had to be managed and associated public duties performed. A leisured and cultivated lifestyle carried on in ample premises amidst abundant servants might once have existed at the highest levels, but not after 1951.

1. MONARCHY MOVES WITH THE TIMES

None of the class models can fully accommodate the monarchy. Though popularly associated with aristocracy, with the hereditary principle integral to both, the royal family was consigned to a sort of classless limbo where privilege inspired little resentment. Its role was sufficiently distinctive for its fate not to depend on aristocracy's overt vitality.

The long-term decline in the monarchy's political and constitutional importance freed it to perform its social role even more effectively. Monarchy's very existence reflected and reinforced continuity and stability in Britain. George VI was shooting in the country with friends and staff on the day before he died,

[3] D. Butler and D. Stokes, *Political Change in Britain: The Evolution of Electoral Choice* (2nd ed. 1974; 1st publ. as *Political Change in Britain: Forces Shaping Electoral Choice*, 1969), 69.

and the public reacted very differently from hard-boiled politicians and intellectuals. 300,000 people queued on three wintry days during February 1952 to attend his lying-in-state, and more than 200,000 queued for his widow's half a century later.[4] Elizabeth II found herself Queen at an unexpectedly early age: 'it was all very sudden . . . ', she recalled long afterwards, 'taking on and making the best job you can'.[5] The new monarch's image for youthful innocence belied the strong pressures towards continuity, if only because her mother remained active in public life for another half century. Queen Elizabeth the Queen Mother, her new title, was slow to move out of Buckingham Palace, continued to refer to her late husband as 'the King', and remained in close daily contact with her elder daughter. Because she combined her personal extravagance and traditionalist outlook with charm and an infectious zest for life, she endeared herself to the public; and with her discretion and stamina for even the most tedious of public functions, she created a distinctive role for herself which in no way threatened the Queen.

Continuity was reinforced by the new Queen's conservative temperament. Like her father and grandfather, Elizabeth II relished annual and family routines; nor would a taste for innovation have befitted a figurehead required to embody tradition and avoid controversy. The need for continuity was widely felt by a nation whose world status seemed threatened, and the sequence of televised royal weddings and anniversaries with Richard Dimbleby as BBC compère was reassuring. In the Buckingham Palace staff the Queen inherited a highly traditionalist structure led by the handsome, self-effacing, but meticulous and upright Sir Alan Lascelles, private secretary to George VI from 1943 and to the Queen during the first year of her reign. Slow to take initiatives, seldom to the fore in resolving a family dispute, lacking spontaneity on public occasions, and nervous of the camera, the Queen was at first content to deliver speeches that were almost totally free of content. Given her parents' rather recent success in restabilizing the monarchy, little more than that was needed or wanted at first. Even Labour critics of class privilege saw debate about the monarchy as a side-issue; besides, its popularity with working-class voters[6] ensured that Labour's left had nothing to gain by stirring things up.

In private the Queen differed markedly from her public image. She was a good mimic, with a sharp sense of humour, and had inherited her mother's forthrightness, spontaneity, and sense of fun. In public, though, she often seemed stiff and rather severe, especially in her Christmas broadcasts. The monarchy's ceremonial role, however well managed, did not always convey a helpful image of Britain. 'What is it that packs the customers in?' asked Lord Samuel in 1964, discussing the 'British weeks' abroad, of which there

[4] *G* (8 Apr. 2002), 6; *Ind.* (8 Apr. 2002), 8. [5] *G* (6 Feb. 1992), 4.

[6] See the sample survey material in R. McKenzie and A. Silver, *Angels in Marble* (1968), 150.

were twenty in that year: 'in a word, it is Beefeaters'.[7] In complementing the Queen with his less formal manner, the Duke of Edinburgh was somewhat precariously helpful: his bluff and bantering style had at first disconcerted his future father-in-law, and the marriage had not been readily approved. Yet the Duke, like Denis Thatcher later, ably demonstrated how a decidedly masculine consort could play a subordinate role without becoming a non-person; it was a role difficult enough even for a 'new' man, let alone for two 'old' ones. Initially restive, the Duke soon carved out a niche for himself and enlivened the monarchy with his down-to-earth, commonsensical, and sometimes controversial remarks. 'Politically incorrect' before the phrase was invented, he was a lightning conductor: like his eldest son he reached across officialism and protocol to articulate sentiments widely held. He was able to identify the monarchy with significant initiatives that the Queen could not herself take, some of them imaginative and forward-looking: Outward Bound, the conservation movement, and his award scheme, which by 2000 had attracted as participants nearly three million young people.

The indecision shown in 1953–5 by the Queen's younger sister Princess Margaret on whether to marry the divorced but much-decorated wartime RAF pilot and commoner Peter Townsend can be interpreted as simultaneously looking backward and forward. In highlighting the conflict between love and duty, the episode replicated the abdication, an event that was no doubt uppermost in the Queen Mother's response, for if the Princess could marry a divorced man and yet retain her status, why had a divorced woman been impossible for the Duke of Windsor? This semi-public debate, together with the Princess's subsequent activities, also illustrates a new way in which the royal family was becoming representative. It was itself about to reflect changing British attitudes to personal relationships, and in her marital problems Princess Margaret anticipated those of the Queen's children from the 1980s onwards. From the 1950s the fun-loving and party-going princess evolved a distinctive trend-setting fashionable role for herself, probably less from design than from personal taste. Like the Prince of Wales under Queen Victoria, she moved in circles quite different from the Queen's, thereby extending the reach of a royal family that might otherwise have seemed rather staidly overdomesticated. After Princess Margaret had married the photographer Antony Armstrong-Jones (created Earl of Snowdon), the Snowdons became the most fashionable couple in London, exemplifying the 'swinging sixties'.

In the longer term, it was not sufficient for the Queen to move with the times only through her sister. In 1957 Lord Altrincham, in a critique that seems mild in retrospect but was startling at the time, regretted the stilted phrasing and banal subject-matter of the Queen's early speeches, together with

[7] *HL Deb.* 17 June 1964, c. 1218.

the narrowly 'tweedy' company she kept.[8] The monarchy needed henceforth to tread the delicate line between seeming on the one hand archaic and out of touch, and on the other hand losing dignity and continuity by pursuing the latest fashion. Here the media could help, and wisely the Queen had already revoked her initial hostility to the idea of televising the coronation in 1953;[9] its lush pageantry constituted a breakthrough for British television, and seven-eighths of the adult population heard or viewed the service. Its blend of ceremonial, traditionalism, religion, and music—memorable for all who heard it, and for the 20 million people who saw it[10]–was the apogee in more than a century's refinement of the British monarchy's talent for public display. Noel Coward, an expert on such matters, thought it 'most excellently done. The English State Ballet at its best.'[11] It was the last great moment when the Church of England, patriotism, and Britishness came together [Plate 6]. Its impact was all the greater because—unlike that other great ceremonial occasion of the reign, Churchill's funeral in 1965—the ceremony seemed optimistic rather than nostalgic, forward-looking rather than merely clinging to the past. Thereafter, for at least a generation, the monarchy kept ahead of parliament in exploiting television. This was all the easier because the universal life cycle was so central to its ceremonial function—from weddings (Princess Margaret in 1960, Princess Anne in 1973, Prince Charles in 1981) to comings-of-age (Prince Charles in 1969) to birthdays (the Queen Mother's in 1980) to anniversaries (the Queen's silver wedding in 1972 and silver jubilee in 1977) to funerals (Earl Mountbatten in 1979, the Queen Mother's in 2002).

The Queen broadened her impact in several ways. From 1956 she invited a few guests to the Palace for an informal lunch; with about five such lunches a year, about 1,200 people had enjoyed such hospitality by 1983.[12] There were also significant media initiatives. Collaborating on publicity was a dangerous but inevitable game for the monarchy to play. Dangerous, because monarchy needed to preserve dignity and distance, whereas the media instinct was immediately to expose all; inevitable, because without media exposure, the monarchy risked being sidelined. In a democratic society the monarchy needed simultaneously to seem both extraordinary and representative. Friction inevitably resulted, especially while the rather starchy Commander Colville remained press secretary, from 1947 to 1968. Relations were especially stiff when the publicity was unauthorized. The royal family's once-loved employee Marion Crawford ('Crawfie'), whose unofficial *The Little Princesses* (1950) now seems innocuous, in effect pioneered the inside revelation of the royal family's 'human' dimension, but she was ostracized thereafter. So long as it could retain

[8] Altrincham *et al., Is the Monarchy Perfect?* (1958), 9; see also 11, 116.

[9] Cockerell, *Live from No. 10*, 19.

[10] A. Briggs, *Sound and Vision* (Oxford, 1979), 467.

[11] Coward, *Diaries*, 214 (12 June 1953).

[12] E. Longford, *Elizabeth R: A Biography* (1983), 207.

control, the royal family (and especially the Queen Mother) had readily made itself available to photographers—moulding its image through Beaton, 'Baron', or Armstrong-Jones. But Ray Belissario, pioneer of the wide-angle lens, was thought too intrusive with his unauthorized published photographs, though they soon came to seem harmless enough.[13]

Lord Altrincham's critique chimed in with views privately held by younger members of the Queen's staff and by Prince Philip, who edged the Queen forward into making her first televised Christmas broadcast in 1957, watched by more than 16 million people.[14] Attack was for monarchy the best form of defence, and invented or enhanced traditions could attract the media on the monarchy's own terms. Even before William Heseltine replaced Colville as press secretary, a 'media spectacular' was engineered in July 1967 when the Queen knighted round-the-world yachtsman Francis Chichester at Greenwich, using the sword that Elizabeth I had used for knighting Francis Drake after circumnavigating the globe in 1580.[15] Much trouble was taken over the investiture of Prince Charles as Prince of Wales at Caernarvon Castle in July 1969. In 1966 the monarchy plunged in even more deeply with the pioneering hour-long television film on *The Royal Palaces of Britain.* This paved the way for the more substantial *Royal Family*, shown three years later, which admitted the cameras into the royal palaces for the first time,[16] and was followed by *Elizabeth R* in 1992. The monarchy was forsaking the reticence hitherto associated with good breeding, and was now dallying with populism. This did not distance it from the upper classes because they were doing just the same.

Something similar could also be said of marital relations. A monarchy responsive to middle-class family values had existed only spasmodically in modern Britain: during the marriage of Victoria and Albert and in the twentieth century since George V's accession. In retrospect the marital patterns of the Queen's children from the 1980s represented a return to conduct long accepted in aristocratic circles, among many of Queen Victoria's predecessors, and by Edward VII and Edward VIII. In one other important respect the royal family and the upper classes were at one. When Jock Colville asked Churchill what he and the Queen talked about during their (lengthening) weekly audiences, 'Oh, mostly racing', was the reply. Both the Queen and the Queen Mother loved the sport, and whenever Elizabeth II needed to unwind, it was to horses that she turned. 'Jumping in and out of Land Rovers with great wet Labradors is her idea of a perfect afternoon', wrote Robert Lacey: 'or trudging across ploughed fields in Wellington boots'.[17]

[13] B. Pimlott, *The Queen: A Biography of Elizabeth II* (1996), 413.

[14] Ibid. *The Queen*, 291–2.

[15] Obituary of Chichester, *T* (28 Aug. 1972), 8.

[16] For a penetrating analysis of monarch and media see C. Dunkley, 'Monarch of All Who Survey Her', *FT* (20 Apr. 1986), 19.

[17] Pimlott, *The Queen*, 194. Lacey, *Majesty*, 408.

2. UPPER-CLASS RESILIENCE

The monarchy's sustained popularity between 1951 and 1970 illustrates the complexity of its link with aristocracy, for in these years aristocratic values were seriously challenged. Several close relatives of the Queen married not only outside European royal families, but outside the British aristocracy. And if the system of lords lieutenant still continued to symbolize the monarch's social authority in each locality—with Eton producing thirty of the forty-six male lords lieutenant in 1990[18]—it offered little political power. Furthermore, if the aristocracy and gentry had never constituted more than a segment of the upper classes, their salience dwindled still further after 1951. But whereas the concept of aristocracy had earlier brought cohesion, self-confidence, leadership, and visibility to the upper classes, it now went into decline and found no successor. The 'upper classes' existed after 1951, but the fact that they were usually referred to as plural rather than singular signifies their diversity and lack of clear identity. Two significant frontiers were left unclear: between aristocracy and upper classes, and between upper and middle classes. In social surveys only a tiny minority placed themselves in the upper-class category: a mere 1–2 per cent in Gallup polls of 1952, 1956, and 1957, and a mere 0.1 per cent of those surveyed in the sociologist Peter Townsend's project of 1968–9. He noted that 'while the great bulk of the population adopts class imagery which assumes the existence of an upper, or a ruling class, practically no one claims to belong to such a class'.[19]

After 1951, as in medieval England, social standing 'was made up of multiple elements, which were not always consistent'.[20] There were important shifts in the balance within the constellation of six qualities required for membership of the upper classes: lineage, title, wealth, lifestyle, merit, and power. These shifts occurred all the more easily in Britain where class boundaries were so vague. Lineage and title were waning as an upper-class qualification, and few now possessed the expertise to distinguish even between aristocracy and gentry, let alone between their various titles. From the late-Victorian period peerages had been opening up to businessmen and civil servants, and by 1962 Sampson could comment on the fact that knighthoods now went to cricketers, advertisers, and horseracers: 'it is doubtless only a matter of time before there will be bingo knights'. Harold Wilson came near to obliging quite soon, for with him as with Lloyd George, a somewhat carefree distribution of honours reflected personal indifference to them. 'His reformism consists not of altering the conventions like Honours', wrote Castle, 'but in using them in unorthodox ways.'[21]

18 J. Paxman, *Friends in High Places: Who Runs Britain?* (1st publ. 1990, paperback edn. 1991), 65.

19 *Gallup Polls*, i. 274, 390, 407. P. Townsend, *Poverty in the UK* (1979), 372, 374.

20 M. Prestwich, *Plantagenet England, 1225–1360* (Oxford, 2005), 353.

21 A. Sampson, *Anatomy of Britain* (1962), 295. Castle, *Diaries 1964–70*, 74–5 (12 Dec. 1965).

In the UK's long history of honours, the years between 1951 and 1970 were unresourceful, and such distinctions as were awarded seemed increasingly archaic. There was no Labour Party enthusiasm for the 'logical Labour alternative to the honours list' on which Benn was working in May 1963.[22] What did occur was reform in the reality beneath a scarcely changing appearance: a slow and only half-explicit decoupling of honours from the class system so as to reward voluntary work, celebrity, and economic achievement—and thus in some sense, merit. During Wilson's first two terms all four Beatles received MBEs, together with television stars Violet Carson (of *Coronation Street*) and Jack Warner (*Dixon of Dock Green*). There were knighthoods for footballers and CBEs for the comedian Peter Sellers and the actor Harry Andrews. Footballers, television stars, journalists, and comedians also flourished in the honours distributions of Wilson's final term.[23] What had once been a symbol of aristocratic status, public service, or royal approval had now become a badge of success in almost any area of British life.

Unlike titles, the third upper-class quality—wealth—percolated downwards only slowly. The fact that it percolated downwards at all between 1914 and the late 1970s was a striking change, for during at least 250 years before 1914 personal wealth's distribution had remained surprisingly stable, with the top 5 per cent of adults owning a steady 80–5 per cent.[24] The percentage of British marketable net wealth held by the richest 1 per cent of the adult population fell from 55 in 1936 to 34 in 1960/5 to 27 in 1971/5, and the fall among the richest 5 and 10 per cent was likewise slow but steady.[25] In all three periods inequalities of wealth were far greater than inequalities of income, given that wealth represents past income saved and invested, and that taxation of income under all governments in the 1950s and 1960s enhanced redistribution. Before tax the percentage of total national income in Britain held by the top 1 per cent fell steadily from 11 in 1949 to 5 in 1976/7, and the percentage held by the top 10 per cent from 33 to 26. After tax the percentage held by the top 1 per cent fell from 6 to 4 and by the top 10 per cent from 27 to 22.[26] Also relevant to the distribution of wealth were three other factors, of which only the first was partly within the politicians' control. For the smaller wealth-holders, the growing importance of state and occupational pension rights was significant.[27] But largely beyond the politicians' control, and sometimes even countervailing it, were two other developments: the trend in the housing market after 1951 towards owner-occupation, and the fact that egalitarian government policy

[22] T. Benn, *Out of the Wilderness: Diaries 1963–67*, ed. R. Winstone (1987), 16 (12 May 1963).

[23] J. Walker, *The Queen has been Pleased: The British Honours System at Work* (1986), 148, 150.

[24] C. H. Feinstein, 'The Equalizing of Wealth in Britain since the Second World War', *Oxford Review of Economic Policy*, 12/1 (1996), 96, 104.

[25] Ibid. 101; cf. W. D. Rubinstein, *Wealth and Inequality in Britain* (1986), 51.

[26] Rubinstein, *Wealth and Inequality*, 80.

[27] For more on these see below, pp. 284, 318.

during these years was accompanied by voluntary egalitarian trends within the family. Death duties were important in the redistribution of wealth as much for their indirect as for their direct effects: they could be evaded by the individual's decision to redistribute wealth within the family, not just from the eldest son to other sons, but from sons to daughters. This last trend helps to explain why in the 1950s and 1960s the top 10 per cent's share of wealth fell more slowly than that of the top 1 per cent.[28]

From 1900 to 1939 country houses were destroyed at an accelerating rate. Large-scale destruction resumed in the late 1940s, and about a twelfth of the nation's stock of country houses seems to have been lost between 1945 and 1960. Many surviving houses became institutions; Victorian houses, relatively new and with large rooms, were especially suitable for schools.[29] Indeed, but for the private schools, which in the first half of the twentieth century found such premises cheap and convenient, the obsolescent Victorian country house would scarcely have survived.[30] Some landed families decided to cut costs by substituting a smaller home for the larger: in 1961–3, for example, the fifth Duke of Westminster almost completely destroyed Alfred Waterhouse's magnificent Eaton Hall, supplanting it by an undistinguished modern house. The art sales prompted by death duties were extensive enough to enhance the London art market's worldwide influence; and with an overseas boost from Sotheby's Goldschmidt sale of 1958 London gained markedly over its rivals: Paris and Berlin. The gains were consolidated in 1964 when Sotheby's chairman Peter Wilson established the firm in New York through buying the American auction house, Parke Bernet, and Christie's soon followed suit. This, together with its role as home for refugees and as cultural intermediary between America, Commonwealth, and mainland Europe, helps to explain why London in the 1960s became so important in the world of art, conservation, and design. Its commercial galleries more than doubled in the 1950s and increased still further in the 1960s, their number reaching almost 100 by mid-decade.[31]

Yet under the cover of retreat from public life, many landed families quietly preserved their country houses from the predicted collapse. The process was made easier by the network that then linked Oxbridge with Whitehall and the City: forty-six of the 148 directors of the 'big five' banks, for instance, had in 1958 been to Oxford, as had thirty of the 149 directors of eight major insurance companies.[32] The upper classes collaborated with or co-opted two types of

[28] Feinstein, 'Equalizing of Wealth', 100–1.

[29] P. Mandler, *The Fall and Rise of the Stately Home* (New Haven and London, 1997), 259. See also the histogram in G. Worsley, *England's Lost Houses from the Archives of 'Country Life'* (2002), 16.

[30] M. Girouard, *The Victorian Country House* (Oxford, 1971), p. vii.

[31] D. Sandbrook, *White Heat: A History of Britain in the Swinging Sixties* (2006), 71.

[32] T. Lupton and C. S. Wilson, 'The Social Background and Connections of "Top Decision Makers"', *Manchester School* (Jan. 1959), 37.

newcomer within the network. Elite universities were increasingly becoming meritocratic, and were drawing others besides the well-to-do towards the City. And within the City, the well-connected in the 1960s had as colleagues financial experts often much humbler in origin. Sampson considered the pension-fund managers very powerful figures in 1962, for instance, but they were unobtrusive, and rarely from an Oxbridge or independent-school background. As for the actuaries, they were 'mostly quiet men from grammar schools'. Leslie Brown, 'sometimes talked of as the most powerful man in the city', had been to a grammar school in Croydon and had then taken a correspondence course.[33]

With such connections, the upper classes did not depend solely on land for their income, and among UK tangible assets land's share fell markedly between 1900 and 1960 from nearly a quarter to less than a tenth. There was, however, a close link between wealth and landowning: in England and Wales in 1954/5, the larger the proportion of the individual's total wealth held in land the wealthier he was likely to be.[34] Land was by no means the only route to upper-class self-defence, but it remained an important continuing source of influence for the old rich, if only because many newcomers were now moving into the land market. Labour governments proved unexpectedly friendly to landed estates, perhaps because their tax policy reflected their pursuit of national agricultural self-sufficiency. Labour also knew that Conservative voters were not alone in their deference: even between 1958 and 1963 a fifth of Labour voters—young as much as old—favoured a prime minister from an elite background.[35] With the aid of the National Trust (whose owned acreage rose threefold between 1945 and 1965) many country-house owners discovered a new role and income as guardians of what came to be called the national 'heritage'. The Gowers report on *Houses of Outstanding Historic or Architectural Interest* (1950) exposed the threat to the country house, recommending private ownership. Three years later the Historic Buildings and Ancient Monuments Act established quasi-independent Historic Buildings Councils for England, Scotland, and Wales, and the taxpayer helped to fund repairs where the public were admitted.[36] A further bonus was the generous compensation paid to shareholders when such ill-paying assets as mines and railways were nationalized. Country houses were being destroyed at the annual rate of eight in 1900–49, but twenty-five from 1950 to 1975,[37] yet the Devonshires were somehow able to move back

[33] Sampson, *Anatomy of Britain*, 408, 411; A. Sampson, *The Changing Anatomy of Britain* (1982), 288, 291.

[34] J. Revell, 'Changes in the Social Distribution of Property in Britain', *Third International Conference of Economic History* (1968), 369. A. Carr-Saunders *et al., A Survey of Social Conditions in England and Wales* (1958), 179.

[35] McKenzie and Silver, *Angels in Marble*, 156, 158, 227–8, 251.

[36] Hewison, *Heritage Industry*, 62.

[37] M. Girouard, 'Country House Crisis?', *Architectural Review* (Oct. 1974), 243.

into Chatsworth, the Ancasters into Grimthorpe, and the Fitzwilliams into Milton. Much could be raised by selling off a picture, a few books, or pieces of silver, given their soaring value. Surveying the lifestyle of the twenty-seven surviving non-royal dukes in 1962, Sampson found that they had retreated to their estates from almost all aspects of public life except horse-racing, yet 'to an extraordinary extent' had 'succeeded in continuing a feudal, rural, pre-industrial existence in the midst of an urban, bourgeois country'.[38]

More importantly, high taxation almost compelled their owners to find ways of making country houses pay. Looking back in 1959 on *Brideshead Revisited* (1945), Waugh admitted that when writing the book in spring 1944 'it was impossible to foresee . . . the present cult of the English country house'. Such houses then seemed doomed to decay, whereas 'Brideshead today would be open to trippers', because 'the English aristocracy has maintained its identity to a degree that then seemed impossible'. The book had turned out to be 'a panegyric preached over an empty coffin', because after its publication in 1945 the landed families rose again.[39] For if there was a long tradition in Britain of successful business moving into land, there was an equally long tradition of land successfully moving into business or itself becoming businesslike. Through the nation's concern for its 'heritage' after 1945, as earlier through the Victorian elaboration of the honours system, the aristocracy drew the middle classes towards them and learnt from them. So the pace of country-house demolition slowed in the 1960s, and houses which in the 1950s would have been doomed were now being saved, partly through 'spot listing' (or instant protection) under the Town and Country Planning Act (1968), but more importantly through once again becoming financially viable.

In L. P. Hartley's *Go-Between* the Maudsley family in 1950 were living in only a corner of Brandham Hall, the scene of such spaciously dramatic events fifty years earlier; the rest was let to a girls' school.[40] But the wealthier and shrewder landed families, shedding political and social power, focused on converting their homes into profitable cultural and recreational centres.[41] For John, thirteenth Duke of Bedford, reopening Woburn Abbey in 1955 was bound up with his family's future, and 'became an obsession'; an obituarist portrayed him as converting himself into 'a superb showman, stopping at almost nothing'. In friendly rivalry with him was the equally publicity-conscious Lord Montagu of Beaulieu, who built up his leisure centre from

[38] Sampson, *Anatomy of Britain*, 12.

[39] Preface (1959) to E. Waugh, *Brideshead Revisited* (1st publ. 1945, rev. edn. 1960, paperback edn. Harmondsworth, 1962), 8.

[40] L. P. Hartley, *The Go-Between* (1953, paperback edn. 1958), 272.

[41] F. M. L. Thompson, 'English Landed Society in the Twentieth Century, iv. Prestige without Power?', *TRHS* (1993), 5.

1951, introduced professional managers in 1959, encouraged film-makers to use his home in the 1960s, and built a motor museum there in 1972.[42] No fewer than 43 million people visited country houses in 1973.[43] Mid-century House of Lords debates often stressed their tourist value, boosting invisible exports. 'The historic house is a very major feature in the menu or the bill of fare which is offered to our overseas tourists', Lord Montagu told the Lords in 1968. 'If pageantry is the soup, and London is possibly the main course, then historic houses are certainly a very varied and excellent sweet trolley.'[44]

Lifestyle, the fourth upper-class quality, loomed larger after 1951 among the country house's roles. The alliance of Nancy Lancaster and John Fowler in the firm of Colefax & Fowler brought comfort to the country house in the 1950s, with generous chintzes, French wallpapers, and en-suite carpeted bedrooms. The British landed aristocracy, now occupying only parts of the family mansion or much smaller houses on its estate, no longer displayed its wealth in personal expenditure but instead propagated its culture at one remove, within the much smaller homes, whether in Britain or abroad, occupied by people who had visited country houses. The newly fashionable art history interacted with the new aristocratic commercialism, while the magazine *Country Life* under Christopher Hussey and John Adams[45] persisted with its interwar role of educating country-house owners in the value of their possessions. A veritable school of architectural historians opened out from the magazine's long series of articles on country houses. Its articles were not concerned only with exteriors. Many now recognized that country houses had often been designed to display the patron's collections, with the Royal Academy exhibition on 'Italian art and Britain' in 1960 as a landmark; to transfer such objects to a museum was to rip them from context. Hence the growing number of curators and scholars in the area, and the growing collaboration between museums and country houses;[46] the focus could now rest on keeping house and contents together. This valuation and propagation of aristocratic display was not at all what the socialist pioneers had envisaged: their vision of the future had been somewhat puritanical, deploring inequality, whether in lifestyle or wealth. In 1920 the Webbs had predicted for country houses a role as local-authority welfare premises or as 'the holiday homes and recreation grounds of the urban toilers by hand or by brain'. Crosland in 1956 thought that mass production was cheapening invented products so fast that no rich person would attract publicity by consuming conspicuously more than the less wealthy, and that

[42] John, Duke of Bedford, *A Silver-Plated Spoon* (1959), 195; obituary, *DT* (28 Oct. 2002), 25. For Montagu, *T* (5 Apr. 1977), 16; see also Hewison, *Heritage Industry*, 63.

[43] *HL Deb.* 26 Jun. 1974, c. 1486.

[44] *HL Deb.* 15 May 1968, c. 332.

[45] Obituary of Adams, *T* (13 Mar. 2003), 35.

[46] J. Cornforth, *The Country Houses of England* (1998), 72, 80, 82.

'ostentation is becoming vulgar';[47] egalitarian lifestyles were spreading, and such inequality as survived was more likely to be shared only by domesticated adults in private. Social success was now thought to require hard work rather than effortless superiority amidst luxury.

Still less would the socialist pioneers have expected a postwar revival of the upper-class social round. Entry to London 'society' could no longer be closely policed, however, and the monarchy, in broadening its social connections, slowly adjusted to a new and more democratic reality. By the early 1950s the annual upper-class social cycle had returned with a vengeance. The private view of the Royal Academy's summer exhibition which launched the London season was 'less an exhibition than a huge midday cocktail party without cocktails, a gathering of the aristocracy and diplomats, the politicians, artists and literary figures who comprised the then establishment in days when the great and good were standing fairly firm';[48] when not energetically conversing, they could scrutinize the portraits of themselves and friends adorning the Academy walls. The annual round ensued: the Chelsea Flower Show, the 4th of June at Eton, Royal Ascot, Henley Regatta, Harrow speech day, the Eton and Harrow match at Lords, Cowes Week, Goodwood, the International Horse Show at White City, the Dublin Horse Show, and the St Leger, together with wartime reunions, old boys' gatherings, winter holidays in Madeira or Switzerland, and dinners and social functions in London, photographed in full swing with the usual shots of celebrities in the *Tatler*. In 1959 the Duke of Beaufort invented the annual horse trials at Badminton, and by 1971 this too had been incorporated into the annual upper-class social schedule.[49]

Presentation at court simultaneously signified social arrival and availability for marriage, with virginity sedulously husbanded. Madame Vacani trained generations of debutantes in the faultless curtsey at her School of Dancing in Knightsbridge, and 'Jennifer', the *Tatler*'s social diarist, helped to minimize clashes of date for the dances organized by the debs' mothers in London and in country houses. Anxious, pushy, and sometimes ruthless, they 'launched' their girls—already 'finished' at finishing schools at home or (preferably) in France—into a social world rendered hazardous by numerous unwritten rules about dress, accent, and conduct. For decades, growing numbers had negotiated this social ascent—during the 1950s, more than 1,300 women a year. For Lord Altrincham in 1957 all this tied the royal family to 'a grotesque survival', lending the Queen 'the appearance of standing at the apex of an aristocratic and plutocratic pyramid'. It could not last, if only because people had begun to purchase admission. 'We had to put a stop to it', Princess Margaret recalled:

[47] S. and B. Webb, *A Constitution for the Socialist Commonwealth of Great Britain* (1st publ. 1920, Cambridge, 1975), 266. Crosland, *Future of Socialism*, 280–4.

[48] F. MacCarthy, *Last Curtsey: The End of the Debutantes* (2006), 111.

[49] M. Bowen, 'So What's Happened to the Season?', *Sunday Times Magazine* (17 Oct. 1971), 18.

'Every tart in London was getting in.'[50] There was a last-minute push in 1958 when 1,441 curtseying young women rushed in for the positively last performance;[51] thereafter the Queen substituted additional garden parties. An unofficial successor event was devised, however, in the exclusive annual Queen Charlotte's charity ball (which survived till 1994), and when in the 1960s the royal guest of honour no longer came, curtseys were transferred to the gigantic cake which fashionable caterers had presented [Plate 12].[52]

The world of the country house and the London salon, with political hostess presiding, survived well beyond the 1950s. Important Liberal and Social Democratic Party (SDP) gatherings occurred at Kiddington Hall in Oxfordshire, home of the Swedish-born Stina Robson, designer-clothed political hostess. When Pam Berry, prominent political hostess and wife of the *Daily Telegraph*'s proprietor, persisted with a long-standing vendetta against Anthony Eden as prime minister, his wife Clarissa thought it worth trying to end it, but was cut dead at the dinner where she made the attempt.[53] 'I am a Pam Berry person', wrote Crossman, a devotee of her parties. The parties thrown by Ann Fleming, widow of James Bond's creator Ian, were by contrast 'full of a kind of smartness and cultural elegance, quite different from Pam's hard-boiled, political, journalistic atmosphere'. At these Victoria Square parties a dinner was held for ten downstairs and then adjourned upstairs to the drawing room where everyone else assembled.[54] Gaitskell as Labour leader mixed widely in fashionable society, paying court to Ann Fleming and lunching with Lady Diana Cooper, but on such occasions he saw himself as off duty, and his social tastes were not advertised within his class-conscious party.[55] Labour could not or would not buttress its political leaders by this route, and in 1964 Crossman thought its unity suffered as a result. 'How important it was for the Tories when they were in Government to relax for the weekend in those great country-house parties!', he wrote. 'How much we in the Labour Party miss the country houses which we don't have!' He thought that Harold Wilson's domesticated lifestyle, with all the respectability of keeping himself to himself, damaged the party, but Wilson strongly disliked his ministers attending such gatherings, suspecting that plots were hatched there.[56]

Merit, the fifth upper-class quality, was a middle-class identifier, but it was far from absent higher up, though less advertised and less formally certificated.

[50] Altrincham *et al.*, *Is the Monarchy Perfect?*, 8–9. For Princess Margaret, see McCarthy, *Last Curtsey*, 14. This paragraph owes much to her splendidly evocative and amusing yet serious combination of history and autobiography at this point.

[51] M. Pringle, *Dance Little Ladies: The Days of the Debutante* (1977), 77.

[52] Thompson, 'Prestige without Power?', 11.

[53] D. R. Thorpe, *Eden: The Life and Times of Anthony Eden* (2003), 460.

[54] *Cabinet Diaries*, iii. 357 (4 Feb. 1969). See also R. Strong, *Diaries 1967–1987* (1st publ. 1997, paperback edn. 1998), 122 (30 Jan. 1973), 285 (1981).

[55] Pimlott, *Wilson*, 214.

[56] *Cabinet Diaries*, i. 98 (13 Dec. 1964). Castle, *Diaries 1964–70*, 172 (7 Oct. 1966).

For the upper classes, merit was not enough: experience, cultivation, and 'character' were also required. Polished public-school manners kept merit under reticent wraps, staving off 'difficult' questions, and holding the elite together. Among aristocratic women, merit was prized in the form of personal beauty and poise, nourished by good diet, contraception, and a leisured lifestyle; beauty could also be enhanced by portraitists, couturiers, and servants of every kind. 'Eligible' young women continued to blossom in the pages of *Country Life*, but by the 1960s they increasingly sought a career other than, or at least supplementary to, marriage. And well before then, the opportunities (hitherto limited) for cultivating beauty were democratizing. The interwar music-hall artiste and the film star had already competed in this arena with upper-class women, and after 1945 there was a long-term and cross-cultural tendency to standardize dress. It eliminated distinctive regional or national clothing, but also threatened (especially among the young) dress that identified people by social class and even by sex; from the late 1950s the rapid and worldwide diffusion of denim jeans consolidated the trend.

The social conditions moulding personal appearance also converged, given growing access to baths and piped water, labour-saving household equipment, and jobs physically less taxing;[57] at all social levels, women could now age more slowly.[58] Morale was also involved: childbearing and housework had once been so taxing that on marriage many women simply gave up, resigning themselves to a slovenly destiny. New worlds were now opening up. The advertisement headed 'which twin has the Toni?', ubiquitous on the London underground in the 1950s, invited the public to pronounce on which of two apparently identical female heads of hair had been home-permed. Women could now more easily and cheaply banish for good the long, dank hair that had hitherto been the mark of the slum.[59] Children in 1950 in all classes were taller and heavier than in 1936, but age and weight were still correlated with social status. In slum schools of the 1960s, fourth-year boys were on average 63.2 inches tall, but 64.5 inches tall in secondary modern schools, with average weights at 112.5 and 116.9 pounds, respectively.[60] As for upper-class men, their training, diet, and strenuous sports fostered physical strength and courage rather than beauty and poise. As long as sporting achievement rested primarily on superior physique and training, upper-class young men had a built-in sporting advantage.

[57] See e.g. Carr-Saunders *et al.*, *Social Conditions*, 44; Rowntree and Lavers, *Poverty and Welfare State*, 83.

[58] See e.g. Orwell, 'The Art of Donald McGill' (1941), in *Complete Works*, xiii (1998), 27; 'War-Time Diary' (13 Apr. 1941) in *Complete Works*, xii. 469; R. Blythe, *Akenfield: Portrait of an English Village* (1st publ. 1969, paperback edn., Harmondsworth, 1972), 188.

[59] See Hulton Press, *Patterns of British Life* (1950), 133–8, for use of cosmetics and permanent waves by women in 1949.

[60] Rowntree and Lavers, *Poverty and Welfare State*, 94–5. Ministry of Education, *Half Our Future: A Report of the Central Advisory Council for Education (England)* (1963), 25.

Yet in sport as elsewhere, privilege was increasingly at risk from mounting professionalism. The public schools had lost their primacy at football in the 1880s, and from the 1950s onwards professionalism in cricket and rowing dethroned Oxbridge blues from their pedestals in those sports too.[61] With his four-minute mile in 1954 the medical student Roger Bannister was perhaps the last Oxbridge undergraduate to set a really significant sporting record. University students were increasingly required to choose between sport and study, otherwise they would be doomed to amateurism in both senses. By the 1970s the Oxford and Cambridge cricket match aroused so little interest that there were proposals to discontinue holding it at Lord's. Perhaps only in field sports did the landed classes retain any sporting prominence. There the link between sport and warfare had been especially strong, but the increasingly complex equipment of modern warfare meant that bravery and physical strength would not suffice. A democracy of valour had for decades been promoted through the military and civil decorations that rewarded bravery. The Victoria Cross, instituted in 1856, was awarded to four British men (three officers and one private) between 1951 and 1970, all in the Korean war; and the George Cross, instituted in 1940, was in this same period awarded to nineteen British people for bravery in such episodes as fires, sea-rescue, defusing bombs, or tackling armed robbers.[62] There was also now a mounting meritocratic military demand for technical skills.

Distinction in these five areas—lineage, title, wealth, lifestyle, and merit—bestowed power, for which training was provided first at a 'prep' school, and then at one of the closely linked leading independent (or 'public') schools. In the 1950s secure upper-class membership went only to boys who attended not only a public school, but the right public school—at the very least, one of the nine 'Clarendon' schools: Charterhouse, Eton, Harrow, Merchant Taylors', Rugby, St Paul's, Shrewsbury, Westminster, or Winchester. Among these a boarding school was preferable for elite status, though between 1946 and 1971 the proportion of public-school boys who boarded was in slow decline: from 72 per cent in 1946 to 69 per cent in 1961 to 65 per cent in 1971.[63] Public schools were 'comprehensive' in the sense that intellectual merit was only one among their several admission requirements. Their links with the Oxbridge colleges were close, and their entry qualifications were narrowing only gradually towards the purely intellectual.

Through their links with the debating unions and political clubs the political parties had long recruited young Oxbridge talent. Their teachers' links with

[61] For Oxford's changing outlook on sport, see D. J. Wenden, 'Sport', in B. Harrison (ed.), *The History of the University of Oxford*, viii. *The Twentieth Century* (Oxford, 1994), 519–29.

[62] See *The Register of the George Cross* (1st publ. 1985, 2nd edn. Cheltenham, 1990); *The Register of the Victoria Cross* (1st publ. 1981, 3rd edn. Cheltenham, 1997). For help on this point I am most grateful to Dr Mark Curthoys.

[63] R. Lambert, *The Chance of a Lifetime?* (1975), 288.

government were weaker than in the USA except perhaps during the two world wars, but the governmental preoccupations of Oxford and the LSE were particularly strong,[64] and remained so well into the 1960s. That decade saw the Wilson governments heavily recruited from Oxford, with a marked outflow of university talent from the social sciences to Whitehall. Thereafter the relationship cooled somewhat,[65] with both major political parties reaching out more widely into the community. The social class of vice-chancellors' fathers had declined sharply early in the century, and their links with the social elite were weakening.[66] University teachers were becoming more self-consciously professional, and the cultivated but amateur mood which had earlier encouraged their easy interaction with government was less in evidence by the 1980s and 1990s.

As long as Churchill was prime minister, the link persisted between lineage and political power, and at least six members of Macmillan's cabinet together with several other ministers were related to him through his wife; in January 1958, 40 per cent of the cabinet and 39 per cent of Conservative MPs were relations (admittedly sometimes distant) of Macmillan, as were the Macmillan appointees Sir Arthur fforde (new BBC chairman) and Hugh Trevor-Roper (Oxford's Regius Professor of Modern History).[67] The aristocratic factor's ongoing importance in British debate emerged from the exchange between Wilson and the new Conservative prime minister Lord Home in October 1963: 'after half a century of democratic advance, the whole process has ground to a halt with a 14th Earl', said Wilson in a speech. Home's reply in an interview two days later, was mild: 'I suppose Mr Wilson when you come to think of it, is the 14th Mr Wilson'.[68] But meritocratic and socially inclusive tendencies were advancing within the Conservative Party, as evidenced by Heath's election as party leader in 1965. As for Wilson's governments after 1964, they had been self-consciously meritocratic from the start.

At least since the 1930s labour leaders had accepted peerages, not for their class connotations but as testifying to personal achievement and to the rising status of those they represented. The purpose in 1958 of extending the life-peerage concept beyond the law lords was even more overtly utilitarian: it was a staging post on the way towards reinventing the House of Lords as a classless working assembly which could usefully complement the lower chamber without weakening the government party. By 1970 there were 163 life peers in a House

[64] See B. Harrison, 'Politics', in Harrison (ed.), *History of the University of Oxford*, viii. 386–9.

[65] See below, pp. 268–9.

[66] W. D. Rubinstein, 'Education and the Social Origins of British Elites 1880–1970', *Past and Present*, 112 (Aug. 1986), 184.

[67] D. J. Heasman, 'The Prime Minister and the Cabinet', in R. Benewick and R. E. Dowse (eds.), *Readings in British Politics and Government* (1968), 172; cf. Benn, *Diaries 1940–62*, 263 (29 Jan. 1958).

[68] D. R. Thorpe, *Alec Douglas-Home* (1996), 323.

containing 862 (less active) hereditary peers, twenty-six bishops and eleven law lords. The hereditary peerages lingered on, becoming extinct at the rate of about five a year, and others were disclaimed.[69] By 1959 the 13th Duke of Bedford, for one, felt that there was 'very little justification' for the hereditary peers to retain any political role, given that they had 'ceased to be representative of the governing class any more'; instead he favoured the idea of life peerages.[70] From 1964 both Labour and Conservative leaders ceased for the time being to award hereditary honours.

The upper classes had long been retreating from public administration as well as from politics. There was a long-standing trend for members of the elite (bishops and leading civil servants, though not leading industrialists) to reflect the middle class in its geographical distribution, and to come disproportionately from London and the south-east.[71] The mid-Victorian introduction of civil-service entry by examination was seen at the time as a setback for privilege, and thenceforth civil servants came from a markedly lower social level. Permanent secretaries from 1900 to 1986 were diminishingly likely to come from Clarendon schools and more likely to come from fee-paying schools not classed as public schools. Between the wars the familiar pattern had grown up whereby the hard-working grammar-school scholarship boy who did well at Oxford or Cambridge took the civil service examination, thereafter progressing steadily into the elite. 'Very quick, Brook', Warden Bowra of Wadham College Oxford recalled of Norman Brook, who had arrived there from Wolverhampton Grammar School in 1921 and served as secretary to the cabinet from 1947 to 1963. 'Learned the tricks, learned the tricks. Came up with a front pocket stuffed full of pens. Soon disappeared inside. Learned the tricks.' Macmillan was impressed by Brook's good judgement, given that 'he had no background', whereas Benn six years later saw in Brook 'a perfect example of an Establishment figure—Tory in every instinct'.[72] In the Second World War, as in the First, the urgent need for expertise and talent brought still more middle-class talent to the civil service's higher regions. When state scholarships and an increasingly meritocratic entrance examination after 1945 broadened Oxbridge recruitment, Oxford drew in three future general secretaries of the TUC: George Woodcock, Len Murray, and Norman Willis.

All the tendencies after 1945 within the civil service worked to broaden recruitment and promotion still further. The pressure came partly from the

[69] Butler, *BPF* (8th edn.), 224. See also *Econ.* (6 Jan. 1973), 18.

[70] Bedford, *Silver-Plated Spoon*, 233.

[71] Rubinstein, 'Education and Social Origins', 183, 196–201. K. Theakston and G. K. Fry, 'Britain's Administrative Elite: Permanent Secretaries 1900–1986', *Public Administration* (Summer 1989), 132.

[72] P. Hennessy, *Whitehall* (1st publ. 1989, paperback edn. 1990), 145; Benn, *Diaries 1963–7*, 290 (12 July 1965).

sheer complexity of modern government, with its mounting need for experts of every kind: lawyers, statisticians, economists, scientists, and accountants. It was reinforced by growing concern that British governments were delivering economic growth more slowly than several other industrial societies, and also perhaps by distrust of an elite which could produce spies such as Maclean, Burgess, and Philby. From 1963 onwards it owed much to the meritocratic reaction against Macmillan's style of government and to the conviction in Wilson's Labour Party that by attacking privilege it could simultaneously improve government, enhance economic efficiency, and attract middle- and working-class voters. In the Fulton report (1968), urging on the civil service still broader and more expert recruitment and still more effective use of talent, three former grammar-school boys (Wilson, Fulton, and Norman Hunt) brought this train of thought to a head.[73]

With the advance of professionalism, specialization, and expertise came the fragmentation and dilution of the upper classes. The amateur was forced on to the defensive, together with anyone whose social status and role required him to combine activities that now seemed more efficiently conducted separately. Chairmen of the largest industrial companies, top civil servants, and churchmen between 1880 and 1970 were increasingly drawn from the lower part of the middle class, with little family wealth behind them. The social class of bishops' fathers had been declining since the 1880/99 cohort, and was still declining between 1940 and 1970.[74] Secularization and Anglican decline were gradually converting church leaders into critics of the establishment. War-making and diplomacy had once been fully built into the preoccupations of the landed classes. In 1950 and 1960 ten major public schools contributed nearly a fifth of Sandhurst's entrants and in 1959 two-fifths of the British army's lieutenant-generals, generals, and field marshals.[75] The army's informal affinity with the Conservative Party had long been well developed. MPs from this shared background, reinforced in both parties by the Second World War, remained numerous as long as the services required abundant conscripts and volunteers. Here again professionalization exerted a fragmenting impact: with the steady decline in defence expenditure and responsibilities, and with the armed services' mounting professionalism, these political links, too, were weakened. It was becoming increasingly difficult to see the British upper classes as anything other than a loose and very permeable elite, diverse in its composition, and endlessly absorptive.[76]

73 See esp. *Fulton Report*, i. 95.

74 Rubinstein, 'Education and Social Origins', 183–4; cf. D. H. J. Morgan, 'The Social and Educational Background of Anglican Bishops: Continuities and Changes', *British Journal of Sociology* (1969), 299.

75 C. B. Otley, 'Public School and Army', *New Society* (17 Nov. 1966), 756.

76 Paxman, *Friends*, 8.

How, then, does one explain the revived use in the mid-1950s of that nineteenth-century radical term 'the establishment'? The catalyst was Henry Fairlie's article in the *Spectator* in 1955, written in the context of the Burgess/Maclean spy case, and evoking a flurry of indignant correspondence. For Fairlie the term meant not just the centres of official power, 'but rather the whole matrix of official and social relations within which power is exercised'. Power in England, he emphasized, 'is exercised socially', and involves the chairman of the Arts Council and the director-general of the BBC as well as the prime minister and the Foreign Office. The term's vagueness was, for its time, a major virtue. To refer to 'the establishment' was to assume that the contest for power was not between the social classes, but between government and its critics. Such a term was more useful than Marxism as a way of broadening the attack on Macmillan's Conservative government.[77]

More objective observers, by contrast, saw British government in less polarized terms, as a cluster of interacting semi-autonomous groups. When preparing his influential survey of the UK's power structure, *The Anatomy of Britain*, Sampson 'had a growing impression of having visited not a single country but a loose federation of institutions, each threatening, not to coalesce, but to conflict or break away'. So he dismissed the 'establishment' concept, and preferred to think in terms of 'a cluster of interlocking circles, each one largely preoccupied with its own professionalism and expertise, and touching others only at one edge'. He emphasized that power often rested with obscure people, though these still included many among the well-born; they retained their wealth partly by refraining from overtly defending it, thereby not inviting attack. Crosland had reached similar conclusions in trying in the 1950s to divert Labour towards a less narrowly economic agenda. Economic power, he claimed, 'now poses fewer problems than other forms of power', such as 'the power of the enlarged and bureaucratic state', 'the power of a small hierarchy of Court, Church, and influential newspapers' and 'the power of those who control the bureaucratic mass organisation, whether public or private'.[78] Observation of other countries showed that the redistribution of wealth did not necessarily require changes in ownership, and he directed the egalitarians towards such policy areas as taxation, economic management, and unionization—that is, towards the political, social, and even cultural dimensions of power. Gaitskell made much fun of Macmillan's taste for stuffing his cabinets with relatives and aristocrats,[79] but as a revisionist himself, he knew that the British elite was more complex than that.

[77] *Spec.* (23 Sept. 1955), 380. See also A. Sisman, *A. J. P. Taylor: A Biography* (1st publ. 1994, paperback edn. 1995), 427; Paxman, *Friends*, 9.

[78] Sampson, *Anatomy of Britain*, 625, 624. Crosland, *Future of Socialism*, 40.

[79] Williams, *Gaitskell*, 695.

Upper-class fragmentation in the 1950s and 1960s emerges clearly from trends at Westminster. In 1951 there were still many knights of the shire on the Conservative back benches, sent to parliament because they had already made their careers or did not need to make them; likewise with many of Labour's trade-unionist backbenchers. The two parties could then be clearly distinguished by their dress, with the Conservatives sporting their Trumper's haircut, cream silk shirt, and Brigade or Old Etonian tie.[80] MPs on both sides, however, were becoming more careerist in outlook, increasingly distant from both privilege and from the trade-unionist attack upon it, aiming to win ministerial status through preserving a certain aloofness from the fray.[81] The Labour Party's advent after 1918 as leading party of the left in itself constituted a massive dilution of the political elite, and between the wars Labour had recruited many progressively meritocratic and undeferential members of the middle class. The Attlee governments in implementing their ambitious programme of 1945 had been forced into streamlining the procedures of a somewhat gentlemanly parliament. During the 1960s the escalating demands on MPs' time, the growth in constituency and committee work, the increasing need to match the government's expertise, and the need even for the Conservative Party to appear meritocratic forced amateurism in parliament, too, on to the defensive.

Fragmentation within the elite is also reflected in the dwindling national importance of London's clubland. In the 1950s top people were already segregating themselves between clubs, with civil servants preferring the Reform, politicians the political clubs, financiers Brooks's, and so on. The clubs were now becoming less central to the elite social round. Whereas more than four-fifths of Edwardian MPs belonged to one or more London club, only two-thirds of Conservative and 8 per cent of Labour MPs belonged by 1974.[82] And whereas the worlds of law and politics had once closely interacted, Crossman's comment in 1968 after attending the Lord Chancellor's annual reception for leading lawyers is revealing: 'it struck me once again how separate we keep ourselves in Britain. There is the legal world, the doctors' world, the artistic world, the dramatic world, the political world. We are tremendously separate.'[83]

Newspapers, too, were diverging from the elite. The radical press was refining its traditional muck-raking role, with the postwar *Daily Mirror* to

[80] Julian Critchley, quoted in Paxman, *Friends*, 74–5.

[81] For more on this, see A. King, 'The Rise of the Career Politician in Britain—and its Consequences', *British Journal of Political Science* (1981), 249–85.

[82] Lupton and Wilson, 'Social Background and Connections of "Top Decision Makers"', 36–7. M. Rush, 'The Members of Parliament', in S. A. Walkland (ed.), *The House of Commons in the Twentieth Century: Essays by Members of the Study of Parliament Group* (Oxford, 1979), 118.

[83] *Cabinet Diaries*, iii. 206 (1 Oct. 1968).

the fore, confronting snobbery with its irreverently cheeky tone. Warning the nation that it must tighten its belt, R. A. Butler as Chancellor of the Exchequer was unwise enough to say that 'the easy evenings of drinking port and eating over-ripe pheasant' must come to an end. Few *Mirror* readers had experienced such food, and the paper organized a Butlerian dinner for a dozen people at the Savoy; the pheasant was not enjoyed, and a classic *Mirror* article was the result.[84] The less radical press was becoming less respectful of upper-class secrets, and the public was encouraged to watch the vulgar antics of Lady Docker in the 1950s, for example, with awed fascination. Sir Bernard's Daimler, gold-plated on the basis of a sketch by his wife, a former dance hostess, stole the motor show for 1951—though the company disliked such publicity, and Docker survived as chairman of the BSA Group only until 1956.[85] Still more sensational was the amply reported divorce case of Margaret, third wife of the 11th Duke of Argyll, between 1959 and 1963, with its treasured glimpses of promiscuity at the highest levels.[86] In 1963 John Profumo's lie to the House of Commons about his affair with Christine Keeler provided a sort of culmination, during which the press eagerly devoured a scandalously tasty morsel with three commingled flavours: sex, spies, and aristocrats.

The controversy in the 1950s about how to identify upper-class speech forms was only half facetious: it illustrates the disparate nature of the British elite, and perhaps also the growing middle-class move into it. The socialite 'Chips' Channon noted in 1952 that terms hitherto thought middle-class were now accepted in good society: 'we all now say "bus" and admit "week-end"—both formerly very common . . . all agreed that "note-paper", "mantelpiece", "mirror", "radio", are now often heard in "Good Society"'. The social elite had by 1954 lost so many of its distinguishing features, wrote the philologist Alan Ross, that 'it is solely by its language that the upper class is clearly marked off from the others'.[87] His article was first published in a little-known philological journal, but reached national attention in 1955 when its revised form appeared in the magazine *Encounter*; it evoked much correspondence, so was again republished, this time as the first item in the compendium *Noblesse Oblige* (1956). Early in 1957 its 'u' and 'non-u' terminology was sufficiently established to feature in Macmillan's diary, when he described the factors needing to be balanced when recruiting his new government.[88] Between the 1940s and the 1970s the upper-class word 'loo' was travelling socially downwards only to hit

[84] *Tickle the Public*, Radio 4 programme, 4 Mar. 1996.

[85] 'Lady Docker', *T* (12 Dec. 1983), 10. See also B. M. D. Smith's memoir of Sir Bernard in *Dictionary of Business Biography*, ii (1984), 121–7.

[86] Obituary, *DT* (28 July 1993), 19.

[87] *Chips: The Diaries of Sir Henry Channon*, ed. R. R. James (1967), 466 (4 Mar. 1951). A. S. C. Ross, 'Linguistic Class-Indicators in Present-Day English', *Neuphilologische Mitteilungen*, 55 (1954), 20.

[88] *Macmillan Diaries*, ed. Catterall, 615 (3 Feb. 1957).

the lower-class word 'toilet' travelling up, so that by the 1980s a boundary was demarcated between the two somewhere within the lower levels of the middle class.[89] But lower down we must now travel, for it was there that the main thrust in social change during the 1950s and 1960s was making itself felt.

3. MIDDLE-CLASS EVANGELISM

Whereas unity was the strength of both upper and lower classes, the middle classes flourished on their diversity and divisions. They highlighted the fact by usually referring to themselves in the plural, and their business structures assumed competition more than collaboration. And whereas upper-class prosperity required access to resources such as capital and land which were scarce, middle-class growth patterns required skills and expertise which could in principle become abundant in a meritocratic society. So the middle classes could take the world as their parish, expanding through a powerful combination of exclusion and evangelism. Exclusion could take the form of elocutionary concern: amusement at the occasional malapropism and the dropped 'h' had long been a device for fending off boarders from below. Labour's Foreign Secretary Herbert Morrison gave much pleasure in some quarters by failing in August 1951 to pronounce Middle East place names correctly, as did the socially aspiring Joe Lampton when he mispronounced 'brazier' at the Warley Thespians: 'I joined in the laughter', Joe recalled, 'but it was a considerable effort.'[90] In addition, professional exclusiveness at work, by contracting the supply of services, kept up middle-class incomes and led the unprotected either to set about joining the existing charmed circle, or to annexe to it new charmed circles of their own.

The aim of the middle classes' continuously evolving professional structures was formally to exclude rather than overtly to proselytize. Hierarchy, not equality, was the middle-class mood. At any one time the professions maintained a clear pecking order. Asked in 1964 for its most admired profession, a Gallup sample placed the doctor way ahead with 47 per cent, the teacher won 12 per cent, the scientist 10 per cent, the clergyman 8 per cent, and the lawyer 5 per cent; social observers were surprised at the wealth that a leading professional person could accumulate.[91] Because not dependent on birth, the professions' pecking order was adjustable, as was that characteristic middle-class locale, the suburb, dispersed and deliberately separate from work. Forever nervous about

[89] As pointed out by K. Hudson, *Teenage Revolution*, 119. On 'loo' see Viscount Ridley, *HL Deb.* 2 July 1974, c. 204.

[90] Nicolson, *Diaries and Letters 1945–62*, 208 (1 Aug. 1951). Braine, *Room at the Top*, 49.

[91] *Gallup Polls*, ii. 743 (July 1964). For wealth, see e.g. Townsend, *Poverty in UK*, 358–9, 368.

slipping in social status, the suburbans condemned neighbours who 'let down' the estate by selling to an aspirant from below, particularly if drawn from an ethnic minority. The British habit, unusual elsewhere, of giving streets and even houses a name rather than a number reflected a pride in ownership, an identification with locality and a settled outlook replicated in the absence of revolutionary dates from British urban street names.[92]

Yet exclusion was complemented by evangelism. The middle classes possessed the self-confidence and know-how that prompted a taste for volunteering and for taking initiatives. These aptitudes they had long deployed in selectively recruiting their class from below, for they gained from fluidity and vagueness at their lower as well as at their upper boundary; some middle-class professions (welfare workers, schoolteachers, and religious activists, for example) specialized in making converts from lower down. This middle-class evangelizing was sometimes insensitive: the mid-century professionalization of social work, for example, entailed what the social scientist Barbara Wootton called a 'pseudo-psychiatric approach'[93] at the expense of common sense and practical knowledge. But middle-class evangelism was working with the grain, and was all the more powerful for being unobtrusive and self-generating. Between 1951 and 1971 the proportion from the higher professions in the workforce almost doubled, and there were marked increases for the lower professions, for managers and administrators, for clerical workers, and for foremen and supervisors. By contrast, the number of employers and proprietors, sales staff, skilled manual and semi-skilled manual workers declined, and there was only a small increase for unskilled manual workers.[94] In their share of the total occupied population in Great Britain, manual workers fell from 64 per cent in 1951 to 55 per cent in 1971, whereas in the same period white-collar workers rose from 31 to 43 per cent; the rise was particularly marked among managers, administrators, professionals, technicians, and clerks. The same trend was apparent even within manufacturing industries, where the administrative, technical, and clerical staff as a proportion of total male employees in work rose between 1951 and 1968 from 16 to 25 per cent, and among women employees from 19 to 27 per cent.[95]

Education and examinations enabled the middle classes both to consolidate their existing status and to recruit from below. Status anxiety did not normally begin at the elementary-school stage, though some parents sought to protect their child through the private 'prep school' even then. Serious worries began after the age of 11, when examinations loomed and when class location gradually

[92] *Ind.* (15 June 1994), 13, contrasts street-naming in USA, Japan, and Europe.

[93] *HL Deb.* 17 Feb. 1960, c. 106; see also Baroness Swanborough, c. 123.

[94] See the useful table in *TCBST* 288.

[95] R. Price and G. Bain, 'Union Growth Revisited', *British Journal of Industrial Relations* (1976), 346. *BLS* 276–7.

crystallized. At this point the clever child could grasp the secure middle-class status that had eluded the parent. The traditional vehicle of middle-class hopes had long been the grammar school, which provided the examination-passing, parentally encouraged child with the chance to 'get on' once the 'eleven-plus' entrance examination to the grammar school had been passed. Thereafter the scholarship child, self-distanced from more easy-going and less ambitious contemporaries, was on course for status confirmation or ascent, sometimes simultaneously losing contact with family and neighbourhood. Failure at the eleven-plus presented parents with three options: scrimping and saving for an independent school, moving house (with associated expense) so as to qualify for a satisfactory state school, or risking the child's status by staying put.

If the last option were chosen, an alliance between parent and teacher in the 'secondary modern' school might precariously hold the child, located on a class frontier, on its middle-class course. It was above all through passing examinations and staying on beyond the compulsory school-leaving age that social status could be retained or social mobility won.[96] The 'secondary modern' of the early 1960s might still be located in the forbidding and cramped building which had once been a late-Victorian elementary board school, planted in the inner city to crusade for respectability, and whose mid-twentieth-century task was now all too often hopeless. But from the late 1940s many such schools were being rebuilt in the modern style and sometimes also relocated, often in conjunction with espousing the new 'comprehensive school' ideal then gathering pace.[97] With no selection at 11, this type of school aimed at equal opportunity for all, its larger size enhanced flexibility, and better facilities did much (at least in theory) to resolve the middle-class parent's dilemma. These schools' broader choices and facilities made the middle-class child's status less precarious, especially if the classes were 'streamed'. 'Any superficial glance through the window at a "C" or "D" class will tell you at once that these are low stream children', wrote John Partridge: 'The boys from the poorest homes seem always to be in the lower streams . . . boys in "A" classes wear the School uniform, but most "D" boys come in dirty, torn jackets and trousers or jeans.'[98]

Behind middle-class educational evangelism lay a selection process which substituted formally assessed achievement for birth and personal connection, thereby converting schoolteacher and examiner into allocators of life-chances. The radical middle-class battle cry from the 1940s onwards was 'modernization': the need to promote national security and prosperity through invoking

[96] The Crowther report, Ministry of Education, *15 to 18: A Report of the Central Advisory Council for Education (England)*, i (1959), 8, was impressed by the clear correlation between social class and propensity to stay on. See also below, pp. 353–4.

[97] See below, p. 353.

[98] J. Partridge, *Middle School* (1966), 85.

measured merit. For Jonathan Browne, the hero of David Lodge's novel *Ginger, You're Barmy* (1960) who in national service spurned officer-training, the army was 'the last surviving relic of feudalism in English society', run by entrenched but inefficient upper ranks requiring unquestioning obedience from the serfs beneath.[99] Nobody questioned the need for meritocratic promotion among doctors or among individuals and teams in the footballer's world, which in the 1960s was reconstituting itself into a nationwide meritocratic hierarchy.[100] In such areas, as in industry and commerce, it seemed in the 1960s that professionalism might soon fend off national decline by destroying classbound barriers to personal achievement. Both major political parties reflected this outlook: Wilson with his utilitarian pursuit of planning, efficiency, institutional reform, and social opportunity; Heath with his acceptance of European innovation and his pragmatic pursuit of the centre ground. The meritocratic thrust persisted for the rest of the century, from the 1960s transforming university admission criteria, in the 1980s moulding the careers of SDP voters and parliamentary candidates,[101] and pervading Thatcher's reshaped Conservative Party. In the 1990s it shaped the tone of 'New Labour', lay at the heart of collaboration between the Liberal and Labour party leaders Ashdown and Blair,[102] and ensured that by 2000 the honours system had shed most of its feudal connotations.

One book, however, subtly struck a discordant note: Michael Young's ingenious *The Rise of the Meritocracy* (1958). Unstylish and somewhat confusingly laid out, it was none the less reprinted three years later by Penguin Books because its theme was undeniably important. Not only did it sell 500,000 copies in twelve languages;[103] it coined a new word for the English language, and helped to prompt the foundation of the open-access Open University.[104] The book surveys British history since 1914 through the eyes of an enthusiast for meritocracy who looks back from AD 2033. He explains that Labour governments had substituted equal opportunity for heredity, and in the 1970s had used a capital levy to make the grammar schools more attractive and thus undermine the 'public' schools, but had obstructed meritocracy with their continuing faith in socialist equality. The Conservatives then saw that to render the UK economy internationally competitive, they needed to steal Labour's clothes by promoting meritocracy more efficiently. Having got into power, they promoted a regime entirely oriented towards merit (defined as IQ + Effort). Grammar-school values then triumphed, intelligence tests were refined, and clever children were

[99] D. Lodge, *Ginger, You're Barmy* (1960), 76, cf. 87. [100] See below, pp. 388–9.

[101] I. Crewe and A. King, *SDP: The Birth, Life and Death of the Social Democratic Party* (Oxford, 1995), 274, 281, 293.

[102] See the 'joint statement' signed by Blair and Ashdown on 11 Nov. 1998 in P. Ashdown, *The Ashdown Diaries*, ii. *1997–1999* (2001), 168–9. [103] Young's obituary in *G* (16 Jan. 2002), 20.

[104] G. Dench *et al.*, *Young at Eighty: The Prolific Public Life of Michael Young* (Manchester, 1995), 6.

paid to prolong their education, while the stupid departed to jobs matching their limited intelligence. In the 1980s the British economy therefore flourished, the trade unions weakened, and Labour had to rebrand itself as the Technicians Party. Yet old Labour egalitarianism lingered on, unmeritorious members of the old elite pined for lost status, and some idealists valued qualities other than tested merit—kindliness, diversity, courage, imagination, and sensitivity, for example. With the meritocratic regime thus unstable, and with its elite in practice largely self-recruiting, right-wing Conservatives felt in the early 2030s that nothing would be lost by restoring a hereditarian structure. The regime's critics, however, gained adherents and built up to a mass protest in 2034. The author's hopes for a peaceful outcome were presumably defeated, as Young concludes with a wry footnote: the author, killed during the protest, had been unable to check the proofs of his manuscript before publication.

Young's middle-class meritocratic trumpet therefore gave forth a very uncertain sound, identifying a dilemma that was particularly acute for mid-century bourgeois socialists, but also highlighting ambiguities in the social outlook that enabled the twentieth-century middle class to recruit so widely. Young did to Marx what Marx had done to Hegel: stood him on his head. Young's bourgeoisie, far from being hurled down into the proletariat, energetically sucked up talent from below. Young's mood was tongue-in-cheek, not idealistically utopian, and his was not a prediction but a warning. The revolutions ushering in the classless utopias of Marx and Morris were now redundant, he implied, for the crucial revolution (gradual, anti-aristocratic, and largely economic in nature) had already enthroned the middle class. Still less credible at mid-century was H. G. Wells's surreal extension of class conflict—in his *Time Machine* (1895) set in the year AD 802702—whereby the flesh-eating Morlock descendants of the proletariat emerged at night from their underground caverns to terrify the effeminate vegetarian Eloi descendants of the bourgeoisie. Young's revolution of 2034 did not involve an attack on the middle class, but a split within it, and in the real world of 1958 Young thought no such split inevitable if only the middle class took care not to overvalue measured merit. The new post-industrial society would have ample jobs for people with few qualifications; as Sir George Thomson pointed out in 1955, when discussing what he felt able to describe as 'the future of the stupid': 'there are plenty of jobs—tending the aged is one—where kindness and patience are worth more than brains'.[105] Young hoped that meritocratic selection would be entrenched without empowering a caste-like hierarchy even more arrogant than its precursor.

Meritocracy's ambiguities left ample scope for both parties to espouse 'modernization': to cater for those already in the middle classes as well as

[105] Thomson, *Foreseeable Future*, 139–43.

for those who aspired to join them. Like the Victorian aristocracy, the mid-twentieth-century middle classes were the more secure because of their hold on both major political parties—a hold whose strength was masked by the two-party system's advertised conflict over policy. Conservatives resting their values and appeal on a concern with tradition, nation, community, neighbourhood, and personal relationships saw social-class preoccupations as fragmenting and destructive. This made it easy for them in the 1950s to identify with those taking the deferential route to self-help: with the respectful and naturally Conservative employee who as retailer, servant, or professional person sought status through associating closely with superiors. Many tasks once tackled by domestic servants—cleaning, cooking and laundering, for example—might now be performed by home-based equipment such as vacuum cleaners, food mixers, and washing machines, or were jettisoned altogether. Yet in 1960 there were still 30,000 men and 275,000 women in 'private domestic service', including daily helps and gardeners; there were even 600 butlers still in service.[106] Domestic servants had not vanished from the UK, but had reappeared in a new guise, for the living out supplanted the living in. Cleaning ladies, child-minders, 'housekeepers', au pairs, waiters, and butlers now buttressed or even temporarily entered the better-off home for specific purposes, but lived elsewhere.

Still, by the 1950s the deferential route into Conservatism was a waning asset, and the party supplemented it by catering for the mid-twentieth-century variant of self-help: for the more assertive and individualist worker (once predominantly Liberal), whose social mobility was self-propelled. In the late 1950s and early 1960s at least half the working-class Conservatives in the most urban constituencies were not at all deferential. To cater for them Churchill at the general election of 1951 recommended the ladder over the queue,[107] and in its manifesto of 1955 the party aimed 'to develop in our country the idea of a property-owning democracy', whereby 'people should be owners as well as earners. Our theme is that property, power and responsibility alike must not become absorbed into the State machine, but be widely spread throughout the whole of the community.'[108] Tax cuts, free enterprise, deregulation, and owner-occupation were the watchwords. This was the party which attracted the young John Major (Rutlish School), and the young Norman Fowler (King Edward VI School, Chelmsford), who had been shocked during his national service officer-training to hear one public-school cadet saying of another: 'he's very proud of his school—best not to tell him that it's not a very good one'.[109] Opinion surveys showed that the upwardly mobile were keener to

[106] Sampson, *Anatomy of Britain*, 18.
[107] McKenzie and Silver, *Angels in Marble*, 158, 160. D. E. Butler, *The British General Election of 1951* (1952), 66–7.
[108] Dale (ed.), *Conservative Manifestos*, 118.
[109] N. Fowler, *Ministers Decide: A Personal Memoir of the Thatcher Years* (1991), 40.

embrace the party than were the downwardly mobile to abandon it; those who rose into the middle class were drawn disproportionately from the children of working-class Conservatives; people who owned their homes were twice as likely to vote Conservative as those who rented them; and the upwardly mobile tended to support the party of the class they aimed to join. Working-class Conservatives in the 1950s were not to be underestimated: they were well-informed and alert to their own interests.[110] Both types of working-class Conservative merged in Katie McMullen, who under the name Catherine Cookson had by the 1990s become well known as Britain's most borrowed popular novelist. Illegitimate daughter of an alcoholic Tyneside barmaid, she was told by an aunt that her well-spoken father had worn an astrakhan collar and carried a silver-topped cane. Katie set to with a powerful combination of thrift, elocution, and ambition, and in her late twenties became a landlady in Hastings. Marrying the schoolteacher Thomas Cookson in 1940, she then had four miscarriages and steadied herself by writing two novels a year. These historical pageants, 'usually involving a doughty heroine betrayed by a toff', displeased metropolitan critics by assuming a working-class need to move quickly into the middle class, but she made a fortune, much of which she gave away in later life.[111]

Labour, too, held an appeal for actual or aspirant members of the middle class. Already by 1939 the sociologist T. H. Marshall could note that 'the professions are being socialised and the social and public services are being professionalised': the professions were, he claimed, learning both to work together and to acknowledge their wider social obligations.[112] The middle-class mansion's many rooms readily accommodated the government employees, scientists, and technologists attracted by postwar Labour's rationalistic interventionism. Whereas the Attlee government's welfare and nationalization measures at first alarmed many middle-class people, the enterprising among them soon detected a new opportunity: self-interest complemented altruism and idealism in leading professional people to collaborate with and even exploit the state. The number of scientists, engineers, draughtsmen, and lab technicians in Great Britain almost tripled between 1931 and 1951, and more than doubled between 1951 and 1966.[113] Labour's social-democratic 'revisionists' had recognized the need to cater for such people at least since Durbin published his *The Politics of Democratic Socialism* (1940), a powerful influence on Hugh Gaitskell, Tony Crosland, and Roy Jenkins. But only with further electoral setbacks after 1951 could the revisionists effectively challenge the party's entrenched 'labourism'.

[110] Butler and Stokes, *Political Change* (2nd edn.), 98–9, 181. McKenzie and Silver, *Angels in Marble*, 95, 192–3.
[111] 'She's Marched a Long Way from Jarrow', *ST* (15 Jun. 1997), v, 3.
[112] T. H. Marshall, *Citizenship and Social Class* (1939), 147.
[113] *TBS* 114.

At least until the 1970s Labour's corporatism seemed to offer the middle classes much. The Conservatives were not yet ready for a major assault on state employment, nor did their support for free enterprise extend far beyond generalized sympathy. Even in 1958 a tenth of the 'solid middle class' and a quarter of the lower middle class were Labour voters, and by 1964 Labour could attract a tenth of the business class, a fifth of the professionals, more than a quarter of the office workers, and more than a third of the shop assistants.[114] There was much talk by Gaitskell and others in the late 1950s about the 'embourgeoisement' of the working class, whose newly won consumer goods allegedly fostered middle-class politics, yet the newly affluent might not win social acceptance, and might be radicalized by rejection. 'I always had the fear of doing the wrong thing', Joe Lampton recalled: 'of making a fool of myself in front of the higher grades. Saying the wrong thing to the waiter or picking up the wrong fork or not being able to find the cloakroom immediately wouldn't have mattered in an ordinary café . . . The rich were my enemies, I felt: they were watching me for the first false move.'[115] Such resentments were often sharpened by the important middle-class divide between the products of public and grammar school, a contrast central to the plot of Braine's *Room at the Top*. 'The cry of the scholarship boy angrily knocking at the bolted door of the bourgeoisie', a strand in Wilson's socialism, fuelled the intellectuals' assault on the 'establishment' in the mid-1950s, the meritocratic repudiation of Macmillan in the early 1960s, and the Wilson governments' espousal of institutional reform after 1964. A Labour leader who like Wilson regularly re-read Carl Sandberg's life of Abraham Lincoln[116] was socially incorruptible, and felt no special reverence towards the civil service and local government, parliament, and the legal and educational systems—all reformed by his governments. The public schools, too, had their malcontents: a Gaitskell or a Crossman could cultivate Labour sympathies, and when asked by old ladies how it was that he became a Communist, John Strachey's stock answer was 'from chagrin, madam; from chagrin at not getting into the Eton Cricket Eleven'.[117]

The pervasive concept of the 'lower middle class' made it all the easier to move upwards out of the working class. The phrase was anomalous to the extent that its mirror image, 'upper middle' class, was less prevalent, and the term 'middle middle' class was hardly used at all. Nor were there enough small-scale entrepreneurs even in British towns, let alone in the countryside,

[114] J. Blondel, *Voters, Parties and Leaders: The Social Fabric of British Politics* (Harmondsworth, 1963), 57. R. Rose, 'Class and Party Divisions: Britain as a Test Case', *Sociology* (1968), 144.

[115] Braine, *Room at the Top*, 74–5; cf. D. Lockwood and J. H. Goldthorpe, 'Affluence and the British Class Structure', *Sociological Review* (July 1963), 138.

[116] Foot, *Politics of Harold Wilson*, 327. *ST* (15 Feb. 1970), 13.

[117] Quoted N. Wood, *Communism and the British Intellectuals* (1959), 113 cf. Crosland, *Future of Socialism*, 200–1. For Gaitskell see D. E. Butler and R. Rose, *The British General Election of 1959* (1960), 13.

to require an Anglicized version of the French term 'petit bourgeoisie', a phrase that hovered only on Marxist lips. As much a cultural concept as a class category, the lower middle class was even vaguer than most British social-class terminology: it conjured up visions of routine clerical occupations, nonconformist chapels, and regular commuting in a somewhat faded suit from modest inner-city suburban terraces. Each lower-middle-class house would be distinguished from the next by some small architectural, gardening, or furnishing detail. Less likely now to be privately rented, more likely to be owner-occupied and mortgaged, it was safely distanced from any nearby council estate. By the 1960s, however, sociologists and trade unionists were increasingly likely to apply the imported American term 'white-collar' at such social levels.

Here too there was much political ambiguity. In clerical occupations, the values of work and residential community were not in serious tension. Home was less likely to be in a council house or in an industrial estate near the firm than in a rented or (increasingly) owner-occupied house located at a distance within an occupationally diverse suburb. Office machinery's advance did not necessarily radicalize. A clerical proletariat might in theory exist, but it was not nursed into self-consciousness—least of all by an office organized by function rather than by status, planned in egalitarian fashion so as to conceal the firm's lengthening office hierarchy, its growing size and its mechanization. Tasteful partitions, pot plants, and pleasant perks captured at work something of the furnishing, lighting, heating, décor, and fitted carpets of the modern middle-class home.[118] Service-sector employers were, after all, bidding for scarce high-quality employees. In such a context, easy relations readily grew up within the office hierarchy, and recruits to the middle-class lifestyle were readily won. Further nourishing domesticated values was women's growing proportion of clerical workers in Great Britain: only a fifth in 1911, but rising continuously to three-fifths by 1971. As a proportion of all women in employment in Great Britain, clerical workers had risen continuously to 28 per cent by 1971, whereas (at between 5 and 6 per cent) they hardly rose at all as a proportion of all men in employment.[119] Women, part-timers, white-collar workers, and service-sector employees were much less class-conscious than male manual workers in large factories. Women's unionization in the twentieth century broadly followed male trends, but at about half the male level. Women were less likely than men to join the non-manual unions and still less the manual;[120] USDAW, the union for retail workers, many of them women, actually lost members between 1950 and 1970.

[118] For a good discussion see A. Forty, *Objects of Desire: Design and Society 1750–1980* (1986), 140–3.

[119] *BST* 166. J. H. Goldthorpe, *Social Mobility and Class Structure in Modern Britain* (Oxford, 1980), 60.

[120] *BST* 187–8. Price and Bain, 'Union Growth Revisited', 349.

Yet white-collar workers did not inherently differ in their work situation from organized manual labour. Wage costs in white-collar concerns were high as a proportion of the firm's outgoings, leaving ample scope for disputes with the employer. In some large white-collar work units, employers could be remote, especially in the largest of all: the local and national government machine. Hence white-collar unionization, whose social-class significance pointed in two directions: on the one hand it could be seen as merging middle and working classes within structures resembling those pioneered by organized labour, but it could also be viewed as the middle class reaching out once more for new recruits by appropriating structures not their own. Similar middle-class colonization was occurring elsewhere—through joining the Workers' Educational Association (WEA), for example, to pursue middle-class recreational advantage; through launching organizations concerned with public welfare; and through moving into urban localities hitherto predominantly working-class. By 1962 Ruth Glass had invented the term 'gentrification' to describe what was occurring in London: in the mid-1960s the middle classes were overflowing from fashionable areas like Chelsea, Hampstead, or South Kensington into adjacent Fulham, Camden Town, and Notting Hill.[121]

State employees were not discouraged from unionizing: quite apart from trade-union pressure, the sheer size of the government's workforce made unionization managerially convenient for the employer.[122] White-collar unions grew fast between 1950 and 1970: the local-government workers more than doubled their union membership and Clive Jenkins's ASTMS (the scientific, technical, and managerial workers) escalated from a mere 12,000 to 221,000; the pattern recurred with other unions strong in public and welfare services.[123] Growth in union membership and in union density among male (though not female) white-collar workers was much faster than among male manual workers between 1948 and 1974, and white-collar unions contributed almost the entire growth from 1948 to 1964 in TUC-affiliated membership.[124] Private-sector white-collar workers were much more weakly organized; numerically, as well as in other ways, bodies like the National Union of Bank Employees or the National Union of Insurance Workers carried little weight within the trade union world or anywhere else. Of the trade union membership affiliated to the TUC in 1966, less than a fifth could properly be described as attached to white-collar unions, though there were small groups of white-collar workers buried within the big manual-labour unions, especially among clerical employees who worked closely with manual workers—with railwaymen, miners, engineers,

[121] R. Williams, *Politics and Letters: Interviews with 'New Left Review'* (1979), 80. J. Greve, 'London's Homeless', *Occasional Papers in Social Administration*, 10 (1964), 41.

[122] Bain, *Trade Union Growth and Recognition*, 1, 20–1, 67, 91.

[123] *BPF* (8th edn.), 395.

[124] Price and Bain, 'Union Growth Revisited', 349. Bain, *Trade Union Growth and Recognition*, 18.

or dock workers, for example.[125] The overall picture, then, is for mid-century white-collar unionization and Labour voting to reflect, if anything, an agile middle-class self-interest. Instrumental and tactical in motive, it had little to do with working-class solidarity, and was distant indeed from the middle-class social slippage preceding Marx's final revolution.

4. WORKING-CLASS ECLIPSE?

The British labour movement's aims from the outset included elevating working people collectively, but also individually through its educational and community-based structures. In 1976 Benn noted the pride felt by Pat Duffy, a former able seaman, at becoming a minister for the navy; for such people, 'socialism *was* people like them getting to the top, not actually changing the top, just getting there'. Recording his pleasure when the Queen invited him to the naval review at Spithead in 1977, Callaghan wrote: 'my father had taken me aboard the *Victoria and Albert* when I was a toddler, but I do not suppose it ever crossed his mind that one day his son would be invited to return as the Prime Minister of the United Kingdom'.[126] Already by the 1960s, however, the Conservative commitment to home-ownership and an 'opportunity society' was helping to focus the social-mobility options: individually with the Conservatives and collectively with Labour. Furthermore, whereas the Conservative approach seemed increasingly feasible and attractive, Labour's seemed diminishingly so. The working-class move upwards into the 'service class' (professionals, administrators, managers, and large proprietors) had indeed been collective,[127] but resulted less from political action than from technical change, enhanced educational provision, and newly emergent job opportunities. When writing about the general election of 1959, psephologists were beginning to detect a significant number of skilled workers who were what 'may be called class hybrids', working class by occupation and culture, but middle class in terms of income and lifestyle.[128]

Labour's collective route to social mobility was still much needed. To take only one example, half of the employed professional or managerial men sampled in 1968–9 were entitled to more than a month's notice of dismissal, but only 2 per cent of employed male manual workers.[129] Yet the heavy-industry communities in the north and west which benefited from government expenditure were diverging markedly by 1964 in their employment patterns from the two net

[125] A. Flanders, *Trade Unions* (1st publ. 1952, 7th edn. 1968), 25–7. D. Lockwood, *The Blackcoated Worker: A Study in Class Consciousness* (1958), 153, 197.

[126] T. Benn, *Against the Tide: Diaries 1973–6*, ed. R. Winstone (1st publ. 1989, paperback edn. 1990), 564 (6 May 1976). J. Callaghan, *Time and Chance* (1987), 461.

[127] Goldthorpe, *Social Mobility and Class Structure*, 39–40.

[128] Butler and Rose, *British General Election of 1959*, 15.

[129] Townsend, *Poverty in UK*, 452–3.

contributor regions: the west midlands and the south-east.[130] Between 1911 and 1951 manual workers fell in their proportion of Great Britain's occupied population from three-quarters to below two-thirds:[131] agriculture's employees had been declining for decades, the trend had extended to mining by 1951, and thereafter to manufacturing. The war had only briefly revived traditional labour patterns, and manual labour's decline resumed, increasingly recruiting only from its own offspring, and showing little of the middle-class capacity to recruit more widely.[132] The unionization and nationalization so prevalent in heavy industry after 1951 slowed down the search for expanded markets, and between 1931 and 1971 men in unskilled manual occupations fell from an eighth to an eleventh of employed men in England and Wales, and those in partly skilled manual occupations from a quarter to less than a fifth.[133] In the 1950s Labour's revisionists, alert to these changes, became the party's latest group to follow the Fabians in emphasizing socialism's classless appeal. For Crosland, their leading author, class preoccupations were diminishingly salient in a society with less scarcity and more leisure; cultural, libertarian, and recreational issues were destined to advance.[134] Influential research on the affluent industrial workers in Luton of the early 1960s showed how this increasingly pluralist outlook operated in practice. Work was viewed instrumentally, for the purposes of the domestic and recreational life which received first priority. Friends were not normally made in the factory, nor did social life focus there. Trade unions' role was utilitarian, to maximize income: they were not seen as part of a social movement or as a vehicle of social-class values. The demanding nature of work did not prompt a conflictual view of society: it was the price paid for high wages in a society that was seen as inevitably and naturally divided more by income and wealth than by access to power. The affluence of these 'privatised workers' did not lead them to merge with the middle class, nor did they compete for the privilege, if only because they shunned the responsibility attached to the best-paid posts.[135]

All this was slow to shape public debate and party policy. The class-conscious mood of British politics from the 1950s to the 1970s reflects how substantial was the time lag before economic realities reconstructed party-political stances.

[130] A. H. Birch, *Political Integration and Disintegration in the British Isles* (1977), 43; cf. the regional analysis of exposure to polluted air in the late 1960s in Townsend, *Poverty in UK*, 536.

[131] *BST* 164.

[132] Goldthorpe, *Social Mobility and Class Structure*, 259–60, 262, 268. A. H. Halsey, *Change in British Society: Based on the Reith Lectures* (Oxford, 1978), 52.

[133] Townsend, *Poverty in UK*, 143.

[134] Crosland, *Future of Socialism*, 173, 284–6, 520.

[135] J. H. Goldthorpe *et al.*, *The Affluent Worker*, i. *Industrial Attitudes and Behaviour* (Cambridge, 1968), 108–9, 114, 120, 125–6, 136–8, 142–3, 145, 146, 149, 176; ii. *Political Attitudes and Behaviour* (Cambridge, 1968), 26–8, 79; iii. *The Affluent Worker in the Class Structure* (Cambridge, 1969), 80–1, 105–7, 115, 147, 149, 154, 159. See also D. Lockwood, 'Sources of Variation in Working Class Images of Society', *Sociological Review* (Nov. 1966), 256–62.

In politics as in war, old strategies were being mistakenly pursued in entirely changed circumstances. 'Class consciousness is at its peak', wrote Zweig in 1952, 'at a time when the separateness of the classes is growing less pronounced.'[136] It is easy in retrospect to see that a traditionalist allegiance to an unreconstructed classbound Labour Party was doomed, together with the associated escalating trade union membership and Labour affiliation—but at the time the signs were far less clear [Plate 13]. UK trade unions were able to attract a steady 44 per cent of their potential membership between 1951 and 1970, and from the late 1960s this rose fast, reaching 51 per cent in the 1970s to an unprecedented peak in 1979. Union members in these years were solidly behind both TUC and Labour Party. In 1951–70 the TUC managed to affiliate from the total trade union membership a scarcely fluctuating average of 86 per cent, once more rising to unprecedented peaks in the 1970s, and the Labour Party secured a steady and historically high 55 per cent of them.[137] The long-term twentieth-century tendency was for trade unions to amalgamate into ever larger units: their number fell from 1,325 in 1900 to 726 in 1950, and to 540 in 1970,[138] so that the leading unions' general secretaries became nationally known figures. The corporatist policies in vogue during the 1960s and 1970s ensured that the TUC/Labour Party partnership was seldom out of the headlines. In 1960 the five areas of employment with the highest proportion of unionized employees were all either governmental or nationalized: mining, railways, local government, national government, and transport/communications.[139]

Furthermore, the proportion of the partly skilled and unskilled in the male workforce declined more slowly in the 1960s than in the 1950s,[140] and Labour's philosophy of economic planning operated within a nation state which was far less constrained then than later by what was becoming known as 'globalization'; some even thought globalization could be reversed, or at least fended off. It was not at all obvious before the 1980s that the long-term decline in British heavy-industry communities was permanent. The proportion of the UK workforce employed in firms of 1,500 employees or more rose from 24 per cent in 1951 to 36 per cent in 1973, and it was not clear that these firms might later shrink or fragment.[141] The large mid-century manufacturing concerns, whether nationalized or not, inevitably distanced managers from employees, and interposed the newly flourishing profession of 'personnel manager' between the two. Many managers in effect delegated organizing the workforce largely to trade union officials, whose dues the firm helped to collect and in whose closed

136 F. Zweig, *The British Worker* (Harmondsworth, 1952), 207.

137 Calculations from *BST* 187–8. 191–2.

138 *BPF* (8th edn.), 400–1. Flanders, *Trade Unions*, 24, analyses trade union membership by union size as at 1966.

139 See the table in Flanders, *Trade Unions*, 179.

140 Townsend, *Poverty in UK*, 667–8.

141 See the useful table in J. F. Wright, *Britain in the Age of Economic Management* (Oxford, 1973), 40.

shop they acquiesced. Concessions to trade unions were not always difficult: the very size of the large industrial concern both required and enabled it to invest heavily in capital equipment, which rendered the employee's hard physical labour less central to profits.

The language of class conflict was publicly heard in the 1960s at least as frequently from the white-collar workers' leaders as from the manual workers' more pragmatic and seasoned spokesmen, though it was the latter who established the ethos of British trade unionism, if only because they and the skilled craftsmen had created it. It was the big manual labour unions—especially the huge TGWU and Amalgamated Engineering Union—whose bloc votes and muscle power dominated TUC and Labour Party assemblies. In some parts of the economy select groups of workers held a crucially strategic role. Macmillan worried about this in his diary: concerned in 1961 about a possible strike in power stations, he felt that these 150,000 Communist-led workers 'have the whole country in pawn', and knew that the government could not (as in 1926) generate enough alternative power 'to meet the needs of a nation now wholly geared, industrially and domestically, to electricity'.[142] In other areas the urgency of getting maximum return on heavy capital investment gave trade unions considerable power within the firm: the American phrase 'wildcat strike' became domesticated in Britain in the mid-1950s.[143] In vehicle manufacture, managers introduced machinery which threatened both industrial relations and the quality of the product. Workers felt they had two bosses, one of them human, but the other mechanical and impersonal: 'it's the track, the track, the track . . . your guv'nor is that track', exploded one worker in the early 1960s, highlighting the tyranny of the assembly line whose speed provoked so much dispute.[144] These strikes and threats of strikes received much publicity then and later, and within the industries affected absorbed a quite disproportionate amount of managers' time. They eventually led the Labour government into a failed attempt at reform which prepared the way for the Heath government's failed attempt and later for Thatcher's successful alternative.[145]

Labour was not alone in misinterpreting the signs. Deference to organized labour was widespread among intellectuals in these years, and Conservative governments were keen to stave off trouble with timely concession. None the less, the long-term trend later became clear: it lay towards what sociologists in the 1960s often called 'embourgeoisement', though there was then much debate on how far middle-class values would prosper within seemingly middle-class situations. With the middle classes unstoppable, the social extremes withered.

[142] H. Macmillan, *At the End of the Day* (1973), 44 (26 Oct. 1961).

[143] The *Oxford English Dictionary*'s first British reference is to *Encounter* (7 June 1954).

[144] G. Turner, *The Car Makers* (1963), 163.

[145] For a full discussion of this, see below, pp. 310, 457–60.

We have seen how an attenuated upper class managed somehow unobtrusively to survive: something similar was happening at the lower end. 'Instead of being two nations, one of the rich and one of the manual workers', said *The Times* in a leader of 9 December 1972, urging the Labour Party to move on, 'we are increasingly becoming a single nation of middle class people, with a tiny fringe of privilege and a minority of poverty'. This may have anticipated the pace of change, but not by much. Affluence was now so widespread, and there were now so many upward routes into the middle class, that working-class communities felt diminishing need for the earlier and somewhat moralistic institutions designed to encourage individual social mobility: for friendly and temperance societies, savings banks, mission halls, Sunday schools, and self-improvement structures of every kind. The choice between rough and respectable lifestyles, even where it persisted, was now much less stark. Besides, advancing home-centredness more frequently concealed such lapses from respectability as occurred: the family quarrels, the personal untidiness, the overdrinking, the gossiping with the neighbours, and the children roaming free.

Poverty's marginalization in the 1950s and 1960s did not signal a time when the poor would no longer be with us because the sociologists were redefining poverty as a relative rather than an absolute concept: rising living standards drew the poverty's definition upwards, and deprivation became relative.[146] Those left behind included a minority of rather miscellaneous deprived groups who had either never been securely integrated into the working class, or who had appeared only recently. Clustering as they often did in the inner city, such class identification as they possessed was often cut across by age, sex, and marital status. The subgroups were too small and disparate to acquire a class label, and the integrating concept of an 'underclass' was not yet available. The groups' relationship with working-class institutions had always been equivocal. They included the homeless, the impoverished one-parent family, the unemployed, the criminal, and the opters-out from an accumulative society.[147] Public welfare and extended education were still widely expected to reduce their number, and three influences combined in the 1950s to enable a relatively small police force (still on the beat) to operate effectively: the social cohesion bequeathed by the war, the ongoing tradition of civic responsibility, and the persisting values of respectability. Britain was still a face-to-face society, the privatizing impact of mass car ownership was not yet fully felt, domesticated affluence had not yet denuded the streets, and the civilizing work begun nearly two centuries earlier by humanitarians and evangelicals in penal reform was still bearing fruit. So

[146] P. Townsend, 'Measuring Poverty', *British Journal of Sociology* (1954), 136. P. Townsend, *The Social Minority* (1973), 43, 48. Townsend, *Poverty in UK*, 38. See also above and below, pp. 14–15, 150–1, 266, 329–30 (homeless); 247, 295 (one-parent families); 316 (unemployed); 329, 513–17 (opters-out).

[147] Townsend, *Poverty in UK*, 285, 302, 543, 545.

shaming did a criminal conviction seem in the 1950s that employers felt free to dismiss an employee for offences unrelated to work. So crime in the 1950s was politically neither salient nor controversial. The nineteenth-century term 'mugging' had yet to return to Britain from its American refuge, and in the UK the realities of terrorism and 'hijacking'—an American word from the 1920s which came into general use in Britain in the 1960s, often in hyphenated form—were not yet being experienced.

Yet the first sentence of the Home Office's important report of 1959 on *Penal Practice in a Changing Society* found it 'a disquieting feature of our society that, in the years since the war, rising standards in material prosperity, education and social welfare have brought no decrease in the high rate of crime reached during the war: on the contrary, crime has increased and is still increasing', with a particularly worrying growth in juvenile delinquency.[148] Competitive accumulation did not necessarily take legitimate forms. For example, the new supermarkets and better packaging, by making consumer goods more accessible and attractive, combined with advertising pressure to nourish shoplifting: offences of this type in England and Wales rose fast from the 1950s and doubled in the 1960s.[149] Crimes known to the police, which notoriously understate real crime levels, rose more than threefold in absolute terms and in relation to population between 1950 and 1970. Violence against the person rose nearly sixfold, offences against property more than threefold, sexual offences by two-thirds.[150] There was much concern about juvenile delinquency in the 1950s, mounting concern in the 1960s about drug trafficking, and by 1970 the deteriorating relations between young people and the police had produced riots on the south coast.[151] The number of police in England and Wales rose by 28 per cent between 1950 and 1970, from 1.65 to 1.90 per thousand population;[152] the daily average prison population almost doubled between 1950 and 1970—to 39,000, almost all of them men.[153] Public concern about crime, at first more powerful on the right, but gradually spreading across the political spectrum, was sharpened by at least three striking episodes. The first was the Bentley shooting in 1953.[154] The second was the violence between thousands of mods and rockers in seaside towns in the south and east during March and May 1964, which led to 278 convictions.[155] Middle-class and grammar-school in background, the scooter-driving mods were well turned-out, influenced by European fashions

[148] Home Office, *Penal Practice in a Changing Society: Aspects of Future Development (England and Wales)*, *PP* 1958–9 (Cmnd. 645), xxv. 1

[149] See table 2 in D. P. Walsh, *Shoplifting: Controlling a Major Crime* (London and Basingstoke, 1978), 29.

[150] T. Morris, *Crime and Criminal Justice since 1945* (Oxford, 1989), 91.

[151] e.g. in Folkestone, *G* (16 May 1970), 18.

[152] Statistics calculated from Central Statistical Office, *Annual Abstract of Statistics*.

[153] N. Walker in *BST* 627.

[154] See below, pp. 292–3.

[155] R. S. Grayson, 'Mods, Rockers and Juvenile Delinquency in 1964: The Government Response', *Contemporary British History*, 12/1 (Spring 1998), 26.

and sophisticated. The working-class, motor-cycle-driving, leather-jacketed, greasy-haired rockers were, by contrast, rough, with a pedigree going back to the Teds of the 1950s and to the USA's Hell's Angels.[156] The third episode was most shocking of all: the so-called 'moors murders' of at least five young people in 1962–5 by Myra Hindley and Ian Brady. It was shocking for several reasons: because children were involved, because the murders were preceded by torture and sexual molestation, because these activities were photographed and tape-recorded, and because a woman had played so prominent a part. The photograph of Hindley, with her dark eyes and peroxide bouffant hair, became 'a timeless icon of evil'.[157]

There was a growing gulf from the 1950s between the public reaction evoked by this situation and the rationalistic and humanitarian pressures that still powerfully inspired penal reform, especially the abolition of hanging.[158] Important to the humanitarian case was the belief that brutal punishments degrade society. Flogging had been banned in the army in 1906, birching as a judicial punishment in 1948; flogging in the navy ended in 1957, corporal punishment in prisons and borstals ceased in 1967. A major humane influence at this time was the jurist Glanville Williams.[159] Courageous, versatile, and pioneering, this austere and agnostic Welshman was Professor of English Law at Cambridge from 1966 to 1978. In the 1950s criminology advanced markedly as a subject of academic study in Britain. In 1948 its UK pioneer, the Polish immigrant Leon Radzinowicz, published the first volume of his *History of English Criminal Law* (completed in five volumes in 1986). Criminology was deeply penetrated in its early years by psychoanalytic approaches, but in the 1960s moved closer to sociology and social anthropology. It interacted with lay influences such as progressive lawyers and politicians, as well as with humanitarians at home and abroad, to produce a rather hopeful reforming climate in the 1950s. Although of limited practical and short-term value, this new discipline did at least reinforce the trend for dealing with crime empirically rather than through moralistic prejudice—especially within the Home Office, whose criminological climate improved considerably in the late 1950s. R. A. Butler claimed that when Home Secretary in 1957–62 he had informed its work with 'the same spirit of reform and zeal for progress as had called into being the Education Act of 1944'. In 1957 he thought it 'a matter . . . of first importance' to base penal policy on precise information: 'we must know what is happening and why'. His 'biggest initial shock' on becoming Home Secretary had been his ministry's failure to sponsor sufficient research: 'we must . . . make the best use of the tools which the sciences of statistics

156 See Sandbrook, *White Heat*, 196–8, for a useful discussion.

157 Hindley's obituary, *T* (16 Nov. 2002), 9.

158 See below, pp. 291–3.

159 See below, pp. 248, 291.

and sociology have put into our hands'.[160] Butler was a key figure in getting Cambridge's Institute of Criminology established two years later.

It was important to widen access to the law. Legal aid grew out of servicemen's need for free legal advice during the Second World War, and made less impact than had been expected because introduced only very gradually. None the less, by extending the categories of case requiring adjudication it highlighted new areas where the law seemed defective or obscure, prompting further improvements. There was another burst of penal reform in the late 1960s: the Criminal Justice Act (1967) extended eligibility for parole and introduced the concept of the suspended sentence with the aim (not at first realized) of reducing prison numbers; and the Children and Young Persons Act (1969) liberalized the treatment of juvenile offenders. In Lord Denning the legal system even found an influential (though controversial) judicial activist unwilling to wait for parliament to ensure that the law delivered justice; 'I develop the law, I don't bend it', he told his critics: '. . . I believe in developing the law to meet the needs of the time'.[161] By 1970, however, the progressives were in retreat. It was alleged that their enlightened views had undermined some of the moralistic but civilizing influences hitherto painstakingly accumulated. In emphasizing the environmental causes of crime, for example, they risked undermining the sense of personal responsibility. Shoplifting was a prize example of a new crime for which determinist excuses were offered, and whose terminology some thought too soft. The concept of kleptomania fell out of fashion with psychiatrists after the 1940s, and in 1983 some members of the Home Office Standing Committee on Crime Prevention wanted the phrase 'theft from shops' substituted for 'shoplifting', though they did not prevail.[162] Many thought that the progressive outlook chimed in too closely with, and even informed, the criminal's excuses. 'Time after time', wrote the Morrises, investigating Pentonville in 1958–60, 'prisoners cite as being at the roots of their criminality, unloving parents, step-parents, orphanage life, the death of parents, fathers in gaol, and mothers on the streets.'[163]

While social-class identity retained much of its intensity in the 1950s and 1960s, its social basis was being slowly undermined from several directions. We have seen in this chapter how both monarchy and aristocracy were becoming more approachable, but also how landed wealth was becoming less visible and often less confident. Middle-class expansion entailed growth for a class so broad and fragmented as almost not to be a class at all. As for the working class, its spokesmen remained visible and articulate enough, but in the long term

[160] R. A. Butler, *The Art of the Possible: The Memoirs* (1971), 199. *HC Deb.* 13 Mar. 1957, cc. 1142–3.

[161] *T* (6 Mar. 1999), 20.

[162] Home Office, *Shoplifting, and Thefts by Office Staff: A Review by the Home Office Standing Committee on Crime Prevention 1983* (1983), 1.

[163] T. and P. Morris, *Pentonville: A Sociological Study of an English Prison* (1963), 311.

their position was weakening, if only because working people themselves were less easily identified. Observant writers, following up in the 1950s the insights pioneered by Durbin and Orwell in the 1940s and even earlier, commented on modern Britain's growing classlessness. They sometimes struck a nostalgic note: Hoggart's *The Uses of Literacy* feared lest the superficiality of a media-based mass culture might supplant a 'more genuine class culture'.[164] Concurrent ironings-out of class contrasts abounded elsewhere: mass-produced clothing's long war against the second-hand clothing shops was turning into a rout; improved health and dental care were standardizing the human face; a clannish electoral loyalty to party was in decline;[165] class contrasts in housing and diet were diminishing;[166] family size, propensity to marry, and age at marriage and retirement were becoming more uniform;[167] and a new distraction from class loyalties was now making a domestic cultural impact: mass immigration.

5. MINORITIES OLD AND NEW

In Chapter 2 we saw the immigrants arriving; here the concern is with how they settled. Of the overseas-born living in Great Britain by 1951, 34 per cent had been born in 'Ireland' or the Irish Republic, 8 per cent in the 'Old Commonwealth' (Australia, New Zealand, Canada, and South Africa), 14 per cent in the 'New Commonwealth' (Africa, the Caribbean, India, Cyprus, Malta, Gibraltar, and other), and 36 per cent in Europe (France, Germany, Austria, Italy, Spain, Poland, Hungary, the USSR, and other). By 1971 the 'Irish' had fallen to 24 per cent, the 'Old Commonwealth' to 6 per cent, and the Europe-born to 23 per cent, whereas the 'New Commonwealth' had risen to 39 per cent.[168] The geographical reach of the category 'New Commonwealth' was too broad to capture genuine loyalties. Immigrants to all appearances from the same ethnic background could on closer inspection turn out to be very diverse in origin. For example, nearly half Britain's Chinese population in 1981 not born in the UK were born in Hong Kong, but the rest came from mainland China, Malaysia, Mauritius, the Caribbean, Vietnam, and Singapore.[169] Most immigrants did not think of British society in 'horizontal' class terms, if only because many came from societies where the 'vertical' categories of family,

[164] R. Hoggart, *The Uses of Literacy: Aspects of Working Class Life with Special Reference to Publications and Entertainments* (1957), ch. 7; see also his 'Speaking to Each Other', in N. Mackenzie (ed.), *Conviction* (1958), 121.

[165] Butler and Stokes, *Political Change* (2nd edn.), 206.

[166] Burnett, *Social History of Housing*, 296, 305. J. P. Greaves and D. F. Hollingsworth, 'Trends in Food Consumption in the United Kingdom', *World Review of Nutrition and Dietetics*, 6 (1966), 72.

[167] M. Anderson, 'The Emergence of the Modern Life Cycle in Britain', *Social History* (Jan. 1985), 80–1, 86. Anderson, 'The Social Implications of Demographic Change', in F. M. L. Thompson (ed.), *The Cambridge Social History of Britain* (1990), ii. 66–7.

[168] Haskey, 'Ethnic Minority and Overseas-Born Populations', 16.

[169] *TCBST* 160, where the percentages do not add up.

neighbourhood, tribe, ethnic group, region, and religion were salient. Even immigrants accustomed to 'horizontal' categories often found a 'vertical' ethnic identity more relevant on arrival; it might take years to recover lost 'horizontal' status, whereas numerous immediate practical advantages resulted from moving among one's own kind.

Assimilation can move from uncompromising loyalty to minority values, feasible if a low profile is kept, through their qualified acceptance (perhaps in the second or later generations) with or without private reservations, towards the full integration that occurs when the minority disappears into the majority. The immigrant's journey towards assimilation in the UK after 1945 usually entailed gradually substituting 'horizontal' for 'vertical' perceptions. Immigrants understandably banded together in mutual help rather than disperse among strangers. By no means all immigrants sought status in the UK, especially those who saw their migration to the UK as only temporary; if status was important for them at all, it was in the communities whence they had come. For the rest, though, what the sociologists call 'status inconsistency'—society's failure to offer people the status to which they felt justified by their past background or present income—could hold Britain's twentieth-century immigrants politically on the left for longer than might otherwise have been expected. As for the immigrants' impact on British social-class and party-political categories, it was (to say the least) complicating, and for the British labour movement somewhat puzzling, given that ethnic origin inevitably influenced political responses among the socially deprived. The immigrant response could also puzzle Conservatives, who were tempted simultaneously by the idea of uniting all classes in Britain against the outsider, but also by their affinities with the immigrant through imperial loyalties and later through the incomer's proved entrepreneurial zeal.

Some opponents of immigration can fairly be described as racist. Among them was Larkin, whose diary in 1962 recorded a distaste for the large number of blacks now in London: 'I can hear fat Caribbean germs pattering after me in the Underground', he privately grumbled.[170] But immigrants' arrival in large numbers—from the twentieth-century 'New Commonwealth' as from nineteenth-century Ireland and Eastern Europe—presented their white neighbours with genuine problems. Dismissively and indiscriminately to label multi-layered anti-immigrant protest within Britain as Fascist or 'racist' would indeed be facile. The friction resulting from cultural contrast must be distinguished from the friction prompted by immigration as such. When the 16-year-old future general secretary of the TGWU Bill Morris looked out of the window on a cold November morning in 1954 after arriving from

[170] Quoted in A. Motion, *Philip Larkin: A Writer's Life* (1st publ. 1993, paperback edn. 1994), 309.

Jamaica the day before, he saw only row upon row of terraced houses in a treeless chimney-potted urban landscape, not the luscious vegetation he had grown up to expect: 'I felt like going back to bed', he recalled.[171] By no means all immigrants shared his rural background, but many saw their initial home as only temporary; the resultant social problems anticipated those later familiar in the parts of university towns occupied by transient student populations.

Other difficulties resulted not from immigration as such but from its concomitants: a high proportion of the early immigrants were young and unattached males. Immigrant communities were younger than average; as late as 1994 a third of Great Britain's ethnic-minority population was under 16, but only a fifth of its white population, and the birth rate among most immigrant groups was much higher than for the UK population.[172] Friction with white neighbours inevitably stemmed from the overcrowded inner-city rented accommodation occupied by West Indian communities, whose notions of hospitality were more generous and less formal than was usual in Britain.[173] Not surprisingly, property values were affected, and a carefully husbanded respectability within British working- and lower-middle-class localities often seemed threatened. Already by 1950 the cabinet anticipated problems with inner-city housing, though they did not act.[174]

The liberal-minded, well-intentioned, and somewhat rationalistic people who shaped the British official response to immigrants between 1951 and 1970 operated from the Institute for Race Relations. Fabian in mood, and deeply influenced by social anthropologists and American sociologists, they sought to solve problems by persuading the newcomers and their white neighbours to adapt.[175] Where such methods failed, they hoped that enhanced welfare would lubricate trouble away; hence Wilson's commitment in May 1968 to special subsidies for immigrant areas.[176] Powell denounced the environmental determinism of this approach as 'the hoariest of fallacies',[177] claiming also that some would see it as encouraging collective blackmail. The liberals

[171] Interview, *O* (29 June 2003), review section, 3.

[172] *Social Trends* (1995), 19. Table 12.11 in Coleman and Salt, *British Population*, 509.

[173] K. Fitzherbert, 'West Indian Children in London', *Occasional Papers on Social Administration*, 19 (1967), 50–1.

[174] K. O. Morgan, *The People's Peace: British History 1945–1990* (1st publ. Oxford, 1990, 2nd edn. 1999), 96.

[175] C. Waters, ' "Dark Strangers" in Our Midst: Discourses of Race and Nation in Britain, 1947–1963', *Journal of British Studies* (Apr. 1997), 209, 217–18, 232.

[176] Speech to Birmingham Labour rally, *T* (6 May 1968), 1. For the impact on government policy see Crossman, *Cabinet Diaries*, iii. 125 (9 July 1968), 129 (10 July 1968), 138–9 (16 July 1968), 160 (29 July 1968).

[177] Scarborough speech 17 Jan. 1970, reported in *T* (19 Jan. 1970), 4; cf. his speech in *HC Deb.* 8 July 1976, c. 1668.

hoped, however, that the assimilationist precedent set by earlier waves of immigrants—the Huguenot and other seventeenth-century Protestant refugees from Catholic Europe (who had become invisible), and the nineteenth- and twentieth-century Irish and the Jews (who were slowly becoming such)—would apply here too.

Yet this latest wave of immigrants differed in one important respect: as non-whites, they were relatively visible (in Powell's phrase, 'literally marked people'[178])—potential scapegoats for resentful inner-city populations. Whereas proportionately few white people married black, quite a high proportion of black people married white: in the 1970s Britain's mixed-race population numbered about 250,000, though partnerships between minority ethnic groups were rare. Gallup polls in 1958, 1968, and 1973 showed increasing acceptance of mixed marriages.[179] None the less, anti-immigrant feeling began to build up from the late 1950s. MPs for Midlands constituencies felt particularly pressed: 'if you want a nigger neighbour vote Labour' was the slogan allegedly used by Conservative campaigners at Smethwick during the general election of 1964, when Labour supplanted the Conservatives in power; Smethwick's Conservative candidate proposed a ban on all immigration for at least five years.[180]

Labour and Conservative leaders in the 1960s struggled to pursue their agreed and relatively liberal strategy against dissidence within both parties, and it was Powell who suddenly threw the whole subject open to public debate. His speech to the eighty-five people present at the annual general meeting of the West Midlands Area Conservative Political Centre in Birmingham on 20 April 1968 surprised Powell's shadow cabinet colleagues because he had kept his intentions secret, and had hitherto neither advocated immigration curbs publicly nor pushed for them privately. Predicting for British cities race riots like those recently seen in the USA, he said (in a much-quoted passage) 'as I look ahead, I am filled with foreboding. Like the Roman, I seem to see, "the River Tiber foaming with much blood"'. With Kenyan Asians threatening to arrive in such large numbers, it seemed to him 'like watching a nation busily engaged in heaping up its own funeral pyre'. With language like this, Powell hardly needed the publicity he carefully orchestrated. In his role as Cassandra he was as much concerned with the future as with the present, as preoccupied with immigrants' likely location and fertility as with their present absolute numbers. In November 1968 he predicted (in this respect accurately, as it turned out) that the coloured population in Britain would rise above 4.5 million by 2002, but also that 'there would be several Washingtons in England' as a result, and that the British people would not stand for it. Seven months later he

[178] *T* (22 Jan. 1977), 2.

[179] Coleman and Salt, *British Population*, 514–15. *Gallup Polls*, i. 478; ii. 994, 1271.

[180] D. E. Butler and A. King, *The British General Election of 1964* (1965), 361. See also Crossman, *Cabinet Diaries*, i. 270 (8 July 1965), 299 (2 Aug. 1965).

claimed that whites would vacate 'whole areas' of the inner cities and be replaced by blacks. 'There are at this moment parts of this town', he pronounced at Wolverhampton at the general election in 1970, 'which have ceased to be part of England'.[181]

Powell had upstaged all his colleagues in the shadow cabinet, and within three days of his 'Tiber' speech had received at his home more than 45,000 letters, all but a few thousand favourable, with four more large sacks awaiting him at Westminster.[182] Crucial as an influence upon him were his Wolverhampton constituents; as a good parliamentarian he felt bound to ventilate if not advocate their views. For him, the politician's role was not to suppress thoughts widely held, but vividly to articulate them. Gallup found in May 1968 that of those polled, 74 per cent agreed with Powell's remarks and only 15 per cent disagreed, with 11 per cent undecided; in its polls of December 1968 and February 1970 Gallup found twice as many agreeing as disagreeing with him.[183] Powell instantly acquired all the popularity and notoriety attaching to someone with the courage single-handedly to breach the conventions and to expose conspiracies in high places. He saw himself as the de Gaulle who sided with the people against the system, the Winston Churchill to whose warnings on appeasement nobody listened until it was almost too late. London dockers and Smithfield porters severely embarrassed fashionable metropolitan opinion by signing petitions and marching to Westminster in Powell's support singing 'I'm dreaming of a white Christmas'.

Attempts were made to label Powell's championing of national identity as Fascist. True, his policy was supported by the National Front, organized in 1967 from patriotic and right-wing groups, and with about 4,000 members; and among the leaders of the Smithfield meat porters was Dennis Harmston ('Big Dan'), who had stood for parliament as Union Movement candidate at Islington South-West two years before.[184] Yet the Front did not organize the campaign in Powell's support,[185] and Powell was decidedly un-Fascist. A highly rationalistic and passionate parliamentarian and libertarian who repudiated economic corporatism, he aimed to draw his constituents towards parliament, and in his outlook could hardly have been further away from the Dachau and Belsen with which Benn tried to associate him.[186] Does the Fascist label (then uncritically deployed on the left against its enemies) fit Powell's supporters?

[181] Quotations from S. Heffer, *Like the Roman: The Life of Enoch Powell* (1st publ. 1998, paperback edn. 1999), 454; *T* (22 Apr. 1968), 2; *T* (18 Nov. 1968), 3; J. Wood (ed.), *Powell and the 1970 Election* (Kingswood, Surrey, 1970), 101. See also *T* (26 Nov. 1970), 8; (9 Apr. 1973), 3 (speech at Brent); (22 Jan. 1977), 1 (speech to Stretford Young Conservatives).

[182] Quotations from P. Cosgrave, *The Lives of Enoch Powell* (1st publ. 1989, paperback edn. 1990), 250, 247; see also 252.

[183] *Gallup Polls*, ii. 984, 1026, 1090.

[184] *ST* (4 July 1976), 17. *T* (27 Apr. 1968), 8 (Harmston).

[185] M. Walker, *National Front* (1977), 110–11.

[186] T. Benn, *Office without Power: Diaries 1968–72*, ed. R. Winstone (1988), 287 (3 June 1970).

Powell's position on immigration did of course attract the linear descendants of Mosley's blackshirts, but a random sample of about 4,000 letters written in support of Powell's Birmingham speech was found to be crosser with the authorities than with the immigrants. His correspondents were 'concerned with quite definite and limited problems: the effect of alien minorities on British culture and traditions, the strain on the social services, over-population and the possibility of race riots on the American scale'.[187] Powell had now established his platform, and used it to denounce civil servants, especially those in the Foreign Office, for distorting immigration statistics. The figures were certainly defective: Crossman privately confessed at this time to 'the astonishing lack of information' available within government on immigration and emigration statistics: 'everything is guesswork'.[188]

All this brought Powell massive media coverage at the general election of 1970, helping to mobilize the immigrant vote behind Labour.[189] But many who shared Powell's view on the MP's relationship with constituents thought he was abusing his position. They thought MPs should be more than mere megaphones: they should guide and even educate their constituents, whereas Powell merely harped upon the problem without proposing constructive remedies. The counter-argument was that only through vivid language could immigration be forced as an issue into public debate. This would empower politicians to defuse the fears which nourished the National Front by legislating to cut the numbers admitted, and then to cater more effectively for the immigrants who had already arrived. Such was the twin strategy eventually adopted by 'middle opinion', though Powell did not himself use these arguments. By contrast, liberal Conservatives, the Liberals, and many Labour politicians saw themselves as inheriting British liberal multi-racial traditions, and few socialists carried their enthusiasm for planning beyond strictly economic matters to population control. The all-party strategy eventually promoted by Labour and Conservative governments aimed to moderate white fears by extending controls over immigration, while simultaneously helping to ensure full citizenship for the non-whites already admitted, and promoting special measures where needed to enhance welfare and restrict discrimination.

The Commonwealth Immigrants Act (1968)[190] was rushed through parliament in three days as a response to the escalating incursion of Asians expelled from Africanizing East Africa. 'We had to do this job', wrote Crossman in his diary, 'and there is no public opposition to it . . . The intellectuals who were denouncing it . . . are a small minority'. In arguing for the Act, Lord Hailsham pointed out that 'racial prejudice is often based on insecurity, and insecurity

[187] Diana Spearman, *T* (14 June 1968), 9; cf. Crosland, *O* (21 Jan. 1973), 8.

[188] *Cabinet Diaries*, iii. 38–9 (1 May 1968); see also iii. 589 (23 July 1969), 609 (7 Aug. 1969), 828 (20 Feb. 1970).

[189] Butler and Pinto-Duschinsky, *British General Election of 1970*, 406.

[190] See above, p. 84.

is largely the result of want of control, and want of control is precisely the thing which the Government are trying to get rid of by what admittedly is a measure which none of us like'.[191] As usual, exclusion was accompanied by efforts fully to integrate those already admitted. The Race Relations Board had been set up in 1966 to investigate complaints about unlawful discrimination, and in 1968 with extended powers was complemented by the Community Relations Commission, a body created to coordinate public authorities' promotion of racial harmony in such areas as education, housing, employment, and social services. The Race Relations Act (1976) made it illegal to treat workers less favourably because of race or origin, abolished the Board, and to promote equal opportunities and good race relations set up the Commission for Racial Equality, which in 1977 merged with the Community Relations Commission.

The immigrant's day-to-day experience is not best viewed through the lens of social problems and civil liberties, if only because mutual help and self-help usually prevented immigrants from becoming social problems, and because their self-respect or their relief at finding a refuge prompted much stoicism. Cypriot immigrants to Britain in the 1950s, for example, thought it a point of honour to help relatives, and in their absence substitute relatives could be formally created; this enabled a patron or future employer in Britain sometimes to build up a large personal following.[192] Immigrants do not mentally locate themselves in a broad ethnic category, but in much smaller units. With twentieth-century immigrants to Britain, as with Irish immigrants to early-Victorian Preston[193] or nineteenth-century British emigrants to the USA, clusters of settlers would at any one time move from a small area in one country to a small area in another. Chains of mutually assisting personal relationships spread out from the family to tightly knit neighbourhood and thence to region, with young males in the vanguard. This localism, or 'campanilismo', as postwar Southern Italy's immigrants to Britain called it, helped to ease transit and ensure security on arrival. Likewise West Indian immigrants arrived, not as West Indians, but as inhabitants of particular Caribbean islands; immigrants from St Vincent clustered in High Wycombe, and those from Nevis in Leicester; within London, Jamaicans tended to settle south of the Thames, Dominicans chose Paddington, Montserratians Finsbury Park.[194] Even a small island was

[191] *Cabinet Diaries*, ii. 689 (4 Mar. 1968). Hailsham, *HC Deb.* 27 Feb. 1968, c. 1267.

[192] R. Oakley, 'Cypriot Migration and Settlement in Britain' (Oxford D.Phil. thesis, 1971), 112–13, 326.

[193] M. Anderson, *Family Structure in Nineteenth Century Lancashire* (Cambridge, 1971), 101.

[194] T. Colpi, 'The Social Structure of the Italian Community in Bedford, with Particular Reference to its Places of Origin and Migration' (Oxford D.Phil. thesis, 1987), 91, 97–8, 419. C. Peach 'The Force of West Indian Island Identity in Britain', in C. G. Clarke, D. Ley, C. Peach, and P. Paget (eds), *Geography and Ethnic Pluralism* (1984), 215, 221, 223.

too large an immigration unit for many, and in the mind's eye a single village was more relevant.

Religious institutions diversified immigrants still further. They provided contacts, a refuge, and a source of identity; but they also encouraged immigrants to segregate themselves and perhaps also perpetuate distinctive features or conduct. The Catholic Church performed this double role for nineteenth-century Irish immigrants, as for Polish and Italian immigrants from the 1940s. By the 1990s Poles were the largest foreign-language grouping among Catholics in Britain, well ahead of the next largest groups: the Ukrainians and the Italians. Pope John Paul's visit of May 1982 was a major event for the Polish exile community, with 25,000 people gathering in the Crystal Palace stadium at the meeting held specially for them.[195] By the 1960s neo-Pentecostalist churches were springing up to perform a rather similar role for Afro-Caribbean immigrants, and often met in the chapels vacated by defunct white nonconformist congregations; in 1990 the 965 Afro-Caribbean congregations in Britain could attract about 70,000 members.[196] With the Afro-Caribbeans there was no question of distinctive religion: they were often more Christian than the British, and many were surprised and disappointed on arrival to find Britain so secularized. Whereas even among Afro-Caribbean religious groupings the chapel catered for only a minority, and for only a segment of their life—for Asian groupings the Muslim mosque, the Hindu temple, and the Sikh gurdwara were multi-functional, and attracted majority loyalty within the relevant community.[197] During the 1960s it became apparent that for social as well as educational reasons British schools would need to consider teaching religions other than the Christian, and to divorce such teaching from any encouragement to belief. At a more mundane level, diet (itself often owing something to religious commitment) could nucleate the immigrant community: retailing and welfare roles were combined in the Italian coffee shops and Cypriot restaurants of the 1950s,[198] or in the Chinese food stores of the 1980s.

To distinctiveness in religion, immigrants often for religious or practical reasons added distinctive family structures. With Polish and Turkish or Greek Cypriot immigrants, for example, young males dominated the early stages of immigration, but were later balanced by newcomers predominantly female. Among each successive wave of 'New Commonwealth' immigrants—from 1956 West Indians, from 1959 Indians, and from December 1964 Muslims from East Africa and South Asia—the male percentage fell steadily from its high initial

[195] K. Sword, *Identity in Flux: The Polish Community in Britain* (1996), 52, 93.

[196] G. Davie, *Religion in Britain since 1945: Believing without Belonging* (Oxford, 1994), 63.

[197] D. G. Pearson, 'Race, Religiosity and Political Activism: Some Observations on West Indian Participation in Britain', *British Journal of Sociology* (Sept. 1978), 352.

[198] Colpi, 'Social Structure', 419, 422. Oakley, 'Cypriot Migration', 313–14.

level. Up to 1964 nine-tenths of the Pakistani population in Britain was male, a much larger imbalance than with the other groups.[199] The women's arrival was sometimes organized through the arranged marriage or marriage of convenience, whether for cultural reasons or to overcome immigration restrictions.[200] In 2001 no fewer than 55 per cent of British Pakistani couples involved marriage between first cousins, a partnership forbidden to Sikhs.[201] Muslim immigrants from South Asia and Cypriots shared a relatively conservative view of the family, requiring marriage within the group and daughters to be more secluded than sons.[202] These groups shared with London's West Indian settlers a commitment to the extended family that among whites had long been in decline, but in family patterns West Indians had little else in common with South Asian immigrants. The early Jamaican immigrant, accustomed to a looser family structure even before arriving, led a 'stag life' centred on clubs, bars, betting shops, and Jamaican barbers from which black (though not always white) women were excluded, and adjusted only slowly, if at all, to British marital patterns.[203] The pattern among Maltese immigrants contrasted again, and partly because of the Messina Brothers affair in 1947 the Maltese became well known in London during the 1950s for organizing prostitution.[204]

The Notting Hill carnival, the remarkable London street festival that spontaneously emerged in 1965, illustrates the continuous tension within immigrant communities between unity and diversity, but also the continuously syncopating tension between the desire to remain separate from the wider society, yet also fully to belong. Initially aiming to draw whites and blacks together, the carnival had by 1973 become almost exclusively West Indian, with a growing emphasis on Trinidadian steel bands; in 1975 it was opened to Jamaican reggae groups, and soon became an advertisement for the rich diversity of black cultures now active in London, attracting hordes of white spectators.[205] If immigrants tend at least initially to be 'splitters', alert to what divides them, the widespread fear of the 1960s was that the British people would

[199] See the useful table in D. J. Smith, *Racial Disadvantage in Britain: The PEP Report* (Harmondsworth, 1977), 29.

[200] Sword, *Identity in Flux*, 85, 204–5. Oakley, 'Cypriot Migration', 54, 57, 60.

[201] C. Peach, 'Islam, Ethnicity and South Asian Religions in the London 2001 Census', *Transactions of the Institute of British Geographers* (Oct. 2006), 354.

[202] Oakley, 'Cypriot Migration', 287–94. J. Eade *et al.*, 'The Bangladeshis: The Encapsulated Community', in C. Peach (ed.), *Ethnicity in the 1991 Census*, ii. *The Ethnic Minority Populations of Great Britain* (1996), 150, 158–9.

[203] K. Fitzherbert, 'West Indian Children in London', *Occasional Papers in Social Administration*, 19 (1967), 33–9.

[204] G. Dench, *Maltese in London: A Case-Study in the Erosion of Ethnic Consciousness* (1975), 1, 67–8, 75–6.

[205] A. Cohen, 'Drama and Politics in the Development of a London Carnival', in R. Frankenberg (ed.), *Custom and Conflict in British Society* (Manchester, 1982), 316–17, 331–2. B. King, *The Internationalization of English Literature* (Oxford, 2004), 77.

become 'lumpers', mentally corralling the immigrants into a single category. In a downward vortex, white hostility would then gradually unite people from any one ethnic minority in self-defence, and then blur its frontiers with other non-white groups so as to unite non-whites against whites. With an equal and opposite white response, the opponents of immigration would then have manufactured the ethnic solidarity they claimed to fear.

Immigrants were diversified further by the varied motives for their move. Economic motives inspired many of the Irish women who after 1945 sought jobs in personal services, especially nursing, hoping also for better marriage prospects in the UK than at home. An eighth of the entire British hospital nursing staff in 1946 had been born in the Republic, and this had equalized the Irish-born sex balance in the UK by 1951.[206] In this they were followed by many Caribbean women, whose nursing skills in the 1950s and 1960s helped to keep the NHS afloat, as did many Asian immigrant doctors. In 1968 Crossman, then responsible for the health service, said that the cabinet 'has a bad conscience about the way we are sucking the best skills out of the Commonwealth and keeping them here because it is in our best interest to do so'.[207] This was but one instance of the many skilled employees attracted from South Asia after 1961, when the British criteria for admission became more selective. Only 12 per cent of West Indian men had a job definitely arranged before arriving in the UK, but even fewer Indians (9%), Pakistanis (7%), and African Asians (2%), though direct recruitment often provided the initial stimulus for their move.[208] By the 1970s immigrants from South Asia had also moved into the engineering trade in the Midlands and into textiles in the north of England, were running London's electronics retailing centre in Tottenham Court Road, and had taken over numerous car parks and corner shops in West London.

The immigrant has a special incentive to succeed. Often with only his own initiative and energy to draw upon, and often restricted in occupational choice by practical considerations or prejudice, he is forced to exert himself. The immigrant student's lifeline is the examination as route to meritocratic success. The entrepreneur's initial small-scale self-employment is a way of breaking through the barriers, and is powered by flexible and underpaid cooperation from relatives. Alternatively, there is the sort of hard manual work that the British were no longer prepared to do. From their Irish immigrant predecessors, 'New Commonwealth' immigrants took over many heavy jobs, given that both groups had arrived in search of higher pay than was available at home. Both arrived relatively young[209] and often unmarried. If hard work is defined as willingness to work, women in the ethnic minorities in 1974 worked harder

[206] B. Abel-Smith, *A History of the Nursing Profession* (1960), 215. See also *BST* 575–6; *TBS* 471.
[207] *Cabinet Diaries*, iii. 212 (4 Oct. 1968).
[208] Smith, *Racial Disadvantage*, 24–5.
[209] For the youth of New Commonwealth immigrants, see *TBS* 462, 498–9.

than British-born women: 74 per cent of West Indian women were in paid work within an average of only 43 per cent. Of non-Muslim Asian women 45 per cent were in paid work, and if they were joined in this by only 17 per cent of Muslim Asian women, this was because their traditional attitudes to marriage confined them within the home and limited their language skills.[210] For Caribbeans, sporting achievement offered opportunities, especially as by the 1950s a combination of personal social advancement and fewer unskilled occupations drained off the Jewish and Irish boxers from the East London halls, leaving a gap for black immigrants to fill. The regulations against black boxers representing Great Britain were eventually removed, and blacks became as prominent in English boxing as Jews and Irishmen earlier.[211] Wherever sport was meritocratic, black players had a better chance: more so in Rugby League, for example, than in Rugby Union. Even in Rugby League, though, black players attracted their share of racist abuse in what was seen as a white sport; they were slow to reach the central, decision-making positions on the sports field, and Asian communities, though located in Rugby League areas, were not enlisted at all.[212]

The Jewish immigrant has special incentives to achieve, and if entrepreneurship does not attract, scholarship may gain. The need to root themselves in their new community, no doubt often reinforced by gratitude for receiving a refuge, lent Jews an energy that soon bore much fruit. Jewish immigrants from the 1930s onwards brought a rich and immediate infusion of European ideas and methods to British studies in sociology, criminology, physics, statistics, the classics, and the history of art, architecture, and photography. They included the refugee lecturer in the history of art and architecture who arrived from Göttingen in 1933, Sir Nikolaus Pevsner, whose Teutonic energy and rigour ensured that the forty-six volumes of his remarkable *Buildings of England*, launched in 1951, were completed in 1974;[213] the leading government statistician from the 1960s onwards, Sir Claus Moser, who arrived as a refugee from Germany in 1936; the neurosurgeon Sir Ludwig Guttmann, who arrived in 1939 and soon founded the annual games for the paralysed at Stoke Mandeville; and Sir Karl Popper, who arrived from Vienna by way of New Zealand in 1945 in the midst of making his major contribution to the study of political theory and the philosophy of science. Some of these immigrants eventually penetrated to the heart of British life. 'Everybody who is anybody is there', wrote Castle in 1975 of the London

[210] Smith, *Racial Disadvantage*, 64–6.

[211] R. McKibbin, *Classes and Cultures: England 1918–1951* (Oxford, 1998), 367.

[212] For a good discussion see T. Collins, 'Racial Minorities in a Marginalized Sport: Race, Discrimination and Integration in British Rugby League Football', *Immigrants and Minorities* (Mar. 1998), 156–9, 165–7.

[213] Sir John Summerson wrote the memoir of him in *Dictionary of National Biography 1981–1985* (1990), 313–15.

parties thrown by an immigrant now thoroughly established, the publisher George Weidenfeld. Straddling the worlds of business and academic life was the pioneer of the opinion survey Mark Abrams, son of Latvian and Lithuanian Jewish parents and a key figure after 1951 in making the new medium available to politicians.[214]

Entrepreneurship in moneymaking often gains from the special insights and skills the immigrant imports from his place of origin. Pakistani immigrants, for example, came not from the poorest areas, but from the relatively prosperous localities which supplied recruits to the British armed forces; Gujerati immigrants from India came from relatively literate groups in Baroda, Surat, and Bharuch, with a long tradition of trading and migration.[215] The immigrant refugee's entrepreneurial skill before arrival could even provide his enemies at home with the excuse for his expulsion; the initiative, energy, and adventurousness that inspire the young economic migrant of the first wave are in themselves entrepreneurially useful. In business, the Jewish immigrants' contribution to British life was formidable. 'Opportunity is everywhere', said Charles Clore, pioneer of the take-over bid and son of a Whitechapel tailor who had emigrated from Russia; when asked the secret of his success; he replied that 'you have to find it and work hard'. The Jewish achievers included the long-standing managing director of the General Electric Company (GEC) Arnold Weinstock, son of Jewish immigrants from Poland; Alan Sugar, the self-made chairman of the computer manufacturing firm Amstrad; Arthur Katz, from Germany's toy-making aristocracy, who founded Mettoy and launched Corgi toy cars in 1956;[216] and the three sons of the Ukrainian Jewish tailor's presser Boris Winogradsky, who as Bernard Delfont and Lew and Michael Grade became impresarios in the entertainment world. Joseph Kagan should also feature in this story, for his Gannex raincoat became a hallmark of Wilson, and was presented to Nikita Krushchev when Wilson visited the Kremlin in 1963.[217]

The Italian, Cypriot, and Chinese immigrant required similar personal qualities but owed much to a cross-cultural and highly entrepreneurial perception of serious gaps in provision. With a long history of settling in Britain, the Italians were relatively few and unobtrusive, yet distinctive in their impact. They posed no threat, and so were readily accepted. By 1981 there were 90,000 Italian-born residents in the UK, but if children born to Italian parents in

[214] B. Castle, *The Castle Diaries 1974–76* (1980), 467 (16 July 1975). For Abrams see the obituaries in *DT* (4 Oct. 1994), 27; *T* (29 Sept. 1994), 21.

[215] P. Lewis, *Islamic Britain. Religion, Politics and Identity among British Muslims* (1st publ. 1994, 2nd edn. 2002), 16.

[216] *DT* (27 July 1979), 17 (Clore). Obituary, *Ind.* (27 July 1999), 6 (Katz).

[217] For Lord Kagan's extraordinary story see Tam Dalyell's memoir in *Ind.* (19 Jan. 1995), 16. See also A. Morgan, *Harold Wilson* (1992), 208–9.

Britain are added the total rises to about 140,000;[218] nor does this include the many third- or fourth-generation Italians in the larger cities. Heavy labour was widespread within the third (that is, postwar) phase of Italian immigration to Britain, with concentrations in the south midlands (brickmaking), South Wales (steel manufacture), and the Lea Valley north of London (horticulture).[219] But by comparison with Italians settling elsewhere, Italians in Britain were unusually entrepreneurial, making a distinctive impact in catering. Low-paid Italian, Spanish, Greek, and French workers abounded in London's low-priced restaurants from the 1950s to the 1970s. Coffee shops emerged surprisingly early in South Wales to cater for local postwar Italian immigrants; from there they could branch out more widely, and on this foundation the notable career of restaurateur Frank Berni was built. Opening his first licensed restaurant in Bristol in 1948 with his brother Aldo, he soon established a chain of restaurants whose tight quality-control and standardized menu and furnishings brought major economies of scale; Berni Inns soon became the largest food chain outside the USA.[220] In 1911 Rocco Forte, an economic migrant, joined the family's ice-cream firm in Dundee, and by 1951 his son Charles owned a string of cafés in London, was one of the two caterers for the Festival of Britain, and was still moving up. Ice cream did not necessarily cramp aesthetic talent. The war had not begun well for Eduardo Paolozzi, eventually to become a distinguished sculptor: both his father (sympathetic to Mussolini) and his grandfather were deported to Canada and drowned on the way there, and Eduardo was interned for three months in 1940. Nothing daunted, he combined studying calligraphy at the Edinburgh College of Art with helping to run his mother's ice-cream shop in Leith.[221]

Small firms specially attracted Cypriot immigrants, who numbered 74,000 at the end of 1966, or 101,000 if first-generation children are included. Inner London clothes workshops mobilized male tailoring and female dressmaking skills, but equally suited to mobilizing the family as a work unit were the café and the restaurant, whose number grew fast in the 1940s; in the 1960s the catering trade accounted for between a quarter and a fifth of Cypriot men. Cypriot culture valued the personal independence involved in running one's own business, often with the family as workforce; in 1966 about a fifth of all Cypriot men at work were self-employed, more than twice the average in Britain.[222] They too launched their businesses on the secure basis provided

[218] M. Stubbs (ed.), *The Other Languages of England: Linguistic Minorities Project* (1985), 56–7. See also di Blasio, 'Italian Immigration to Britain', *ATI* (1979), 17, 25; Haskey, 'Ethnic Minority and Overseas-Born Populations', 15.

[219] R. King, 'Italians in Britain: An Idiosyncratic Immigration', *ATI*, 29 (Autumn 1979), 9. Stubbs (ed.), *The Other Languages of England*, 55–7.

[220] Obituaries, *T* (20 July 2000), 21; *Ind* (14 July 2000), review section, 6.

[221] Obituary, *G* (23 Apr. 2005), 25.

[222] Oakley, 'Cypriot Migration', 231, 286, 311, 322.

by meeting the needs of their own kind. The Scottish Cyprus-born hotelier Sir Reo Stakis was the apogee of their catering achievement. Opening his first steakhouse in 1947 in Glasgow, he profited from the hotel boom of the 1970s, and went public in 1972; the firm when sold to Ladbrokes in 1999 employed 14,000.[223] As for Chinese restaurants, we have already seen how rapidly they spread in the 1950s and 1960s, and John Koon, born in 1926, can stand for the many other entrepreneurs powering this culinary revolution. His father had founded Maxim's, London's first Chinese restaurant, but it was the son who founded London's first up-market Chinese restaurant (Lotus House) in 1958, as well as the first Chinese takeaway restaurant in Queensway. A bachelor whose staff was his family, he eventually sold his restaurants to them.[224]

Immigrants' voluntary geographical dispersal usually denotes their assimilation, and was encouraged by business success and movement into the professions. In 1951 many Irish still clustered in big-city inner suburbs, especially in parts of London such as Paddington or Hammersmith where in the 1960s they constituted almost a tenth of the population. But by then they and the Jews were well on the way to dispersing both geographically and socially.[225] By the early 1950s the Poles were settling for a life in Britain and were gravitating to areas of economic growth; almost a quarter lived in Greater London. They settled in the cheaper inner-city areas and began setting up their own businesses: garages, delicatessens, and small craft firms. The occupation so often chosen by Italian and Chinese immigrants specially encouraged dispersal. After getting launched in the big cities, their restaurants and coffee shops spread out, gathering small groups of Italians and Chinese in most towns; dispersal was pushed further by the need to avoid mutual competition. The Hungarian refugees of 1956, mostly young single men well able to get a job, were successfully encouraged to disperse,[226] but the Cypriot immigrants were more clustered: in 1966 just over three-quarters lived in Greater London, with the Turkish Cypriots settling south of the Thames, and the Greek Cypriots spreading northwards from the Soho area as time elapsed. If they settled elsewhere they usually chose urban localities, and were more prone than any other Commonwealth immigrant group to buy their own homes, often from Cypriot property agents.[227]

'New Commonwealth' immigrants moved in to replace the British and earlier generations of white settlers who had decamped into the suburbs, and by 1984 all were far more likely than the whites to live in the metropolitan counties: 31 per cent of whites, 51 per cent of Chinese, 67 per cent of Pakistanis, 69 per cent

[223] Obituary *T* (29 Aug. 2001), 15. [224] Obituary, *DT* (12 Feb. 1997), 25. [225] *TBS* 470.

[226] S. E. Hale, 'The Geography of Vietnamese Secondary Migration in Britain' (Swansea Ph.D. thesis, 1991), 114–19.

[227] Oakley, 'Cypriot Migration', 230–2, 256, 258, 262, 336, 340.

of Indians, 78 per cent of Africans, 81 per cent of West Indians.[228] Whereas Caribbean immigrants in the 1950s settled in the inner London suburbs, those from South Asia who settled in London clustered further out to the west near Heathrow.[229] Assimilation was not always the immigrant's aim—certainly not in the first generation, where the need for mutual help and shared facilities made urban clustering likely. The Chinese in any generation keep themselves to themselves, partly because the catering trade makes for long hours, family-centredness, and geographical dispersal; partly because they tend not to compete with whites for jobs; partly because they rarely seek state benefits.

Political dispersal is another index to integration. On arrival, immigrants naturally back a libertarian and internationalist party that champions free immigration and civil liberties—that is, in the Edwardian years the Liberal Party, and later a Labour Party that inherited this aspect of the Liberal tradition, together with its welfarist accompaniment. So Labour held a double attraction for the immigrant; for Caribbean immigrants it was a natural voting destination after 1951, with Bill Morris exemplifying the bond. On the other hand, many of the East African immigrants of the 1960s and later had been entrepreneurs in their country of origin, and once they had re-established their status were likely to see attractions in a Conservative Party which had inherited the individualist dimension of Liberalism. Such an evolution is implied in John Rex's claim that in Britain the West Indians faced an Irish and the Asians a Jewish future.[230]

Rex's comment does not capture the full diversity of the Asian grouping. While immigrants from East Africa and from South Asia were both Muslim, the former were refugees with no desire to return, whereas the latter adopted a quite different lifestyle and outlook within the UK in order to build up credit and assets in the country from which they had come, and where they ultimately intended to resettle.[231] For the Irish and Italian immigrant, too, home had never been far away, and improved air transport made it seem psychologically close even for Afro-Caribbeans. Assimilation may for all immigrant groups be a long-term destination, but it is by no means always their initial aspiration, and when it does occur, the impulse may be necessity rather than choice, as with the UK's Polish immigrants. For them, the cold war had changed everything, confining them in Britain for up to half a century; for although in theory it might thaw at any time, the permafrost did not clear till 1990. Already by the 1950s Polish immigrants were assimilating so fast that they felt the need deliberately to preserve their distinctive culture.[232] Their experience

[228] *BST* 564. [229] *TBS* 460. Peach, 'West Indian Island Identity', 229. [230] *BST* 609.

[231] See V. Robinson, *Transients, Settlers, and Refugees: Asians in Britain* (Oxford, 1986), 157–9, for the clear contrast drawn between the two types of Muslim in Blackburn.

[232] Sword, *Identity in Flux*, 39.

became ever more multi-layered with each successive influx of Polish refugee: anti-Nazis from wartime, postwar economic migrants, political refugees from Communism, then economic migrants within a liberalized European Union, which Poland joined in 2004. Not till 1991, soon after Lech Walesa had been sworn in as President of Poland, did the exiled former President, Ryszard Kaczorowski, feel able to travel to Warsaw's Royal Castle formally to hand over his office to his successor, taking with him the presidential insignia that had remained in Britain since the Polish government had arrived from France in 1940.

Sidney Webb used to say that in Britain 'it is easy for good reason to change the form of an institution without changing the substance, or the substance without changing the form, but . . . one should never try to change both the substance and form of anything at one and the same time'.[233] We have seen in this chapter how the evolution of monarchy and House of Lords in the 1950s and 1960s exemplified the second of these strategies, and changes in the upper classes the first, while the middle-class practice of growth through fragmentation was advancing fast at the expense of both upper classes and working class. At the same time the growth of ethnic minorities was slowly complicating the 'horizontal' class hierarchy with the 'vertical' loyalties of race. The motif of substantial social change amidst apparently unchanged political institutions (the sixth) has thus already emerged. So have four more of the eight motifs. The UK's tension between receptive and hermetic tendencies (the second motif) had been exemplified under King George V in the monarchy's retreat from participating directly in an international diplomatic network while expanding its imperial role. After 1951 the monarchy was very slowly shedding even that, and had come to epitomize Britishness. So much so, that despite its progressive aspects it could have become the centrepiece of a new worldwide role for the UK (the eighth motif) as exemplifying traditionalist ceremonial. Modernizing pressures dictated otherwise, and the monarchy's imperial role was turned naturally to advantage in helping to integrate ethnic minorities within Britain, though the EEC remained politically too controversial for it to develop a significant role there too. On both issues working people showed themselves relatively conservative: hostility to unconstrained immigration and the EEC connection was stronger among them than among Labour's middle-class supporters—understandably so, given that on both fronts middle-class interests were less likely to suffer from change. As for the ethnic minorities themselves, the tension between receptive and hermetic tendencies lay at the heart of their daily experience. Both the relativism fostered by their growing presence and worries about crime's failure to decline with affluence created worries about trends in a secularizing society: fragile indeed now seemed

[233] As cited in Lord Beveridge, *Power and Influence* (1953), 72.

the social discipline that had earlier prevailed within the face-to-face society that was being slum-cleared away (the fifth motif). Austerity and narrowness might have been the hallmarks of such a society, but its accompanying virtues were increasingly appreciated. As for the politicians, shifting class relations in the 1950s and 1960s gave alert political parties ample scope to exploit social change with their flexibility on policy and image. The Conservatives at first set the pace, with Labour in the early 1960s belatedly and less overtly catching up. The politicians' task was also complicated by growing specialization and fragmentation within the UK's elite. Not only did politicians now need to coordinate growing voluntarist pressures (the seventh motif): coordination at the centre was becoming more difficult.

CHAPTER 5

Family and Welfare

Family and welfare are topics that go naturally together, especially in the 1950s and 1960s when public welfare aimed to integrate them. After considering in the first two sections changes in sexual attitudes and conduct, and a shift in women's role, the discussion will broadly follow the life cycle. It will consider changes in childhood and the evolution of public welfare and health before moving to old age and death. Its concluding section will evaluate claims that the changes discussed threatened the family's very existence.

1. SEXUALITY IN QUESTION

Revolutions do not require bloodshed and barricades: indeed, gradual and peaceful revolutions produce changes that are the more profound and far-reaching for reflecting the uncoordinated and unplanned decisions of individuals. Thus it was with personal relations in the UK after 1951. The radical shift in attitudes and conduct in this area had been launched from several directions well before then, accelerated thereafter, and is still in progress, but not until the end of the century did it become clear how complete the transformation had been, or how cumulative had been the revolution's diverse components: in attitudes to sexuality, legitimacy, divorce, birth control, child rearing, and the role of women. The politicians, the lawyers, and the authorities could do little more than run behind these events and belatedly make the necessary institutional adjustments. The revolution was by no means peculiar to Britain, yet its impact was specially intense in a country whose persisting puritan traditions in 1951 entailed much self-deception and even hypocrisy, and whose expectations of personal relations seem in retrospect paternalist, inflexible, and simplistic.

Britishness in the 1950s came somehow to be identified with the fictional Giles household, whose exploits, launched in 1945, featured regularly in the *Daily Express*. Giles had himself begun life at the social level of his fictional family, but by the 1960s he was himself—as a shy and childless Ipswich-based farmer fond of fast cars, horses, and sailing—socially far removed from it. The fictional Giles family centred upon a suburban heterosexual married and somewhat harassed but domesticated lower-class couple pursuing distinct but complementary family roles. They presided somewhat precariously over legitimate but unruly children and family pets, and endured a grumpy live-in grandmother. Giles's cartoons, like Strube's earlier, placed family life centre stage, edging Whitehall and Westminster out of view. But whereas Strube in the 1930s extracted humour from rather abstractly juxtaposing the male and female mentality, Giles in the 1950s focused on the family's day-to-day activities. His hard-pressed housewife shows mild resentment that her increasingly leisured husband still assumes her continuance in the woman's traditional domestic role [Fig. 4]. Yet she is not oppressed: she uses worldly-wise diplomacy and a sardonic tongue to call her husband's bluff and puncture his pretensions. In the areas of traditional heavy industry, the working-class wife might still in the 1950s focus on despatching her man to work with a good meal and on greeting him with a hot meal on his return,[1] but elsewhere 'women's two roles' (the title of Viola Klein's book published in 1962) were coming under challenge from the 'symmetrical family'. Geoffrey Gorer coined the phrase in 1971 to denote a family whose roles remained mutually supportive but had become less distinct, and Michael Young and Peter Willmott employed it two years later to highlight mounting equality within the family.[2]

Many of the conventions associated with the traditional separation of spheres between the sexes persisted in the 1950s, and without women's votes the Conservatives would not have won the general election of 1951, and perhaps not those of 1955, 1959, and 1970 either.[3] The idea that women were destined for a relatively decorative role was encouraged by their perceived relative physical weakness, which limited their freedom of movement and choice of career. The gap between male and female records in athletics and swimming steadily narrowed worldwide during this time,[4] demonstrating the role of cultural factors in women's alleged incapacity, but it still had far to go. The sanitary towel, patented in 1892 and promoted by the Tampax Company (founded in New York in 1936), was available only discreetly even in the 1950s, and was certainly not discussed in public until well after 1970. Its convenience did much to moderate the effects of a menstruation that was still widely labelled as 'the curse'. Prominent among the impulses leading Chad Varah to found the Samaritan was his memory of conducting his first funeral as an assistant curate in 1935 in Lincoln: a 13-year-old girl had killed herself from misunderstanding her menstruation as a sign that she had contracted

[1] Dennis *et al.*, *Coal is our Life*, 181.

[2] M. Young and P. Willmott, *The Symmetrical Family: A Study of Work and Leisure in the London Region* (1973, paperback edn. 1975), 31.

[3] J. Curtice, 'The Electoral System', in V.Bogdanor (ed) *The British Constitution in the Twentieth Century* (Oxford, 2003), 493.

[4] K. F. Dyer, 'Social Influences on Female Athletic Performance', *Journal of Biosocial Science*, 8 (1976), 123–4.

venereal disease, and thereafter he made sex education one of his causes;[5] a very similar event prompted the foundation of Lincoln's Samaritan branch in 1966.[6] Menstruation was still not publicly discussed in the late 1960s when Katharina Dalton was opening up the subject. Children's first names reflected the separation of spheres: parents in England and Wales drew by comparison with later decades on a small stock of names for their sons but were far more resourceful when naming their daughters.[7]

The girl's relatively decorative role shaped educational attitudes. Parents remained readier to discontinue her schooling either temporarily for domestic duties or permanently through discouraging her from entering the sixth form, where at every parental social level boys were in a majority.[8] Women's share of full-time students at British universities increased only slowly (from 23% in 1948/9 to 30% in 1971/2) and in these years women's share of part-time students was significantly smaller at all universities except the Welsh.[9] This contrast persisted into curricular choice: girls were far less likely than boys in the 1950s and 1960s to enter for O- and A-level papers in science subjects, with implications for the university career.[10] Many women in the 1950s viewed the male career as a shared achievement: they rarely envisaged competing with men for reputation or fame, but saw the wife's privacy and reticence as womanly. In 1953 women attending a Labour Party branch in a mining village seemed ignorant of procedure, and were treated 'with amused tolerance' by the men; if they ventured to speak, they did so 'rather apologetically' and risked a firm male rebuttal.[11] The male courtship novel, still widely read in the 1950s, tended to portray the powerful heterosexual male as romantically sweeping off his entranced virgin bride into a relatively humdrum domesticity and preoccupation with personal appearance. Women could assume decidedly public roles, though not if unduly disrupting to male self-esteem. Women readily exhibited themselves in the 'Miss World' competition, held every November at the Royal Albert Hall and televised from 1959. On 17 March 1971 *The Times* published its first photo of a naked model (the popular page-three girl from the *Sun*, Vivien Neves) in a Fison's advertisement over the caption 'What's a nice girl like you doing in a firm like this?' and sold all the paper's editions.[12]

[5] Obituary, *G* (10 Nov. 2007), 40.

[6] M. Sutton, *'We Didn't Know Ought': A Study of Sexuality, Superstition and Death in Women's Lives in Lincolnshire during the 1930s, '40s and '50s* (Stamford, 1992), 25; see also 19–21.

[7] E. Merry, *First Names: The Definitive Guide to Popular Names in England and Wales 1944–1994* (1995), 10, 20.

[8] H. Silver, *Equal Opportunity in Education: A Reader in Social Class and Educational Opportunity* (1973), 134.

[9] W. A. C. Stewart, *Higher Education in Postwar Britain* (1989), 279. *TBS* 218.

[10] E. W. Jenkins, *From Armstrong to Nuffield: Studies in Twentieth-Century Science Education in England and Wales* (1979), 193–4; and see below, p. 363.

[11] *Coal is Our Life*, 165, 207.

[12] Obituary of Neves, *T* (31 Dec. 2002), 26.

The respectable married woman was the public face of traditional family attitudes, but behind her lurked the female prostitute, who unofficially and in practice satisfied unmet male sexual needs. Sociologists claimed for London's 10,000 women prostitutes the heavy workload in the late 1940s of more than 250,000 male clients a week.[13] Earlier marriage, fewer pregnancies, and easier divorce, however, rendered prostitution less integral to the conventional family's operation after the 1960s than in the Victorian years, if only because the family had by then opened up in its sexuality: men were more likely to find sexual satisfaction within their marriage, or could more easily remarry. The permissive society had eroded prostitution, claimed Baroness Birk in 1970, because 'many young men who would previously have had recourse to prostitutes are now finding stable, or not so stable, sexual relationships with their girl friends'.[14] The female prostitute of the 1950s was no pioneer of sixties permissiveness, given that sixties romance was supposed to be spontaneous and certainly not commercial. Pre-feminist and highly traditional in her role, she was an unacknowledged and relatively unobtrusive buttress of the traditional family values that were now increasingly under challenge. Also under challenge in the 1950s was the Victorian vision of the prostitute as social outcast hurrying down-market to her doom. In 1955 the British Social Biology Council's researcher portrayed the profession's new recruit as being initially isolated and socially disoriented, but as finding among fellow professionals a new sense of community through their kindness, generosity, and mutual support, however volatile their temperament might sometimes be.[15] Also changing was the pimp's image: from being an idle and exploitative bully he was becoming integral to what was now seen as the woman prostitute's substitute family: a voluntarily chosen protector, helping to stabilize her life.[16] If London convictions for living on immoral earnings are any guide, he was likely to come from Malta or the West Indies.[17]

The better class of female prostitute aimed to attract enough private custom to work entirely indoors. The less fortunate had to seek male clients by street soliciting in well-known areas of the larger cities, approaching passers-by who lingered. Men temporarily or permanently without family attachments seemed particularly temptable, and prostitutes had long clustered in seaports and garrison towns. By the 1960s, however, institutions catering for unmarried men—religious orders, the armed services, teaching in single-sex residential institutions—were in slow decline, whereas newly arrived male immigrants were on the rise.[18] Prostitution as such was not an offence: it was not thought

[13] B. S. Rowntree and G. R. Lavers, *English Life and Leisure* (1951), 209–10.

[14] *HL Deb.* 3 Feb. 1970, c. 602.

[15] C. H. Rolph (ed.), *Women of the Streets: A Sociological Study* (1955), 94, 133, 135.

[16] Ibid. 112–16, 209; [Wolfenden] Committee on Homosexual Offences and Prostitution, *Report* (Cmnd. 247, 1957), 99–100.

[17] Dench, *Maltese in London*, 75, convictions 1951–69.

[18] N. Swingler, 'The Streetwalkers Return', *New Society* (16 Jan. 1969), 82.

practicable or even desirable for the law to enforce the official morality. The police intervened with arrests and fines only to discourage indecent conduct and over-energetic or offensive street soliciting. The working relationship often established between police and prostitute assumed that she would go along with a law which she thought mistaken and which did not deter. When in court she would plead guilty and pay her periodic fine, angry only when she felt unfairly picked upon. For many prostitutes the fine was in effect a tax, which some favoured formalizing into a system of state licensing. No such system was politically feasible, though, given the long-standing British feminist and religious hostility to implicating the state, and given the gradual twentieth-century retreat of such systems elsewhere in Europe.[19] Soliciting gave offence in certain parts of London during the 1950s, however, and the Street Offences Act (1959) by raising the penalties reduced the prostitute's visibility, and greatly curbed prosecutions.[20]

Integral to changed attitudes was a much more open approach to sexuality. The first popular sex manual was Dr Eustace Chesser's influential *Love without Fear* (1947), which went so far as to recommend and discreetly describe sexual 'foreplay'. But in retrospect the major influence, in Britain as in America, was Alfred Kinsey, who complemented his earlier study of the human male with his *Sexual Behavior in the Human Female* (1953). By thoroughly documenting the sheer diversity of human sexual conduct, inside and outside marriage and in every age group, he chased away mythology and uninformed moralism, so that both the *Lancet* and (somewhat nervously) the *British Medical Journal* welcomed his book.[21] The pretences which before the 1950s had masked the reality—the pregnant unmarried mother's furtive seclusion, the spiriting away of her child for adoption, the carryings-on under assumed names, the discreet Harley Street abortions—were now vulnerable. Adam Faith was the first teenage idol publicly to acknowledge his pre-marital sexual experience,[22] and after the Legitimacy Act (1959) the sins of the fathers could no longer be visited upon the children.[23]

The erosion of sexual taboos in the 1950s and 1960s helped to emancipate the many groups for whom the nuclear-family structure had never catered, most notably those with same-sex inclinations. In the 1950s homosexual conduct seemed so obviously despicable, so obviously tainted by the squalid locations where it often occurred, that its critics felt no need to explain themselves; the homophobic outlook must now be re-created in all its lost intensity. The parallels

[19] Rolph (ed.), *Women of the Streets*, 18–19, 24, 74. *Wolfenden Committee Report*, 85, 97.

[20] *HL Deb.* 8 Feb. 1968, c. 1289; 3 Feb. 1970 c. 546.

[21] 'The Human Female', *Lancet* (14 Nov. 1953), 1032–3; T. N. A. Jeffcoate 'The Kinsey Report', *British Medical Journal* (30 Jan. 1954), 259–60. See also Claire Rayner in *O* (9 Nov. 1997), review section, 15.

[22] G. Melly, *Revolt into Style: The Pop Arts in Britain* (1970), 56.

[23] *HC Deb.* 30 Jan. 1959, cc. 1405, 1409 (John Parker); *HL Deb.* c. 1198 (Baroness Wootton).

with the anti-paedophile panic half a century later in Britain are strong. The integrity of the family—foundation of the state and source of the desired rising birth rate—was thought to be at risk. The hated minority was seen as numerous but unnumbered because concealed; in 1968, thirty years before homosexuality ceased to be a disciplinary offence, the Admiralty acknowledged that if every sailor shown to have performed homosexual acts were discharged, the Fleet could not be manned.[24] The paedophile analogy extends further: the male homosexual's conduct was assumed to be voluntary and predatory, particularly among the young; indeed, homosexual and paedophile were not always clearly distinguished, and the homosexual's 'victims' were seen as touchingly innocent. Serious problems of definition reflected the widespread ignorance about the hated practice. A clear but simplistic contrast was drawn between homosexuality and heterosexuality. Intruding a 'bisexual' category between the two might cater for the many in Britain then and later with both homosexual and heterosexual experience,[25] but even that could not hope to capture the broad spectrum and subtle gradations of conduct and attitudes involved, nor could it accommodate the elusive impact of environmental and cultural factors. Homosexuals were not encouraged to enlighten their critics, and if more had been known about lesbians, they too might have been discouraged from sharing a household or from publicly displaying mutual affection. Ample scope therefore existed for conspiracy theories, popular scares, and blackmail.

Britain has changed so completely in this area since the 1940s that imagination is needed to conjure up the half-forgotten world of same-sex relations as they then were. The term 'gay' was being casually used by Kenneth Williams in 1947–8,[26] and the alleged dichotomy between 'gay' or 'straight'—familiar among American homosexuals by 1951—was catching on in Britain by the mid-1960s.[27] But more widely used were the pejorative terms 'queer', 'deviant', or 'pervert'. In the 1950s the pressures on the homosexual towards conventional heterosexual conduct were in some ways growing. The pressures towards heterosexual marriage had been weaker in earlier years when some occupations required or encouraged celibacy, and when sexual fulfilment was less discussed because seen as less urgent. Hence much misery. Suicidal responses to sexual problems launched Chad Varah on creating the Samaritans, whose attitude of acceptance towards potentially suicidal clients was, he wrote, 'particularly important in the case of those with sexual problems, which clients may be

[24] 'Over Half the Navy had Homosexual Experiences', *Ind.* (31 Oct. 2002), 8.

[25] K. Wellings, J. Field, A. Johnson, and J. Wordsworth, *Sexual Behaviour in Britain: The National Survey of Sexual Attitudes and Lifestyles* (1994), 211.

[26] R. Davies, 'Introduction', to K. Williams, *Diaries*, p. xxii.

[27] 'D. W. Cory' [pseud. for E. Sagarin], *The Homosexual Outlook: A Subjective Approach* (London, 1963 edn.), p. xiv (preface of 1951). A. Sharpley, 'London's Hidden Problem', *Evening Standard* (20 July 1964), 7. See also 'G. Westwood' [pseud. for M. Schofield], *A Minority: A Report on the Life of the Male Homosexual in Great Britain* (1960), 207–8.

ashamed to speak of at all'.[28] Homosexuality was, in short, viewed as a 'problem', even by many homosexuals. Unsurprisingly, some male homosexuals—Peter Wildeblood, for example, before his public exposure[29]—eagerly sought a cure, and psychologists and medical experts hurried to provide it. The traditional 'cure' was to encourage the homosexual towards the sympathetic prostitute and towards experimental marriage with an understanding wife, a 'remedy' that perhaps made its small contribution towards further elevating early twentieth-century divorce statistics.[30] Of the medicalized 'cures', oestrogen injections and aversion therapy were decidedly unpleasant options: the distinguished mathematician Alan Turing, in court in 1952 for his relations with a young Manchester man, escaped prison by agreeing to a year of oestrogen injections, but killed himself two years later.

For homosexuals who accepted their orientation, there were several options, of which the first was discretion or even deceit. The Queen's dress designer Hardy Amies lived with one man for twenty-two years, but was prudent enough to view it as 'just too common' for the couple to be regularly seen together.[31] Though often inspired by homosexual situations, the plots of Terence Rattigan's plays were rendered safely heterosexual, and he compartmentalized his life between a debonair, affluent, golfing, cricket-loving exterior and a consistently homosexual inner life. 'I was forced to be deceitful', Wildeblood recalled, 'living one life during my working hours and another when I was free. I had two sets of friends; almost, one might say, two faces . . . My whole life became a lie.'[32] A second option was 'adjustment': repression sublimated through fulfilment in the diminishing number of suitable careers. For Bishop Stockwood of Southwark, with his sexual orientation well known to intimates, the two most intense but platonic relationships were with schoolboys who remained in grateful contact throughout his life. A third option was to opt out of 'normality', and travel along what could then be an exceedingly lonely road. Failing in teenage years to move with contemporaries through heterosexual friendships towards marriage, nervous about confiding in unsuspecting associates, denied the satisfactions of parenthood—the male homosexual who took this third route had with much solitary soul-searching to seek out what was virtually an alternative and classless society with its own private language and codes of conduct, shuttling in and out of it as circumstances required.

Safety lay in numbers and anonymity, and large towns (especially London) provided a refuge, as did more tolerant societies overseas for those who could

[28] C. Varah (ed.), *The Samaritans in the '70s to Befriend the Suicidal and Despairing* (1st publ. 1965, 3rd edn. 1977), 56.

[29] P. Wildeblood, *Against the Law* (1st publ. 1955, paperback edn. Harmondsworth, 1957), 185.

[30] Dept of Health and Social Security, *Report of the [Finer] Committee on One-Parent Families* (Cmnd. 5629, 1974), i. 25.

[31] Obituary, *Ind.* (6 Mar. 2003), 22.

[32] Wildeblood, *Against the Law*, 37.

afford to visit them. Caution was essential, even in London; a male prostitute on a London bus in 1953 gave Lees-Milne 'one of those sidelong looks I know so well, expressionless and full of deep meaning; a second look was of the most languishing and seductive nature, yet one which if seen by a third person would not be noticed'.[33] There may have been only 1,938 'unnatural offences' and 3,087 attempts to commit them known to the police in 1952,[34] but police surveillance was capricious, and opportunities for blackmailing and robbing the homosexual abounded. In 1963 both Kenneth Williams and Noel Coward noted in their diaries that John Vassall, then at the centre of a spy case, would probably never have photographed secret documents for the Russians if the law had not made blackmail feasible.[35] In a little-known urban struggle of the 1950s, the police laboured to render public the lavatories that homosexuals, for lack of a better meeting place, viewed as private 'cottages'.[36] Even what were later designated as 'gay bars' could not be overtly such in 1964: in that year Anne Sharpley found them always 'full of silent, standing, staring males. An intense mating struggle goes on in these roomfuls of stock-still, dark-suited, workaday-looking men, as they eye one another.'[37] London homosexuals extended their safe space further by sharing with actors and some working-class East Enders a semi-private language, polari, which enabled them both to recognize one another and to converse more freely in public areas.[38]

Leading a double life was an excellent training for some professions: Sharpley declared that 'the West End stage would come to something of a halt if every homosexual writer, actor, producer or designer were suddenly banished'.[39] Indeed, the American Dr Edward Sagarin, in his impressively pioneering and well-balanced *The Homosexual Outlook* (1951), published under the pseudonym Donald Webster Cory, wondered whether their emancipation would remove the stimulus which had elicited their substantial cultural achievement.[40] Necessarily adept at closely observing fellow human beings, the homosexual could capitalize upon his unusual perspective. Here is one source of the brilliance with which Joe Orton's plays captured the paradoxes of gentility, together with the surreal Pinteresque conversations overheard every day on a London bus. Orton's homosexual escapades attuned him to the contrasts between appearance and reality, and alerted him to the strange worlds concealed beneath convention's surfaces. From there it was but a short distance to writing plays which subverted respectable values in the most powerful way possible: through high farce. Yet

[33] Lees-Milne, *Mingled Measure*, 45 (24 Aug. 1953).

[34] Earl Winterton, *HL Deb.* 19 May 1954, c. 737.

[35] *Kenneth Williams Diaries*, 206 (18 Jan. 1963). *Noel Coward Diaries*, 528 (10 Feb. 1963).

[36] M. Houlbrook, 'The Private World of Public Urinals: London 1918–57', *London Journal*, 25/1 (2000), 52–3, 61.

[37] 'London's Hidden Problem', 10.

[38] P. Baker, *Polari: The Lost Language of Gay Men* (2002), 68.

[39] 'London's Hidden Problem', 7.

[40] Cory, *Homosexual Outlook*, 156.

the overall impression conveyed by the law's workings in this area is one of tragic waste, for Turing was not alone. In 1953 the actor John Gielgud was arrested for importuning a few months after being knighted, and his anguish lasted a lifetime, though he pleaded guilty, and with staunch backing from fellow actors forced himself back on to the stage; the prominent stage director John Dexter was briefly imprisoned for homosexual conduct in the 1950s, a 'cure' worse than the disease; and fear of exposure deterred the brilliant and homosexual student of social policy Brian Abel-Smith from seizing the opportunity of a safe parliamentary seat.

Gaitskell as Labour leader told the Macmillan government he wanted the law on homosexuality reformed by all-party agreement; given its members' traditionalism, Labour could not then risk campaigning alone on the issue.[41] Homosexuality remained sufficiently controversial in 1967 for MPs keen to uphold their public image to welcome the reforming involvement of an unelected House of Lords. Given the scale of this hostility, how did liberalization ever occur? 'When the earth is fully peopled', the philosopher Jeremy Bentham had written, 'then will the policy of the statesman be directed to the arrestment of population, as now to the increase: and what is now stigmatised as vice will then receive the treatment, if not the name of virtue.'[42] Such a situation was now being realized, together with greatly improved understanding of sexuality. Kinsey had exposed the contrast between public image and private practice, had excluded prescriptive notions of 'normality' from his analysis, had viewed the heterosexual sex act within marriage as only one item on a menu of sexual 'outlets', and had undermined the stereotype of 'the homosexual' as a distinct type of person: 'there were no homosexual persons, but only homosexual acts'.[43] His ideas gradually shaped intelligent British comment on the subject—from Michael Schofield, for example. Sometimes using the pen name 'Gordon Westwood', Schofield was a Cambridge-trained social psychologist whose absorption in relativist zoological, psychological, and social-anthropological literature gradually freed him from traditionalist notions, enabling him to conduct several important surveys in this area. But for change to occur, insight must interact with opportunity. This conjuncture arrived in 1953, when two boy scouts accused Lord Montagu of Beaulieu and Kenneth Hume of homosexual offences. Wildeblood, also implicated in the case, advertised the prevailing danger of blackmail when he published his *Against the Law* (1955) after release from prison. With some difficulty, a few homosexuals (including Wildeblood) gave evidence to the Wolfenden committee on homosexual offences

[41] On this see Williams, *Gaitskell*, 390. P. Thompson in Coopey *et al.*, *Wilson Governments*, 139.

[42] Bentham seems to have had homosexuality rather than birth control in mind—see L. Campos Barolevi, *Bentham and the Oppressed* (Berlin, 1984), 47.

[43] P. Robinson, *The Modernization of Sex: Havelock Ellis, Alfred Kinsey, William Masters and Virginia Johnson* (1976), 67.

and prostitution (1954–7), appointed to investigate the law in this area. A small delegation from the committee interviewed Kinsey, but the committee's report rather oddly questioned whether his findings on homosexuality in America applied in Britain. This painstaking committee—alert to expert opinion, cross-cultural in its perspectives, measured in judgement, and probably well ahead of prevailing attitudes—recommended that homosexual acts between consenting adults over 21 should not be illegal, thereby in effect proposing equality before the law for all male or female adult same-sex relationships.

The ideas, the opportunity, and the evidence were now in place: only a reforming campaign was required. One of its key figures, A. E. G. Wright, who assumed the pseudonym Antony Grey, was already committed to reform before Wolfenden reported. With same-sex leanings as a teenager well before embarking on any close relationships, he had been deeply influenced by Havelock Ellis's *Studies in the Psychology of Sex* (1897–1910) and by Sagarin's *Homosexual Outlook*. On 2 April 1954 the *Sunday Times* published Wright's long and forceful anonymous letter: the homosexual's sense of personal responsibility and self-respect could be attained, he argued, only through liberty, with full social integration as the objective. In a letter to *The Times* on 7 March 1958 drafted by the lecturer in English A. E. Dyson, influential liberal and intellectual opinion—which included Clement Attlee, Isaiah Berlin, Lord David Cecil, Trevor Huddleston, J. B. Priestley, and Bertrand Russell—backed Wolfenden's recommendations. From there grew the earnest, moderate, and highly responsible Homosexual Law Reform Society, keen to transcend the role of pressure group run by and on behalf of homosexuals; Wright was its treasurer and then from 1962 to 1970 its paid part-time secretary. His rare combination of high-serious commitment, shrewd political effectiveness, and total lack of self-advertisement was precious indeed. Dirk Bogarde's courageous decision to act in *Victim* (1961), a film showing some sympathy with homosexuality (still then illegal), publicized the issue further, and the non-party Sexual Offences Act (1967), legalizing homosexual acts in private, was the outcome.

Even less is known about the chronology of attitudes to transsexuality, a category which in the 1960s was hardly yet understood. Originating in an American medical context during the 1950s, the term was at first used to denote people who combined the physical characteristics of one sex with the psychological characteristics of the other, and transsexuals were not at first clearly distinguished from transvestites or even homosexuals.[44] The transvestite, in the form of the 'pantomime dame', had long been familiar on the British stage, but in the 1950s the distinct term 'transsexual' began rapidly to subdivide, and soon designated people whose sex had been changed by surgery. This operation

[44] D. King, 'Gender Confusions: Psychological and Psychiatric Conceptions of Transvestism and Transsexualism', in K. Plummer (ed.), *The Making of the Modern Homosexual* (1981), 166–73, 175.

was rare and unpublicized until Roberta Cowell exploded into the popular press in 1951–2. In her autobiography (vague on names and dates, though otherwise remarkably frank), this former fighter pilot and father of two claimed that hers was the first surgical sex-change operation in Britain. Certainly the change of sex on her birth certificate (1951) antedates the much-publicized similar transition of Christine Jorgensen, patient of the Danish doctor Christian Hamburger. During the 1960s a gender identity clinic was established at Charing Cross Hospital by Dr John Randell, author of *Sexual Variations* (1973); by the 1970s he was performing between eight and twelve sex-change operations a year.[45] Neither the terms 'transvestite' nor 'transsexual' featured in book titles before 1965, but thereafter they became more common,[46] and research on transsexuals greatly increased.

Meanwhile birth control's advance was from another direction blurring what had hitherto been a relatively well-defined separation of roles between men and women. This had been among the earliest aspects of sexuality forced (by early nineteenth-century Malthusians) into public discussion. In 1929 Bertrand Russell envisaged governments rescuing population 'from the blind operation of instinct', and in 1949 the Royal Commission on Population aimed to ensure 'that in all relevant branches of policy and administration the population factor will be taken into account'.[47] The spontaneous decision by millions of couples to have fewer children reflected people's mounting desire in a relatively affluent and secular society to win more control over their lives. Public anxiety about their decisions diminished as the armed forces' resort to sophisticated technology rendered cannon fodder less integral to national security. By 1950 a third of local health authorities provided birth-control clinics, a third made grants to voluntary agencies, and only a third did nothing.[48] Public concern was shifting to anxiety about teenage pregnancy. Attitudes in the early 1960s were particularly casual among sexually active adolescents, with fear of pregnancy usually too weak among women for them to choose the contraceptive used; besides, less than half such adolescents regularly used one.[49] A survey of 1963 showed that the resort to the contraceptive sheath, cap, or other device as sole contraceptive method declined with each descent in the social scale, and that withdrawal as the sole method rose with each such descent.[50] 'If you take a walk up Greenacres Estate', said a working-class informant in the late 1950s of a middle-class area in

[45] D. King, 'Gender Confusions', 173. [46] COPAC book-title search.

[47] B. Russell, *Marriage and Morals* (1929), 199. Royal Commission on Population, *Report* (1949), 233; see also 149–50.

[48] C. Webster, *The Health Services since the War*, ii. *Government and Health Care: The National Health Service 1958–1979* (1996), 245.

[49] M. Schofield, *The Sexual Behaviour of Young People* (1st publ. 1965, 2nd edn. 1968), 88; based on 1,873 interviews with 16- and 18-year-olds of both sexes in seven areas.

[50] Sir D. Baird, 'A Fifth Freedom?', *British Medical Journal* (13 Nov. 1965), 1143.

Woodford, 'they look at you and say, "Oh, look at all those children" '.[51] Those who were alert to the role of intellect and physical fitness in the struggle for world influence, and who thought intellect and health genetically determined, had special reason to worry about class differentials in birth control.[52] But the labour movement, with its environmentalist diagnoses, had always repudiated the eugenic approach to social problems, and Conservatives bidding in the 1950s for the centre ground were hardly likely to diverge.

Britain was not unique among Western societies in finding its birth rate's long-term decline temporarily masked by an unexpected 'baby boom' from the early 1950s to the mid-1960s, reflecting women's decision to bear children earlier. In Britain the boom added about two million births to the number which might have occurred if fertility had remained at the level of 1955 through to the 1970s.[53] This put great pressure upon primary schools and housing in the 1960s, on secondary schools in the 1970s, on higher education and (again) on housing in the 1980s, as the baby boomers worked their way through the life cycle. They unconsciously contributed something to the high-rise housing and the mounting welfare expenditure of the 1960s. But the earlier correlation between prosperity and childbearing was weakening in the mid-1960s: by then an unprecedented proportion of married women and mothers had begun to take paid work.[54] The birth rate's long downward trend therefore resumed, and families at every social level became progressively smaller and much more uniform in size: by the 1970s there were only two children in nearly a third of all families.[55]

The campaigners' role in spreading birth control was probably small, and their mounting prominence in the 1950s (boom period for the Family Planning Association) was probably consequence rather than cause of a more profound change. By 1961 the contraceptive pill had become generally available in Britain: nearly half a million used it by 1964, with a threefold rise by 1971, and a nearly fivefold rise by 1975.[56] Yet during the quarter-century after 1945, as before, changes in the birth rate reflected change in attitudes rather than in birth-control technique. Better and more accessible contraceptives did not change parental priorities, but facilitated them. Those priorities had not changed: higher expectations of health and comfort for all members of the family, male and female, combined with minimizing avoidable uncertainty. The gradual twentieth-century advance of public welfare reduced the need for children as family earners or as an insurance against old age; and now that

[51] Willmott and Young, *Family and Class*, 120. See also J. M. Mogey, *Family and Neighbourhood: Two Studies in Oxford* (1956), 142–5.

[52] See table 2.8 in *TCBST* 47.

[53] *BST* 49.

[54] Coleman and Salt, *British Population*, 139, 145, 525.

[55] Anderson, 'Modern Life Cycle', 80–1.

[56] M. Murphy, 'The Contraceptive Pill and Women's Employment as Factors in Fertility Change in Britain 1963–1980: A Challenge to the Conventional View', *Population Studies* (July 1993), 224.

schooling lasted longer and children began work so late, their earnings were less important to the parents; the decision to conceive them (and conception did increasingly flow from a decision) competed with desire for the consumer goods now increasingly available. An earlier incentive to larger families, the fear that young children might die, declined concomitantly with the growth in public welfare; infant mortality plunged throughout the twentieth century[57] because of the mother's improved diet and environment, together with better ante-natal and post-natal care. The contraceptive revolution had now set up a virtuous cycle: with smaller families came an improved income and environment, and a concentration of such births as there were on what was physiologically the most suitable time.

Birth control was rapidly losing its earlier associations with rationalistic 'causes', with prostitution, and with preventing births, and between the wars had moved on towards the more positive concept of 'planned parenthood' and the aim of promoting conception where desired. It still required courage from Iain Macleod and prominent medical sympathizers to back the Family Planning Association in the mid-1950s,[58] but the birth controllers continued to move on—to the unmarried mother. In the late 1940s a tenth of the births even to those practising birth control had been unwanted, and in the 1950s—the last of legitimacy's golden decades—an annual average of 10,000 illegitimate children (about a third of the total) were adopted into two-parent families in England and Wales.[59] The Marie Stopes Clinic held its first evening session for unmarried women in 1959, and two years later the Brook Street Advisory Centre was founded to promote this cause more widely, creating a storm in 1967 by deciding to advise girls under 16. To the pioneer birth controller Dr Helena Wright, it seemed a major breakthrough when, at her clinic in the 1960s, a patient asked 'are *married* women accepted in this clinic?'[60]

Behind all this lay a concern, more humanitarian than feminist, to widen women's opportunities. Ancient fears were under challenge: of unwanted conception, of being involuntarily childless, of not finding a husband, or of being yoked to an unwanted husband. New opportunities were emerging: of sexual fulfilment and of full recognition and reward for talent. In a lecture of 1965 the distinguished consultant gynaecologist Sir Dugald Baird began by citing Roosevelt's speech of 6 January 1941 on the 'four essential freedoms', but now thought a fifth should be added: 'freedom from the tyranny of civilized man's excessive fertility'. Man's survival might once have required high fertility,

[57] For figures see *BST* 409.

[58] Author's tape-recorded interview with Dr David Pyke on 19 July 1977.

[59] Royal Commission on Population, *Report* (Cmd. 7695, 1949), 77. Dept of Health and Social Security, *Report of the [Finer] Committee on One-Parent Families* (Cmnd. 5629, 1974), i. 60–2.

[60] Author's tape-recorded interview with Dr Helena Wright, 27 Feb. 1977. See also *G* (3 Jan. 1991), 13. For Helen Brook see P. Ashdown-Sharp, 'A Singular Lady', *G* (19 June 1974), 9.

he said, but not in present-day advanced societies whose death rates were so low. By distributing the pill from his Aberdeen birth-control clinic Baird had brought a special emancipation to lower-class women, leading him to recommend free contraceptive advice and tubal ligation to women who saw their families as complete.[61] In its fourth phase, beginning in the mid-1960s, British feminism lost much of its earlier reticence about sexuality,[62] and from the mid-1950s novels were increasingly seeing the world through the eyes of the liberated young woman who accepts male advances more confidently because more firmly in control of the consequences. Even in Mills and Boon novels the heroine in the 1960s became more assertive and independent, and found romance in more exotic locations with heroes not British.[63] Women were now less frequently viewed as doomed to childbearing, though in Lynne Reid Banks's novel, *The L-Shaped Room* (1960, filmed in 1962), the pregnant Jane Graham deliberately opts for unmarried motherhood despite the doctor's patronizingly paternal assumption that she will prefer an abortion. Singing and dancing in her new-found independence, she 'felt wonderfully alive and capable', exclaiming 'I can do anything! I can do anything!', fitting 'the exultant words to my tune'.[64]

The L-Shaped Room resembled Shelagh Delaney's *A Taste of Honey* (1958) in several respects: the unmarried but pregnant young woman is befriended by people then marginal to mainstream society: blacks, loners, and homosexuals who none the less provide warm support and understand how complex moral decisions really are. The film censors took considerable trouble to tone down the backstreet abortion episode in the filmed version (1960) of Alan Sillitoe's *Saturday Night and Sunday Morning* (1957), and in his study of abortion Paul Ferris admitted in 1966 that his was 'not a polite topic'.[65] Abortion in the 1940s and 1950s was widespread, but its precise incidence was unknown, though the estimate of 100,000 abortions a year was widely accepted. Highly coloured and exotically packaged 'female' pills and potions had for generations fraudulently exploited women's fears, and in the mid-1960s at least twenty-two varieties were still being sold.[66] Ferris stressed that abortion had long been accessible to those able to pay, and that millions must have some personal knowledge of it.[67] In the early 1960s he closely observed the socially diverse women who sat in Harley Street London waiting rooms contemplating paying the going rate of £100: 'pretty, dressed-up, well-scented women,

[61] Baird, 'A Fifth Freedom?', 1141–8. [62] See above, pp. 30–1 for phases 1–3.

[63] J. McAleer, *Passion's Fortune: The Story of Mills and Boon* (Oxford, 1999), 258.

[64] L. R. Banks *The L-Shaped Room* (1960, Vintage edn. 2004), 57. See also D. J. Taylor, *After the War: The Novel and England since 1945* (1993, paperback edn. 1994), 247–8, 254.

[65] J. Richards and A. Aldgate, *Best of British: Cinema and Society 1930–70* (Oxford, 1983), 134–6, 142. P. Ferris, *The Nameless: Abortion in Britain Today* (1966), 10.

[66] Murphy, 'Contraceptive Pill', 230. Ferris, *Nameless*, 55–6, 60. [67] Ferris, *Nameless*, 9–10.

mostly aged between twenty and thirty, looking stonily into space'.[68] During the 1960s, however, the unmarried mother began to move in from the fringes, for the stigma of bearing children outside wedlock was beginning to follow the stigma of illegitimacy itself into oblivion. The number of children available for adoption might then be rising fast, but so was the proportion of mothers wishing to keep their illegitimate children. Still, Jane Graham's doctor, however mixed his motives, was understandably concerned, for his profession had not yet won control over an operation which (through the self-induced miscarriage or backstreet abortion) had long brought women untold suffering.

With abortion, as with birth control, the mounting prominence from the late 1950s of a sympathetic movement was consequence rather than cause of a profound social change. At first sight, prosecutions and convictions for causing illegal abortion do not appear to support this: rising slowly throughout the century, the rate of increase had slowed by the 1960s, with only 59 in court in 1961, 69 in 1964. Yet it was the patient's serious illness that had caused abortionists to be prosecuted, and because sulphonamides had greatly reduced the risk, these statistics were compatible with a large increase in the number of illegal abortions.[69] Abortion laws were relaxing outside Britain in the 1950s. Within a secularizing society a pragmatic preoccupation with health gained over the older and principled restrictive morality. In 1958, in one of his many boldly humane assertions, Glanville Williams noted that 'the chief evil of an abortion is no longer thought to be the loss of the unborn child, but the injury done to the mother by the unskilled abortionist'.[70] Although most obstetricians and gynaecologists remained conservative, a small minority of consultant gynaecologists (most notably W. C. W. Nixon at University College Hospital, Baird at Aberdeen, and Peter Diggory at two Surrey hospitals) pioneered a new outlook, partly feminist in inspiration, and the number of therapeutic abortions in NHS hospitals in England and Wales rose sixfold between 1958 and 1967.[71] The courageous and committed Baird, with all the prestige of a Scottish university doctor, made Aberdeen a mecca for rational, pioneering, and managed policies on birth control, sterilization, and abortion.[72] Then in 1963–4 thalidomide was prescribed as a sedative, but turned out to have disastrous side effects: more than 250 grossly deformed children alive in 1964 were expected to survive to maturity.[73] This tragedy overcame opposition to legalized and medically supervised abortion from all but the most principled traditionalists, and injected young talent into the ageing

[68] Ferris, *Nameless*, 112. For fees, ibid. 100, 103–5.
[69] Ibid. 36–7.
[70] G. Williams, *The Sanctity of Life and the Criminal Law* (1958), 146.
[71] K. Hindell and M. Simms, *Abortion Law Reformed* (1971), 49; see also 51–6.
[72] Ferris, *Nameless*, 145.
[73] Hindell and Simms, *Abortion Law Reformed*, 108.

Abortion Law Reform Association which humanitarians had founded in the 1930s.[74]

With unobtrusive help from Labour ministers, David Steel's Abortion Bill (1967) became law. It legalized abortion if justified by the risk of a seriously deformed child being born or by danger to the woman's physical or mental health, taking her environment into account. Medical pressure ensured that the doctor's clinical autonomy was upheld and that the profession's control over the operation greatly extended. In these circumstances, still wider access to birth-control information could hardly be resisted, and the National Health Service (Family Planning) Bill went through parliament in the same year, making local-authority services available on a permissive basis to all women, regardless of medical or marital status. The Abortion Bill almost immediately became controversial. Crossman, prominent among the Bill's advocates, was himself concerned by July 1969 that the reform was being exploited by 'money-making commercial doctors', and there were rumours that Scandinavian women eager for abortions were descending upon London.[75] By the 1970s even legal (let alone illegal) abortion in England and Wales was terminating more than a third of conceptions outside marriage; but for birth control, the number would have been much higher. The close relation between the two was revealed in 1970, when the number of abortions soared as soon as medical doubts about the pill temporarily diminished the demand for it.[76]

2. WOMEN'S TWO ROLES

To the traditional motives for limiting family size the 1950s added a new one: married women's growing potential as wage earners at the same time as heavy labour's falling share of the workforce made them eligible for more jobs. Birth control's impact on women's life cycle, reinforced from the late 1960s by wider access to safe abortion, reduced the period devoted to bearing and rearing children. By the 1970s the pattern was established whereby more than half all babies were born within the first five years of marriage and more than three-quarters within the first eight years.[77] With earlier marriage, childbearing beyond the mother's twenties had by the 1960s become rather unusual,[78] and half of her lifespan remained for other projects. The Victorian woman's pregnancies, recurring until well into her forties, were now consigned to a far-off age. Women, emancipated from their biological clock,

[74] K. Hindell and M. Simms 'How the Abortion Lobby Worked', in R. Kimber and J. J. Richardson (eds.), *Pressure Groups in Britain: A Reader* (1974), 154.

[75] Crossman, *Cabinet Diaries*, iii. 549–50 (4 July 1969), 606 (5 Aug. 1969).

[76] Coleman and Salt, *British Population*, 128. Crossman, *Cabinet Diaries*, iii. 877 (2 Apr. 1970).

[77] *Finer Report*, i. 32.

[78] Coleman and Salt, *British Population*, 151. See also the table in *TBS* 50.

could now adopt the male's more linear outlook on life, and contemplate a lifetime's career. Between the wars Eleanor Rathbone's great scheme for raising women's status had been to reward motherhood by paying adequate family allowances, but in Britain her scheme was bypassed, together with Beveridge's social insurance ideas, when successive governments failed to maintain the allowance's real value; in its share of the occupied population's income as at 1960, the family allowance's role was far smaller in Britain than in France, Italy, Belgium, the Netherlands, and West Germany.[79] So British mothers had less incentive than many European mothers to keep out of the labour market.[80]

For more than a century, some areas of the economy (most notably textiles) had depended on married women's willingness to take up paid work, and in the two world wars patriotism and opportunism further extended women's occupational reach. In the tight labour market after 1945 the government encouraged many to remain in paid work, but respectability still required the married woman to stay at home, especially when also a mother. So the pacesetting for married women's paid work came from lower down in society. Consumerist pressures, however, gradually secured a similar outcome higher up, for during the 1950s consumer goods gravitated from luxuries into essentials, and after 1955 were energetically promoted on commercial television. So the home's needs often prompted the middle-class woman also to make the move, if only to pursue more effectively a domestic role that was still seen as primary—though women were far more likely to be part-timers than were married men.

The cornucopia of consumer goods and services available in the 1950s included items despised by some prominent pioneer feminists: fine clothes, cosmetics, and hairdressing, for example. For many interwar middle-class feminists, women had nothing to lose but their powder compacts, whereas postwar women felt that they had everything to gain from the permanent wave. It became an aid to self-confidence, a badge of female self-help, a symbol of respectability by comparison with the unkempt greasy hair of social inferiors who had lost hope. Half the women over 16 in Great Britain in 1949 had at some point experienced a permanent wave, and those without it clustered at the very bottom of society. Those who could afford it were permed by their hairdresser, but elsewhere the 'home perm' spread fast. The younger the woman and the higher her social status, the more likely she was to use

[79] J. F. Sleeman, *The Welfare State: Its Aims, Benefits and Costs* (1973), 139.

[80] For levels of payment see C. M. Stewart, 'Family Allowance Statistics in Great Britain', *Population Studies* (Mar. 1963), 210. See also Harris, 'Enterprise and Welfare States: A Comparative Perspective', *TRHS* (1990), 183.

cleansing preparations, rouge, nail varnish, and mascara. Ownership of cars, the ultimate in consumer goods, grew fast after the 1940s, but for women it grew from a very low base: in 1949 cars were registered in the name of 13 per cent of men in Great Britain, 2 per cent of women.[81] In the longer term the car, like birth control and the sanitary towel, carried further the freedom of movement for women pioneered by the late Victorian bicycle and the Edwardian teashop, and finally consigned the chaperon to history. Even the paid and employed working-class wives of employed husbands in 1950 seem often to have felt emancipated: a fifth said they went out to work to lead a less restricted life and meet other people.[82] Liberation carried a price: between the early 1950s and early 1970s women's average annual death rate in the age group 15–24 from road accidents nearly trebled, whereas the male figure less than doubled.[83]

Both the proportion of women in Great Britain who were economically active, and (in England and Wales) the proportion of married women in the total workforce, almost doubled between 1951 and 1971, whereas in the same period the proportion of men at work in Great Britain fell from 88 to 81 per cent.[84] Manual labour steadily declined as a proportion of both sexes at work throughout the century. The heavy-industry occupations had always been those least likely to employ women—mining and construction work least of all.[85] Women responded more flexibly than men to mid-century demands: they benefited from the twentieth-century trend towards reducing the number of employees in textiles and personal service and towards increasing it in clerical, commercial, retailing, and financial work.[86] The new pattern of married women's work was at first much more common in London and the south-east than in Wales and the north, where a smaller proportion of the workforce was female, and even that proportion more likely to be under 20.[87] None the less, from the late 1950s women's magazines, which had focused heavily on woman's domestic role and on her twin goals of finding and keeping a husband and raising a family,[88] began to lose circulation.[89]

81 Hulton Press, *Patterns of British Life* (1950), 134–8, 118.

82 Rowntree and Lavers, *Poverty and Welfare State*, 57.

83 Office of Population Censuses and Surveys, *Trends in Mortality 1951–1975* (1978), 31; cf. OPCS, *Mortality Statistics 1975* (1978), 67.

84 *Econ.* (4 Jan. 1975), 60. Figures for married women from Moroney, *Family and State*, 19.

85 See table 1 in *Econ.* (26 July 1975), 27 for the situation in 1971.

86 E. James, 'Women at Work in Twentieth Century Britain' *Manchester School*, 30 (Sept. 1962), 291—a useful and somewhat neglected article.

87 Ibid. 288.

88 C. L. White, *The Women's Periodical Press in Britain 1946–1976* (1977), 11; cf. 60–1.

89 J. D. Halloran, *The Effects of Television* (1970), 143. White, *Women's Periodical Press*, 23, 25, 49.

When the wife took paid work away from home, the family's traditional separation of spheres was adjusted, but not abandoned. The difference between the married woman's role before and after the 1950s was not between idleness and work, but between work that was unpaid and paid. Working-class women had slaved for generations at childbearing, child rearing, and house-cleaning, with few enough of the aids that were now becoming routine; their move into paid retailing, laundering, nursing, and dressmaking grew naturally out of that. Before the 1950s the well-to-do woman-at-home had also usually been 'employed' in unadvertised and unpaid family duties and good works—as witnessed the large gaps left in Britain's informal welfare structure when she too took up paid employment. The mother deserted by the father of her children was now becoming more prevalent at precisely the time when help was diminishingly available from the maiden aunt and the unmarried daughter at home. Their role had fallen out of fashion, and in 1965 when the veteran Labour MP Edith Summerskill assembled in the House of Commons single women with older dependants, she was 'struck by the general shabbiness undoubtedly stemming from a life of self-denial; at the sad, unsmiling faces, for a life dedicated to the care of the elderly leaves little room for cheerful social contacts with younger people'.[90]

Both a problem and its solution were thus created. A paid substitute for women's unpaid voluntary work within the family was now required, especially as the National Assistance Act (1948) had contracted the family's welfare responsibilities. Hitherto a citizen had been statutorily obliged to support spouse, children (young and even adult), and grandchildren who could not support themselves: thereafter, spouses were liable only for each other and for their children under 16. In every census year from 1911 to 1971, however, the 'pool' of potential carers (that is, the married and unmarried female age group from 45 to 59) for the rising proportion of elderly in the population was in marked decline.[91] Women's paid work in public welfare was the solution, and accounts for many of the paid occupations that married women increasingly took up in the 1950s and 1960s: they were being paid for performing more anonymously tasks which they would earlier have tackled unpaid and in a more personal way. The educated woman's paid work from the 1950s to the 1970s often centred on spheres for which her traditional domestic role had seemingly prepared her: as doctor, solicitor, schoolteacher, social worker, and office worker. All that happened after the 1940s was women's transfer of locations for a role that remained separated, though less directly

[90] E. Summerskill, *A Woman's World* (1967), 234.

[91] Moroney, *Family and State*, 20–2.

SEVEN AGES OF WOMAN

Fig. 3. *Manchester Guardian* (28 Jan. 1955), 9.

subordinate to men financially and in other ways. As for manufacturing, women preferred jobs that were 'light' in a double sense—physically and intellectually undemanding, but also clean and where possible part-time. Men understandably kept away: 'many firms told me', wrote Zweig, 'that they had failed in putting some men on women's jobs side by side with them. The men could not stand being ridiculed by women for doing a job which befits women only.'[92]

Women experienced their paid work differently from men. Their status at work suffered from preferring to work part-time, from the nature of the occupations requiring it, and from the levels at which women were customarily employed. Even in manufacturing industries during the 1960s a rising proportion of the total number of women in each industry chose to work part-time.[93] The proportion of women in paid clerical work rose throughout the twentieth century, but was accelerating in the 1950s and 1960s, by which

[92] F. Zweig, *Women's Life and Labour* (1952), 88. [93] *BLS* 275.

time it far exceeded the proportion of men in paid clerical work. Women were increasing their share of shop workers too, though more slowly; and there too their proportion was far higher than the men's.[94] With part-time status came relative inactivity in trade unions, whether manual or white-collar. Union membership as a percentage of the total eligible in 1948 and 1970 was for men 53 and 55, respectively, but for women only 26 and 33.[95] Partly for this reason women were paid less than men. The politicians were divided: Conservatives were socially conservative, yet sought women's votes; Labour wanted to deter women from undercutting men in the labour market, but the party's heavy-industry base led it to focus on improving welfare benefits for the mother who stayed at home. None the less, R. A. Butler made a modest advance in 1955 when as Chancellor of the Exchequer he announced that women civil servants would move towards equal pay in seven annual instalments, reaching their goal in 1961 [Fig. 3]. The EEC set a faster feminist pace in the 1960s, and British desire for membership encouraged it to follow suit. None the less, by 1971 women's status at work was relatively low, not just for the reasons outlined, but because women were less likely to get the top jobs, and because within lower-grade occupations they tended to cluster in lower-status activities: as typists not office managers, as physiotherapists not doctors.[96]

Postwar women's taste for part-time work reflected their tendency to acquire two roles in place of one, for their traditional and unpaid domestic role did not decline concomitantly with their new and paid non-domestic role [Fig. 4]. Furthermore, the home's enhanced need for paid help (usually female) perpetuated the separation of spheres at another level. The domestic servant lived on even in middle-class families after 1951, pursuing a somewhat shadowy existence without the name, not unionized and usually absent from national statistics. Fewer of these domestic employees were male or British than in earlier years, au pairs being imported after the 1940s from Scandinavia, Spain, and the Philippines. In place of the live-in nanny, the less affluent resorted to the childminder, the babysitter, and the playgroup. Still less obtrusively, there persisted the part-time and often moonlighting gardener, and the cleaning lady: the redesignated charwoman and 'treasure' of earlier years.

Pre-feminist attitudes survived long after 1945, and when launching Cruse, her movement to help widows in 1958, Margaret Torrie had been shocked at the helplessness of married women forced by bereavement out of their hitherto sheltered lives 'like crustaceans without a shell'.[97] From the 1950s onwards,

[94] Goldthorpe, *Social Mobility and Class Structure*, 60.
[95] Price and Bain, 'Union Growth Revisited', 349.
[96] See the intelligent discussion in *Econ.* (26 July 1975), 27.
[97] M. Torrie, *My Years with Cruse* (Richmond, Surrey, 1987), 61.

however, paid work brought a new independence: the women who had earlier entered the labour market had usually been spinsters or widows except in rather limited areas of employment such as textiles. Single non-widowed women contributed four-fifths of Great Britain's female workforce in 1911, over a half by 1951, and only a quarter by 1981.[98] Feminist pioneers had broken into the professions (law, civil service, medicine, teaching) several decades earlier, and now a modest harvest could be gathered: the female proportion of managerial posts in Great Britain rose between 1951 and 1981 from a sixth to a fifth, and in higher professional posts from one-twelfth to one-eighth.[99] Feminist attitudes did not necessarily prevail at such high levels: the historian of the British College of Obstetricians and Gynaecologists might see Hilda Lloyd's election as its first woman president (1949–52) as 'a revolutionary step', for example, but as it turned out 'there was no need for fear'.[100]

In 1961 the Women's Freedom League (another offshoot from the suffragettes) thought it time to disband, and it was some years before the younger and much less politicized fourth phase of British feminism sprang up, inspired from the USA. There is no necessary relation between agitation for a cause and its success, which sometimes arrives by unexpected routes. The impulse behind the postwar emancipation of married women through paid work owed little to contemporary feminist pressure. British feminists usually went along with the widely held view that wives and mothers should stay at home, and in so far as they were concerned to promote women's paid work at all, they had the unmarried woman in mind. In truth, the impulse to postwar change seems to have been largely economic, even non-feminist, in nature. The Second World War, unlike the First, was followed by full employment and by a government keen to keep women war workers in paid peacetime employment. With heavy industry still in slow retreat and with the service sector on the advance, the opportunity for women was there, together with the growing supply of consumer goods and services that encouraged them to seize it.[101]

3. A NEW MAP OF YOUTH

The changes so far discussed had profound implications for children, and by 1960 the term 'latch-key child', originating in the USA in the 1940s, had crossed the Atlantic. Anyone familiar with Britain after 1951 visiting Britain in earlier centuries would have been astonished at the abundance of children, for during the twentieth century their proportion of the British population had

[98] *BST* 169–70. [99] *BST* 166.
[100] F. Shaw, *Twenty-Five Years: The Story of the Royal College of Obstetricians and Gynaecologists 1929–1954* (1954), 159.
[101] This discussion owes much to M. Pugh, *Women and Women's Movement 1914–1959* (1992), 286–9.

been falling—from a third under 14 in 1901 to a quarter in 1971 to a fifth in 1991.[102] It was unusual for a married woman in 1951 not to have children, then a deliberate choice for only about half the childless.[103] In 1951 most parents wanted children, and whereas 19 per cent of women married in 1926–30 were childless in 1961, only a tenth of those married in the late 1940s and late 1950s were childless in 1971.[104] The yearning for children could not yet be tackled: the great advances in treating infertility were still to come. Yet childlessness was now more rarely thought discreditable; indeed, the balance of opinion was beginning to shift the other way, with compassion or even disapproval extending to parents of three or more.[105] In England and Wales the 9,692,000 children under 15 in 1951 were reared in smaller families: in 1911 three-fifths of the population had lived in households of five or more, but sixty years later only just over a quarter did so. By then the really large household had almost vanished: only 1 per cent lived in households of eight or more, but 20 per cent in 1911.[106] Few indeed were the families that could show a Victorian recreational self-sufficiency, let alone boast family newspapers. Parents with fewer children could give, and perhaps also wanted to give, more attention to each child, and fewer children were now left to bring up one another. After the 1940s parents possessed or made the time and money to share recreation with their children, the family car carried off the whole family at weekends, and dispersed children's recreations further afield.

Childhood is not an objective category: it is socially defined, its boundaries change and subcategories emerge. Hints on baby care were still passed on informally from mother to daughter, and few consulted books on the subject. The *Common Sense Book of Baby and Child Care* (1946) by the American paediatrician Benjamin Spock did not reach Britain from America till 1955, though through women's magazines its reassuring and relatively relaxed approach to parenthood arrived rather earlier than that.[107] During the 1950s pregnancy was beginning to lose some of its seclusion and mystery, and such rituals as the expectant mother's buying in of the 'layette' and the prestigious 'pram' were giving way to the more varied and self-chosen strategies practicable for the busy working mother. The first portable and collapsible pushchair or 'stroller' was patented in 1965, and in 1999 Silver Cross, once the Rolls Royce of perambulators, went into administration.[108] Douglas Gairdner's influential article of 1949 discredited the medical arguments for another babyhood ritual: male circumcision. Clearly correlated with social class, this monument to the medical credulity of the well-to-do, this caricature of the professional classes' enthusiasm for long-term planning, had for decades lopped off foreskins in their tens

102 *TCBST* 75. 103 *BST* 56. 104 *TCBST* 44–5.
105 E. M. Hubback, *The Population of Britain* (West Drayton, 1947), 71. 106 *BHS* 15, 118.
107 D. Sandbrook, *Never Had It So Good: A History of Britain from Suez to the Beatles* (2005), 388.
108 *FT* (15 May 1999), 11.

of thousands annually at great expense;[109] by the 1990s one in five British males were still being circumcised, though by then rarely for medical reasons.[110] Given the marked UK fluctuations in the late-twentieth-century incidence of surgery for children with 'glue ear', and given the marked cross-cultural contrasts in the incidence of tonsillectomy and Caesarean section—a combination of affluence, fashion, and cultural factors may likewise have ensured that surgery elsewhere was not always medically justified, though by 1980 the UK was by no means internationally in the van for luxury operations of this type.[111]

The designation 'toddler', increasingly employed in Britain from the 1960s and escalating from the mid-1990s,[112] marked the transition period between babyhood and delivery for pre-school care outside the home. This brief interval was of growing interest at a time when young mothers increasingly took paid work, and when wartime experience shifted theories of child rearing towards the idea that both mother and child might benefit from being apart for some of the day. Investigating women's work in 1952, Zweig 'came to realise what a great blessing to a working mother a good granny can be',[113] but the Royal Commission on Population (1949) had recommended more family services, home helps, day nurseries, and nursery schools. Government funds for new day nurseries were cut in the late 1940s, however, and family services suffered through poor coordination between the public authorities at national and local level.[114] Education in the late 1940s had to compete with other pressing claims on resources, and within the educational budget the main postwar priority was to get schools built and class sizes reduced for children aged 5 and above. The proportion of children aged between 2 and 5 in state schools actually fell: from 16 per cent in 1938 to 12 per cent in 1950 to 10 per cent in 1965.[115] Furthermore, the distinctive needs of children under 5 suffered by an administrative change which if anything blurred the distinction between children of school and pre-school age: whereas the interwar trend had favoured building distinct nursery schools, the postwar trend was to tack nursery classes on to a three-stage

[109] D. Gairdner, 'The Fate of the Foreskin: A Study of Circumcision', *British Medical Journal* (24 Dec. 1949), 1433–7; cf. leading article, 1458–8 and correspondence *BMJ* (Sept.–Nov. 1935). For its social-class incidence as at 1950 see D. MacCarthy *et al.*, 'Circumcision in a National Sample of Four-Year Old Children', *BMJ* (4 Oct. 1952), 755–6.

[110] *T* (23 Sept. 1997), 6.

[111] A. Gray, 'International Patterns of Health Care, 1960 to the 1990s', in C. Webster (ed.), *Caring for Health: History and Diversity* (2nd edn. Buckingham, 1993), 179. For Caesarian section *Caring for Health* (3rd edn. Buckingham, 2001), 305. I am most grateful to Dr Webster and Professor Gray for generous help on this matter.

[112] For advice on this, based on COPAC searches, I owe much to John Simpson, chief editor of the *OED*.

[113] Zweig, *Women's Life and Labour*, 71.

[114] V. Randall, 'The Irresponsible State? The Politics of Child Daycare Provision in Britain', *British Journal of Political Science* (July 1995), 337–8, 341, 344–5.

[115] N. Whitbread, *The Evolution of the Nursery–Infant School* (1972), 112. Figures for children under 5 in maintained primary schools 1947–65 also register a decline, see T. Blackstone, *A Fair Start: The Provision of Pre-School Education* (1971), 69.

schools system whose first stage was 'primary'. In state schools in 1969 there were nearly 200,000 more children aged 3 and 4 in nursery classes than in nursery schools.[116]

All this left ample room for self-help. In the 1960s the state was far less prominent in educating and caring for children under 5 than for older children: only a fifth of the children in the age group between 2 and 5 were in playgroups or schools in 1969, and of those only three-fifths were in the state sector.[117] The need felt by young mothers, whether in paid work or not, was great: with smaller families and fuller female employment there were fewer relatives around to help, and more dispersed patterns of settlement often distanced the mother from such leisured relatives as there were. Growing traffic made streets more dangerous, and high-rise housing made play areas more remote. Enhanced middle-class demand ensured that by the 1960s part-time places for children under 5 were growing fast in prep and nursery schools; by the mid-1960s a third of children from the professional middle classes were attending nursery school.[118] There was mounting demand, too, for childminders, yet in 1973 there were only 30,000 registered childminders charged with 92,000 children in England and Wales, whereas by then 600,000 working mothers had children under 5, so childminders must often have been unregistered.[119] Reinforcing them was the pre-school 'playgroup', less formal and less narrowly educational than the nursery school or class. Owing much to efforts for handicapped children, this movement was boosted by a letter published in 1961 in the *Guardian* by the London mother Belle Tutaev, concerned for her daughter's needs. The playgroup movement owed little to professional skills or formal school structures, much to parental and voluntarist energies. By 1970 playgroups catered for more than three times as many under-5s as were in part-time attendance at state and private nursery schools and classes combined, and covered about 5 per cent of the age-group.[120]

There were other signs that children were being taken more seriously. Peter and Iona Opie began their comprehensive research into the culture of early childhood in the 1940s, and in the 1950s published important books on nursery rhymes and childhood lore and language, moving on in the 1960s to childhood games. Children's fiction was treated by reviewers with growing seriousness, and in Harold Williamson the BBC found a journalist brilliant at getting young children to talk spontaneously; his long sequence of programmes on *Children Talking* began in 1968.[121] *Whistle down the Wind*, the film (1961) based on Mary Hayley Bell's novel, showed that 'social realism' could as brilliantly illuminate the adult's timeless incomprehension of the child as the more

[116] Whitbread, *Nursery–Infant School*, 129. [117] Ibid. 133. [118] Ibid. 115.
[119] B. and S. Jackson, *Childminder: A Study in Action Research* (1979), 174–7, 182.
[120] Whitbread, *Nursery–Infant School*, 130.
[121] Obituaries in *DT* (14 Mar. 2001), 31; *Ind.* (23 Mar. 2001), review section, 6.

timebound incomprehensions arising from social class. Discovering 'Blakey', on the run because wanted for murder, hiding in a barn, the local children convince themselves he is Jesus Christ, and touchingly protect him against his persecutors until the film's denouement when the police move in.

To the extent that a child's happiness requires continuous access to its natural parents, the first half of the twentieth century was in some ways a golden age for children. Parents were then diminishingly likely to die young and were not yet prone to divorce, nor had mothers yet begun to flock into paid work away from home. Childhood then seemed both freer and more secure. Relatives were more likely to live nearby, more children had direct access to the countryside, road traffic had not yet eroded the street as a play area or rendered the bicycle unsafe, and because parents were by later standards unconcerned about sexual hazards, children were freer to roam unsupervised. From the 1950s children's life in some ways improved still further. Affluence and birth control made the home seem more spacious and comfortable, and central heating (spreading from the 1960s) enhanced privacy by dispersing the family into more rooms. Parental discipline grew less harsh, and children's fiction was vibrant. Several leading authors from its golden age died between 1951 and 1970: A. A. Milne in 1956, Arthur Ransome in 1967, W. E. Johns and Enid Blyton in 1968, Richmal Crompton in 1969. Their creations—Winnie the Pooh, the Walker and Blackett children, Biggles, the Famous Five, and Noddy, and William Brown—lived on to delight children for much longer. Alison Uttley (who died in 1976) with her 'Little Grey Rabbit' books carried forward the long British tradition which lent human traits to animals and which Beatrix Potter (who died in 1943) had carried to perfection. The careers of Uttley, Crompton, and Blyton exemplify the rich creative brew that the combination of schoolteaching and storytelling could foster among early-twentieth-century English women, and Johns and Ransome enthralled the boys by conjuring up outdoor adventures and brave episodes in exotic locations. Then in 1967 Roald Dahl's *James and the Giant Peach* brought a refreshingly surreal subversiveness into Christopher Robin's relatively suburban world. Children's fiction often first appeared in the numerous children's magazines, complemented by the world of the comic strip. Desperate Dan, Lord Snooty, and the Bash Street Kids in the *Dandy* (1937–) and *Beano* (1938–) occupied a world decidedly further down-market than the *Eagle* (1950–69), launched by the clergyman-publisher Marcus Morris and greatly enjoyed by the young Prince of Wales after his uncle had given him a subscription to it.[122]

The new media brought new recreations. The puppet programme *Muffin the Mule* lasted from 1946 to 1955, by which time Muffin, operated by the puppeteer Ann Hogarth, had become a national institution. As a medium for children, television was at first constrained by the so-called 'Toddler's Truce'

[122] Dimbleby, *Prince of Wales*, 39.

from 6 to 7 p.m., the interval between programmes that aimed to encourage younger children into bed and older ones to do their homework; ITV's commercial pressures prompted its abolition early in 1957. The children's radio slot from the BBC's earliest days had been *Children's Hour*, from 5 to 6 p.m., reinforced from 1950 by the weekday quarter-hour *Listen with Mother* at 1.45 for the youngest children. When *Children's Hour* was abolished in 1961 with the claim that children no longer liked the label, nostalgic adults raised an outcry. Childhood after 1951 was being eroded at both ends, with the infant's distinctive claims increasingly asserted and with adolescence beginning ever earlier. Engaged in self-criticism in 1966, the boy scout movement admitted that the word 'boy' presented 'a juvenile image', given that the word 'tends to be used today to describe those below adolescent age'. Given that the movement sought to attract teenagers, and given that 'the older boy and youth is most anxious to be regarded as adult', the Boy Scouts Association became the Scout Association in the following year.[123]

Long before the advent of teenage culture, inner-city teenage boys had in their recreation slowly gravitated away from parents towards their contemporaries. This was one aspect of growing up—'not because boys reject their parents. It is merely that *being seen* with parents makes them feel self-conscious.'[124] What was occurring in the 1950s, however, was a powerful combination of educational, physiological, and cultural change which commercialized teenage, lending it a new symbolism and a sharpened distinctiveness. With the age of menarche in Europe falling on average by three to four months in each decade for well over a century, there was a physiological basis for this adolescent consciousness.[125] There was ample room for friction between the generations when children reached physical maturity earlier yet stayed in school for longer. More of them further prolonged dependence on parents by attending university and by extending their training in other ways. Between 1950/1 and 1970/1 children in maintained secondary schools who stayed on beyond 16 rose from less than a fifth to more than a half, and in the direct-grant grammar schools from 88 to 96 per cent.[126]

The commercializing of teen age arrived from several directions. On the one hand, teenagers had more to spend. Part-time weekend jobs for schoolchildren were rare in 1951, but full employment and declining apprenticeship ensured that teenagers who had left school but were not yet parents were getting richer. Given that middle-class children stayed on at school, the new teenage

[123] The Chief Scout's Advance Party, *Report* (1966), 14–15.

[124] J. B. Mays, *Growing up in the City: A Study of Juvenile Delinquency in an Urban Neighbourhood* (Liverpool, 1954), 88.

[125] J. M. Tanner, 'The Trend Towards Earlier Physical Maturation', in J. E. Meade and A. S. Parkes (eds.), *Biological Aspects of Social Problems: A Symposium held by the Eugenics Society in October 1964* (Edinburgh and London, 1965), 51.

[126] *TCBST* 194–5.

fashions were established lower down in society. Men's clothing, eating out, confectionery, holidays, films, bicycles and motorcycles, cosmetics, and records all attracted a markedly above-average share of the teenage budget.[127] American influences were important: James Dean established his image as archetypal moody adolescent rebel with his first major film *East of Eden* (released in 1954). Marlon Brando, with his tougher image, lies behind the 'Teds' of the 1950s, who merged in the 1960s with the motorbiking 'Rockers'. By 1977 the pop singer Elvis Presley was so important to his decidedly middle-aged fans that even *The Times* devoted a leader to his death, and pronounced the BBC's breaking into its programme schedule to announce it as 'not inappropriate'.[128] Commercial pressures shifted the teenage frontier to ever-younger ages, and boys eagerly substituted long trousers for short. The terms 'teenage' and 'teenager' (American in origin) came into widespread use from the mid-1950s, and teenagers in Western industrial societies began to feel that they had more in common with one another than with their parents. Observers comparing Ilford children in 1958 and twelve years earlier found that they had abandoned traditional children's games for activities which they shared with adolescents, and which were promoted in the magazines they were now reading.[129] Hair length and styles grew more varied, causing friction between the generations. Parents had hitherto chosen their children's clothes, often handed down from older children to younger, and often cut-down versions of adult clothes. But now teenagers began to distinguish themselves both from children and from adults by following their own fashions. School uniforms became less formal, were more casually worn, and were sometimes discontinued. The young middle-class male's initiation into a suit, like the opening of a bank account, had been a social indicator and rite of passage, but both lost their symbolism during the 1960s.

Such tendencies threatened organizations for young people, especially those with uniforms and religious links—all the more damagingly because adult volunteers for activity with young people were dwindling. National service had provided a major opportunity for an adult counter-attack in defence of hierarchy and discipline among the young, but the last national serviceman departed in 1963, and with the advent of a smaller professionalized army, young people had less reason to apprentice themselves through structures like the Combined Cadet Force. Youth organizations had long shown imagination in harnessing a youthful taste for adventure, but by the 1960s they had become unfashionable in self-consciously progressive circles.[130] Scouting and Wolf-Cub numbers had risen fast in the UK between the wars, and this growth had resumed in the 1950s,

[127] See M. Abrams, 'The Teenage Consumer', *London Press Exchange Papers*, 5 (July 1959).

[128] 'A Singer of Social Significance', *T* (18 Aug. 1977), 13.

[129] M. Stewart, *The Leisure Activities of School Children* (WEA, n.d.), 5, 22.

[130] e.g. M. Archard, 'Cold Showers and Unfurling the Flag', *Evening Standard* (20 July 1967), 8; N. Mackenzie, 'Sweating it out with B-P', *NS* (15 Oct. 1965), 555. See also below, pp. 486–7.

but recruitment declined in the 1960s and merely stabilized thereafter. The pattern was rather similar for Brownie and Girl Guide membership, but their decline began rather later, in the 1980s—though in 1990 the Scouts and Guides could still jointly attract 1,366,000 members. The Outward Bound movement also grew fast in the 1950s but retrenched thereafter. Youth organizations such as the Boys' Brigade and the Combined Cadet Force with more directly religious and military connections had never attracted such numbers, and by the 1960s their growth rate was slowing down.[131]

A further problem long dormant for youth organizations (as well as for single-sex schools) surfaced from the 1960s: the fear that adults would abuse children sexually. This concern fuelled debate in the 1990s about the boundary line delimiting adolescent from adult, but of more immediate concern before 1970 was regulation of the child's sexuality, one among three areas in the 1960s where the child's status became a political issue. Michael Schofield brought ample evidence and a calming tone to such debate. Outlining in 1952 the lack of alternative sexual outlets for teenage boys, he felt that adults fussed unduly about the sexual activity that they misinterpreted as homosexual.[132] Praising Kinsey in his pioneering *Sexual Behavior of Young People* (1965), Schofield emphasized that men under 20 were at their peak of sexual potential; indeed, given the constraints, it was, he thought, surprising that the young did not embrace premarital intercourse more energetically.[133] The Wolfenden Committee's open-mindedness did not extend this far. It cited the unanimity of medical witnesses that sexual orientation is determined by the age of 16, but was led to recommend 21 as the age of consent (implemented by the Act of 1967) because of its concern for what public opinion would accept, given the widespread belief that boys' sexual orientation was not determined until well after 16, and that homosexuals were weak-willed and predatory.

Discipline made the child of some political interest. Parental discipline over children in 1951 could still be harsh: two-thirds of mothers surveyed in 1958 said they smacked even their one-year-old children, let alone older ones,[134] and many parents still wielded canes. Michael Croft's best-selling novel *Spare the Rod* (1954, filmed in 1961) marks a stage in corporal punishment's prolonged late twentieth-century retreat. The novel vividly describes how a new teacher, John Sanders, surrounded by disillusioned colleagues, struggled in vain against the practice and, after embarrassing the regime by publicly deterring a colleague from inflicting an unjust punishment, was encouraged to move to a better and cane-free school. In Ken Loach's film *Kes* (1969) the cane still features—in a memorably brutal scene involving Mr Gryce,

131 Table 17.20 in *TCBST* 612–13.

132 'G. Westwood', *Society and the Homosexual* (1952), 159–60, 174,

133 Schofield, *Sexual Behaviour of Young People*, 14, 253–4.

134 J. and E. Newson, *The Extent of Parental Physical Punishment in the UK* (1989), 1.

the bullying headmaster at Billy Casper's state secondary school—and with no conviction that it would do any good. On this issue Conservatives after 1951 went along with conservative pressure from the teachers' unions, and a Gallup poll of 1967 suggests that the parents backed the teachers: 70 per cent wanted the cane retained and 81 per cent 'believed in' parents slapping their children.[135] Here, as elsewhere, humanitarian causes benefited at least indirectly from a Labour government's advent, and in 1967 corporal punishment was discontinued in prisons and borstals. In the same year the Plowden report on primary schools opposed recognizing any independent school which authorized beating children. Savage beatings of boys at the Court Lees approved school, publicized in 1967, roused opinion further: the school was closed and canings in such schools halved during the following year.[136] Children in care were now being more frequently entrusted to foster-parents,[137] and in 1971 the Inner London Education Authority committed itself to banning the cane in London's maintained primary schools from January 1973. More importantly, the overall trend in schools had long been shifting towards making education more enjoyable. Earnest late-twentieth-century parents carried these attitudes into the home by purchasing educational toys along the lines that the Abbatts had introduced in the 1930s;[138] to cater for them, toyshops in some towns were by the 1970s becoming 'early learning centres'.

Children benefited from the growing international preoccupation in the 1960s with civil rights, and from the advancing notion that children were rational enough to be at least consulted. The state moved only slowly from paternalist protection to extending rights to the child, especially against parents. The nearest approach to the latter was to lower the age of majority to 18. In recommending this, the Latey Committee (1965–7) was influenced by young people's greater knowledge and experience, and by earlier physical maturity; the media, part-time work, and wider travel now made them much better informed. Also influential with the Committee was the fact that 18 was the qualifying age for many activities, including liability for conscripted military service, full national insurance contribution, eligibility to drink in public, and access to a vehicle licence.[139] The Labour government helped to defeat a House of Lords attempt in 1968 to retain 21 as the age beyond which parents' consent to marriage was no longer required, and in the following year Labour Party support for enfranchising all at 18 (accumulating at least since 1959[140]) at last bore fruit.

135 *Gallup Polls*, ii. 946 (Sept. 1967).

136 P. Newell (ed.), *A Last Resort? Corporal Punishment in Schools* (Harmondsworth, 1972), 31–2.

137 *TBS* 378, 388.

138 Obituary of Marjorie Abbatt (1899–1991), *Ind.* (13 Nov. 1991), 27.

139 [Latey] Committee on the Age of Majority, *Report* (Cmnd. 3342, 1967), 40, 161–4.

140 Hansard Society, *Parliamentary Reform: A Survey of Recent Proposals for the Commons* (1st publ. 1961, 2nd edn. 1967), 1.

4. A WELFARE CONSENSUS

Adapting as best it could to these remarkable and spontaneous changes, Britain's mid-century welfare structure faced ineluctably rising expenditure, given that demographic trends delivered ever larger numbers into categories which earlier generations had decided were eligible for benefit: prior commitments must be honoured whichever party was in government. In most countries, social-security systems 'mature', in that more people become eligible for welfare schemes already established, and precedents are established for future expenditure.[141] The trend operated in all industrial societies. Indeed, if total welfare expenditure is taken into account, most West European countries spent more than Britain in the 1950s and 1960s; in the 1960s they also devoted more of their gross national product to social-services expenditure, and their social-security benefits bore a higher ratio to average earnings.[142] In Britain in the 1950s and 1960s the baby boom raised the 'dependency ratio' (persons under 15 and over 65 expressed as a ratio of those aged between 15 and 64) slightly at the younger end, while longer life and the ageing of the pre-birth-control generations also raised it at the older end to levels far higher than between the wars, though the ratio was still in 1971 lower than in child-abundant mid-Victorian Britain.[143] Reinforcing all this were continuously rising expectations, regardless of what the economy could afford, most notably in education, whose spontaneous take-up was advancing into the sixth form and beyond. Because sociologists from the 1950s were concerned to prevent social exclusion, and thus to define poverty in relative terms, there were pressures for benefits to rise in parallel with overall incomes rather than in relation to Beveridge's objective individual need. So total expenditure on social-security benefits rose in real terms, regardless of the party in power: from 0.6 per cent of the UK's gross national product in 1910 to 5.6 per cent in 1950 to 8.8 per cent in 1970. The share of government grants (often for welfare) in total local-authority expenditure rose from 13 per cent in 1910 to 35 per cent in 1950 to 36 per cent in 1970.[144]

Welfare expenditure helped to ensure that taxation absorbed a growing proportion of Britain's gross national product, despite the latter's massive increase since the 1860s. People were increasingly willing to claim their benefits, and the middle classes were at least as alert to their interests here as elsewhere: in seizing educational opportunity, for instance, their children were in the forefront.[145] The Attlee governments were committed simultaneously to paying old-age pensions and national insurance commitments as of right without

[141] H. L. Wilensky, *The Welfare State and Equality: Structural and Ideological Roots of Public Expenditures* (Berkeley, Calif., 1975), 10.

[142] Harris, 'Enterprise and Welfare States', 180–2. See tables 8–9 in Sleeman, *Welfare State*, 136, 138.

[143] Coleman and Salt, *British Population*, 544, and see the interesting table in Moroney, *Family and State*, 20.

[144] Rose, 'Class and Party Divisions', 156. *BST* 501. *BPF* (8th edn.), 474.

[145] See the useful discussion in Townsend, *Poverty in UK*, 155–60, 221–2.

means-testing, and at levels higher than the Beveridge scheme envisaged; because the scheme's requirement for contributions was not acted upon, there was throughout the 1950s and 1960s an ongoing taxpayer subsidy of pensions and of means-tested supplementary national-assistance benefits. Beveridge had strongly opposed what he called 'the Santa Claus state': he favoured state machinery only as a way to encourage self-provision, and preferred the concept of the 'social service state' to 'welfare state', yet by 1981 an eighth of the population were receiving means-tested relief.[146] Meanwhile, the more prosperous were through their own and employers' contributions supplementing the state pension with an insurance-based occupational earnings-related pension; so powerful was its impact by the 1960s that any earnings-related state substitute had already become politically impossible.

Labour's economic planning and public-welfare measures assumed the continuance of citizen initiative: 'we must have an active democracy in this country', said Morrison in 1948, 'and we must whip up our citizens to their responsibilities just as we canvass them in elections or just as the air-raid wardens did in the war'.[147] The middle classes were active in the many organized groups with an altruistic but also often direct interest in public welfare. Whereas the Victorian volunteer often aimed to supplant the state, his twentieth-century successor tended rather to skirmish on the welfare state's frontiers in the hope of extending them, sometimes even aiming from the start (as did the birth controllers, for example) for the state to take over. Many professions—teachers, doctors, lawyers, social workers—felt drawn by their daily work into recommending public welfare's further advance. In the 1950s and 1960s the new counselling professions were booming, urged on by Hans Hoxter, a refugee from Nazism.[148] The concept of the marriage counsellor, however, originated in the USA,[149] whose affluence supported psychiatrists, psychoanalysts, and social workers in abundance. In Britain the counselling professions, secular substitutes for the priest, mobilized energetically. Narrowing the welfare focus from social engineering towards needs specific to the individual,[150] they were very labour intensive.

Poverty was rediscovered during the late 1950s, and pressures from without made it a political issue. Its rediscovery owed much to Labour sympathizers who pushed forward the LSE's distinguished tradition of social administration. In *The Poor and the Poorest* (1965), Abel-Smith and Townsend challenged

[146] P. Johnson, 'The Welfare State', in R. Floud and D. McCloskey (eds.), *The Economic History of Britain since 1700*, iii (2nd edn. 1994), 290; cf. Harris, 'Enterprise and Welfare States', 182, 184, 188.

[147] H. Morrison, *The Peaceful Revolution: Speeches* (1949), 51 (18 May 1948 to Labour Party Conference).

[148] 1909–2002, obituary in *T* (28 Nov. 2002), 45.

[149] D. R. Mace, *Marriage Counselling* (1948), 9.

[150] This discussion owes much to Paul Halmos's interesting and somewhat neglected *The Faith of the Counsellors* (1st publ. 1965, 2nd edn. 1978), esp. 6–7, 18, 39, 41, 43, 49, 202.

complacency by showing how poverty persisted despite twenty years of public welfare, especially among the young and the old. Sociology, with the rapidly growing subdiscipline of social administration as its empirical arm, seemed a powerful prop for the planners, especially given the central contribution towards it made by the Labour intellectual Richard Titmuss. By the 1960s poverty was ceasing to be viewed as a single problem, and campaigners against it were tackling its separate dimensions in specialist groups, as well as becoming more adept at handling the media. Thence emerged the Child Poverty Action Group, of whose pressure in the late 1960s Crossman at the Department of Health and Social Security (DHSS) was continuously conscious.[151] Thence also emerged 'Shelter', launched in 1966 on the ample publicity attending Jeremy Sandford's play with a real-life basis, *Cathy Come Home*, directed by Kenneth Loach for the BBC and broadcast that summer. The film made such an impact because it lent a human scale to a generalized campaign for better housing. With voice-overs providing the necessary generalizations and statistics, the film followed Cathy (Carol White) and Reg (Ray Brooks) in their downward path. With a new baby and low income, and then Reg's injury in an accident, they could not afford to buy a house. They moved in with his parents, friction resulted, then a search for rented accommodation. Many landladies would not take babies, and a sequence of evictions from ever-lower-grade accommodation followed for failure to pay the rent, ending on a caravan site. Unsympathetic officialism allowed only Cathy and her two children to occupy its temporary accommodation, so the marriage broke up, Reg drifted away, and the film ended tragically, with a distraught Cathy torn from her young children at a railway station.

The professions provided an interventionist state with ample social information. Supplementing it were the census, royal commissions, government inquiries, and parliamentary select committees. They had been accumulating facts for a century and more, and Britain's well-developed tradition for empirical social investigation has already been discussed.[152] Demographic and actuarial research had been integral to national insurance; Seebohm Rowntree's investigations of poverty lay behind the Beveridge report in 1942; and the Royal Commission on Population set a new standard of research in this genre when published in 1949. Royal commissions were not normally so professional, however, and by the 1950s the departmental or inter-departmental committee had become a more regular resort; as for the reports of parliament's select committees, they seemed amateur by comparison, at least until the committees were reformed in 1979. In 1951 the census's punch-card techniques

[151] *Cabinet Diaries*, iii. 140 (16 July 1968), 791 (27 Jan. 1970), 809 (8 Feb. 1970), 888 (16 Apr. 1970).

[152] See above, pp. 176–7. For a longer-term perspective, see B. Harrison, 'Finding Out How the Other Half Live: Social Research and British Government since 1780', in B. Harrison, *Peaceable Kingdom: Stability and Change in Modern Britain* (Oxford, 1982), 260–308.

did not represent much advance over 1931, but in 1961 the main operations were processed by electronic computer, the IBM 705 system used by the Royal Army Pay Corps, and more questions were included. Inexperience with the new methods, together with the need to answer planners' numerous questions, at first delayed publication, but better computing technology improved matters in 1971 and 1981, and users' requirements were better catered for.[153]

In the 1950s and 1960s the academic study of sociology grew so fast and interacted so well with the computer's new facilities that high hopes of governmental 'planning' seemed justified. By the 1950s demography had become integral to school-building and pensions policy, as was educational sociology to educational policy: sociologists of education increasingly alerted the Labour Party in the 1950s to education's role in perpetuating class barriers. Statistical awareness was markedly advanced in 1963 by the Robbins report on higher education, whose statistical adviser prepared its unusually informative appendices. Here, as with the Royal Commission on Population in 1949, the LSE's 'political arithmetic' was enhancing the quality of public debate. In Oxford H. A. Clegg and A. Flanders were establishing the systematic study of industrial relations. Empirical in outlook and keen to guide government towards planning wages and full employment on foundations laid by G. D. H. Cole, they aligned themselves with progressive employers, trade unions, and the Ministry of Labour. Social information advanced most strikingly in opinion polling. Its techniques had evolved through the Anglo-American interwar market survey, and its acceptance in Britain owed much to the wartime coalition government's urgent need to gauge morale—whence sprang the career of the survey's leading practitioner Mark Abrams, who founded Research Services in 1946. The opinion survey was integral to a democratic society: its politicians needed continuous guidance between elections on voters' wishes, especially when increasingly interventionist governments required substitutes for or supplements to the information provided by the free market. Labour governments were particularly keen to harness universities to government, and in the 1960s the party needed the economists' help in its ambitious schemes for planning the economy. Econometrics seemed integral in the 1950s to shaping economic policy: at a time when inflation and unemployment were low and oil prices relatively stable, fiscal devices held out high hopes of fine tuning the economy. In such matters the Treasury was more practised than the Germans and Americans.[154] In Harold Wilson, Labour prime minister from 1964, Britain

[153] This paragraph is based on General Register Office, *Census 1951: England and Wales. General Report* (1958); General Register Offices, London and Edinburgh, *Census 1961 Great Britain: General Report* (1968); Office of Population Censuses and Surveys, *Census 1971 England and Wales: General Report*, part 2. *Administration, Fieldwork, Processing* (1983). See also P. Redfern's letter in *T* (10 Jan. 1975), 15.

[154] S. Brittan, *Steering the Economy* (1989), 313.

was led by a statistician whom Beveridge had trained, and who in 1970 became president of the Royal Statistical Society.

On forming his government Wilson aimed to supplant Conservative amateurism with the new professionalism of socialist planning. A sudden influx of economists arrived in Whitehall, and all this culminated in the so-called 'National Plan' of 1965. The Plan's failure[155] did not halt the process. In 1965 a new 'economist class' of administrative-grade civil servants was established, and in the subsequent ten years employees in the government economic service grew from 42 to 317. The number of government statisticians rose from 175 in 1966 to 315 in 1970, distributed widely through the civil service.[156] In 1967 Wilson appointed Moser director of the Central Statistical Office, and from then until 1978 as head of the government statistical service he greatly improved the government's information,[157] though when ministers pressed Moser to massage the content of statistics or the timing of their presentation, he refused.[158] The aim was to integrate statistical information into a single framework, emphasizing speed and accessibility of information as much as quantity. Statistics would henceforth be systematically generated instead of arising as an incidental by-product of administration. With *Economic Trends* (1953–) as the model, the *Abstract of Regional Statistics* (1965–), *Trends in Education* (1966–), and *Social Trends* (1970–) sprang up to improve access. The amalgamation in 1970 of the General Register Office for England and Wales with the government social survey at last embedded the census within a coherent and continuous government machine for collecting population data. What with this and the General Household Survey (launched in 1973), the needs of several government departments for information between censuses were met simultaneously. Graphs and statistics entered into public debate as never before. Investigating British society in 1962, Sampson noted how the prewar research institutes, supplemented by the Institute for Strategic Studies (founded in 1958) had evolved into 'a kind of shadow civil service', monitoring the Foreign Office, the Treasury, and the ministries of Defence and Education.[159] The routine publication of statistics influenced almost every election campaign from the 1950s onwards. By making balance of payments statistics the test of his government's achievement, Wilson during the campaign of 1970 unintentionally ensured that when unfavourable statistics unexpectedly appeared, the maximum amount of damage was done.[160] This powerful machinery culminated after 1965 in the

[155] See below, pp. 310–11. [156] *T* (24 Nov. 1975), 1. *Econ.* (19 Dec. 1970), 24.

[157] For its progress see e.g. *T* (23 May 1968), 26; *G* (13 Nov. 1969), 15.

[158] Jenkins, *Life at the Centre*, 299–300. *STel.* (11 Dec. 1988), 8.

[159] A. Sampson, *Anatomy of Britain* (1962), 242–3.

[160] D. E. Butler and D. Kavanagh, *The British General Election of October 1974* (1975), 110. For the 1970 general election see Crossman's remarks in the Radio 4 broadcast about the election on 15 Apr. 1971.

Prices and Incomes Board's formidable engine; its inquiries by the time it was disbanded in 1970 had covered 18 million people, three-quarters of the workforce,[161] and it pioneered systematic and regular surveys of earnings.

None the less, the 1960s revealed the severe limits to what planning and the associated collection of information could achieve, and never subsequently have social statistics aroused such enthusiasm. Even at the time there was significant resistance. We have already seen[162] how dissatisfied was Crossman in 1968 with the statistics on immigration and emigration. He hoped for much from the census's new questions in 1971,[163] but the ethnic minorities were uncooperative, nor was participation universal elsewhere. In that year 3,675 households refused to cooperate with the census and the refusal rate was rising: from 0.003 per cent of all households in 1961 to 0.022 per cent in 1971 to 0.03 per cent in 1981.[164] The tension between a thirst for more information and a fear of antagonizing informants had never been absent from the social investigator's mind, but 'statistical fatigue' resulted from the mounting number of market surveys and opinion polls, and the sheer difficulty of empirical sociology's interventionist aims was becoming apparent.

There were problems still more serious. This elaborate planning structure was expensive, and in the 1960s nourished a distaste for paying taxes which often took the form of opposing subsidies for the undeserving. When in 1964 and 1968 Gallup asked people to choose between 'lack of effort on his part' and 'circumstances beyond his control' in explaining a person's poverty, the answers were roughly divided three ways, between these two options and 'both equally'.[165] Devices for fending off higher taxes included charging for teeth and spectacles, introduced by the Labour government in 1951, and prescription charges introduced by the Conservatives, then abolished in 1964 by Labour, only to be restored by Labour in 1968. They also included failing to update old plant, so that public welfare began to conjure up a seedy image very different from the smart and colourful premises of commercial firms keen to attract custom. There were Victorian poor-law hospitals, run-down post offices, and the sort of supplementary benefit office which Crossman observed in the roughest part of Manchester during 1968, where 'the seats had been slashed to pieces by the toughs and there was a smell of the slum'.[166] It was with good reason, too, that the poor had long been wary of officials, if only because their lower ranks often felt threatened socially or in other ways by the claimant, and showed it. The attempt to limit costs through comprehensively restructuring

[161] A. Fels, *The British Prices and Incomes Board* (Cambridge, 1972), 39.

[162] Above, p. 222. [163] *Cabinet Diaries*, iii. 38–9 (1 May 1968), cf. 589–90 (23 July 1969).

[164] Office of Population Censuses and Surveys, *Census 1971 England and Wales: General Report*, part 2. *Administration, Fieldwork, Processing* (1983), 57–8. *Census 1981: General Report. England and Wales* (1990), 35.

[165] *Gallup Polls*, i. 740; ii. 1014.

[166] *Cabinet Diaries*, iii. 212 (4 Oct. 1968).

welfare services was foreshadowed by Crossman at the DHSS in the late 1960s, but was not seriously attempted till the 1980s. It was 'not good enough', he declared in 1970, 'simply to pour extra money into the national health service with its present organization unchanged'.[167]

Criticism of welfare structures as they were in the 1960s also came from privatizers on the right, and their influence grew from the 1970s onwards. But voluntarism was also gaining ground on the left. Labour was alert to charity's capricious and even quirky priorities, and had for decades dismissed volunteering and self-help as reflecting misdirected religiosity and outworn attitudes to social class. Yet volunteering was more integral to effective social welfare than had been envisaged, for the volunteer is adaptable and cheap. A public welfare starved of voluntary input would be clumsy, introverted, and unenterprising. The WVS, for example, launched its meals-on-wheels to deal with an emergency in Welwyn Garden City, and legislation in 1946 and 1948 authorized local authorities to promote such schemes. By June 1960 the WVS was delivering 88 per cent of the total, and between 1958 and 1976 its delivered meals rose from 1.4 to 13.5 million a year.[168] Crossman at the DHSS in the late 1960s was impressed with the scale of voluntary provision in the social services, but also with the need for more,[169] given that by 1969 he thought universal welfare provision could be funded 'only . . . if we have an enormous amount of community and voluntary organization'.[170] He found Whitehall unenthusiastic,[171] but came to see the volunteer as offering a less regimented, more flexible, and more resourceful route to welfare, and preached the new gospel in his lecture on *The Role of the Volunteer in the Modern Social Service* (1973). The volunteer might seek more public funding, but a state-run monolith was neither Crossman's nor the volunteer's objective.

Such attitudes geared in well with the American preoccupation with civil rights and avoidance of discrimination, then newly fashionable in Britain, and some volunteers were important in the 1960s for criticizing or even superseding institutionalized welfare. Aided by new drugs and new ideas in psychiatry and geriatric medicine, voluntarism was integral to getting the institutionalized back into their homes and to encouraging self-help groups, fostering their members' self-confidence, and mobilizing public concern. The subordination of ends to means and the growth of institutional self-interest in large state-run concerns

[167] *T* (24 Mar. 1970), 8.

[168] K. B. Beauman, *Green Sleeves: The Story of the WVS/WRVS* (1977), 63–4, 67, 71, 74.

[169] See his comments in *T* (8 Aug. 1973), 14.

[170] *Cabinet Diaries*, iii. 433 (9 Apr. 1969); cf. 848 (8 Mar. 1970).

[171] Crossman, *Cabinet Diaries*, iii. 67 (17 May 1968), 433 (9 Apr. 1969), 848 (8 Mar. 1970). See also his 'The Role of the Volunteer in the Modern Social Service', in A. H. Halsey (ed.), *Traditions of Social Policy: Essays in Honour of Violet Butler* (Oxford, 1976), 259–85.

could be challenged only from outside in a sequence of highly damaging mid- and late-twentieth century reports on hospitals, asylums, care homes, and prisons. Crossman at the DHSS, for example, was much worried in 1969 by 'the terrible danger to us' from Barbara Robb's *Sans Everything*, which exposed inhumane treatment in hospitals.[172]

Voluntarism prompted new disadvantaged groups—even new categories of citizen, seeking a more complete involvement in society—continuously to reveal themselves. The visually impaired had been early among these because themselves so visible. Between 1900 and 1950 people over 70 contributed a growing proportion of the blind, nearly half in 1951, but they benefited considerably from the cataract operations pioneered against medical opposition by Sir Harold Ridley[173] after 1949; by the 1970s the operation had become routine, and useful as a palliative were the large-print books that by the 1960s were being widely distributed. Less easy to identify were mentally handicapped people who looked normal. Not until 1943 was autism first diagnosed in the USA, and not until about 1960 was the National Society for Autistic Children founded. By 1970 about 5,000 autistic children had been identified in England and Wales, and while it was agreed that subnormality hospitals were inappropriate, it was not always clear where else the children should go, nor was there agreement on whether educational segregation was best.[174] Socially less damaging but educationally a major hindrance was dyslexia. Research into the problem was pioneered in Britain and took off in America; by 1964, when Macdonald Critchley published his *Developmental Dyslexias*, the numbers in Britain who questioned the concept were dwindling—so much so, that the British Dyslexia Association came into being in 1972.

From the 1960s the disabled, the deaf, the blind, the autistic, the dyslexic, and many who suffered from specific diseases were encouraged to pool their expertise and mobilize for self-defence in specialist organizations that raised participation to a new plane. Townsend became a one-man campaigner for and theorist about defending these newly perceived minorities, by no means all in public institutions. Late-twentieth-century disability in Britain owed less to war and more to the growing number of old people and to modern medicine's capacity to keep people alive. But disability is also a social and political category, and what the volunteers achieved was to advertise disability's sheer extent[175] and to cultivate in the disabled self-awareness and self-confidence. In a society increasingly preoccupied with perfecting health and physique, this was not easy; the disabled had to focus simultaneously on improving public facilities

[172] *Cabinet Diaries*, iii. 727 (12 Nov. 1969), cf. 859 (16 Mar. 1970).

[173] A. Sorsby, *The Causes of Blindness in England* (1953), 25. For Ridley see obituaries in *T* (29 May 2002), 15; *G* (29 May 2001), 23.

[174] *HL Deb.* 17 Feb. 1970, c. 1115.

[175] For their number see P. Townsend, *The Disabled in Society* (1967), 1.

and on changing people's attitude to disability. It was important to prevent disability from being seen as the central ingredient of personality: hence the importance of name changes. By the 1960s the once familiar noun 'incurable' had long been abandoned, and 'disabled' had ousted the word 'crippled'; for similar reasons the Royal National Institute for the Deaf was renamed 'Royal National Institute for Deaf People' in 1992. A balance had also to be struck between on the one hand encouraging the disabled to mobilize in mutual association, and on the other hand to integrate with society at large by moving about more freely. Would disabled children do better, for instance, if educated separately or if merged with others in their age group? Self-help for adults was increasingly encouraged through home help, and through access to the many gadgets that medical engineering, one of medicine's growth points in the 1960s, was making available—gadgets quite disproportionately beneficial in relation to their cost. Many firms with twenty or more employees were not meeting their statutory obligation to assign 3 per cent of their jobs to the disabled, yet by 1983 there had been only ten prosecutions under the statute of 1944.[176] Should access to public facilities and jobs therefore be widened? Welfare's claims on the taxpayer were greater even than this, for the major impulse to welfare expenditure has yet to be discussed: the ever-growing claims of medicine.

5. NATIONAL HEALTH TRIUMPHANT?

Britain's welfare structure in its health dimension after 1951 needed to accommodate notable changes in family structure, but also unpredictable and worldwide shifts in medical advance and in the virulence of disease. Influenza's long-term undulating decline since 1919 seems to reflect declining virulence,[177] and by 1951 new drugs and vaccines had prompted a therapeutic revolution which sent other infectious diseases into retreat. There was a striking decline in diphtheria from 1940 and in paralytic polio after the mass immunization of the mid-1950s.[178] Between 1948 and 1958 annual deaths in Great Britain from tuberculosis fell from 25,000 to 5,000, and patients no longer went for treatment to Swiss sanatoria.[179] In 1951 the notification rate in England and Wales for scarlet fever, measles, typhoid, and tuberculosis was already falling, and by 1970 had fallen much further; in the same period whooping cough's notification rate declined by nine-tenths. The 1950s also saw venereal diseases in marked decline, with the long-dreaded syphilis almost disappearing (in 1992

[176] Townsend, *Disabled in Society*, 15, 18; John Hannam, *HC Deb.* 11 Feb. 1983, c. 1251.

[177] Sir R. Doll, 'Major Epidemics of the Twentieth Century', *Journal of the Royal Statistical Society*, series A, 105 (1987), 388–9.

[178] See the graphs in I. Loudon *et al.* (eds.), *General Practice under the NHS* (Oxford, 1998), 300.

[179] Webster, *Health Services since the War*, ii. 22.

there was only one case), though changes in sexual conduct later slowed the waning of gonorrhoea.[180]

These remarkable improvements enhanced the image of the doctor and the NHS, but the diseases and disabilities that became more salient within an ageing population—most notably cancer and bronchial and heart diseases—were more tenacious.[181] The statistics showing a rising death rate from cancer (which for men in England and Wales peaked about 1973, and for women continued rising for longer) were inflated by better diagnosis, but there was also a real increase which owed much to previous smoking habits.[182] Deaths from heart disease, too, rose during the 1950s and 1960s but fell in the 1970s, partly reflecting changing fat levels in diet and changing levels of physical exercise.[183] Chronic disease and disability also proved intractable before 1970: in that year half Great Britain's population wore glasses, 94 per cent had shed at least one tooth, and arthritis (the greatest single cause of handicap) affected nearly 200,000 men and nearly 700,000 women.[184] The NHS's introduction had presented dentists with a massive backlog, frequently involving extraction and providing false teeth for quite young people as well as for the old. In the 1960s, however, fluoridation of water was cautiously introduced piecemeal despite critics' libertarian complaints against 'mass medication',[185] and by 1970 seventeen local health authorities covering two million people had adopted it.[186] Thus did preventive dentistry set about improving young teeth, helping to ensure that dental (like ophthalmic) services absorbed a declining proportion of NHS gross expenditure throughout the second half of the twentieth century.[187]

From the 1860s the female mortality rate (adjusted for age differences) improved steadily by comparison with men's, and speeded up markedly in 1900–50.[188] The improvement in women's average expectation of life at age 65 continued between 1950 and 1970, perhaps partly because women more readily consulted doctors,[189] whereas men's marginally worsened.[190] The continued spread of birth control reduced pregnancies at any one time, but also curbed the illnesses associated with repeated childbirth. Maternal mortality in childbirth fell markedly—from 1.01 per thousand births in 1949 to 0.18 in 1970—and the perinatal mortality rate fell from 38.2 per thousand live births in 1948 to

[180] M. Adler *et al.*, *The Health of Adult Britain 1941–1994* (1997), ii. 22–4.

[181] For the contrasting trends see the table in Loudon *et al.* (eds.), *General Practice*, 290.

[182] Doll, 'Major Epidemics', 377–8. [183] Ibid. 381, 384.

[184] A. I. Harris, *Handicapped and Impaired in Great Britain* (1971), 2, 9.

[185] e.g. from Lord Douglas of Barloch, *HL Deb.* 26 Jan. 1966, cc. 84, 98.

[186] Webster, *Health Services since the War*, ii. 242.

[187] For useful figures, see table C1 in Loudon *et al.* (eds.), *General Practice*, 302.

[188] W. J. Martin, 'A Comparison of the Trends of Male and Female Mortality', *Transactions of the Royal Statistical Society*, series A, 114 (1951), 296.

[189] T. McKeown and C. R. Lowe, *An Introduction to Social Medicine* (2nd edn. Oxford, 1974), 72. For consultation rates see A. Carr-Saunders *et al.*, *A. Survey of Social Conditions in England and Wales* (Oxford, 1958), 235.

[190] Townsend, *Poverty in UK*, 797, cf. 172.

28.2 in 1964.[191] The interwar trend towards medicalizing childbirth continued in these years, and by 1980 in England and Wales only 1.3 per cent of babies were born at home.[192] Doctors' attitudes to female patients were also changing. Professor Norman Morris at Charing Cross Hospital from 1958 pioneered a less authoritarian attitude to women in childbirth, for example. He was the first obstetrician to allow husbands to attend the birth of their children, and introduced many other changes to moderate women's fears of childbirth,[193] as well as braving much controversy by successfully challenging the need for such frequent hysterectomies.[194] Birth control generated an unprecedented succession of menstrual cycles during the twentieth-century European woman's reproductive life; had these countries not been affluent, serious iron deficiency would have resulted. In Britain after 1951 women's image as the 'weaker sex', so integral to the Victorian anti-feminist case, was becoming suspect, and still more so were the political conclusions drawn from it. Women's emancipation did not bring undiluted health benefits: although women remained less liable than men to accidents of all types, even within the home, their growing mobility ensured that their proportion of deaths in road accidents rose steadily throughout the twentieth century; by 1967 it had reached 30 per cent.[195]

'Extraordinary thing about the lower classes in England', said Lord Goring in Wilde's *Ideal Husband*: '—they are always losing their relations'.[196] After 1951 marked social-class inequalities in life chances persisted. Death from bronchitis and tuberculosis in 1949–53 was more likely lower down in society than higher up, and class differentials in mortality from disease actually widened after the NHS was established.[197] Manual labour's retreat moderated class contrasts in health after 1951:[198] occupational hazards in marked decline were noise (boilermaker's ear), the lifting of heavy weights (hernia), air pollution (bronchitis), and accidents. The decline in fishing and agriculture also diminished the health problems resulting from outdoor work. By no means all the new occupations after 1951, though, were desk-bound. When BP's drilling rig 'Sea Gem' capsized in rough weather on 27 December 1965, for example, thirteen men died; only three months earlier, rig and crew had made the first gas strike in the North Sea.[199]

191 Dept of Health and Social Security, *Health and Personal Social Services Statistics for England 1977* (1977), 13. C. Webster, *The National Health Service: A Political History* (Oxford, 1998), 136.

192 V. Berridge *et al.*, 'Mobilisation for Total Welfare, 1948 to 1974', in Webster (ed.), *Caring for Health* (3rd edn.), 181–2.

193 N. Morris, 'Human Relations in Obstetric Practice', *Lancet* (23 Apr. 1960), 913–15, and controversy throughout the May issues.

194 Obituary, *DT* (11 Mar. 2008), 23.

195 *Econ.* (4 Jan. 1975), 60. P. E. H. Hair, 'Deaths from Violence in Britain: A Tentative Secular Survey', *Population Studies* (Mar. 1971), 9.

196 *The Works of Oscar Wilde*, ed. G. F. Maine (1948), 508.

197 *BST* 418–25. P. Johnson 'Welfare State', 308–9.

198 *BST* 418–21.

199 B. Cooper and T. F. Gaskell, *The Adventure of North Sea Oil* (1976), 10.

NHS staff doubled between 1948 and 1979 to reach more than a million. The ratio of nurses and doctors to population in England and Wales, already rising fast earlier in the century, rose further still after 1951, and the number of university students in Britain studying medicine and dentistry doubled between 1950/1 and 1980/1.[200] Although between 1949 and 1969 the ratio of general practitioners to population was static, the ratio of medical and dental personnel in hospitals to population rose by 74 per cent and of nurses by 70 per cent.[201] The number of child-welfare clinics rose steadily in England and Wales from the 1920s to the 1960s, as did the number of health visitors and the proportion of children in local-authority schools receiving milk and school meals.[202] What had become an inverse relationship between concern with physical and spiritual health is reflected in the inverse relationship between the numbers employed in medicine and in (Protestant) religion.[203] After the 1950s Christian Science was increasingly redundant as a halfway house between the two: its practitioners dwindled by a third between 1951 and 1970.[204]

The NHS's creators, when estimating its likely cost, assumed that prewar trends would persist, with costs falling as the population grew healthier and more health-conscious. Yet ill-health did not passively await its erosion by preventive measures, better nutrition, and more efficient health care: its demands on the NHS proved dynamic, even insatiable. With each new drug, each new piece of equipment, expectations rose further. The NHS's therapeutic revolution unpredictably escalated prescription costs, especially as the newer drugs were relatively expensive,[205] and new and often costly treatments proliferated. In 1948 one antibiotic was available: thirty-three in 1968. In 1948 there was no effective drug therapy for hypertension or mental depression: in 1968 there were fifteen antihypertensives and eighteen antidepressants.[206] Urging on the process were yet more pressure groups, their moral authority flowing from their altruistic attack on suffering: the Spastics Society, for example, founded in 1952 by Ian Dawson-Shepherd, his first child born with cerebral palsy; or Mencap, founded by Judy Fryd, whose autistic child could find no school. There was even a 'technological imperative' at work, whereby medical equipment was developed, sales were pushed, the doctor's scientific pretensions were harnessed, the equipment was bought, and it had then to demonstrate its worth.[207]

[200] C. Webster, *The National Health Service: A Political History* (Oxford, 1998), 112. *TBS* 326, 353. Table 7.17 in *BST* 293.

[201] *TCBST* 114.

[202] *TBS* 396, 399. See also B. Harris, *The Health of the Schoolchild* (Buckingham, 1995), 197.

[203] For statistics see *BST*, 452, 525.

[204] R. Currie, A. Gilbert, and L.Horsley, *Churches and Churchgoers: Patterns of Church Growth in the British Isles since 1700* (Oxford, 1977), 210–11.

[205] See Loudon *et al.* (eds.), *General Practice*, 305, for statistics.

[206] Webster, *Health Services since the War*, ii. 754.

[207] I. Kennedy, *The Unmasking of Medicine* (1981), 143–4.

During its first ten years the NHS came to be accepted as a national institution, even a national treasure.[208] Major economies of scale had been expected from it, yet in the haste and confusion of its creation, with a backlog so large and the Ministry of Health so lacking in leadership during the 1950s, the desired coordination and rationalization—let alone sustained planning—proved elusive.[209] The NHS's cost rose more slowly than in several other industrialized countries,[210] but in the UK this did not prevent it almost doubling between 1950 and 1970 in real terms; and whereas in 1950/1 the NHS took 4.1 per cent of gross national product, by 1970/1 it took 4.8 per cent. Though health's share of total public expenditure was falling slowly, social security's demands remained at a plateau during these years and education's steadily rose.[211] The British system whereby the state provided health care directly was unique until 1969, though Sweden, Italy, and Spain later adopted it. Theoretical alternatives elsewhere were to base health care on state-subsidized private insurance, or on a national insurance scheme funded by compulsory levy.[212] In practice the NHS had no option but to evolve pragmatically: there was no significant demand even from the Conservatives for significant structural change, nor was there time to consider it. So in the 1960s the easiest and in the short term the most effective approach was adopted: to continue on the existing basis, somewhat reorganized at the margins, adapting the old structures to the new framework, the old buildings to their new purposes. Fully planned reallocation of resources between different aspects of medicine or between regions was impossible.[213]

This did not preclude substantial changes. Until the advance of health statistics and the double-blind trial in the 1940s, medicine had been regarded as art rather than science, and hospitals had been only loosely associated with universities. General practitioners were expected to know their patients in the round, and hospitals then relatively small collaborated closely with them to provide treatment locally. Between 1948 and 1965 the 'cottage hospitals' waned from 2,800 to 2,500,[214] however, reflecting the NHS's main thrust: away from the general practitioner and public health through the local authority, and towards centralization and specialization through the large general hospital. A coordinated system of regional teaching and research hospitals aimed to create centres of excellence which would promote hi-tech medicine nationwide.[215] Universities and hospitals drew closer, and clinical medicine was harnessed

[208] Webster, *Health Services since the War*, ii. 2–4.

[209] On this see C. Webster, *The Health Services since the War*, i. *Problems of Health Care: The National Health Service before 1957* (1988), 393–4; *The Health Services since the War*, ii. 27–9, 766–7.

[210] See figure C2 in Loudon *et al.* (eds.), *General Practice*, 303.

[211] Apps. 3.2, 3.3, and 3.4 in Webster, *Health Services since the War*, ii. 802–3.

[212] See the useful discussion in Webster, *NHS: A Political History*, 1.

[213] For more on this see Webster, *Health Services since the War*, i. 292–3, 296; ii. 8–9, 23, 26, 766–7; *NHS: A Political History*, 57.

[214] Loudon *et al.* (eds.), *General Practice*, 124–5.

[215] Webster, *NHS: A Political History*, 38–9.

more closely to medical progress. Benefiting most from this expansion in the 1950s were the new surgical specialities and the hitherto ill-developed medical specialisms such as anaesthetics and pathology; the number of radiographers, medical lab technicians, and pharmacists within the NHS grew fast. This structure could boast many trophies, including the first successful organ transplant in the UK: on 20 October 1960 Michael Woodruff, Professor of Surgery at Edinburgh University, conducted a kidney transplant between twins.[216]

General practitioners were pushed out of the hospitals into their consulting rooms. They lacked the medical prestige that increasingly flowed from research, and were at risk of becoming mere gatekeepers allocating admission to hospital-based treatment. Whereas between 1950 and 1970 the hospitals' share of NHS gross expenditure rose from 55 to 65 per cent, the general-practitioner services' share fell from 10 to 9 per cent, and community health services from 8 to 7 per cent.[217] The number of hospital doctors doubled, overtaking the (static) number of general practitioners and far outnumbering the (static) number of doctors in community health services.[218] The Medical Officer of Health's local role went into decline: in 1948 he lost control of the municipal hospital, and his links with the general practitioner became distant and even somewhat fraught. When the health centre modestly revived in the 1960s, it was the general practitioner, and not the Medical Officer of Health, who benefited.[219] Hospital out-patient attendance, by contrast, grew slowly in relation to population throughout the second half of the twentieth century.[220]

With the decline in infectious disease, the general practitioner was thrown back on to diseases which could be palliated but not cured. Professionalization depersonalized what he could offer, with home-based consultation less likely, whether the home was his own or the patient's; a purpose-built health centre for the practice seemed more suitable, with consequent decline in the role of the doctor's wife in the practice. Partnerships with colleagues became common, and the percentage of GPs who were single-handed fell from 43 in 1952 to 24 in 1965. Doctors then distanced themselves from patients by employing nurses, receptionists, and other specialists within the practice—and out of hours by setting up duty rotas.[221] The foundation in 1952 of the College of General Practitioners, with its royal charter gained twenty years later, helped to ward off threats to the professional pride of the GP, who even began to reclaim some medical areas ceded to hospitals.[222] This was because the NHS soon lost some

[216] Obituary in *G* (16 Mar. 2001), 20.

[217] Loudon *et al.* (eds.), *General Practice*, 302. See also Webster, *Health Services since the War*, ii. 17. S. Taylor, *Good General Practice: A Report of a Survey* (1954), 530.

[218] For useful statistics see app. 3.29 in Webster, *Health Services since the War*, ii. 828.

[219] See V. Berridge's excellent *Health and Society in Britain since 1939* (Cambridge, 1999), 17, 44.

[220] Fig. D2 in Loudon *et al.* (eds.), *General Practice*, 308.

[221] Ibid. 48, 52, 57–8, 61, 310.

[222] Ibid. 52, 61, 144, 168.

of its early enthusiasm for large specialist hospitals. The tripartite division between hospital specialist, general practitioner, and public-health authority made it difficult to coordinate health-service resources within any one locality,[223] and medical progress was shortening average hospital stay, so that from the 1950s in England and Wales the ratio of hospital beds to population declined; home nursing, home-help services, and hospital out-patient work expanded accordingly.[224] Iain Macleod as Health Minister in 1954 acknowledged that emphasizing the curative side of medicine risked downgrading the preventive and social sides of health care.[225]

In medicine as elsewhere in the late 1960s, the difficulties of controlling and motivating large structures became ever more apparent: 'nobody knows to within thousands how many doctors are at work in this country', Crossman noted in December 1968.[226] Professionalization supplanted or downgraded many of the socio-medical roles voluntarily performed (often by women) within neighbourhood and family, so that dependence and anonymity advanced at the expense of self-reliance and personal care. Beveridge had assumed in 1942 that public welfare would be reinforced by voluntary help at neighbourhood, community, and family levels, and his favoured variant of voluntarism was altruistic. In his first party-political broadcast, Macleod, too, emphasized how important was the NHS's voluntary dimension.[227] A very widespread form of self-help lay in self-medication. A study in the 1950s found that two-thirds of those interviewed took some form of self-prescribed medicine, most commonly swallowing laxatives and aspirins; a survey at the end of the 1960s showed that during the two weeks before the interview 80 per cent of the sample had taken some medicines, two-thirds of them self-prescribed.[228]

The thalidomide tragedy heightened scepticism about the link between the medical profession and medical progress. By the 1960s more people were willing to challenge the doctor's authority. Authoritarian and conservative attitudes still prevailed within hospitals, especially in the relationship between doctors and nurses, but the nurses had a powerful weapon: among the many exposures of NHS abuses during the 1960s it was the marginal people—orderlies, student nurses, and part-timers—who were the whistleblowers. Particularly vulnerable were the long-stay patients in relatively isolated and routinized institutions staffed by self-insulated people in the medical profession's backwaters. So it was in mental health and geriatric medicine that the reaction against institutionalization began.[229] Less complex societies often reserved special roles

[223] Webster, *Health Services since the War*, ii. 322–3.
[224] *TBS* 349, 352, 390–1. [225] N. Fisher, *Iain Macleod* (1973), 335.
[226] *Cabinet Diaries*, iii. 279 (2 Dec. 1968). [227] Fisher, *Macleod*, 93.
[228] Berridge, *Health and Society*, 41.
[229] J. P. Martin, *Hospitals in Trouble* (Oxford, 1984), 82, 87, 245, 247.

within the community for the eccentric, the mentally subnormal, and the very old, but industrial societies tended to put them in institutions—often huge and bleak Victorian buildings whose tall chimneys and water towers seemed slightly sinister when glimpsed from distant locations through the trees. As far as the patients were concerned, it was out of mind out of sight, out of sight out of mind, and they were treated like children.

Their patient numbers reached a peak in the mid-1950s, but then everything began to change: the discovery of the first tranquillizers in 1952 and of the antidepressants in 1960 opened up major new libertarian possibilities. Humane values, new attitudes in psychiatry, and the need to cut costs interacted to ensure that many of the mentally ill could now re-join society—one reason for the declining average length of hospital stay.[230] The Mental Health Act (1959) embodied these attitudes and increased local health authorities' role in caring for the mentally ill. So the number of long-term in-patients at mental hospitals in England and Wales fell sharply between 1954 and 1969.[231] In 1964 Townsend, discussing those who remained, noted how 'ill-fitting and cheaply made hospital clothes hang from human frames which are further derided by clumsy uniform haircuts'.[232] Friern Barnet psychiatric hospital shook Crossman, when at the DHSS, with the stench of the incontinent and the soaking walls; it was, he wrote, 'the worst kind of Dickensian, Victorian loony bin'.[233] He publicized staff cruelty at Ely Mental Hospital, Cardiff, to alert the public about the scale of the problem; this was because he wanted to prepare the ground for shifting funds towards the old and subnormal, while keeping them in hostels or at home where possible.[234] He thought improvement also required a shift in vocabulary. 'One of the things that we could do', he told parliament in 1970, 'is to get rid of the word "subnormality" . . . It is a shocking word . . . We should call these people what they are—mentally handicapped people. They are not subnormal or sub-human or sub anything. They are fellow citizens.'[235]

Crossman was not alone in recognizing the need for public education on health, for further successes in medicine now required lifestyle changes. Television had begun to demystify medicine with fictional serials like *Emergency Ward 10* (1957–67), *Dr Kildare* (1961–6), and *Dr Finlay's Casebook* (1962–71). Also helpful was Dr Gordon Ostlere ('Richard Gordon'), with his humorous *Doctor in the House* (1952) and its many televised successors. Advertisements were by no means always otiose: television's first commercial (on 22 September 1955) for Gibbs SR toothpaste, could hope for much, given that a third

[230] For figures on this see Office of Health Economics, *Compendium of Health Statistics* (2nd edn. 1977), ss. 3, 14.
[231] *T* (2 Sept. 1971), 2. *TBS* 331, 367.
[232] Townsend, *Social Minority*, 135.
[233] T. Dalyell, *Dick Crossman: A Portrait* (1989), 177.
[234] *Cabinet Diaries*, iii. 408–13 (10–13 Mar. 1969), 429 (27 Mar. 1969). Webster, *Health Services since the War*, ii. 741–2.
[235] *HC Deb.* 11 Feb. 1970, c. 1350.

of the British population did not then clean their teeth.[236] The television commercial 'snap, crackle and pop' launched Rice Krispies in the same year, but breakfast's improved fibre intake owed more to haste than to health concern; by the late 1960s ready-cooked cereals had become the staple for weekday breakfast, consigning bacon and eggs to weekends.[237] There was a special role for government education where willpower was involved. In 1950 Richard Doll's epidemiological research exposed the link between smoking and lung cancer, at which time 80 per cent of men between 45 and 75 were smoking.[238] On seeing the results, which had surprised him, Doll at 37 gave up smoking for good.[239] In 1954 his influential article appeared in the *British Medical Journal*, and in 1957 the government launched its steadily broadening campaign against smoking. In 1965 it banned cigarette advertising on television, though this did not deter tobacco companies from the growing practice of sports sponsorship, and from 1972 government required health warnings on cigarette packets. The marked rise in cigarette smoking among men until the 1940s levelled off thereafter until the 1970s and then plunged; women's smoking rose almost continuously till 1970 and then began to fall.[240]

On heart disease it was the fashion in the 1960s to blame a fatty diet, so the well-known poster advertisements of the 1950s—the Egg Marketing Board's 'Go to work on an egg' (1957), and the National Milk Publicity Council's 'Drinka pinta milka day' (1958)—disappeared, and the distribution of free milk to schools in England and Wales (still reaching four-fifths of day and boarding pupils in 1967) was scaled down.[241] Vegetables, fruit, and 'fibre' were promoted at the expense of sugar and fat, but government was hampered by nutritionists' disagreements. John Yudkin set up Europe's first academic department of nutrition at Queen Elizabeth College, London, in 1954, and in an article of 1957 shook the arguments of those who blamed heart disease on fatty diet. Instead, he stressed the need to secure a balance between quantity of food eaten and exercise taken, but in the 1960s overreacted by launching a crusade against sugar which infuriated the sugar industry.[242] Behind everything, however, lay the need to win over the public, especially in the UK's more conservative areas. It was in northern England and Scotland, for instance, that diet was at its most traditional and least healthy, with more resort to suet and dripping, less to poultry and fresh green vegetables.[243]

[236] J. Potter, *Independent Television in Britain*, iii. *Politics and Control 1968–80* (1989), 209. <www.whirligig-tv.co.uk/tv/adverts/commercials.htm> consulted 30 Aug. 2005.

[237] D. Oddy and D. Miller (eds.), *The Making of the Modern British Diet* (1976), 36.

[238] S. Connor, 'Sir Richard Doll: A Life against Tobacco', *IOS* (10 Jan. 1993), 23.

[239] Ibid. J. Laurance, 'The Man Who Declared War on Lung Cancer Lives to See Millions Saved from the Enemy', *Ind.* (3 Aug. 2000), 3.

[240] *TCBST* 119.

[241] Harris, *Health of the Schoolchild*, 199.

[242] *DT* (19 July 1995), 23. *G* (15 July 1995), 30 (obituaries).

[243] J. Yudkin and J. C. McKenzie, *Changing Food Habits* (1964), 27.

Several new fashions speeded on the healthier lifestyle favoured by the doctors. Small but significant was the growth of vegetarianism. The influential Cranks vegetarian restaurant opened near Carnaby Street in 1961, and prospered sufficiently to open branches in several other towns before overextending itself and ceasing to exist in 2001. Whereas in 1968 there were sixteen vegetarian restaurants in London and eighteen elsewhere, by 1977/8 there were fifty-two in London and eighty elsewhere.[244] The impulse was more often humanitarian than medical. A further non-medical impulse lay in concern for personal appearance. Women, freed from recurrent childbearing, could now take a pride in their shape, and at her peak Eileen Fowler, whose career as radio health broadcaster began in 1954, reached half a million listeners at 6.45 a.m.[245] Fashion dictated a slim figure, especially in the 1960s, and in moderation this promoted health, and nourished the market for special slimming foods. The attack on the plump, rubicund male physique had begun early in the nineteenth century, and physical self-improvement had long featured in the self-help movement's repertoire. By the 1970s this preoccupation was accelerating, reinforced by admiration for sporting heroes, now often televised.

By the 1950s a powerful government machine was monitoring accidents at work through the mechanism built up since the Factory Act of 1833. Without public awareness, however, the campaign could not extend fully into the home. The statistics reflected many social changes: safer forms of fuel were superseding the coal fire, for example, and birth control ensured that fewer unsupervised young children fell into such coal fires as remained. None the less in 1959, when the roads claimed 6,520 deaths and 327,000 people injured, the home's equivalents were 8,157 and 1,260,000, respectively.[246] Double white lines were introduced in 1959 to deter dangerous overtaking. A combination of manufacturers' self-regulation and publicity markedly reduced firework injuries during the 1960s,[247] and the breathalyser, introduced in 1967, increased convictions for drinking-and-driving threefold between 1968 and 1980.[248] An overwhelming majority of those polled by Gallup in 1952 and 1963 favoured compulsory crash helmets for motorcyclists,[249] and these were introduced in 1973, with compulsory front-seat safety belts for motorists ten years later. There was progress, too, on resuscitating accident victims when John Bullough in 1963 performed the first recorded kiss of life in place of external heart massage to restart the heart of a girl whom others had assumed dead.[250] There were even more direct reasons for doctors to involve the public: new trends in

[244] J. Twigg, 'The Vegetarian Movement in England, 1847–1981: With Particular Reference to its Ideology' (LSE Ph.D. thesis, 1981), 309.

[245] See obituaries, *G* (11 Mar. 2000), 24; *DT* (13 Mar. 2000), 23.

[246] *HL Deb.* 12 Apr. 1961, c. 262.

[247] *HL Deb.* 14 Apr. 1970, c. 398.

[248] T. R. Gourvish and R. G. Wilson, *The Brewing Industry 1830–1980* (Cambridge, 1994), 569–70.

[249] *Gallup Polls*, i. 305, 694.

[250] Obituary, *DT* (20 Mar. 1999), 27.

surgery demanded more blood donations, and donors rose more than threefold between 1950 and 1970.[251] Family backing was integral to health care, and in April 1951 the single, the widowed, and the divorced were revealed as using hospitals far more heavily than married people.[252] Nowhere were welfare problems so acute as those posed by smaller families with working mothers and perhaps also absent fathers, especially as the number of old people was growing proportionately as well as absolutely.

6. LIFE AND DEATH

The young and the old were the greatest charge on the health and welfare structure, but all age groups benefited from its pooling of risks. The middle aged were too diverse and too subjective a category to attract much research, but with rising affluence, full employment, and better health, life improved for them in the 1950s and 1960s, especially for middle-aged women. The spread of birth control and of pride in appearance narrowed contrasts in the ageing process between the sexes, with some men now even laying claim to a mid-life crisis or 'menopause'; the phrase 'male menopause' first appeared in 1949, and by the 1960s was widely used.[253] There were growing contrasts at different social levels in the experience of late middle age. The physical strength integral to manual occupations inevitably waned with age, as did pay; at a time of fast-moving technology, accumulated craft skills did not necessarily bring dividends. In the better-paid occupations, by contrast, accumulated knowledge and experience remained assets, postponing any decline in status and pay till rather later.[254] In an inflationary age, these differentials in middle-aged wealth were enhanced by the wider diffusion of the middle-class financial life cycle: thereby a low income accepted early in life could generate a much higher income later on, especially after expensively educated children had departed and the tax-subsidized mortgage had been paid off.

Furthermore, in professional occupations age still brought authority: during staff meetings and meals in Partridge's 'Middle School', for example, 'seldom does a junior member initiate conversation or voice strong opinions other than or contrary to those of his seniors'.[255] Politics and government in the 1950s saw no cult of youth. People liked their statesmen seasoned, and old men abounded in the cabinets of Attlee and Churchill; not till the satire of the early 1960s did Macmillan's age cease to be an electoral asset. Thereafter, pensioners' growing share of the electorate did not preclude a growing political and cultural cult of youth reminiscent of the 1890s or the 1920s.[256] In his iconoclastic Reith Lectures

[251] *TCBST* 608. [252] Carr-Saunders *et al.*, *Survey of Social Conditions*, 230.
[253] J. Benson, *Prime Time* (1997), 13. [254] Townsend, *Poverty in UK*, 676.
[255] Partridge, *Middle School*, 34. [256] See below, pp. 473–4, 484–91.

of 1967 the distinguished social anthropologist Edmund Leach recommended the young to enforce a retiring age of 55 in those areas of education, industry, and politics involving research and technological development. 'In our runaway world' human beings like machines rapidly become obsolete, he said: the young should not be 'loaded down with the out-of-date clutter of useless information which is all that traditional scholarship has to offer', and nobody much over 45 'is really fit to teach anybody anything'.[257] The sheer scale of late-twentieth-century electronic revolutions lent such notions some retrospective credibility.

From 1921 to 1991 the pensioners' share of Great Britain's population rose steadily, more than doubling between those years,[258] so for growing numbers the label 'middle-aged' was no misnomer: it was reasonable now to expect a relatively prolonged retirement. Nowhere more heavily than in the history of population does the past hang over the present, for only a cataclysm can prevent those born in one generation from advancing ineluctably towards the next. In 1871 the distribution of age groups in England and Wales had looked rather like a pyramid, with the most numerous age group (those under 5) lending it a wide base, but with each older age group progressively shrinking; at its topmost tiny pinnacle were those of 85 and more. In 1921 for the first time there were fewer children in England and Wales under 5 than between 5 and 9. Thereafter, as birth control's effects gradually worked through, young people declined and old people rose in their share of the population—a trend reinforced by mounting longevity. In the twenty-first century the population's pyramid will be inverted, on a narrower base and with a higher and less sharply pointed peak.[259]

This long-term ageing of the population seemed worrying in the 1930s and 1940s, and the government's encouragement after 1945 for old people to retire later[260] owed nothing to concern about 'ageism', much to the supposed needs of an overtight economy and an overstrained national budget. In the 1950s and 1960s the workforce was rendered more youthful by young immigrants and by married women's growing taste for paid work, reinforced later by a 'bulge' of young indigenous 'baby boom' workers. So the 1950s and 1960s, despite the continued and marked decline in the proportion of over-65s in paid work, gradually began worrying more about the young than the old.[261] In Britain the trade union desire to keep younger people in work combined with rule-based pensions systems and more formalized relationships between

[257] E. Leach, *A Runaway World? The Reith Lectures 1967* (1968), 74–6.

[258] A. M. Warnes and R. Ford, *The Changing Distribution of Elderly People* (1993), 4.

[259] For the pyramids see Coleman and Salt, *British Population*, 77–8.

[260] S. Harper and P. Thane, 'The Consolidation of "Old Age" as a Phase of Life, 1945–1965', in M. Jefferys (ed.), *Growing Old in the Twentieth Century* (1989), 48–9.

[261] Townsend, *Poverty in UK*, 659.

employer and employee to encourage retirement at 65 for men and 60 for women.[262] The state pension's advance was important not just for its own sake, but because it defined categories: it provided an administrative reason for demarcating the working life from old age. The proportion of men in England and Wales aged between 65 and 70 who were still at work fell steadily (65% in 1931, 31% in 1971), and likewise for those between 70 and 74 (42% in 1931, 16% in 1971).[263] Those working beyond age 65 tended to come from relatively low-skill, low-paid, and weakly unionized areas of employment such as agriculture, clothing, sales, and service. Women were expected to retire at 60, five years earlier than men; given that by 1970 women could expect to live for six years longer than men, however, this anomaly remained surprisingly undiscussed.[264] Behind the differential lay two attitudes soon called into question: that the married heterosexual couple constituted the normal social unit (because most men reached 65 with a younger wife, it was argued that the differential made it easier for both to retire together); and that a national insurance scheme should pool risks throughout the entire nation rather than within its subcategories.

Public pensions in their share of gross national product rose from 0.44 per cent in 1910 to 5.4 per cent in 1981, yet whereas in 1968–9 the elderly comprised only one-sixth of the UK population, they comprised one-third of those in poverty.[265] Conservative governments in the 1950s had carried further the Attlee governments' policy of combining a low basic rate of state pension with national assistance benefits for those in need. More pensioners between 1951 and 1971 were willing to claim these benefits, fewer were deterred by pride, inertia, or lack of information. From 1948 to 1976 the state pension hovered at around a fifth of average gross male industrial earnings, and for a married couple remained below a third—a fact that the trade union leader Jack Jones deployed at the TUC in 1972 to back his view of Britain as a 'pensions slum'.[266] Powered by full employment, tax incentives, and initiatives from the insurance companies, privately funded earnings-related occupational pensions grew apace after 1951 to complement the state system. Such pensions covered 36 per cent of employees in the UK by 1956, 49 per cent by 1971, but covered far fewer manual employees than non-manual, far fewer part-timers than full-timers, far fewer women than men.[267]

[262] P. Johnson, 'The Employment and Retirement of Older Men in England and Wales, 1881–1981', *Economic History Review* (Feb. 1994), 125, 127. See also Townsend, *Poverty in UK*, 654–61.

[263] C. M. Law and A. M. Warnes, 'The Changing Geography of the Elderly in England and Wales', *Town Planning Review* (1976), 455.

[264] T. McKeown and C. R. Lowe, *An Introduction to Social Medicine* (2nd edn. Oxford, 1974), 70.

[265] Johnson, 'Employment and Retirement of Older Men', 125. Townsend, *Poverty in UK*, 788.

[266] Townsend, *Poverty in UK*, 789. *G* (6 Sept. 1972), 9 (Jones at TUC); cf. *T* (4 Sept. 1974), 2.

[267] Miller, 'Retirement Pensions Policy', 62, 68, 70, 150–1, 275. See also L. Hannah, *Inventing Retirement: The Development of Occupational Pensions in Britain* (Cambridge, 1986), 55–6.

In 1951 there were 5,467,500 people over 65 in the UK, rising to 7,306,300 in 1971.[268] Commercial interests did not quickly recognize this diverse but important market. Not until 1949 did Sidney de Haan, the owner of a small hotel in Folkestone, spot the pensioner market for cheap out-of-season holidays, though he soon diversified into organizing tours, and in 1966 launched his *Saga Magazine*. Any public discussion of old age came not from mobilized pensioners but from altruistic social workers and sociologists. Townsend, the sociologist most interested in the old, published his pioneering *The Family Life of Old People* in 1957, stressing that the old were sharply polarized between the affluent and the poor.[269] Although some were rich, an increasing number were excluded from paid work, were prevented by disability from organizing in self-defence, and when on fixed incomes were particularly vulnerable to inflation. An increasing number of old people had never had children, had outlived them, or were geographically separated from them, and this in 1940 had led to the creation of the pressure group which in 1971 became 'Age Concern'. The pressure group 'Help the Aged' emerged in 1961 from the world of Christian concern about refugees that had earlier created OXFAM, but both Age Concern and Help the Aged were more concerned with aid than empowerment: by American standards the old were slow to mobilize. This contrast did not reflect any shortage of old electors in the UK, but perhaps reflected the opportunities the American political system offers pressure groups through its voluntarist mood, its relatively fragmented legislature, and its relatively vague party platforms.

With old as with young, subgroups grew up within the wider category: among the young the impulse came from extended education, among the old from postponed death. Death rates in each age group over 65, as in all other age groups, fell steadily for both sexes between 1851 and 1951 and continued falling thereafter;[270] the number of people over 80 in England and Wales rose more than ten times as fast as the overall population between 1901 and 1971.[271] With some help from earlier marriage and parenthood, women, at least, could for the first time know all their grandchildren, though grandmothers now more rarely brought them up. So the family of three generations was giving way to the family of four, and already by 1966 Townsend could predict that the woman in her sixties would increasingly need to look after an infirm mother in her eighties,[272] for whereas the sex balance among the young was levelling off, among the old it was opening out. The male share of the population over 60 fell consistently from 1851, and among people over 85 in the 1980s there were more than three times as many women as men; of the women in England and

[268] Calculated from *BHS* 15–17. [269] Townsend, *Poverty in UK*, 794–5; see also 285, 302.
[270] See figures in Carr-Saunders *et al.*, *Survey of Social Conditions*, 11. *BST* 402–3.
[271] Calculated from *BHS* 15.
[272] Anderson, 'Modern Life Cycle', 75. Townsend, *Social Minority*, 308.

Wales aged 65 and over in 1951 and 1961, half were widows.[273] This was not just because women lived longer, but because the older age groups, especially the First World War generation, still included the generations when young males were less prone to survive.

The life of the old was becoming increasingly solitary, though not necessarily lonely. Governments since 1908 had deployed state pensions to keep the aged poor out of institutions, and birth control's advance left any one parent with fewer descendants, among whom the women were more likely to take up paid work and to get divorced. Better transport dispersed families, and diminished the casual and regular contact between the generations that had earlier been so widespread, especially between mother and daughter. From 1911 to 1951 the average household contained fewer per room because families were getting smaller and servants now lived out. The average size of household in England and Wales had been stable for centuries near its level in 1901 of 4.6 persons, but thereafter began falling fast—to 3.0 in 1961 and 2.4 in 1994.[274] After 1951 the trend was accentuated by the growing tendency throughout Western Europe for the old to live alone. This reflected demographic and divorce trends, but also the desire among the old for independence and privacy—sentiments the authorities welcomed because it was cheaper to keep old people in their own homes.[275] Home helps and meals-on-wheels, substitutes for an extended family now in decline, came into their own: full-time-equivalent home helps more than doubled between 1960 and 1980, and between 1954 and 1980 their beneficiaries rose more than threefold.[276] The home became recreationally much more self-sufficient in the 1950s. In 1961 the over-65s in Great Britain, when compared with all those aged 15 and above, stayed in bed on weekdays for longer, but got their shopping done earlier in the day; they socialized more in the afternoons and less in the evenings; and they spent more time in the evening listening to the radio, yet also watched television at least as much as the rest of the adult population, despite going to bed earlier. On weekdays and Saturdays the over-65s spent far more time with the media, and on Sundays only marginally less, than the overall population; the balance of their media time slanted far more firmly towards radio, however, partly because they were freer to listen during the mornings, when television was not then available.[277] Already by the 1960s the media had become boon companions for the old.

[273] M. Britton and N. Edison, 'The Changing Balance of the Sexes in England and Wales, 1851–2001', *Population Trends*, 46 (Winter 1986), 22–3. D. C. Marsh, *The Changing Social Structure of England and Wales* (rev. edn. 1965), 39.

[274] *TCBST* 76. For pre-industrial household size see P. Laslett, *The World We Have Lost, Further Explored* (1983), 64, 69, 95–6.

[275] For figures, see *BST* 118. See also Coleman and Salt, *British Population*, 233.

[276] M. Dexter and W. Harbert, *The Home Help Service* (1983), 210.

[277] BBC Audience Research Department, *The People's Activities* (1965), tables 1.23 and 1.29. Survey based on activity diaries kept by a regionally balanced sample of 2,643 people aged 15 and above.

'Everyone wishes to live as long as possible', wrote Margaret Hill in 1961, 'but no one wants to be old'.[278] This was partly because being old still ultimately meant moving into an institution, and the exposure in the 1960s of hypothermia as a social problem warned the authorities against leaving this transition too late. A far larger proportion of the elderly had been in state residential care in 1911 than in 1952, but a slowly rising proportion were drawn into care thereafter, and by 1970 their absolute number had doubled.[279] Although more people were now long-lived, the long-lived were not living for much longer: what increased the pressures on public institutions was the replacement of infectious disease as the cause of death by the chronic diseases of old age such as cancer, and bronchial, arthritic, and circulatory disorders. In Britain as in all industrialized countries a growing minority were living into extreme old age. The over-eighties' share in the population of England and Wales rose by 2 or 3 per cent each year from 1911 for the rest of the century, with the number of centenarians roughly doubling in each decade.[280] Even the frontiers of death seemed to be advancing: eight people in England and Wales survived until 105 or more in 1951, thirteen in 1961, thirty-two in 1971, and ninety-two in 1981.[281] Geriatric medicine had to evolve from merely caring for a category of patient into a medical specialism with a distinctive expertise, and given Crossman's distress at how his mother had died in a somewhat squalid nursing home, Barbara Robb's campaign of the late 1960s to improve the care of old people was well timed in its Secretary of State.[282] The advance of geriatric medicine may have ensured due medical attention to the problems of the old, but its lack of glamour and ultimate lack of curative power no doubt led some doctors to specialize elsewhere.[283]

Three women after the 1960s were notable for subverting reticence about death: Mother Teresa, Elizabeth Kubler-Ross (who encouraged openness in American hospitals), and Cicely Saunders (founder of what in the 1960s became the hospice 'movement'). The hospice's pedigree ran from the medieval haven for the sick and destitute to the modern Roman Catholic hospice such as St Joseph's Hospice, Hackney, where Saunders pursued research before branching out. In 1957–8 the Gulbenkian Foundation comprehensively surveyed the hospice scene in a report which did not use the word, though it noted that the phrase 'homes for the dying' had 'largely gone out of use', and it included

278 M. N. Hill, *An Approach to Old Age and its Problems* (Edinburgh, 1961), 55.

279 Figures in Moroney, *Family and State*, 47–8.

280 *BST* 299, 408, 411. Thatcher, 'Trends in Numbers', 414–16. See also Moroney, *Family and State*, 36.

281 Thatcher, 'Trends in Numbers', 415.

282 Dalyell, *Crossman*, 175. On Robb's campaign see Webster, *Health Services since the War*, ii. 228.

283 As argued in P. Thane, *Old Age in English History: Past Experiences, Present Issues* (Oxford, 2000), 451, 456.

institutions concerned with 'terminal care'.[284] Nearly half the deaths outside mental institutions in 1956 occurred at home, two-fifths in NHS hospitals, and the rest in religious, charitable, and profit-making homes. Often inadequately inspected, under-equipped, under-staffed, and under-funded, the last three approaches to care could sometimes provide sympathetic nursing, but many were austere and crowded, and some had to unload on hospitals patients close to death. The Foundation's ideal was for the long-stay and chronic-sick patient to be nursed either within purpose-built general hospitals or in affiliated homes, but it foreshadowed the hospice movement in its threefold objective: hospital care, a 'homely atmosphere', and pain control through drugs.[285]

Saunders often said that 'there are not many original ideas in the world. One only brings together things culled from here and there, shakes the kaleidoscope and finds a new pattern.'[286] She owed much to Christian inspiration, whether Catholic or Protestant, but much also to the growing medical expertise at relieving pain in its psychological as well as physiological dimension: she was 'wedding the professional scientific rigour with the Christian foundation'.[287] She favoured collaboration for a shared objective: between medical and social (including religious) workers, between professional and lay people, between nurses and family members who wanted to get involved, and above all between all these and the informed and alert patient. Her articles in the *Nursing Times* for 1959 on care for the dying made enough impact for her to set up at St Christopher's, Sydenham, the first hospice to combine research, teaching, and care; its first patient arrived in 1967. Among the old people with no option but institutional care, the late-twentieth-century trend was to discourage a resigned defeatism, provide stimulus, and encourage activity; but once the aged person's options closed in, acceptance was the very different mood which the hospice fostered. Whereas the Gulbenkian Foundation was uncertain whether people should be told they were dying, the hospice movement leaned towards openness.[288] Saunders's initially evangelical impulse gradually broadened, and she aimed to attract doctors into extending medicine's frontiers beyond the hunt for cures: death should be seen not as a professional failure but as a prize opportunity for a multi-disciplinary sharing of expertise. Hospices were soon incorporated into a campaign, in 'a characteristic mixture of tough clinical science and compassion',[289] reuniting and adapting for new purposes

[284] H. L. G. Hughes, '. . . *Peace at the Last': A Survey of Terminal Care in the United Kingdom. A Report to the Calouste Gulbenkian Foundation* (1960), 9. The *OED*'s first citation of 'hospice' in its modern specialist sense is for 1967, and for 'hospice movement' 1979.

[285] Hughes, *Peace at the Last*, 16. 59, 61, 31, 39.

[286] Letter to Grace Goldin, 28 Oct. 1980 in C. Saunders, *Selected Letters 1959–1999* (Oxford, 2002), 205.

[287] Author's tape-recorded discussion on 1 Sept. 1997 with Dame Cicely Saunders, to whom this discussion owes much.

[288] Hughes, *Peace at the Last*, 41–2.

[289] Author's collection: Saunders to author, 15 Sept. 1997, quoting *British Medical Journal*.

specialisms which had unhelpfully diverged. Like Torrie's organization, Cruse, hospices were quietly challenging taboos about death—counteracting the attitude experienced by a dying patient whose remark Saunders recalled long afterwards: 'it's very strange; nobody seems to want to look at me'.[290]

Many who welcomed such openness in the hospice context wanted reticence elsewhere. For Kenneth Williams it was shocking, for instance, that *The Times* could on its front page in 1968 publish the famous close-up photograph of the Saigon chief of police shooting a young Vietcong officer.[291] Reticence also attended the hastening of death, whether by the dying person or by the doctor. Saunders rejected euthanasia in principle, and even thought it redundant, but growing longevity and the doctor's growing capacity to influence death's timing alerted many to the new ethical dilemmas doctors now faced. To take only one example: antibiotics could now cure 'the old man's friend', pneumonia, which had hitherto released the dying patient without medical intervention.[292] Joseph Fletcher (1905–91) helped to crystallize opinion with his influential *Morals and Medicine* (1955). This one-time Protestant clergyman was a prolific pioneer of bioethics in the USA, a eugenist, and an advocate of compulsory sterilization, as well as president of the Euthanasia Society of America (1974–6). Many of the theological arguments he repudiated seemed antique later, but his counter-arguments remained relevant. Aiming to protect the patient against secretive professions and to ensure better-informed choices, he advocated rational self-direction through birth control, artificial insemination, and voluntary medical euthanasia.

Launched in the 1870s, the small but significant British movement for euthanasia had hitherto attracted little publicity and only wavering twentieth-century support: it confronted powerful vested interests and entrenched attitudes, its platform was complex and easily misrepresented, and its aims were difficult to present positively.[293] Among the many plausible counter-arguments, Nazi conduct in the 1940s lent force to 'slippery slope' reasoning.[294] 'There must be very few doctors', said Professor Henry Miller in 1967, 'who have not from time to time felt uneasiness, if not revulsion, at the spectacle of some stuporous ancient in hospital being maintained in a state of suspended animation by all the sophisticated paraphernalia of modern resuscitation'; yet he went on to stress the dangers of abandoning the doctor's overriding commitment to strive by all possible means to keep alive. Two years later, however, Kenneth Vickery, Medical Officer for Health for Eastbourne, created a stir by proposing to the Royal Society of Health's congress

290 Saunders interview with Cherie Blair, *DT* (5 Sept. 2002), 25.

291 Williams, *Letters*, 79 (6 Feb. 1968).

292 *Medical Press* (18 Aug. 1954), 147.

293 For a valuable and full discussion of the movement see N. D. A. Kemp, *'Merciful Release': The History of the British Euthanasia Movement* (Manchester, 2002).

294 e.g. Archbishop Garbett, *HL Deb.* 28 Nov. 1950, c. 564; c. 577 (Lord Amulree).

an age limit beyond which doctors should refrain from artificially preserving life.[295] The euthanasia movement had two powerful long-term allies, however. First, medical science had so greatly advanced by the 1950s that death more often needed to be formally pronounced and even planned—involving decisions which should arguably be reached more openly, taking fuller account of the patient's known wishes. Second, the humanitarian concern to uphold the individual's dignity, personality, and autonomy, to which Christianity's other-worldly concerns had once contributed so much, now owed more to a secularized preoccupation with this-worldly priorities. Belief in other-worldly compensation for unavoidable pain was giving way to the increasingly feasible this-worldly aim of removing avoidable pain; quality as well as quantity of life in this world seemed of mounting importance. 'Surely', wrote Fletcher, '. . . we are not as persons of moral stature to be ruled by ruthless and unreasoning physiology, but rather by reason and self-control'. Against such arguments Saunders could deploy doctors' growing control over pain through new combinations of drugs:[296] all the more reason, then, for preserving a life which can benefit both self and others right up to the moment of death.

In March 1958 Gallup asked people their views on suicide: 49 per cent thought it should no longer be viewed as a crime, 27 per cent wanted no change, and 24 per cent did not know.[297] Sociologists had for decades been emphasizing the social (rather than individual) causes of suicide, which as Baroness Wootton pointed out in 1961 was more common in some parts of London and among the gifted young: 'it is not so much individuals but society which is responsible', she said.[298] Responding to this climate, the police were no longer enforcing suicide law; hence suicide was not deterred, under-recording was substantial, and relatives' distress enhanced. When suicide was decriminalized in 1961, the individual's right to decide when to end his life was in effect conceded. Euthanasia was not thereby advanced, because the Suicide Act (1961) simultaneously strengthened the penalty for assisting suicide. After rising in the 1950s, suicide levels for men and women fell markedly in the 1960s in all age groups above 24. The shift to non-toxic North Sea gas explains why suicide in England and Wales by domestic gas plunged in the 1960s and 1970s for both sexes and all age groups. Replacing it was poisoning with solid or liquid substances, rising quite fast, together with a steady overall rise throughout the 1950s and 1960s in self-poisoning by other gases (especially car exhaust for men) and by hanging or strangulation. There was a long-term

[295] H. Miller, 'Economic and Ethical Considerations', *Proceedings of the Royal Society of Medicine. Symposium No. 9: The Cost of Life*, 60 (Nov. 1967), 1216. *T* (30 Apr. 1969), 3 (Vickery).

[296] J. Fletcher, *Morals and Medicine* (1955), 208, and see the letter from C. Saunders and A. Winner in *T* (27 Mar. 1969), 11.

[297] *Gallup Opinion Polls*, i. 459.

[298] *HL Deb.* 2 Mar. 1961, c. 267.

slow decline, however, in suicide by drowning.[299] Somewhat paradoxically, the decriminalizing of suicide was accompanied by greater efforts to prevent it. When Chad Varah launched the Samaritans in 1953, inviting people in distress to telephone MAN 9000, the scale of the response surprised him. A branch structure soon spread far beyond London: from seven branches in 1960 to 115 in 1970, dealing with new clients whose number mounted rapidly in the 1960s year by year. By 1970 there were 12,832 Samaritan volunteers in the UK, and the suicide rate per thousand population fell as the number of branches rose.[300]

Attitudes to death were changing kaleidoscopically in the 1950s and 1960s, and people's priorities on how to prevent it diverged, sometimes along party-political lines. The right was more confident than the left that preparing for nuclear war would best prevent it, and that humane values would benefit from hanging convicted murderers. Other issues involving death—abortion, euthanasia, contraception, and suicide, for example—were emotive and/or controversial, so a non-party approach was thought appropriate. Uncontroversial between the parties, because operating at the level of individual choice, was the growing preoccupation with saving and prolonging life through international food aid, dietary reform, and attacks on smoking. What united reform in all these areas was a secularized, rationalistic, and utilitarian humanitarianism that pursued justice and a long and fulfilling life for all in this world rather than requiring any belief in a compensatory after-life. As Wootton pointed out, 'those of us who believe that the brief interval between birth and death is the only certain experience that we know are not likely to attach less importance to that period than those who believe that there is a greater future beyond'.[301] She was among those who helped to change attitudes to death in all its aspects, but by far the most influential was Glanville Williams, whose *Sanctity of Life and the Criminal Law* (1958) did for the legal background of medicine what Fletcher had done for medical ethics: Williams's became the classic textbook on death-related legal topics.

Significant shifts in opinion emerged from the debate of the mid-1950s on hanging. In 1956 the House of Commons on a free vote backed its suspension, but was overruled by the Lords. When the government introduced the Homicide Act in the following year, Archbishop Fisher shifted his position: whereas in 1948 he had taken an absolutist position, advocating selective hanging according to the degree of iniquity, in 1957 he adopted a utilitarian stance whereby hanging would apply only to those types of murder where it was likely to deter. The Act divided murder into capital and non-capital categories, the former being murder as a calculated means to an end, but the distinction proved so difficult

[299] L. Bulusu and M. Alderson, 'Suicides 1950–82', *Population Trends*, 35 (Spring 1984).
[300] Varah (ed.), *Samaritans in the '70s*, 15, 139.
[301] *HL Deb.* 12 Feb. 1976, c. 296.

to operate that the experience of attempting it converted some judge advocates of hanging into abolitionists.[302] This further reinforced the case for complete abolition: capital punishment was suspended for five years in 1965, abolished in 1969.

Concern for the sanctity of human life influenced both sides in this debate. Abolitionists argued that a practice inhumane in itself weakened society's respect for human life, and glamorized the killer through demonizing him, precluding not only reclamation, but also correction for error. They also argued that it failed to deter—a view taken even by Albert Pierrepoint, chief public executioner from 1946 to 1956.[303] The conviction rate for murder shot up from about 58 per cent in 1962 to 90 per cent in 1970 after hanging had been abolished;[304] with murder as with suicide, the penalty's earlier severity had deterred convictions. When Pierrepoint resigned in 1956 the authorities asked him to keep his reasons confidential, but in 1974 his autobiography branded hanging as 'an antiquated relic of a primitive desire for revenge which takes the easy way and hands over responsibility for revenge to other people'.[305] By contrast, the retentionists claimed that deterrence through hanging saved far more innocent lives than criminals executed. In retrospect the abolitionists seem unduly optimistic. Koestler, for instance, attached an unreal importance to the symbolism of the gallows, which for him were 'not only a machine of death, but a symbol . . . the symbol of terror, cruelty and irreverence for life', standing 'for everything that mankind must reject'. In his passionate attack on hanging, the publisher Victor Gollancz even hoped that abolition would cause murder to 'progressively cease (it may never cease altogether) as a habit of spiritual and physical gentleness becomes more and more instinctive in the human mind'.[306] Such claims were as absolutist in their moralism as the retributionist arguments so readily deployed by the retentionists, buttressed as they were till the mid-1950s by the bishops. By then, however, the shrewder abolitionists were adopting the increasingly pragmatic and secular mood of the times. Bishops contributing to the Lords debates were three to one against abolition in 1948 but unanimously for it in 1956.[307] The more effective abolitionist arguments emphasized the practical and empirical case against hanging, whose strength had been highlighted by three recent and questionable hangings for murder: of Timothy Evans in 1950, subsequently proved unjust; of the unarmed 19-year-old Derek Bentley in 1953, but not the 16-year-old Chris Craig who had the

[302] For a good discussion see C. Davies, *The Strange Death of Moral Britain* (Brunswick, NJ, 2004), 70–5.

[303] *T* (13 July 1992), 15.

[304] BBC Radio 4 programme *The Law in Action*, 13 June 2003.

[305] A. Pierrepoint, *Executioner: Pierrepoint* (1st publ. 1974, paperback edn. 1977), 204; see also 207.

[306] A. Koestler, *Reflections on Hanging* (1956), 170. V. Gollancz, *Capital Punishment: The Heart of the Matter* (1955), 5.

[307] H. Potter, *Hanging in Judgment: Religion and the Death Penalty in England from the Bloody Code to Abolition* (1993), 175, 193–4.

gun; and of Ruth Ellis in 1955 for shooting a lover whose kicks in the abdomen had caused her to miscarry.

Joe Orton's play *Loot* seemed so shocking when first performed in 1965 partly because it humorously treated death, then far more subject to prudery and traditionalism than sex.[308] Nothing more strikingly displays British conservatism about death than the UK's willingness to assign so much of its scarce urban space to graveyard monuments. After 1951, however, funeral celebration became less of a public occasion: from being a protracted celebration of community relationships and religious loyalties organized by the family, funerals were shrinking into relatively cursory and private ceremonies. They were becoming secularized, bureaucratized, and managed by professionals: doctors, funeral directors, and local-government authorities. The percentage of people dying in their own homes fell in Britain from 49 in 1954 to 35 in 1969.[309] The new pattern was for segregation from the family steadily to advance as the old person moved to the retirement home, the hospital, the hospice, and ultimately the mortuary. Even after death at home, the corpse seldom now stayed there for long, nor did the funeral procession often start from the home. Rarely, too, was the corpse returned for burial within the community, marked by a gravestone near the parish church. Instead, dispersed and more loosely knit communities and a car-owning population found suburban crematoria increasingly convenient. Theological notions on the resurrection of the body proved adaptable, and with the Catholic acceptance of cremation in 1964 the last theological barrier succumbed. During the 1950s cremation in the UK became a public service funded by the local authority, and by 1959 a third of all funerals involved cremation in 121 crematoria; in England and Wales the number of cremations first overtook burials in 1967.[310] Death was slowly being denied its one-time reverence; people ceased to wear black armbands, and slow-moving hearses ceased to raise hats or stop the traffic. The almost universal emergence of black ties on George VI's death later seemed inconceivable, and not just because ties were slowly going out of fashion—there was from the 1960s a growing tendency at funerals to celebrate life rather than mourn over death.

Changes within the British funeral industry secularized death ceremonial from another direction. In the late 1950s a tenth of the population were covered by funeral insurance policies, of which 280,000 were still being taken out annually. Inevitably reflecting the supposed wishes of the elderly, undertakers responded only slowly to economic and social trends. In England

308 J. Lahr, *Prick up your Ears: The Biography of Joe Orton* (1978), 228.

309 P. Gore, 'From Undertaker to Funeral Director: Development of Funeral Firms in East Kent' (University of Kent M.Phil. thesis, 1993), 117–18, 134.

310 P. C. Jupp, 'The Development of Cremation in England 1820–1990: A Sociological Analysis' (LSE Ph.D. thesis, 1992), 348; P. C. Jupp, *From Dust to Ashes: The Replacement of Burial by Cremation in England 1840–1967* (Congregational Lecture 1990, n.d.), 1.

and Wales in 1951 the industry employed 4,262 people, three-fifths classified as employers or managers. The family firm, with sons following fathers into the trade, lasted longer here than elsewhere,[311] and the industry was slow to professionalize or commercialize. Self-regulated, self-consciously respectable, and with growing claims to expertise, the undertaker as at 1951 possessed some of the profession's attributes, but not four that are crucial: a secular tone, a clearly identified specialism, and strictly regulated recruitment through an overall control exerted by a single professional body. Under American influence the 'undertaker' had in the 1940s become the 'funeral director'. His continuing responsibility for disposing of the corpse inevitably involved him in 'trade', but to that he now annexed a 'professional' or 'service' role by cultivating a confidential, supportive, and even expert relationship with the client. As with Cruse Bereavement Care, his evolution harmonized with the emergence of the new counselling professions.[312] He was collaborating, even competing for control, with professionals from the law, medicine, local government, and the churches; and without any unseemly squabble, the churches were slowly succumbing to the legal and medical expertise and bureaucratic know-how that he was learning to deploy.[313]

7. THE END OF THE FAMILY?

This chapter has shown the family in the 1950s and 1960s evolving autonomously, but also in response to wider social change. Its transformation predictably prompted continuous, vigorous, and multi-dimensional controversy, for no revolution in the intimacies of daily life can be painless. There was growing and sometimes apocalyptic talk about the breakup of the family, for which at first sight this chapter provides ample support. The central principle of the British family in the 1950s, the lifelong loyalty of a heterosexual couple to one another and to their children, seemed undermined when single-sex relationships, illegitimacy, and abortion lost their stigma, and when birth control for the unmarried woman was in effect endorsed. Many other changes seemed to work in the same direction, some in unexpected ways. Easier communication, far from enlarging the extended family, coincided with its continued contraction. Affluence enabled the old to choose independence in their own home, propped up by volunteers from outside the family; or when that proved impossible, it was to institutions and not the family that they turned. Public welfare was

[311] 'The Business of Burial', *Econ.* (5 Apr. 1958), 8–9.

[312] For a good discussion see B. Parsons, 'Change and Development in the British Funeral Industry during the Twentieth Century, with Special Reference to the Period 1960–1994' (University of Westminster Ph.D. thesis, 1997), 249, 253, 263–4.

[313] This discussion owes much to M. J. A. Naylor, 'The Funeral: The Management of Death and its Rituals in a Northern Industrial City' (University of Leeds Ph.D. thesis, 1989), 157, 163–4.

slowly eroding the family's mutually supportive role; health care, childbirth, and even death were increasingly professionalized out of the family and into the hospital. Birth control enabled women to vacate the home for paid work, leaving the mother less time for the children. Schools and universities competed with the family for influence over children of all ages and both sexes, and teenage culture further distanced parent from child. Meritocratic ideals undermined the family's traditional role of choosing the child's employment and even (given the family firm's decline) of creating it. The attack on aristocracy was only the most visible end of a much wider attack on inherited status and wealth, seemingly eroding the family's loyalty to its past and future.

Britain's divorce rate till the 1960s was among the lowest in the world,[314] but rising divorce statistics nourished pessimism. Such figures are a poor guide to the number of unhappy marriages, and the attempt to eliminate such marriages prompted each stage in the spread of divorce, always with the hope that the latest relaxation would mop up remaining problems and at last send the trend downwards. Yet petitions for divorce rose slowly up to the 1940s, then rapidly to a new plateau of about 30,000 a year in England and Wales during the 1950s. Each subsequent decade saw a higher plateau reached, so that by the 1970s there were 142,000 a year.[315] The absolute number of divorces exaggerates the trend slightly because the number of married couples also rose markedly in these years, and because some of the apparent increase represented marriages exposed as broken only once the divorce law had been further relaxed. The rate of divorce was rising too. Only 2 per cent of the marriages embarked upon in 1926 ended in divorce after twenty years, 6 per cent in 1936, 7 per cent in 1951, but 24 per cent by 1966 and 28 per cent by 1971.[316] By the 1970s divorce had even in some circles become fashionable, yet given the assumption by then prevalent that marriage should be for love, with state and parents as mere bystanders, divorce levels might have been expected to stabilize or fall.

A similar escalation in divorce was occurring elsewhere, but in Britain it was accelerated by the legal aid available since 1949, of which more than three-quarters went towards funding matrimonial cases.[317] Given all this, the benefits from widening access to divorce seem in retrospect less obvious than they did at the time. Happiness benefited, to the extent that miserable relationships ended, but easier divorce also encouraged the idea that marriage was ephemeral, terminable at the first sign of difficulty—a development from which many earlier feminists thought women might lose much. The 'nuclear' family now all too often gave way to the 'one-parent family'. The phrase, together with 'lone parent' and 'single parent', was imported from America during the 1970s, and the lone parent was much more likely to be female than male. Many serious

[314] See the figures in W. J. Goode, *World Revolution and Family Patterns* (Glencoe, Ill., 1963), 82.
[315] Figures from *BST* (1988), 80. [316] *TCBST* 63–4. [317] *Finer Report*, i. 73.

people were understandably disturbed that changes so large were occurring so fast. The dynamic seemed so powerful and so alien that they suspected coordinated conspiracy, and in this area accused the media of being more than intermediaries. Often Roman Catholic in origin, the pessimists were rightly aware that these changes were secularizing in their impact, and feared the apparent cultivation of false and even inhumane values. They rightly worried about the implications of these changes for the child, and here their concerns were more widely shared. To take only one relevant statistic: the number of adoption orders for children in Great Britain almost doubled during the 1960s, though a growing proportion of the adoptees joined the family set up by a parent and step-parent rather than joining a family of strangers.[318]

None the less, the view so far painted is historically insensitive and too gloomy, and each of the fears discussed craves a rejoinder. To begin with, the changes under discussion were part of a revolution so widespread in developed societies as to elicit from demographers a special label: the 'second demographic transition', the first being the spread of birth control. The transition is to a situation where both mortality and fertility fall from high to low, and in which birth control, reinforced by abortion, postpones both conception and marriage; premarital cohabitation then becomes so widespread as often to supersede marriage, thereby reducing the need for divorce, and greatly extending choice in personal relationships.[319] With this transition came what the demographers called the 'demographic bonus', whereby during a thirty- or forty-year period, as in the UK between 1900 and 1950, the dependency ratio falls markedly: birth control reduces the proportion of children, but medical advance and longer life temporarily and simultaneously reduce the proportion of dependent old people. A change widely adopted is not necessarily right, but its diffusion reflects a cross-cultural and spontaneous felt need and opportunity which owed little to governments or the media, much to the free choice it reflected. When in October 1954 Gallup asked its sample whether Princess Margaret should be allowed to marry the divorcee Group Captain Townsend, 24 per cent were not interested, 17 per cent disapproved, but 59 per cent were in favour,[320] and this at a time when no divorcee at Ascot could enter the royal enclosure. Public opinion in its deeds as much as in its words, endorsed trends in 'the family' whose new flexibility catered better for the rich diversity in human nature and circumstance. To cramp all adults into a single monogamous heterosexual mould had never been practicable. Human diversity, now more fully and openly acknowledged in the UK, would if ignored simply cause endorsed appearance

[318] *HL Deb.* 21 Jan. 1975, c. 18.

[319] D. J. van de Kaa, 'Postmodern Fertility Preferences. From Changing Value Orientation to New Behavior', in R. A. Bulatao and J. B. Casterline (eds.), *Global Fertility Transition* (New York, 2001), 302. I owe this reference to Dr Coleman.

[320] *Gallup Polls*, i. 357.

and practical reality to diverge. The pessimists could counter this with little beyond a longed-for but unrealistic return to the past, without sufficiently allowing for the religious and irreligious pluralism of modern Britain, which in a democratic society government and the media had to reflect.

The pessimists did not always appreciate how unattractive some aspects of the traditional family that they favoured had been, or how extensive had been the family changes preceding its precarious and relatively recent predominance. Much of its warmth and intimacy had reflected the surrounding society's austerity, whereas affluence and public welfare now generated a salutary pooling of risks and extension in privacy. Not choice, but the privations of war and poverty, were what had often created such prized features of earlier family structures as the closeness of mother and daughter, the neighbourhood's sociability, and such security as the extended family could provide. Affluence after 1951 invalidated earlier feminist predictions of communal living, or at least of facilities shared between families, because each family could increasingly fund facilities of its own. This was welcome, because the objective even of those living in local-authority rented housing, let alone of owner-occupiers, was privacy, self-sufficiency, and independence. All this made it easier for the late twentieth century to revert to the freedom of the earlier family relationships that the authorities had temporarily pushed underground. Relaxation in the UK's family structure after 1951 echoed the informality prevailing before Lord Hardwicke's Act of 1753; up to that point (and afterwards in Scotland till 2006), informal or 'common-law' marriage could be entered into purely by mutual consent in what later seemed a remarkably casual manner.[321] A family which had changed so much and so often in the past could and perhaps should change in the future. The family is, after all, made for man, not man for the family.

Traditionalists underplayed the narrowness and intolerance of the traditional family, together with its concern to keep up appearances and to avert unpredictable social descent. They chose not to dwell upon the overcrowding, the subordination of women within the home, the prominence of drink and prostitution on a Saturday night, and the parental exploitation of children, sometimes harsh. Idealization of the traditional family owed much to its being so defined as to exclude many of its concealed accoutrements: the prostitute, the mistress, the trapped daughter-at-home, and the exploited or neglected child. Then there were the misfits: the intelligent unmarried woman with no career, the oppressed but trapped wife, the homosexual with no acknowledged social role. With some justice Edward Sagarin declared that 'if homosexuality were a force destructive of our family institution, it would be because the family

[321] S. Cretney, *Family Law in the Twentieth Century: A History* (1st publ. Oxford, 2003, paperback edn. 2005), 4–7. I am most grateful to Dr Cretney for generous help on this point.

has been built in such manner as to exclude the homosexual from its rank'.[322] The child would not necessarily be happier if confined within a broken but formally unbreakable family. The one-parent family and the more complex successor structures now emerging had their drawbacks for children, especially in a transitional period; but children are resilient and resourceful, society has a marked and spontaneous capacity for self-repair, and widely shared problems generate new supportive structures and attitudes.

Rising divorce levels did not indicate that the family was in decline: rather that more was expected of it. Indeed, from the 1930s to the 1970s marriage became much more prevalent than before: the mean age at marriage plunged for both sexes to levels lower than had been seen for centuries, with manual workers setting the pace, and age at marriage became much more uniform.[323] This may owe something to the more equal balance between the sexes before the onset of old age—a change reflecting the more balanced pattern of emigration, the boy's improved chances of survival at birth, and the waning demographic impact of two world wars. By 1961 there were for the first time in England and Wales more males than females in the age-group from 15 to 19.[324] Marriage's continued prevalence must also denote its popularity, all the more striking given that the risks of failure were palpably increasing. The divorced were eager to remarry: age at remarriage fell for both sexes in England and Wales in the 1960s, and between 80 and 90 per cent of the divorced had remarried before they were 50. If divorce became more frequent, this was partly because marriages were now tested more stringently: given that the 1950s and 1960s saw earlier marriage and longer life, marriages had to last longer, and divorce rates in the 1960s were much higher for brides who had married young.[325] Women now expected more from marriage, and their easier access to paid work equipped them better to protect themselves when it failed. Whereas in earlier years decrees were granted more often to husbands than wives, by the 1960s divorce petitions were more than twice as likely to come from wives than from husbands, and by the 1970s and early 1980s decrees awarded to wives were rising fast—from 60 per cent in 1971 to 72 per cent in 1983, the highest ever recorded.[326]

The family in the 1950s and 1960s demonstrated its flexibility and resilience in other ways. It became more self-sufficient through taking on new roles or resuming old ones. The transition (except in some immigrant groups) from the arranged to the romantic marriage made sexual fulfilment more central to its function, whereas this had often earlier required surreptitious 'affairs'

[322] *Homosexual Outlook*, 36.
[323] Coleman and Salt, *British Population*, 181, cf. 179. Anderson, 'Modern Life Cycle', 82.
[324] *TBS* 34; cf. Coleman and Salt, *British Population*, 180. [325] *Finer Report*, i. 54, 47.
[326] *BST* 80. J. Haskey, 'Trends in Marriage and Divorce in England and Wales: 1837–1987', *Population Trends*, 48 (Summer 1987), 16–17.

with mistresses and prostitutes in relationships that now seemed hypocritical. With the more openly relaxed outlook on sexuality that was developing in the 1960s, sexual fulfilment could be secured through the 'open' marriages and cohabitations that now became more common, or through marriages embarked upon only after cohabitation. The family was also resuming some of its earlier recreational self-sufficiency. In an urban context the separation of spheres had led male breadwinners more often to take their recreation away from home, which led the wife to cultivate even closer relations with other women—as neighbours, friends, or relatives. From the 1950s this situation changed again: with more women in paid work outside the home, and geographically more distant from relatives in an increasingly mobile society, female companionship had to be sought either at work or within the family. The latter was more feasible now that affluence, birth control, car ownership, and the new media were domesticating recreation: the family that played together stayed together. As for the family's educational role, this was if anything enhanced by the children's lengthening dependence on and residence with their parents. Parents might no longer directly determine their children's careers, but they could help them get the necessary qualifications—by moving house to extract the most from state schooling, providing and funding additional help and stimulus out of school hours, attending parent–teacher meetings, and (if the state facilities seemed inadequate) scrimping and saving to fund an independent schooling.

The growing shift in attitudes to and understanding of sexuality in the 1950s and 1960s, complemented by married women's changing employment prospects, prompted widely ramifying changes in family structure. In so far as children's lives deteriorated in these years, shifts in family structure were only partly responsible: also relevant were physiological, environmental, and commercial changes quite distinct in origin. Besides, in many respects children's lives were improving—most notably in disciplinary methods, recreation, education, and privacy. All age groups benefited from the pooling of risks involved in public welfare and the NHS—not least the old, who were living longer and more independently.

Of the four motifs thrown into relief by this chapter, the first must be the prolonged influence of the Second World War (the first motif), which had accelerated the paid employment of married women, the advance of public welfare, and alertness to the distinct interests of the old; in none of these instances was much need later felt for back-tracking. The seventh motif has also been highlighted: the politicians' limited room for initiative. In family matters politicians responded as best they could to changes that took them by surprise, and on welfare issues they often found themselves beset by high-minded voluntarist pressures and trapped in commitments entered into by predecessors: public-welfare expenditure was powered by an engine whose momentum they restrained with only the greatest difficulty. The elusiveness of time-saving devices (the fourth motif) was exemplified in the new pressures introduced by the paid work for married women that such devices made possible. And in many of the areas under discussion, most notably health and welfare, the individual experienced greater certainty. Minorities welcomed the growing understanding of their distinctive problems and the growing tolerance of wider lifestyle choices. For them, at least, there was no such thing as 'the family'—fixed for all times, people, and circumstances—but an evolving set of relationships which adapted to new situations and perceptions. These major changes in the family owed much to humanitarian, materialistic, and even hedonistic reforms, and exemplified the fifth motif: the vulnerability amidst social change of structures which owed so much to religious sanctions. Many people experienced all the pain involved at no longer seeing an unchanging family as their one secure haven within a rapidly changing world: the ground seemed to be moving beneath their feet. Yet when confronted in 1777 by a prediction of national ruin through the defeat of British forces at Saratoga, Adam Smith was unflustered: 'be assured, my young friend', he replied, 'that there is a great deal *of ruin* in a nation'.[327] As an economist, he knew that political and economic institutions when challenged respond spontaneously with flexibility and with resilience. So did the twentieth-century British family, both before 1970 and after.

[327] *The Correspondence of the Right Honourable Sir John Sinclair, Bart.*, i (1831), 391.

CHAPTER 6

Industry and Commerce

Nowhere more powerfully than in the economy did the UK feel the Second World War's legacy. In the aftermath of a divisive 'national' government, considerations of sheer national survival had in the early 1940s dictated government coordination of producers through employers' organizations and trade unions. Corporatist strategies, participatory and voluntarist in nature, were combined with curbs on consumer demand. This overall strategy provided the basis for economic policy under postwar Labour and Conservative governments until well into the 1970s. The attempt to operate this structure in peacetime conditions is the theme of this chapter's first section, culminating in the pursuit from the mid-1960s of an incomes policy. The second section, on the shift from manufacturing to services, is important for its own sake, but also (together with the third section, on the changing experience of work) for exposing growing difficulties with prolonging the wartime system. Employers' organizations and trade unions had less influence in a service sector whose firms were smaller and less unionized, where hours were more flexible, and where women (often part-timers) were more prominent in the workforce. The advance of consumerism, discussed in the chapter's final section, compounded the difficulty, given that consumers were more dispersed and less organized than producers; the attempt was made from the 1950s to draw consumers into the central planning structure, but never very plausibly.

1. CONSENSUS CORPORATISM

For British governments between 1951 and 1970, unemployment was a nightmare to be avoided. In its manifesto of 1950, Labour saw the depression years as 'unhappy years for our country and our people' which 'must never come again'.[1] The memory remained vivid for key Labour and Conservative politicians alike: for Harold Macmillan the interwar MP for Stockton just as much as for Harold Wilson, whose 48-year-old father's sudden loss of employment in 1930 had plunged the family into despair and had left his son with a lifelong fear

[1] I. Dale (ed.), *Labour Manifestos*, 64.

of sudden dismissal.[2] Postwar governments of both parties assumed that this evil could be warded off through planning and rationalization by an interventionist government alert to its moral as well as economic responsibilities. The Conservatives committed themselves to full employment in their manifesto of 1945, and in their bid to retain the centre ground after 1951 they recognized the electoral benefits of being seen to keep unemployment low, and went along with fashionable views about how interwar unemployment had arisen.[3] Interwar governments were seen as callous in their welfare policy, and postwar governments interpreted Keynes reassuringly as encouraging public welfare among a battery of cures for unemployment. Churchill, never securely partisan in outlook, had helped to pioneer public welfare in his Liberal days, and as prime minister from 1951 to 1955 recognized the need to neutralize welfare as Labour's winning electoral card: both party interest and personal inclination dictated his acceptance of the Attlee governments' major welfare achievements.

Full employment seemed essential not only for economic growth, but also for enabling Britain to compete with the USSR on the moral plane: the British economic and political system must be seen to combine fairness with liberty, redistributive taxation with enterprise. Avoidable unemployment seemed inhumane: R. A. Butler when Chancellor of the Exchequer said that 'those who talked about creating pools of unemployment should be thrown into them and made to swim'.[4] Conservative governments of the 1950s committed themselves still more deeply by endorsing what was a historically unusual presumption, though by then widely accepted: that both the nation and its citizens should enjoy an annual increase in their real income. Somehow the means had to be found. When in November 1967 Callaghan, then Chancellor of the Exchequer, said that 'the real problem . . . was not the question of the total level of unemployment but the distribution of that unemployment', he sent his party into an immediate flurry.[5] Full employment in the short and longer term remained a top priority for governments of all parties right up to 1979. Even after that, full employment was not rejected as a long-term aim—only the belief that its short-term incidence should be avoided at all costs.

In the 1950s even under a Conservative government central planning in some form seemed integral to full employment; the party had not fought the general election of 1951 on any other platform. State planning had apparently succeeded during the war, its structures were still in place, and the economists liked it. Their subject was becoming increasingly mathematical in approach, with multiple regression as their standard tool. More and better economic statistics could now be processed by ever more sophisticated equipment, with the new

[2] Pimlott, *Wilson*, 36. Wilson, *Memoirs 1916–64*, 48–9.
[3] Following the analysis by N. Ferguson and G. O'Hara, *FT* (28 Apr. 1997), 12.
[4] Butler, *Art of the Possible*, 61, cf. Crossman, *Backbench Diaries*, 108 (20 May 1952).
[5] *T* (8 Nov. 1967), 9.

subdiscipline of 'econometrics' (pioneered at the LSE) interpreting them.[6] Econometric models of the British economy, mathematical representations of the relations between the economy's major variables, were developed both inside and outside the Treasury. With inflation low and no oil crisis, Macmillan in 1958 could liken the economy to a car for which both brake and accelerator were required: 'their use is a matter of judgement but their purpose must remain essentially the same—to go forward safely; or, in economic terms, expansion in a balanced economy'.[7] Computers were already opening up vistas of planning potential: they had 'already done invaluable work in astronomy, in physics and in engineering, as well as in pure mathematics', wrote the future physics baron B. V. Bowden in 1953; 'they may help to make weather forecasting into an exact science; they bid fair to revolutionize accountancy and book-keeping and the analysis of Government statistics . . . Time alone will show if this will help a government to forecast cycles of boom and slump and perhaps to control them.'[8]

Whatever the long-term and abstract merits of a move towards the free market, the political and intellectual climate was not yet ripe for it, if only because the drawbacks of managed capitalism were not yet apparent. From the free-market viewpoint, things had to get worse before they could get better. Besides, faith must be kept with the electors, and after 1945 the Conservatives had publicly clutched a hold of the centre ground for fear of something worse. The furious small-shopkeeper hostility that greeted Heath's abolition of resale price maintenance in 1964 showed how warily even Conservative electors viewed a free-market strategy. Hence what many Conservatives in the 1980s saw as their predecessors' timidity on privatization. Only road transport and iron and steel were selected for denationalization, and many government controls were retained even there. The government was in retrospect surprisingly lukewarm in championing the changes. When in 1953 the iron and steel shares made available were three times oversubscribed, no ongoing privatization dynamic followed. The resulting growth in the number of shareholders was welcome, but it had neither been expected, nor intended.[9] 'Popular capitalism' was not yet even a gleam in the Conservative eye. What might anachronistically be described as a 'Thatcherite' policy for the Conservative government after 1951 would have encountered a hostility from Labour in opposition far more intense

[6] C. L. Gilbert, *The Development of British Econometrics 1945–85* (University of Oxford, Institute of Economics and Statistics, Applied Economics Discussion Paper, 8, Apr. 1986), 10–20. Obituary of Denis Sargan, *G* (13 May 1996), 11.

[7] H. Macmillan, 'The Middle Way: Twenty Years After', in his *The Middle Way* (1st publ. 1938, 1966 edn.), p. xxv.

[8] B. V. Bowden (ed.), *Faster than Thought: A Symposium on Digital Computing Machines* (1953), p. ix (preface).

[9] K. Burk, *The First Privatisation: The Politicians, the City, and the Denationalisation of Steel* (1988), 11, 135.

than anything offered after 1979, and a Labour victory in 1955 or earlier might well have resulted.

After 1945 British governments were less willing than European to use tariffs for promoting selected industries. Instead, the Conservatives after 1951 relied upon demand management; this involved a manipulation of the bank rate which Labour critics thought clumsily undiscriminating. Central planning in the 1950s carried to a deliberate and higher plane the integration and amalgamation within industrial concerns that were spontaneously occurring lower down: factories with 1,500 or more employees employed 24 per cent of total manufacturing employees in 1951, but 36 per cent in 1973.[10] Desire for economies of scale ensured that during the 1960s mergers were all the rage, in government departments as well as in businesses. It was thought that captains of industry like Kearton, Ryder, Stokes, and Weinstock could maintain overall strategic control of the huge structures that emerged, and that they would be able to respond flexibly to events. Nationalization, a sort of state-sponsored merger, harmonized well with this corporatist outlook. In 1951 it was by no means discredited: indeed, for years afterwards even private-sector employers when in trouble (leading shipbuilders in 1967, for example) were keen to extend it.[11] Trade unionists liked it too, not because they wanted to run the nationalized industries or abandon free collective bargaining within them, but because nationalization seemed likely to promote job security, to redistribute wealth, and ensure humane treatment of employees. Even under Conservative governments, nationalization seemed likely to stay.

Driving the planners forward was the pursuit of economic growth, given widespread apprehension about economic and moral competition from the USSR's planned economy. In the 1950s Labour's social democrats were propagating Durbin's message of 1940: that capitalism could deliver mass abundance, and in 1956 Crosland no longer viewed questions of growth and efficiency 'as being, on a long view, of primary importance to socialism'.[12] It was now feared, however, that the British economy was not even comparing well with democratic economies. Fear reinforced envy when the UK in the late 1940s viewed superior American productivity. Then in the 1950s, as the shattered European economies recovered, growth rates first in West Germany, then in France, then in Italy seemed intimidating. Spurring on the UK's search for economic success were publications, corporatist in mood, mostly from outside the universities, on 'political economy': in periodicals such as the *Financial Times* and *Economist*, and in books written for a lay readership by authors literate in economics such as Andrew Shonfield, Samuel Brittan, and Michael Shanks.

[10] J. F. Wright, *Britain in the Age of Economic Management* (Oxford, 1973), 40.
[11] Wilson, *Labour Government 1964–1970*, 423.
[12] *Future of Socialism*, 515. See also G. F. M. Durbin, *The Politics of Democratic Socialism* (1940), 142.

Particularly influential were the increasingly accessible comparative statistics on national economic performance, together with Political and Economic Planning's *Growth in the British Economy* (1960).[13] These publications sought to answer such questions as the following. Was the British national share in world trade rising or falling? Where did Britain stand in the international league for productivity growth? If the British economy was in relative decline, why? And what was the cure?

Britain was steadily slipping in the world league for gross domestic product per head: from seventh place in 1950 to ninth in 1960 to twelfth in 1965 to eighteenth in 1970 to twentieth in 1975 to twenty-first in 1981. In 1950–73 it was the nations defeated in the Second World War—Japan, Germany, and Italy—which grew fastest; Canada, France, and the USA lagged behind somewhat, with the UK trailing furthest behind of all.[14] When Crossman returned to London from Vancouver in September 1956, a remark from the Canadian-born political scientist R. T. McKenzie 'hit me in the stomach': what a relief, McKenzie had said, to have been in a country without a dollar crisis and with good prospects of economic growth. On returning to England Crossman had 'the sense of restriction, yes, even of decline, of an old country always teetering on the edge of a crisis, trying to keep up appearances, with no confident vision of the future'.[15] The cliché 'the envy of the world', so often complacently applied to British institutions in the past (and future), for the moment carried less conviction, especially for British travellers abroad. Long gone were the days when their standards had been so pacesetting as to shame European hotels into installing English sanitation.[16]

To explain this relative decline, at least four theories were current from the mid-1950s. According to the 'early start' theory, the UK's European rivals could draw upon reserve armies of agricultural and self-employed labour which UK industry had mopped up long before. The 'rejuvenation by defeat' theory argued that victory in 1945 had denied Britain the German and Japanese incentive to re-equip and rethink. The third, 'imperial distraction', theory pointed to the UK's special handicap by comparison with its leading trade rivals: its worldwide responsibilities. The Macmillan government's 'future policy study' of February 1960 included Treasury estimates on the share of gross national product at factor cost that these absorbed; defence, economic aid, diplomacy, civil defence, and overseas cultural services had risen to a

[13] For valuable commentary on this see J. Tomlinson, *The Politics of Decline: Understanding Post-War Britain* (Harlow, 2000), 12–21; and his 'Inventing "Decline": The Falling Behind of the British Economy in the Postwar Years', *Economic History Review* (Nov. 1996), 735, 738, 740–1, 743.

[14] D. Sanders, *Losing an Empire, Finding a Role* (1990), 117. Table 1 in S. N. Broadberry, 'The Impact of the World Wars on the Long Run Performance of the British Economy', *Oxford Review of Economic Policy*, 4/1 (1988), 26.

[15] Crossman, *Backbench Diaries*, 507 (5 Sept. 1956).

[16] J. Pemble, *The Mediterranean Passion: Victorians and Edwardians in the South* (Oxford, 1987), 44.

peak of 12.3 per cent in 1952, and had then slowly but steadily fallen to 8.4 per cent in 1959.[17] The 'institutional failure' theory reacted against wartime pride in the continuity and longevity of British political institutions, and argued instead that their ritualized conflict injected into the shaping of policy three harmful ingredients: discontinuity, unpredictability, and class envy. The theory's social-class ingredients, fashionable from the 1950s to the 1980s, included demonizing the trade unions and blaming the public schools and universities for perpetuating an 'anti-industrial culture' in Britain. The alleged outcome was to privilege the professional and financial life over manufacturing. Radicals on left and right found a remedy in the meritocratic challenge to an allegedly amateur and backward-looking 'establishment' which allegedly squandered national resources on propping up outdated colonial commitments.

There was a regional dimension to the 'institutional failure' theory. The central planning fashionable in the 1950s and 1960s incorporated a regional planning structure whose pedigree stretched back to the Special Areas Act (1934), after which the areas eligible for grants and tax incentives gradually extended. In the 1950s and 1960s it seemed only common sense to protect declining regions from a decay that would squander their infrastructure and push their populations into more prosperous but overcrowded and alien areas. Regional planning might instead tempt new employers into the areas of declining manufacture with government grants, concessions, and an improved infrastructure. Regional planning reached its peak under Labour in 1966: a fifth of the working population then lived in the so-called 'development areas', including almost the whole of Scotland's insured population. At the same time the Highlands and Islands Development Board was established to develop the region with grants and loans.[18] Successive governments reinforced such schemes by the policy, which had originated for defence reasons in the 1940s, of dispersing their own and other offices away from London and into the assisted areas.[19] Regional policy had allegedly generated a tenth of Scotland's manufacturing jobs by 1975, more than three times as many as Scottish oil up to that date.[20] By 1970 the development areas covered almost the entire UK outside the Midlands and south-east.

The development areas were Labour's heartland, the areas its welfare measures benefited most, at least in the short term. 'In this crowded island', said Wilson in 1967, 'the new industrial frontier for the next generation depends on opening up again the areas of the first Industrial Revolution, which the Tories

[17] Hennessy, *Having It So Good*, 588.

[18] Ponting, *Breach of Promise*, 114–15. R. Saville (ed.), *The Economic Development of Modern Scotland 1950–1980* (Edinburgh, 1985), 69.

[19] For a fuller discussion see C. M. Law, *British Regional Development since World War I* (Newton Abbot, 1980), 198.

[20] As claimed by J. N. Randall in Saville (ed.), *Economic Development of Modern Scotland*, 255.

allowed to decline into grime and decay.' By July 1966, however, Crossman was already arguing privately that retreat from intervention would produce 'massive growth', whereas 'almost all our social policies ran counter to the idea of rapid growth'; he thought the 'old development areas' were over-represented in the cabinet, and were reinforced by MPs from Labour's heartlands, so that when government funds were distributed, the growth areas lost out.[21] Politics affected which areas were chosen for favourable government treatment, and while the jobs that regional policy 'created' in the designated areas were advertised, the jobs lost through diverting resources to them from elsewhere were not.

By the late 1950s the consensus between employers, trade unions, and government that had been integral to wartime corporatism was ebbing.[22] The 'money illusion', whereby employees appraised nominal pay increases without taking taxation and inflation levels into account, was beginning to fade, and wage negotiations were becoming more difficult. Churchill's policy of avoiding industrial conflict broke down with the Associated Society of Locomotive Engineers and Firemen (ASLEF) strike of May 1955, the first national strike for over twenty years seriously to inconvenience the public. In 1957 the government tried to enforce wage restraint, yet would not back the employers in resisting the trade unions opposing it.[23] In an age of growing inflation the corporatist settlement of 1944 was all the more needed, yet it could precariously generate the necessary collaboration only in a real or convincingly alleged national emergency. Statist in overall outlook but voluntarist in execution, corporatist wage settlements even when secured could not ensure that efficiency would in the longer term be maximized or that the consumer's interests would not suffer by comparison with the producer's. Self-regulation was at risk of degenerating into short-term pragmatic compromise and an inertia which persisted under Labour governments allied with the trade unions and under Conservative governments reluctant to offend them.

There were growing doubts, too, even within the labour movement, about nationalization, that major component of the postwar planning mechanism. Productivity gains were patchy, workforce morale did not gain much from knowing that the state was now the employer, and management often forsook Labour's heartlands for London, becoming still more remote.[24] Labour's revisionists in the 1950s noted James Burnham's emphasis in his *Managerial Revolution*

[21] Wilson, *T* (5 Oct. 1967), 7. Crossman quoted in Benn, *Diaries 1963–7*, 453 (14 July 1966); Crossman, *Cabinet Diaries*, i. 410 (13 Dec. 1965); Benn, *Diaries 1968–72*, 161–2 (21 Apr. 1969).

[22] I acknowledge here the four important books written in this complex, neglected, and important area by Keith Middlemas: *Politics in Industrial Society: The Experience of the British System since 1911* (1979) and *Power, Competition and the State* (3 vols., 1986–91).

[23] H. A. Clegg, *How to Run an Incomes Policy and Why We Made a Mess of the Last One* (1971), 2.

[24] For figures see L. Hannah, 'The Economic Consequences of the State Ownership of Industry, 1945–1990', in R. Floud and D. McCloskey (eds.), *Cambridge Economic History of Britain*, iii (2nd edn. 1994), 176–7.

(1941) on the increasing divorce between ownership and control, and sought more flexible alternative routes to planning. Crosland denied that nationalization was an end in itself. As a means—for example, in counter-cyclical investment, redistribution of wealth, or advancing the classless society—it was either redundant or inefficient or both. Nationalization was, he declared, 'bad for liberty, and wholly irrelevant to socialism'. When surveyed in 1960, public opinion was pragmatic on nationalization, and only a fifth of Labour supporters wanted more of it, a marked decline on 1949.[25]

Much of the shift reflected dissatisfaction at nationalized industries' defence of producer against consumer. Benn saw how a state concern worked at close quarters when Postmaster General in 1964–6. In annual wage negotiations, the director general would suggest a maximum figure, the general secretary of the Union of Post Office Workers would suggest his alternative, and with many nods and winks the two would work through to the middle.[26] The two producer 'sides' of the monopolistic nationalized concern colluded against the consumer. Hence a steady shrinkage in the nationalized segment of an economy that was already encumbered enough. Often originating in loss-making private concerns, the nationalized industries incurred political interference (especially from governments allied with trade unions) in their management, and statutory curbs on their sphere of activity. Benn was impressed in 1965 with American capitalists' enthusiasm for private enterprise, absent from Britain's public sector.[27] In the nationalized world, Galbraith's phrase 'private affluence, public squalor' retained much relevance. By contrast, Felixstowe, through not joining the National Dock Labour Scheme of 1948, could grow from nothing during the 1950s into a major port, pioneering the use of forklift trucks (1956), completing an oil jetty (1964), becoming the first East Anglian port to build a container holder for roll-on/roll-off ferries, and from 1976 operating a regular passenger service.[28] Nationalization advanced in only two areas between 1951 and 1970: when the denationalization in 1953 of iron and steel and road transport was reversed in 1967.

Up to 1970 and beyond, the immediate corporatist response to these setbacks was not retreat, but more energetic attempts to advance. Such aspirations were not narrowly partisan: employers' organizations in 1960 were attracted to French methods of 'indicative' planning, which involved target-setting consultation between civil servants, trade unionists, and representatives of industry. The Conservative government was enthusiastic: what distinguished the parties was not the destination but how best to get there, given that Labour seemed best placed to 'deliver' the trade unions. The National Economic

[25] Crosland, *Future of Socialism*, 496. M. Abrams and R. Rose, *Must Labour Lose?* (Harmondsworth, 1960), 31–7.
[26] Benn, *Diaries 1963–7*, 245 (12 Apr. 1965).
[27] Ibid. 241 (5 Apr. 1965), cf. 264 (28 May 1965).
[28] 'Ian Trelawny (1917–98)', *ODNB*.

Development Council, established in 1961 as a forum to bring government and the two 'sides' of industry together, published in the following year a national plan which chose a figure for the desired rate of national economic growth and spelt out its implications for exports, imports, investment, and other sections of the economy. Such efforts foundered on the trade union refusal to collaborate with what they mistakenly saw as a free-market Conservative government. Here, as in welfare and decolonization in the 1950s, Labour exploited its built-in advantage over the Conservatives, integrally linked as Labour was with powerful and relevant interest groups.

The Labour government's attempt in 1965 to set up a 'national plan', together with trying to operate an incomes policy, saw corporatism at its apogee. It was promoted through a new government department (the Department of Economic Affairs, DEA) which was designed to foster economic growth and counterbalance the Treasury's shorter-term and allegedly less constructive influence. On 16 September 1965 the Plan was published, aiming to increase the national output by 25 per cent between 1964 and 1970. The Plan's authors assumed that central government, like individual firms, needed to make 'forecasts or projections' for particular industries, and that these would sometimes be wrong; but that 'this does not mean that it is useless to make them', because when an industry falls below the projection, 'it will be valuable to discover why'.[29] It was hoped that the desired outcome would emerge from enhanced productivity combined with employing labour more efficiently through regional planning. More workers would be freed to work in engineering, construction, and the public services through cutting employment in agriculture, mining, inland transport, textiles, aircraft, clothing, and footwear. Such policies would be reinforced by cutting defence expenditure, discouraging investment abroad, and encouraging economies of scale through government-induced mergers and rationalization. A virtuous cycle would then set in whereby expectations of growth would enhance confidence, generate high investment, and thereby produce growth.

Yet the Plan lacked guidelines on mechanisms. How would its targets be reached? What were the government's powers of enforcement? The Plan was in effect stillborn. Wilson's initial strategy in 1964 was reasonable enough: to revitalize British industry not through the soft and short-term option of devaluation, which anyway would have stirred unfavourable recollections of the Attlee governments' failures and austerities, but through the sort of voluntary 'physical' planning which could invaluably exploit Labour's close trade union links. He hoped consultatively to mobilize trade union loyalties behind a more fundamental restructuring of British industry under a Ministry of Technology (Mintech) headed by the most powerful trade unionist of the

[29] *The National Plan*, 3; cf. 74.

day, Frank Cousins. Unfortunately for Wilson, there were contradictions within government economic policy: the Plan required growth, whereas balance-of-payments worries dictated deflation; and trade unionists disliked his strategy's necessary accompaniment, an incomes policy. From the earliest days of incomes policies some Labour ministers had been attracted by their participatory aspect; Crossman's vision in 1966 was even that they might realize R. H. Tawney's democratic dreams.[30] But in practice incomes policies readily drifted from wage planning into wage restraint, and cruelly exposed the tension within the labour movement between the pursuit of equality and the rewarding of merit. Far from reviving the wartime corporatist consensus, they eroded it still further. The free market, for all its clumsiness, did not complicate decisions on wage differentials with semi-moralistic exhortation: it merely signalled impersonally the short-term implications for pay of an abundant labour supply.[31]

Worse, Wilson sought to win credit with middle opinion in 1969 by planning to force trade unions to reform themselves through the proposals outlined in the white paper 'In Place of Strife'.[32] But Castle, enthusiastic at the Department of Employment and Productivity for a full-blown socialist interventionist policy of manpower planning,[33] was too late on the scene. When between 1970 and 1974 Heath's Conservative government demonstrated conclusively that the Conservatives could not work a corporatist policy either, his failure was in effect preparing the ground for something completely different. Wilson's governments after 1964 were caught in several dilemmas: without full trade union collaboration in planning and modernization they could not secure economic growth, yet only economic growth could deliver the welfare and other benefits that would render such collaboration attractive. There were now too many middle-class voters to render electorally feasible the theoretical alternative: using an incomes policy to redistribute wealth between the classes. Besides, the weak balance of payments exposed the government to continuous uncertainty after its election victory of 1966, and its inevitably Treasury-led focus subordinated long-term plans to the tackling of short-term emergencies. Britain did not possess the elaborate administrative structure and independence of overseas trade that would have made a protectionist 'fortress Britain' approach feasible. Profits after mergers did not vindicate economies of scale,[34] whereas the prosperity of Scottish whisky and Italian textiles demonstrated

[30] Crossman, *Cabinet Diaries*, ii. 50 (24 Sept. 1966).

[31] For more on this see B. Harrison, 'Incomes Policies in Britain since 1940: A Study in Political Economy', in K. Bruland and P. O'Brien (eds.), *From Family Firms to Corporate Capitalism: Essays in Business and Industrial History in Honour of Peter Mathias* (Oxford, 1998), 269–96.

[32] This is fully discussed below, pp. 212, 458–60.

[33] See e.g. her *Diaries 1964–1970*, 755 (26 Jan. 1970).

[34] T. R. Gourvish and R. G. Wilson, *Brewing Industry 1830–1980* (Cambridge, 1994), 499–500. See also Middlemas, *Power, Competition and the State*, i. 305; ii. 166–7; Sampson, *Changing Anatomy of Britain*, 317–18, 424.

the small firm's virtues;[35] in the latter case, the innovative, design-conscious small firm that focused on adding value and catering for a European market could achieve great successes.[36] Besides, the National Plan's enthusiasm for size conflicted with the consumer's interest in breaking up monopolies. By the late 1970s smallness was becoming beautiful. So the outcome of Labour's Plan was profoundly disappointing. Among the industry groups, productivity grew faster than planned only in food, drink, and tobacco, and output per head even there fell well below earlier trends.[37] In this situation Jewkes decided to republish his *Ordeal by Planning*: 'I wish to add nothing to what I then said', he wrote, when introducing its reprint of 1968. 'This original essay is reprinted, virtually unchanged. . . . I have nothing to retract from the doctrine I then enunciated—that when Governments begin to claim that they know of short cuts to prosperity, economic trouble is in the offing.' For him 'one of the most surprising things' about the resurgence in the 1960s of socialist planning was that nobody wanted to learn from past failure.[38] Until well into the 1970s both Labour and Conservative front-bench insiders hugged the interventionist centre ground, and in their informal centrist union they precariously prevailed—for the moment—over the outsiders: libertarian trade unionists to the left, free-market Conservatives to the right.

2. FROM MANUFACTURING TO SERVICES

The underlying trend in the British economy after 1951 was from manufacturing to services. In so far as government perceived it, they did not welcome it and even tried to discourage it. The Second World War's temporary revival of heavy industry had helped to mask the long-term trend—and, if anything, enhanced the prestige of the trade-union-dominated northern-based heavy industry, with its masculine image. The Labour Party's regional strength gave it a strong interest in reviving manufacture, and Wilson's first speech as leader to the Labour Party conference in 1963, identifying socialism with technology, aimed both at this and at winning votes from the growing number of scientists and technologists;[39] Conservatives eager to shed their interwar image were forced to tag along behind. Shipbuilding after 1945 succumbed throughout Europe, even in Sweden, to competition from the Far East. How

[35] S. Broadberry, 'The Performance of Manufacturing', in R. Floud and P. Johnson (eds.), *The Cambridge Economic History of Modern Britain*, iii. *Structural Change and Growth, 1939–2000* (Cambridge, 2004), 79–81.

[36] As argued in G. Owen, *From Empire to Europe: The Decline and Revival of British Industry since the Second World War* (1999), 57.

[37] *The National Plan*, 8. M. J. C. Surrey, 'The National Plan in Retrospect', *Bulletin of the Oxford University Institute of Economics and Statistics* (Aug. 1972), 261.

[38] Introduction to 2nd edn. (1968) of his *Ordeal by Planning*, p. ix.

[39] Wilson, *Memoirs 1916–64*, 197; cf. Foot, *Politics of Harold Wilson*, 151.

was the once-mighty Scottish shipbuilding industry fallen! Its three-fifths of the world's merchant shipping tonnage launched in 1913 was a mere 2 per cent in 1980, and its contribution to shipbuilding even within Britain had shrunk.[40] Late twentieth-century improvements in the Scottish economy stemmed from the spontaneous growth of new industries—most notably oil, oil rigs, and computers—not from politicians' attempts to preserve old ones.

In 1951 Britain was the world's leading exporter of motor vehicles: it had 44 per cent of the world's car exports, 30 per cent of commercial vehicles.[41] British car manufacture kept up well until the 1960s, greatly increasing its share of the world market by 1950, and responding well thereafter to a rapidly growing home market. It could still develop highly successful new models, most notably the Morris Minor (launched in 1948, and the first British car to sell a million units), and the 'Mini' (launched in 1959, and reaching its first million in 1965). Both were brilliantly designed by Alec Issigonis, son of a Greek living in Smyrna; Alec had come to England in 1922 as a refugee with his mother. In 1955 Britain manufactured only a tenth as many cars as the USA, but more than Germany, and far more than Italy and France. Yet the last three countries were rapidly catching up, especially in exports, and by the late 1960s Japan was racing ahead. With faster manufacturing growth elsewhere, the British share of world exports in manufactures declined from 25 per cent in 1950 to 9 per cent in 1973.[42] High hopes were placed in enhanced expertise and economies of scale. In 1952 the amalgamation between Austin and Morris Motors at Longbridge and Cowley made the British Motor Corporation the largest builder of private cars in Europe, and a further clutch of mergers produced British Leyland in 1968. Mergers did not cause either cars or textiles to prosper. Even huge British textile conglomerates could not ward off low-cost imports.[43]

On energy, the record was more mixed. A nationalized coal industry was able to humanize and slow down decline, but could not prevent it. In 1950 coal accounted for the UK's entire fuel production and for 90 per cent of its consumption, but its role fell continuously in both respects thereafter, despite the National Coal Board's readiness to develop and adopt the latest technology. Whereas the number of Board collieries fell by three-quarters between 1951 and 1981, output fell by less than half, and manpower by two-thirds, so productivity more than doubled.[44] Huge new power stations stood like sentinels in the Trent

[40] Saville (ed.), *Economic Development of Modern Scotland*, 80.

[41] R. Millward, 'Industrial and Commercial Performance since 1950', in Floud and McCloskey (eds.), *Cambridge Economic History of Britain*, iii (2nd edn.), 141.

[42] See the table in E. J. Hobsbawm, *Industry and Empire: An Economic History of Britain since 1750* (1968), 220. C. Feinstein, 'Success and Failure', in R. Floud and D. McCloskey (eds.), *Cambridge Economic History of Britain*, iii (2nd edn. 1994), 108.

[43] Owen, *Empire to Europe*, 57, 77, 87–9.

[44] P. Johnson (ed.), *The Structure of British Industry* (1988), 29, 63. W. Ashworth, *The History of the British Coal Industry*, v. *1946–1982: The Nationalised Industry* (Oxford, 1986), 672–6.

valley, catering through the supergrid for growing demand in the south of England, but coal ran into growing competition from oil and nuclear power. For even within the manufacturing sector what Schumpeter had called waves of 'creative destruction'[45] were at work, though less dramatically so than in the 1930s or 1980s. Britain's Magnox gas-cooled reactors, developed in the 1950s, were the first effective commercial nuclear power stations. In retrospect, coal's defenders in the 1950s rightly highlighted the hidden costs of nuclear power; though great care was taken with safety, setbacks were not publicized. The fire of 10 October 1957 in the Windscale plutonium plant endangered human health far more than the better-known Three Mile Island partial meltdown in 1979. When told that one of the eighty-foot piles was on fire, Thomas Tuohy (deputy to the general manager) ignored safety regulations, repeatedly climbed to the inspection holes at the top, and eventually decided to take the risk of recommending dowsing the fire with hoses.[46] Brave, blunt, and forceful, he had found the answer, but Sir William Penney's report on the fire severely criticized the plant's management, and nearly half his report was kept secret; thirty-five workers had been irradiated, and its effects in Cumbria were still apparent half a century later.[47] Politicians were ill-equipped to challenge prevailing scientific orthodoxy, which in the 1950s and 1960s assumed that oil was a mere stopgap, especially after the Suez crisis in 1956 had shown how insecure was its supply, and how the future lay with nuclear power; the meltdowns at Three Mile Island (1979) and Chernobyl (1986) had yet to advertise its hazards. In October 1956 the Calder Hall nuclear reactor became the first in any country to deliver electricity for commercial purposes to a national grid system. Thereafter, new nuclear power stations opened almost annually, all located for safety reasons on remote coastal sites. By 1967 Britain had generated more electricity by nuclear means than the rest of the world (including the USA) put together, and had a greater installed capacity for nuclear power than any other nation.[48]

Yet the first-generation Magnox and second-generation gas-cooled reactors did not prove commercially viable, and in the 1960s the rising relative cost of nuclear power decelerated the building programme. Elsewhere the returns from governments' promotion of new science-based jobs proved even more disappointing. Investment in defence-related research and development, seemingly inflated in retrospect, concentrated science-related expenditure on aviation, nuclear physics, and atomic energy—rendering skilled manpower scarce

[45] J. A. Schumpeter, *Capitalism, Socialism and Democracy* (1st publ. 1943, 5th edn. 1976), 83; cf. 68.

[46] Obituary of Tuohy, *Ind.* (26 Mar. 2008), 34.

[47] *DT* (25 Apr. 2006), 10. See also Hennessy, *Having It So Good*, 582.

[48] Pierre, *Nuclear Politics*, 127. Hannah, 'State Ownership', 186–7. R. Williams, *The Nuclear Power Decisions: British Policies, 1953–78* (1980), 342.

elsewhere.[49] Even in the defence-related areas there were major setbacks. The 1950s saw serious failures in Britain's rocket programme, and the spectacular failure of the Comet 1 airliner, launched in 1952 as a symbol of national self-confidence and recovery, was but one among several unprofitable high-altitude, high-speed jet aircraft developed with government funds after 1945, culminating in the supersonic plane Concorde. After three of the seven Comet 1s had crashed within two years, all seven had to be grounded. Sir Raymond Streat, chairman of the Cotton Board, voiced distress in his diary: amidst the humiliations of national decline, 'our leadership in the jet aeroplane brought comfort to the heart of the meanest citizen'.[50] Metal fatigue was diagnosed, and the USA's Boeing 707, which could carry more passengers, was launched in 1958 and eventually captured the market.

At least as disappointing were governments' attempts to build up a powerful British computing industry. The Wilson government's National Plan in 1965 aimed to accelerate 'automation', as it was then called: computerized control of plant processes and automatic data processing for management and design. The term was first used in 1936 in an American car-manufacturing context to denote 'the automatic handling of parts between progressive production processes',[51] and was first used in Britain in 1953 at a time when electronic control was distancing human physical agency even further from the manufacturing process. If Britain had fully exploited her disproportionate impact on the early history of computers, huge new manufacturing opportunities for a world market would have opened up. Britain had done much to develop the basic concepts as well as the research and development that led to computer manufacture, and in the mid-1950s there were eight British computer manufacturers. In the late 1940s mainframe computers had been developed at Manchester University, and smaller machines with commercial links at the universities of Cambridge and London. By 1954 LEO (Lyons Electronic Office) was computing the weekly payroll for the food and catering firm's 10,000 employees; LEO Computers Ltd, established in the same year, became Britain's leading manufacturer of commercial computers.[52] LEO had originated in a visit to the USA by Lyons executives investigating office technology, and already in 1953 the USA had more computers in use than the rest of the world combined. Thereafter the

[49] J. Agar, 'The New Price and Place of University Research: Jodrell Bank, NIRNS and the Context of Post-War British Academic Science', *Contemporary British History*, 11/1 (Spring 1997), 5. For a useful table of overall expenditure on research and development, see P. Gummett, *Scientists in Whitehall* (Manchester, 1980), 39.

[50] Sir R. Streat, *Lancashire and Whitehall: The Diary of Sir Raymond Streat*, ii. *1939–57*, ed. M. Dupree (Manchester, 1987), 706 (17 Jan. 1954).

[51] L. L. Goodman, *Man and Automation* (1957), 24.

[52] T. Kelly, *The British Computer Industry: Crisis and Development* (1987), 40–1. M. Campbell-Kelly, 'The Development of Computer Programming in Britain (1945 to 1955)', *Annals of the History of Computing* (1982), 127–8.

number of computers in the UK grew fast: 23 in 1955, 306 in 1960, 1,424 in 1965, and 5,470 in 1970.[53] Not fast enough: Britain by 1964 had 800 computers in operation, but to match the USA's usage per head of population it should have been using 5,000. Of the 40,000 computers in the world early in 1966, Britain had more than any European country, but it already had fewer than Japan, and was entirely dwarfed by the USA.[54] With computers, as earlier with office technology, the USA's larger domestic market and relatively entrepreneurial climate enabled the Americans in the early 1960s to pull rapidly ahead.[55] Wilson's government fully acknowledged the need for the government to encourage the British computer industry through the Ministry of Technology, but by 1968, when the early British computer manufacturers merged into ICL, it was dwarfed by IBM.[56]

Exploitation of gas and oil resources, by contrast, saw dramatic growth from the 1960s. Between 1950 and 1973 UK energy consumption increased by nearly 2 per cent a year, yet coal's share fell from 90 to 38 per cent:[57] the need for a home-produced alternative was clearly great. We have already seen how a nationalized concern exploited North Sea gas resources during that decade;[58] the 1960s launched the dramatic growth in extracting North Sea oil. Pioneered in the Gulf of Mexico, worldwide submarine exploration had been spreading fast from the 1950s, and ever deeper wells were being drilled: from a maximum of 20 feet in 1950, but routinely reaching 350 feet by 1973.[59] Given the USA's proportionately declining contribution to the world's oil resources and the consequent growing worldwide dependence since the 1940s on the Middle East's less predictable resources, economic considerations and even national security made a discovery highly desirable for the UK. Fortunately, with oil discovered at Ekofisk in September 1969, the balance of North Sea exploration could shift from gas to oil. This shift was particularly timely in Scotland, whose share of UK output in both coal and steel was falling fast—by almost half between the mid-1940s and the late 1970s.[60] Although the areas of decline and growth in Scotland were not exactly matched, oil rigs could emerge from the old shipbuilding areas, and oil could help to replace fish as a source of jobs in the north-eastern coastal areas, with all the encouragement to profitability

[53] Bowden (ed.), *Faster than Thought*, 173. P. L. Stoneman, 'On the Change in Technique: A Study of the Spread of Computer Usage in the United Kingdom 1954–1970' (Cambridge D.Phil. thesis, 1973), 27.

[54] Viscount Astor, *HL Deb.* 8 Apr. 1964, c. 192. H. A. Rhee, *Office Automation in Social Perspective: The Progress and Social Implications of Electronic Data Processing* (Oxford, 1968), 11.

[55] M. Campbell-Kelly, *ICL: A Business and Technical History* (Oxford, 1989), 208–9.

[56] *The National Plan*, 50. J. Kavanagh, 'History Often Repeats Itself', *FT* (16 Mar. 1994 supplement on 'Information and Communications Technology'), p. xiii.

[57] Band, 'Fifty Years of UK Offshore Oil and Gas', 179.

[58] See above, p. 125.

[59] Chapman, *North Sea Oil and Gas*, 35.

[60] Saville (ed.), *Economic Development of Modern Scotland*, 80.

stemming in the 1970s from OPEC price rises and political embargoes. By 1980 Britain was self-sufficient in oil.

These long-term changes profoundly influenced where people lived. For more than 4,000 years after the neolithic period it was the more readily accessible lowland areas close to Europe that were most often invaded, and where the most significant cultural, economic, and technological development took place. The industrial revolution had disrupted this pattern, with its flow of population, ideas, and self-confidence to the north and west, but in the eye of history this regional shift was no more than an interruption to the longer-term trend which resumed after 1951, complemented by resumption of the population's interwar drift from north-west to south-east.[61] This drift reflected the resumed growth in the service sector: that is, in such areas as banking, professional services, retailing, leisure, education, welfare, transport, and communications. Service employment had been strong in the south of England even before the industrial revolution, and persisted there throughout manufacture's nineteenth-century rise and twentieth-century fall. After 1951 some Scots moved southwards to growth areas within England, but others moved within Scotland from Clydeside's heavy engineering into the new electronic and oil-related industries to the east and north-east of Scotland. The industrial and mining areas of England and Wales in 1951 were predominantly in the Midlands, the north and Wales, whereas the service and defence sectors were strongest in the south.[62] The regional distribution of those registered as unemployed mirrored these changes; unemployment was consistently higher in the north and in Scotland throughout the 1950s and 1960s, and in Northern Ireland highest of all. This regional contrast grew increasingly stark as unemployment mounted in the late 1960s,[63] and as the balance of Britain's overseas trade shifted towards the regions closest to Europe. Regional analyses of poverty, environmental and educational deprivation, and dependence on council housing tell a similar story.[64]

Because affluent modern societies demand more leisure, and better education, welfare, and transport, labour-intensive service occupations eat up more and more of the workforce: 47 per cent of its total employment in 1951, 49 per cent in 1961, 53 per cent in 1971.[65] In the 1960s the many local branches of the major national banks still stood like sentinels in the high streets, advertising their dependability with their external pillars and porticos and internally with their mahogany counters and protective grilles. The 'bank manager', respected within his community, still cultivated a

[61] R. H. Best and J. T. Coppock, *The Changing Use of Land* (1962), 21. For a fuller discussion, see C. Law, *British Regional Development since World War I*, 59.

[62] See the useful tables in Carr-Saunders *et al.*, *Survey of Social Conditions*, 48–9.

[63] *BHS* 126.

[64] Townsend, *Poverty in UK*, 551–2.

[65] F. Cairncross, 'Into Services Everyone', *G* (15 May 1976), 16.

professional and confidential relationship with customers as individuals, but there were signs that this apparently stable and secure world was breaking up. By the 1960s the large clearing banks were democratizing the bank account, now diminishingly a middle-class preserve. Successful American precedents prompted Barclaycard's introduction to Britain in 1966; by the end of the year there were a million Barclaycard holders. Initially available only for Barclays customers, the dispenser's purpose was to relieve bank staff of routine operations. On 17 June 1967 the world's first cash dispenser attracted a large crowd to Enfield, dispensing £10 to customers issued with special cardboard vouchers.[66]

By the 1960s banking in London was changing fast. The City's national role both preceded and outlasted the industrial revolution, but in retrospect its function in the late 1940s seems modest and its morale low. The two world wars and the resort in 1931 to exchange control had seriously damaged it as a national and international source of commercial information and expert financial services, and London's commodity markets opened only slowly after 1945. In the 1950s the London Stock Exchange was relatively sheltered and insular: a reticent and respectable body aiming primarily to meet the needs of the British government and economy, both in relative decline. Run informally on a basis of trust through a network of small, socially exclusive groups, the City policed itself, while the Treasury managed a Bank of England that by later standards was remarkably secretive. 'If I want to talk to the representatives of the . . . whole financial community', said the Governor of the Bank of England in 1957, 'we can usually get together in one room in about half-an-hour'.[67] Within the year, however, the so-called 'aluminium war' of 1958 exposed the mounting power of player versus gentleman in the City: the American firm Reynolds Metals joined Tube Investments and triumphed over the old banks when it bought up British Aluminium, Britain's only aluminium company.[68] In the 1950s the building societies' growing financial power helped further to prise open the City's intimate world. The City's critics tended to exaggerate its cohesion. To Labour's cabinet ministers after 1964 it seemed formidable: in December 1967 Crossman pronounced the government's distance from the world of the City 'terrifying', and in the following February Jenkins as Chancellor of the Exchequer pronounced the Bank of England 'a closed book to us all'.[69]

In the 1950s it was becoming fashionable to say that the banks neglected British industry, yet among City priorities its needs were far more salient then

[66] *FT* (27 June 1997), 11. *Ind.* (14 June 1996), 3.

[67] Governor Cobbold (1957), quoted by M. Moran, 'Finance Capital and Pressure-Group Politics in Britain', *British Journal of Political Science*, 11 (1981), 390.

[68] Sampson, *Anatomy of Britain*, 387–90.

[69] Crossman, *Cabinet Diaries*, ii. 603 (14 Dec. 1967); 667 (6 Feb. 1968); cf. i. 155 (11 Feb. 1965).

than later, and British industry's access to the stock market was broadening. The merchant banks—which before the war had focused on raising capital for governments and countries, especially overseas—were shut out by exchange control from such business for many years after 1945, and focused instead on advising businesses on mergers, acquisitions, and takeover bids. None the less, a multi-layered banking revolution was unobtrusively occurring in the 1950s and 1960s. Insurance, banking, and finance accounted for 3.01 per cent of the UK's gross domestic product in 1951, 3.19 per cent in 1961, and 7.31 per cent in 1971.[70] The deposit banks attracted the deposits of most British residents, but the 'wholesale' banks (merchant banks, overseas banks, foreign banks in London) attracted a growing share of overall deposits because companies and financial institutions were alert to their better interest rates; by 1971 they held 43 per cent of total deposits, whereas the deposit banks held 27 per cent and the building societies 23 per cent.[71]

Meanwhile, the spread of occupational pensions after 1945 created huge pension funds, of which the largest in the early 1960s belonged to the National Coal Board. The pension funds were increasingly involved with industry and property and, because they had no reason to invest in firms with bad labour relations, had the effect of fostering class harmony. The Conservatives' denationalization of iron and steel in 1953 depended for its outcome largely on how far the insurance companies would take up the shares, and by 1962 they owned more than a third of the Steel Company of Wales's ordinary shares.[72] The pension funds' advent attracted little attention partly because the pension-fund managers, inexpert in management and fearing nationalization, did not advertise their new-found power. Sampson in 1962 portrayed them as an obscure cabal whose association issued its twice-yearly journal *Superannuating* from above an ironmonger's in Kensington.[73] He found Leslie Brown, the Prudential's chief investment manager and company secretary, 'stocky, quietly-spoken, with a neat bristly moustache and twinkling eyes', a man 'who talks in a frank, humorous way about the problems of his job'. Brown had worked his way up through the Prudential from Selhurst Grammar School with the aid of a correspondence course, yet was 'sometimes talked of as the most powerful man in the city', and 'in the stock exchange, his name is a legend: for a new issue can depend on the raising or falling of his eyebrows'. When necessary, though, the insurance companies were quite prepared to come out into the open: in 1956, for example, when at an exciting shareholders' meeting the Prudential (with 260,000 shares in BSA) ousted Sir Bernard Docker (with only 100,000) as chairman.[74]

[70] *BHS* 824. [71] R. Pringle, *A Guide to Banking in Britain* (1973), 131.
[72] Sampson, *Anatomy of Britain*, 409. [73] Ibid. 411.
[74] Quotation ibid. 408, see also 410.

The friendly societies between 1950 and 1970 continued in their long twentieth-century retreat, their branches declining by half, their members by two-thirds, but significant change came from the building societies' continued growth. Their number had been falling steadily throughout the century, and between 1950 and 1970 it almost halved, but the number of depositors remained stable and borrowers more than doubled.[75] The middle classes by the 1960s had discovered that an inflationary age makes renting uneconomic, especially when the taxman concedes mortgage interest relief: better to buy with a mortgage, incur the interest payments, but claim for yourself the house's enhanced capital value. Patterns of personal banking were changing too, and big mergers were as prevalent in banking as elsewhere in the 1960s. As a source of loans, the building societies and hire-purchase firms now far outclassed the pawnbroker. Together with public welfare and affluence, they were gradually pushing him out of business, earlier in London than elsewhere; his numbers fell during the 1940s and 1950s by three-quarters to about 1,000 by 1959.[76] Faster inflation alerted savers to the importance of interest rates, and small savers, hitherto catered for by savings banks and building societies, turned to the big banks for better returns, shifting the overall balance of their accounts from current to deposit.[77]

By the 1960s the public were becoming much better informed on financial matters. This was all the more necessary because in the 1950s the self-confident pension-fund manager George Ross Goobey, carnation in buttonhole, led the move away from relying on gilt-edged stock towards investment in equities by demonstrating that a large but diversified equity portfolio was less risky than earlier supposed.[78] The art of investment analysis, well developed in the USA, and pioneered in Britain by the increasingly meritocratic stockbroking firm Phillips & Drew, now became crucial. The insights of Goobey, son of a haberdasher and Primitive Methodist preacher, were complemented by the expertise of the firm's unassuming research leader Denis Weaver, boilermaker's son and former Quaker, socialist and wartime conscientious objector.[79] Broader financial comment was required, and in the 1960s the national broadsheets began to carry business supplements, city editors (together with labour correspondents) rose in status, the *Financial Times* advanced in scope and impact, and leading investors and entrepreneurs became better known. Paradoxically, it was under a Labour government that public interest in the workings of capitalism mounted apace.

After 1945 there were in effect two cities of London: the first restrictive, closely regulated, shrinking, conservative, and insular; the second open,

[75] *TCBST* 605. Building Societies Association, *Building Societies Yearbook, 1992–3* (1992), 301–2.

[76] A. L. Minkes, 'The Decline of Pawnbroking', *Economica*, 20 (1953), 18–22. *HC Deb.* 27 Nov. 1959, cc. 813, 820.

[77] For figures see Pringle, *Guide to Banking*, 134.

[78] Obituary, *DT* (31 Mar. 1999), 29.

[79] *FT* (27 Feb. 2002), 24.

international, and expanding.[80] This second city owed much to the City's relative freedom, by world standards, from government interference, and much also to its flexibility and ingenuity in solving new and unexpected problems. Empire had never cramped the horizons of City bankers, whose international outlook had preceded its rise and outlasted its fall. Empire even bequeathed to British banking an extensive overseas retail branch network; it was built up most notably by such London-based British banks as Barclays, and decolonization rendered Barclays Bank International truly international. Furthermore, London had long welcomed bankers as economic or political refugees, and could also offer its high reputation, the advantages of the English language, and a location conveniently within the time zone between Europe and USA. So for the City in the 1950s the international money market was a further powerful growth engine. In 1951 the City reopened as an international market for foreign-exchange dealing and commodity trading, and several liberalizing measures followed. In 1954 several exchange controls were removed, enabling non-residents of the UK to deal more freely in sterling; in 1958 sterling was freed for conversion into other currencies during trade transactions; and 1962 saw the end of control on foreigners' sterling deposits. The growing instability of the world's currencies, accentuated from the late 1960s by the retreat of fixed exchange rates, increased the need for some way of covering international transactions against future movements of one currency against another. Then the oil crisis of 1973–4 brought new opportunities with the need for facilities which could recycle petrodollars.

American, Japanese, and European investors, over-regulated by their own governments, gravitated instinctively to the relative freedom of London's money markets, earning interest there on balances that would otherwise have remained idle. American dollars transferred to London for deposit ('Eurodollars') gave London's money markets a special boost. Looking back on these developments in 1979, Citibank's Walter Wriston pointed out that 'national borders are no longer defensible against the invasion of knowledge, ideas or financial data. The Eurocurrency markets are a perfect example. No one designed them, no one authorised them, and no one controlled them. They were fathered by controls, raised by technology and today they are refugees . . . from national attempts to allocate credit and capital for reasons which have little or nothing to do with finance and economics.'[81] So the City called into existence a new non-sterling role to redress a balance upset by the retreat of its one-time sterling role. Many American banks set up in London during the 1960s, and by the 1970s there

[80] Here I follow the argument of B. Jessop and R. Stones in L. Budd and S. Whimster (eds.), *Global Finance and Urban Living: A Study of Metropolitan Change* (1992), 172–3.

[81] At the International Monetary Conference in London in June 1979, quoted in D. Kynaston, *The City of London*, iv. *A Club No More 1945–2000* (2001), 583.

were more American banks in the City of London than in New York.[82] They were followed by the Japanese, and between 1957 and 1969 the number of foreign banks directly represented in London almost doubled. Their deposits (largely in foreign currencies, not sterling) rose more than three hundredfold, and by 1973 far more foreign banks were represented in London than in any of the world's other financial centres.[83]

Such major changes demanded significant shifts in the City's banking structures. Professionalization and amalgamations were driving out family members and shareholders from the London merchant banks, which were losing something of their gentlemanly flavour, as Warburgs demonstrated during the 'aluminium war'. By the early 1970s their staffs ranged from about fifty to about a thousand in a large merchant bank like Hambros or Kleinwort Benson.[84] The professions gained much from all this, and in doing so felt little need for the government help so prominent in the postwar history of British manufacturing. Accountants grew far faster during the twentieth century than any other major profession in Britain. With their numbers roughly doubling every twenty years they outdistanced doctors, lawyers, teachers, and engineers/scientists. Their expertise was as near as Britain came to a professional qualification for meritocratic business management, and boardrooms recruited them in steadily growing numbers.[85] London firms of solicitors, too, attracted international business. The complexity of the financial world pushed forward the familiar pattern of professional specialization and diversification, and in the professions there were many (often Anglo-American) equivalents of the multinational company. In such ways did the City lose its interwar introversion and in the early 1960s resume, first in bonds and later in equities, its Victorian and Edwardian prominence in world finance.[86]

3. A NEW LIFE AT WORK

The British people in the 1950s and 1960s were often accused of being relatively lazy, and early in 1968 such attitudes encouraged a much-publicized but ephemeral movement endorsed by the prime minister to 'back Britain'

[82] J. Plender and P. Wallace, *The Square Mile: A Guide to the City Revolution* (1985), 13.

[83] R. C. Michie, *The City of London: Continuity and Change, 1850–1990* (London and Basingstoke, 1992), 92—an excellent book, concise and lucid on all City matters. See also Pringle, *Guide to Banking*, 82–9.

[84] M. Lisle-Williams, 'Merchant Banking Dynasties in the English Class Structure: Ownership, Solidarity and Kinship in the City of London', *British Journal of Sociology* (Sept. 1984), 335, 337. Pringle, *Guide to Banking*, 60.

[85] D. Matthews, M. Anderson, and J. R. Edwards, 'The Rise of the Professional Accountant in British Management', *Economic History Review* (Aug. 1997), 409, 423. D. Matthews, 'The Business Doctors: Accountants in British Management from the Nineteenth Century to the Present Day', *Business History* (July 1998), 74–6.

[86] Michie, *City of London*, 143.

through working extra hours without extra pay, a notion which the trade unions did not favour.[87] The section which follows will show that the accusation grossly oversimplified a complex picture, and that after 1951 a rising proportion in the population of working age took paid work, and responded readily and flexibly to shifts in the type, timing, and location of the work available. The British workforce expanded steadily between 1911 and 1966, not just because there were more people of working age, but because more people seized the increased opportunities for taking up paid work. This was despite the growing claims of schools and universities on the young and despite pensioners' tendency to leave the labour market; only 5 per cent of the British male labour force in 1950–68 were under eighteen, only 4 per cent 65 or over.[88] The share of the female labour force in the female population of working age rose from 33 per cent in 1951 to 43 per cent in 1971.[89] In the 1950s and 1960s the people eligible for work but registered as unemployed never rose above 2.6 per cent and averaged at only 1.9 per cent—far below interwar levels, though these figures concealed much overpaid underemployment. Other Western democracies, except the USA, had unemployment levels equally low at this time.[90]

The move from manufacturing to services was gradually reshaping the workforce, and in this golden age for Western industrial economies the British economy grew faster even than between 1856 and 1913, and benefited from both milder fluctuations in and favourable terms of trade. This pleased the Conservatives, whose manifesto of 1955 claimed that the British people had 'a real chance during the coming twenty-five years to double their standard of living. The future beckons to this generation with a golden finger.'[91] The prediction was not unduly optimistic: the national income grew by roughly 250 per cent between 1945 and 1990, and earnings in real terms grew if anything even faster, with each decade registering rises in production and productivity.[92] Fewer of the UK workforce undertook heavy manual labour. Agriculture, despite its marked increase in productivity, continued its long-term diminuendo: contributing 5.8 per cent of gross domestic product in 1951, 3.9 per cent in 1961, and 2.9 per cent in 1971.[93] By 1951 the agricultural workforce had already shrunk so far that its further decline could not fuel productivity elsewhere in the British economy

[87] Wilson speech at Burnley, *T* (9 Jan. 1968), 1, cf. Frayn's criticisms of the movement in *O* (7 Jan. 1968), 9. For a full discussion see Sandbrook, *White Heat*, 573–6.

[88] *BLS* 206–7, 297.

[89] *BST* 168.

[90] *BST* 174. For overseas comparisons see the useful table in S. Broadberry, 'Employment and Unemployment', in Floud and McCloskey (eds.), *Cambridge Economic History of Britain*, iii (2nd edn.), 201.

[91] Dale (ed.), *Conservative Manifestos*, 105.

[92] A. Cairncross, 'Economic Policy and Performance, 1964–1990', in Floud and McCloskey (eds.), *Cambridge Economic History of Britain*, iii (2nd edn.), 93.

[93] *BHS* 824.

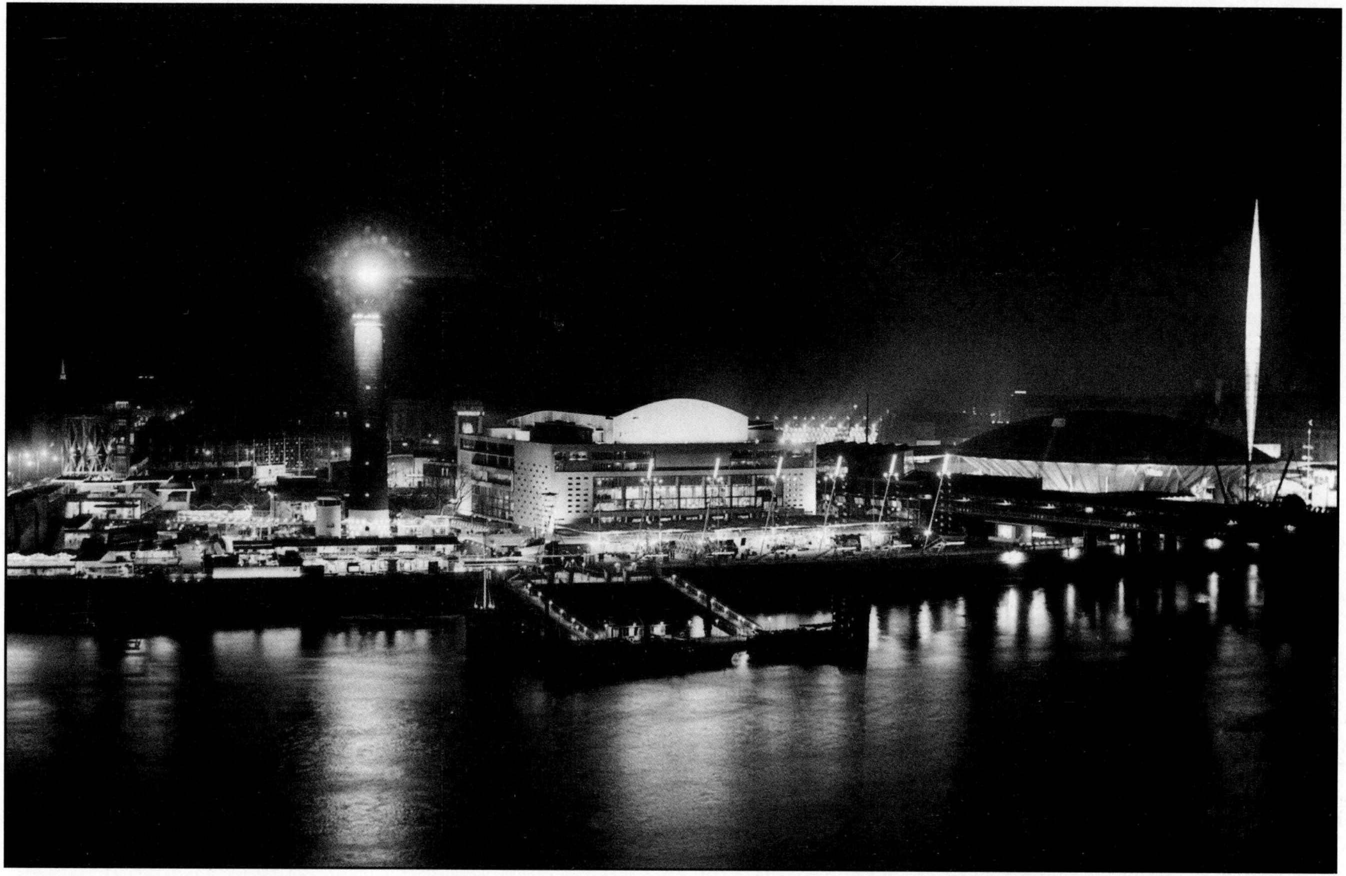

Plate 1. The Festival of Britain buildings (Skylon, Dome, Festival Hall). *See p. xv.*

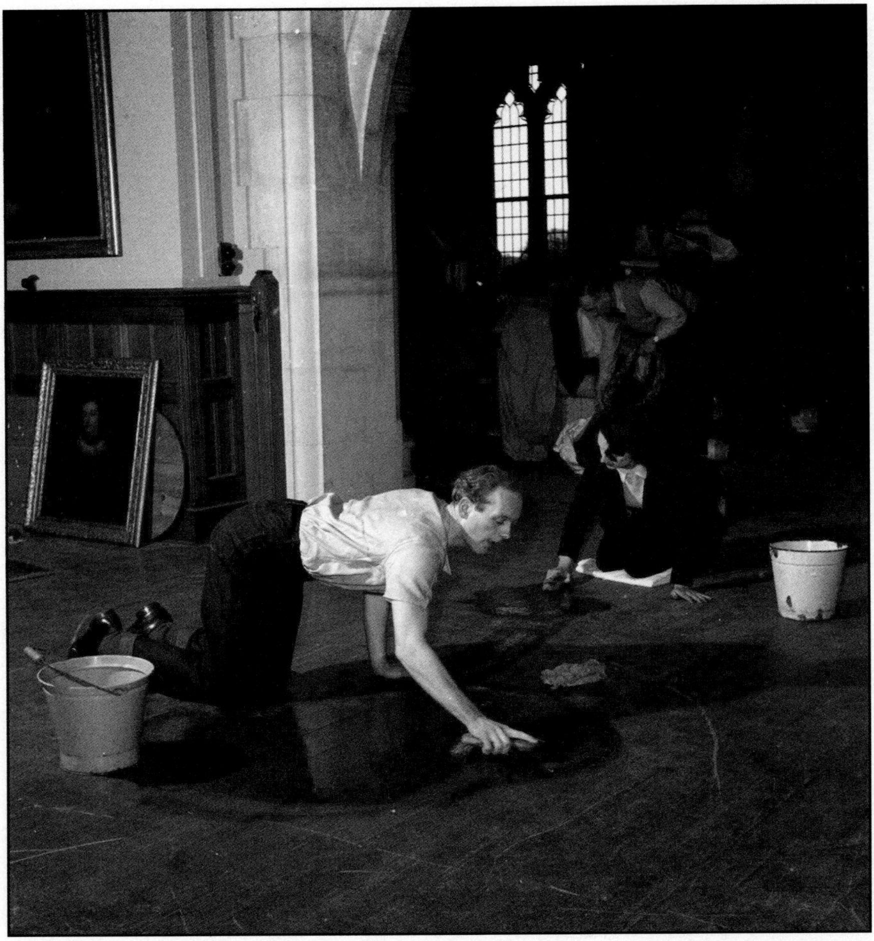

Plate 2. Lord Montague of Beaulieu kneeling on the floor scrubbing it with inexpert movements in 1952. *See p. 18.*

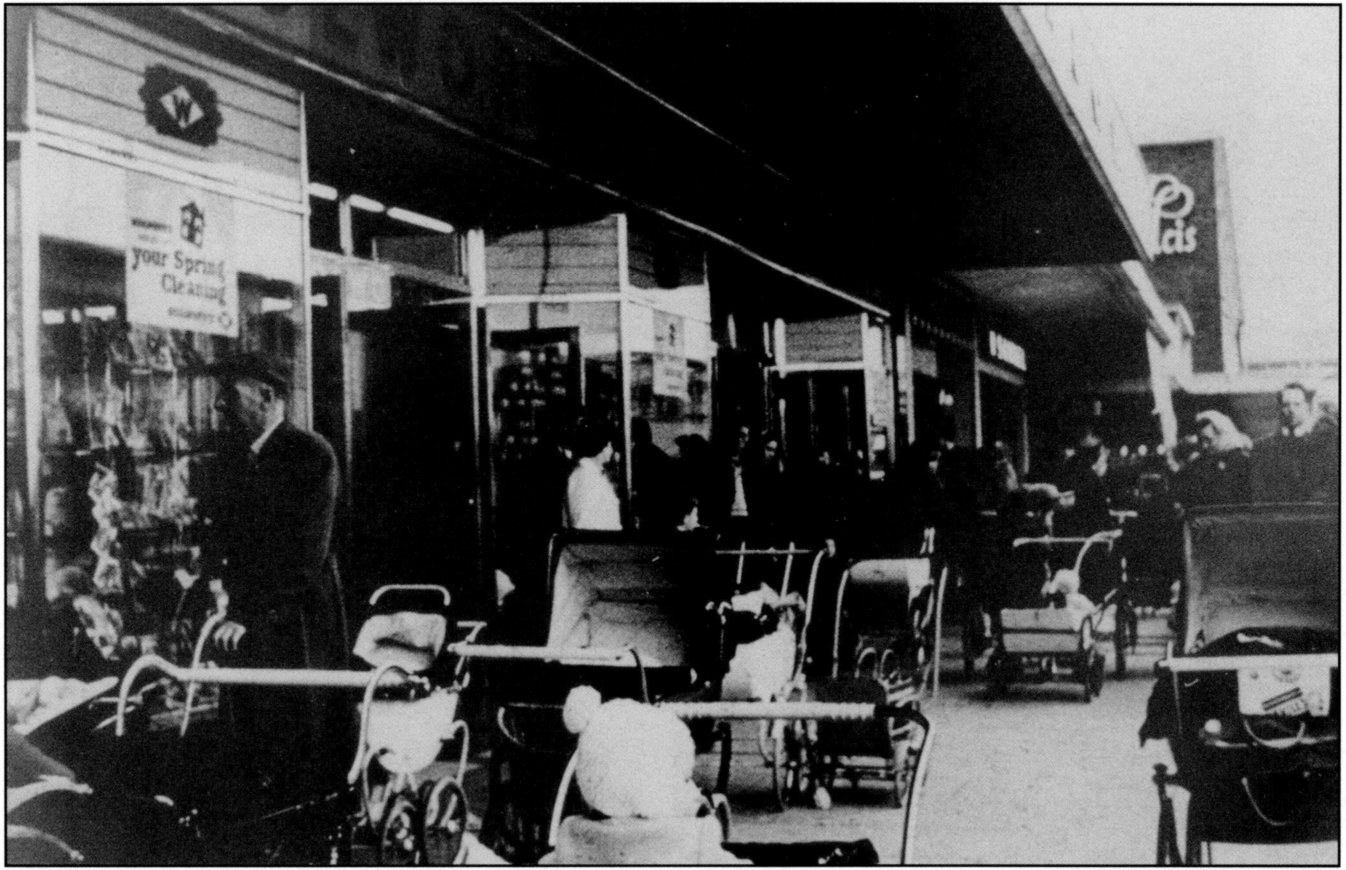

Plate 3. 'Pram Town' outside Woolworths in 1950s Harlow illustrating its youthful age structure. *See p. 155.*

Plate 4. Harold Macmillan speaking at the opening ceremony in March 1952 for six houses built in seven weeks. *See pp. 161, 413.*

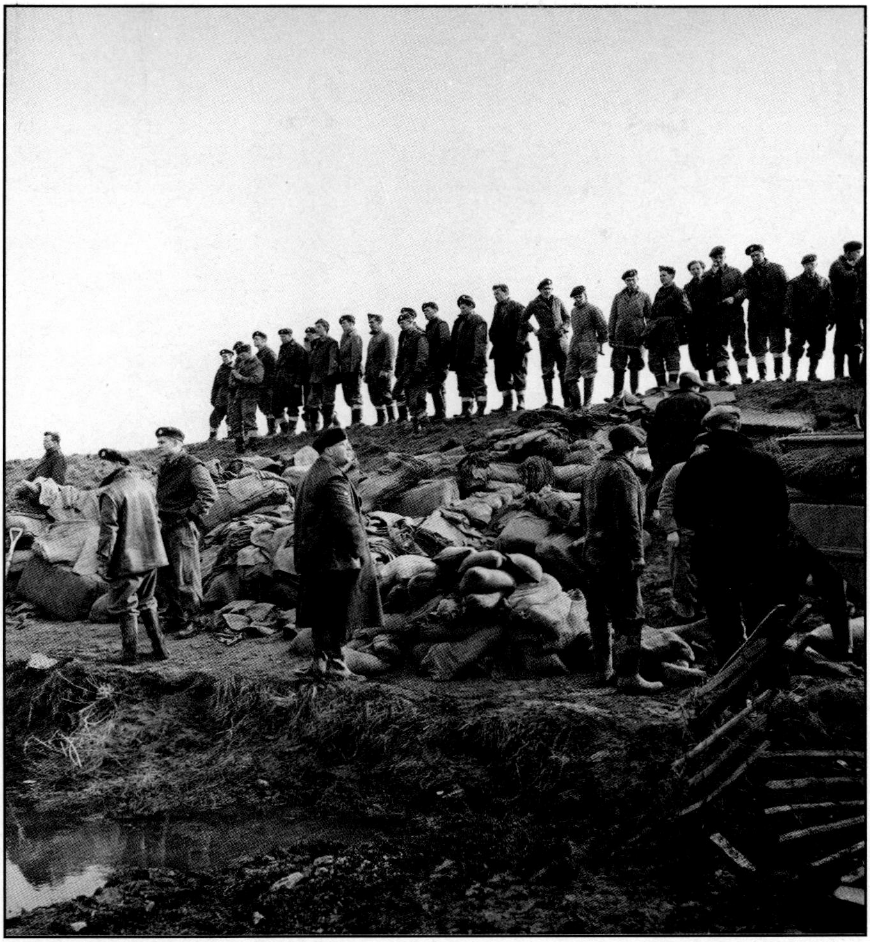

Plate 5. Troops with sandbags, Canvey Island floods, 21 Feb 1953. *See p. 125.*

Plate 6. Coronation (2 June 1953), Queen and Bishop Ramsey of Durham. *See pp. 49, 181.*

Plate 7. Excitement at the sweetshop as sweet rationing ends, 5 Feb 1953. *See pp. 332, 337.*

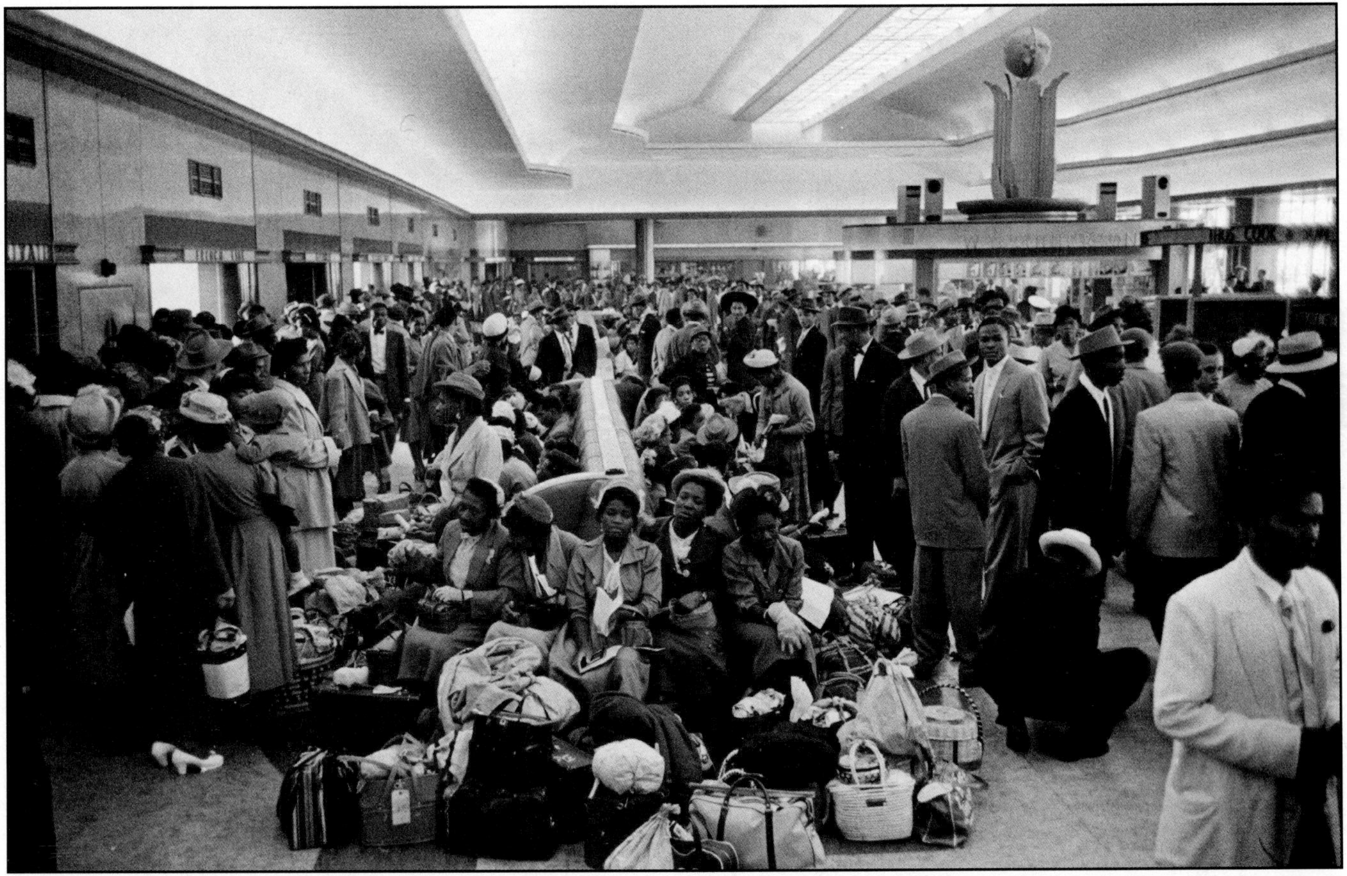

Plate 8. A crowd of 700 West Indian immigrants in the customs hall at Southampton, 27 May 1956. *See p. 82.*

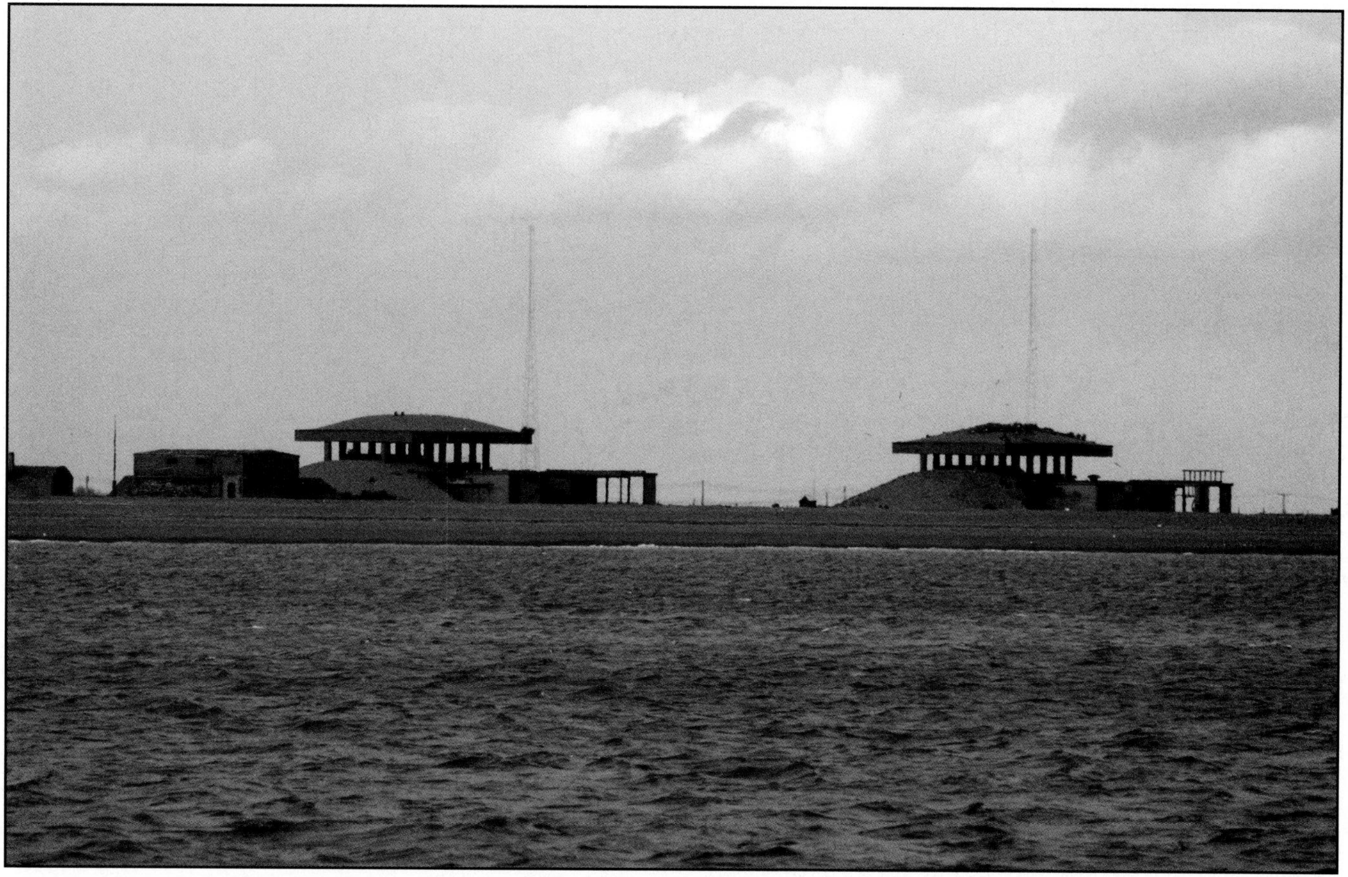

Plate 9. Pagodas at Orfordness, Suffolk, used for vibration testing. *See p. 97*.

Plate 10. CND march from Aldermaston to London (1960) showing Canon Collins and Michael Foot leading the way. *See pp. 448, 483.*

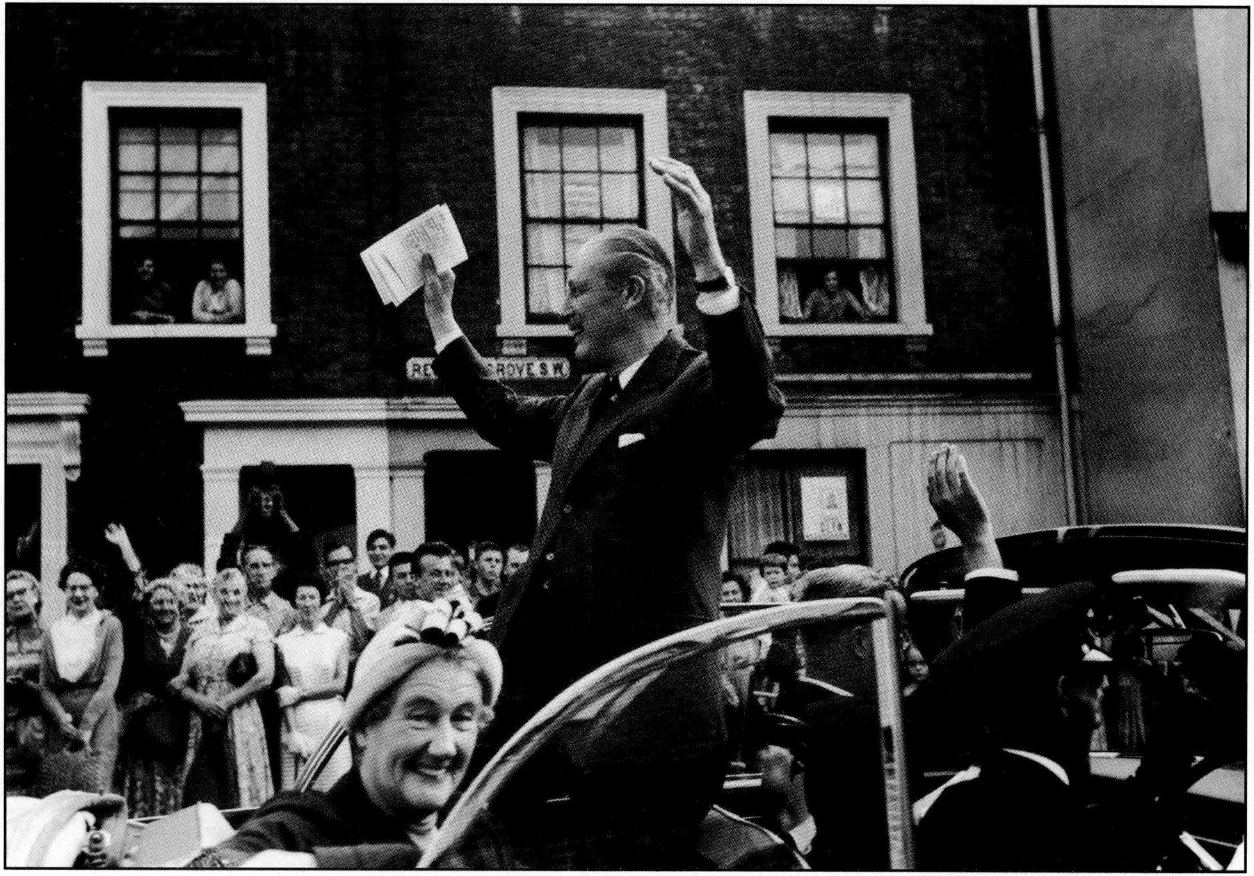

Plate 11. Harold Macmillan campaigning at the 1959 general election with his wife Dorothy. *See p. 412.*

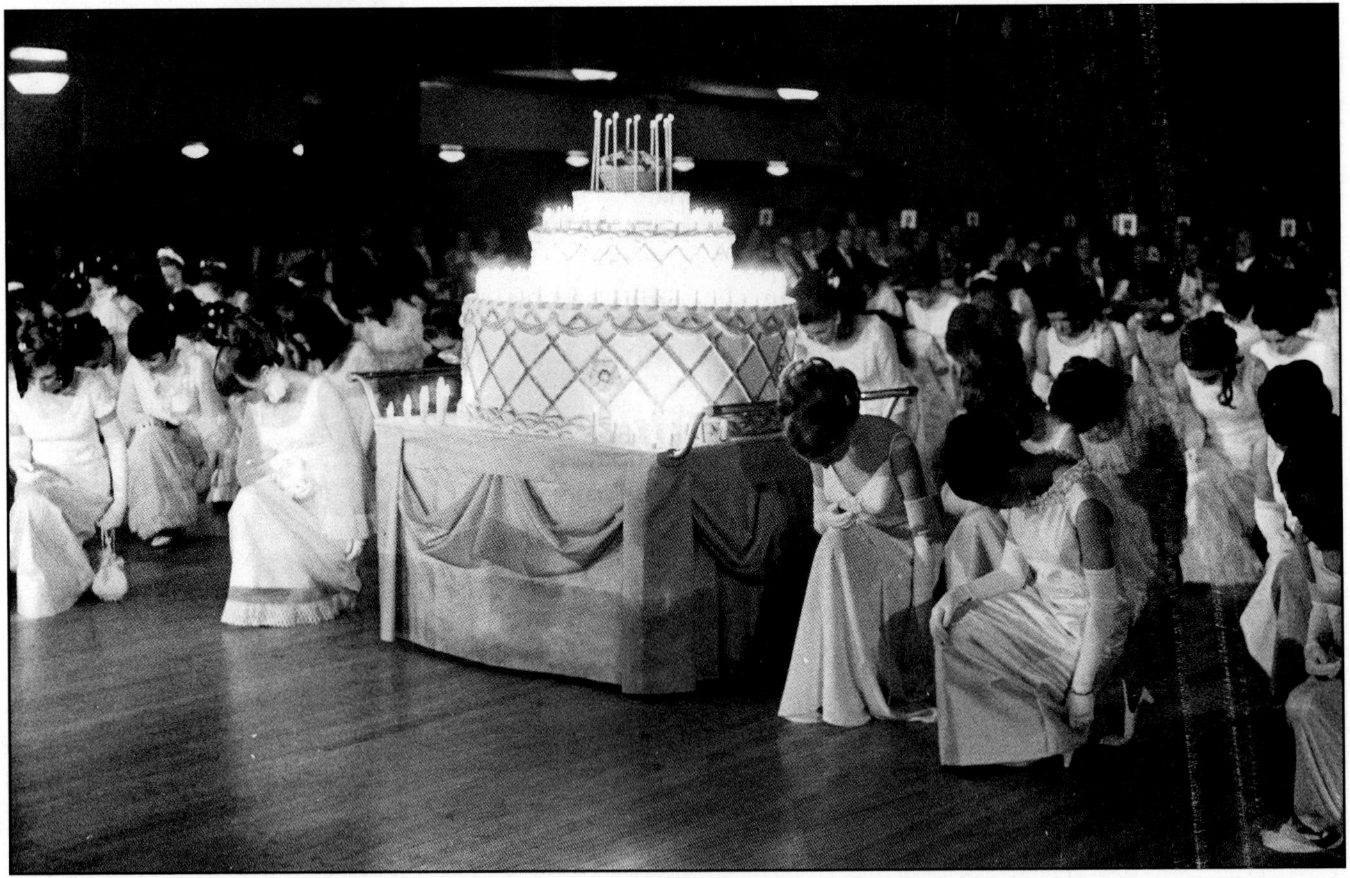

Plate 12. Queen Charlotte's Ball, 1967. *See p. 190.*

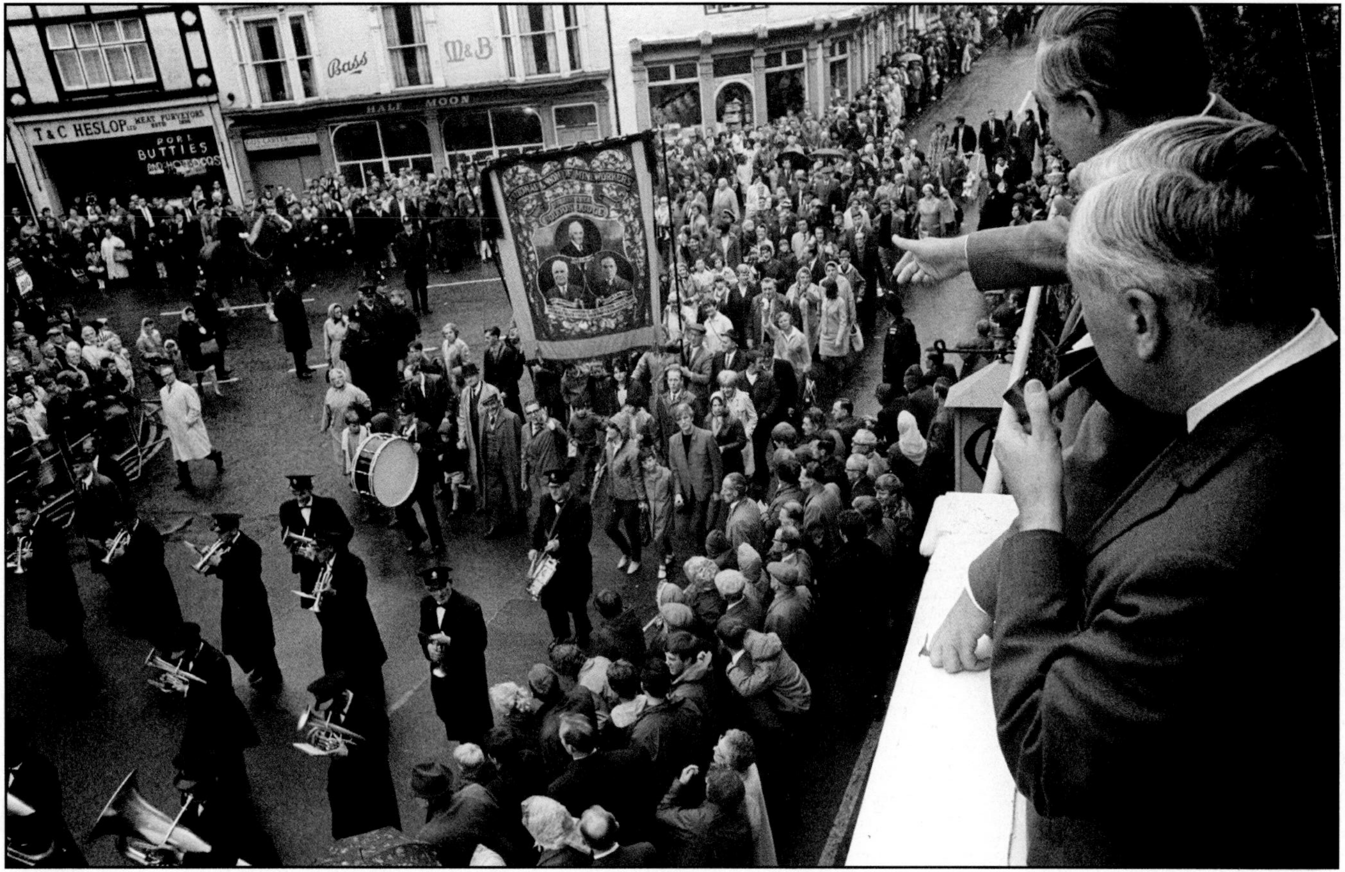

Plate 13. H. Wilson watching the Durham miners' gala procession in July 1965. *See p. 211.*

Plate 14. Rescue workers digging into the coal slack at Aberfan after the avalanche on 22 Oct 1966. *See p. 131.*

Plate 15. Ronan Point: aerial view of the collapsed flats at Beecher's Road, Newham, London, May 1968. *See p. 154.*

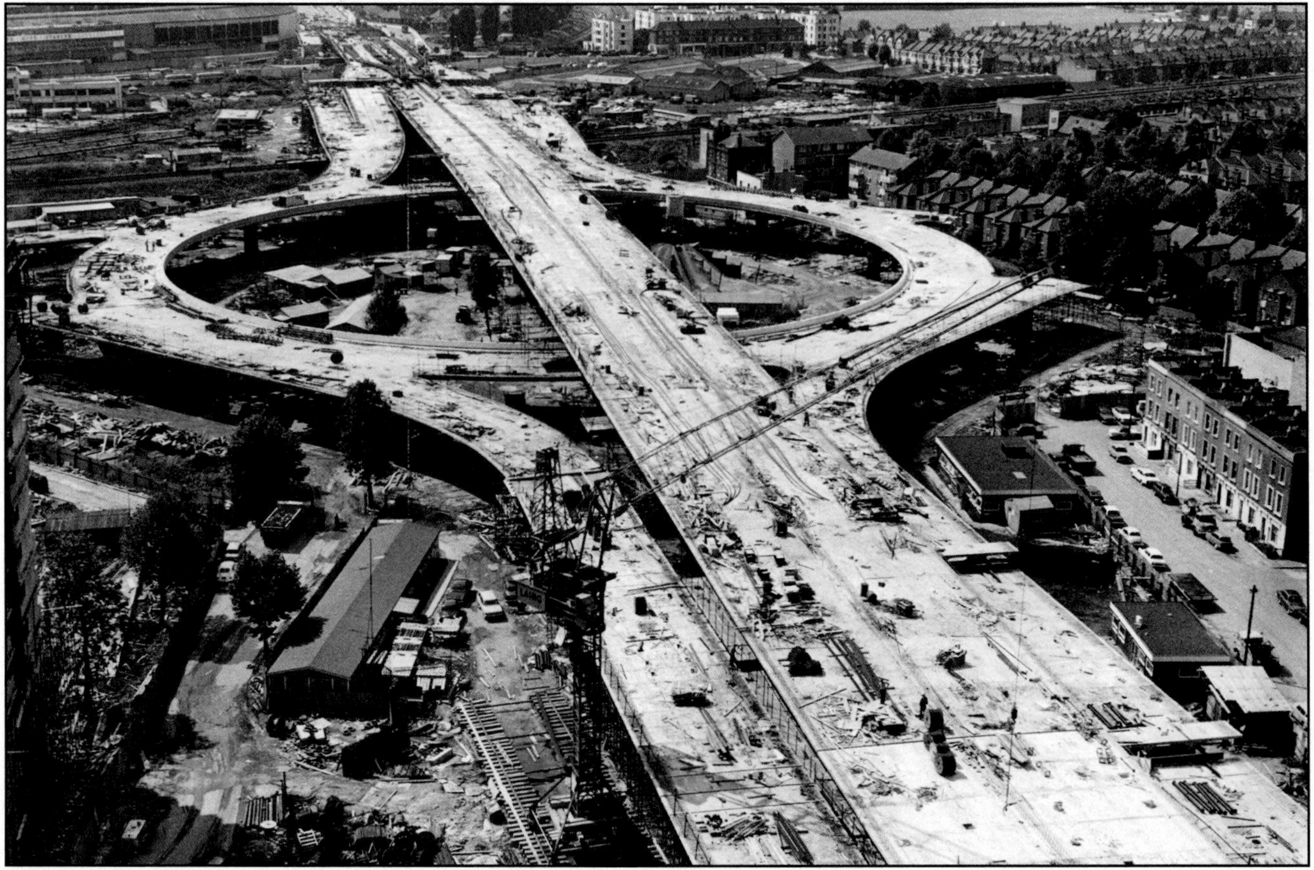

Plate 16. The Western Avenue extension, part of the Latimer Road Interchange, under construction in west London

by providing the influx of rural labour that aided European competitors.[94] Nor was war damage so serious in Britain as to require re-equipment on the scale of some manufacturing rivals.[95] Furthermore, regional employment policies encouraged workers in the declining industries of the north and west to stay put instead of moving to the growth areas south and east; it was the 'New Commonwealth' immigrant and the married woman who met many of the growth areas' needs.

Manufacture's share of the UK's employed population began declining during the 1960s, and the proportion of semi-skilled and unskilled manual workers in the British male workforce fell between 1951 and 1971.[96] The future lay with the service sector. Its growing importance in Western Europe as well as in Britain marked a transformation whose long-term significance is comparable only with industrialization itself. The non-manual workers' share of the total occupied population in Great Britain grew steadily throughout the twentieth century—19 per cent in 1911, 31 per cent in 1951, and 44 per cent in 1971—whereas the equivalent figures for manual workers were 75, 64, and 56 per cent, respectively.[97] All this had implications for the experience at work. Physical labour's retreat helped to ensure that the number of those killed each year in industrial accidents—falling throughout the century—fell further, by a quarter between 1948/57 and 1958/67.[98] Deaths per manshift among coalminers fell steadily from the 1950s to the 1980s.[99]

In manufacturing, larger firms (especially when nationalized) meant fewer self-employed entrepreneurs and a remoter, more diffused, and anonymous management structure. Continuing mechanization left less room for skill in the employee. By the mid-1950s there was much talk of automation, which promised a second industrial revolution—a revolution which, like the first, would greatly enhance productivity, but with much less drudgery and routine. The trade unions were understandably worried at the likely loss of manual jobs, whereas the prime concern of government and employers was to obtain a more flexible and better-qualified workforce: 'it is a matter of urgency', said the National Plan in 1965, 'that the present position should be improved and that automation technology should be developed and applied more rapidly'.[100] Already by the 1960s the computer revolution seemed likely to sweep through the service sector as well, processing statistical information with unprecedented speed, providing management with a new wealth of data, and there too

[94] As Healey pointed out in cabinet on 4 Aug. 1975 when Crosland said that other countries seemed able to prosper more than Britain while channelling into public expenditure at least as high a proportion of gross national product. Castle, *Diaries 1974–6*, 482 (4 Aug. 1975).

[95] Feinstein, 'Success and Failure', 117–21.

[96] Wright, *Britain in the Age of Economic Management*, table 2.3. Goldthorpe, *Social Mobility and Class Structure*, 60.

[97] *BST* 164.

[98] From an annual average of 1660 to 1201, as calculated from *BLS* 399–400.

[99] Ashworth, *Coal Industry*, v (1986), 677–81.

[100] *The National Plan*, 50.

requiring better educated, more adaptable employees. Electrically powered punched-card machines were proliferating in the City by the late 1950s, electric typewriters and closed-circuit television were appearing, and in 1960 Linklaters and Paines got its first Rank Xerox photocopier and its first telex machine. By the early 1960s punched-card machines were succumbing to the electronically powered digital computers which government statisticians were using.[101] Whereas manufacturing employers were becoming more remote from their employees, service-sector managers were coming closer, for their working units were small, however large their firms.

From the 1950s design was increasingly salient in public discussion, and Gordon Russell, knighted in 1955, remained active. He drew together past and present, theory and practice, local and national, private and public, and successfully established the Design Centre in London in 1956. It compiled an index of well-designed products submitted by manufacturers, and selected from them an evolving exhibition of consumer goods. Design education expanded greatly after 1945. In an excitingly experimental and classless mood, publicly funded art colleges in the 1960s formed new constellations of artistic skills, generated excellence in such areas as typography, photography, and stage design—and infused metropolitan high culture with populism. Yet there were difficulties. Richard Hammond had explained to William Morris in *News from Nowhere* that the socialist utopia which supplanted the old regime of painfully competitive work pressure needed no word for art 'because it has become a necessary part of the labour of every man who produces'.[102] Such instinctive harmonization was particularly elusive in Britain where, in contrast to Scandinavia, designers identified more with 'art' than with 'business': the two interacted less fruitfully in the UK, especially given the art schools' diminished emphasis during the 1950s on skills in drawing and painting. Instead of working together, art school and technical college espoused separate values, the art school carefully distancing itself from the general public, from the local community, and from the taxpayer who funded it. The problem lay also with the affluence, the shifting fashions, and the revived commercialism of the 1950s: the simplicity of modern design was ascribed to wartime austerity, and in the 1950s 'utility' succumbed to an over-ornamented, reproduction-antique reaction. The Festival of Britain might juxtapose Scandinavian and Bauhaus styles with the traditional British folk art of the pub in the 'Lion and Unicorn' pavilion, but it was not then clear how seriously the modernists would be weakened by internal divisions. In 1951 it seemed to the Bauhaus's

[101] Kynaston, *Club No More*, 145. HM Treasury, *Government Statistical Services* (1st publ. 1953, 2nd edn. 1962), 9.

[102] W. Morris, 'News from Nowhere', in W. Morris, *Selected Writings and Designs*, ed. A. Briggs (Harmondsworth, 1962), 299.

purist devotees that machine art could alone be the style of the future, both economical and morally superior.

When it came to training the workforce, secondary schools embraced vocationalism only slowly. The academic child's needs moulded the entire schooling system, partly because of the link between democracy and meritocracy. There was much discussion in the 1950s and 1960s about the interaction between schooling and social class, and the labour movement thought that an educational system which emphasized such subjects as engineering, domestic science, or purely practical skills would neglect liberalizing objectives; it even feared that vocationalism would consign the child too early to a lifelong inferior status. Reinforcing this was the anti-vocationalism of the ancient universities, a powerful influence on the school and university system. As for the (London-based) professions, their younger recruits came directly from outside the university system, whereas their older recruits came increasingly from university graduates—though only after their more academic studies were complete. Not until the 1980s was education in school and university related more closely to the type of work most young people were likely to do.

In manufacturing, the tight postwar labour market ensured that the trend was if anything towards training less formal than before: young people could get jobs without it. Besides, there was a pragmatic preference in many areas of British life for training only 'on the job', employers wanted an uncomplicated if short-termist focus directly on production, and trade unionists were keen to simplify wage bargaining. In 1955 only 37 per cent of the boys who began paid work at 15 in Great Britain embarked upon apprenticeships or systematic training, and far fewer of the girls.[103] This low figure also reflected the fact that teenagers were staying on at school for longer, more technical colleges were providing vocational training through 'day release' schemes and 'sandwich courses', and alternatives to the traditional type of apprenticeship were extending. This was especially necessary for the more complex types of skill that the growing service industries required. And since people were usually apprenticed for five years, employers (especially small employers) had little incentive to train a 15-year-old boy who was destined for national service at 18 and might never return, still less a girl expecting a career break on marriage or no career at all. Alertness by the 1960s to competition from West Germany, where vocational qualifications were more formal, prompted the growing late-twentieth-century British move towards state-fostered and better organized training, but it began from a low base. The British tradition was for apprenticeship to be work-based and self-organized within industry groups, whereas in France and West Germany the state played a larger role. Hence the complaint in 1958 by the Ministry of

[103] Carr-Saunders *et al.*, *Survey of Social Conditions*, 78–9.

Labour's inquiry on the subject that its 'main difficulty' lay in 'the almost complete absence of reliable statistics'.[104]

The move from manufacturing to services changed attitudes to working hours. Here as elsewhere, the weather had long been retreating as a powerful influence on daily life in Britain. The natural rhythms of the day, the year, and the seasons as a major and direct influence on the quality of life had been moderated ever since industrialization had roofed over most of the workforce. Artificial light freed recreation from its natural constraints, roads and weather forecasts improved, and electronic communication warded off hazards. With better ways of preserving food commercially and in the home, produce hitherto available only 'in season' became continuously available. Cheaper and easier overseas travel in the 1960s made a hot climate increasingly accessible at any time of year, but nowhere did the weather retreat more strikingly as an influence than in the timing and duration of work. Cheap artificial lighting made it easier for employers to organize shift working at night. With fewer in agriculture and more in white-collar work, working hours could be more precisely defined, rendering work less subject to uncertainties and waiting about. The latest twist in Britain's long journey towards precise timing came in 1971, when radio's six equal pips for the Greenwich time signal were reduced to five, with a longer one at the exact second.

The period of 'summer time' varied from 1947 to 1964, and was fixed annually a year in advance by Order in Council. From the late 1950s, however, pressure was building up to extend it, and Euro-zeal led some even to recommend all-the-year-round permanent summer time for Britain so as to harmonize with Central European Time. Urban interests, with ready access to artificial light, were gaining over rural interests, where natural light was more important; and England's interests were gaining over Scotland's, where mornings were darker. Neither farmers nor the construction industry nor the Scots wanted to exchange lighter mornings for lighter evenings. Leisure's claims were advancing over those of work, however, for as one summer-time enthusiast in parliament argued in 1962, 'the long-term objective should . . . be to secure the maximum amount of free time during daylight and the maximum amount of work done during the hours of darkness'.[105] In 1961 the government introduced the compromise of extending summer time at each end for a total of seven weeks, an arrangement fixed for three years in 1964. After further surveys of opinion, the government in 1968 introduced summer time by putting the clocks forward by an hour all the year round for a three-year period, thus harmonizing with Central European Time. With maximum use made of daylight, road accidents declined. The

[104] Ministry of Labour, *Training for Skill: Recruitment and Training of Young Workers in Industry. Report by a Sub-Committee of the National Joint Advisory Council* (1958), 10.

[105] B. T. Parkin, *HC Deb.* 11 Dec. 1962, c. 369.

further north and west opinion was tested, however, the more hostile it became, and the interests of Scottish children and farmers moving about outdoors on dark mornings eventually prevailed over the counter-arguments: abolition of the twice-yearly clock change, lighter evenings for sport and leisure, European harmonization.[106] In 1971 summer time all the year round succumbed to a large parliamentary majority with its somewhat angry spokesmen. Rather surprisingly, at no point in the parliamentary debates did anyone—not even nationalists later—suggest freeing the Scots to arrange their day as they chose, though this would have benefited both local autonomy and the old people in Broadstairs playing their afternoon bowls. The much-advertised plight of Scottish children going to school in the dark thus prevailed over UK interests futher south.

Working hours for all employees were slowly contracting: for manual workers in the UK, normal weekly hours (for which overtime rates were not paid) had been declining since 1945, and between 1951 and 1970 fell from 44.6 to 40.3. Weekly hours actually worked fell from 46.3 to 43.9, and both figures continued falling after 1970, the persisting gap between the two reflecting what was in effect a device for boosting low wages.[107] Non-manual workers put in fewer hours than manual, with a much smaller gap between nominal and actual hours worked.[108] The shift from manufacturing to services heralded major change because the latter required relatively flexible working hours. With smaller firms divided into smaller working units, with less capital tied up in costly equipment than the manufacturing sector, and with closer responsiveness to customer needs, service-sector employers were keener on part-time working. This meant more women: even in manufacturing between a fifth and a third of women in the 1960s worked part-time, but fewer than 3 per cent of men.[109] The BBC's survey of 1961 showed that on weekdays nearly three-quarters of the men surveyed (but less than a third of women) were out at work, a third (but only a tenth of women) on Saturday mornings, tailing off during the afternoon, and under a tenth (but only 1 per cent of women) on Sundays.[110]

The move from manufacturing to services accelerated change in the relationship between work and leisure. The manual worker had long been more vulnerable to involuntary leisure—that is, unemployment—with consequent damage to industrial relations. The bitter memory of casual docklands employment, for example, fuelled Liverpool's tenacious late-twentieth-century reputation for bad industrial relations. For some time, however, decasualization had been the trend, together with a shift to continuous employment, specified working hours, and overtime payment when these were exceeded. There was

[106] *Gallup Polls*, ii. 931 (June 1967), 1035 (Feb. 1969), 1087 (Jan. 1970). [107] *BST* 178.
[108] National Board for Prices and Incomes, *Hours of Work, Overtime and Shiftworking* (Report No. 161), *PP* (Cmnd. 4554), xlv. 50. [109] *BLS* 275.
[110] *The People's Activities* (1965), 1/24–5.

as yet no significant move towards repudiating the conventional working day, but there was growing restiveness with it, especially among retailers and their customers. The law on shop closing hours contained so many anomalies that it was widely ridiculed, quite apart from the fact that the growing number of women in paid work found the shops open when they were working, and closed when they were not. The BBC's survey gave a snapshot of how adults aged 15 and above were spending their time in 1961. Of the men, 2 per cent at most shopped on any one weekday, less than a tenth on Saturdays, and not at all on Sundays. Limited opening hours prevented women's shopping pattern from diverging as much as might have been expected: about a tenth shopped on a weekday morning, tailing off in the afternoon, rather more shopped on Saturdays, but none at all on Sundays.[111] All this was soon to change.

The BBC's survey revealed interesting class contrasts. By 8 a.m. on weekdays a third of the 'working class' were out at work but only 6 per cent of the 'upper middle class', though the latter worked for rather longer in the evenings. In manufacturing trades, reduced working hours encouraged shift working in the 1950s, given the need for capital-intensive industries to extract the most from their plant by keeping it running. Comparing 1954 with 1964, metal manufacturing stood out above the rest, with 42 and 44 per cent of its employees, respectively, doing shift work, but also prominent were vehicle manufacture (13 and 33) and chemicals (24 and 29).[112] This type of flexibility on hours differed markedly from that in the upper middle class, whose relatively variable hours were self-chosen. In the BBC's survey the upper middle class were more prone to take Saturdays off, and were less likely to work on Sundays,[113] but the survey could not take account of the paid work often done at home. The French commentator on postwar Britain, Bertrand de Jouvenel, after discussing contemporary pressures on teachers, civil servants, and technicians, claimed that 'today, when the workers are having leisure guaranteed them, the rulers are being stripped of what leisure they had'.[114] These pressures did not go away, but they were less burdensome for professional people because often in some sense self-chosen. Even in service-sector work away from home, hours were loosening up: in the City from the 1960s, for example, the American working breakfast and the snatched midday sandwich gradually edged out the late-morning arrival and the heavy alcoholic lunch. 'Today, the more important the man, the less his leisure', wrote the *Times Literary Supplement* in an editorial of 1970: ' "leisure" now belongs to the not-so-important'.[115]

[111] *The People's Activities* (1965), 1/24–5. [112] *BLS* 401.

[113] *The People's Activities*, 1/30, 1/32. The social-class aspect of the survey does not differentiate between the sexes.

[114] B. de Jouvenel, *Problems of Socialist England*, tr. J. F. Huntington (1949), 152.

[115] *TLS* (29 Jan. 1970), 108. See also Kynaston, *Club No More*, 712.

In the days when the home or small workshop was the workplace, work and recreation were not clearly distinct, but when working units grew larger and noisier in the nineteenth century, the contrast was sharpened. Progressive interwar employers sought to consolidate loyalty to the firm by reuniting the two in a new way, through works clubs and sports facilities. The trend did not persist after 1945: in larger firms paternalism seemed less appropriate, trade unions did not want to complicate wage bargaining further, and employees preferred home-based leisure. The affluent car workers in Luton investigated by sociologists in the early 1960s distinguished clearly between work as the sphere of necessity and non-work as the sphere of freedom and self-realization, and made their friends outside the factory.[116] So substantial and significant had the time and resources for leisure become that holidays almost became the purpose of work, thus inverting earlier priorities. Between 1951 and 1976 paid annual holidays for manual workers lengthened from one and three-quarter weeks to three and a half,[117] but the number of bank holidays in England and Wales (since 1871 reinforcing the traditional holidays on Christmas Day and Good Friday) remained unchanged until the 1970s: Easter Monday, the first Monday in August, Boxing Day, and Whit Monday.

Not everyone was willing to work for fixed hours at regular times in a specified location at a distinct occupation. Indeed, the culture of the 1960s slowed down the trend towards such conformity. Busking, begging, squatting, and a migrant lifestyle then became fashionable with some young people, but with the Romany people this was a way of life rather than a lifestyle. Symbolic of changing attitudes was a willingness by the 1970s to apply to a people hitherto labelled 'gypsies' their own name, 'traveller'. These migrant dissidents from accumulative values, declining in number, were often confused with two other migrant groups: the itinerant scrap-metal dealers, Irish in origin; and the people who lived semi-permanently in a caravan park because they could afford nothing better. In England and Wales by the late 1960s about 200,000 people lived on caravan sites, whereas there were about 15,000 travellers, mostly in the urban fringes of the south-east, the west midlands, and the south-west. There were by then only 300 horse-drawn caravans left in the country.[118] Despite their poverty and illiteracy, the travellers were not an 'underclass' because their lifestyle had been deliberately chosen, and because for them the social-class hierarchy was irrelevant. Some felt threatened by travellers, but in 1961 the Labour MP Norman Dodds championed their interests in parliament. In 1966 the Gypsy Council was founded, asserting their right to pursue a distinct way of life and seeking official provision of caravan sites. Much of the mid-century concern about homelessness reflected the assumption that most

[116] Goldthorpe *et al.*, *Affluent Worker*, i. 91–2; iii. 65, 72.
[117] *BST* 17.
[118] *HC Deb.* 1 Mar. 1968, cc. 1949, 1978.

people had a home, or yearned for one when beyond their reach. Many even among the travellers' friends in the 1960s still hoped that they would eventually settle down on fixed sites and conform; the immediate problem, however, was to ensure their access to sites for temporary stops, and under the Caravan Sites Act (1968) local authorities were providing 50 sites by 1972 and 142 by 1977.[119]

4. MANAGED CONSUMERISM

The home market was changing fast during the 1950s and 1960s. The share of wages and salaries in UK national income had been rising since the First World War, whereas profits, interest, and mixed incomes had been falling since then, and rents had been falling since the 1880s—trends which continued into the 1970s.[120] Although real national income per person grew more slowly in Britain than in most other industrial countries, even manufacturing growth was impressive by British historical standards.[121] By the early 1950s consumers' expenditure per head at constant prices had returned to the level of the late 1930s, and thereafter went on rising fast.[122] The demand for furniture, clothing, and private motoring, curbed during the war, now recovered.[123] As the *Daily Express* headline pointed out in 1955, in a phrase Macmillan (impressed by the contrast with his interwar Stockton constituency) repeated in 1957, and which became famous and much misinterpreted at the general election of 1959, 'the British people never had it so good'.[124]

By 1951 the foundations for a consumer society were being laid. Ever more remote areas were criss-crossed by telephone lines, sewage pipes, electricity cables, and above all, by beams from radio and television transmitters. Urban facilities were thus extended into the heart of the country. In 1951 86 per cent of British households were wired for electricity, 96 per cent ten years later. Only 3 per cent of the population lacked both gas and electricity at home in 1949, but in that year only 4 per cent of households used refrigerators, and of those with electricity supply only 40 per cent used vacuum cleaners and 4 per cent washing machines. Between 1951 and 1970 gas sales in Great Britain more than doubled, and electricity sales nearly quadrupled; sales of

119 J. Okely, *The Traveller-Gypsies* (Cambridge, 1983), 22, 105.

120 P. Deane and W. A. Cole, *British Economic Growth* (2nd edn. Cambridge, 1969), 247. *BST* 144.

121 See table 4.1 in Feinstein's 'Success and Failure', 98.

122 I. Zweiniger-Bargielowska 'Consensus and Consumption: Rationing, Austerity and Controls after the War', in H. Jones and M. Kandiah (eds.), *The Myth of Consensus: New Views on British History, 1945–64* (Basingstoke and London, 1996), 80.

123 See the useful table in I. Zweiniger-Bargielowska, *Austerity in Britain* (Oxford, 2000), 53.

124 A. C. H. Smith, *Paper Voices: The Popular Press and Social Change 1935–1965* (1975), 150. For Macmillan's speech at Bedford on 20 July 1957 see vol. iv of his autobiography, *Riding the Storm 1956–59* (1971), 350.

electricity for domestic and farm use, however, went up fivefold.[125] The British were keener than the Americans on time-using appliances, less keen on time-saving appliances. None grew as fast as black-and-white television, whose ownership in Britain rose so quickly that by 1970 saturation coverage had almost been reached, and colour television was beginning to move up fast. Although television owners at first clustered at the higher social levels,[126] this soon changed. By December 1955 95 per cent of the population had access to television and by 1970 its average audience in Great Britain had reached a third of the population.[127]

By encouraging home-centredness, television accelerated the advance of all the other consumer goods, but also directly promoted their sale once commercial television arrived in 1955. This coincided with and doubtless helped to accelerate rapid growth in the advertising industry, especially as viewing was more regular at lower social levels.[128] Commercial television was politically all the more powerful for not being overtly political at all. Although the Conservatives were far more than a mere party of business, they benefited considerably in the 1950s from the Americanization of British life, which demonstrated among other things what public-relations skills could achieve. After 1945 American advertising agencies bought out the relatively uncompetitive British agencies, and from the 1930s to the 1970s focused on quite a narrow range of products: tobacco, confectionery, soap, and washing powder.[129] In the 1950s the prewar growth rate in British advertising expenditure resumed, and in one of Britain's three twentieth-century advertising booms rose threefold in real terms between 1947 and 1970.[130] Press advertising absorbed four-fifths of total advertising expenditure until the late 1950s, but 'display' (as distinct from classified) press advertising declined after commercial television was introduced in 1955.[131] Many in press and cinema understandably opposed ITV's advent, and anti-American feeling helped to inspire the defence of the BBC monopoly by the paternalist National Television Council. It marshalled the Great and the Good, including both archbishops and fourteen vice-chancellors; nor were Churchill, Eden, and Macmillan enthusiastic for change.[132] But to no avail: the Popular Television Association—anti-establishment, populist, relatively wealthy, heavily backed by public relations experts, sophisticated in technique—was championed by the small group of Conservative backbenchers who pushed

[125] T. A. B. Corley, *Domestic Electrical Appliances* (1966), 19. Hulton Press, *Patterns of British Life* (1950), 103–6. *BHS* 264.

[126] S. Bowden and A. Offer, 'Household Appliances and the Use of Time', *Economic History Review*, 47 (1994), 729–32. For figures on this see Briggs, *Sound and Vision*, 251, 262.

[127] A. Briggs, *The BBC: The First 50 Years* (1985), 386. *TBS* 556.

[128] For growth figures see J. D. Halloran (ed.), *The Effects of Television* (1970), 155. *TBS* 557.

[129] West, 'Advertising Industry', 94.

[130] T. R. Nevett, *Advertising in Britain: A History* (1982), 177.

[131] *Advertising Statistics Yearbook* (1990), 10–14.

[132] *T* (3 Jan. 1984), 2.

through the change, 'a victory for money over breeding, of corporate power over paternalism'.[133]

Contesting in 1946 the idea that the British people were lazy, Robert Barrington-Ward, editor of *The Times*, pointed out that they 'have nothing to buy with what they earn. Once there are things in the shops, then they will work well enough.'[134] There soon were 'things in the shops', engines of economic growth far more powerful for the Conservatives after 1951 than anything the Attlee governments envisaged. Television was not the only aid to the consumer which emerged or re-emerged in the 1950s. The end of sweet rationing [Plate 7] brought back the slot machine, bolted and barred during the war. With the car in the garage, eating out became more convenient; in the owner-occupied home, stylish entertaining could occur; and from the television in the drawing room new ideas poured forth on what to eat, how to cook it, how to present it. Significant shifts in the balance of consumers' expenditure resulted: clothing took up less of it after the late 1940s, food less after the late 1950s, but from the late 1950s housing took up more, cars notably more, and consumer durables far more than between the wars.[135] Ownership of electric irons and radios had already approached saturation point in the late 1940s, but in 1953 annual income still held back ownership of cars, television sets, refrigerators, and washing machines.[136] Each new consumable fuelled the desire for more: the market for consumer goods rose so fast from the 1950s that former luxuries became necessities, and take-up approached saturation point. This was a boom period for the mail-order firms, whose share of retail sales by value rose from 0.9 per cent in 1950 to 4.1 per cent in 1970.[137] With an agency structure staffed by capable working-class women who knew their neighbours, these firms could safely but selectively extend credit within traditional working-class communities for purchase either directly or (through clubs) by subscription. Deploying their ever larger and glossier catalogues, these women were drawn disproportionately from the families of skilled manual workers, and could mobilize friends, neighbours, and relatives in a consumer network which united mutual convenience with moneymaking and pleasant companionship.[138] Of all women over 16, 46 per cent had been or still were mail-order agents in 1980.[139]

The labour movement disliked much of this, and Labour voters from every social class disliked the world of advertising and mass consumption.[140]

133 Quoted from Paxman, *Friends*, 111. See also Briggs, *Sound and Vision*, 902–6, 912.

134 Nicolson, *Diaries and Letters, 1945–62*, 55 (11 Mar. 1946). See also p. 46 above.

135 *BST* 150.

136 For a valuable graph showing take-up of new appliances, see Bowden and Offer, 'Household Appliances', 731. See also Carr-Saunders *et al.*, *Survey of Social Conditions*, 181.

137 Coopey *et al.*, *Mail Order Retailing*, 53.

138 Ibid. 59–61, 78–81, 87, 96, 100, 101, 111–12, 121, 129, 233–4.

139 Ibid. 108.

140 e.g. Williams, *Gaitskell*, 390. F. Pethick-Lawrence in *HL Deb.* 26 Apr. 1960, c. 80.

The Attlee governments had risked their popularity by holding back present consumption in pursuit of a stronger economy in the longer term, said Bevan, whereas the Conservatives after 1951 'retained political popularity at the expense of the industrial resources of the nation'.[141] Labour saw the advertiser as fostering a disconcerting hedonism and preoccupation with the short term—moods thoroughly alien to the serious-minded people who had created the labour movement, and to their rather austerely rational middle-class sympathizers. Advertising seemed in itself wasteful, at the same time as encouraging consumers to be wasteful; Labour's high-toned union between a secular pursuit of reason and a nonconformist anti-materialism was wary. The advertiser was manipulative, pandering to people's lower instincts, whereas Labour sought cultural and moral improvement. Crossman began to wonder whether capitalist prosperity left the Labour Party as 'missionaries without a mission', but by the mid-1950s socialists had (with Crosland) begun to question whether, amidst the prevailing abundance, self-denial really was integral to economic or moral growth.[142] Labour's working-class supporters were rapidly moving into the income-tax-paying bracket, and by the 1960s the party could no longer assume that its supporters would gain if it preferred taxes on income to taxes on spending. And given the flattening of income differentials since the 1930s, the party could no longer assume that the poor would benefit appreciably if income from the rich was redistributed.[143] By no means everyone gained from this prosperity: inflation capriciously caused the real incomes of some (the well-organized and the employed, for example) to rise, whereas others (for example, pensioners, the unemployed, and people on fixed incomes) lost out. This prepared the ground for what could have become a new socialist cause in the 1960s: a national incomes policy that would distribute wealth more fairly. Yet to carry socialism into this area was to expose the tension between Labour's egalitarian and trade union traditions.

Few could contest the convenience that stemmed from the new materials (nylon, plastics, Formica, denim), or the attractiveness of the new packaging and design. When Orwell in hospital in 1947 wanted a ballpoint pen, he had to pay £3 (about £70 as at 2005) for it.[144] After 1951 towels and fabrics became more artistic, pots and pans more colourful, detergents protected the hands, and cupboards were increasingly fitted. The departure of gas stoves or ranges meant no more rakings of ashes and brushings with black lead. While this change carried with it the coal fire's gradual departure from living

141 *HC Deb.* 3 Nov. 1959, c. 863.

142 Crossman, *Backbench Diaries*, 437 (15 July 1955). Crosland, *Future of Socialism*, 288, 293, 518.

143 As Crosland pointed out in *Future of Socialism*, 190.

144 Crick, *Orwell*, 371. I am most grateful to the late Andrew Glyn for enabling me to update the original price.

rooms, together with all the emotive connotations of hearth and home, the television soon provided a substitute focus there. No end seemed in sight to material comfort's advance. By 1970 wall-to-wall carpets, electric blankets, double glazing, and central heating were extending within the home a year-long freedom of movement hitherto available only in warmer months. One could move about freely instead of continually fending off draughts and huddling close to fires in the home's small heated area, periodically dashing out to a cold bedroom or an outside lavatory. The average living room was over 5°F warmer in 1970 than in 1950, with or without central heating. This did not necessarily mean that people had become 5°F hotter when indoors, because many preferred to wear fewer clothes in a higher temperature than more clothes in a lower; but there seem to have been limits to this disrobing because the temperature in centrally heated homes ceased in the 1960s to rise faster than in other homes.[145] Central heating had penetrated a majority of households by 1977.[146]

Mass home-ownership was another television-boosted Conservative policy which promoted both the party and a privatized materialism. Labour, by contrast, had emerged from the public life of working-class communities: from co-op, chapel, trade union, and workplace. 'When . . . a working class family buys a motor car', said Gaitskell in July 1959, '. . . it may produce a feeling of a more individual and independent status. Its loyalty ceases to be the simple group loyalty. It begins to function as an independent unit.'[147] By the mid-1960s the home with a television had become for almost everyone what it had hitherto been for only a minority: a place comfortable enough and sufficiently stocked with the supermarket's bottled and canned beer to supplant the recreational and communal roles of pub and cinema. The living room supplanted the bedroom as the room in the house on which most was spent,[148] and householders with a stake in the country were all the more tempted to leave their mark on nature with a carefully kept garden. Catering for such tastes were *Gardeners' Question Time* (first broadcast in 1947) on radio and a host of televised garden programmes.

Meanwhile the wife, and increasingly the husband, were profiting from television's many cookery programmes, with their associated glossy cookery books. We have already seen[149] how culinary opportunities were broadening in the 1950s, even though food absorbed less of the consumer's overall expenditure. Growing culinary inspiration came from holidays overseas and

[145] See the extraordinary article by D. G. Hunt and M. R. Steele, 'Domestic Temperature Trends', *Heating and Ventilating Engineer* (Apr. 1980), 9–12.

[146] J. Obelkevich and P. Catterall (eds.), *Understanding Post-War British Society* (1994), 147.

[147] Interview in *Daily Mail* (30 July 1959), quoted in Butler and Rose, *British General Election of 1959*, 13.

[148] Burnett, *Social History of Housing*, 275.

[149] See above, pp. 85–7.

from more diverse restaurants at home, while the frozen vegetable launched an assault on seasonally fluctuating supply.[150] The Second World War had narrowed class contrasts in diet, with the poor consuming more milk and the rich consuming more margarine. By the early 1960s the poor had also pushed up their sugar consumption, though by comparison the rich were still consuming more milk, cheese, meat, fish, vegetables (other than potatoes), and fruit. Unfortunately for Labour, it had been free to relax rationing only at the point of vacating power to the Conservatives, who reaped much of the credit for a relaxation that would have occurred under any government. But because young people in 1951 had no recollection of Britain's growing interwar affluence, and because the labour movement had no interest in reminding them of it, the limited affluence of the 1950s under the Conservatives was thrown into even sharper relief, giving them the credit for the cornucopia which the Attlee governments' upright and short-term austerity had helped to ensure.

In service occupations, relatively labour-intensive by manufacturing standards, relations with the customer were at first relatively close—most notably in leisure, welfare, and finance. Market stalls and even market halls had been steadily retreating since 1945, but the Victorians would have felt quite at home in Britain's shops of the 1950s: small concerns managed by the proprietor, working through assistants who knew him, the goods he sold, and his customers. Many items were still weighed out, wrapped according to the customer's instructions, and put in shopping baskets. The supermarket emerged out of self-service within the same Express Dairy or Tesco which had earlier given personal service. Alan Sainsbury introduced the supermarket idea from the USA after a visit there in 1949, two years after Tesco's first (ephemeral) self-service shop opened in St Albans. Sainsbury's first supermarket opened at Croydon in the following year, and Tesco's first at Maldon in 1956. There were 2,500 self-service outlets by mid-1955, many of them co-ops, and by mid-1957 more than eighty supermarkets.[151] Liberalization combined with commercial pressure to accelerate supermarkets' expansion. Food rationing and building restrictions ended in 1954, and the Restrictive Practices Act (1956) required resale price maintenance agreements to be vetted and then selectively registered before taking effect. This freed the multiples to engage in the price-cutting they and their customers craved; price restrictions were not popular, and by mid-1958 retail price maintenance on most branded groceries had ended.[152] By 1959 there were 286 supermarkets, and 572 two years later. In 1961 supermarkets

[150] J. P. Greaves and D. F. Hollingsworth, 'Trends in Food Consumption in the United Kingdom', in G. H. Bourne (ed.), *World Review of Nutrition and Dietetics* (1966), 66, 71–2.

[151] J. F. Pickering, 'The Breakdown of R.P.M. in the Grocery Trade: Cause and Effect', in J. Benson and G. Shaw (eds.), *The Retailing Industry*, iii (1999), 29. W. G. McClelland, 'Economics of the Supermarket', ibid. iii. 15.

[152] Pickering, 'Breakdown of R.P.M.', 29–31, 33–4.

when related to population were most prevalent in the south-east of England, especially in the home counties and their outer fringe, least prevalent in Wales and Scotland.[153] Shops gradually became larger and less intimate, and the supermarket chains grew in the number and size of their premises, and in the range of goods they stocked. Large retail concerns claimed an ever-larger share of the market. Of 11,000 grocery outlets in 1970, the 3,500 supermarkets accounted for more than a quarter of the total grocery business, and were diversifying into hardware, drink, clothing, and household goods generally.[154] In the following year there were far more of the multiples (including the Co-op) in the south-east than in any other region, but their share of total shops was highest in Scotland (20.2 %), and in no region of Great Britain did they contribute less than an eighth of the total.[155] Victims of the change were the specialist food shops, especially dairymen, fishmongers, butchers, bakers, confectioners, and greengrocers.[156]

This conjuncture of abundant choice, increasingly complex products, and diminishing personal guidance gave the Consumers' Association (founded in 1957) and its much-consulted periodical *Which?* (launched in the same year) their moment. The Association was founded by an American on the model of the USA's Consumers' Union, which provided an initial subsidy.[157] The first number of *Which?* surveyed electric kettles, sunglasses, aspirin, cake mixes, scouring powders and pastes, no-iron cottons, and cars. The British pedigree for consumer protection was longer than was realized at the time, and its natural home on the left would have been more readily recognized if the co-op movement had not then been in marked relative decline, if the trade unions had not focused so firmly on producer interests, and if the public monopoly had been less central to Labour policy. The Association from its earliest days was highly participatory, issuing questionnaires to its members about what should be investigated. It grew fast, built up a branch structure, and by September 1959 had 140,000 members.[158] Thereafter the movement was slowly drawn into the all-party interventionist consensus of the 1960s and early 1970s: government ministers and civil servants struggled within a planning environment to curb price rises, whereas growing numbers saw the free market as the consumer's best defence. 'The price side of the prices and incomes policy', wrote Crossman privately in October 1966, 'is as much a fraud as the workers suspect.'[159]

Volunteers sprang to defend particular types of consumer. For the foreigner, said Orwell in 1945, England's 'two worst faults' were 'the gloom of our

[153] Pickering, 'Breakdown of R.P.M.', 15–16, cf. 30.

[154] *T* (16 Feb. 1970, supplement on 'Food in Britain'), p. vi. *T* (5 May 1978, supplement on 'Grocery Retailing'), p. iii.

[155] *T* (21 May 1973), 19.

[156] For useful statistics see Walsh, *Shoplifting*, 9.

[157] *Which?* 1/6 (Winter 1959), 35.

[158] *Which?* (Sept. 1959), 103.

[159] *Cabinet Diaries*, ii. 58 (1 Oct. 1966).

Sundays and the difficulty of buying a drink'. It was not, he added, 'a law of nature that every restaurant in England should be either foreign or bad', and from the late 1960s government promoted better hotel standards.[160] By then British food puritanism had been subverted by the end of rationing in the early 1950s and from 1951 by the Good Food Club's annual *Good Food Guide*. In the following year tea, gammon, and ham were derationed; in 1953 chocolate, sweets, and sugar [Plate 7]; in 1954 cheese, butter, margarine, cooking fats, bacon, and meat. As the state retreated, so the volunteer advanced. The Club depended entirely on volunteered reports, and with minimal administrative structure it was, said its president, 'the creation, and the creature, of its members'.[161] In the 1950s the *Guide* surveyed 700–800 restaurants; continuously refining its criteria, and gravitating towards organizing its material by region, its good-humoured prefaces were optimistic in mood. It was setting standards from the top, as exemplified in that prototype of the country-house hotel, the Sharrow Bay Hotel, which opened with five rooms in 1949.[162] In 1970 Raymond Postgate, the *Guide*'s editor, noted 'the enormous improvement in British catering' since 1949; the 'unending and never-varying sequence of sullen and ill-managed hotels and unfriendly restaurants, serving over-cooked meats and sodden vegetables' had already become a distant memory.[163] We have seen how immigrant minorities were improving food standards lower down, too, and by the 1960s the distinction between pub and restaurant was becoming blurred. Pubs were now losing their name for minimal and poor-quality food, and mergers between the big brewing, catering, and leisure concerns during the 1970s were the natural consequence. Food retailing improved in parallel. To take but one example: cheese. Orwell had pronounced Stilton 'the best cheese of its type in the world, with Wensleydale not far behind', and with the renaissance of English cheeses during the coming half-century the names of James Aldridge, Patrick Rance, and Randolph Hodgson are imperishably linked.[164]

The corporatist years of the 1950s and 1960s, then, were by no means stagnant or unenterprising. Their growth rate was high by British standards, and both inflation and unemployment were relatively low, though slowly rising. The recurrent gloom about the economy in public discussion was not at all replicated in the attitudes or conduct of the general public, who had as yet little reason to repudiate a regime compatible with a prosperity so tangible. They felt it at work, given the growing employment opportunities for women, the shorter and more flexible working hours, and the transition from manufacture

160 Orwell, 'In Defence of English Cooking', 446, 448. Stewart, *Hoteliers and Hotels*, 11.

161 R. Postgate (ed.), *The Good Food Guide 1961–1962* (1961), 18 (preface).

162 Obituaries of Francis Coulson, *T* (18 Feb. 1998), 25; and Brian Sack, *T* (5 Jan. 2002), 27.

163 *Good Food Guide 1969–70*, p. vi (preface).

164 'In Defence of English Cooking', 447. 'James Aldridge', *T* (19 Feb. 2001), 21 (obituary).

to the service sector's relatively attractive working conditions. They felt it also in the shops, freed at last from rationing and with supermarkets extending ever more choice, diversity, and abundance. As yet, relatively few travelled abroad within Western Europe to see how much faster prosperity was growing there, and if newly available comparative statistics alerted the politicians to worrying comparisons, British corporatist resources had yet to be exhausted. Politicians did not change course: they strained all the harder to prop up manufacturing and make interventionist structures work better.

So six of the Introduction's motifs are relevant here: the politicians' continued endorsement of the Second World War's corporatist legacy (the first motif), and the notable contrast between politicians' and popular perceptions about the economy (the third). Only towards the end of the 1960s was there any significant move towards irrelevantly blaming the electoral system or adversarial politics for such economic problems as existed: institutional stability (the sixth motif) persisted amidst substantial socio-economic change for many years more. In seeking to operate a corporatist economy the politicians were not of course in full control (the seventh motif): skills in persuading, coordinating, energizing, and conciliating remained integral to British political leadership in the corporatist years. But corporatist approaches seemed more popular and less anarchic than a free-market alternative which few thought existed, and fewer still advocated. An overridingly materialist political agenda lay behind all this, and given that acquisitive values can prompt illegal as well as legal responses, there was an associated challenge to traditional Christian values and structures (the fifth motif). Also relevant is one last motif (the fourth): the failure of shorter working hours and time-saving devices to moderate the busy-ness of daily life. Dual-career families required careful timetabling; the transition from manufacturing to services involved working hours less clearly delimited; and abundance outside working hours involved time-consuming planning and choice. Prominent within this abundance were the diversified cultural and recreational activities next to be discussed.

CHAPTER 7

Intellect and Culture

Though in the 1950s and 1960s religion played a diminishing role in British education and culture, it was still important, not least because its influence in the schools was considerable. The chapter's first section, on religion, therefore leads naturally into the second, which outlines the full flowering of the state schools structure after the austerities and disruption of the war, together with the persistence of the independent sector. Schools expansion flowed naturally into expanding universities, discussed in the third section. In these years they grew into a nationwide 'system'. Increasingly dominated by the ideas and values of natural science, they were none the less of great cultural significance locally and nationally, so in the chapter's fourth section the discussion moves towards prosperity in literature and the arts. The chapter concludes with a section on recreation in the wider sense, also greatly enriched and diversified.

1. CHRISTIANS IN DIFFICULTY

The UK in 1951 was still to all appearances a Christian country. Asked in January 1950 whether they believed in prayer, 69 per cent said they did, and there was as yet no need to specify whether their god was Christian; 90 per cent of the population in February 1954 said they owned a Bible, and more than a third said they would take it to a desert island, far more than would take its nearest rival: Dickens.[1] Christianity was still much involved with rites of passage: in 1968 four-fifths of the population had their children baptized, and in 1970 only a third of those eligible to marry in church preferred a register office. In the areas of England and Wales where civil marriage had been most popular a century earlier, its popularity had actually declined by the 1960s, and in 1970 a religious burial was almost universal.[2] Christians were well entrenched in intellectual and cultural life, with T. S. Eliot and John Betjeman prominent in literature, and Stanley Spencer painting at Cookham. Symbolic

[1] *Gallup Polls*, i. 648, 316.

[2] W. S. F. Pickering, 'The Persistence of Rites of Passage: Towards an Explanation', *British Journal of Sociology* (Mar. 1974), 64, 65–8. O. Anderson, 'The Incidence of Civil Marriage in Victorian England and Wales', *Past and Present* (Nov. 1975), 55. Pickering, 'Rites of Passage', 68.

of the continuing affinity between art and religion was the performance of Britten's 'War Requiem' at the opening in 1962 of Basil Spence's Coventry Cathedral, adorned as it was with John Piper's stained glass and Graham Sutherland's tapestry.

Christian apologetics attracted many readers. C. S. Lewis and Dorothy L. Sayers were prominent in popular theology, and there was a lively market for the paperback versions of Lewis's *Screwtape Letters* (1942) and Albert Henry Ross's *Who Moved the Stone?* (published under the pseudonym Frank Morison in 1930). Christianity had not yet vacated the intellectual high ground. Overtly Christian scholars—Jacob, Knowles, Powicke, Southern—were distinguished medieval historians, and under Edward Evans-Pritchard (converted to Catholicism in 1944) the social anthropologists were becoming less distant from Christianity. Religion deeply influenced political leaders, too. A Wilson without Congregationalism was as impossible as a Thatcher without Methodism; when controverting Christians during her third term she was well able to swap text for text.[3] In 1992 Callaghan vividly recalled his terror three-quarters of a century earlier when, returning home to find his mother unexpectedly absent, he thought she had ascended to heaven, and that he had been too wicked to accompany her.[4]

Yet if Christianity had been really powerful, it would have evoked the sort of equal-and-opposite reaction that emerged in the Victorian period; militant irreligion was not prominent in the UK after 1951, however—though humanism, its milder and more cultivated variant, was more in evidence. Even humanists were not numerous, and in 1970 the British Humanist Association had only 3,020 members.[5] In 1963 only 9 per cent of those polled said they did not think there was any sort of spirit, god, or life force, and when asked in 1965 'what is your religion?' only 3 per cent of respondents said 'atheist, agnostic, or no religion'.[6] When Margaret Knight, a psychology lecturer at Aberdeen, gave three talks on the BBC Home Service in 1955 from a humanist point of view, Churchill joined in the national outcry. The agnostic Barbara Wootton claimed in 1967 that the penalties for being overtly non-Christian were still then serious enough in the UK to require 'those who (like myself) have nothing to lose by frankness . . . to let their opinions be freely known'.[7]

There were, in truth, reasons for Christian concern, not because Christianity was being overtly attacked, but because of a quietly growing indifference. The

[3] See e.g. *STel.* (28 June 1987), 23. *FT* (26 May 1988), 1.

[4] Callaghan quoted in BBC2's programme, *Labour's Last Premier* (25 Apr. 1992).

[5] Currie *et al.*, *Churches and Churchgoers*, 194.

[6] P. G. Forster, 'Secularization in the English Context: Some Conceptual and Empirical Problems', *Sociological Review* (May 1972), 159.

[7] A. Briggs, *Sound and Vision* (Oxford, 1979), 800. B. Wootton, *In a World I Never Made: Autobiographical Reflections* (1967), 163.

Church of England's educational role continued to decline, from responsibility for 37 per cent of primary schools in 1950 to 26 per cent in 1971; by that year at the secondary level it had fallen to 4 per cent, with only the Roman Catholic proportion rising.[8] The rising number of books published on religion between 1946 and 1976 could not raise its proportion: about 5 per cent of the total.[9] The audiences for religious programmes on BBC radio and television plunged after 1945,[10] and on every measure—baptisms, Sunday school scholars, confirmations, or numbers on the electoral roll—the Church of England was in absolute decline between 1951 and 1970. In the forty years before 1960 38 per cent of Anglican ordinands were drawn from Oxford and Cambridge graduates, but only 16 per cent by 1971, while 57 per cent by then had no degree at all.[11] The religious challenge to Oxford philosophy's secular mood was on the wane, and the agnostics Ayer and Russell had by the 1960s become the heroes of progressive youth. Symbolizing the Church's gradual loss of its nationally integrating role was the advent in 1961 of an Archbishop of Canterbury (Michael Ramsey) who assumed a purple cassock instead of the gaiters that his predecessor had expected from his bishops. It was in 1957 that Robert Milburn, probably the last dean to wear them, took office,[12] and the archbishop's new garb, while revealing perhaps a certain personal holiness, also signified the narrower professional status that was now superseding an earlier and broader social role.

Membership figures tell the same story for all other Protestant groups in the UK, and when adult membership figures are related to adult population, the decline becomes more like a plunge.[13] The population's growing social and geographical mobility particularly weakened the nonconformist denominations, whose recruitment depended so heavily on loyalty to a particular chapel and on cultivating respectability within a face-to-face community: many nonconformist chapels found new roles as furniture stores, cinemas, and homes for non-Christian religions new to the British Isles. National identity could help to prolong religious allegiance. Hence the three major exceptions to religion's overall decline in the UK: the Roman Catholics, the Protestants in Northern Ireland, and the smaller sectarian churches throughout Great Britain. Presbyterianism was noticeably stronger in Scotland, nonconformity in Wales, than were either in England, and in the Irish Republic Roman Catholic dominance was overwhelming. Furthermore, their prior religious allegiance helped to insulate migrants to Britain from its predominantly secular environment:

[8] *BST* 238.

[9] *Bookseller* (4 Jan. 1947), 5; (5 Jan. 1957), 10; (31 Dec. 1966), 2677; (25 Dec. 1976), 2839.

[10] Currie *et al.*, *Churches and Churchgoers*, 235.

[11] A. Hastings, *A History of English Christianity 1920–1985* (1986), 614.

[12] O. Chadwick, *Michael Ramsey: A Life* (Oxford, 1990), 363. Obituary of Milburn, *T* (25 Feb. 2000), 27.

[13] *BST* 524, 541. Currie *et al.*, *Churches and Churchgoers*, 65–7, 167–8.

Catholicism for the southern Irish, Presbyterianism for Northern Ireland's Protestants, and Protestant sects for Christian immigrants from abroad.[14]

Secular values were so pervasive that they shaped church organization. There was a decidedly secular preoccupation in the 1950s and 1960s with rationalization: with how best to deploy the Church of England's resources. By then it was clear that its predominantly rural parish structure must adapt to population change and ongoing urbanization. Team ministries for enlarged parishes and group ministries for amalgamated parishes were seen in the 1960s as the solution. But what of the buildings? 'I trust we shall be relieved of mountains of masonry that at present divert almost all energy from mission to maintenance', wrote Bishop Robinson of Woolwich, sketching out his hopes for a revived inner-city Christianity in 1966.[15] In the outcome, the secularization of redundant rectories and even churches helped to fund something very different: the continued institutional existence of a somewhat attenuated established church. Given the growing secular touristic and aesthetic roles of the great English cathedrals, there was also a good case not only for the appeals launched by 1967 to restore nine of the twenty-eight, but even for boosting state aid beyond periodic grants for repair, so as to match the public funding that their European equivalents received.[16] Fewer nonconformist chapels were architectural treasures, so their 'rationalization' could be faster: whereas Anglican buildings or congregations shrank by 3 per cent between 1950 and 1970, the equivalent nonconformist shrinkage in England and Wales was 14 per cent.[17]

Individual moral reform, the traditional Christian preoccupation, ran into thickets between 1951 and 1970: the world was becoming more complex. Gwen Raverat in 1952 applied the phrase 'Christian parasites' to her Victorian-born Cambridge intellectual relatives:[18] they had rejected Christian dogma while retaining Christian ethics. The next generation had the best of both worlds: Keynes told Virginia Woolf in 1934 that 'we destroyed Christianity and yet had its benefits'.[19] By the 1960s pragmatism and empiricism were ousting principle from public debate about moral issues. In 1969 Archbishop Ramsey, predicting further Anglican decline, took comfort from the persisting social influence of Christian attitudes separately from Christian belief, which to the museum director Roy Strong 'sounded a pretty grim scenario'.[20] There was now less room for that high-toned abstract confrontation on values that the clergy had

[14] *TBS* 409, 414, 449. Currie *et al.*, *Churches and Churchgoers*, 28–9, 36, 158.

[15] Quoted in E. James, *A Life of Bishop John A. T. Robinson: Scholar, Pastor, Prophet* (1987), 146.

[16] As argued by Earl Jellicoe, *HL Deb.* 25 Apr. 1967, cc. 506–11.

[17] Adapted from table 19.12 in *TCBST* 669 by aggregating as 'nonconformist' the figures for Congregational, Presbyterian Church of Wales, Baptist, and Methodist.

[18] G. Raverat, *Period Piece: A Cambridge Childhood* (1st publ. 1952, paperback edn. 1960), 189.

[19] *The Diary of Virginia Woolf*, iv. *1931–5*, ed. A. O. Bell (1982), 208 (19 Apr. 1934).

[20] Strong, *Diaries*, 45.

earlier found congenial: experts now populated the field with their statistics, social engineering replaced moral uplift, and concern with the short-term subordinated longer-term (let alone other-worldly) perspectives.[21] In these years the behavioural sciences' wealth of knowledge about human motivation, in alliance with a humanitarian ethic, was sending personal moral responsibility into retreat before a growing acceptance of environmental determinism.[22] In March 1969 *The Times* claimed that debate about euthanasia could no longer assume an absolute ban on taking human life in all circumstances: such discussion must accept that 'human happiness, the avoidance of suffering, compassion, and the full realization of human capacities are the chief goods to be sought in inter-personal behaviour'.[23] Even Mary Whitehouse's non-denominational National Viewers' and Listeners' Association in effect transferred blame for individual misconduct to the pressures of a polluted moral (rather than unjust social) environment. The traditional religious emphasis on girding up the individual to resist inner temptation was giving way to the pursuit of more earthly causes.

For one distinguished social investigator, 'the struggle against Communism' was 'a religious struggle': Seebohm Rowntree, who in 1946 enlisted a colleague half his age in Commander Russell Lavers, a former naval intelligence officer with a good war record. Together they embarked on research for a book at first called 'English Life and Character', but published in 1951 as *English Life and Leisure*. William Beveridge, reviewing the book, found it 'frightening' to think that the equal votes of 'the mainly deplorable human beings' revealed in the book's case histories as 'so irresponsible and so ignorant' could now shape British government.[24] Their research moved forward in the early 1950s to planning a book on 'the spiritual life of the nation'. It was never published, but included a census of church attendance in York and interviews with many influential people willing to pronounce on the moral issues which had lain behind Rowntree's research throughout his long life. Despairing of the churches as guardians of socially responsible conduct, and as bulwark against Communism, and showing only a brief postwar interest in Moral Rearmament, Rowntree (first President of the Outward Bound Trust) sought salvation through promoting community-based character-building organizations such as youth clubs and the Women's Institutes, and through army and factory chaplains and personnel workers.[25]

21 This discussion owes much to C. Davies, *Permissive Britain: Social Change in the Sixties and Seventies* (1975), 14–24, 36.

22 As Archbishop Runcie complained in his interview with Bernard Levin, *T* (30 Mar. 1987), 10.

23 *T* (24 Mar. 1969), 9 (leader).

24 *Spec.* (8 June 1951), 756.

25 See Mark Freeman's important 'Britain's Spiritual Life: How can it be Deepened? Seebohm Rowntree, Russell Lavers, and the "Crisis of Belief" c.1946–54', *Journal of Religious History* (Feb. 2005), quotation from 31; see also 27, 28, 33, 34, 38, 40–1.

The revivalist Billy Graham's objectives were similar, but his methods very different. Did he and the sharp-suited, somewhat glamorous young American men who accompanied him on his evangelistic crusades to Britain (most notably in 1954) benefit religious observance in the longer term? In three pages of quiet but concentrated reasoning, Ramsey in 1956 expressed doubts. Evangelical fundamentalism in its Bible-centredness, in overemphasizing Christ's taking upon himself the punishment for human sin, and in calling for an immediate decision of will and emotion 'for Christ', subordinated both the individual's intellect and the church's guidance. He concluded by hoping 'that the stream of conversions will not be followed by a backwash of moral casualties and disillusioned sceptics'.[26] Graham's huge meetings may well have confirmed in their faith the many churchgoers who attended, and his visit may even have drawn together British evangelicals, hitherto divided, lending them a self-confidence recently lacking[27]—but he did not arrest the long-term British decline in religious observance. There was religious as well as political good sense (though no long-term remedy) in Churchill's warning to Graham, despite their shared anti-Communism, 'not to allow mundane considerations to bulk too largely in his mission, and to stick to the spiritual side'.[28]

What hope for the faith lay, then, in the political option? The Methodist leader Donald Soper noted in a Lords debate of 1974 how morality had evolved during his lifetime from 'a purely personal relationship between man and his neighbour or man and his God' into a much more complex 'social morality'.[29] Christians from T. H. Green onwards had for decades been seeking impact through displaying their 'relevance' in political and reforming activism. In the mid-1950s Trevor Huddleston's enormously successful *Naught for your Comfort* (1956) reinforced the Christian assault on apartheid, and the Suez sermons of Labour councillor Mervyn Stockwood filled Cambridge's university church. CND later fostered much debate on collective ethics, and attracted two well-known clergymen who had earlier campaigned against apartheid: Canon John Collins, who became its chairman, and Canon Michael Scott, who as a vice-president of the direct-action 'Committee of 100' served two prison sentences. Quakers were central to launching the pressure groups Shelter and Child Poverty Action Group in the 1960s.[30] Yet political work diverted effort from the Christian's distinctive contribution, for such activism could as well be secular as Christian in its impulse. The humanitarian values pioneered by Christianity's critics from the eighteenth-century Enlightenment onwards risked consigning Christians to cheering from the sidelines. Worse, such values

[26] M. Ramsey, 'The Menace of Fundamentalism', *The Bishoprick* (Feb. 1956), 24–6.

[27] As argued in I. M. Randall, 'Conservative Constructionist: The Early Influence of Billy Graham in Britain', *Evangelical Quarterly* (Oct. 1995), 309–33.

[28] Quoted in M. Gilbert, *'Never Despair'* (1988), 979.

[29] *HL Deb.* 10 Dec. 1974, c. 607.

[30] A. G. Jordan and J. J. Richardson, *Government and Pressure Groups in Britain* (Oxford, 1987), 76.

might pollute the substance of their faith: with hell discarded, and with God radiating benevolence, beliefs once seen as central to Christianity (the last judgement, the atonement) slowly lost their appeal. Besides, it was not clear that politicized Christians had anything distinctive to offer. In an increasingly specialized world, the Christian's emphasis on sin seemed unduly simplistic and unaccompanied by useful expertise. The social sciences had by the 1950s already exposed the complex of motive and impulse that in practice governs decision-making, whether political and social or personal and moral: the choice between right and wrong no longer seemed straightforward. The political option also risked dividing congregations: for example, by the 1960s the more regular the attender at Anglican services, the more likely was the Conservative allegiance likely to be.[31]

Even more subversive from the 1960s, because strategically more central, was the intrusion of secularized attitudes into theology. In 1962 Alec Vidler, Dean of King's College Cambridge, and a self-described 'sceptic in faith's clothing',[32] assembled ten Cambridge theologians in his volume *Soundings* (1962). Unlike the 'liberation theology' then prominent in Latin America, this movement was not socially radical, but its intellectual radicalism seemed subversive enough at the time, especially when publicized by Bishop Robinson. 'My God, John Robinson's written a book which is going to cause mayhem', Hugh Montefiore told the future Archbishop Runcie,[33] '—he's going to tell the world the sort of things *we* believe!' Robinson's controversial *Honest to God* (1963) included much autobiography and thinking aloud, noting that in any debate between Christians and humanists 'most of my sympathies are on the humanist's side': the Christian position was, he thought, being inappropriately defended[34] through using outmoded language and unhelpful images, thereby alienating people quite unnecessarily. God should no longer be portrayed as 'an old man in the sky', if only because space research seemed now to be leaving him 'no vacant spaces': God was not 'out there', but within each of us. Opposing any clear distinction between God and man, between the religious and the secular, Robinson felt that the church should not be 'a walled garden'; instead, he aimed to extend lay influence within it and project the Christian message beyond the experts and the professionals to the many outsiders who could yet be drawn in.[35] Describing the Christmas story as myth, dismissing black-and-white approaches to sexual morality as too simplistic, sceptical about the continued vitality of the institutional church, he weakened support for any one of his good causes by championing too many others. His loosening

[31] Butler and Stokes, *Political Change in Britain* (2nd edn.), 157–8.

[32] Obituary, *T* (29 July 1991), 16.

[33] As cited in H. Carpenter, *Robert Runcie: The Reluctant Archbishop* (1st publ. 1996, paperback edn. 1997), 159.

[34] Robinson, *Honest to God*, 8.

[35] Quotations ibid. 13–14, 140.

of the barriers to faith did not produce the desired religious revival, and by the late 1960s he feared that the clergyman remained a mere 'manager of a religious club', stripped of educational, cultural, and welfare roles that were now performed more effectively elsewhere—and reduced to offering only 'one line, which nobody much wants'.[36]

From a less cerebral direction came the sort of challenge that nineteenth-century Christians had encountered in the overseas mission field but seldom at home: the relativism prompted by the coexistence of different religious beliefs all held fervently. This problem, also central to Victorian education debates, had subsequently faded, but in the 1960s the Asian immigrants unexpectedly revived it. To quote *The Times* in 1969, 'nobody's interest can be served by teachers of doubtful religious faith trying to provide traditional Christian instruction to Sikh and Muslim children', so 'what is required is to move more towards the comparative study of different religions'.[37] University students of religion were reaching a similar destination for less practical reasons. Central to this shift was Ninian Smart, professor of religious studies at Lancaster University from 1967 to 1982. He estimated that in the mid-1950s only sixteen people in British universities taught religions other than Christianity, whereas by the end of the century his approach (initially controversial) was taken for granted.[38] Given the scale of worldwide migrations, he was working with the tide, and helped to advance it by using his political influence and media skills in the 1970s to get comparative religion into primary- and secondary-school syllabuses. His energy ensured that Lancaster became a powerhouse for promoting worldwide the multi-dimensional study of his subject.

The Roman Catholic Church was not immune from these changes. It had long shed any taint of political disloyalty, its schools in the 1960s gained equal access with Protestant schools to state funds, and its congregations had for decades been slowly moving out of their Irish ghetto and back towards the centre of British life. Catholics were upwardly mobile and were spreading out in their patterns of residence from north to south and from inner-city to suburb. Symbolic of their wider contacts was the growing prevalence of mixed marriages, whose number first overtook exclusively Catholic marriages in 1963.[39] With the Second Vatican Council (1962–5), the barriers between the Christian churches were lowering remarkably fast, so that Archbishop Ramsey could be far less furtive when visiting Rome in 1966 than Fisher had been six years earlier. For many Catholic intellectuals impatient with their church's deferential culture and respect for papal infallibility, these changes could not come soon enough; several, among whom Charles Davis in 1966 was the best

[36] 'The Exploding Church', *O* (14 Apr. 1968), 7.

[37] *T* (19 Nov. 1969), 11 (leader).

[38] Obituary, *Ind.* (5 Feb. 2001), 6.

[39] Hastings, *History of English Christianity*, 563. Hastings is excellent on Roman Catholic history in these years.

known, chose to leave. On the other hand, for many in the congregation, the changes were coming too fast, and it was amidst much bewilderment and some controversy that the full mass in English rather than Latin arrived in 1968. The decline of UK anti-Catholicism outside Northern Ireland represented in one respect sheer gain for the British Catholic community, but tolerance can denote indifference as much as respect, nor do ecumenical enthusiasms necessarily prove lasting or bring new recruits.

Much of the energy and idealism which had hitherto fuelled religious institutions now found secular outlets. It was both consequence and, in its turn, cause of diminished religious observance that recreation diversified so markedly after 1951. This change did more than compete with religion for time: in its hedonism it also competed with religious values. 'Wealth and luxury are constantly held out to be desirable ends in themselves', the sociologists Rowntree and Lavers complained in 1951, reserving a special distaste for the materialistic values in the many American films now being imported.[40] Add to this the influences that had long been cumulatively undermining religious belief and observance in Western societies. The nineteenth-century conflict between religion and science had not gone away: it had merely gone underground, and it occasionally resurfaced—in the irreligious impulses motivating the distinguished biologist Francis Crick, for example.[41] Human self-confidence gained, too, from the advance of affluence, the removal of uncertainty through the growth in state and private insurance, the big city's banishing of the dark, the specialization of function subtracting from religious institutions so many of their traditional roles, the diversion by feminism and birth control of women's energies into fulfilment through careers rather than through religious observance, and the broadening Christian exposure to other religions through worldwide migration and travel.

And yet belief in the supernatural did not decline contemporaneously with organized religion. Emancipated from guidance by relatively educated religious leaders, belief in the supernatural could henceforward take exotic and even anti-social directions. *Old Moore's Almanack* still circulated widely, catering for the working-class belief in luck, and belief in ghosts still attracted as many as a fifth of those questioned in Gallup polls of 1973 and 1975, though in the same surveys ghosts had allegedly been seen by only 4 and 5 per cent respectively.[42] In his survey of 1955 Gorer could cite many other examples of supernatural belief as influences on daily life: a seventh of the population then owned a lucky mascot, a sixth believed that special days automatically brought good or bad luck, and a quarter thought some numbers especially lucky or unlucky for them. Two-thirds of the women and just over a quarter of the men in his

[40] Rowntree and Lavers, *English Life and Leisure*, 249.

[41] Obituary, *T* (30 July 2004), 38.

[42] *Gallup Polls*, ii. 1283, 1417.

sample had visited a fortune-teller at least once, and about half the respondents to a questionnaire issued by *The People* said they regularly followed the paper's astrologer.[43] By 1967 Donald Soper in a House of Lords debate could declare that 'we are living in what is the first genuinely pagan age . . . there are so many people, particularly children, who never remember having heard hymns at their mother's knee, as I have, whose first tunes are from Radio One, and not from any hymn book'. It was because there was truth in his remark that John Lennon gave enormous offence in 1965 by claiming in an interview that the Beatles were 'now more popular than Christ'.[44]

2. HIGH HOPES FOR THE SCHOOLS

By the 1950s the link between religion and education, once so close, had greatly weakened, and in a secularizing society economic priorities might have been expected to fill the void. 'If we are to hold our position among men of our own race or among the nations of the world', the Liberal education minister W. E. Forster told parliament in 1870, when launching Britain's national education system, 'we must make up the smallness of our numbers by increasing the intellectual force of the individual'.[45] Yet in its schools, its universities, its religious attitudes, and its culture, Britain after 1951 kept moneymaking at bay: its educational driving force was never narrowly utilitarian or vocational. Instead, a secularized idealism among policy-makers higher up, uniting civic to democratic values, ensured a ready response to the continuous pressure for expansion emerging from below. The expansionary impulse came from the liberal concern for individual self-realization and democratic participation which extensions of the franchise had earlier nourished. We have already seen[46] how this was reinforced by an internal educational dynamic; it prompted almost as spontaneous a growth in state education as in public welfare—responding to demographic trends and individual hopes rather than to any firm political direction. The entire system reflected a concern to encourage the able child to climb an educational ladder. The values inspiring that climb, the more deeply inculcated the higher the child rose, were academic and meritocratic, not vocational. Prestige within the system lay not with polytechnics and technical schools but with the arts-based courses of the grammar school, and with the unworldly values of Oxford and Cambridge which presided somewhat remotely over the whole. Liberal values pervaded the British educational system, and educational pluralism reigned supreme. Through mediating bodies

[43] Gorer, *Exploring English Character* (1955), 265–7.

[44] Soper, *HL Deb.* 15 Nov. 1967, c. 734, debate on religious teaching in schools. Lennon quoted in Davies, *Beatles*, 287. For his interviewer's claim that the remark was misinterpreted see T. Benn, *More Time for Politics: Diaries 2001–2007*, ed. R. Winstone (2007), 36.

[45] *HC Deb.* 17 Feb. 1870, c. 466.

[46] See above, pp. 52–3.

such as the UGC and local authorities, every effort was made to shield schools and universities from centralized political interference. So decentralized was educational power by European standards that British ministers of education could hardly have implemented an 'educational policy' even had they wanted one.

Government spending on UK education rose threefold in real terms between 1950 and 1980, and until the late 1970s rose also in its share of gross national product. This was partly because more children were going to school: 5.3 million in England in 1951, 7.6 million in 1970. Children in school between the ages of 2 and 4 in England and Wales rose from 8 per cent of their age group in 1950/1 to 41 per cent by 1983/4.[47] The long-term trend was for provision at one level to prompt eventual demand for expansion higher up. So while the share of government's total educational expenditure spent on primary education (age group 5–10) had been declining at least since the 1920s, the share that went on secondary education (age group 11–15) and the universities had been rising, and these trends continued after 1951;[48] 13 per cent of children between 15 and 18 in England and Wales were in school in 1951, 21 per cent by 1970/1. This was partly because the numbers staying beyond 16 had risen threefold, a shift consolidated in 1972/3 when the statutory leaving-age rose to 16.[49] Both in 1950 and in 1961 girls in every region of England and Wales were much less likely than boys to stay beyond 16, but in every region the proportion staying on had increased, and for both sexes had more than doubled overall; in both years children of both sexes were more likely to stay on in the south of England and in Wales than in the Midlands or north.[50]

Educational expenditure rose partly because school buildings were improving. By 1962 in England and Wales new schools accounted for nearly a fifth of primary and secondary schools, accommodating nearly a third of all pupils. Although the number of state-inspected primary schools in the UK fell by 3 per cent between 1951 and 1970, about a fifth more children were attending them by 1970; the number of secondary schools fell by 4 per cent in the same period, while their pupils increased by 73 per cent,[51] so schools were getting bigger. They set the pace in architectural fashion. Because their architects worked closely with the teachers,[52] and designed the buildings round the children's activities, the schools' growing size was compatible with a far less forbiddingly institutional mood. Rising expenditure also reflected the larger workforce: in this labour-intensive area, more pupils meant more staff. Between

[47] DES, *Statistics of Education: Schools in England 1996*, 14–15. *BST* 230.

[48] *BST* 241–2. See also D. Wardle, *English Popular Education 1780–1975* (Cambridge, 1976), 36, 146, 177.

[49] *BST* 230, 236.

[50] *TBS* 175.

[51] Calculated from *BHS* 800–9.

[52] Calculated from table 1 in M. Seaborne and R. Lowe, *The English School: Its Architecture and Organization*, ii. *1870–1970* (1977), 154.

1951 and 1970 the number of teachers in England rose by two-thirds, but their composition changed markedly to reflect secondary education's rapid growth: whereas primary-school teachers rose by more than a third, secondary-school teachers more than doubled.[53] Classes were getting smaller: in England and Wales classes of 41 and more in primary schools fell from 29 to 3 per cent between 1951 and 1971, and in secondary schools from 7 to 2 per cent. In all types of school in England and Wales the number of teachers per pupil rose during the twentieth century, a rise that persisted between 1951 and 1971; and in all of them the proportion of graduate teachers also rose, with Wales notably in the lead.[54]

More teachers do not necessarily mean better teaching. On teaching methods the physicist Sir George Thomson yearned for the precise research that was customary in his own subject. Current knowledge of educational principles was, he thought, 'a disgrace'; on how best to teach reading, for example, there was 'far less real evidence . . . than there is on the best sort of potato to grow'.[55] Instead, shifting fashions prevailed, and the 1950s and 1960s were a liberal period which carried forward the interwar child-centred 'progressive' approach. The dominant emphasis (later controversial) was for the child to discover things for itself in a relatively informal setting, lending priority to inquiry over memory. The aim was to release the child's abundant hidden talent, thereby simultaneously enhancing personal fulfilment and promoting democratic values. This would also advance the interests of a country beset by nations better endowed with national resources and a cheaper workforce: Britain must live off her wits. The teacher's achievement depends profoundly on the mood and composition of the school and its classes, and between 1951 and 1970 these evoked major concern. Of the three types of school established in 1944, the technical schools did not last long: the experiment was later seen as a major lost opportunity for raising the status of industry and science by comparison with the grammar school's promotion of the professions and the humanities. Given Labour's backing,[56] the grammar schools were secure enough.

Very different was the fate of the secondary modern schools. The initial intention had been that they would differ from the grammar schools without being inferior. Yet over John Partridge's secondary modern 'Middle School' in the early 1960s there hung 'heavily across the general school work' during the first year the shadow of the second chance for eleven-plus failures to get into grammar schools. Its pupils who failed again would be stigmatized: doomed to see out their time in a school that was in effect a second-rate grammar school,

[53] DES, *Statistics of Education: Schools in England 1996*, 14–1

[54] *BST* 252–4. *TBS* 172 (figures for 1967).

[55] Thomson, *Foreseeable Future*, 145.

[56] See above, pp. 23, 51.

especially if its classes were streamed according to ability. 'What we teachers are trained to present to the boys in the classroom is a watered-down version of the minority, and to these boys, alien, culture', wrote Partridge. Michael Croft described the grim day-to-day realities within many such schools in his *Spare the Rod* (1954), whose fictional Worrell Street secondary modern school reflected Croft's own teaching experience. The background to his story is the teacher's ceaseless form-filling and ill-equipped struggle in seedy premises to foster civilized values among sullen and disorderly pupils. 'You've got to be hard while you're here', the headmaster Mr Jenks tells the somewhat idealistic new teacher John Sanders at the outset: 'hard and heartless. Otherwise you're certain to go under.' 'You don't need a degree for this job', his disillusioned colleague Mr Gubb tells Sanders. 'In fact, at Worrell Street you're better off without one. It's common sense you need here. Common sense and discipline.'[57]

Kenneth Loach's deeply depressing film *Kes* (1969) offers momentary optimism when Casper, the 15-year-old no-hoper, suddenly displays intelligence and initiative in training his kestrel, and bursts into unexpected eloquence when talking about Kes to the class, with encouragement from his enlightened English teacher Mr Farthing. Even in a drab working-class one-parent family in 1960s Barnsley, talent awaits discovery. And yet Casper's impossible environment drags him down, his bullying brother kills the bird, and in the impressively understated concluding burial scene, Casper's hopes die with Kes. More hopeful in one respect was the experience of Ricardo Braithwaite—projected from George Town, British Guiana, into East London's Greenslade School in his autobiographical *To Sir, With Love* (1959, film 1967): by treating as adults pupils initially only half civilized, by relating their lessons to their daily lives, and by getting to know them as individuals and helping them out when in trouble, he very quickly gets results which seem to validate the rather high-flown liberal ideals of the headmaster, Mr Florian. The book's title echoes the inscription on the present his pupils give him on leaving school. On the other hand, Braithwaite is shocked by the entrenched race prejudice his pupils absorb from their environment. Two years later he was lost to teaching, becoming a welfare officer, and later taking up a diplomatic career which culminated with him as Guyana's ambassador to Venezuela.

Edward Blishen's influential *Roaring Boys* (1955) eloquently portrayed the plight of the conscientious secondary-modern-school teacher, beset by his pupils' alien and anti-intellectual out-of-school culture, yet conscious of their academic potential if only he could find the time and energy needed to elicit it. With such limited resources, it was an uphill battle: even the fictional raw material for teaching working-class boys was lacking, for how could they

[57] Partridge, *Middle School*, 57, 153. M. Croft, *Spare the Rod* (1954), 11, 79.

ever be enthused by stories whose class background was so alien to theirs? Blishen's four years teaching art and English at Stonehill Street School were a voyage of self-discovery. Demoralized in his first year by the humiliations and sheer grind of struggling to keep order, he gradually found that by being himself, and by developing his own highly individual teaching style, he could precariously win respect from his pupils and seduce a handful even into respecting his values. Teaching is 'the cunning employment of one's own natural resources', he wrote. 'One uses creatively what one brings into the room.' If the teacher's energy could somehow surmount the large classes and somehow make time to comprehend his pupils as individuals, there was hope. Flexibility, ingenuity, resourcefulness, and even eccentricity must be deployed, the alien culture had somehow to be turned to advantage, the role of martinet forsaken, and the cane wielded only as a last resort and always with guilt. At the end of four years Blishen had surfaced, but his success merely substituted a new form of exhaustion for the old, the exhaustion that springs from the need to avoid disappointing the high expectations raised: 'now it was the fatigue of always having to be on top, of having to be endlessly lively, patient and explanatory. At times it felt like offering oneself as a feast for leeches.'[58]

What Blishen so vividly evoked with a novelist's imagination, Basil Bernstein translated into the austerities of sociological prose. In a sequence of influential articles he emphasized the divergence between the 'formal language' of classroom, teachers, and textbooks—logical, grammatical, economical, highly structured—and the looser 'public language' of many children.[59] If to this middle-class advantage was added parental encouragement—home-based books, conversation, private space, and longer in the sixth form—examinations would be passed and social status won. By the 1960s the idea was gaining ground that in 'educational priority areas' deprived children should be edged forward by benefits such as new schools, more nursery-school places, better pupil-teacher ratios, better pay for their teachers.[60] Otherwise when these children got to the secondary modern school, energetic but semi-literate, and consigned to its lowest forms, their only hope lay in extra-curricular achievement, whether on the sporting field or in overtly challenging the rules through indiscipline and truancy, and then to leave at the earliest opportunity. In 1961 a total of 35,000 children (0.5%) were at least occasional truants, absence for this reason being almost twice as common in secondary modern as in grammar schools.[61] Some commentators now thought a more vocational curriculum might enthuse

[58] Quotations from E. Blishen, *Roaring Boys: A Schoolmaster's Agony* (1955), 104, 230.

[59] See e.g. B. Bernstein, 'Social Structure, Language and Learning', *Educational Research*, 3 (June 1961), 169.

[60] J. S. Maclure (ed.), *Educational Documents: England and Wales. 1816 to the Present Day* (1st publ. 1965, 3rd edn. 1973), 282, 309, 311, 317, 318.

[61] M. J. Tyerman, *Truancy* (1968), 9, 19.

the less academic teenager, whose plight the raised school-leaving age might otherwise even worsen.

A more immediate response in the 1950s, however, was to attack the tripartite distinction of 1944, which apparently squandered so much buried talent, and to move towards 'comprehensivization': to bring all children into a single school so large as to make it possible to diversify the curriculum, to ensure a sufficiently large sixth form, and to procure economies of scale when buying better equipment. A larger school could also arrange the pupils so that no one child would always be at the bottom of the form. As long as the numbers taking the grammar schools' 'eleven plus' examination remained small, the pain of rejection was muted; but when increasing numbers attempted it, the comprehensivization option became politically as well as intellectually plausible, and the first purpose-built comprehensive school (Kidbrooke) opened in 1954. The relationship between social class and educational opportunity became central to British sociology's educational aspects, and for Labour's egalitarians promoting educational opportunity became a substitute for, or even an alternative route to, the economic opportunity that the party had hitherto pursued directly and without the predicted success. Whereas Labour's general election manifesto in 1951 did not mention the comprehensive-school idea, the party within four years had become publicly committed to it, though without at first combining this with repudiating the grammar school. For Conservatives the comprehensive school as route to social cohesion and equal opportunity may not always have seemed attractive in itself, but sheer political prudence dictated the Conservatives' continued bid, here as elsewhere, for the centre ground at the price of allowing the left to set the political agenda. Comprehensivization now advanced under governments of both parties, and received full backing from a Labour government in 1965. Early during Crosland's time as Secretary of State for Education (1965–7) his missionary zeal for the comprehensives was captured in his late-night casual remark to his wife: 'I'm going to destroy every fucking grammar school in England'. In England and Wales by 1970, comprehensive schools accommodated 31 per cent of schoolchildren in the state sector, and had significantly shrunk the other three main types of school: 'modern' (now only 41% of the total), grammar (20%), and technical (1%).[62]

Given that social status now depended more directly on educational manœuvre than on wealth or marriage, middle-class parents were becoming increasingly adept at benefiting their children by 'working' the state educational system, even allowing educational aims to determine family size and home location. Otherwise they might be forced into all the self-sacrifice involved in buying the type of education they thought their children required. Between 1951 and 1970 the state system as a whole steadily encroached upon territory

[62] S. Crosland, *Tony Crosland* (1982), 148. *BHS* 806–7.

once the preserve of private schools, and its share of schoolchildren aged 16 and above rose from three-fifths to four-fifths. Secondary-school children outside the state sector were grouped into state-subsidized or 'direct-grant' schools (with 9% of schoolchildren aged 16 and above in England and Wales in 1951, 7% in 1971), and fee-funded private schools misleadingly named 'public' (with 29% in 1951 and 11% in 1971). There were markedly more teachers per pupil in the private than in the state secondary schools, which helps to explain why 34 per cent of pupils in private or direct-grant schools in 1971, but only 7 per cent of state-school pupils, obtained three or more A-level passes.[63]

In England and Wales the private schools' share of the age group between 5 and 10 fell from 7 per cent in 1951 to 4 per cent in 1971,[64] but the private/state divide was more significant for older children—numerically and, still more so, qualitatively. By 1964 the IAPS's 505 member schools were educating 54,000 children, mostly under 13. The prep schools' influence transcended their small numbers, if only because four-fifths of their leavers in that year went on to private secondary schools.[65] A prep school would prosper if it met several conditions: it must get its pupils into the private secondary schools, the best of them in the Headmasters' Conference (HMC); the local state schools must be low-grade; parents must be eager for that or other reasons to avoid the state system; talented people must be available as staff; and the overall climate must favour educational entrepreneurs. Prep-school teachers were recruited as much for character as for formal qualifications, and often through personal contacts. The weakened entrepreneurial climate after 1945 helps to explain why fewer prep schools were being founded, and why by the 1960s others were being converted into non-profitmaking trusts;[66] the latter were the resort of the ageing proprietor who could no longer keep going, even with his wife's unpaid help. None the less, the prep school's great strength lay in its flexibility, for unlike state or endowed private schools it could survive only by catering for every parental whim. Less than half in 1966 felt the need for an entrance exam, so within their privileged sphere they could take pride in being in some sense comprehensive. In that year about a tenth of prep-school pupils were on reduced fees, and the boarding facilities taken up by more than half the pupils[67] were a boon to parents working overseas, whose pay often incorporated a schooling subsidy. The Prince of Wales attended two prep schools, Hill House and Cheam. At the first he encountered in the headmaster that prize educational entrepreneur Lt Col. H. Stuart Townend. To launch the school in Knightsbridge in 1951 he had sold his car, and his wife her jewellery. He

[63] *BST* 252, 260. [64] *BST* 236.
[65] P. L. Masters, *Preparatory Schools Today* (1966), 34, 91, 108.
[66] Ibid. 25–8. [67] Ibid. 56, 90, 108.

'combined pre-war officer-class brusqueness with an eccentric, superhuman energy', wisely viewed a child's mind as 'not a vessel to be filled but a fire to be kindled',[68] and was still running the school in his nineties. However impoverished the prep schools' facilities, they nourished young talent to the utmost: nearly a fifth in 1966 were starting their pupils on Latin before the age of 9, and half were teaching Greek.[69] Alert to their interests in the late 1950s, they launched education's entire private sector into self-defence through engaging public-relations consultants.[70]

In an age when faster and cheaper travel enabled one or more parents increasingly to work overseas, the private schools' boarding facilities met an important parental need; only a seventh of the 153,000 children in England and Wales who boarded in 1967 were at schools outside the private sector.[71] To the extent that they were usually located in rural parts of the south of England, private boarding schools were cut off, but in other respects they were joining the mainstream. During the 1960s a growing proportion of private-school masters married, and contacts with girls' schools were extending; by 1979 nearly a third of HMC schools had admitted girls, and more than a tenth had become fully co-educational.[72] This change was associated with the private schools' waning emphasis on sport and growing interest in the arts. Their curriculum was broadening too. In 1965 thirty-seven masters at Eton taught classics, nineteen taught other languages (including English), nineteen science, and thirteen mathematics.[73] Latin fell steadily in its share of the papers attempted at O level in all schools in the 1950s and 1960s, and ancient Greek's share was tiny from the start; by 1971 only 1,890 schoolchildren were taking it at O level, and A levels tell a similar story. Very different was the fate of O-level physics (holding its own in all schools amidst escalating overall numbers at about 5% of the papers attempted) and chemistry (4%);[74] private-school science teachers were influential through writing science textbooks, and in 1955 the Industrial Fund for the Advancement of Scientific Education was set up to modernize and expand private schools' science facilities. In this as in other changes, the private schools were responding to growing parental pressure for academic success, given the universities' increasingly meritocratic admissions policy. Open days exposed private schools to the parents' modernizing impact: 'mothers went into the dormitories and often did not like what they saw'.[75] If it was concern for the underperforming child which drove on comprehensivization, it was

[68] Obituary, *Ind.* (30 Oct. 2002), 18. [69] Masters, *Preparatory Schools Today*, 67.

[70] J. Rae, *The Public School Revolution: Britain's Independent Schools. 1964–1979* (1981), 61–3.

[71] R. Lambert, *The Chance of a Lifetime?* (1975), 16–17.

[72] Rae, *Public School Revolution*, 129–31.

[73] F. Campbell, 'Latin and the Elite Tradition in Education', in P. W. Musgrave (ed.), *Sociology, History and Education* (1970), 251.

[74] Dept of Education and Science, *Education in 1951*, 116–19; *Statistics of Education 1971*, 69, 71.

[75] Rae, *Public School Revolution*, 144.

concern to protect the gifted child that drove on the private schools. The USSR was establishing special boarding schools for special children, and the Yehudi Menuhin School showed what could be achieved in Britain. 'Clever people educate each other . . .', said Lord Snow: 'it is no use distributing either very bright children or very good teachers in penny packets'.[76]

If anything, these improvements exposed the private schools still further to Labour attacks on privilege. It is surprising that there had not been more such attacks before 1951, and not at all surprising that after 1951 Labour's revisionist and Bevanite wings both focused on the matter. For Crosland in 1956 the private schools' very existence entailed 'the most flagrant inequality of opportunity, as it is cause of class inequality generally, in our educational system'. If socialism entailed a classless society, entry to these schools must be democratized so as to integrate them into the state sector, and this should be 'the front on which the main attack should now be mounted'.[77] In the early 1960s, with the party committed to comprehensivization, the private-school issue revived with a vengeance because the abolition of grammar schools risked despatching middle-class refugees from the comprehensive alternative to the nearest private school. Should Labour's affluent middle-class supporters now promote what often seemed their children's best interest by choosing private schooling? Or should they act upon principle and help to leaven the state sector with articulate and demanding middle-class parents and children? It was a painful middle-class progressive dilemma of the time.

With private schools, as with the landed families, it was threats from politicians on the left[78] that prompted potential victims to organize in self-defence. In 1962 the private schools appointed a public relations consultant; in 1964 they launched their own magazine, *Conference*, to combat hostile views; and by 1967 the public-school headmasters had hired a full-time public relations firm. The Labour government after 1964 gave forth as uncertain a sound as the parents of school-age children. There were some such parents inside the cabinet. Crossman, for one, repeatedly asked himself in the late 1960s whether he should have sent his only son to the local state school; there was what he called 'a filthy row' in May 1968 with Wayland Young, who argued that one's children should come first, and that one should do the best possible for them.[79] Wilson's in 1964 was the first Labour government bound by a manifesto commitment to tackle the private schools, and in the following year the Newsom Commission was asked to advise on how they could best be integrated into the state system. The whole issue was sidelined, however, by lack of pressure from Wilson and the party's mass following, by distraction

[76] *HL Deb.* 14 May 1969, cc. 127, 163.
[77] *Future of Socialism*, 261, 518.
[78] e.g. from Hattersley, *T* (8 Sept. 1973), 2.
[79] *Cabinet Diaries*, iii. 68 (17 May 1968), cf. iii. 121 (7 July 1968).

from problems thought to be more urgent, and by the Commission's impolitic recommendations. Furthermore, Labour's Catholic connections, alert to the interests of Catholic schools, set limits to practicable reforms, which could never anyway countervail the central problem: the home background which gave the middle-class child an educational head-start. If the parents went further and bought their child special education, they consciously incurred the penalty: double payment (once for the state sector in taxes, and once for private-school fees). Given the liberal pluralism of British education, it seemed neither practicable nor desirable for politicians to restrain parents from struggling to advance their children's interests. So although between 1951 and 1971 the private-school share of full-time pupils in England and Wales from age 5 upwards fell from 8 to 5 per cent,[80] the schools lived on to fight another day.

Educational achievement can be captured only crudely through statistical analysis, but if the school system in 1951–70 is viewed as a whole, examination results seem to indicate progress of a sort. With the creation in 1951 of the three-level 'General Certificate of Education', the components of the two school certificates were disaggregated, pupils were allowed to select individual subjects, and could now carry them to the lower 'O' (ordinary, taken at 16), the higher 'A' (advanced, usually taken two years later) level, and the 'S' (scholarship) levels. The whole system opened up, and the number of O-level papers attempted in the summer examination in England and Wales rose fivefold between 1951 and 1971, and A levels threefold,[81] It was not simply a matter of more people attempting the examinations: the numbers passing both O levels and A levels almost doubled in the 1950s.[82] The examination system opened up further in 1965 when buttressed at its lower levels by the 'Certificate of Education': increasingly detailed information provided on the grades attained removed the crudeness of the simple pass/fail distinction, and a wider swathe of schoolchildren now experienced an examination incentive.[83]

3. UNIVERSITY BONANZA

Pressure from below produced unprecedented university expansion after 1945, if only because more pupils and higher standards required more teachers. Twentieth-century universities claimed a rising percentage of Britain's relevant

[80] A. H. Halsey *et al.*, 'The Political Arithmetic of Public Schools', in G. Walford (ed.), *British Public Schools: Policy and Practice* (1984), 14.

[81] DES, *Education in 1951*, 116–19; *Statistics of Education 1971*, 69, 71.

[82] See tables 45–6 in DES, *Education in 1961*, 200–3.

[83] This paragraph owes much to *TCBST* 207. R. Montgomery, *A New Examination of Examinations* (1978), 47, 49, 73.

age group: 0.8 in 1900, 3.2 in 1954, 4.0 in 1962. Add on teacher training and further education, and these percentages double.[84] Already by 1945/6 the prewar number of full-time students in British universities had been surpassed, and after rapid expansion in the late 1940s the growth rate slowed until the second postwar boom in the mid-1950s; after a further lull, a third postwar boom occurred in the mid- and late-1960s.[85] Full-time and part-time university students in Great Britain rose by nearly a quarter in the 1950s and by an unprecedented three-quarters between 1961 and 1968: by the late-1960s there were more than three times as many as in 1939.[86] The universities were now beginning to provide, in a formal and even certificated way, the preliminary training the professions and even the skilled trades had traditionally provided less formally. Young people who had once taken apprenticeships, part-time training, and evening courses were now full-time university students. Educational institutions were replacing the family, employers, and the community in assigning talent to the different areas of national life. Grammar-school entry might no longer determine life's opportunities, but university entry had become crucial to them: for the discarded eleven-plus, substitute the eighteen-plus.

This university expansion was largely spontaneous and unplanned, but in so far as it was deliberate it owed much to the same idealistic complex of fairness, democracy, and 'citizenship' that had earlier expanded the schools, together with the same internal dynamic. If more children were staying on in the sixth form, and if the baby-boom children were now coming of age, the influential Robbins report on higher education (1963) could easily show that universities were not accommodating all those qualified for entry.[87] In 1960 the Anderson committee favoured universal national entitlement to a grant for those with a university place, and Robbins wanted a place for every qualified person keen to take it up. The outcome was a system of funding that by world standards was very generous, though deployed more efficiently, given that the British drop-out rate was only 14 per cent by comparison with 40–50 per cent in France and America.[88]

Before expansion on this scale could occur, the government must provide the wherewithal and carry the electorate with it. Valuable in this was to allege a direct relationship between university growth and economic prosperity. This seemed more plausible in the early 1960s than later, and seemed to justify expansion on utilitarian grounds, but it also required better pay and opportunities for university teachers. Of British natural scientists with recent doctorates between 1952 and 1961, 16 per cent moved permanently abroad, a growing number to

[84] *TCBST* 225–7.
[85] Figures from W. A. C. Stewart, *Higher Education in Postwar Britain* (1989), 268.
[86] *TBS* 217–18.
[87] Committee on Higher Education (Chairman: Lord Robbins), *Report* (Cmd. 2154, 1961–3), 12.
[88] Ibid. 190.

the USA, which absorbed 7 per cent of the total, and by 1963 the USA had permanently recruited twenty Fellows of the Royal Society.[89] Whereas with the Commonwealth there was a balance between intellectual exports and imports, few American scientists thought it worth moving permanently to Britain. 'If, as we believe, a highly educated population is essential to meet competitive pressures in the modern world', said the Robbins report, 'a much greater effort is necessary if we are to hold our own'.[90] British science and technology seemed then to be falling behind: the UK's share of all patents granted in the USA to patentees within other countries was still as high as 36 per cent in 1950, by far the largest, but it fell steadily thereafter to only 11 per cent in 1979, with Britain overtaken by Germany in 1958, and by Japan in 1973.[91] For intellectual, defence, patriotic, and economic motives, university expansion was arguably needed to keep up with Russia, America, and Western Europe, defence motives being entwined with industrial.[92]

In the early 1920s fees had generated a third of UK university income, but thirty years later only an eighth. Parliamentary grants rose concomitantly with this decline, and by the early 1950s were contributing two-thirds of the universities' income; the share derived from endowments, donations, and local authorities was also in marked decline.[93] The universities were, in short, becoming dependent on central government. Close interaction between a university and its local industry and commerce had been integral to the nineteenth-century origins and success of many British universities. Such interaction persisted, and was familiar enough to the natural scientist in the 1950s. The decade witnessed a remarkable rise in the number of commercial benefactions to British universities, and a still more remarkable boost to university revenues from their payments for research, whose importance in university finances grew apace in the 1960s.[94] By 1970 such business links seemed significant enough to the Marxist historian E. P. Thompson to justify his publishing an attack on what he called *Warwick University Ltd*—a book which left 'an uneasiness in the mind' even of the *Times* leader writer.[95] J. B. Butterworth, the first vice-chancellor of this new university, perhaps deferred to power and success too enthusiastically for his own good, but by the 1980s the climate was moving in his direction, and in later career he resumed forging his university's business links with none of the earlier fuss: the ongoing

[89] *Emigration of Scientists from the United Kingdom: Report of a Committee Appointed by the Council of the Royal Society* (1963), 10, 12.

[90] *Robbins Report*, 268.

[91] K. Pavitt and L. Soete, 'International Differences in Economic Growth and the International Location of Innovation', in H. Giersch (ed.), *Emerging Technologies: The Consequences for Economic Growth, Structural Change and Employment* (Tübingen, 1982), 109.

[92] White Paper on Technical Education (1956), quoted in Maclure (ed.), *Educational Documents*, 239.

[93] *TCBST* 246–7.

[94] M. Sanderson, *The Universities and British Industry 1850–1970* (1972), 358. *BST* 281 ('other sources').

[95] *T* (16 Apr. 1970), 11.

growth of natural science had rendered Thompson's a lost cause. We have seen how central to the so-called 'Oxford school' of industrial relations was the assumption that labour, capital, and intellectual inquiry could readily be reconciled;[96] ironically, Warwick during the 1970s replaced Oxford at the heart of industrial-relations research.

None the less, the trends led away from localism. If Oxford distanced Thatcher from her Grantham background in the early 1940s, most students soon shared her experience. 'Redbrick' English universities, originating in their local communities and initially recruiting local home-based students, fell under Oxbridge's spell: they recruited increasingly on a national rather than local basis, and became residential. Some even adopted collegiate or pseudo-collegiate structures, seeking thereby to provide a total environment for students distant from home. The proportion of university students living in colleges or halls of residence rose from a quarter to nearly half between 1950/1 and 1979/80, and those living at home fell from more than a third to a seventh. As for part-time students, their numbers, falling from the First World War onwards, halved between 1950/1 and 1967/8.[97] A national student culture, even a national student marriage market, was emerging. Counterbalancing the many benefits of these centralizing trends were at least two losses: greater cost to the taxpayer, and a university-fuelled recycling of talent away from the student's home region.

Expansion occurred initially through upgrading to autonomy the former provincial university colleges hatched into maturity through apprenticeship to established universities—at Nottingham (1948), Southampton (1952), Hull (1954), Exeter (1955), and Leicester (1957)—and through expanding the existing universities. By 1957 there were twenty-one British universities, but the foundation of the University College of North Staffordshire at Keele (which gained university status in 1962) anticipated a new wave of university promotions and foundations in the 1960s. The high-minded but cloudy idealism of Keele's founder, A. D. Lindsay, the Oxford philosopher, may have fallen entirely from fashion with philosophers after 1951, but his influential disciples ensured that his university impact persisted posthumously in more practical ways. John Fulton's creative work as principal and vice-chancellor, first at Swansea and then at Sussex, showed what an energetic man of action could achieve in university administration if he could negotiate round central government. Also within this network were Eric James at York, Charles Morris at Leeds, and his brother Philip at Bristol. The decision in 1959/60 to launch a new university (Sussex) without preliminary apprenticeship to an existing university marked the advent of the instant university. The new foundations were Dundee, East Anglia, Essex, Heriot Watt (Edinburgh), Kent, Lancaster,

[96] See above, p. 267. [97] *TCBST* 239. *TBS* 222.

Stirling, Strathclyde (Glasgow), Sussex, Warwick, York—leaving the country with forty-six universities (including UMIST and the Open University) in 1970. In addition, the government responded to the Robbins report by raising the ten Colleges of Advanced Technology to university status. Such rapid growth resulted in what was in effect a national system of higher education with some approach towards a division of investment between recognized national centres of excellence: Edinburgh for medicine, Manchester for engineering, Imperial College London for the natural sciences, Reading for agriculture, and so on. Aiming at a national reputation from the outset, Essex adopted what its first vice-chancellor called 'the Montgomery technique', involving 'attack on a narrow front, and where there is a break-through go hell-bent ahead'.[98]

Oxford and Cambridge retained considerable influence over British universities. In 1960 they had between them educated 39 per cent of the Fellows of the Royal Society in British universities, in 1961/2 twice as many Fellows of the British Academy as all the other British universities combined, and in 1967 59 per cent of the vice-chancellors and principals in British universities.[99] In publishing, journalism, and the media, their metropolitan links were close; and their debating unions and political clubs drew talent towards Westminster and Whitehall.[100] Leading politicians of the 1950s and 1960s—Macmillan, Crossman, Douglas Jay—had a recurrent nightmare that they were once more taking their Oxford entrance or final examinations.[101] Oxford and Cambridge saw themselves as national or even international rather than local universities. Between the wars they had held aloof from encouraging any national structure of 'higher education'. Not so by the 1950s, however, if only because their share of university students and staff in Great Britain was plunging throughout the century. Their interest now lay in collaboration,[102] especially with the new coordinating bodies springing up everywhere: annual conferences of university registrars and university surveyors, associations of university librarians, trade unions for university employees. The UGC in the late 1950s was building up its staff, and by 1966 the Association of University Teachers had enrolled about three-quarters of all university teachers.[103] Universities, like schools earlier, experienced piecemeal and uncoordinated expansion followed by state-sponsored collaboration and coordination.

[98] A. E. Sloman, *A University in the Making* (1964), 27.

[99] A. H. Halsey and M. A. Trow, *The British Academics* (1971), 163, 217–18.

[100] For fuller discussion of the Oxford aspect, see Harrison (ed.), *History of the University of Oxford*, viii, chs. 14–15.

[101] Crossman, *Backbench Diaries*, 1010–11 (17 July 1963). D. Jay, *Change and Fortune: A Political Record* (1980), 32. H. Macmillan, 'Oxford Before the Deluge' (tape-recorded talk at Oxford, 14 Mar. 1973, in University Archives).

[102] See e.g. Harrison (ed.), *The History of the University of Oxford*, viii. 580–2, 694–6.

[103] *Oxford Magazine*, Trinity Term, 3 (1966), 385.

University students did not quickly diversify in their recruitment: as in schools, the children of professional and managerial fathers performed disproportionately well,[104] and this huge university expansion left working-class children on the margins. The traditional (and rarely travelled) working-class route into university study had been through adult education, often in association with the trade union movement and the WEA. This had endowed Oxford with two future general secretaries of the TUC, George Woodcock (1960–9) and Len Murray (1974–83). The WEA's influence was almost as profound on its lecturers, who included Labour leaders such as Gaitskell and Crossman, both of whom carried their lecturing careers into lecturing from a national political podium. Also from this stable came two scholars whose impact on their disciplines was profound: Raymond Williams on cultural studies, and E. P. Thompson on history. The number of registered students in adult education was still rising in the 1960s,[105] afforced by middle-class people seeking recreational stimulus. Working-class children had now to rely on the increasingly meritocratic mood of the secondary-school system, while overcoming all the obstacles already discussed. The search for working-class talent later on in life prompted a new and remarkably successful extension of the adult education movement. Devised by Michael Young from 1962 onwards, and energetically pushed by Wilson as Labour prime minister, its planning owed much to Russian and American models, and it emerged as the Open University, established in 1969.[106] Like more and more other universities, it was formalizing, enhancing, and more fully integrating the provision for adult education that had earlier taken place outside universities, in adult education departments and voluntary classes. It too found itself catering largely for a middle-class clientele.

Many new universities were on greenfield sites, but the British university system retained something of its intimacy by keeping the new universities' overall size low by world standards. The largest university of the thirty in Great Britain in 1962/3 was London, with 22,644 full-time students, but the median size was only 2,630.[107] Like their seniors, British students in the 1960s were encouraged to work within existing power structures. Growing out of the culture of the 'student union', a concept then unfamiliar to Oxbridge 'undergraduates', the National Union of Students (NUS) in the 1960s emerged from relative obscurity to represent students nationwide. The UGC's chairman addressed a conference of its delegates in 1960 about his plans for future expenditure, and its officers met the Committee of Vice-Chancellors and Principals (CVCP) for

[104] For figures on this see *BST* 291. Stewart, *Higher Education*, 281.
[105] There are figures in *TBS* 570.
[106] For its gestation see Pimlott, *Wilson*, 514. Wilson, *Memoirs 1916–64*, 190, 195.
[107] Calculated from Halsey and Trow, *British Academics*, 512. See also Stewart, *Higher Education*, 275.

the first time in 1966.[108] For the so-called 'redbrick' universities outside Oxford and Cambridge the NUS offered an alternative career ladder into politics, and to the national scene it contributed (among others) two future Labour cabinet ministers, Roy Hattersley and Jack Straw. But a deracinated student culture was by this time opening out still further into a worldwide lifestyle, with much international exchange. Overseas students contributed about a tenth of full-time students at British universities from the 1930s to the 1980s,[109] of whom 6 per cent in 1960/1 came from the Commonwealth, 4 per cent from foreign countries.[110]

Student life was changing too, even the buildings where they lived and worked. In their famous engineering building at Leicester (1959–63), Stirling and Gowan blazed the trail with an overtly technological structure that would then have been inconceivable in more traditional universities. The new universities were often located on pleasant sites near ancient cities: York could offer its ornamental lake, Essex its tower blocks, Sussex its Spencean combination of brick and concrete pseudo-vaulting, Kent its superb hilltop view of the cathedral city, the University of East Anglia Lasdun's extraordinary ziggurat residential terraces. Students relished what was a new freedom of association between the sexes. Women's share of the British university population rose from 23 per cent in 1950/1 to 27 per cent in 1967/8; Oxbridge tapped only slowly into the trend, but the 'redbrick' share was much higher, and the new universities attracted the largest share of all: 37 per cent of their intake in 1967/8.[111] Women were much less likely than men to study the natural sciences, which made it difficult to reconcile the Robbins committee's twin objectives of boosting the proportion of science students and the proportion of women among full-time students.[112] Among the courses available in the 1950s and 1960s, women were twice as likely as men to choose arts, equally likely to choose the social sciences, less likely to choose pure science and medicine, and far less likely to choose technology.[113] Further boosting the arts and social sciences were their relative cheapness and the fact that they were fashionable with students; hence some prominent scientists argued that less specialization within the sixth form would prolong natural-science study, thereby retaining it as a university option.[114] So despite the speed of university growth, these years saw no striking shift in the balance of studies. In the 1950s and 1960s more than a third of students and staff were in arts/social studies departments, though within those departments

[108] E. Ashby and M. Anderson, *The Rise of the Student Estate in Britain* (1970), 95–8.

[109] Stewart, *Higher Education*, 279. [110] *TBS* 220. [111] *TBS* 218.

[112] J. Carswell, *Government and the Universities in Britain: Programme and Performance, 1960–1980* (Cambridge, 1986), 43–5, 106.

[113] *BST* 292–3. For statistics on full-time postgraduate students at British universities 1910–81 see R. Simpson, *How the Ph.D. Came to Britain: A Century of Struggle for Postgraduate Education* (Guildford, 1983), 166.

[114] e.g. the Dainton report (1968), quoted in Maclure (ed.), *Educational Documents*, 329.

the 1960s witnessed a marked growth in social studies; those studying pure science rose from a fifth in 1949/50 to more than a quarter; the applied sciences consistently took up about a sixth, medicine and related subjects a fifth.[115] The new universities' attempts to offer something distinctive generated courses involving new combinations of the old subjects, with a strong interdisciplinary emphasis, but most eventually succumbed to the powerful thrust of the specialist department.

First-degree courses now taken by so many inevitably lost their earlier cachet, and academic status increasingly required a higher degree. In all British universities the postgraduate student was gaining ground: whereas 11 per cent of male and 10 per cent of female full-time UK university students were doing research degrees in 1950/1, these figures by 1967/8 had risen to 17 and 13 per cent, respectively.[116] Between 1950/1 and 1970/1 the number of full-time postgraduate students at British universities rose fourfold, and the number of higher degrees awarded almost sixfold.[117] The taste for graduate study also reflected the need felt by a growing academic profession for recruiting itself in a more standardized way. British universities by world standards operated on an unusually high staff/student ratio. In 1951/2 there were 9,869 full-time staff in British universities, but three times as many twenty years later. Inevitably the proportion of staff drawn from Oxford and Cambridge declined, and as the academic hierarchy elongated, the proportion of readers and senior lecturers rose.[118] A career ladder had emerged within and between universities with increasingly standardized procedures, structures, and funding arrangements.

Given the twentieth-century expansion of pure science in British universities and the continued strength of applied science, the typical university teacher was now a technologist[119] There was an enhanced interest in applied science, especially engineering, given the growing concern in the 1960s about Britain's relative economic decline. Lord Hailsham, as Conservative minister responsible for science, thought pure scientists now looked down on engineering rather as interwar classicists had looked down on natural science, and equally mistakenly.[120] There was all-party recognition of the need for a changed outlook. The Wilson government's national plan in 1965 ascribed much of British manufacturing weakness to 'a shortage of engineers and . . . insufficient attention to the importance of engineering design'; it aimed through Mintech to raise their status, improve their training, and deploy them more effectively.[121] Scientists required massive investment in capital equipment and in the people who could operate it, so that scientific and technical workers were proliferating

[115] *TBS* 216. [116] *TBS* 222. [117] Simpson, *Ph.D. to Britain*, 165–6.
[118] Stewart, *Higher Education*, 284. *BST* 283, 286.
[119] Halsey and Trow, *British Academics*, 156–7.
[120] *HL Deb.* 9 Nov. 1960, c. 429. [121] *The National Plan*, 49.

faster than any other white-collar occupations: the number of lab technicians almost doubled between 1951 and 1966, and the number of scientists and engineers more than doubled.[122]

Research now moved up among the university teacher's priorities, and natural science provided the fashionable model for collaboration in government-funded interdisciplinary and group projects. The 1940s had been the physicists' great moment: the Hiroshima bomb alone sufficed to advertise their influence. Refugees from Hitler made a major contribution here as well as to the arts and social sciences[123]—in building up Oxford's Clarendon Laboratory as a centre for the study of low-temperature physics, for example. There was a long postwar afterglow: wartime radar research, for instance, prompted major and ongoing advances in spectroscopy, and research in nuclear physics helped to build up an important scientific research complex south of Oxford. The government's defence priorities ensured that some scientific subjects (ballistics, meteorology, oceanography, and aerodynamics, for example) 'were state sciences and technologies, in a way which chemistry or medicine were not'.[124] Physicists and engineers also gained from the efforts in the 1950s to switch from coal to nuclear fuels. As with all rapidly growing subjects, physics after attracting huge investment in capital equipment and personnel, dissolved fruitfully into subspecialisms.

Yet natural science, at its moment of triumph, had serious worries. There was first the problem of communication. By 1955 Sir George Thomson thought specialization so far advanced that 'professional liaison officers between specific fields' would be needed to enable scientists to communicate even with each other; as for the general public, popularizers would be essential.[125] Fred Hoyle met the need in astronomy, with broadcasts and books beginning with *The Nature of the Universe* (1951), an outcrop of his Third Programme broadcasts in 1950. There he coined the phrase 'big bang' to describe the idea that the universe had been created in a massive explosion. By advertising Russian scientific prowess, the launch of the Soviet Sputnik satellite on 4 October 1957 made the democracies all the keener to encourage their own scientists. Radio astronomy's advance led to the eye-catching Jodrell Bank radio telescope; it came into operation in 1958 and symbolized Britain's continuing intellectual vitality. Television was particularly helpful to zoology, with spin-offs into popular books like Michaela Denis's *Leopard in my Lap* (1957) and Joy Adamson's *Born Free* (1961).

The scientists felt vulnerable in British public life. Fragmented between their specialisms, preoccupied with their research, they were less adept at

[122] *TBS* 114. See also above, p. 208. [123] See above, p. 4.
[124] D. Edgerton, *Warfare State: Britain, 1920–1970* (Cambridge, 2006), 112.
[125] Thomson, *Foreseeable Future*, 147.

self-defence in the 1950s and 1960s than their increasingly unionized technicians. C. P. Snow's lecture on *The Two Cultures and the Scientific Revolution* (1959) made a wide impact with its complaint that in Britain only arts people tended to be described as 'intellectuals'.[126] In the 1960s the scientist's distance from the establishment, his identification with merit and modernity, and his rationalistic affinity with the ideal of planning, made an alliance with the Labour Party seem natural. Snow, son of a clerk in a shoe factory, was one among many twentieth-century socialist enthusiasts for science from H. G. Wells onwards. 'If there had never been a case for socialism before', said Wilson in his first speech to the Labour Party conference as leader in 1963, 'automation would have created it', for technological progress 'left to the mechanism of private industry and private property, can lead only to high profits for a few, a high rate of employment for a few and to mass redundancy for the many'.[127]

Yet 'big science' already had its critics. The late-Victorian concern about vivisection had not gone away, and Hiroshima reinforced doubts about whether science and progress were inextricably linked. Orwell in 1946 had detected a link between science and totalitarianism,[128] and CND both divided the scientists and drew its best-known supporters from the arts—so much so, that in the first Aldermaston march in 1958 the publisher Victor Gollancz claimed to have done more business than in the entire previous year.[129] Even when nuclear physics was deployed for peacetime purposes in nuclear power stations, the authorities were nervous of alienating the public by saying too much about accidents.[130] University students by 1959 were becoming wary of cooperating with mass radiography,[131] and in the same year the Nobel-prizewinning biologist Peter Medawar decided that his Reith lectures must counter the growing gloom about the natural sciences' impact on ordinary life. Also in 1959 H. K. Beecher's *Experimentation on Man* made much impact with its claims—inflated in M. H. Pappworth's *Human Guinea Pigs* (1967)—that scientific experiment was not confined to animals,[132] and soon afterwards medical science was hit by the thalidomide tragedy.[133] The sheer cost of 'big science', given the British economy's problems in the 1960s, evoked doubts; nor did the Wilson governments' combination of intellect, social science, and interventionism succeed as much as had been hoped. Yet natural scientists knew that the complaints against 'big science' need not entail no science at all,

[126] C. P. Snow, *The Two Cultures and the Scientific Revolution* (Rede lecture, Cambridge, 1959), 3.

[127] Wilson, *Memoirs 1916–64*, 197.

[128] G. Werskey, *The Visible College* (1978), 287–9.

[129] Ian Rodger, quoted in *The Road to Aldermaston* (BBC programme, 30 Mar. 1978).

[130] See above, p. 313.

[131] University of Oxford, *Hebdomadal Council Papers*, 232 (Jan.–Apr. 1959), 299; 238 (Jan.–Mar. 1961), 283.

[132] See L. J. Witts's review of Pappworth in *British Medical Journal* (10 June 1967), 689.

[133] See above, p. 248.

but rather a shift towards new areas of scientific growth: problems in one area of natural science would be answered in another. We have seen how by the 1960s the ecological sciences had already begun to inform the public's growing preoccupation with the environment, just as epidemiology and nutrition were by then shaping debate about preventive medicine.[134]

The history of classical studies indicates how fruitful non-utilitarian university research could be. The leading public schools could still train their sixth-formers to impressive levels of classical virtuosity. Fewer now took Oxford's 'Greats' degree, but it still carried considerable prestige, and although House of Commons speeches had long abandoned the classical tag, Macmillan could still privately cite classical references at crisis moments.[135] In the self-consciously progressive climate of the 1960s, however, anti-elitist critics of the 'establishment' bracketed the classics with a despised gentlemanly amateurism,[136] and from the 1960s Latin was no longer required for admission even to Oxford.[137] Far from this being the death of the subject, refugees from Hitler had from the 1930s infused it with a new and Germanic professionalism;[138] the future of classical studies lay not in holding the nation's elite captive but in captivating other highly professional academic specialisms. Many fruitful directions were taken: E. R. Dodds's *The Greeks and the Irrational* (1951) linked classical with social-anthropological studies, and the combination of imperial and classical influences lent vitality to the study of social anthropology, and fertilized the close study of medieval texts. In archaeology, flourishing in both its Romano-British and medieval departments after 1945 and eventually extending into 'industrial archaeology',[139] the funds and perhaps even the need for a professionalized exclusiveness did not exist, so that in these subjects lay enthusiasm was more fully enlisted in Britain than in continental Europe.[140] Philosophy, which also owed much to classical studies, was in its abstractness not obviously useful, yet philosophers were prominent in British public life, partly because from the 1940s to the 1960s the Oxford variant of analytical philosophy exerted worldwide influence, and partly because its precise use of language helped the authorities to clarify the public mind through official inquiries. A. J. Ayer followed C. E. M. Joad in becoming a well-known national figure on the Brains Trust; and with Bertrand Russell philosophers came to epitomize for the general public the intellectual's endearingly clever eccentricity and wit. With their combination of irreverence and precision they also enlivened the humanist challenge to Christianity. Philosophy was valuable, too,

[134] See above, pp. 134–5, 280–1.
[135] e.g. Sampson, *Macmillan*, 91.
[136] See e.g. the sociologist Flann Campbell, *T* (4 Oct. 1968), 12.
[137] For the crucial debate in Congregation on 23 Feb. 1960 see *Oxford Magazine* (25 Feb. 1960), 210.
[138] On these see H. Lloyd-Jones, *Greek Studies in Modern Oxford: An Inaugural Lecture* (Oxford, 1961), 14.
[139] For more on this see above, pp. 126–8.
[140] K. Hudson, *A Social History of Archaeology* (1981), 143.

for fertilizing other subjects—to great effect in H. L. A. Hart's contribution to the scholarly study of jurisprudence.

We have already seen how British sociology retained its empirical liveliness in the 1950s.[141] During the 1960s, however, university departments of sociology ingested theory from the USA and from Marxism, and subordinated that tradition—even demoting it into associating with lower status 'social work'. Continental Europe's probings into the roots of social cohesion, however fashionable, seemed less appropriate to Britain's more stable structure, but had been highly relevant in the colonial context, within whose structure social anthropology flourished;[142] at several points in the Second World War the academic career of its leading exponent, Edward Evans-Pritchard, had interacted with colonial administrative and defence requirements. This was by no means the only area where Britain's colonial connections proved intellectually stimulating. To take only one example, the ethnologist and art historian William Fagg spent his career in the British Museum devoting to African sculpture the close scholarly attention hitherto reserved for European works, and became the leading English-speaking authority. Keynes's governmental impact in the 1940s, and the apparent success of 'Keynesian' policies in curbing unemployment thereafter, help to explain the strongly empirical and policy orientation of economists in the 1950s and 1960s; we have seen how their involvement with 'planning' prompted fast growth in the subdiscipline of econometrics.[143] In the 1960s the prestige of economics reached its apogee, but suffered from that decade's setbacks to central planning, as well as from an escape into extremes of abstraction where politicians and electors were unable to follow. The powerhouse of the social sciences remained the LSE, which showed itself adaptable, given that Lionel Robbins had attracted there some economists with a decidedly practical purpose: the pioneers in Britain of neo-classical economics (though the influence of St Andrews was at least as important here). The social sciences had now grown so fast, however, that their fate was not determined by the successes of any one set of specialists: Baroness Wootton predicted in 1967 that the term 'social science' would eventually fall into disuse, as had already happened with the term 'natural philosophy': social science like natural science would eventually dissolve into separate specialisms.[144]

Within the study of politics, a new empiricism subordinated legalistic and constitutionalist approaches, most notably in electoral studies,[145] but also in the study of international relations, where American abstractness was contained by a strong dose of realism under the historically informed influence of Alastair

[141] For more on this see above, pp. 176–7.

[142] As argued in P. Anderson, 'The Components of the National Culture', *New Left Review* (July–Aug. 1968), 47.

[143] See above, pp. 42, 302–3.

[144] Wootton, *In a World I Never Made*, 210.

[145] See below, pp. 464, 467.

Buchan, Hedley Bull, and (later) Michael Howard. None the less, in the UK too the study of politics was diverging from its original home in modern history. The impish radicalism of that pioneer 'tele-don' A. J. P. Taylor did not curb this divergence: it merely concealed the traditionalism of his approach to the study of international relations as a high-political diplomatic story. His *Origins of the Second World War* (1961), however, most courageously pioneered a revisionist and historically sensitive view of 'appeasement' in the 1930s, and with his volume on British history from 1914 to 1945 he brought to completion in 1965 the 'Oxford History of England', whose fifteen magisterial volumes shaped the study of British history for half a century. In this and other ways he helped to move forward the chronological frontier of what historians could respectably study. Something similar was happening in the revaluation of the Victorians that George Kitson Clark encouraged at Cambridge in the 1960s, reinforced by the conservationist energies of the Victorian Society and the non-metropolitan cultural insights of the prolific Asa Briggs.

The intellectual impact of Marxism in Britain, much less formidable than in Europe, is nowhere more striking than in historical writing, where it left a permanent memorial in the broad-ranging historical journal *Past and Present*. Marx's rich capacity for synthesis fertilized E. P. Thompson's exhilarating *Making of the English Working Class* (1964); the book's covert traditionalism did not prevent it from somehow catching the radical and irreligious mood of the time, for it geared in with the reaction against parliamentary socialism after 1964. More sharply original were the essays of Eric Hobsbawm, deeply permeated by a rich European cultural awareness. The Marxists by no means dominated the flourishing subdiscipline of 'labour history', which owed much to the pioneeringly empirical monographs of Henry Pelling and to the leading figures in the Oxford school of industrial relations. Christopher Hill was doing something similar for anti-establishment groups in the seventeenth century, and masterpieces of empathy were achieved for medieval studies by scholars such as R. W. Southern and Peter Brown. British historians did not confine their research to Great Britain. The advent of scholarly Irish history owed much to the Protestant Anglo-Irish tradition exemplified in the work of T. W. Moody and F. S. L. Lyons; Denis Mack-Smith was renowned in Italy, Raymond Carr in Spain, and the historians of modern Germany included several British stars, most notably Alan Bullock, whose biography of Hitler became a classic.

Two Jewish-born immigrants deeply influenced British historical writing. The great days of creativeness in Polish-born Lewis Namier had long passed, but as re-creator from 1951 of that huge historical project, the *History of Parliament*, he bequeathed a major legacy to his adopted country. Geoffrey Elton, born in Tübingen, not only revolutionized the study of Tudor England, but became industrious and sociable statesman to the entire historical profession. It was to the history of the fine arts that the refugees contributed most distinctively. Musicology was rejuvenated, and musical and operatic taste greatly enriched, by the transfer from Germany of important collections, expertise, and trading and publishing firms.[146] And in a fusion of British country-house aesthetic amateurism with Germanic systematic scholarship, British architectural history in the 1950s became fully professional. What with the Warburg Institute's achievement in art history, Gunnis's *Dictionary of British Sculptors* (1951), and Colvin's *Biographical Dictionary of English Architects: 1660–1840* (1954), this was a breakthrough period for these neglected scholarly areas. With his 'Buildings of England' series, Nikolaus Pevsner, a Jewish refugee from Hitler, made himself into something of a British institution. Adept with the media, and adding a new dimension to Englishness, he wrote thirty-two of the volumes in the series, collaborated with others on ten more, and delegated to others only the remaining four.[147]

The 1950s and 1960s, then, were a bonanza time for British universities, a brief interval between austerities. There is no limit to the claims on funding that knowledge-based institutions will make, but by earlier and later standards the 1950s and 1960s saw rapid and well-funded expansion. The universities were reinforcing their earlier links with the political and social elite by annexing a claim to promote national economic and scientific self-defence, and yet remained small enough for their staff to enjoy generous funding. Three developments in the late 1960s eroded these assets: the nation's accelerating retreat from worldwide ambitions, its growing doubts about centralized expert-assisted planning, and an impolitic unconcern among student radicals about the universities' image with taxpayers and potential donors.[148] Politicians after 1970 could no longer back universities without risking their seats.

4. AESTHETIC CORNUCOPIA

Fast-growing universities helped to fill the cornucopia of cultural opportunity that enriched British life from the 1950s. University Bookshops, Oxford (UBO) and other consortia set up or nourished high-quality bookshops in university towns.[149] Thirty new theatres were built in the 1960s,[150] usually with their companies supported by local authorities or centrally funded through the Arts Council. The anti-vocationalism of British higher education had traditionally

[146] For an informative account see E. Levi, 'The German-Jewish Contribution to Musical Life in Britain', in W. E. Mosse (ed.), *Second Chance* (Tübingen, 1991), 186, 190, 193, 295.

[147] B. Cherry, *The Buildings of England, Ireland, Scotland and Wales: A Short History and Bibliography* (Henley-on-Thames, 1998), 7–13. See also D. Watkin, *The Rise of Architectural History* (1980), 161.

[148] For which see below, pp. 491–2, 499–502, 506, 518–19, 524–5.

[149] *Mumby's Publishing and Bookselling in the Twentieth Century* (6th edn.), 185, 188.

[150] Elsom, *Post-War British Theatre*, 132.

identified the performing arts with 'trade', assigning them (in contrast to the USA) to an extra-curricular role, but this did not prevent the universities from culturally leavening their localities. Intermediaries sprang up to interpret the university to society and society to the university, most notably Richard Hoggart and Raymond Williams, but the growth of academic professionalism and the decline of a leisured class with a private income combined after 1951 to make the 'man of letters' seem unfashionably amateur. The Harold Nicolsons, Philip Toynbees, and Cyril Connollys could survive for a time as broadcasters on the Third Programme and as literary critics in weeklies or Sundays like the *New Statesman* and the *Observer*, but the integrated and educated elite that had once spread out from country house to subscription library, from country rectory to London club and London Library, was now fragmenting and fading.

Hence the widespread concern in the 1950s about whether 'popular culture' would fill the gap. University teachers in English literature, especially when influenced by the Cambridge academic F. R. Leavis, showed a growing part-time interest in producing and reviewing fiction, as was advertised when reviewers in the *Times Literary Supplement* lost their anonymity in 1974.[151] Peter Hall claimed that Leavis, despite disliking the theatre, wielded even there 'more influence . . . than any other critic'. Creative writers did not always welcome Leavis's pronouncements. When he declared D. H. Lawrence alone worth consideration among modern novelists, J. B. Priestley expressed alarm at this 'sort of Calvinist theologian of contemporary culture' with his acolytes forcing authors 'to undergo some kind of customs and passport examination . . . with narrowed gaze, tight lips, service revolvers'.[152] Larkin regretted that academic professionalism had since the 1920s called forth the kind of poetry that required elucidating: for him, twentieth-century English poetry had 'gone off on a loop-line that took it away from the general reader'. He rejected the modernist view that Betjeman was commonplace and old-fashioned because instantly intelligible: there were all too few Betjemans and Dylan Thomases to hold poetry and the general public together.[153] So successful were Betjeman's *Collected Poems* (1958) that by February 1960 'this awful publicity' was 'getting me down'.[154]

Professionalism was also spreading through publishing, where a quiet revolution occurred between 1951 and 1970. The history of firms such as Faber and the Hogarth Press illustrates how blurred had been the interwar boundary between author and publisher, an attractively amateur affinity which persisted well into the 1950s. Authors and publishers did not qualify as professionals because

[151] D. May, *Critical Times: The History of the 'Times Literary Supplement'* (2001), 425.

[152] P. Hall, *Peter Hall's Diaries: The Story of a Dramatic Battle*, ed. J. Goodwin (1984), 347 (18 Apr. 1978). Priestley, *NS* (10 Nov. 1956), 580.

[153] Betjeman, *Letters*, ii. 201. Motion, *Larkin*, 344–5.

[154] Betjeman, *Letters*, ii. 183 (to Martyn Skinner, 23 Feb. 1960).

they lacked the professional person's exclusive entry, formal qualifications, and standardized career pattern. Yet neither were they committed entrepreneurs: author and publisher both relied on personal flair, but by no means all sought to maximize profits, and many authors needed the income that came from a second occupation, so were part-timers. The strength of British postwar publishing, amateur or not, emerges from the figures for 1952. In the total number of volumes produced, only the USSR surpassed the UK, which produced far more volumes than any other country, including the USA. Volumes published in English accounted for a fifth of the world's total production, and a third of the volumes produced in the UK went overseas—a higher proportion than any other country exported.[155] British publishers almost doubled their output of titles in all categories between 1951 and 1970, including reprinted or new editions, which in both years contributed more than a quarter of them.[156] The utilitarian share of the book titles published by a country declines as its industrialization advances, and by 1953 44 per cent of the titles produced in the UK fell into the non-utilitarian categories of fine arts, recreation, and literature.[157]

Three developments from the 1950s onwards brought significant change to what later came to seem the gentlemanly and amateur world of small British publishing firms. There was first the linked decline of the private circulating library and the rise of the public library. In 1937 Mudie's had been the first private circulating library to go, and in 1957 was followed by Day's Library; W. H. Smith succumbed in 1961, the Times Book Club in 1965, and Boots Book Lovers' Library in 1966. By then most of the small shop-based twopenny libraries had also vanished, and only Harrods' Subscription Library remained.[158] The rise of the public library, much faster in Britain than in France, increasingly complemented its initial self-improving purpose by catering for leisure needs. In the late 1950s some still refused to use them for fear that their books would be soiled or would carry infectious disease, but by the mid-1960s they had become 'one of the great middle-class institutions in this country'[159]. The public library could well have killed off book-buying but for the second major publishing development: the paperback. Allen Lane, its leading pioneer, had always seen himself as 'converting book-borrowers into book-buyers',[160] and in the 1950s Penguin's educational thrust had not

[155] Barker, *Books for All*, 22–3. [156] *Mumby's Publishing*, 220.

[157] Barker, *Books for All*, 20. See also Escarpit, *Book Revolution*, 37; the book contains fascinating statistics.

[158] J. G. Olle, 'The Lost Libraries', *Library Review* (Autumn 1966), 455–6. R. Findlater [pseud. for K. B. F. Bain], *What are Writers Worth? A Survey of Authorship* (n.pl., 1963), 9 claimed that in that year there were still about 4,000 shops lending books at a weekly charge.

[159] Lord Francis-Williams, *HL Deb.* 30 Jun. 1964, c. 544; see also Baroness Wootton, c. 539.

[160] Quoted in S. Hare, *Penguin Portrait: Allen Lane and the Penguin Editors 1935–1970* (1995), 117–18.

yet wilted. The first Penguin classic, Homer's *Odyssey*, translated into modern English by E. V. Rieu, came out in 1945 and by 1960 had sold a million copies—a total also reached by Orwell's *Animal Farm*, and in 1978 by Coghill's rendering of Chaucer's *Canterbury Tales*.[161] Penguin eventually got caught up, however, in the third major publishing development: the Americanized commercialism of the 1960s. Penguin by the late 1950s faced stiff competition from paperback publishers further downmarket, and hardback publishers were by then publishing paperbacks from their own backlists. After shifts among Penguin's top personnel, Tony Godwin, who in Charing Cross Road's 'Better Books' had established a modern and more stylish bookshop, moved into and up Penguin's hierarchy. The firm transformed itself from a private limited company to a public company in 1961, and Americanized glossier covers swept through the paperback trade, whose total number of titles grew sixfold during the 1960s; in 1970 paperbacks accounted for two-fifths of the sales revenue in book publishing.[162] Few people now bought a book primarily because it was a Penguin book: the brand had lost its distinctiveness, and in 1970 the firm was gobbled up by the huge Longman Pearson Group.

Some complained that the paperback had ended the earlier reverence shown towards books, which were now readily left lying open face down, dog-eared, and treated as disposable, but the mergers and commercialization of the 1960s were irreverent in a more important sense. By then Paul Hamlyn was well launched on promoting books for a mass market, and American publishers viewed small British publishers with their large Commonwealth export market (especially for educational books) as fair game: they rapidly disappeared into large consortia. Godwin announced in 1967 that the upper classes were no longer custodians of culture: 'the distinguished amateur in publishing was . . . being supplanted by the passionate professional'.[163] By 'professional' he did not mean skill at discovering and nurturing authors with something to say, but skill at discovering what the market seemed to want and then finding writers who could be trained to write best-sellers; these books would then be 'professionally' packaged and marketed. From the early 1960s Mills and Boon, which for decades had applied this formula to romantic fiction, discovered that paperbacks could greatly enlarge their trade; the firm would continue to prosper, John Boon pronounced many years later, 'provided someone doesn't do anything silly. Someone might suddenly decide they want to *educate* the public. Bloody disaster.' All this centralized publishing even more firmly on the London area, broadly defined,

[161] *Mumby's Publishing*, 163. J. Sutherland, *Reading the Decades: Fifty Years of the Nation's Bestselling Books* (2002), 22.

[162] Stevenson, *Last of England?*, 137. S. Laing, 'The Production of Literature', in A. Sinfield (ed.), *Society and Literature 1945–1970* (1983), 128.

[163] See his 'Is Publishing a Worthwhile Profession?', *The Bookseller* (14 Oct. 1967).

and by the 1960s English publishers had virtually wiped out any independent Scottish publishing industry.[164]

Also making for changes in British publishing during these years was the impact of overseas firms. European immigrants' importance as publishing entrepreneurs, especially in transforming art history, has already been noted.[165] None the less, the empire lasted longer in publishing than on the ground: 18 per cent of British-produced volumes in 1952 were exported to Australia, 15 per cent to the USA, 12 per cent to South Africa, 7 per cent to Canada, 6 per cent to India, and 6 per cent to New Zealand.[166] Although cultural fashion in the 1950s and 1960s turned away from Henty and Buchan, the imperial stiff upper lip persisted into the novels of Ian Fleming (who taught himself to write partly by reading Buchan) and Nevil Shute (who emigrated to Australia in 1945), in the postwar wealth of Second World War autobiography, and in John Le Carré's spy fiction. None the less, European influences had already begun to impinge on literature through the revived fashion for 'modernism', whose priorities included preoccupation with the individual's inner life, together with a taste for allegory and structural experiment. During the 1950s it once more became fashionable to embrace the modernist option: Iris Murdoch's *Under the Net* and William Golding's *Lord of the Flies* were both published in 1954, and Muriel Spark's *The Comforters* in 1957. Britain's relatively conservative cultural mood, however, led many twentieth-century British novelists to continue along the Victorian and Edwardian narrative and descriptive groove, Kingsley Amis being among those who relished repudiating any other course.

Where Europe and radical America made their greatest impact on the arts in Britain during the 1950s and 1960s was in the theatre. The London stage had for years been dominated by the concept of 'the well-made play', with its grammatical syntax and logical progression through three acts. It provided Noel Coward with an elegant arena for his polished performances, and 'drawing-room sets were clapped on opening nights by audiences who had dressed up for the occasion'.[167] All this had become stifling. Samuel Beckett's *Waiting for Godot*, first performed at London's Arts Theatre in 1955, was startling in its impact because revolutionary in its bleak staging and unfamiliar subject matter: 'waiting, repetition, silence' were its themes, and audiences were not told what it all meant: they were required to make up their own meanings.[168] The year 1956 saw one of those sudden and unexpected bursts of irreverence that often prompt cultural creativity: in May *Look Back in Anger* was first performed and *The Outsider* by Colin Wilson was published, the briefly

164 Obituary of John Boon, *DT* (16 July 1996), 21. J. A. Sutherland, *Fiction and the Fiction Industry* (1978), 52.
165 See above, p. 4.
166 Barker, *Books for All*, 21–4, 27.
167 Elsom, *Post-War British Theatre*, 205.
168 M. Billington, *The State of the Nation: British Theatre since 1945* (2007), 78–80, 83.

fashionable philosophical treatise and first book written by a shoe-factory worker's self-educated 24-year-old son who had left school at 16.[169] Then in August came the influential visit by the Berliner Ensemble to the Palace Theatre with *The Caucasian Chalk Circle*, *Mother Courage*, and *Trumpets and Drums*; with its austere costumes and scenery, brilliant lighting, and broadened appeal, it liberated British theatrical style. Brecht's influence helped to blur the clear distinction hitherto made between the 'musical' and the 'straight play', and edged the performance away from the formal, the elaborate, and the apolitical and towards the sincere, the austere and the politically committed. With Osborne's *The Entertainer* (1957) and Harold Pinter's *The Caretaker* (1960), the theatregoing middle class was pushed off the sun-drenched terrace of a big house in the south of England and into a Brechtian cavern of 'kitchen sink' realism.

The new did not oust the old, but even the old was infused with its revolution in acting style and stage design. From the USA came the influence of Tennessee Williams, Arthur Miller, and the 'method' school of acting. Originating with Stanislavsky, this school expected the actor to grow into his part through the improvisation that flowed from emotional conviction. Especially welcoming to these new developments were the Royal Court Theatre in Sloane Square and Joan Littlewood's Theatre Workshop at the Theatre Royal, Stratford, East London, where improvisation was all the rage: 'I'd like to throttle that tiresome talented woman for not taking more trouble', wrote Coward, discussing Littlewood's 'calculated lack of discipline'.[170] None the less, it was she who discovered Brendan Behan and who in 1958 put on *A Taste of Honey* by Shelagh Delaney, a 19-year-old playwright from Salford who had seen Rattigan's *Variations on a Theme* and rightly thought she could do better. There were associated important technological innovations embraced by architects, entrepreneurs, and stage directors. It was a time for experiment, with thrust stages, raked stages, open stages, theatre-in-the-round, pub theatres, lunchtime theatres, studio theatres, warehouse theatres. Lighting design became a specialized skill in itself,[171] and Oliver Messel (himself a revolutionary stage designer in his day) sent himself into exile in Barbados to develop a new career as an architect.

A simultaneous semi-official endorsement of the new tendencies and an individual self-reinvention occurred in 1957 when that national icon Laurence Olivier edged his career forward by becoming Archie Rice in Osborne's *The Entertainer*, which made the seediness of the decaying music-hall tradition a metaphor for British imperial grandeur in decline. 'Don't clap too hard', says

[169] Wilson is fully discussed in Sandbrook, *Never Had It So Good*, 153–61.

[170] Coward, *Diaries*, 539 (21 July 1963).

[171] P. Mudford, 'Drama since 1950', in M. Dodsworth (ed.), *The Penguin History of Literature*, vii. *The Twentieth Century* (1984), 376.

Rice, 'we're all in a very old building'.[172] The first major British playwright to emerge from this new world was Harold Pinter. Owing much to Beckett and Ionesco, Pinter took a leap forward in 1956 when his *The Room* was praised by the *Sunday Times* reviewer Harold Hobson. Pinter's ear for the illogicalities and non-communications of day-to-day conversation was sharp enough to prompt the epithet 'Pinteresque'. He knew that words, far from uniting and clarifying, are used to divide and conceal, and to establish who is master and who is servant. He deployed the comfortable absurdities of ordinary talk to enhance the air of menace that pervades his plays, and carried to a higher power the routine stage conventions present in standard whodunit repertory fare. It was a humdrum bed-and-breakfast encounter in 1954, for instance, during a tour in Eastbourne, that inspired the most terrifying of his plays, *The Birthday Party* (1957), which begins with a landlady fussing over a strangely laconic guest. In its classless portrayal of anonymous loneliness and isolation, of the fragility of personality in the face of an intimidating unknown, Pinterism was a world away from the West End's comfortable middle-class certainties dominant only a few years before, and carried to its ultimate the theme of violence so frequently taken up by British playwrights at the time.[173] Many years later the actress Sheila Hancock recalled how Pinter's enigmatic style had changed audience attitudes since the 1950s: 'audiences back then wanted a beginning, middle and end. They wanted to know exactly who the characters were. Audiences now are more open to going away and arguing afterwards'.[174]

Ballet provided the bridge between music and the stage, and nobody in 1945 could have predicted that half a century later there would be classical ballet companies based in Birmingham, Glasgow, and Leeds, with the Ballet Rambert revitalized and an English National Ballet touring the country. But it was in music that changing technology made the most direct impact. In 1944 the British company Decca introduced 'full frequency range recording', to be followed in the 1960s by stereo recording. The American company Columbia launched the long-playing record in 1948 in the USA. Each side of the record could now offer twenty-five minutes rather than only four, and Decca introduced it to Britain in 1950—all the more appealing for being sold in attractive and informative cardboard record sleeves. With at most only one turnover break, records of whole symphonies could now be comfortably enjoyed. Each new type of record reached its peak and fell back with the rise of its successor, 78 rpm records peaking at 1957 and virtually vanishing by 1970, 45 rpm records rising fast from the late 1950s to a high plateau in the 1970s, 33 rpm records rising steadily throughout the period, and tape cassettes rising fast in the early 1970s.

172 Quoted in Billington, *State of the Nation*, 106.

173 M. Billington *The Life and Work of Harold Pinter* (1996, paperback edn. 1997), 75–7, 79–80, 82, 109–10, 371.

174 Interview with Brian Logan, *IOS*, 4 May 2008, 'the new review', 26.

British record sales rose fourteenfold between 1950 and 1970, a growth rate comparable with North America, France, and Germany, and rather faster than for the world as a whole.[175] Particularly important for classical music were the quality and range of recordings.

Easier travel and competition between the record companies greatly improved the range and standards of performance, and the sheer scale of the music boom in the 1960s, together with the falling production costs which the tape recorder made possible, destroyed the Decca/EMI duopoly of the 1930s, freeing many independent record companies to emerge.[176] Deutsche Grammophon and several small record companies were by then making available much hitherto unknown or virtually inaccessible classical music. William Glock, as BBC Controller of Music from 1959 to 1972, was encouraging London's Prom Concerts to break out of the rather conservative repertoire fostered by Malcolm Sargent, the much-loved Proms conductor-in-chief from 1957 to 1966. Essential to the Proms repertoire in the 1950s were symphonies by Beethoven, Brahms, Tchaikovsky, and Sibelius, and piano concertos by Beethoven, Tchaikovsky, and Rachmaninov. The Proms did not offer Orff's 'Carmina Burana' till 1958 or Berlioz's 'Grande Messe des Morts' till 1960 (Glock's first season); nor did eight of Mahler's ten symphonies and five of Bruckner's nine arrive till the 1960s.[177] The long-playing record raised expectations of performance and repertoire, and Glock brought to the Proms international performers and contemporary music, some of it commissioned by the BBC. Sargent was not pleased and, prompted by (of all things) Tippett's 'Fantasia on a Theme of Corelli', expressed his intention 'to get the intellectuals out of music'.[178] Glock somehow survived.

An enlarged audience for music was all the more necessary because three great nurseries of British musical talent—the army, the churches, and (in areas of heavy industry) the brass bands—were all shrinking. The wider repertoire made available by the record companies greatly eased the task of such innovators as the trumpeter Philip Jones, launched through the brass band at Battersea Grammar School and founder of the Philip Jones Brass Ensemble in 1951; its success interacted with the revival in baroque and renaissance music, and its first recording dates from 1965. Europe's major influence on music in Britain lay through opera. The idea in 1946 of Anglicizing opera at Covent Garden was abandoned after a decade: opera was now international, and visiting stars could not be expected to memorize the English versions. By the late 1960s opera in Britain had transformed in at least three respects: in the number of

[175] D. Harker, *One for the Money: Politics and Popular Song* (1980), 81, 226. L. G. Wood, 'The Growth and Development of the Recording Industry', *Gramophone* (Nov. 1971), 795.

[176] A. Peacock and R. Weir, *The Composer in the Market Place* (1975), 102–3.

[177] D. V. Cox, *The Henry Wood Proms* (1980), 155, and its valuable appendix at 280–96.

[178] D. Wright in J. Doctor and D. Wright (eds.), *The Proms: A New History* (2007), 175; see also 172.

opera facilities available, the training opportunities on offer, and the quality of performance.[179] Several smaller music festivals complemented the larger. At Aldeburgh's, founded by Benjamin Britten and Peter Pears in 1948, many of Britten's works were first performed; and at the Swiss Dolmetsch family's Haslemere festival, Carl Dolmetsch promoted his own speciality, the recorder, through his summer school launched in the same year.

Electronic advances from the late 1940s made it possible not only to reproduce music more effectively, but to create new types of music by mixing sounds from different magnetic tapes, thus blurring the distinction between composer and technician. Originating in the world of classical music with so-called 'musique concrète', this new approach did not attract the head of the BBC's chamber music and recitals department, Hans Keller. The Third Programme in June 1961 mischievously broadcast a bogus 'mobile for tape and percussion', allegedly by a young Polish composer Piotr Zak; the reviewers may not have liked it, but they took it seriously.[180] By then the BBC's Radiophonic Workshop had been operating for three years, and from there came the famous theme music for the series *Dr Who*, which widely advertised electronic music's potential. The first instalment in the series was broadcast on 23 November 1963, and in the following year the signature tune was issued as a record.

Traditional jazz, which experienced revivals in the early and late 1950s, was far removed from the new technology, but resembled pop music to the extent that enthusiasm for it marked off the generations and captured the young. The clarinettist Acker Bilk built up a national following, and Chris Barber made a big impact with his first success, 'Petite Fleur', in 1959; in that year 10,000 people attended the fifth of the annual jazz festivals held at Beaulieu.[181] Several progressive intellectuals developed a sideline as jazz critics, to which the New Left added its enthusiasm for folk music. Jazz, folk, and pop music may in retrospect be seen as allied causes, but at the time they saw themselves as rivals, and the Beatles were not welcomed by the jazz enthusiasts dominant at the Cavern Club in Liverpool.[182] Traditional jazz was a minority taste, whereas pop music had a wider appeal, was more open to the new technology, and was distanced politically from the British left by its Americanized commercial mood.[183] On 15 November 1952 Percy Dickins published in the *New Musical Express* the first ever pop chart based on the sales of records rather than sheet music, initially the 'top twelve' but from 1954 the 'top twenty'. In the five years from 1955 to 1959, 60 per cent of the records in the British top ten hits came

[179] As Lord Donaldson noted in *HL Deb.* 26 Feb. 1969, cc. 1163–4.

[180] H. Carpenter, *The Envy of the World: Fifty Years of the Third Programme and Radio 3. 1946–1996* (1st publ. 1996, paperback edn. 1997), 200.

[181] M. Clarke, *The Politics of Pop Festivals* (1982), 22.

[182] Davies, *Beatles*, 132.

[183] I gratefully acknowledge the generous and expert help I have received here from Dr Andrew Callingham.

from the USA.[184] While their parents in the 1950s were increasingly hooked on television, teenagers espoused the radio programmes developed in the USA by disc jockeys influential with record sales.

Given the frenetic jiving it provoked, Bill Haley's 'Rock around the Clock' (1954) could hardly be described as passive entertainment, but it was the charismatic Lonnie Donegan, banjo player with Chris Barber's jazz band, whose music-making first prompted widespread imitation. Donegan's 'Rock Island Line', by topping the charts in May 1956, made the skiffle boom into the precursor of the national pop music craze. His performance was not technically innovative, but that in itself encouraged imitation, and amateur groups henceforth cultivated their mid-Atlantic accents in skiffle cellars backed by tea-chest bass, washboard, and acoustic guitar. For British teenagers in the 1950s, as for New Orleans blacks in the 1920s, the simplicity of the skills and the cheapness of the equipment required were major attractions. Paul Johnson might denounce the 'bottomless chasm of vacuity' he observed in the teenagers who appeared in televised programmes about pop music in 1964,[185] but he did not recognize how for some pop groups enhanced musical technique was the route to status, money, and creative opportunity. The Beatles aspired to something more than their contemporaries who were content with Saturday afternoon in the local football terraces, and were still further removed from teenagers who in the late 1960s 'dropped out'. The worlds of self-help and pop music somewhat improbably interacted: skiffle could produce quick results, stirred widespread self-instructed creativity, and was something one could do as well as consume;[186] the guitar now began to rival the upright piano as the essential aid to music in the middle-class home. Technique was refined through listening closely to records of admired performers, scrutinizing them on television, and experimenting among groups of friends. An informal venue—the small-time pub, for example, or a garden fete—could provide a first chance of public performance and financial return.

Like that other pop-singing pioneer Tommy Steele, troubadour beneficiary of pubescent shrieks with his 'Singing the Blues' in 1957, Donegan eventually gravitated to modern equivalents of the music hall, but among Donegan's fans were members of the Quarrymen skiffle band, later the Beatles: 'we studied his records avidly', Paul McCartney recalled: 'we all bought guitars to be in a skiffle group'.[187] The USA was still in the ascendant: shortly

[184] *T* (22 Mar. 2002), 44 (Dickins obituary). C. Gillett and A. F. Davis, 'Big Noise from across the Water: The American Influence on British Popular Music', in A. F. Davis (ed.), *For Better or Worse: The American Influence in the World* (Westport, Conn., 1981), 63.

[185] 'The Menace of Beatlism', *NS* (28 Feb. 1964), 327.

[186] For a good discussion see C. Cutler, 'Progressive Rock in the U.K.', in his *File under Popular: Theoretical and Critical Writings on Music* (1985), 174. I owe this reference to Dr Callingham.

[187] Obituary of Donegan, *Ind.* (5 Nov. 2002), 7.

after the cinema had advertised James Dean and Marlon Brando as sultry misunderstood teenage rebel heroes, Elvis Presley burst on the scene with his desolate 'Heartbreak Hotel', recorded in January 1956. He came to exemplify the teenage rock star as sex god, briefly inspiring Cliff Richard into imitation before respectability descended. Popular music's themes had of course included romantic love, but only as one among many, and with a much less hormonal emphasis: the teenagers were ousting their parents, and using music to add to the many other burgeoning generational barriers growing up at the time. For the Quarrymen, Buddy Holly and the Crickets were an important influence and, sporting piled-up and sleeked-back hair, they first appeared in the back of a lorry at an Empire Day fete in 1956. Several British rock musicians who won through in the 1960s—John Lennon, Keith Richards, Ray Davies, and Pete Townshend, for example—were simultaneously rejecting middle-class conventionality and a working-class destiny, with art school as their alternative to university.[188]

The Beatles did not deliberately diverge from the predominantly working-class pedigree that led from the velvet-collared Teds to the leather-jacketed rockers, if only because this would have been imprudent when both Teds and rockers were potentially among their audiences. But the Beatles were aiming at success, and after being repackaged by their Liverpool impresario Brian Epstein, dressed so as to acquire a distinctive clean-cut image. The rock world's competitive and macho individualism stemmed less from its American inspiration than from the realities of the rock group's daily life. Travelling along the new motorways to perform at all hours, depending heavily on confidentiality and trust between friends, rock groups could hardly have held their acts and their audiences together if beset by owner-occupied homes, regular habits, and monogamous female ties: the Blue Boar at Watford Gap service station, mecca for late-night pop-group gossip, was no haven of domesticity. Despite Liverpool's centrality to their image, the Beatles inevitably moved on to a wider stage, first in Hamburg, then to London, and thereafter moved out into the world at large. With their exhausting first major American tour in 1964 they achieved the unprecedented among British groups: entry into the American market. By comparison with 1955–9, American items in the British lists had halved by 1960–4, and fell further still in 1965–9.[189] This helped the balance of payments when under strain, and influential people felt that the Beatles had earned the MBEs they received in the following year.

In painting, no technological change could compare with photography's nineteenth-century impact, and in the mid-1940s the Tate Gallery had already launched regular temporary exhibitions at the major galleries. Television,

[188] S. Frith, *Sound Effects: Youth, Leisure and the Politics of Rock* (1983), 75.
[189] Gillett and Davis, 'Big Noise', 63.

however, brought art education a much wider following, culminating in 1969 with the programmes on *Civilization* presented by Kenneth Clark, a twentieth-century Ruskin without the moral and socially reforming uplift. Particularly relevant for art galleries was the steady advance of the state, powered by the conviction that subsidies could popularize elite culture. In earlier periods the churches and the private philanthropist had been major patrons of the arts, but by the 1970s the closing of choir schools threatened choral music, and high taxation had undermined the private philanthropist. By contrast, government grants to art museums and galleries rose fourfold in real terms between 1945 and 1964, to the Arts Council sixfold, to other arts bodies ninefold, to royal commissions in this area tenfold, and to historic buildings and ancient monuments twentyfold;[190] to these should be added the Ministry of Defence's substantial hidden subsidy to music through funding military bands. The Festival of Britain had greatly raised the status of the Arts Council as guide to public taste, and it enjoyed much freedom in spending its resources. Throughout the 1950s and 1960s more than half its expenditure went on music (including opera and ballet) and about a fifth on drama.[191] The demand for taxpayer subsidy was as insatiable here as elsewhere, and in this instance was reinforced by politicians' reluctance to seem philistine: the experts were predictably enthusiastic, and the causes proposed for subsidy seemed so obviously good.

During the 1960s regional pressures impinged rather more. Public subsidy of the fine arts had arguably been hitherto unduly focused on England, and towards London. In Germany, Italy, and the USA, a fusion of diverse cultures stemmed from the distinct cultural roles of several regional capitals, but England's political system was unitary in origin, its build-up towards a united kingdom had been relatively continuous, and its metropolitan culture correspondingly powerful. Still, non-metropolitan cultural initiatives had advanced apace since 1951,[192] and by the 1960s there was growing pressure to devolve aesthetic patronage beyond and within England. To ease the pain of redistributing the balance of arts funding away from London, an overall rise in subsidy was desirable; and given Labour's strength outside the south-east and her moral claims upon the prime minister, Baroness Lee (in effect minister for the arts from 1964 to 1970) carried public funding of the arts to a new height. With her encouragement, regional arts associations gradually covered the country, civic theatres owned and subsidized by the local authority proliferated, and she 'measured her achievement by the size of the Treasury contributions she extracted'.[193]

[190] Calculated from HM Treasury, *Government and the Arts 1958–64* (1964), 24, inflation-proofed from the 'ready reckoner' in *TCBST* (2000), 712.

[191] J. S. Harris, *Government Patronage of the Arts in Great Britain* (Chicago and London, 1970), 86.

[192] See above, pp. 168–72.

[193] Lord Goodman, quoted in P. Hollis, *Jennie Lee: A Life* (Oxford, 1997), 285.

The British 'are always faintly apologetic about the arts', said Baroness Gaitskell.[194] Yet taxpayer funding is not inevitable as a way of funding the arts, and may not ultimately generate as much as private funding or deploy it with as much impact. As early as 1949 the high hopes of public funding uppermost in 1945 evoked doubts even within the Royal Academy in an after-dinner speech of its president, Alfred Munnings, which must have embarrassed all who were there. Addressing in Churchill's presence what was later nicknamed the Academy's 'bump supper', he attacked 'highbrows' and 'experts' who 'think they know more about Art than the men who paint the pictures'. Munnings accused the Academy of 'shilly-shallying' when it compromised with 'this so-called modern art', and grumbled that the millions spent on art education did not prevent the display of 'bloated, heavy-weight monstrous nudes' in public places. 'If you paint a tree', he said he had told some art students, '—for God's sake try and make it look like a tree'.[195] His boozy outburst of unreasoning prejudice discredited his case, and on the surface, at least, the supposed experts now had it all their own way. Even Churchill felt obliged to conceal his distaste for Graham Sutherland's portrait of him: on receiving it in 1954 he pronounced it 'a remarkable example of modern art' combining 'force and candour', but he privately saw it as 'malignant', and his wife secretly destroyed it.[196] Munnings was ineptly speaking up for a large dissident group whose sentiments did not go away. They re-emerged in the public stir of 1972, for instance, when the Tate Gallery bought a pile of 120 firebricks entitled 'Equivalent VIII' by the American minimalist sculptor, Carl André.

The drawbacks of public funding for the arts on the scale that built up during the 1950s and 1960s became apparent only slowly. First, government patronage risked distancing the subsidized arts still further from the public who funded them. Patronage by expert committees weakened the artist's incentive to seek a wider following, and encouraged some even to take a pride in their unpopularity: 'defiance or a certain bravado about being misunderstood is very common . . . among artists', Lord Eccles told the House of Lords in 1963.[197] Much populist criticism of the arts stemmed less from objection to art as such than to the type of art that the alleged experts were funding in the taxpayer's name. The distinction was less between highbrow and lowbrow than between well-organized experts who knew their own mind and an undifferentiated general public whose minds were open. Private funding, by contrast, would at least require the patron to pay for and live with his acquisitions, would

[194] Maiden speech, *HL Deb.* 3 June 1964, c. 529.

[195] Quoted in P. Fuller, 'The Visual Arts', in B. Ford (ed.), *The Cambridge Cultural History of Britain*, ix. *Modern Britain* (Cambridge, 1992), 103. A. Munnings, *The Finish* (1952), 144.

[196] Moran, *Struggle for Survival*, 648 (30 Nov. 1954), 652.

[197] *HL Deb.* 11 Mar. 1963, c. 652.

diffuse patronage more widely, and (by ensuring plural funding) would limit the damage that patronage by any small coterie could do. Furthermore, here was another instance of public expenditure having the effect of channelling resources upwards from the worse off; subsidized art by definition had not attracted the masses, and this aspect of government expenditure increased much faster than overall government expenditure between 1945 and 1991.[198] These doubts about public patronage were widely held, but awaited articulation later. In retrospect, the interest of the arts funding scene in the 1960s is enhanced by the dogs that did not bark: the arguments for commercial sponsorship, the case for tax relief on charitable donations, and serious debate about how to close the wide gulf now existing between the artist and the general public.

5. RECREATION DIVERSIFIED

With diversified recreation complementing enhanced cultural opportunity, Britain in the 1950s and 1960s was doubly enriched. We have seen how growing professionalism and administrative complexity at work ensured that higher up in society there was if anything less leisure than before. Lower down, however, leisure—through longer statutory holidays and shorter working hours—was extending, even allowing for the significant divergence between real and statutory hours worked, and for women's frequently performing two roles in place of one.[199] In the 1950s anxiety about 'the problem of leisure' became widespread, especially now that television absorbed so much of it, though few were as melodramatically anxious as the Earl of Arran. In 1960 he informed the House of Lords that, though Sweden and Switzerland might have few national worries and the highest living standards in Europe, happiness does not necessarily result: 'what happens? They shoot themselves, my Lords; they shoot themselves in great numbers. Their suicide rates are the highest in the world.'[200]

Attempts to explain British economic decline in terms of national laziness (especially by contrast with the Germans) usually ignored the enormous energy the British people put into productive activity, hidden from the official statistics, outside working hours. Machinery had forsaken the home when the industrial revolution mechanized craft work,[201] but it returned by an unexpected, semi-recreational route. Women's productive work within the home had

[198] D. Sawers, *Should the Taxpayer Support the Arts?* (Institute of Economic Affairs, 1993), 14–15, 19–20, 39–41. For a well-informed and irreverent discussion of the whole subject, see D. C. Mason, *Expounding the Arts* (Adam Smith Institute, 1987).

[199] See above, pp. 254, 328

[200] *HL Deb.* 2 Mar. 1960, c. 655.

[201] For a good discussion see Willmott and Young, *Family and Class*, 26–7.

never been thought worth measuring, but now that men and women spent more of their leisure together, home-based activity was seen to be of growing economic significance. Televisions, washing machines, refrigerators, cars, and electric tools purchased from do-it-yourself (DIY) stores gradually caused the home more closely to resemble a workshop. Work done there by householders, friends, or moonlighters was often exchanged for cash or favours, and the authorities knew little about it. Men and women did not choose the same activities within the home, but the car encouraged joint outings, and television brought them together, with each devoting equal time to it. Women read more than men, and spent much longer on crafts and hobbies, but gave less time to sport, gardening, or maintaining the home. Men with allotments in England and Wales in the late 1960s were devoting ten hours a week to them in spring, twelve and a half in summer. Even when gardening, many men were performing a social duty rather than a hobby, given that the prized suburban house often had an unwanted garden attached.[202] Cooking remained in the woman's sphere, though men's interest was growing. Standards of cooking rose from the 1930s to the 1960s, an advance compatible with only the weak variant of feminism that sought prestige for semi-professionalized (usually unpaid) household tasks. The more radical style of feminism either required the man to cook, or both partners to compromise by eating out, and did not gain ground till the 1970s. Of the many best-selling cookery books published from the 1940s, the first was Philip Harben's. His plump, bearded, and genial personality exemplified the televised cookery series from the mid-1940s to the early 1950s, at which point the irruption of Fanny Cradock introduced theatre and more than a pinch of snobbery. Appearing in evening dress with her unobtrusive partner (not then her husband) 'Johnny', she yoked social status to 'kitchen magic' (her programme's title) within the suburban home.[203]

The prize new male hobby was DIY, an American term which by the late 1950s had crossed the Atlantic,[204] capitalizing upon a fourfold conjuncture: between growing male leisure, rising labour costs, growing pride in the home, and an armoury of new and more convenient tools and materials such as power drills, sanders, emulsion paint, paint rollers, improved and more accessible wallpapers. The former factory hand Robert Appleby's DIY career involved joining the insignificant British subsidiary of the American firm Black & Decker in 1953 and—with advertising skill, energy, and entrepreneurial flair—thereafter capturing about 90 per cent of the booming British market in tools for the amateur handyman. David Quayle had the idea for the B&Q do-it-yourself store in 1968 when visiting a Belgian hypermarket with a section

[202] *TBS* 553. McKibbin, 'Work and Hobbies in Britain', 132. 'Down with the Crazy Paving', *Econ.* (21 June 1958), 1052.

[203] See Paul Levy's obituary, *Ind.* (29 Dec. 1994), 12.

[204] As indicated by a COPAC search.

selling DIY tools; on returning home he got his brother-in-law to join him, borrowed from the bank, secured family help, and was launched.[205] Enthusiasts were egged on by DIY magazines and television programmes. Television's first DIY expert was W. P. Matthew (1947–55), and his successor Barry Bucknell soon became television's most popular personality. The annual DIY exhibition at Earls Court was four times as large in 1957 as its precursors, and united instruction to entertainment, bargain hunt to international trade fair; it attracted 248,932 visitors; and in 1963 *Do It Yourself* pronounced the exhibition 'the Mecca of DIY'.[206] The magazine was by then thoroughly practical in mood, stripping away self-interested craft mysteries and displaying on its cover proud male and female householders wielding their power tools. Confirmed in their domestication, they stepped back to view their cupboard-fitting, double-glazing, fireplace-installing, patio-laying, extension-building feats.

Watching and playing sport was another decidedly male recreation. A poll in 1986 showed that men were then eight times more likely than women to attend a football game and five times more likely to attend a county cricket or test fixture.[207] Diversification is the first among six interlocking trends that transcend the many contrasts between individual sports to bring this area of British life into focus. Affluence enables a society to diversify its sports by bringing them money, time, training facilities, equipment, and easy access at home and abroad. These ensured that in any one area enough people could foregather to make a sporting event viable; after 1965 the Sports Council's provision of shared sporting facilities in multi-sport recreation centres specially benefited the smaller sports. Wider car ownership helps to explain the great increase by the mid-1960s in adventure sports such as mountaineering, rambling, sailing, ski-ing, canoeing, and camping. More and more leisure consisted in solitary motion, whether in sailing boats, in gliders, or on skis. By 1968 badminton clubs in England and Wales had more than doubled since 1939, gliding clubs had more than doubled since the war, and since the late 1940s squash clubs had doubled, and climbing clubs had risen tenfold.[208] Arguing in 1967 for a Brighton marina, Earl Jellicoe claimed that 'in many places now along our South Coast it is just as difficult to park one's yacht or one's dinghy as it is to park one's car'. By the early 1970s inland water was also being colonized, 'as a glance on any fine summer evening at some of our great reservoirs in this country will show'.[209]

[205] *T* (13 Dec. 1996), 21 (Quayle obituary). *DT* (5 Dec. 1998), 3.

[206] *Do It Yourself* (Nov. 1957), 795; (Sept. 1963), 983. See also *T* (27 Feb. 2003), 44; *Ind.* (22 Feb. 2003), 24 (Bucknell obituaries).

[207] MORI poll of 1,913 respondents aged 15+ in 171 British constituencies, *T* (30 June 1986), 4.

[208] *HL Deb.* 7 Feb. 1968, cc. 1141, 1187.

[209] Jellicoe, *HL Deb.* 20 July 1967, c. 459; 21 May 1973, c. 977.

Not all sports were growing: by the 1950s greyhound racing was in absolute decline, though it remained the second largest spectator sport after football;[210] and by the 1960s traditional school team games were losing ground. By the late 1950s grouse had 'become a term of sarcastic reproach', and symbolized the alleged Tory amateurism under Macmillan as prime minister;[211] field sports none the less persisted alongside the growth of urban sports like football, or suburban ones like tennis. In 1951 their organ, *The Field*, breathed in its advertisements an air of opulence. Non-political but traditionalist in mood, it abounded in people on horseback, included lively correspondence columns, and its broad interest in animals and birds readily overflowed into farming and gardening. The rich were by no means alone in combining sport with an interest in birds: eight million birds were marshalled into the long-distance pigeon racing which in the early 1970s attracted quarter of a million people.[212] The overall tendency was not to supersede older or unfashionable sports, but rather to add a new layer to them, so that the diversification cumulated. It advanced also through well-established sports improving their facilities. In 1950 the Football Association rescinded its rule (abolished in 1956) against floodlighting matches; with its permission, mid-week winter matches could now be organized. The floodlit game, with its white ball and with tall pylons marking the corners of stadia, introduced a touch of drama; televising the game now became more feasible, 'and the crowds in their thousands were drawn to the lights like moths attracted to a flame'.[213] Clubs grew attached to their 'home' grounds, and after the 1920s preferred to rebuild on them rather than move, especially in the 1960s, with the aid of the pools which from the late 1950s they had been authorized to run. Higher and higher the new stadia soared, presenting architects with interesting challenges: from glorified warehouse sheds they had by the 1960s become cantilevered constructions dwarfing mean streets, supplanting the cathedral as symbol of the city's identity and aspirations, and their fixtures surpassed saints' days in their national impact.[214]

Football's history exemplifies the second overriding postwar sporting trend: internationalism—tragically symbolized by the death of eight 'Busby babes' in Manchester United's air crash at Munich on 6 February 1958. Success in international competitions tended to boost a sport's take-up at home. British mountaineering profited from Edmund Hillary's scaling of Everest in 1953 just as British sailing gained by Francis Chichester's single-handed round-the-world voyage in 1967. Internationalism brought political difficulties: disruption of

[210] M. Clapson, *A Bit of a Flutter* (Manchester, 1992), 154.

[211] P. Ferris, *The City* (1960), 9. See also Lord Ferrier, *HL Deb.* 7 Feb. 1968, c. 1249.

[212] J. Mott, 'Miners, Weavers, and Pigeon Racing', in M. A. Smith *et al.* (eds.), *Leisure and Society in Britain* (1973), 92.

[213] G. Green, *Soccer in the Fifties* (Shepperton, 1974), 27.

[214] S. Inglis, *The Football Grounds of Great Britain* (1st publ. 1983, 1987 edn.), 14, 20.

sporting links with South Africa, for instance, proved a powerful weapon against apartheid, and with his 'Stop the Tour' movement of 1969–70 the young Liberal Peter Hain showed how even cricket could get entangled in politics.[215] International pressures made most impact in British football, whose self-confidence was seriously dented in 1953 when Hungary defeated England by six goals to three at Wembley; of the nine international games thereafter, England won only two. In 1955 the Football Association was as reluctant as the Foreign Office to embrace Europe, and slow to endorse English participation when what became the European Cup was launched, though the Scots were less shy. European competitions greatly enhanced interest in the game. Overseas competition even re-shaped English football, which became more defensive (the number of first-division goals scored in the 1960s plunged); shorts became shorter; vests, boots, and the ball became lighter; and play became less violent, more theatrical, more balletic, more intelligent.[216] By 1966 the Post Office was issuing special stamps to celebrate Britain's footballing victory in the World Cup, with police warding off the crowds seeking to buy them on the first day of issue. Crossman took a distanced view, claiming that this victory would strengthen sterling and help the Labour government, but two years later Wilson disparaged his total indifference to the European Cup match: 'Harold clearly felt this . . . makes me incapable of being a great political leader because the mark of a leader is to be a man who sees football or at least watches it on television.' When planning the timing of the general election in 1970, Wilson told Cabinet colleagues in March that 'one of the problems was the World Cup. If it wasn't for that, he would favour the end of June, and was now trying to find out at what time of day the match was played, because he felt this was a determining factor.'[217] By the 1970s the World Cup contest had become British football's equivalent of judgement day.

Through meritocratic recruitment, the third major sporting theme of these years, nations brushed aside social-class, ethnic, sexual, and regional hindrances to fully exploiting their talent. The racial barriers against sporting meritocracy remained formidable, but in the 1960s and 1970s the respected boxing coach George Francis specialized in promoting Commonwealth-born fighters against hostility from the British Board of Boxing Control, with John Conteh and Frank Bruno among his trophies. It was in the predominantly working-class Rugby League, not in the amateur Rugby Union, that black players made their earliest progress, given that teams requiring commercial success thirst

[215] For Hain's career see *FT* (6 Apr. 1991), 6. For his own account of 'Stop the Tour' see *G* (1 Apr. 1991), 15.

[216] C. Critcher, 'Football since the War', in J. Clarke *et al*. (eds.), *Working-Class Culture: Studies in History and Theory* (1979), 181. Green, *Soccer in the Fifties*, 24.

[217] *Cabinet Diaries*, i. 594 (31 July 1966); iii. 91 (29 May 1968), 846 (8 Mar. 1970).

"Hark who's telling us the trouble with our Olympic team is that they don't train hard enough."
Sunday Express, September 4th, 1960

Fig. 4. Giles in *Sunday Express* (4 Sept. 1960)

for talent wherever it can be found.[218] Sporting women had to battle against discouragements allegedly endorsed by science, but by the mid-twentieth century the gap between male and female sporting records was narrowing, especially in swimming, athletics, and long-distance cycling, where the case against segregated competition was mounting. By the early 1980s women had achieved eight of the ten fastest swims across the English Channel in either direction.[219]

It was football that most notably subverted regional obstacles to talent in these years. 'Above all other sports', wrote J. B. Mays in his study of Liverpool boys in 1954, 'football occupies a paramount position in the estimation of these youngsters. They will play football whenever they get the opportunity.'[220] Opening out from the casual backstreet game was a ladder of sporting opportunity that passed through school and youth club to local football teams throughout

[218] *Scotsman* (11 Apr. 2002), 14 (Francis obituary). Collins, 'Racial Minorities in a Marginalized Sport', 156–7, 167.

[219] K. F. Dyer, *Catching up the Men: Women in Sport* (1982), 135, 166, 168, 174. E. Cashmore, 'Women's Greatest Handicaps: Sex, Medicine and Men', *British Journal of Sports Medicine*, 33/2 (Apr. 1999), 76.

[220] Mays, *Growing up in the City*, 48; see also 169–77.

the country. But before the talent could flow freely, football clubs needed to be clearly ranked on merit. The Football League gradually organized its divisions meritocratically rather than regionally, and increasingly in practice (and not just, as earlier, in theory) encouraged relegations and promotions between divisions. With the creation in 1958 of the third and fourth national divisions out of two third-division regional groupings, this process was complete, so that free competition could transcend the local loyalties that were gradually weakening.[221] Reinforcing this tendency were the media, which gradually eroded the appeal of the smaller clubs while building up a national following for superclubs like Manchester United—clubs which had earlier depended only on local support. Talent flowed even more freely when clubs ceased virtually to own their players, with associated restrictions on their conduct and freedom to move: this liberation occurred in 1961 when the maximum wage was abolished. This reform also recognized that the best players would not stay in Britain unless better paid. Wealth and showbiz celebrity had now arrived with a vengeance, and in 1965 when Stanley Matthews became the first footballer to be knighted, he seemed almost old-fashioned in disclaiming hero status.

Meritocracy and internationalism combined to accelerate a fourth sporting development: professionalism. Sports training was becoming much more demanding. In retrospect, Bannister was surprised at how amateurishly he had trained for his great achievement;[222] sporting and scholarly professionalism were beginning to compete for the student's time and energies. Sporting contests between Eton and Harrow, Oxford and Cambridge, lost status within the sporting calendar, and by the early 1960s the distinction between amateur and professional was in many sports becoming artificial. The attractions of British amateurism were very great: this was sport for its own sake, reflecting British voluntarist traditions, and undiluted by moneymaking and chauvinism. Yet in most sports only the well-to-do could afford to be genuinely amateur amidst tougher training standards. Eventually international sporting competition from self-consciously meritocratic countries such as USA and USSR killed British amateurism in high-grade sport. Internationally the British, who had pioneered so many sports worldwide, were surprised and peeved to find their prowess increasingly challenged by foreigners; in sport, at least, British traditions of gallant failure were not relished.

The amateur's retreat was slower in cricket than in most sports, if only because the professional's minimization of risk made the game less entertaining to watch. But the combination of higher taxation, changed attitudes to social

[221] See above, p. 171. I am most grateful to Professors Dick Holt and Tony Mason for generous help at this point, and also to Dr John Davis of Queen's College Oxford for patient overall guidance on footballing matters.

[222] As interviewed in E. Whitley (ed.), *The Graduates* (1986), 124.

class, and ever-more demanding jobs undermined the amateur cricketer at the same time as fewer came to watch him. Attendance halved at county cricket matches in the 1950s, and fell by a third at the Ashes series between 1948 and 1964, reflecting also the decline of Commonwealth loyalties.[223] The abolition in 1962 of the social distinction between (amateur) gentlemen and (professional) players was necessary if only to retain the gentlemen in the game. None the less, it was now on the football pitch, not on the cricket field, that national achievement was measured. The football team's manager, an occupation which had scarcely existed before the war, had to evolve from training underpaid workers to scouring the schools for younger talent and bringing off financial deals with well-paid professionals. In athletics, as in that other amateur preserve—mountaineering —working-class professionals were also on the advance.

With intensified competition came a fifth sporting development: bureaucratization. A register of sporting achievement was now required. Sporting 'record' is a term which in its modern sense dates from 1884, and the register arrived in the shape of *The Guinness Book of Records*, first published in 1955. It was an instant success, and in its first year 'correspondents from all over the world . . . sent comments and suggestions' to improve and swell the next edition.[224] Ten years later the McWhirters envisaged annual publication, 'such is the pace of modern record breaking', for during the past year 'man has travelled faster and higher, probed deeper, built larger, run and swum faster . . . than ever before. Now there have been 23 men who have stood on the summit of Mount Everest and more than 200 conquests of the four-minute-mile.'[225] The growing number of rules now had to be codified and enforced, coaching and facilities provided and coordinated, international competitions organized, and funds raised, not least from government. The Wilson government in 1964 was quick to establish the Sports Council, with its network of eleven regional sports councils. Government funding could be justified on grounds of boosting national morale, growing participation among the less affluent, and the need to cultivate Britain's overseas image and trade. 'May I remind your Lordships', Baroness Burton told the House of Lords in 1963, 'that in 1954, when Roger Bannister broke the four-minute mile, the Foreign Office rushed him off to the U.S.A.?'[226] Professionalism entailed more power for commercial sponsors, trainers, and managers, and sponsorship from the mid-1960s brought higher wages for cricketers.[227] The pioneer

[223] R. Holt and T. Mason, *Sport in Britain 1945–2000* (Oxford, 2000), 4, 171–2.

[224] *Guinness Book of Records* (1956 edn.), preface by the compilers, n.p.

[225] *Guinness Book of Records* (12th edn., 1965), preface, n.p.

[226] *HL Deb.* 22 May 1963, c. 289 (Burton). For the Sports Council, 8 Dec. 1965, c. 301; 7 Feb. 1968, cc. 1140–3.

[227] M. Cronin and R. Holt, 'The Imperial Game in Crisis: English Cricket and Decolonisation', in S. Ward (ed.), *British Culture and the End of Empire* (Manchester, 2001), 117. I received generous help on cricket's history from the late Dr G. M. D. Howat.

was Denis Compton, whose alliance much earlier with Bagenal Harvey, the pioneering sporting entrepreneur, had produced his famous advertisement for Brylcreem.

So publicity was the last of the six sporting themes, with television the main influence. Some sports gained considerably from the screen's total view of the action and from the advent of colour: tennis, snooker, and show jumping, for example. The last of these became a national enthusiasm in the 1950s for both sexes, and by 1969 was second only to football in its popularity on television.[228] In sports reporting the BBC set the pace over ITV in the 1950s and gradually built up its expertise at presenting and interpreting the week's events. The BBC's longest-running regular magazine programme, *Sportsview* (later, *Sportsnight*) was launched in 1954, at first fortnightly and then weekly, laying much stress on sporting personalities; the BBC's *Match of the Day* began in 1964. Television technique and technology were advancing fast, television channels leapfrogged over one another to advance and exploit innovation, and sports commentators became household names. Sport had long been defended on moral grounds, as encouraging self-discipline, sobriety, and teamwork; nor had the interwar press been keen to advertise breaches in the ideal. Billy Wright, the first England player capped a hundred times, with five autobiographies published between 1950 and 1962 and with a Beverley Sister for his wife, in some ways anticipated the football superstar, but the maximum-wage structure held him in check.[229] Its abolition enabled George Best to blow all this apart. His career was central to the transition in the 1960s from the footballer as local working-class hero to deracinated superstar. A regular member of Manchester United's championship side from the age of 18, Best had his head turned by his role in Manchester's European Cup victory, and thereafter the journalists pursued him, his fast cars, and his beautiful women. 'I couldn't hide, and I tried', he recalled of his periodic vanishing acts to exotic parts: 'that's why I disappeared so many times. I kept packing in just to get away from it all, trying to find havens to disappear to, and I couldn't.'[230]

The escalating role of the media itself helped to diversify recreation. Taking first the press, the twentieth century witnessed a sequence of newspaper mergers, initially accompanied by rising circulation, but after the 1960s by decline—though in that decade the 'quality' papers were still gaining ground.[231]

[228] Holt and Mason, *Sport in Britain 1945–2000*, 98.

[229] See Dave Russell's memoir of him in *ODNB*.

[230] R. Taylor and A. Ward (eds.), *Kicking and Screaming: An Oral History of Football in England* (1995), 215.

[231] Circulation statistics here and later from Bertrand (ed.), *The British Press*, 202. J. Cunningham, 'National Daily Newspapers and their Circulations in the UK, 1908–1978', *Journal of Advertising History* (Feb. 1981), 16. A. Smith (ed.), *The British Press since the War* (Newton Abbot, 1974), 97.

Among national papers the important casualty was the *News Chronicle* in 1960; lacking enough well-to-do readers, the paper could not retain its advertisers.[232] Among London evening papers, the *Star* also died in 1960, leaving only the *Evening News* and *Standard*, though under its distinguished editor Charles Wintour (1959–76, 1978–80), the *Standard* became central to London's cultural life. Among the eight popular Sunday papers of 1947, four had died by 1967; and from the 1,307 provincial papers extant in 1947 there had been a net loss by 1967 of 43. There were two significant gains, though: the *Manchester Guardian*'s transition in 1959 from provincial to national paper, and the creation in 1961 of the *Sunday Telegraph*. The *Financial Times* could also perhaps be classified as a gain because, with its circulation doubled between 1947 and 1967, it was transcending its earlier role as a purely 'City' paper.

The 'quality' papers held a small but growing share of the market between 1947 and 1967, with the dailies rising from 2 to 3 per cent of total national and provincial circulation. *The Times*, despite its small circulation (only about a fifth even of the quality dailies' total), was unique—its circulation unrivalled for quality. Its advertisement of 1957, 'Top people take *The Times*. Do you?', did not seem absurd: people in public life conversed on its correspondence page, where a well-placed and timely contribution could carry weight. Not till 1966 did the paper drive classified advertisements off its front page. The mood of all the 'quality' papers, emphasizing fine writing and clear reasoning, was well captured by the *Guardian* editor Alastair Hetherington: 'the atmosphere of the office was that of a senior common room: collegiate, thoughtful, friendly, and at once both intensely serious and cheerfully irreverent'.[233] Circulation of the Sunday 'quality' papers rose even faster than the quality dailies, from 1 per cent of the market in 1947 to 5 per cent in 1967, with the *Sunday Times* dominant. The quality Sundays were influential: for example, in the 1950s the dialogue between the theatre reviewers Harold Hobson in the *Sunday Times* and Kenneth Tynan in the *Observer* was an important feature of British cultural life.

With wartime restriction on newsprint slowly relaxing, British newspapers in the 1950s could get bigger. By the 1960s it had become feasible for the *Sunday Times* to introduce Americanized detailed investigative reporting, and its 'insight' pages grappled with such subjects as the Profumo affair, Rachmanism, and the thalidomide tragedy. The quality Sundays boosted their growing circulation and visual emphasis with so-called 'colour supplements'; the *Sunday Times*'s was the first in 1962, followed more than two years later by the *Observer*'s. Far more than mere vehicles for commercialism, these glossily up-to-date advert-stuffed magazines wielded direct cultural influence,

[232] Smith (ed.), *British Press since the War*, 42.
[233] D. Ayerst (ed.), *Guardian Omnibus 1821–1971* (1973), 755.

and American-style 'supplements' proliferated thereafter. Gradually filching advertising revenue from traditional magazines, the colour supplements by the 1980s had absorbed more than a fifth of the total for all magazines.[234] A populist intellectual such as Crossman in his *Daily Mirror* column from 1955 to 1959, or A. J. P. Taylor in the *Express*, could straddle the divide between 'quality' and 'popular' papers, though in so doing they risked their reputation for being 'serious'. The weeklies were still culturally significant, most notably the *New Statesman* for its literary coverage, and the BBC's influential *Listener* for consolidating radio's impact. The popular national dailies retained a fifth of the total national and provincial circulation in 1947 and in 1967, but within the category the *Daily Mirror* was moving up fast, whereas the *Daily Express* (which in 1938 and 1948 had been well ahead of the rest[235]) was not. In the 1950s and 1960s the *Mirror* owed much to the 'cheeky populism' of Hugh Cudlipp, 'an artist in the shaping of a tabloid front page, delighting to say in bold black type what he thought ordinary people would like to hear—but other newspapers were too polite to publish'.[236] The popular Sundays retained about a third of the total national and provincial circulation in 1947 and 1967, with the *News of the World* dominant, but chased by the *People*, the *Sunday Pictorial* and the *Sunday Express*. In the same two years the provincial papers retained their share, just over a third, of the slowly falling total national and provincial circulation.

The journalist's status was changing. Till the 1960s he was often anonymous and lacked his later glamour. There was lively controversy in the *Times Literary Supplement* in 1957 about whether reviews should be anonymous,[237] but the cult of openness did not make strides till the 1960s. Then the *Times* journalists, after initially offering stiff resistance, had to accept named reporters and a less reflective and more instant news-gathering style, as well as a distinct business section set up in 1967. In the New Year honours list of that year space was set aside for publishing and journalism, a development which *The Times* thought potentially corrupting, and Wilson's honours for journalists were generous, to say the least.[238] Some influential people thought Robin Day mistaken in 1981 when he accepted a knighthood: journalists should be seen to retain their independence.[239] Something of television's glamour was now rubbing off on the journalists, many of whom performed in both media. The growth in newspaper circulation was slowing, however, partly because television was the medium for up-to-the-minute news; it forced journalists into retrospective magazine-style commentary and into feature articles more ruminative than revelatory. Television hit the evening papers hardest because up-to-the-minute

[234] *Advertising Statistics Yearbook 1995*, 134.

[235] Cunningham, 'National Daily Newspapers', 17.

[236] Obituary, *T* (18 May 1998), 25.

[237] *TLS* (22 Nov. 1957), 705; (29 Nov. 1957), 721; (13 Dec. 1957), 757; (20 Dec. 1957), 773; (10 Jan. 1958), 19; (17 Jan. 1958), 31.

[238] *T* (1 Jan. 1967), 9. Jenkins, *Life at the Centre*, 253.

[239] e.g. David Wood, *T* 5 Jan. 1981, 13.

sports news had been central to their role: in London their circulation halved between 1947 and 1967.

By 1951 radio had created a national electronic family. The BBC's survey ten years later showed that on all weekdays including Saturday people were most likely to switch on the radio as they were getting up; listening at its peak, 9.30 a.m., included about a quarter of the nation. Sundays were rather different, with listening attracting at least a fifth of the population throughout the morning, and reaching a higher peak at lunchtime than on any other day: 45 per cent at one o'clock. In 1961, on all evenings, when competition from television was at its peak, there was far less listening than earlier in the day: for both sexes radio took up less than a fifth of the household's total evening 'media time' after 6.30 p.m. on weekdays and Sundays, and only an eighth on Saturdays. On all days women's morning listening lasted for much longer than men's, and reached higher peaks: on weekday and Saturday mornings about a third of women were listening between 9 and 10 a.m. but only half as many men, and at lunchtime on Sundays more than half the women were listening but only a third of the men. In this, women resembled the over-65s, whose leaning towards radio has already been discussed.[240] The 'upper middle class' in 1961 spent less time than the 'working class' in listening to radio on all days of the week, but devoted marginally more of its total media time to radio.[241]

BBC radio serials helped to hold the nation together. From 1948 to 1969, when amidst much protest it was discontinued, *Mrs Dale's Diary* like the royal family epitomized continuity amidst change; and when Grace Archer in the popular radio serial launched in 1950 was permitted to die rescuing a horse from a blazing stable in September 1955, hundreds rang Broadcasting House to protest.[242] *The Goon Show* (first broadcast on 28 May 1951) built up a devoted and entirely aural following, and with *The World at One* (first broadcast on 4 October 1965) radio staked out its continuing claim for influence on news broadcasting. There were well-known national radio personalities: the somewhat irascible former schoolteacher Gilbert Harding, who became question master in *Round Britain Quiz* and managed other prominent programmes; Richard Dimbleby, high-toned radio ringmaster of great state occasions; and Jack de Manio, endearing because so incapable of interpreting the studio clock, became despite his name 'the epitome of the middle-class, middle-brow Englishman' and in 1958–71 made the *Today* breakfast programme a national forum.[243] *Any Questions*, too, could convert its panellists into national names:

[240] See above, p. 286.

[241] This paragraph draws upon BBC Audience Research Dept, *The People's Activities* (1965), 1.23–5, 1.29–30, 1.32.

[242] Briggs, *Sound and Vision*, 1013.

[243] A. Baker in C. S. Nicholls (ed.), *The Dictionary of National Biography 1986–1990* (Oxford, 1996), 104.

Bob Boothby and Mary Stocks, for example. From the advent of commercial television in 1955, however, the BBC began to lose its nationally integrating role, and by 1964 ship-based pirate radio stations were forcing BBC radio into competition; local radio's advent in the 1970s carried fragmentation still further.

Reith's idea of using radio to educate was more salient in the 1950s than later. Radio's mood became more relaxed, partly because tape recording, with its portability and flexibility, made broadcasting much more versatile. *People Talking*, for example, Denis Mitchell's programme of the 1950s, pioneered the idea of taping people as they talked, rather than taking down their remarks in shorthand and getting an actor to utter them from a tidied-up text.[244] As the nation's largest employer of musicians, the BBC took seriously its policy of broadening listeners' musical tastes, and in the late 1940s its 'Third Programme' owed much to refugees from Europe, and so was better insulated against American influences than most areas of British life.[245] Under the Glock regime the Third Programme greatly extended the time span of broadcast music, and commissioned much new orchestral music. Glock was once asked what he aimed to offer listeners: 'what they will like tomorrow', he replied.[246] This was stretching the BBC's educational function to the limit, but at least Britain could no longer be described as a land without music. The BBC also developed close relations with creative writers, guiding them towards writing plays for radio, as well as tempting distinguished scholars such as Nikolaus Pevsner and Isaiah Berlin to become 'public intellectuals' and make this the great age of the radio talk. There was always a running-fire of populist hostility to the Third Programme, however, and any programme tarred with its brush was heard by more people if broadcast on another channel. When the 'Third Programme' became 'Radio 3' in 1970 the cultural establishment (mobilized against the change in the Campaign for Better Broadcasting) once more failed to prevail.

The cinema was more important to the British than to any other nation in 1950; the average person saw a film twenty-eight times a year, more even than Americans. Attendance in Great Britain was five times as large in 1952 as for theatre, football, cricket, and racing put together,[247] and the 5,000 cinemas in the previous year provided nearly five million seats, each occupied on average six times a week. The cinema audience in the late 1940s was broadly representative of the population as a whole, though with a bias towards women and young adults. Even in the early 1960s, it was the natural

[244] J. Corner, 'Documentary Voices', in J. Corner (ed.), *Popular Television in Britain: Studies in Cultural History* (1991), 49–50.

[245] Briggs, *Sound and Vision*, 721, 725. McKibbin, *Classes and Cultures*, 474.

[246] Hugh Wood, in *ODNB*. For Glock's obituary see *T* (29 June 2000), 25.

[247] McKibbin, *Classes and Cultures*, 419. *TBS* 558.

resort for Neasden teenager Lesley Hornby, soon better known as the model 'Twiggy': 'if you went out with a boy you went to the pictures', she recalled. 'That was what going out meant then: the pictures.'[248] The cinema was important enough in social life for David Lodge to centre his first novel, *The Picturegoers* (1960), on the Palladium in Brickley, where it features prominently in the lives of all the leading characters as a focus of cultural activity and courtship for the young, a solace for their seniors, a threat to the values of the local Catholic church, and an abundant source of livelihood. Why did people go? Partly because there were fewer rival recreations, especially within the home; partly because the cinema's architecture and American imports conveyed glamour; partly because the cinema programme could offer a rich bill of fare. People then went to the cinema for an evening out, and not just for a single film. The sort of continuously updated news coverage later customary on television then came from the cinema newsreel—especially in the news cinemas widespread in the larger towns.[249] Films could influence attitudes and conduct in the most complex ways, often incidentally: manners, personal relationships, dress, speech.[250] They also helped to consolidate a view of Englishness, feeding back to its audience selected images of themselves, especially in the Ealing Studio comedies from the first (*Hue and Cry*, 1947) to the last (*The Ladykillers*, 1955).

Cinema-going declined steadily from its peak year for admissions (1946), then plunged in the late 1950s. At that point it received a considerable cultural boost from the provincial literary revival, several of whose major books became memorable films. Shelagh Delaney's *A Taste of Honey*, filmed on location, gained immensely from the backdrop provided by Salford's seedy waterways and decayed tenements. Karel Reisz made his name as a film director with his rendering (1960) of Alan Sillitoe's novel *Saturday Night and Sunday Morning*, set in Nottingham and filmed there. The affluent young labourer Arthur Seaton (played by Albert Finney, with his wild week-ending) is ultimately domesticated by Doreen, and Reisz's move into producing Lindsay Anderson's film of *This Sporting Life* in 1963 followed naturally from it. Yet the British cinema's long-term decline resumed, and by 1966 admissions were only a fifth of their level in 1950.[251] Symbolic of the British film industry's difficulties was its resort to the Dracula and Frankenstein myths, recycled in the 'horror film'; it released more than 1,200 between 1956 and 1973. Hammer Film Productions, founded in 1947, produced about fifty, including *The Quatermass Xperiment* (1955), and dominated the British market till the mid-1960s, giving

[248] [Lesley Hornby], *Twiggy: An Autobiography* (1975), 14. For the audience see Rowntree and Lavers, *English Life and Leisure*, 228–31.

[249] They are usefully discussed in Rowntree and Lavers, *English Life and Leisure*, 251.

[250] For a brilliant evocation of cinema's influence on a suburban London teenage boy in the 1960s see J. Walsh, *Are You Talking to Me? A Life through the Movies* (2003).

[251] *TBS* 559.

way thereafter to even less inhibited American equivalents.[252] When horror was too closely tied to realism, however, public revulsion at the implications for conduct could destroy a distinguished filming career. The ingenious *Peeping Tom* (1960), from the distinguished British film director Michael Powell, has as its central figure the shy young film technician Mark Lewis. Victim of a sadistic upbringing, he is a serial murderer of women, with an inner compulsion to film the terror of their last moments. Recurrently chilling, the film sees everything through the murderer's eyes or lenses, with clever photography, fine acting from a distinguished cast, and an ingenious plot centring on the film within the film. Withdrawn five days after its release, *Peeping Tom* ruined Powell's British career, and in effect he exiled himself in Australia. Not till the 1970s was the film's brilliant originality recognized.

Radio had reached a mass market well before 1951, pioneering home-based electronic recreation, and the cinema had created a mass audience for film. Television united both attractions, thereby ensuring a much larger impact than either could separately have made. It was the major influence in changing patterns of recreation in the 1950s and 1960s. In 1950 only 4 per cent of the UK population could receive it, 40 per cent in 1955, 82 per cent in 1960, and 91 per cent in 1964. As for television licences, only 382,000 had been taken out in Great Britain in 1950, thereafter rising twelvefold within five years, and more than doubling again in the next five. By 1968 television was attracting on average a third of Great Britain's population, and absorbing a quarter of their leisure time.[253] The BBC survey of 1961, when there was no morning television, showed adults on all days of the week rapidly building up their viewing during the mid-afternoon to a peak between 8.30 and 9.30 p.m. and then tailing off. Saturday night was the big viewing night for both sexes, but men watched rather less than women on Sunday and weekday nights. The 'upper middle class' listened to and watched far less radio and television than the 'working class', but their viewing timetable during the week's seven days was very similar.[254] Television helped by the early 1960s to shift the internal geography of the working man's home, gradually replacing 'the kitchen mentality . . . by the living-room mentality', and moving the main entrance from back door to front.[255]

By the early 1950s some television programmes were already becoming national institutions. Landmarks in television's reaching out to new publics were the first *What's My Line?* on 16 July 1951, the coronation on 2 June 1953, the first *That Was The Week That Was* on 24 November 1962, the first *Match of the Day* on 22 August 1964, the first instalment of Galsworthy's *The Forsyte Saga* on 7 January 1967, and the first *Dad's Army* on 31 July 1968. *The*

[252] P. W. Hutchings, 'The British Horror Film: An Investigation of British Horror Production in its National Context' (East Anglia University Ph.D. thesis, 1989), 1, 79, 106, 198, 313, 383.

[253] *TBS* 552, 553, 556. [254] BBC, *People's Activities*, 1.23, 1.24–5, 1.30, 1.32.

[255] F. Zweig, *The Worker in an Affluent Society: Family Life and Industry* (1961), 5.

Forsyte Saga's first showing (on BBC2) attracted six million viewers, its second showing (on BBC1) eighteen million.[256] The first televised 'soap' serial was *The Grove Family*, a North London family named after Lime Grove studios, whence it was broadcast live between 1954 and 1957. The BBC axed it, leaving the field open to ITV's *Coronation Street* launched three years later. *Steptoe and Son* was so popular with Labour voters in 1964 that Wilson got the BBC to postpone it so as to ensure a fair voting turnout, though at the general election of 1966 he failed to get the BBC's popular spy series *The Man from UNCLE* postponed.[257] Television's educational impact in the 1950s was considerable. Its panel game *Animal, Vegetable, Mineral?* made two archaeologists, Glyn Daniel and Mortimer Wheeler, into household names. Zoology was highly telegenic, and gained much attention through Cousteau's under-sea programmes, the African animal programmes of Michaela and Armand Denis, and the nature programmes of David Attenborough, whose *Zoo Quest* series began in 1954. Clark's *Civilization* series inspired many imitators, of which the first was Jacob Bronowski's *The Ascent of Man* (1972), in the same year as Alistair Cooke's *America*. Inevitably the authorities turned frequently for help to so powerful a medium. The task of the census was greatly eased in 1961, for example, after a census enumerator had appeared on television's popular programme *What's My Line?*[258]

The advent of commercial television in 1955 did not prevent the state from regulating broadcasting: it created a complex duopoly whereby the Independent Television Authority granted a regional monopoly to the companies creating the programmes. Not until 1972 was all government restraint on broadcasting hours removed.[259] Commercial television brought a breath of fresh air, especially in news reporting. American ideas were introduced, and what later seemed extraordinarily restrictive attitudes to political reporting were removed; within its first year, ITV was in a position to dominate reporting of the crises in Suez and Hungary.[260] Although ITV initially threatened BBC audience ratings, the BBC fought back in the 1960s and each learnt from the other: while ITV absorbed much of the BBC's culture, the BBC substituted for its public-service ethic the values of media professionalism. Much more was now heard about 'the mandate of autonomous judgement' and 'professional integrity' within the BBC,[261] which by the 1970s felt more vulnerable and obliged to lobby in its own defence.

[256] *T* (25 Apr. 2002), 34. [257] Cockerell, *Live from No. 10*, 107, 129.

[258] General Register Offices, London and Edinburgh, *Census 1961 Great Britain: General Report* (1968), 9.

[259] A. Briggs, *The History of Broadcasting in the United Kingdom*, v. *Competition* (Oxford, 1995), 5, 158–9.

[260] B. Sendall, *Independent Television in Britain*, ii. *Expansion and Change, 1958–68* (Basingstoke and London, 1983), 123, 283–6. For the restrictions, see below pp. 461–2.

[261] Briggs, *Competition*, 380.

The major changes in the media world emerge from studying changes in humour, which thrives on its quick response to new situations. Quickfire conversational repartee has always been prized at every social level. For Zweig, the worker's language was 'often vigorous, sharp, and pungent', ripe with parables and proverbs; he was 'astonished to find how great are the wit and sense of fun, common sense and intelligence of the vast majority', with 'humour and wit . . . the most popular qualities'.[262] Radio enhanced still further the music hall's megaphone for working-class wit. The royal family's music-hall favourites were Tommy Trinder, son of a tramdriver and baker, and the Crazy Gang with their fifteen official royal variety performances. The transition to the mass media's relatively classless world was natural enough, and in 1955 Trinder became the first host of *Sunday Night at the London Palladium*, among television's most successful variety shows. But not all music-hall stars made the transition in the 1950s from the dying music-hall tradition into the new media. Ted Ray did so, and the ten years of his radio programme *Ray's a Laugh* launched in 1949 roughly coincided with the music hall's demise. There was a price to pay: the mass media needed performers with a wide appeal, which entailed a flattening of contrast such as was already occurring with accent and dialect. Max Miller's quickfire humour could not travel far beyond London and the south-east, though the success of Wilfred Pickles in running the radio quiz show *Have a Go* for twenty-one years until 1967 showed how a skilful northerner could without undue compromise build up a national following. The accent of many Scottish comedians was too strong for that, and Harry Lauder and Will Fyffe attracted an English following partly for reinforcing an English image of Scotland that was disliked nearer home. Humour was not uniform between the regions: death could be joked about in Scotland but not (at least until Orton) in England, and whereas English comedians could joke about the vicar, the Scottish minister was sacrosanct.[263] The 'family entertainment' factor flattened contrasts in another dimension: 'humour must be clean and untainted directly or by association with vulgarity and suggestiveness', pronounced the BBC's 'Green Book' in 1949: 'Music hall, stage, and to a lesser degree, screen standards, are not suitable to broadcasting . . . There can be no compromise with doubtful material.'[264]

Radio's music-hall input was refracted through wartime experience. The Entertainments National Service Association (ENSA) was there to boost the morale of the other ranks, and honed the talents of many key figures in postwar comedy. An unsubversive ridiculing of those in authority arose naturally in such

[262] Zweig, *British Worker*, 228; *Life, Labour and Poverty*, 61.

[263] For a good discussion see R. Wilmut, *Kindly Leave the Stage! The Story of Variety 1919–1960* (1985), 169.

[264] B. Took, *Laughter in the Air: An Informal History of British Radio Comedy* (1st publ. 1976, rev. edn. 1981), 87.

a context, together with the hilarious lower-rank situations generated within tight hierarchical structures. ENSA, the wartime gangshow, and the NAAFI concert party trained a new generation of postwar comedians drawn from rather higher social levels than the interwar music-hall performers. They helped to evolve a new comic vehicle, the 'sitcom', or serialized interplay between distinctive characters and bizarre situations. The influential comedy writers Frank Muir and Denis Norden, both in the RAF in the Second World War, developed further the role of scriptwriter which Ted Kavanagh had performed for *ITMA*, Tommy Handley's postwar radio comedy programme *It's That Man Again*. One of *ITMA*'s regular characters was 'Colonel Chinstrap', a boozy caricature of the army officer who briefly reappeared in *The Goon Show*. From Muir and Norden's radio show *Take It From Here*, which ran from 1947 to 1958,[265] the pedigree moved forward to the influential radio programme *Hancock's Half Hour* (1954–9). It centred on the ENSA-trained Tony Hancock, whose resentful combination of inner insecurity and bravado at 23 Railway Cuttings, East Cheam, transferred readily to television (1956–61), given his genius for conveying nuances of mood through subtle changes in his jowly facial expression. Hancock's scriptwriters Ray Galton and Alan Simson, essential to his performance, carried their skills into such subsequent sitcoms as *Steptoe and Son* (1962–74), and *Till Death Us Do Part* (1966–75).

ITMA's abundant sound effects and surreal dimension were carried forward in the 1950s by the four ex-servicemen Spike Milligan, Peter Sellers, Michael Bentine, and Harry Secombe into *The Goon Show*, vehicle for their alertness to authority's absurdities. Sellers did wartime gang-show work in India, and Secombe had participated with Milligan in wartime concert parties in Italy. *Crazy People*, the radio comedy programme which later became *The Goons*, first broadcast on 28 May 1951, reacted for nine years against the high-flown tone of war films and imperial rhetoric. As John Cleese put it, the *Show* 'was the very clever NCOs making jokes that the officers wouldn't quite have understood'.[266] The *Show*'s bizarre plots often involved pursuing some impossible overseas mission reminiscent of imperial legend, yet with Major Dennis Bloodnok, a cowardly deserter from the British army, to the fore. If the criticism of empire had been overt, the BBC would have banned the programmes, nor would the Prince of Wales later have publicized his taste for them. The *Show*'s anti-imperial message probably carried no stronger significance than Milligan's personal repudiation of the values he had observed in Poona, as son of a sergeant major.

In puncturing pomposity and challenging authoritarian stereotypes and values, *The Goon Show*'s pedigree went back to the cartoonist David Low's interwar character 'Colonel Blimp', and in turn helped to generate the less

265 D. Nathan, *The Laughtermakers: A Quest for Comedy* (1981), 19–20.
266 Billington, *State of the Nation*, 56.

muted variant of satire that emerged in the 1960s, beginning with *Beyond the Fringe*, which opened at the Edinburgh Festival in 1960.[267] Comedians were by then being recruited from Oxbridge graduates and from a younger generation. If they had earlier tripped the boards at all, such people would have gone into straight theatre, and would not have braved the social hazards of comedy's music-hall connections. The early 1960s were also a time when colonial openings for educated members of the middle class were rapidly closing down, and when humour could therefore play upon a combination of irreverence and nostalgia—though in its links to *Private Eye* and still more to the radical journalist Paul Foot, humour could become sharper-edged. The line from *Beyond the Fringe* into the television show *That Was the Week That Was* (*TW3*) was direct, but the satire was as notable for its location as for its content, given that television had hitherto been shy of irreverent political and social comment.

Humour does more than merely reflect context: it has its own internal history. The Goons pioneered the sort of surreal and irreverent humour carried forward by *Monty Python's Flying Circus*; as John Cleese put it, the Goons 'nudged us forward to be even crazier than we were intending to be'.[268] Cleese studied the natural sciences at Cambridge, performed in the Cambridge 'Footlights', and wrote some sketches for *TW3*. The *Circus* grew out of his collaboration with five other men, all but one with an Oxbridge background. Adorned with striking psychedelic and baroque circus or fairground images, the programmes were in effect exuberant televised 'Goon Shows', first broadcast late at night on 5 October 1969. This was a wild and fantastic insider variant on the theme that the outsider Joe Orton had been pursuing more sharply in mid-decade. Rejecting in July 1967 what he called 'the old theatre of reassurance—roses, French windows, middle-class characters', Orton described his writing as 'a deliberate satire on bad theatre'. He felt provoked by the 'ridiculous lines' of *The Desert Song* into an idea for a new play,[269] but a month later he was dead.

This chapter has shown that the 1950s and 1960s were decades of intellectual, cultural, and recreational vitality. Religious observance might be declining, but debate on religious issues was lively. Schools and universities, broadened in recruitment and curricula, were extending their impact as powerhouses of intellectual and cultural activity. It was in some ways the very strength of these institutions that prompted a healthy scepticism: that is, slowly growing doubts about natural science and falling academic standards. Yet technological change, improved transport, growing affluence, and (for many) reduced working hours, were opening up hitherto unimaginable cultural and recreational opportunity.

267 For more on this see below, pp. 478–9.

268 Commenting on the death of Spike Milligan, *T* (28 Feb. 2002), 5.

269 *The Orton Diaries*, ed. J. Lahr (1986, paperback edn. 1998), 256 (27 July 1967), 239 (12 July 1967).

The highest hopes of mass culture may have been disappointed, but the diversification and enrichment were undeniable.

The first two of the Introduction's motifs to be stressed must therefore be the fifth (the recreational and cultural components of the materialist challenge to Christian values and structures), together with the fourth (the contribution to ongoing pressures on daily living that these recreational and educational opportunities supplied). Teachers in schools and universities, together with all professions and the young people themselves, experienced growing demands on their time and energy, nor could amateurism any longer prevail in sport. Also present is the second motif: however easy it might be to turn away from international involvement in other spheres, intellectual, cultural, and sporting competition compelled a receptiveness to worldwide trends that was remarkable by earlier standards; even Christians had to confront the challenge presented by the immigrant religions planted in their midst. As for the Second World War legacy (the first motif), there were as yet few signs of retreat from the prestige it brought to natural science, though the social sciences were by the late 1960s running into difficulty, as was the tripartite educational structure developed in 1944. A further motif (the seventh) is in some ways more relevant here than elsewhere: the democratic politician's dependence on spontaneous developments within the community. We have seen how educational growth was powered by demographic and democratic pressures pushing up from below, forcing the politicians to respond. Furthermore, sport and education were areas where political interference had long been conventionally discouraged in the UK, though their growing salience had important implications for the politician's profession: complicating his access to the universities' expertise and eroding their political involvement. As for the UK's world roles (the eighth motif): sporting leadership had now to be conceded to societies either wealthier or readier politically to capitalize upon sporting prowess. Attitudes increasingly prevalent in cultural and intellectual circles during the 1960s suggested, too, that the British reputation for political aptitude was now at risk. To complaints that his humour was 'sick', Orton replied in 1966 that his plays merely reflected a sick society, and he noted the changed climate since the 1950s, when political solutions to the world's problems had seemed convincing, whereas 'today there is a general sense of despair about politics because we know it can't provide any real solutions'.[270] To politics and government we must now turn.

[270] Lahr, *Prick Up Your Ears*, 166.

CHAPTER 8

Politics and Government

More than once it has been noted so far that while many aspects of British life were changing fast between 1951 and 1970, the political system alone seemed almost unchanging. Since the sixteenth century, British monarchs and politicians had first built up a United Kingdom and then a world empire which had prevailed in two world wars. In 1951, in the guise of the Commonwealth, that empire still seemed largely intact and defensible. By contrast, the political systems of leading European states—Russia, Germany, France, Spain, and Italy—had experienced discontinuity or worse, and even where democratic institutions had been restored they seemed beset by extremists to right and left and destabilized by complex electoral systems, whereas the British two-party, simple-majority electoral system appeared stable. This was not because it had become fossilized—the British political structure was unusually flexible by world standards—but because its critics in the 1950s were few. The mood in an influential textbook such as Morrison's *Government and Parliament* (1954) was decidedly insular and complacent, if only because in practical politics Morrison had himself demonstrated how adaptable the British system could be. He had helped to ensure that parliament complemented its wartime successes with a domestic postwar social revolution without the constitutional discontinuities that earlier socialists had recommended. The Attlee governments had been resourceful in policy and tactics. They had emphasized the civic virtues, with a constructive outlook pursued in a mood of integrity and serious-minded public duty, honouring manifesto pledges to the electors and satisfying public expectations of uncorrupt administration. The system's successes in the 1940s had been so great, and Britain's perceptions of relative economic decline emerged so slowly, that only in the 1960s did the political system become a scapegoat. Then, as in the 1930s, seemingly intractable economic problems prompted the irrelevant diversion that pressure for constitutional reform entailed.

Britain's proud and perhaps complacent self-image in 1951 gradually came to seem remote indeed, yet it was not seriously challenged until the 1970s, and was widely echoed in Europe: British self-confidence had not yet shrunk into a grumpy chauvinism. The one moment when anyone of substance even considered the unconstitutional overthrow of the British political system—Earl Mountbatten's celebrated discussion with Cecil King in May 1968—seems to have got no further than table talk and (given the personalities involved) had no hope of wider support.[1] During the 1960s, however, the UK became more alert to defects in the national self-image, nor had the British structure ever accommodated the Anglo-Irish connection satisfactorily. It was gradually becoming clear how close Britain had come to defeat in both world wars, how much Germany's defeat owed to the Americans, and how crucial was the USSR's contribution towards defeating Hitler. It also became clear how great had been the price of victory: encouragements to anti-colonialism, formidable debts to the USA, worldwide military commitments diverting resources from economic reconstruction at home, and a failure to see both how extensive that reconstruction needed to be, and how it could best be secured. The Commonwealth soon turned out to be far less substantial and secure than it seemed in 1951, and the proclaimed national virtues of common sense and pragmatism soon looked more like excuses for postponing necessary choices.

The national myth may seem fragile in retrospect, but it was sincerely propagated and widely accepted. Nor does the British gradualist approach to institutional change and its valuation of tradition seem so very foolish in the international context of the time or later. Indeed, in the 1950s and 1960s British political institutions still seemed worth exporting to former colonies, and were by no means always rejected. In his final speech before the first Indian parliament was dissolved in 1957, Jawaharlal Nehru, first prime minister of independent India, said that his country had chosen parliamentary democracy partly because it accorded with Indian traditions, but 'also—let us give credit where credit is due—because we approved of its functioning in other countries, more especially the United Kingdom'. For Dr Azikiwe, in his inaugural address as Governor General of Nigeria in 1960, representative government 'based on the rule of law and respect for individual freedom' had been 'bequeathed to us during our political associations with Britain . . . The Westminster model of parliamentary government and democracy has been proved by us . . . to be . . . practicable in this part of Africa'[2]

The aim in this chapter is not to narrate British political history between 1951 and 1970, though this is cursorily done earlier in this book,[3] and the raw material for a more detailed narrative appears in the chronology of events. The aim is rather to analyse change in the political structure's leading components, beginning in the first section with the executive (monarchy, cabinet, prime

[1] A. Morgan, *Wilson*, 331.

[2] Madden (ed.), *Imperial Constitutional Documents*, 100 (Nehru). Azikiwe quoted in J. Callaghan, *Time and Chance* (1987), 131.

[3] See above, p. xix.

minister), and in the second with the two houses of parliament. Discussion turns, in section 3, to the administrative structure: civil service, devolution, regional and local government, and the tension between enforcement through the judicial and penal system and libertarian resistance to it. In sections 4 and 5, changes within the Conservative and Labour parties, respectively, are considered in detail. A concluding section focuses on changed ways of discovering public opinion; these did more than anything else to transform the social context of political life.

1. A FLEXIBLE EXECUTIVE

As a unitary state with an unwritten constitution, a tightly disciplined adversarial parliament and a majoritarian electoral system, the UK in 1951 possessed what was by world standards a very powerful yet flexible executive. For a distinguished backbencher in 1960, parliamentary procedure was 'all the Constitution the poor Briton has, now that any Government which can command 51 per cent. of the House can at any moment do anything they like, with retrospective or prospective intention'.[4] Culture and policy interacted with structures to generate internal compatibility and relatively long-term perspectives in formulating policy. These become possible when one party has a good chance of governing for a sustained period, when the party has generated the necessary conviction, and when the electors can directly endorse the policies promoted. A powerful executive suited both the Conservative Party, with its respect for leadership and strong government, and the Labour Party, with its interventionist instinct and belief in central planning.

Executive power was symbolized, though unobtrusively moderated, by monarchy. Early in 1956 the Queen and Prince Philip helped to change attitudes to leprosy in Nigeria by visiting a leper settlement, but this was the nearest the Queen came to deploying the magic of monarchy once so central to its appeal. Monarchy was now justified increasingly in utilitarian terms, even publicly by the Duke of Edinburgh. Widespread criticism during the Queen's visit to Canada in 1964 led its prime minister Lester Pearson to warn her that the monarchy might not survive there. Four years later the Duke was reportedly resigned to that outcome, and in 1969 told a press conference in Ottawa that 'the future of the Monarchy depends on the national community, and if at any stage the community decides it is unacceptable then it is up to that community to change it'.[5] At home, however, the monarchy seemed impregnable. In the long debate of 9 July 1952 on the civil list, only twenty-five MPs wanted cuts, and only fifty-six voted to reduce the Duke's

[4] Kenneth Pickthorn, *HC Deb.* 8 Feb. 1960, c. 70.

[5] Pimlott, *The Queen*, 392. See also Benn, *Diaries 1968–72*, 38 (23 Feb. 1968).

salary. Though some Labour ministers in the 1960s were embarrassed or even indignant at the social protocol surrounding monarchy,[6] they could not deny the monarchy's popularity. Tactfully passing over the abdication crisis of 1936, Morrison referred in 1954 to 'the steady increase in the esteem of the nation' for George V and George VI, claiming that 'no monarchy in the world is more secure or more respected by the people than ours'.[7] Opinion polls endorsed that view: working-class voters supporting both parties in 1958 overwhelmingly backed monarchy as an institution, and when Gallup asked in 1973 whether the head of state should be a monarch or president, 80 per cent favoured a monarch, 9 per cent did not know, and only 11 per cent favoured a president.[8] None the less, growing inflation in the 1960s prompted a concern with differentials that exposed all pay claims to close scrutiny, the monarchy's no less than the rest. Prince Philip caused a stir in November 1969 by saying that the royal family was going into the red, and that Buckingham Palace might have to be sold.[9] More trouble was brewing for the civil list.

Monarchy's growing social role[10] did not preclude an ongoing political role. The Queen was now only nominally the executive's head, and had in practice delegated most of her powers to the cabinet through a prime minister for whose selection she was ultimately responsible. In what was before 1970 a securely two-party system, both the major parties were sufficiently in control of parliament and sufficiently decisive in choosing their leaders to minimize her powers of selection. Worrying in his diary about how to get Churchill to retire as prime minister, Macmillan felt that 'we are missing an essential part of our constitutional mechanism', whose 'effective working depends on the power and authority of the Sovereign being revived and used': a monarch 'alone could say to Churchill what needs to be said in his interest as well as in ours'.[11] The Queen seems to have been entirely happy with Macmillan's controversial recommendation in 1963 that Alec Douglas-Home rather than R. A. Butler should succeed him, not least because of their shared interest in landowning and field sports.[12] Her last vestige of influence in choosing the prime minister within the two-party system disappeared in 1965 when the Conservative Party entrusted MPs with choosing its leader.

Crossman, who as Lord President of the Council in 1966–8 observed monarchy closely, found no section in Bagehot's famous study of the English constitution published a century earlier that was 'more completely truthful to

[6] e.g. Benn, *Diaries 1963–7*, 187 (16 Nov. 1964), 191 (20 Nov. 1964).

[7] H. Morrison, *Government and Parliament* (1964), 105.

[8] R. McKenzie and A. Silver, *Angels in Marble* (1968), 150, 152. *Gallup Polls*, ii. 1249.

[9] Crossman, *Cabinet Diaries*, iii. 723–4 (11 Nov. 1969).

[10] See above, pp. 178–82.

[11] Macmillan, *Diary*, ed. Catterall, 355 (22 Sept. 1954).

[12] Pimlott, *The Queen*, 332.

real life today' than its chapter on monarchy.[13] The Queen timed her presence in London to reflect parliament's needs,[14] and her accumulating experience, together with her wide connections in British life and her ceremonial role, made her regular confidential audiences with prime ministers useful. Churchill's private secretary found him, on hearing of George VI's death, alone in his bedroom looking straight ahead with tears in his eyes. 'I tried to cheer him up by saying how well he would get on with the new Queen, but all he could say was that he did not know her and that she was only a child.' He soon came to enjoy playing Melbourne to Elizabeth's Victoria, and both found that audiences were enjoyable enough for them to grow ever longer. When the Queen heard that Churchill had decided to retire she told him through her private secretary that she would especially miss occasions 'so instructive and . . . so entertaining'.[15] Macmillan relished the intimacy of the audiences, which became for him an arena for deferential display. As for Labour's Harold Wilson, he soon established easy relations with the Queen, while also realizing the need to be well briefed beforehand.[16] Prime minister and monarch in alliance could be formidable: Tony Benn when Postmaster General in 1964–6 found that he could not even get the Queen's head off the postage stamps.[17]

The prime minister's power within the cabinet after 1951 depended as always on the blend of personality, party, and circumstance. Churchill brought to his second premiership (1951–5) all the prestige of a national icon, and drew powerfully upon his wartime achievement and personal connections. He broke down with emotion when rehearsing for his first broadcast of the new reign which like all his speeches reflected his fine command of the English language: 'I, whose youth was passed in the august, unchallenged and tranquil glories of the Victorian Era, may well feel a thrill in invoking, once more, the prayer and the Anthem, GOD SAVE THE QUEEN.'[18] While prime minister he somehow found the time to publish more volumes in his history of the Second World War, and even slowly to advance his *History of the English-Speaking Peoples*. His premiership gained greatly from the many ceremonial events it witnessed: the funeral of the King in February 1952 and of his mother Queen Mary in March 1953, the coronation in June 1953 with its associated Commonwealth celebrations, his installation as a Knight of the Garter in June 1954, his eightieth

[13] R. H. S. Crossman, *Inside View: Three Lectures on Prime Ministerial Government* (1972), 39.

[14] See Duke of Edinburgh in *Listener* (4 Dec. 1969), 791.

[15] Quotations from J. Colville, *The Fringes of Power: Downing Street Diaries*, ii. *October 1941–1955* (1st publ. 1985, paperback edn. 1987), 194 (6 Feb. 1952). Sir M. Adeane to Churchill, 5 Apr. 1955, in M. Gilbert, *'Never Despair'* (1988), 1117.

[16] Lacey, *Majesty*, 360–2. Wilson, *Memoirs 1916–64*, 2.

[17] Benn, *Diaries 1963–7*, 168–9 (21 Oct. 1964); 231–2 (10 Mar. 1965); 343, 345 (2 Nov. 1965); 364 (31 Dec. 1965); 446 (5 July 1966). Crossman, *Cabinet Diaries*, i. 29 (22 Oct. 1964); iii. 39 (1 May 1968).

[18] W. S. Churchill, *Stemming the Tide: Speeches 1951 and 1952*, ed. R. S. Churchill (1953), 240. See also Moran, *Struggle for Survival*, 397 (7 Feb. 1952).

birthday in November and his farewell dinner for the Queen at 10 Downing Street in April 1955. The width and historical depth of his perspectives lent a certain grandeur to his speeches and to his role within cabinet, and yet also a special piquancy to his jokes and revelations to intimates of the warm human being beneath. Macmillan, for one, was charmed: 'there was hardly a Cabinet, however serious the situation, without some gem'.[19]

Yet with the icon went backward-looking attitudes. These alone could have lent Churchill such courage and determination at his historic moment in 1940, but by 1951 they were waning assets. He was haunted after 1945 by the declining world status of 'poor England', and the thought of it tended to evoke a sigh; he was all too conscious that the UK's fifty million inhabitants were producing enough food for only thirty million,[20] and by no means acquiesced in the UK's loss of world status. Deploring in 1953 Eden's policy of retreat from Egypt, he bitterly said he had not realized hitherto 'that Munich was situated on the Nile', and in the following year when discussing imperial devolution with Eisenhower, he confessed to feeling 'a bit sceptical about universal suffrage for the Hottentots even if refined by proportional representation'. A few months later he thought it would be 'a wonderful thing' if Israel joined the Commonwealth: 'so many people want to leave us; it might be the turning of the tide'. In his final remarks at his last cabinet on 5 April 1955 he wished 'all good fortune' to his colleagues, and success in 'weaving still more closely' the threads binding together the Commonwealth, 'or, as I still prefer to call it, the Empire'.[21]

Between 1904 and 1924 Churchill had been an enthusiastic deserter from his party, and for long afterwards remained a loose cannon. After 1940 his tendency was, even more than with most prime ministers, to see himself as above party. As late as 1952 he spoke of the need for a coalition government, given that 'four-fifths of the people of this country were agreed on four-fifths of the things to be done'.[22] He might arrive at the party conference grandly—with retinue of aides, family, valets, baggage, and canary—for 'the big speech', but by comparison with his successors his visit was brief. For several reasons his last cabinet was restive. His scheme for simplifying control through a smaller cabinet, three of whose 'overlords' were based in the House of Lords, was in effect the war cabinet revived, but it had many drawbacks. It impoverished the cabinet's expertise and divided it by unduly formalizing its internal hierarchy; backbenchers had less chance of promotion; and the House of Commons found it more difficult to call ministers to account. After 1953 the scheme fell into abeyance. There were limits, too, to busy colleagues' appetite for Churchill's wider horizons. 'Winston thinks with his mouth', Asquith had once said,

[19] Macmillan, *Tides of Fortune*, 391. [20] Moran, *Struggle for Survival*, 390–1 (16 Jan. 1952).

[21] Quotations from Gilbert, *'Never Despair'*, 795, 1041 (8 Aug. 1954). Shuckburgh, *Descent to Suez*, 251 (18 Feb. 1955). H. Pelling, *Churchill's Peacetime Ministry, 1951–55* (1997), 175.

[22] Colville, *Fringes of Power*, ii. 303 (16 May 1952).

and although Churchill broadened participation in forming policy through encouraging free cabinet discussion early on, the process was time-consuming and cabinets became more frequent. By August 1954 even for Macmillan 'these interminable Cabinets, full of reminiscences and monologues' were becoming 'an intolerable burden'.[23]

Churchill was backward-looking in a further respect. He had little taste for the complexities of the economic policy-making which by 1951 had moved up among British governments' priorities. And while in the nuclear age his experience in and taste for foreign policy were highly apposite, ministers (especially Eden, his Foreign Secretary) were understandably worried at the thought of one man in his late seventies pursuing the old-fashioned method of what Churchill called 'parleys' directly with other heads of government. In March 1954 he was still making the case to President Eisenhower for man-to-man talks with the Russian leaders: 'I can even imagine', he wrote, 'that a few simple words, spoken in the awe which may at once oppress and inspire the speakers, might lift this nuclear monster from our world.'[24] Only in defence and foreign policy was Churchill reluctant to leave his ministers alone. For four months in 1951–2 he combined the roles of prime minister and minister of defence, and during Eden's illness in 1953 he took on the Foreign Secretary's duties. In July 1954 the cabinet was appalled to learn that after consulting only a handful of colleagues Churchill had decided that Britain should manufacture a hydrogen bomb. Significant resignations were threatened that summer when he committed himself without consulting the cabinet to a summit meeting with the Russian leaders. Macmillan had by then become convinced that Churchill must resign: 'He thinks about one thing all the time—this Russian visit and his chance of saving the world—till it has become an obsession.' Diplomats wisely feared such one-to-one discussions: the participants lacked the necessary expertise, and were likely to be swayed unduly by personal relationships and circumstances, with confusion as the outcome. Yet Churchill insisted on the prime minister's right to consult privately with other heads of government without the cabinet's prior consent. 'The public cared nothing for these constitutional niceties. The issue would be—"Is a top-level talk with Malenkov a good thing or not?"' His looseness to party attachment even at this late stage in his career emerged from his threat to go to the country on the issue with a divided cabinet.[25]

The cabinet's fears were nourished by knowing that Churchill experienced a serious stroke on 23 June 1953. The need to preserve his influence if he recovered ensured that only a few cabinet colleagues knew how serious it

[23] Quotations from R. Churchill, *Winston S. Churchill*, ii. *Young Statesman. 1901–1914* (1967), 341. Macmillan, *Diary*, ed. Catterall, 349 (25 Aug. 1954).

[24] Gilbert, *'Never Despair'*, 960.

[25] Macmillan, *Diary*, ed. Catterall, 332 (10 July 1954), 334 (16 July 1954).

was, and great responsibilities were temporarily entrusted for a month to his private secretary John Colville and to his parliamentary private secretary and son-in-law Christopher Soames as interpreter of the prime minister to his colleagues. Although Churchill made a remarkable recovery, Wilson for one noticed a decline in his parliamentary performance; it was, he wrote, 'a tragic period', and 'as he perceptibly aged, it was pathetic to see him baited by Labour backbenchers'.[26] So powerful did the icon remain that even Eden, eager to succeed him, could hardly nerve himself to raise the topic of Churchill's retirement. In 1951 Eden had failed to get himself officially designated deputy prime minister, and in the cabinet of 14 March 1955, with the succession still unsettled, there was what Macmillan called 'a long and difficult silence' after Eden had blurted out 'I have been Foreign Secretary for 10 years. Am I not to be trusted?' By then Churchill's reluctance to retire seemed to Macmillan 'almost a form of advanced megalomania'. On 2 April Churchill at last informed Eden that he had decided to resign. Two days later, after receiving the Queen to dinner at 10 Downing Street, Churchill was found by Colville on his bed, still wearing his Garter, Order of Merit, and knee-breeches: 'for several minutes he did not speak . . . Then suddenly he stared at me and said with vehemence: "I don't believe Anthony can do it".'[27]

Churchill's combination of qualities was unique, and no successor could match them, though Eden could hardly have been better qualified for the post. With a First in oriental languages from Oxford and a fine record in the First World War, he had a quick intellect and a close grasp of detail. His experience of cabinet office extended as far back as 1935, and though his ministerial experience lay almost exclusively in foreign affairs, he was a well-known and respected public figure, untainted by what had come to be known as 'appeasement'. Elegant, even glamorous, he had recently married Churchill's niece, and for years he had seemed heir apparent. As prime minister he made a refreshing start, with cabinets far more crisply managed than Churchill's. His disqualifications as prime minister none the less came rapidly into focus. His languid aristocratic manner was much less appropriate even for diplomatic purposes in the 1950s than in the 1930s, for the dominant powers (USA and USSR) were now decidedly un-aristocratic and plain-speaking. His image was not improved in his first year by the *Daily Mirror*'s report that his wife had objected when a cottager near Chequers, the prime minister's official country residence, hung out her washing in her front garden.[28] Though Eden shared Churchill's preoccupation with international relations, no prime minister is free to specialize: Eden lacked Churchill's interest in domestic policy, had

[26] Wilson, *Memoirs 1916–64*, 147–8.

[27] Quotations from Macmillan, *Diary*, 405 (14 Mar. 1955), 404 (13 Mar. 1955). Colville, *Fringes of Power*, ii. 379 (Apr. 1955).

[28] Thorpe, *Eden*, 459.

never been responsible for a home department, and was not good at meeting the prime minister's need to shift quickly between problems. Yet difficulties crowded upon his government in 1955–7 from all directions: strikes, economic problems as well as serious issues precisely in the area he had made his own, foreign policy. Besides, diplomacy's continuous search for compromise was a poor preparation for a prime minister's tough decision-making. In the *Daily Telegraph* on 3 January 1956 the deputy editor Donald McLachlan claimed that Eden was 'relying too much in home affairs on the technique of smoothing and fixing which are the essence of skilled diplomacy'. He added a sentence to which Eden took special exception: 'There is a favourite gesture of the Prime Minister's . . . To emphasise a point he will clench one fist to smack the open palm of the other hand—but the smack is seldom heard.'[29]

Eden's sensitivity to criticism reflected his lack of self-confidence. Reluctant to delegate, he displayed a defect the reverse of Churchill's: he got buried in detail. As Foreign Secretary he liked presiding over large gatherings of ministers and officials, and could not work on a speech unless surrounded by secretaries. He had few political friends, and did not seek them through informal sociability: he never entered the House of Commons smoking room, and never sought to penetrate the masculine Tory heartland through joining the London clubs, whereas his successor Macmillan joined five and attended them regularly. We saw in Chapter 2 how uncharacteristic was Eden's alliance in the Suez venture with his party's right wing, for though consistently loyal to the Conservatives, he was a centrist and no partisan. A skilful debater, Eden could not hope to match Churchill for a memorable and wide-ranging parliamentary speech. Debonair and polished in public, he indulged in frighteningly childish tantrums behind the scenes, and these grew worse with his mounting ill-health after the botched operation on his bile duct in 1953. Prone as prime minister to seek action almost for its own sake, he telephoned his ministers frequently and at all hours with fussy inquiries and exhortations. Eden's was a life full of misfortune: unsympathetic parents, an unhappy first marriage, the death in action of two brothers in the First World War, and of his own elder son at the end of the Second World War. It was ironic that it should be on foreign policy that his career foundered. In twentieth-century politics the personal tragedy of this patriotic, industrious, and in many ways brilliant prime minister was perhaps surpassed in profundity only by that of Neville Chamberlain, the prime minister whose career he had himself helped to undermine when as a rising young politician he had resigned from the cabinet in 1938.

Macmillan was better suited by background for a party seeking to broaden its appeal. 'I have it both ways', he used to say: 'my grandfather was a crofter, my

[29] D. McLachlan, 'Waiting for the Smack of Firm Government . . .', *DT* (3 Jan. 1956), 6.

wife's father a Duke'.[30] He drew his cabinets unashamedly from a very restricted circle, nor was his association with grouse-shooting unhelpful in his relations with key figures in his party. The main interest of John Morrison, chairman of the 1922 Committee from 1955 to 1964, was foxhunting, and he would return to London on Monday afternoons and quickly change out of hunting clothes and top boots before driving to the House of Commons. As government chief whip from 1959 to 1964 Martin Redmayne, with a fine war record and with golfing and fishing as his hobbies, ran the whips' office like a military headquarters. In 1962 at least six of Macmillan's cabinet ministers, together with several other ministers, were related to him through his wife.[31] The essential qualifications for joining a Macmillan cabinet were not opinions but loyalty and 'character', and this helped to keep it united and happy. Macmillan made business enjoyable because he could combine Churchill's humorous asides with efficiency in clarifying issues and with masterly summings-up. Unlike Eden, Macmillan could delegate: he left his ministers alone unless they needed help. Just as Churchill had backed Macmillan as housing minister, so Macmillan backed Duncan Sandys as defence minister in 1957–9, otherwise Sandys's important defence cuts[32] would never have overcome the armed services' stiff resistance. Macmillan's unflappable style of leadership enabled him to survive the resignation of Lord Salisbury within three months of becoming prime minister, and a year later of his entire Treasury team. We have seen,[33] too, in how masterly a fashion Macmillan managed to unite the party in 1960–1 behind the decision to apply for membership of the EEC.

Macmillan's apparent traditionalism was a pose. He was a very unusual Conservative, radical in his inclinations, cultural and intellectual in his leisure tastes, and inclusive in his aspirations for the party. Behind this stance lay his deeply etched memory of the First World War, which had drawn together officers and other ranks, together with his interwar experience of representing Stockton-on-Tees, a constituency with serious unemployment. Macmillan could also be ruthless: 'first in, first out' was Wilson's phrase about Macmillan's stance in the Suez crisis, yet an enthusiast for the venture was specially equipped to repair the damage.[34] Macmillan was radical, too, for a Conservative, in so readily keeping abreast of modern publicity devices, and throughout his premiership he usually surpassed his party in his personal Gallup poll rating. This, together with his flair for phrase-making and his unconcealed zest for prosperity, helped the Conservatives to overtake Labour in Gallup's poll of voting intentions during 1958–9 and to engineer in 1959 the third successive electoral victory [Plate 11] that had seemed inconceivable

[30] *Ind.* (23 Feb. 1994), 21.
[31] *T* (29 May 1996), 21 (Morrison). Heasman, 'Prime Minister and Cabinet', 172–3.
[32] See above, pp. 93–4.
[33] See above, pp. 117–18.
[34] Wilson, *Memoirs 1916–64*, 169.

three years before.[35] Essential to media influence then and later was success in the House of Commons. There Macmillan took the offensive, vigorously leading his own side and thriving on the opposition's interjections. He had cultivated the photo-opportunity in 1951–4 when housing minister [Plate 4], and his image gained from his prime-ministerial taste for diplomatic globetrotting. Whereas Eden rejected the teleprompter, an American invention, when addressing the nation during his election campaign of 1955, Macmillan pioneered its use during his first televised broadcast as prime minister in 1957. Thereafter he conducted many pioneering television interviews in London Airport's VIP lounge, and it was there that he famously dismissed the resignation of his entire Treasury team in January 1958 as 'little local difficulties'. In the next month he was the first British prime minister to give an interview in a television studio. Just before the general election of 1959 he invited BBC cameras into 10 Downing Street when President Eisenhower came to dinner.[36] Macmillan's fifteen-minute final television election broadcast directly to camera in that year was widely praised.

Yet Macmillan was inwardly far less confident than he seemed. Ambition had led this nervous and in some ways unstable personality to school himself against anxiety with a sense of humour, an alertness to the ironies of life, and a skill for switching off during a crisis. At the height of the Suez crisis he consumed George Eliot's *Middlemarch* in only four days, and as the crisis progressed he moved through the rest of her works to embark upon Churchill's *History of the English Speaking Peoples*. It was lack of self-confidence, not his ruthless streak, which inspired his damaging decision in 1962 to sack a third of his cabinet, including several loyal friends. Worried by the Liberal revival and by dissidence in his party, and with a general election looming, he wanted a new image and more vigorous economic policies for his government, and this led him on 13 July to jettison his respect for loyalty in what came to be known as 'the night of the long knives'. A prime minister's loyalty to colleagues must always be balanced against the need to ensure more than one candidate for the succession, but thereafter Macmillan no longer seemed unflappable, and in his one prime-ministerial parallel with Eden, illness in the following year forced him out of office. His successor, Alec Douglas-Home, was a respected and upright colleague without Macmillan's taste for media self-marketing, and the general election of 1964 ensured that he was only a stopgap before the advent of Wilson, Labour's first prime minister since Attlee's defeat in 1951.

In several respects Wilson modelled himself on Macmillan, if only because both had to unite a fissile political party. Wilson as opposition leader consciously reacted against the somewhat combative style (though not against the substance) of Gaitskell's party leadership. Wilson's background equipped him admirably to

[35] *BPF* (8th edn.), 268–9. [36] Cockerell, *Live from No. 10*, 36, 54, 57, 61–2, 66–7.

lead a party mobilizing meritocracy against a Conservatism which by the early 1960s seemed permeated by traditionalism, privilege, and even corruption. Provincial, Congregationalist, and lower middle-class, Wilson instinctively tuned in to his party's instincts. For Jenkins he was 'an inveterate provincial', whose reference point lay with the 'real' people north of the Trent.[37] *Private Eye* harped benevolently upon Wilson's provincialism because he was a decent and kindly man, unafraid of power and incorruptible by it, and he really did enjoy eating tinned salmon and offering his friends Nescafé;[38] Crossman found him in bed at No. 10 the morning after addressing a Birmingham meeting of 10,000, breakfasting on kippers and throwing their skeletons on to the carpet for the cat.[39] Uninterested in money or honours, and completely unpretentious, this grammar-school boy had a brilliant career at Oxford, and his wartime government service confirmed him as a classless and unsnobbish half-insider who could confidently take on the establishment. His campaign for modernization and participation prompted high hopes, and his unstuffy, unpretentious demystifying of British government during the 1960s was among his under-rated achievements.

Wilson's loyalty to his party was complete: continuously resilient under daunting hostility, he held it together. Like a seasoned stage performer, he knew at party conferences which emotions to stir, which groups to conciliate, which memories to evoke. He also staunchly and skilfully defended British parliamentary traditions. Such feats could be attained only through an agile and tactical style of leadership—a style so overt and so obviously relished as to deny his moralistic and provincial attacks on the establishment much Gladstonian uplift. For Crossman, Wilson the politician was 'a tight, little, careful, calculating man' who thought that 'in politics, timing is everything';[40] notorious for claiming that 'a week is a long time in politics', Wilson once told Castle that 'footwork is my strong point'. He could have applied to his second government of 1966–70 W. E. Gladstone's description of his second government of 1880–5: 'a wild romance of politics, with a continual succession of hairbreadth escapes and strange accidents pressing upon one another'. Throughout his manœuvres Wilson was as keen as Macmillan to ensure that within the cabinet no single successor emerged, but this involved him in continuous, overt, and somewhat undignified sniffings-out of alleged plots, accusations of leaks, and grumbles about the press. After his reshuffle in August 1966 he proudly told Benn that 'there are now six crown princes instead of just one'.[41]

[37] Reviewing his memoirs, *NS* (30 July 1971), 139.

[38] Crossman, *Cabinet Diaries*, ii. 718 (17 Mar. 1968).

[39] Ibid. i. 480 (17 Mar. 1966).

[40] Crossman, *Backbench Diaries*, 986 (5 Mar. 1963). See also Benn, *Diaries 1973–6*, 421 (22 July 1975).

[41] Quotations from Castle, *Diaries 1974–6*, 32 (3 Mar. 1974). J. Morley, *The Life of William Ewart Gladstone* (1st publ. 1903, 2-vol. edn. 1905), ii. 426. Benn, *Diaries 1963–7*, 477 (23 Sept. 1966).

With each crisis, and especially after devaluation's major setback to his policy in 1967, Wilson's tactical style became even more patent. His weight as prime minister steadily diminished as potential rivals within the cabinet gained experience. Adept at parliamentary manœuvre, he was ideally qualified to cope with small House of Commons majorities like those of 1964–6 and 1974–6, but not to steer his party towards anything other than winning and holding power in the short term. Whereas Gaitskell confronted and defined issues, Wilson preferred to act as Labour's Macmillan, evading and blurring them. Damagingly for a party of the left, this meant that tactics submerged inspiration. Wilson told Benn in 1966 that the public was happy to let the Labour Party worry about the affairs of the nation while it enjoyed its rising living standards. To Benn this seemed 'getting dangerously close to Macmillan's "You've never had it so good" ', whereas Labour should, like all parties of the left, be about campaigning to change opinion.[42]

The mid-twentieth-century Labour Party could have taken two directions. There was what turned out to be the Bennite strategy of carrying further forward the Attlee governments' socialist drive. Alternatively, there was what turned out to be the Blairite strategy of guiding the party towards becoming less doctrinaire and more pragmatic, so as to recover the Edwardian Liberal Party's breadth of appeal. The latter course had several attractions. Socialism could not come by stealth, if only because its ambitions for democratic change demanded full public cooperation. If the Labour Party could not be the vehicle of socialism, its continued access to power—together with the integrity of its leaders and of the political system—demanded the activists' re-education into the gradualist and pragmatic Liberal alignment that the party had in effect deserted in 1917–18. Since this was largely the direction that Wilson took in practice, he could have made a virtue of necessity, but he was disinclined to do so. Yet neither of Labour's two potential directions was feasible under so tactical a leader, given that a socialist party must educate the public at large, and that a neo-Liberal party must re-educate Labour's rank and file. Wilson's pragmatism seemed merely to consign the party to long-term decay, for Labour's largest share of the votes cast under his leadership (48% in 1966) never matched the Conservative votes of 1951, 1955, and 1959, and long-term social trends favoured the Conservatives.[43] His actual, though never overt, course was simply to play off Conservative mistakes and defend Attlee's inheritance without the Attlee governments' high-minded constitutionalist tone. It is difficult, for instance, to imagine Attlee's governments protecting their vulnerable seats by postponing the Parliamentary Boundary Commission's review, as Wilson's did in 1969, on the flimsy ground that local government

[42] Benn, *Diaries 1963–7*, 422–3 (7 June 1966); see also 436 (21 June 1966).
[43] See above, pp. 161–4, 200–1, 209–10.

was soon to be reorganized.[44] For all the similarities between Wilson's private and Gaitskell's overt objectives, Wilson's style of leadership, so different from Gaitskell's, soon disillusioned the Gaitskellites and eventually others too.

These prime ministers' varied and short-term impact on the cabinet between 1951 and 1970 should not conceal longer-term structural changes which elevated the prime minister so far above colleagues as to prompt suggestions in the 1960s that he was becoming 'presidential'. For more than a century the parties had been strengthening their hold on the electors, and hence their party leaders' hold on the country. We have seen how faster international travel enabled the prime minister to conduct a personal diplomacy which somewhat downgraded the Foreign Secretary; how the new mass media enabled him to impinge more directly on public opinion; and how by 1951 the cabinet had become a committee presiding over a complex network of subordinate committees.[45] Some of these committees consisted only of cabinet ministers, some included junior ministers, some included civil servants, and some consisted exclusively of civil servants. Some cabinet subcommittees were high-powered in their composition, and played a central role in formulating government policy. A secret so-called 'steering committee', for example, ensured in 1957–9 that the Macmillan government took full account of party attitudes when deciding on new policy priorities: it was a virtual inner cabinet.[46] In 1967 Wilson told the cabinet that matters could be brought up from subcommittees to full cabinet only with agreement from the subcommittee's chairman. The cabinet's committee structure extended the prime minister's patronage, given that he appointed the chairmen of committees which he could not chair himself, though in doing so he risked losing his grip on them and strengthening potential rivals. The entire structure was buttressed by the cabinet secretary's expanding machine; Churchill's dependence on Norman Brook as cabinet secretary was substantial, especially in the aftermath of his stroke in 1953, and the Cabinet Office staff grew from 186 in 1938 to 565 in 1970.[47]

The cabinet in these years was a flexible structure, partly because so secret. Its subcommittees' very existence was concealed, let alone their membership, for fear of obscuring who was answerable to parliament for what areas of policy. On some issues a prime minister might choose to do business through 'partial cabinets': Eden during the Suez crisis, for example, or Wilson in 1969 with trade union reform. On other issues—negotiations in 1961 for joining the EEC, for example—a prime minister might judge that only regular consultation of the full cabinet could keep it together. Throughout the 1950s and 1960s 'ministerial responsibility' (the cabinet minister's accountability to

[44] See the leader 'Shoddy and Dangerous', *T* (13 Nov. 1969), 9.

[45] For more on these points, see above, pp. 60, 72, 109, 412–13; and below, pp. 440, 462–3.

[46] M. Jarvis, *Conservative Governments, Morality and Social Change in Affluent Britain, 1957–64* (Manchester, 2005), 7.

[47] *BPF* (8th edn.), 310.

parliament for the work of his government department) was fully maintained, together with 'collective responsibility' (the corporate responsibility of the entire cabinet for the government's actions). Also in these years the opposition party's shadow cabinet was formalizing its membership, tightening party cohesion, and clarifying its members' responsibility for policy. What held both cabinet and shadow cabinet together, however, was less a constitutional doctrine, more the power of parliament. Colleagues loyal to their party and regularly facing vigorous parliamentary criticism had every reason to stick together, given that splits or failed policies threatened them all, electorally and in other ways.

2. A PRESTIGIOUS PARLIAMENT

At the heart of the political system lay the House of Commons. Its response to the bomb which destroyed it on 10 May 1941 had been simply to rebuild, not to reform, and the wartime coalition only temporarily interrupted its well-established adversarial mood and structure. The two dominant parties of government and opposition promoted through the adversary system a conflict of ideas, personalities, and values which was carried to the electorate at general elections occurring roughly every four years. Between 1945 and 1951 the Conservative Party exploited the disappointments and resentments inevitably accumulated by a reforming government operating in difficult times, and until the 1970s the two-party system entered a classic period comparable with the years between 1868 and 1914. In 1955, for the first time at a general election, every seat in the country was contested,[48] and the Liberal Party—with only six MPs returned at the general elections of 1951, 1955, and 1959—seemed doomed: the Conservatives would eat up its more individualist and traditionalist members, Labour would consume its collectivists and internationalists. The adversary structure was further advertised by the mounting importance of question time in the House of Commons. Held at a fixed time twice weekly from 1961, it was from this polarized situation that prime ministers rallied their troops against sniping from the opposition.

Britain's adversarial parliament rested securely on a simple-majority single-ballot electoral system purged in 1948 of the university seats and 'business' votes that by then seemed anomalous. There were 625 seats in the House of Commons in 1951 and thereafter 630 until 1974, but because the population was slowly increasing, the number of electors per seat continued on the escalating course it had followed since 1832, reaching 62,448 by 1970, a fifth higher than in 1945. With a little help in 1969 from enfranchising people between 18 and 21, the ratio of electors to population also continued its prolonged upward trend. The Boundary Commission helped to ensure that equal votes did not carry

[48] D. E. Butler, *The British General Election of 1955* (1955), 72.

precisely equal value: both Scotland and Wales received more seats in 1951 and 1971 than their populations would have justified, whereas England and Northern Ireland received fewer. This bias could help to determine national party fortunes; for example, without it Labour would not have been the largest party after the general election of February 1974.[49] The electoral system did not come under serious criticism until the late 1960s; critics then complained that it could not deliver seats in accordance with the rising support for a regionally dispersed Liberal Party, though no similar problem arose with the regionally more concentrated nationalist parties in Wales and Scotland. Whereas by 1970 the third and minor parties could win 11 per cent of the total vote, they could obtain only 2 per cent of the seats,[50] and many thought this too high a threshold to impose before parties stood an equal chance of winning representation. The campaign for proportional representation, which had originated with mid-Victorian Liberals, and was promoted from 1884 by the Proportional Representation Society, now began to take off, with the Society changing its name to Electoral Reform Society so as to avoid being identified with the list-based electoral systems which it did not favour.

The House of Commons, which occupied its rebuilt premises in 1950, became in some ways less representative between 1951 and 1970. Earlier in the century the Labour Party and trade unions drew extensively upon working-class talent for their leaders, but by 1951 this talent was increasingly drawn into public life indirectly through the meritocratic ladder that led through schools to university. Between the wars only 22 per cent of Labour MPs had enjoyed a university education, but 42 per cent from 1964, with Conservatives moving up from 59 to 70 per cent;[51] as the obverse of this, trade unionists by the 1960s were making careers within the trade union movement rather than through politics. The Conservatives, too, were becoming less representative, but not by losing working-class MPs because these had always been rare. Ray Mawby, MP for Totnes from 1955 to 1983, was the first Conservative MP to have been a shop steward and educated at a state school, and was seen by Labour as a class traitor.[52] It was at the opposite end of the social spectrum that the Conservatives after 1951 were losing MPs, from two social groups: the 'knights of the shire', and the middle-aged representatives of significant industries. For the latter, entry to parliament had not been the start of a career but acknowledgement that a successful career had already been pursued.

[49] The discrepancies were not large. For example, calculation from the statistics in *BPF* (8th edn.), 241, 348 shows that England in 1951 had 81.9% of UK population, 81.0% of seats; in 1971 82.9% of population, and in 1970 81.0% of seats. For 1974 see Birch in S. E. Finer (ed.), *Adversary Politics and Electoral Reform* (1975), 65, 68.

[50] D. E. Butler, *British General Elections since 1945* (Oxford, 1989), 72.

[51] S. A. Walkland (ed.), *House of Commons in the Twentieth Century* (Oxford, 1979), 99, 113.

[52] See obituaries, *T* (24 July 1990), 14; *DT* (24 July 1990), 19.

Women's progress was slow, for they had only 3.5 per cent of MPs in the 1950s, 4.4 per cent in the 1960s, and 3.8 per cent in the 1970s.[53] Because the House is a governmental assembly, its composition has never aimed precisely to mirror existing opinion in the short term, let alone in its membership precisely to reflect Britain's adult population in all its variety. It does, however, seek to combine its governmental role with providing government's critics with a platform. The proportion of MPs from the government party who were in post—by 1960, a sixth[54]—rose steadily with the twentieth-century increase in government's responsibilities. Opposition came primarily, not from backbenchers as a whole, but from the opposition party, mobilizing opinion after electoral defeat in the hope of winning next time. In these years at only three elections did this overturn actually occur—in 1951, 1964, and 1970—but the sanction on government is not what happens, but what may happen: the first two of these victories for the opposition party were precarious, and at all times government strategy is partly shaped by the opposition party's continuous counterminings.

Scrutiny of government was all the more needed because the bulk and complexity of legislation rose steadily between the 1920s and 1990s.[55] One lively student of politics, then in his mid-thirties, had a remedy: Bernard Crick's *Reform of Parliament* (1964) was the best known among several treatises then advocating parliamentary reform. Issued with a preface dated December 1963, it was nicely timed to catch the radical breeze which sent Labour into office in the following October. For Crick, Congress provided the expert and professional answer. House of Commons committees before the 1960s were not shaped to accumulate expertise: why not adopt the USA's committee-based, research-equipped approach? Crossman as Leader of the House in 1966 backed the idea of the specialist committee with enhanced powers of inquiry and publicity, but its drawbacks in the British context soon became apparent. Overcomplicating the government's already complex task, and cutting across parliament's party-oriented main line of communication with the electors, it soon ran into trouble from civil servants and cabinet ministers. Michael Stewart even claimed that the committees were unsocialist in so far as they divided the Labour government, limited government's powers, and rendered parliament inefficient. In May 1967 Benn's civil servants were not at all keen for him to be the first minister ever to expound departmental policy before a select committee.[56] That would not perhaps have mattered if the reform had not also

[53] Calculated from *BPF* (8th edn.), 261.

[54] Table 1.1 in R. Rose, 'The Making of Cabinet Ministers', in V. Herman and J. E. Alt (eds.), *Cabinet Studies: A Reader* (1975), 10.

[55] See A. Seldon's useful graph in Bogdanor (ed.), *British Constitution in Twentieth Century*, 160.

[56] Crossman, *Cabinet Diaries*, ii. 308 (11 Apr. 1967), for Stewart. Benn, *Diaries 1963–7*, 498 (11 May 1967).

threatened to generate a consensual non-party mood which would blunt the sharpness of the government's critics.

In his preface of September 1967 to the second edition Crick said that 'nearly everyone had a good word to say for Parliamentary reform' before Labour took power in October 1964, but he also noted that this in itself had 'caused a temporary ebb in reformist stocks', and made it all the more necessary to press the reforming case. By October 1968 Benn was alone among cabinet ministers in still favouring committees of this kind.[57] Another reforming proposal failed in 1968 for similar reasons: getting budgetary proposals discussed in a well-attended committee instead of in an ill-attended full House; the reform did indeed ensure closer scrutiny, but it took up too much parliamentary time to be replicated in 1969.[58] The House combined at least three roles: arena for criticizing the executive, but also reservoir of the talent needed to recruit the executive, and vehicle for mobilizing public consent behind the policies for which it answered to the electors. Crick's proposals might advance the first, but they threatened the second and third. Parliament was admittedly amateur, but in the best sense: more concerned to mobilize opinion right across the policy spectrum, intelligibly to the general public, than to cater for minority tastes by mounting detailed criticisms on specific issues.

More promising were smaller-scale evolutionary reforms. Because technical expertise was not the MP's main priority, the House of Commons library adapted only slowly from the role of country-house leisure facility to professional political information service, but the process now accelerated. Its staff grew from seven in 1945 to thirty by 1955 to fifty-four by 1970. In addition, MPs from 1969 received a secretarial allowance which by 1992 had grown into an 'office cost allowance' worth seven times as much in real terms.[59] Also strengthening parliament was the publication in 1969 of a forecast detailing public income and expenditure to 1973/4; this made it easier to see where the public finances were going.[60] On the other hand, parliament failed to enhance a change that would have built effectively upon its adversarial role. The entire debating procedure of the House of Commons was designed to maximize drama and impact, and it had sensibly enhanced the parliamentary question's power by developing its written dimension, which came into its own in the 1960s.[61] It had opened itself up to the press in the late eighteenth century, but it failed to capitalize on the parliamentary question's spoken version by allowing debates to be broadcast

[57] B. Crick, *The Reform of Parliament* (1st publ. 1964, 2nd edn. 1968), p. ix. For Benn see Crossman, *Cabinet Diaries*, iii. 219 (10 Oct. 1968).

[58] Crossman, *Cabinet Diaries*, iii. 73 (23 May 1968).

[59] For the library see Walkland (ed.), *House of Commons in the Twentieth Century*, 627, 631. For pay see P. Norton, *Does Parliament Matter?* (Hemel Hempstead, 1993), 20, adjusted for inflation using the ready reckoner in *TCBST* 712.

[60] H. Stephenson, 'Public Spending: Now the Chance for a Real Debate', *T* (5 Dec. 1969), 29.

[61] A. Seldon in Bogdanor (ed.), *British Constitution in Twentieth Century*, 173.

on radio or television. By comparison with other assemblies it was coy in this respect, and retained its club-like seclusion well beyond 1970.

It soon became clear that the reformers' case had been misleading in a further respect: it had exaggerated the decline in backbenchers' powers. At crucial points even before the 1960s, back-bench influence had been significant, especially (as in 1950–1) when government majorities were small. This happened again in 1964–6, and even with the government's larger majority after 1966 back-bench rebellions were frequent for lack of a Morrison to impose discipline. Even when a government's majority was large, parliament could intimidate the executive. Peter Rawlinson vividly recalled the fury of the opposition Eden encountered at the height of the Suez crisis: 'in few other national assemblies could the leader of a nation be confronted daily, and for weeks on end, by nearly three hundred shouting and jeering political opponents. That was what Anthony Eden had to endure.' Macmillan as prime minister was no novice, yet even in his heyday when a big House of Commons speech was imminent, he often vomited from nervousness, and so was careful to lunch alone before question time on Tuesdays and Thursdays.[62] There were also at least two new sources of back-bench influence in the mid- and late-1960s. First, non-party humanitarian issues: the 'permissive society' in its political dimension depended heavily on MPs' free votes.[63] But secondly, even on party issues back-bench influence could be important if unobtrusive; when informal channels of influence failed, backbenchers' automatic backing for front-bench positions could not be assumed. When an alliance of backbenchers on both sides of the House in April 1969 defeated front-bench proposals for House of Lords reform, The *Times* political correspondent claimed that 'looking back over nearly 90 years of Commons history, I can find no reasonably comparable backbench achievement'.[64]

By 1951 the House of Lords had become little more than an adjunct to the House of Commons. The Parliament Act (1949) reduced its delaying powers over non-fiscal legislation from two years to one. Benn's successful battle in 1963 to disclaim his peerage and remain in the House of Commons emphasized the Lords' subordination; in leading fourteen others to follow suit, he weakened the Lords' independent sources of talent. Yet the second chamber remained important. With a steadily rising average daily attendance, both in the number of its sitting days and in average length of sitting,[65] it now made itself increasingly useful primarily in two ways: through providing extra scrutiny for draft legislation and through enabling politicians still to pursue their craft when for whatever reason they could no longer stand for election. The House's

62 P. Rawlinson, *A Price Too High: An Autobiography* (1989), 68. Macmillan, *Winds of Change*, 41.
63 See below, p. 511.
64 David Wood, 'May it Please, My Lords', *T* (21 Apr. 1969), 8; cf. 11 (leader).
65 P. Norton (ed.), *Parliament in the 1980s* (1985), 108.

role in reinforcing public life with non-elected talent was enhanced in 1958 when the Conservative government, in a classic instance of reforming in order to preserve, introduced life peers and enabled women to become members. Between 1952 and 1968 the Conservative share of the House fell from 59 to 44 per cent, and given that for many years after 1964 the leaders of neither political party created any hereditary peers, the Conservative proportion of the regular attenders fell still more sharply.[66] By 1984 life peers contributed a quarter of the House's members, and a far larger proportion of its active and informed component. All in all, parliament's reforms in the 1950s and 1960s were piecemeal, gradual, and unflamboyant, yet cumulatively they were substantial, and help to explain how public Acts which in 1900 amounted to less than 200 pages could be implemented without undue fuss in 1974 when ten times as numerous.[67]

3. PLURALISTIC CENTRALISM

With a strong executive came a relatively powerful central-government structure, enhanced by two social changes launched in the late 1950s: a nationwide motorway system, and a national system of higher education.[68] Improving physical and electronic communications drew even southern Ireland, let alone Wales and Scotland, closer to England. The civil service, like all office-based structures, was growing fast in these years, accelerated by enlarged government ambitions. This was reflected, not in the size of the cabinet, which it was convenient to leave at about twenty after 1945, but in the number of paid government political posts, which rose from 81 in 1950 to 102 in 1970.[69] The Conservatives after 1951 retained many of the Attlee governments' economic and welfare structures, and after 1964 the Wilson governments added to them. The 1960s saw big increases in civil service numbers;[70] not until 1979 was the retreat sounded. Local-authority expenditure might absorb a rising share of gross national product, but it drew a rising share of its income from central-government grants, and in spreading out into provincial outposts, the central-government departments set up mini-Whitehalls nationwide. By the mid-1950s two-thirds of non-industrial civil servants worked outside London.[71]

Ministries changed significantly in relative size. Britain's reduced world role prompted amalgamations, and in a meritocratic age the Foreign Office's aristocratic flavour was out of fashion, especially with Labour governments; furthermore, as other ministries increasingly established their own international

[66] Bogdanor (ed.), *British Constitution in Twentieth Century*, 201, 203.

[67] M. Rush in Walkland (ed.), *House of Commons*, 73.

[68] See above, pp. 138–9, 360.

[69] *BPF* (8th edn.), 71.

[70] As G. Rippon complained, *HC Deb.* 29 Jan. 1968, cc. 885, 911.

[71] Willson, *Organization of British Central Government*, 37.

outposts, its distinctive role within the civil service was undermined. Its merger with the diplomatic service had begun in the Second World War, and in the 1960s the commercial sections integrated too. Labour was by no means alone in being wary of the Foreign Office. The Eden government entirely ignored its advice during the Suez crisis in 1956, and the British ambassador to the USSR almost resigned in protest.[72] The four ministries that covered overseas relations before 1947 (India Office, Dominions Office, Colonial Office, and Foreign Office) had by 1968 shrunk into one: the Foreign and Commonwealth Office. Decline also shrank British defence administration; whereas before 1946 the three service ministries were each represented in cabinet, thereafter a minister of defence spoke in cabinet for the entire area, and in 1964 the service ministries merged into a single Ministry of Defence, headed by a Secretary of State.

In welfare matters, by contrast, amalgamation stemmed from growth. The 1960s saw state welfare expanding fast, and (in an all-party trend) the creation of large ministries was expected both to curb the number of cabinet ministers and produce significant economies of scale. So the huge DHSS grew up in 1966–8 out of the various welfare ministries; 'Mintech' was created in 1964 to unite management of trade and industry; and the Wilson government created the Department of the Environment in 1970 from a merger between the Ministry of Housing and Local Government and the Ministry of Public Building and Works to manage housing, transport, and local government—a reform implemented by the Heath government. The trend towards big ministries culminated under the Heath government, but was declining before Labour returned to power in 1974. On the other hand, Labour's eagerness for government-prompted economic growth led it to pare down Treasury pretensions. Morrison had floated the idea of a counterbalancing 'Ministry for Economic Affairs' in his *Government and Parliament* (1954), and after 1964 the Wilson government set up the DEA, whose role and mood was to promote growth not curb expenditure.[73] The Treasury's power was further curbed in 1968 when the Civil Service Department assumed overall responsibility for managing the civil service. With zest for planning came the search for administrative talent, which chimed in well with the meritocratic mood of the time, and culminated in the Fulton report of 1968.[74] It sought to remove barriers within the civil service that were both vertical (between experts and non-experts) and horizontal (between ranks), and in 1971 the clerical, administrative, and executive grades were merged so as to produce a single career ladder. Women were increasingly colonizing the lower ranks in the civil service, but were slow to rise higher

[72] Nicolson, *Diaries and Letters, 1945–62*, 319 (16 Nov. 1956). Hennessy, *Whitehall*, 164–6, 168. For Sir William Hayter's near-resignation, see his obituary in *T* (30 Mar. 1995), 21.

[73] Morrison, *Government and Parliament*, 317. See also Benn, *Diaries 1963–7*, 25 (25 May 1963).

[74] For a convenient digest of its recommendations and the outcome see table 2.2 in G. Drewry and T. Butcher, *The Civil Service Today* (1st publ. 1988, 2nd edn. 1991), 52–3.

up; the first woman ambassador, Dame Barbara Salt, was not appointed till 1963.

British government opened up in the 1960s. Civil servants had long been professionally reticent because required to be politically neutral; the elected politician took responsibility for policy, and the civil servant must go along with that. From 1958, however, the 'fifty-year rule', opening government records to inspection after fifty years, was in operation, and in 1967 the time limit was cut to thirty years. The Wilson governments did much to open up British government. In his first term (1964–6) Wilson showed an almost American 'openness' to journalists.[75] His relations with them soon turned sour, but in his second term the government introduced the 'green paper', a device for publicizing draft legislation before government endorsed its details. It was, in Wilson's words, 'one of our major contributions to the concept of public participation in public decisions'[76]. In 1967 the Parliamentary Commissioner for Administration (colloquially known by his Swedish title 'ombudsman') was appointed to investigate, on instruction from parliament, cases of maladministration. Parliament's new select committees also made civil servants more visible, opening up the formative discussions on policy. Critics in the 1960s, influenced by European models, often recommended a more 'positive' role for British civil servants, but inappropriately in a country without statist traditions. The civil servant's role in Britain was primarily political and domestically diplomatic: to help negotiate his political masters through the UK's complex of semi-autonomous power centres. Governments were always electorally vulnerable, political fashions came and went, panaceas so often failed, so the British civil servant's mood was inevitably sceptical. Cynicism was not the reason, but pragmatism: the civil servant needed continuously to ease a delicate mechanism into working efficiently, and ensure the short-term effectiveness of governments under pressure.

If central government, despite its recent growth, was less powerful than at first sight, it seemed weaker still when viewed from beyond Whitehall. In 1968 two-thirds of the Glaswegians surveyed saw themselves as Scots and only 29 per cent as British; 69 per cent of the Welsh surveyed saw themselves as Welsh and only 15 per cent as British.[77] In 1966 the Red Dragon flag, symbol of the Free Wales Army, was carried through Dublin streets in the ceremonies marking the fiftieth anniversary of the Easter Rising.[78] Yet there

[75] For a good discussion see 'The Prime Minister and the Press', *O* (25 May 1969), 7.

[76] Wilson, *Labour Government 1964–1970*, 380.

[77] R. Rose, 'The United Kingdom as a Multi-National State' (University of Strathclyde Survey Research Centre Occasional Paper, 6, Glasgow, 1970), 10. I am most grateful to Professor Rose for giving me both his paper, and his book *Understanding the United Kingdom: The Territorial Dimension in Government* (1982), which on p. 14 presents figures for 1979.

[78] Obituary of Dennis Coslett, *Ind.* (21 May 2004), 35.

was no integrated Celtic consciousness outside England. It had eluded the late Victorian Liberal Party, for all its strength outside England, and was still more elusive after 1951 when there were only six Liberal MPs. Besides, nationalism is by definition preoccupied with the distinctive features of one nation, and the nationalisms of Scotland, Wales, and Northern Ireland sprang from contrasting impulses. England's relative size and prosperity ensured that internal migration undermined such Celtic solidarity as did exist. Many Irish-born immigrants chose England rather than Wales and Scotland; in their share of Scotland's total population, Irish-born inhabitants fell steadily with each decade after 1861 to only 2 per cent in 1961; as for Wales, only 2 per cent of its population in 1961–81 had been born in southern Ireland.[79]

Welsh and Scottish nationalism were in decline till the 1950s. It had long been widespread, though technically incorrect, to apply the word 'England' to the Tudor union between Wales and England. Still less correct had it been after 1707 to stretch the term to include Scotland, but the term 'North Britain' never caught on, and after 1800 the term 'England' was sometimes used even to include Ireland. Independence in 1922 had removed any Irish impetus behind devolutionary pressure. The UK's success, however precarious, in two world wars had emphasized the benefits of inter-national UK collaboration for larger purposes, as did the continued viability of empire and Commonwealth until the 1950s. The Labour Party's supersession of the Liberals in the 1920s advanced social-class alignments over religious and constitutional issues: Wales and Scotland were Labour's heartland, and the labour movement strengthened the links of both with England. Twentieth-century Labour embraced the majoritarian variant of fairness that results from redistributing wealth from the centre through taxation, nationalization, and public welfare, and felt diminishing sympathy with the locally based and fragmented democracy which elevates self-government above equality. The Council for Wales which Morrison devised in 1948 fed information to central government, but did not aim to lend Wales autonomy from Whitehall. Ten years later Attlee, when asked his view of Scottish and Welsh nationalism, was content to use only three words: 'out of date'.[80] Up to the 1970s and beyond, Labour and nationalism within the UK were not kindred spirits.

By the late 1950s all these discouragements to Scottish and Welsh nationalism were going into reverse: colonialism was in flight, the memory of shared wartime triumphs was fading, socialism was losing impetus, working-class consciousness was losing its edge, nationalism in northern Ireland was beginning to revive, and disillusion outside England with the Conservative government was as likely to take on a nationalist as a Labour guise. In 1951, as in 1901, the numbering of

[79] J. G. Kellas, *Modern Scotland: The Nation since 1870* (1968), 240. *BST* 573.
[80] Author's recollection; Attlee was addressing Oxford University's Labour Club, *c.*1959.

British monarchs proved controversial in Scotland, given that there had been no Elizabeth I as Queen of Scotland; when postboxes bearing the monogram 'ERII' were blown up it was quickly replaced by 'ER'.[81] By the 1970s nationalist consciousness within the UK had become strong enough to confine the term 'England' to the territory south of Hadrian's Wall and east of the Welsh border. The Welsh and Scottish Nationalist vote in British general elections rose steadily from 100,000 in 1959 to one million in October 1974, by which time there were three Plaid Cymru and eleven Scottish Nationalist MPs.[82] As for Northern Ireland, the Labour Party had never got established there, and even the Conservative Party's alliance with Ulster Unionism was somewhat tenuous. In the 1960s, however, Ulster Unionism was increasingly under challenge from an Irish nationalism, to which Labour was rather more sympathetic than were the Conservatives, yet the Conservative pursuit of middle opinion made them wary of backing the Unionists in all-out resistance. In the 1960s some began to wonder whether the phrase 'United Kingdom' might eventually become redundant.

The roots of Scottish nationalism were as much political as social: we have seen that the English migration to Scotland was unobtrusive and gradual, and that the decline of Gaelic had little political resonance.[83] In Wales, by contrast, nationalism fed on resentment at mounting interaction with the English: their 'second homes', the water piped from Wales to England, and the threat to the Welsh language posed by mingled populations. Saunders Lewis in 1962 claimed that restoring the Welsh language was possible 'only . . . through revolutionary methods', wanted it made 'impossible for the business of local and central government to continue without using Welsh', and felt that getting the Welsh language recognized in official documents should precede self-government, which might otherwise not come at all.[84] Plaid Cymru was strongest by 1970 in the least Anglicized areas: in north and west Wales, where Welsh was most widely spoken.[85] It was the language issue which provoked bombs from the Free Wales Army in the 1960s, the decade in which it was thought necessary to meet complaints by extending Welsh-language media provision.[86] The Prince of Wales had to be guarded closely, especially when spending a term at the University of Wales before his investiture.[87]

Since 1920 Northern Ireland had run its own affairs from its parliament at Stormont, and as long as no major abuses were exposed or discontent erupted, British governments of either party let well or ill alone. Although the

[81] Miller (ed.), *Anglo-Scottish Relations*, 24, 29, 31. [82] *BPF* (8th edn.), 236–8.

[83] See above, pp. 173–4. [84] Lewis, 'Fate of the Language', 140.

[85] D. E. Butler and M. Pinto-Duschinsky, *The British General Election of 1970* (1971), 402.

[86] K. O. Morgan, *Rebirth of a Nation: Wales 1880–1980* (Oxford, 1982), 384. Committee on the Future of Broadcasting, *Report* (Chairman Lord Annan, Cmnd. 6753, 1977), 412–15.

[87] Dimbleby, *Prince of Wales*, 120.

Conservatives' unionism aligned them with the Ulster Unionists, Conservative leaders felt no close affinity with them. Apart from Robin Chichester-Clark, chief Conservative spokesman on Northern Ireland in 1964–70, the Ulster Unionists between 1921 and 1970 contributed only one parliamentary secretary and three parliamentary private secretaries to Conservative governments. As for Wales and Scotland, British governments used timely concession to deflate nationalist resentments. From 1939 St Andrew's House in Edinburgh accommodated Scottish administrative departments. Churchill considerably strengthened the Scottish team in his government of 1951–5. With the creation in 1962 of the Scottish Development Department, Scotland acquired a force for extending and coordinating economic and infrastructure planning well before Labour created the DEA. By the 1950s Wales, too, was being treated as a single administrative region; in 1957 it acquired a minister of state, and in 1964 he was promoted to Secretary of State within the cabinet.

When the union came under challenge, there were two ways of preserving it. The 'unionist' tradition, making only cosmetic concessions, was implicitly taken for granted by Labour; Conservatives from the 1880s took up the same position but with more noise, and were still reaping dividends in the 1950s and 1960s from having done so. The alternative strategy—extending beyond administrative decentralization to devolution or even federalism—could have enlisted the anti-statist strain within the Conservative Party if it had not been so corporatist in its outlook during these years. Conservatives could then have simultaneously mopped up much of the sentiment fuelling Welsh and Scottish nationalism while strengthening their impact outside England. But Heath as Conservative leader went no further than suggesting in 1968 that Scotland might welcome its own elected assembly to consider specifically Scottish matters,[88] and left matters there.

Would a federal settlement have been feasible? There were at least two obstacles. In any variant of federalism with only four (Northern Irish, Scottish, Welsh and English) components, England's superiority in wealth, population, and area would have brought undue dominance. On the other hand, if federation arrived in such a way as to bring a rough equipollence to Wales, Scotland, Northern Ireland, and the components of an English heptarchy, the necessary English regional loyalties would have been lacking because the medieval monarchy had done its job too well. In the 1950s and 1960s, as in the eleventh century, England 'was full of local diversity' and yet 'remarkably homogeneous' and 'one of the most uniform political entities' in Europe.[89] And as in thirteenth- and fourteenth-century England, 'the range of liberties in the hands of the king's subjects was immense' despite the absence of any clear distinction between

[88] *T* (20 May 1968), 3.
[89] R. Bartlett, *England under the Norman and Angevin Kings 1075–1225* (Oxford, 2000), 156.

local and central government.[90] Wessex and the Midlands possessed some sort of identity, but their frontiers were vague, and there were important internal divisions; many Cornishmen, for instance were loyal to Cornwall, not to Wessex; nor would Nottingham ever have conceded regional primacy to Birmingham. Any identity the south-east might possess was swamped by London in its midst; and the Pennines cut through the northern region. There were important north–south cultural divides even within Wales and Scotland, and a significant minority of Northern Ireland's population questioned the Province's very legitimacy. Devolutionary sentiment was never strong enough within England for the Liberals to rise beyond their third-party status after 1918, let alone for federalism to be practicable.

To say that Britain lacked tightly nucleated regional identities in the 1950s and 1960s is not at all to say that Britain was politically, let alone culturally, uniform. In the late 1960s the upper classes were over-represented in the south-east of England, which also surpassed the rest in levels of education and ownership of consumer durables.[91] Relative deprivation explains much of the striking continuity in the geographical basis of support between the Edwardian Liberal Party and the twentieth-century Labour Party. This ongoing continuity owed much, though not everything, to the geographical pattern of transfer payments, whereby tax revenue from the relatively prosperous south-east and Midlands in the 1960s funded the higher level of welfare expenditure required in East Anglia, the north, and areas outside England.[92] Twentieth-century regional discrepancies in levels of unemployment were tenacious, and we have seen how all-party attitudes to local-authority housing and regional employment policy in the 1960s deterred the unemployed from moving.[93] In 1969 Crossman impatiently dismissed Wilson's insistence on 'fantastically expensive' attempts to bring work to West Cumberland when 'a few thousand people from Cumberland should move South where there is work'.[94]

The absence from England after 1951 of strong regional political loyalties was the more surprising given that administrative and political pressures all favoured regionalism. The shift to road transport after 1945, and the resulting patterns of settlement, weakened traditional local-government identities. The larger structures fostered by nationalization, planning, and the fair allocation of public welfare seemed to demand bigger authorities, regional in nature; furthermore, a Labour Party which in the first half of the century had moved from municipalism to statism was unobtrusively providing them. So the new towns had not been placed under the local authorities but under the Ministry of Housing, the health service was entrusted to regional rather than local-government

[90] Prestwich, *Plantagenet England*, 68; see also 66.
[91] Townsend, *Poverty in UK*, 552–3.
[92] Table 3.5 in Birch, *Political Integration and Disintegration*, 43.
[93] See above, pp. 161–2, 307.
[94] *Cabinet Diaries*, iii. 538 (26 June 1969).

authorities, it was the Ministry of Transport which built the motorways, and it was through regional planning boards and councils that the Wilson government's National Plan of 1965 was designed to operate. Control over hospitals, roads, sewerage, water, public transport, health services, electricity, and gas was entrusted increasingly to relatively remote and impersonal regional authorities, leaving as substantial items for local-government control only highways, schools, and housing.[95] Furthermore, if Britain had incurred nuclear attack in the 1960s, government would have devolved to twelve regional supremos whose English regions mirrored the Anglo-Saxon kingdoms.[96] There were moves to consolidate regional structures. Government statisticians officially recognized the existence of 'conurbations' in 1951: Greater London, West Midlands, south-east Lancashire, west Yorkshire, Merseyside, and Tyneside.[97] The London Government Act (1963) from 1965 drew together suburbs and inner city into a Greater London Council much larger than the London County Council, which it superseded. For a local authority the Maud Commission thought a population between 250,000 and a million organizationally the most convenient, and 'also appropriate on democratic grounds'. Its recommendations, which fed into the local-government boundary reforms implemented in 1974, reflected its belief that the existing 'local government areas do not fit the pattern of life and work in modern England'. The revised areas, it insisted, 'must be based upon the interdependence of town and country'.[98] Also compatible with larger units was the growing self-consciousness and integration of local-government officials, moving as they were from the 1930s towards a national scheme for pay, promotion, and conditions of employment.[99]

Yet England was both too uniform and too fragmented for regionalism to flourish: the weakness of regional identity reflected the strength not just of central government, but of subregional loyalties. The latter included the county, with which cricketing teams and regiments identified, and which was still central to local government. Its components remained remarkably stable between 1951 and 1969: administrative counties excluding London diminished from 61 to 58, non-county boroughs from 309 to 259, urban districts from 572 to 522, rural districts from 475 to 469, while parish councils rose from 7,300 to 7,500. Cities sufficiently substantial and self-conscious were carved out of the counties as county boroughs, and their numbers remained stable at 83.[100] The stability in the number of rural local-government authorities shows how successfully

[95] For a good discussion see R. Jackman in M. Loughlin *et al.* (eds.), *Half a Century of Municipal Decline 1935–1985* (1985), 148, 153, 157.

[96] *DT* (7 Aug. 1998), 4.

[97] *BST* 328–9.

[98] Royal Commission on Local Government in England 1966–1969, i. *Report* (Chairman Lord Redcliffe-Maud, Cmd. 4040, n.d.), 73, 2, 3.

[99] P. G. Richards, *The Reformed Local Government System* (1st publ. 1973, 3rd edn. 1978), 135–7.

[100] Table 1 in H. V. Wiseman (ed.), *Local Government in England 1958–69* (1970), 11.

they held their ground in an urbanizing society. The UK's pockmarked and irregular pattern of county and borough, which to planners seemed so untidy, attracted tenacious loyalty. Local-government reform suffered in these years from the long-running squabbles and vested interests accumulating round each type of local authority, each entrenched behind its own nationwide association.

These little local authorities were being drawn not into intermediate regional structures but into a centralized framework of mounting power. The local authorities were being asked, especially from the 1960s, to do more—most notably on welfare and education. The taxes to fund their new roles were collected centrally and then distributed as grants-in-aid for approved purposes; their share of total local-government expenditure in England and Wales rose from a quarter in 1950 to more than a third in 1970.[101] This enhanced the power of central government to enforce uniform standards, as well as its moral right to control local-authority expenditure. In its share of total public expenditure, local-government expenditure more than doubled in the twenty years after the war, and by the late 1960s accounted for more than a quarter of the whole.[102] By the mid-1960s a third of local-authority income came from rates, more than a third from central-government grants, and more than a quarter from charges for services.[103] So variegated was the English landscape that the units of loyalty could be smaller still: John Betjeman's England, for example, 'had always been divided into hundreds of areas, each with a fiercely different regional character', and he took pleasure in the distinctiveness of 'old Berks' country and of Southend within Essex.[104] Many took the same view of Hull within Yorkshire or Exmoor within Somerset. Parliamentary constituencies, too, were popular enough as units to reinforce the tenacity of the simple-majority electoral system.

The defence of liberty therefore owed much to the localism of British culture and public life, the tenacity of local-government institutions, and a richly variegated landscape; given such a context, most in the UK found Protestant enthusiasm in Northern Ireland for 'the union' rather puzzling, even slightly disreputable. Complexity was compounded when regional loyalties within the UK were cross-cut by the many pressure groups with which government, whether corporatist in outlook or not, felt obliged to cooperate. Acronyms proliferated in British life, symbolizing the prevalence of voluntary mobilization and interaction with government. In the 1950s and 1960s the two multi-national states, USA and UK, were held together very differently: the USA overtly endorsed localism through its federal structure, informally complemented by a strongly integrating culture; the UK, formally centralist,

[101] *BPF* (8th edn.), 474. [102] Wiseman (ed.), *Local Government*, 12.
[103] There is a good table in Loughlin *et al.* (eds.), *Municipal Decline*, 166.
[104] C. Lycett Green in her edn. of Betjeman, *Letters*, ii. 445.

in practice acquiesced in local diversity. Liberty's informal defence within the UK owed much to cultural rather than institutional factors, most notably to the weakness of statist attitudes: this outlook reflected the religious pluralism that the Reformation had released, together with parliament's seventeenth-century triumph over the monarchy. The two-party system's gradual growth then ensured liberty's defence through an adversarial parliamentary structure. A sequence of formal documents from Magna Carta onwards lent force to British pluralism, but it owed more to the informal pluralistic culture prevailing at several levels—especially within the British political and social elite, and within the parliamentary and judicial system.

Where a pluralist structure cannot defend liberty informally, legal safeguards become necessary, and the USA resorted to them more often than the UK. Cultural rather than institutional mechanisms ensured the major victory for pluralism that the abolition of identity cards in Britain entailed in 1951. Introduced for wartime reasons without significant controversy in 1939, their advent reflected the war's unprecedented intrusions on privacy and civil liberties. The identity card lingered on after 1945, and 235 people were convicted in 1951 under the National Registration Act.[105] However, enough people saw them as un-English to get them abolished. Harry Willcock, a Yorkshire urban district councillor and Liberal Party candidate, was stopped by the police when driving in Hornsey; when asked for his card he refused, and in the lawsuit *Willcock* v *Muckle*, his refusal was endorsed. The cultural outlook that generated conduct like Willcock's helps to explain how in the 1950s UK anti-Communism never acquired the USA's McCarthyite tone,[106] for all the USA's libertarian constitutionalism. Yet British libertarians needed to be watchful, especially when state and medical power were allied with professional self-interest. This somewhat sinister combination explains the death of Ronald Maddison, the 20-year-old RAF engineer who volunteered in a programme of defence research at Porton Down, and died in 1953 from exposure to the nerve gas sarin. 15,000 British and 18,000 Australasian servicemen were present during UK nuclear weapon tests, some of them only 25 miles from the explosions; Australasian governments later pensioned those involved, given that cancer's incidence was higher among those involved, and genetic disorders in their families. Told of radiation's genetic effects in November 1955, Eden—far from callous by temperament—had endorsed the memorandum 'a pity, but we cannot help it'.[107]

105 <http://www.statewatch.org/news/2003/jul/26ukid.htm>, consulted 13 Mar. 2005. See also A. W. Bradley, 'Why National Registration Had to Go: The Judges' Contribution', *Public Administration* (1987), 209–10.

106 J. Mahoney, 'Civil Liberties in Britain during the Cold War' (Cambridge Ph.D. thesis 1989), 321–2, 334.

107 Broad, *Conscription in Britain*, 208–9. For Maddison, see Hickman, *Call-Up*, 257.

Overseas influences from 1951 encouraged in Britain a more overt and formalized preoccupation with civil rights, partly in the hope of warding off Nazi horrors. In that year Britain ratified the European Convention on Human Rights (1950), implemented within ratifying countries in 1953, and in 1966 Jenkins as Home Secretary for the first time enabled British litigants to appeal to the European Court of Human Rights. In the 1950s British law reformers, most notably Thomas Sargant, were prominent in nourishing international concern about prisoners' rights. As secretary during the first twenty-five years of the human-rights organization Justice from its foundation in 1957, he and others collaborated with the BBC in producing the influential television series *Rough Justice*. It was the young barrister Peter Benenson who encouraged Sargant in 1956 to set up an all-party group of lawyers which could monitor trials in South Africa and Hungary. Benenson went on to found Amnesty International, publicized through his 'Appeal for Amnesty' in the *Observer* on 28 May 1961, to defend 'prisoners of conscience' worldwide.[108] The 1960s carried the formal and legal defence of civil liberties rather further. 'The concept is on everyone's lips', wrote Crick in 1964; he thought it 'strange to think' that there had been no comprehensive British book on the subject until Harry Street's *Freedom, the Individual and the Law* (1963).[109] The Labour Party, pursuing a classless yet radical image in the hope of pre-empting Liberal revival, was moving on to libertarian territory. This shift in priorities was nourished by the growing disillusion with British political institutions and a consequential openness to overseas ideas—to Swedish precedents for open government, for example.

By the late 1960s computers, the crowdedness of modern living, and growing media intrusiveness had begun to threaten a privacy that was increasingly prized because growing more scarce. Lawyers had not hitherto seen this as a major concern, if only because respect for privacy had been so instinctive within British culture. When introducing Britain's first 'Right of Privacy Bill' in 1961 Lord Mancroft tried to balance the defence of privacy against the people's right to know. In 1968 *The Times* noted the paradox inherent in the fact that the technical complexity of modern society 'centralizes decision-making but spreads the desire to make decisions'.[110] Politicians and lawyers seeking to defend a right to privacy found themselves drawing together very scattered and inadequate legal provisions to counteract the growing integration and accessibility of personal data. The nightmare of Orwell's *1984* loomed over parliament's debates on privacy in 1967–9. Movements seeking justice for ethnic minorities, women, and Irish Catholics in Northern Ireland became powerful, and their libertarian concerns spread in the 1970s to ever wider

[108] 'Peter Benenson', *Ind.* (28 Feb. 2005), 34.

[109] B. Crick, *Reform of Parliament* (1964 edn.), 182.

[110] *T* (27 May 1968), 9 (leader).

groups: homosexuals, battered wives, hospital patients, armed services' rank and file, children, and the inmates of any large institution.

Outside the monarchy, it was in its judicial system that the British state in 1951 seemed at its most mystical and remote. The system was distanced from the public by its strange ceremonial and attire, as well as by restraints on how far judges could appear on radio or television.[111] Operating through its inward-looking collegial institutions and stylized language, and with gaolers and even hangmen as its agents, it inspired something close to awe, whereas the lawbreaker seemed glamorous to only limited social groups. None the less, the police and prison service were slowly slipping in status. Between 1950 and 1970 total police strength in England and Wales rose by nearly half,[112] yet to cope with escalating crime the police had to shed some of their street-based functions to traffic wardens (introduced in 1960). Increasingly important, too, were commercial security firms; their Scandinavian pedigree went back to 1901 and their British pedigree to 'Night Watch Services' of 1935, renamed Night Guards Limited in 1939, then Securicor in 1951.[113] It was Securicor which pioneered the modern British guard company, and it eventually absorbed the Armoured Car company, modelled on the American cash-transport companies and launched in 1955. When De La Rue formed Security Express in 1960, and Group 4 Total Security (formerly Factoryguards, of Swedish parentage) expanded to London from the north-west of England, the three companies henceforth leading the British field were in place.[114] The uniformed, goggled, and truncheoned private security guard soon became a familiar sight, and by 1970 private-security organizations controlled nearly 13,000 men with more than 1,000 armoured cars.[115]

Specialization and a professionalism of sorts within the police force opened up a gulf between police and public. The public sometimes even identified with the criminal rather than with the police: with the burglar Alfred Hinds, for example, who became sufficiently versed in the law to defend himself in his frequent court appearances after 1953, and acquired a Robin Hood image; or with the train robber on 8 August 1963, 'Buster' Edwards, who acquired a rather similar image, and was subject of the film *Buster* (1988). Several corruption cases in the late 1950s distanced police from public, and in 1964 prompted a reformed system for investigating complaints.[116] The influential image of George Dixon of Dock Green, first projected in the film *The Blue Lamp* in 1950 and carried forward into a long-running television series, grew

[111] For Kilmuir's rules on this see D. Pannick, *Judges* (Oxford, 1987), 173–4.

[112] *Annual Abstract of Statistics 1938–1950*, 58; *1976*, 92.

[113] See <www.g4s.com/home/about/history/history-1950-2000.htm> (consulted 15 Apr. 2006), for valuable chronology.

[114] H. Draper, *Private Police* (Harmondsworth, 1978), 19–20.

[115] *G* (4 Mar. 1970), 13. See also *O* (6 Dec. 1970), 9.

[116] Morris, *Crime and Criminal Justice*, 62, provides a useful discussion.

increasingly out of date. The police resorted to radio-equipped 'Panda' cars, some even to helicopters. The serial *Z Cars*, set (with local police collaboration) in Liverpool where Panda cars had first been introduced, was launched in 1962 and conveyed a much less bland image. With the terrorism of the 1970s even this seemed tame, and dramas like *The Sweeney* and the American cop series *Starsky and Hutch* seemed more appropriate, portraying the police as hard-bitten and glamorous adventurers, hard-drinking and earthy in their language.[117]

The prison's image was not improving. The average daily number of convicted prisoners in England and Wales rose by 37 per cent between 1950 and 1970, from 0.43 to 0.53 per thousand population,[118] and the idea of imprisoning more was popular enough for both parties to embrace it. With informed opinion, though, the system was falling into discredit. For all its harshness, the Victorian prison system had at least been driven by the belief that it could curb crime or cure the criminal, or both; no such belief could survive close investigation of mid-twentieth century British prisons. In 1953 nearly half of the men assigned prison sentences had been imprisoned at least once before, not to mention reoffending former prisoners so far unconvicted.[119] As reformatories, prisons were clearly ineffective, and the trade unions ensured that prisoners could undertake only monotonous work;[120] understaffing ensured that even that was available for only an average of twenty-one hours a week, and shortage of prison accommodation ensured that more than a tenth of prisoners in England and Wales were sleeping three in a cell.[121] In the 1950s the Home Office backed the Morrises in their research on Pentonville prison, yet its prison officers' grumbling determination to prevent change obstructed them. The officers showed a 'despairing cynicism' about prisoners, who received minimal training, let alone rehabilitation. The Victorian bifurcation of the prison between the two cultures of improvers and improved had by the 1950s degenerated into something close to a bifurcated single culture: the prison officer as respectable artisan had virtually disappeared, and bad language pervaded both sides of the continuing divide between prisoner and custodian. Warders could preserve discipline only on the surface. Serving his prison term in 1954–5, Peter Wildeblood later vividly recalled the 'air . . . buzzing with ventriloquial conversations' in the prison workshops, with the older prisoners often removing their false teeth so as the better to communicate with fellow-prisoners unobserved.[122] Short-term order-keeping problems had become the

[117] For a useful discussion see P. F. Turner, 'The Presentation of the Police in English Fictional Television Series: 1954–1984' (Bristol M.Phil. thesis, 1988), 17–18, 22–3, 56, 62.

[118] Population figures for 1950 from *Annual Abstract of Statistics 1938–50*, 7, prisoner figures from *1952*, 63; 1970 figures from *1976*, 7, 99.

[119] C. H. Rolph, 'Prisons and Prisoners', *NS* (2 Feb. 1957), 136.

[120] *HC Deb.* 13 Mar. 1957, cc. 1152, 1180.

[121] *HC Deb.* 13 Mar. 1957, cc. 1143, 1180.

[122] Wildeblood, *Against the Law*, 118–19.

prime concern of the Prison Officers' Association, if only because prisons were pervaded by a continuous undertow of violence between prisoners. And because prisons were not matching growing standards of comfort elsewhere, most notably in sanitation, the prisoners' degradation was compounded.[123] Dangerous prisoners had of course to be locked up, but all hope seemed now to have abandoned these grim fortresses.

4. CONSERVATIVES IN THE MIDDLE

British political pluralism involved policies forcing themselves on the politicians for public discussion, rank ordering, and refinement before being implemented (if adopted) by the administrators. Pressure groups were a major source of ideas, for what eventually came to be known as 'civil society' was already richly developed in Britain in 1951. Volunteering took place not just at the level of practical action: it was integral to advancement in public life and to minority groups' full integration into British society, and was often rewarded through the honours system. Royal commissions and departmental committees were frequently employed to collect evidence from voluntary bodies,[124] and were often themselves recruited from the government's central register of the so-called 'great and good'.[125] But in the UK's system of adversarial parliamentary party government, operating through a simple-majority electoral system, the main channel for voluntarist influence lay through the Labour and Conservative parties, and not through non-party legislative committees or civil servants. Party was integral to the House of Commons: 'bone of its bone, and breath of its breath', as Bagehot had long ago pointed out.[126] Each party's relationship with voluntarism was distinctive, and like other British political institutions after 1951 each disliked change. But both parties disliked the rival party even more, and because each competed for votes, each continuously sought new routes to the electors—hence their flexibility on policy and structure.

Between 1945 and the mid-1970s there were three possible strategies for the Liberal Party: the centre-party strategy of Clement Davies (leader from 1945 to 1956); the attempt under Jo Grimond (1956–67) to create a non-socialist but radical opposition to the Conservatives, with a good chance of profiting from

[123] Morris, *Pentonville*, 101, 183, 199, 215, 240, 255, 257, 258, 262.

[124] Those from 1945 to 1974 are tabulated in T. J. Cartwright, *Royal Commissions and Departmental Committees in Britain: A Case-Study in Institutional Adaptiveness and Public Participation in Government* (1975), 240–61.

[125] P. Hennessy, *The Great and the Good: An Inquiry into the British Establishment* (Policy Studies Institute report 654, Mar. 1986), 19.

[126] W. Bagehot, 'The English Constitution' (2nd edn. 1872), in W. Bagehot, *Collected Works*, ed. N. St John-Stevas, v (1974), 295.

a Labour split; and the attempt under Jeremy Thorpe (1967–76) to present the Liberals as sole radical alternative to two allegedly conservative parties, Labour and Conservative. The first strategy was frustrated by the fact that both Labour and Conservatives homed in on the centre ground, the second by Labour's failure to split. As witness to the Liberal Party's uncertain destiny, Lloyd George's son Gwilym became minister of food in the Conservative government of 1951, whereas his daughter Megan moved leftwards in 1955, and in 1957 became a Labour MP. Because the Liberals at the general election of 1955 put up candidates in only 110 seats they won only 2.5 per cent of the votes cast, and did not advance on their six MPs of 1951. The party seemed doomed, but Churchill, in making overtures to the Liberals in 1950–1, seems to have been aiming for a working alliance between two anti-socialist parties. Much Liberal individualist opinion had already moved rightwards, and as late as 1959 thirty-four Conservative supporters included the word 'Liberal' in their party label; not till 1966 did the last prewar 'National Liberal' leave parliament. Socialism was widely thought to threaten liberty, and when Churchill invited Clement Davies to join his cabinet in 1951, Davies wanted to accept, but his party required proportional representation as the condition of his joining, and that Churchill could not deliver.[127]

The Conservatives in 1951 won fewer votes but more seats than Labour, and never in the 1950s won more than half the votes cast: their strength lay in their vote holding up better than Labour's. Hence their attraction to centrist policies: these might win waverers by scotching Labour-fomented fears that the National Government's unpopular policies of the 1930s would return. Conservatives could then hope to eat up the centrist Liberals, and keep Labour on the run. Churchill labelled this strategy as 'houses, red meat, and not getting scuppered';[128] he would ensure that Macmillan got his housing programme funded, just as he would back his minister of labour, Walter Monckton, in industrial appeasement. 'Walter, you're handling this all wrong', he told Monckton during a strike. 'You should give them the money. I can't have strikes.'[129] When viewed at close quarters, the parties diverged far less on policy than outsiders realized. Two diarists in October 1951 saw how things were going: Crossman noted that Churchill in forming his cabinet had kept out 'the real free enterprisers and deflationists'; Robert Hall, Director of the Cabinet Office's economic section, thought 'one might almost say that Labour would like to conceal pro-Capitalist measures under a cloak of

[127] Bonham Carter, *Daring to Hope*, 88, 90, 105 n. 1 (Davies). See also D. E. Butler, '1945–1977', in D. E. Butler (ed.), *Coalitions in British Politics* (London and Basingstoke, 1978), 96.

[128] As Churchill put it to Jock Colville shortly before the general election of 1951, quoted in A. Seldon, *Churchill's Indian Summer: The Conservative Government 1951–55* (1981), 30.

[129] As reported by Monckton in Benn, *Diaries 1940–62*, 220 (15 Dec. 1956).

anti-Capitalism and the Tories to conceal anti-Labour measures under a cloak of benevolence'.[130]

This shared ground led *The Economist* facetiously to invent a composite Chancellor, 'Mr Butskell' (a merger between Conservative Chancellor of the Exchequer and Labour's shadow Chancellor). But the idea that 'Butskellite' policy in the 1950s reflected an unusual 'consensus' in British politics both misrepresents what happened at the time and misunderstands the British adversarial two-party system. The latter assumes that at any one time there is wide divergence in style, strategy, mood, and personality between the government and opposition parties, and that this may even generate personal distaste between the two front benches. But the system has the effect of producing 'governmental' parties, whether in or out of power, and assumes that on policy the party leaders will usually edge their parties towards the centre. The system would be unworkable if both parties committed themselves to policies markedly different: policy would then be discontinuous if the parties alternated in power, and unstable if they did not. Between 1951 and 1979, as between 1868 and 1914, there were two mature 'governmental' parties in government and opposition, quite close to one another on policy.

Yet government and opposition are not divided solely by policy. Labour and Conservative might agree to use the budget for a broadly Keynesian management of the 'mixed' economy, and steadily to increase welfare expenditure, but consensus here did not preclude major divergence in presentation, tactics, and elsewhere even on policy: on the handling of the Suez crisis, for example; on the Rent Act of 1957; or on the role of 'physical' planning. The two parties diverged markedly too in their mood and aspirations: whereas Labour still claimed to think capitalism outmoded and a permanent Labour electoral majority eventually inevitable, the Conservatives hoped for and eventually secured a pan-class anti-socialist electoral majority. Conservatives saw themselves as in the front line for defending British democratic values against Russian Communism, in which they thought Labour would ultimately acquiesce. If working-class extremists could be fobbed off with industrial conciliation at home, if decolonization could be brought off in time, if reliable non-Marxist leaders could be eased into key positions in the successor states, and if American forces could be retained in Europe, then Krushchev's prediction of 1956—'history is on our side. We will bury you'—might be falsified. As for the gulf between far-left Labour and far-right Conservative, that was wide indeed, not to mention the element of personal distaste that often shaped relations between party leaders

[130] Crossman, *Backbench Diaries*, 30 (31 Oct. 1951). A. Cairncross (ed.), *The Robert Hall Diaries 1947–53* (1989), 177 (31 Oct. 1951).

(between Gaitskell and Macmillan,[131] for example, or later between Heath and Wilson). In the early 1950s there were also important differences between the parliamentary parties in language, class attitudes, and even dress. In 1959 Julian Critchley (a Conservative MP who unwisely sported suede shoes) recalled that 'you could tell a Tory just by looking at him': well suited, Trumper's haircut, cream silk shirt, Brigade or Old Etonian tie,[132] whereas Labour's uniform was deliberately casual.

Because the Conservative Party does not instinctively welcome change, and because it is easier to disagree about the direction of change than about how to prevent it, unity came more easily to Conservatives than to Labour. Conservatives had of course split famously in the past, most notably during the Corn Law crisis of 1846 and in the tariff reform controversy of 1903–5, but by the 1930s Conservative leaders had learnt lessons from those splits and were keen to prevent their recurrence and to welcome refugees from splits in other parties. Conservative Party structure helped in this because it did not formally restrain the leader's powers; also helpful was the Conservative distaste for doctrinaire policies or even for any precise policy at all. Conservative Party activists were relatively harmonious in social background, with no Conservative equivalent of Labour's need to yoke together a traditionalist working class and a progressive middle class. Furthermore, by identifying with established institutions, the party could informally capitalize among all classes upon the routine celebrations of the national and family life cycle, and could also (in a decade of attenuated but persisting deference) attract the many electors who relished following their social superiors. Two of the three street urchins whom Bert Hardy famously photographed as astonished observers of togged-up Harrovian boys outside Lord's in 1937 later became enthusiastic Conservatives.[133]

The middle classes in the late 1950s were much more united behind the Conservatives than was the working class behind Labour.[134] Anyone holding a responsible post in the City in the late 1950s would have been prudent to conceal such socialist views as he possessed,[135] and the party readily attracted those who socially were rising or hoping to rise. We have seen[136] that the middle classes were a growth area: given mounting affluence and an expanded service sector, more people were rising than falling, and the falling were even more likely to retain their Conservative views than the rising were likely to acquire them.[137] Encouraging owner-occupation helped the party continuously to strengthen

[131] See e.g. Williams, *Gaitskell*, 312–13. Jenkins in W. T. Rodgers (ed.), *Gaitskell*, 124. Butler, *Art of the Possible*, 160.

[132] Paxman, *Friends*, 74.

[133] *T* (10 Apr. 1993), 2.

[134] Abrams and Rose, *Must Labour Lose?*, 76.

[135] Ferris, *The City*, 8.

[136] See above, pp. 162–4, 209.

[137] Butler and Stokes, *Political Change in Britain* (2nd edn.), 180–1. McKenzie and Silver, *Angels in Marble*, 97.

its electoral grip on the suburbs at a time when Labour's heartlands where shrinking, while simultaneously realizing the Conservative aim of dispersing power. The more the middle classes predominated in a district, the more likely it was that working-class people living there would also vote Conservative.[138] Tax-cutting policies also helped the Conservatives, given that inflation and mounting affluence had for some time been extending eligibility for income tax. At the same time the spread of public welfare was eroding the personal insecurity that had aligned working-class people behind Labour. 'The simple fact is', said a prominent Labour politician, commenting on the 1959 election result, 'that the Tories identified themselves with the new working class rather better than we did.'[139]

Already by 1955 the Conservatives were attracting at least a quarter of the trade unionists who told pollsters of their party preference,[140] yet the party's lack of an institutional link ensured that only 34 of its 623 candidates were trade unionists. Labour leaders, like the Liberals before them, liked claiming that intelligent working people voted only on the left, but at this time working-class Conservatism owed more to relatively independent circumstances than to being dim. Furthermore, the trade unions were beginning to lose the self-discipline acquired under Bevin and Citrine, thereby unintentionally building up a prize long-term Conservative electoral asset: trade union scapegoats. The ASLEF strike in May 1955, the first postwar national strike seriously to inconvenience the public, marked the end of Monckton's appeasing successes, and in 1958 the TGWU's challenge to government and management in the bus strike seemed to disrupt the organic vision of society then widely held at every social level. By the early 1960s hostility to trade union power was strong even among Labour voters.[141] To all these assets the Conservatives added an assumed competence in foreign policy, a reputation readily cultivated under leaders such as Churchill, Eden, and Macmillan. Viewed objectively, Labour's anti-Communism was more formidable than the Conservatives', but for tactical reasons it had to be less overt, so the Conservative stance was electorally more profitable.

Why, then, did the Suez crisis of 1956 harm the Conservatives so little? A party's electoral successes can flow as much from its leaders' skilful footwork as from deeper-running and long-term tendencies, and sometimes it profits as much from its opponents' weaknesses as from its own strengths. Wilson admired the panache with which Macmillan rescued his party: he at once

[138] Willmott and Young, *Family and Class*, 115.

[139] P. Gordon Walker, quoted in Sampson, *Macmillan*, 166.

[140] BIPO poll cited in Butler, *British General Election of 1955*, 213 n. 1.

[141] R. T. McKenzie and A. Silver, 'Conservatism, Industrialism and the Working Class Tory in England', *Transactions of the Fifth World Congress of Sociology. 1952*, iii. 196. Butler and Stokes, *Political Change in Britain* (1st edn.), 167–8, 170; (2nd edn.), 197–9.

embarked upon covert retreat, and because the party's Suez diehards were by no means right-wing in all areas of policy,[142] his progressive domestic policy possessed healing power. But Macmillan's success also reflected the public's ignorance of how deeply Eden had colluded against Nasser with the French and the Israelis; this emerged only gradually during the next decade, as details leaked out piecemeal, often from overseas sources. Furthermore, Labour had less to gain from exploiting the issue than might at first be supposed. Its policy of countermining Nasser through the United Nations entailed relying on an institution which in a crisis was powerless to act; this risked antagonizing the more robustly patriotic elements within Labour's working-class following, and thereby widening the gulf between them and its progressive middle-class supporters. In the longer term, however, resentment against the Suez venture helped to accumulate within educated opinion the resentment that lent Labour such impetus in 1963–4.

Much of the Conservatives' electoral success in the 1950s stemmed from skilful timing, and from being able to call elections when opinion polls were most favourable. Conservatives felt comfortable with affluence, and unfairly but profitably harped upon the Attlee governments' identification with scarcity and queues; they benefited in 1951 and 1955 from the desire for change, and from the remembered difficulties surmounted by what must in retrospect be seen as one of twentieth-century Britain's two most successful reforming governments. In 1956 Crosland thought Labour 'in grave danger of allowing the Tories to run away with the kudos of being the Party of prosperity and consumption'.[143] Having held his party together, Macmillan could then deploy his publicity skills. His party's membership was beginning the long slide from its high peak of the late 1940s, and by the early 1960s the Young Conservatives had only half the members of their peak year (1949); by 1970 the party's membership had halved since 1953.[144] But such decline mattered less now that the party's appeal could more effectively be presented through the national media than through canvassers knocking on doors, especially as Conservatives in the 1950s were readier than Labour to embrace the new American opinion-forming techniques. Working-class parties might earlier (in a 'contagion from the left') have pioneered mass political organization, but (in a 'contagion from the right') middle-class parties were now pioneering media electioneering.[145] This leapt forward when Lord Woolton, party chairman from 1946 to 1955, employed the public relations firm Colman, Prentis & Varley. Reinforced by a timely burst of prosperity, a major press and public relations campaign in 1957–9 focused on improving the party's image, morale, and appeal. And in so far

[142] Foot, *Politics of Harold Wilson*, 127. L. D. Epstein, *British Politics in the Suez Crisis* (1964), 51–3.
[143] *Future of Socialism*, 293.
[144] J. Ramsden, *The Winds of Change: Macmillan to Heath, 1957–1975* (1996), 403–4.
[145] L. D. Epstein, *Political Parties in Western Democracies* (1967), 257.

as traditional party-branch activism remained important, Conservatives were relatively good at it, especially in mobilizing the postal vote, which Labour itself had introduced in 1948; without it, Labour's majority in the general election of 1964 would have been between twenty and forty, not a mere four.[146]

With a third and even more substantial victory in 1959, Conservatives were unlikely to grumble at the time, but in the 1970s their successors became increasingly alert to the price the party had paid for its electoral success. Articulate Conservatives in the 1950s and 1960s felt 'a sort of moral inferiority complex' in the face of socialist ideas.[147] This led them completely to neglect Hayek's free-market option for the party, and to cling instead to its hierarchical, paternalist, and populist traditions. So policies initially supported only on Labour's left gradually became mainstream: Labour set the agenda on economic and welfare policy matters, and increasingly on colonial policy as well. And if Macmillan implemented the party's promise to build 300,000 houses a year, no wholesale privatization was involved: his achievement rested upon a powerful machine operating from the Ministry of Housing. The denationalizations of 1953 did not anticipate the privatizations of the 1980s: instead they were timid, almost apologetic in tone, and made little impact.[148] Not until the late 1970s did events restore the Conservatives to their fortunate situation of 1931, and place them once more securely in policy's driving seat.

The concessionary strategy of Churchill and Macmillan had never been universally accepted within the party, as indicated by periodic rebellions against its leaders: from the Suez Group in 1956, from Thorneycroft and colleagues when resigning over excessive government expenditure in 1958, and in 1961 from the Monday Club's founders, hostile to Macmillan's 'wind of change' mood on decolonization. The significance of Thorneycroft's resignation was inflated in later years: the iron lady had to wait rather longer for her John the Baptist, and the party's defeat in 1964 did not prompt any major rethink on policy. Among prominent Conservatives between 1964 and 1970 only Enoch Powell was alert to the uncongenially collectivist implications of Conservative centrism. By 1970 a more individualist and entrepreneurial mood was gaining ground, and Conservative corporatism after 1945 soon came to seem an ephemeral sidetrack from the party's individualist main line. From 1940 to 1979, however, it had been Labour's achievement temporarily to divert the Conservative Party in structure, mood, and policy, and to force it into meeting Labour's moral challenge through concession rather than resistance. Conservative leaders could hardly have behaved differently: shaping opinion in a democracy is inevitably slow and inefficient, though in the long term more

[146] Butler and King, *British General Election of 1964*, 226.

[147] The phrase was Samuel Brittan's in his *Left or Right: The Bogus Dilemma* (1968), 51; cf. 123–6.

[148] O. Letwin, *Privatising the World: A Study of International Privatisation in Theory and Practice* (1988), 7.

efficient than any undemocratic alternative. It was first not only politically prudent, but necessary to democracy, for the corporatist strategy's defects to become apparent before alternatives could be tried.

5. LABOUR FACING TWO WAYS

The Labour Party after 1951 experienced a painful transition. It catered for 'labourism': for class-conscious but pragmatic trade unionists and working-class communities keen to assert themselves within the existing political system, yet wary of the state and deeply permeated by Liberal and nonconformist values. It also catered for constituency-based intellectual and middle-class socialists whose views ran all the way from a classless and rationalistic identification with 'planning' to a class-preoccupied and romantic near-revolutionary variant, whether syndicalist or Marxist. The consequent continuous tension between the two was fruitful, but some in both groups (militant and class-conscious trade unionists, Marxist socialists) questioned whether parliament should be the prime arena: in its tactics the twentieth-century labour movement syncopated between gradualist parliamentarism and direct action.

The cold war's international dimension[149] had its domestic concomitant, for it sharpened the continuous dialogue between gradualist labourism and socialism's more revolutionary variants. The dialogue was all the more intense because in the 1950s the labour movement's long-term destination was for so long left ambiguous. If Conservative history between 1940 and 1979 involved a long corporatist diversion from individualism, labour history between the First World War and the 1990s involved an even more prolonged diversion: a statist and class-conscious diversion from the pragmatic, libertarian, and undoctrinaire Edwardian radical/Liberal reforming alliance whence it had come. During the 1950s the Conservatives gained much from Labour's preoccupation with a continuous, half-hidden, and (on both sides) fierce and not always scrupulous internal struggle for control. Churchill, in discussion with Eisenhower in June 1954, praised the anti-Communist stance Labour's leaders were taking, on German rearmament, for example: 'our Labour Party is very sensible. Attlee and Morrison have a very great deal of courage'.[150] Because Marxist socialists did not always fly under their true colours, the frontier between Labour and Communism was unclear, but Labour's experience since the 1920s inspired and equipped its central structures to fend off Communist boarders. From 1930 until the early 1960s the party operated a list of proscribed organizations, continually revised (perhaps with guidance from MI5), which included several Communist 'front' groups.[151] For these and other reasons

[149] See above, pp. 87–101.
[150] Quoted in Gilbert, *'Never Despair'*, 1002.
[151] Mahoney, 'Civil Liberties', 50, 55–7.

the membership figures for the Communist Party of Great Britain (CPGB) are elusive, but the official registered membership declined from its peak of 56,000 in December 1942 to 25,000 in February 1958.[152] Communists remained strong in the trade union movement, most notably in engineering,[153] and their relative commitment brought them disproportionate social as well as political influence. Their stamping grounds were the small meetings, beyond the control of Labour's national leaders and trade union barons, where political, socialist, and trade union ideas and strategies were so often hammered out. In labour disputes the Communists were almost invariably the best disciplined and most enthusiastic—sometimes too much so. Ballot-rigging by the Stalinist general secretary Frank Haxell within the Electrical Trades Union, for example, was exposed in a famous lawsuit of 1961, and helps to explain why the Union thereafter moved so far to the right for so long.[154]

Yet Britain saw nothing to compare with the Marxist pressure which led the anti-Communist Democratic Labor Party to split off from the Australian Labor Party in 1955, nor was there any anticipation in the 1950s of the SDP secession from Labour in the 1980s. Indeed, the split on the left in the 1950s turned out to be within the Marxist camp, when in 1956 the Russian invasion of Hungary prompted the New Left secession from the CPGB. Although Communists were intellectually less influential in Britain than in many European countries, their contribution was not negligible—especially after the New Left secession had released many of them for wider influence and had demonstrated that in Britain one could be a Marxist without being a Communist. The names of intellectuals influenced by Marxism, often eventually to turn against it, speak for themselves: J. D. Bernal, Eric Blair, Christopher Hill, Eric Hobsbawm, Dorothy Hodgkin, Doris Lessing, Ralph Miliband, Raphael Samuel, E. P. Thompson, Raymond Williams, and there are many more. The cultural importance of their meeting places was also important: Collet's Bookshop, the history workshops, the *New Left Review*, and the adult education movement.

The rejoinder from Labour's 'revisionist' social democrats came all the more easily because the New Left's output was too literary, too rarefied, too self-consciously intellectual ever to win mass support. It was also too impatient with the political process to acquire much influence within a Labour Party then securely oriented towards parliament. Crick thought the New Left's *Out of Apathy* represented 'a complete rejection of political values. All is denunciation and sectarian polemic.'[155] The revisionist case against more statist versions of socialism was not new: its combination of reason, passion, and parliamentary

[152] H. Pelling, *The British Communist Party: A Historical Profile* (1958), 192–3.

[153] R. Stevens, 'Cold War Politics: Communism and Anti-Communism in the Trade Unions', in A. Campbell *et al.* (eds.), *British Trade Unions and Industrial Politics*, i. *The Post-War Compromise, 1945–64* (Aldershot, 2000), 183.

[154] For a hostile obituary of Haxell see *DT* (30 May 1988), 19.

[155] B. Crick, 'Labour Publicity', *Political Quarterly* (July–Sept 1960), 371.

gradualism had been present within the British Labour Party from the start, for passion could as well inspire parliamentary gradualism as anti-parliamentarism. The 'revisionism' of the 1950s entailed recovering earlier ethical and humane priorities overlain by the statist and managerial approaches of the 1930s and 1940s. The Christian socialist R. H. Tawney was for Hugh Gaitskell 'the best man I have ever known' and '*the* Democratic Socialist *par excellence*'. Tawney's selfless personal example, his ethical priorities, and his sustained socialist reasoning in many spheres and over many years made him influential with Labour long after his death in 1962. Also influential with Gaitskell was his friend Durbin from New College, Oxford. Drowned in 1948, Durbin lived on through the impact of his perceptive *The Politics of Democratic Socialism* (1940), a work which in 1953 seemed to Gaitskell 'just as relevant to our current problems as it was to those of the thirties'.[156] Humane, intellectually wide-ranging, and courageous in repudiating (unfashionably within the left at the time) Soviet totalitarianism, Durbin was particularly important for evolving a class analysis free from Marxian class categories. Gaitskell wanted Labour's class attitudes adjusted in the light of what the opinion polls revealed about how people actually thought: 'more and more the younger people don't feel class-conscious', he told Crossman in 1959, citing Mark Abrams. Indeed, Marxian preoccupation with class conflict risked subverting the very values socialists sought to foster. As early as 1940 Durbin had emphasized how the middle class was both expanding and recruiting for its values on its frontier with the working class; in such a situation 'the pre-capitalist classes . . . are increasingly important as a group', he argued, with revolution a waning possibility.[157]

Crosland's formidably well-informed *The Future of Socialism* (1956) adorned this revisionist tradition. Crosland did not pull his punches: Marx, he said, 'has little or nothing to offer the contemporary socialist, either in respect of practical policy, or of the correct analysis of our society, or even of the right conceptual tools or framework'. While admitting that Marx was 'intellectually . . . a towering giant amongst socialist thinkers', Crosland urged socialists not to assume that poverty could be cured merely through redistributing wealth, and said he had 'never been able to see why high consumption and brotherly love should be thought incompatible'. Indeed, Danish social democrats in 1960 were to improve their electoral position under the slogan 'make good better'.[158] To the revisionists, the problem of production seemed resolved: mass abundance was approaching, 'and within a decade' the average family's standard of living

[156] Gaitskell's foreword to the 1954 edn., 8. See also R. Terrill, *R. H. Tawney and his Times: Socialism as Fellowship* (1974), 79.

[157] Crossman, *Backbench Diaries*, 742 (19 Mar. 1959). Durbin, *Politics of Democratic Socialism*, 144.

[158] Crosland, *Future of Socialism*, 20–1, 287. J. P. Mackintosh, *British Cabinet* (1st edn. 1962), 486 n. 18.

would be such as to persuade the reformer to focus elsewhere, on ethical and educational issues. Neither 'planning' nor nationalization had been central to early socialism, whereas competition provided valuable stimulus to effort and freedom of choice.[159]

The revisionists—whose leading members included Crosland, Jenkins, Douglas Jay, and Patrick Gordon Walker—aroused resentment in the party because they forced it to think hard about its objectives; in this sense the revisionists were more radical than their Labour critics, who advertised their radicalism more vigorously. The revisionists did not write merely for the library: Labour's important and innovative policy documents *Industry and Society* (1957) and *Signposts for the Sixties* (1961) incorporated their ideas. Labour's tradition for setting up semi-formal intra-party subgroups was well-established: there was a social dimension to the inner lives of both revisionists and their Bevanite rivals. Bevan was a magnetic orator who could never quite decide whether to be a rebel or a man of government. His followers identified themselves on 5 March 1952 when fifty-seven MPs voted against the front bench on the defence estimates.[160] They were irreverent critics of the party's establishment, and tended to back anti-colonial and anti-establishment causes. They included Fenner Brockway, Barbara Castle, R. H. S. Crossman, Tom Driberg, Michael Foot, Jennie Lee, and Ian Mikardo. Both sides wielded a powerful combination of reason and passion. This was not a split between moderate leaders and rank-and-file enthusiasts, but between elements of both, each influential with MPs and constituency parties. Rather separate from both were Labour's town hall and trade union traditionalists on the right of the party led by Morrison. The revisionists might occasionally form an alliance of convenience with the latter, but their close-knit social habits and radical outlook precluded any merger. Partly in self-defence the revisionists gathered tightly round Gaitskell, whose high valuation of political friendship alienated the excluded.[161]

Few such conflicts lack a personal dimension. There is some truth in the polarity between Bevan the flamboyant working-class romantic with imagination and flair and Gaitskell the serious middle-class rationalist with an acute sense of responsibility, but it is not the whole truth. It was not clear at the time whether Bevan's phrase 'desiccated calculating machine' was intended for Gaitskell or for Attlee,[162] but if aimed at Gaitskell it was decidedly ill-judged. Passion unobtrusively inspired the rational party leader who worked so hard to win converts for his viewpoint, and who took such care over the precise drafting of policy documents. Crossman in 1956 thought that 'if challenged to say in

[159] Quotation from *Future of Socialism*, 515; see also 496, 498, 525, 469.
[160] Listed in Crossman, *Backbench Diaries*, 1071–2.
[161] On this see Rodgers (ed.), *Gaitskell*, 159.
[162] Williams, *Gaitskell*, 332.

a single sentence what is wrong with British Socialism, I should reply that it is bookless': books were needed, he thought, to bring busy politicians and trade unionists into touch with reality.[163] Presumably he did not regard the Bevanites' best-known text, Bevan's *In Place of Fear*, published four years before, as a 'book', but the same could not be said of Crosland's *Future of Socialism* published in answer to Crossman's prayer. To compare the two is instructive. Both combine firmly rejecting Soviet communism as a political system with vigorously espousing parliamentary democracy and the mixed economy. Though Bevan had earlier been strongly influenced by Marx, his socialism was deeply rooted in the day-to-day experience of manual labour, while at the same time retaining a commitment to state planning. Crosland's book is more than twice as long as Bevan's, far more tightly argued, better documented, and far better briefed on recent social-science ideas. Bevan's volume covers a rather wider policy range, yet it is slight by comparison: diffuse, uneconomical, and at several points autobiographical. Where Crosland is focused, intellectually innovative, and oriented towards the practical, Bevan is rambling, conventional in his views, and prone to somewhat vapid abstraction. Bevan the author is rhetorical but flat in tone, displaying in prose none of the colour and surprise which delighted those who heard him speak. What Bevan wrote was important less for its inherent interest than because it was he who had written it.

Until the 1930s, if not later, the Labour Party thought time was on its side, and for long after the 1930s Labour's trade union bond remained tight. The trade union movement had grown out of a strong sense of community, and the background of cabinet ministers in the first four Labour governments shows how deeply the party could draw upon a tradition of public service within working-class as well as middle-class families, especially in local government and nonconformist chapels.[164] The proportion of trade union members affiliated to the party rose sharply in the 1940s to half, a level maintained up to the 1980s.[165] Labour's support was strongest in the large unions: although in the 1960s only a minority of the trade unions which affiliated to the TUC were also affiliated to the Labour Party, most of those with no party attachment were small, and Labour attracted a large majority of the TUC's members.[166] Through their affiliation fees the trade unions contributed two-thirds of Labour's finances in the 1950s and 1960s, as well as contributing directly to its election funds during election years.[167] This was a shaky longer-term foundation for Labour: it bred a certain complacency in a competitive electoral situation, for if Labour's long-term victory was assured, Labour did not need to mimic

[163] R. H. S. Crossman, 'John Strachey and the Left Book Club' (1956) in Crossman's *The Charm of Politics* (1958), 139.

[164] J. Bonnor, 'The Four Labour Cabinets', *Sociological Review* (1958), 45–7.

[165] *BST* 191–2.

[166] Flanders, *Trade Unions*, 151.

[167] Pinto-Duschinsky, *British Political Finance*, 163.

the Conservatives' campaigning energy and ingenuity. Besides, public opinion was by the late 1950s turning against the trade unions, and much Labour voting among the organized working class sprang from concentrated patterns of work and residence that by the 1950s had become vulnerable.

The basis of the Labour Party man's allegiance, wrote the American political scientist S. H. Beer, 'is not so much that he *agrees* as that he *belongs*'[168]—at home through occupying a council house in an area of clustered working-class residence, and at work through belonging to a trade union. In Britain, as elsewhere, the larger the firm, the more likely the employee would unionize, and the more concentrated the manual-worker residence the higher the percentage voting Labour.[169] Only within such insulating situations could it seem deviant to vote Conservative.[170] It was rash to assume that the collectivism of wartime and of Labour's postwar heartlands would persist: council-house building might in the medium term be buoyant and factories getting larger,[171] but in the longer term nationalization inhibited growth, and privatization produced contraction, with dispersal and dilution the outcome in both work and residence. The Labour Party perhaps suffered more than the Conservatives from the twentieth-century decline in a sense of community.[172] Partly because of its strong links with the rail unions, partly because it favoured state management, Labour had always believed in an integrated transport system under public ownership; hence its later sympathy with environmentalist ideas for restricting road traffic in city centres.[173] In 1948, however, the number of public-transport vehicles peaked, whereas the number of goods vehicles was still steadily rising, and the number of private cars shot up from 3 million in 1950 to 12.7 million in 1970.[174] Labour in the 1950s needed to open out beyond the organized working class, and the revisionists knew it.[175]

Labour also needed to tackle its structural problems. In the 1950s and 1960s these were advertised by its run-down branch premises and by the heavily masculine and middle-aged composition of its annual conference.[176] Labour's individual membership at constituency level fell almost continuously after its high peak in the early 1950s.[177] Wilson in his report of 1955 on the party's organization claimed to be 'deeply shocked' at its poor state: 'compared with

[168] S. H. Beer, *Modern British Politics: Parties and Pressure Groups in the Collectivist Age* (1st publ. 1965, paperback edn. 1982), 85.

[169] Price and Bain, 'Union Growth Revisited', 348, 350. Blondel, *Voters, Parties and Leaders*, 65.

[170] F. Parkin, 'Working-Class Conservatives: A Theory of Political Deviance', *British Journal of Sociology* (Sept. 1967), 285–9.

[171] For factory size see table in Wright, *Britain in the Age of Economic Management*, 40.

[172] See above, pp. 26, 63–4, 161, 334.

[173] For a lucid exposition see Castle, *Diaries 1964–70*, 83–5.

[174] Halsey, *TBS* 257–8, 280. *BPF* (8th edn.), 372.

[175] As emerges from the discussion reported in Crossman, *Backbench Diaries*, 664 (18 Feb. 1958).

[176] Butler and King, *British General Election of 1964*, 217. L. Minkin, *The Labour Party Conference: A Study in the Politics of Intra-Party Democracy* (1978), 131.

[177] Pinto-Duschinsky, *British Political Finance*, 156–8.

our opponents, we are still at the penny-farthing stage in a jet-propelled era'.[178] Policy, he went on, was receiving too much attention by comparison with organization: it was less important to make converts than to find ways of discovering where support already lay: membership was ageing, volunteers were scarce, and morale was declining. The contrast with the Conservatives (held up as a model throughout Wilson's report) was striking, especially in marginal seats. The party's ward structure, with its dull and sparsely attended meetings, all too easily became club-like and introverted, especially in constituencies where Labour's majority was large.[179] Crossman's diaries in the 1960s were still peppered with affectionate but despairing references to the branches' inward-looking and traditionalist attitudes. The branches were particularly conservative in areas of traditional heavy industry, and in 1965 Crossman noted how unsophisticated were the party's Scottish branches by comparison with Coventry.[180] 'Oh dear, defunct Derby', he wrote in the same year after a visit there: '—that soulless industrial Victorian town with its pathetically ingrained Labour administration terrified of any change'; of the six councillors selected to receive him, all were over 62 and two were over 80.[181]

In the late 1950s this depressing picture was thrown into relief by CND's vitality, idealism, and appeal to youth. Its international significance has already been discussed,[182] but its domestic impact was also considerable. It was good at publicity. CND was a major cultural force among the young in the late 1950s and early 1960s, and attracted authors, journalists, teachers, and communicators of every kind. Like many such movements, CND hovered between adopting a non-party outlook and trying to capture the party of the left. Labour's formal commitment to changing the world and to mobilizing idealism gave it a natural affinity with protest movements of any kind, but the protest movement which had created the party was now being absorbed into the system. As the TUC's general secretary George Woodcock told Congress in 1963, 'we left Trafalgar Square a long time ago' for the committee rooms where power resided.[183] For some in the Labour Party, CND provided a substitute. It was the last outburst of that idealistic, moralistic, semi-religious populism that Gladstone had mobilized in the Liberal Party's great days. With its mass sit-downs and its huge marches from Aldermaston to London [Plate 10], CND was an important stage in the growing disillusionment with natural science, and pioneered many subsequent protesting and participatory attitudes. It also revived the nonconformist tradition of civil

[178] 'Interim Report of the Sub-Committee on Party Organization', printed in *Report of the 54th Annual Conference of the Labour Party, Margate 1955* (n.d.), 65.

[179] McKenzie, *British Political Parties*, 546, 548.

[180] *Cabinet Diaries*, i. 159 (14 Feb. 1965); cf. McKenzie, *British Political Parties*, 546.

[181] *Cabinet Diaries*, i. 254 (18 June 1965).

[182] See above, pp. 96–100.

[183] Quoted in L. Panitch, *Social Democracy and Industrial Militancy: The Labour Party, the Trade Unions and Incomes Policy, 1945–1974* (Cambridge, 1976), 50.

disobedience, and stirred its followers with visions of conspiracy in high places. CND revitalized the British left by assembling a diversely motivated but activist coalition, and by challenging the need for state secrecy. Nuclear weapons, by their very nature, obstructed democracy because parliament and cabinet could say so little about them. The Attlee governments, despite their crucial nuclear decisions, did not promote any House of Commons debate on the subject,[184] and we have seen how leaks from the plutonium plant at Windscale were covered up in 1957.[185] On 24 June 1974 Castle was rather shocked when Wilson told the cabinet that a nuclear warhead test had taken place a few weeks earlier: 'it is a relief to know that the test is in the past', she wrote, 'but appalling that these things can be done without the knowledge of Cabinet'.[186]

CND's original aim was the Fabian one of subjecting government to publicity—hence the choice of the Aldermaston route for its marches. In a campaign spiced with debates over principle and millennial visions, CND could offer all the excitements of opening up what the authorities wanted to hide: mysterious weapons, concealed emplacements, conspiracies against the public. Its loose structure made any tight 'membership' requirement unnecessary, and its inclusiveness mobilized anyone convinced that the individual could by personal effort prevail over large, secretive, and powerful structures. Its apparently simple objective, 'ban the bomb', united very disparate forces: survivors from interwar pacifism and Quakerism; the rationalistic progressivism of the Cambridge scientist and philosopher; and the protest of the radical young against stuffy parents. It included Christians angry about the bomb but also about church leaders' political quietism, together with nonconformists and pacifists who sniffed the potential for martyrdom in non-violent protest. 'From a very early date', wrote A. J. P. Taylor, 'it was obvious that we were preaching to the converted—the gallant stage-army of the nineteen thirties—now reinforced by their grandchildren.'[187] CND also included people on the left who thought Labour's leadership timid and uninspired, and were impatient with politicians' wheeler-dealing. Here was an opportunity for Marxists in the New Left to rediscover the warm commitment they had sacrificed so painfully in 1956. This new cause was for them all the more exhilarating for evoking embarrassment and indecision in the CPGB. A moralistic crusade against war could reunite the British left in a new but non-Communist popular front, and at last heal the wound on the left that the First World War's split between Liberals and Labour had created.

Presiding over the whole was an archetypal Liberal rationalist, the philosopher Bertrand Russell, appealing 'as a human being to human beings' to

[184] See the discussion in K. Harris, *Attlee* (1982), 290–1.

[185] See above, p. 313.

[186] Castle, *Diaries 1974–6*, 121 (24 June 1974); cf. Benn, *HC Deb.* 15 Dec. 1982, c. 331.

[187] A. J. P. Taylor, *A Personal History* (1983), 230. See also C. Driver, *The Disarmers: A Study in Protest* (1964), 60, 128.

'remember your humanity, and forget the rest'.[188] He claimed that 'there is in every great modern State, a vast mechanism intended to prevent the truth from being known, not only to the public, but also to the Governments'.[189] The strategy of 'direct action' was seen as a way to push the media, allegedly biased against protest movements, into conceding them more publicity. At Easter 1961 Ralph Schoenman, Russell's aide, led Aldermaston marchers in an unauthorized sit-down in Grosvenor Square. The government then consolidated the hold on young people of this frail intellectual, well advanced into his eighties, by briefly imprisoning Russell for inciting civil disobedience. Yet Schoenman had launched a controversial strategy which split the movement, and CND for all its inclusiveness was schismatic in the impact made on the British left by its single-issue strategy and apolitical mood. Bevan at the Labour Party conference in 1957 had already dismissed the vague but integrating policy of unilateral disarmament as requiring a British Foreign Secretary to enter 'naked into the conference chamber': it was, he declared, 'an emotional spasm', and no policy at all.[190] Democratic structures were difficult enough to operate within the mass movement which CND had become by 1959; they were entirely incompatible with mounting conspiratorial tactics monitored by the police, nor could civil disobedience mobilize the large numbers attracted by legal demonstrations. So the movement faded temporarily from political prominence paradoxically just when the Cuba crisis advertised the hazards of nuclear escalation. The movement lived on, and fertilized Labour's left with much talent and energy. Some of its supporters were drawn into welfare causes, for example, in the belief that, if poverty were tackled, their hoped-for working-class allies would at last back the cause. Others drifted away from parliamentary politics altogether and towards the many non-party environmentalist and community-action protest movements associated with 'the sixties'.[191]

Schisms often invigorate both sides in a controversy, and in the response it evoked from opponents within the Labour Party, CND's impact was lasting. From the 1920s to the 1950s Labour had kept its activists in harmony with the parliamentary leadership at the party conference by an informal and rather clumsy mechanism. Open to abuse, though effective enough, this involved an alliance between the front-bench Labour politicians and the leaders of the larger trade unions; the latter could deploy the block vote within the TUC and Labour Party conference in the leaders' support. This alliance held the

[188] Quoted from his BBC broadcast on 'Man's Peril' (Dec. 1954) in his *Autobiography*, iii. *1944–67* (1969), 72; cf. 139 the statement of the Committee of 100 in autumn 1960: 'We appeal, as human beings to human beings: remember your humanity, and forget the rest.'

[189] Russell, *Autobiography*, iii. 141.

[190] Quoted from his Labour Party conference speech in 1957 in J. Campbell, *Nye Bevan and the Mirage of British Socialism* (1987), 337.

[191] C. Pritchard and R. Taylor, *The Protest Makers: The British Nuclear Disarmament Movement of 1958–1965, Twenty Years On* (Oxford, 1980), 110.

Attlee governments' incomes policy on course, and in the 1950s at first held the Labour leadership's line against unilateralism. Attlee in opposition in 1951–5 chose not to exert the leader's powers to the full: through contenting himself with balancing off conflicting forces in the party, he allowed matters to drift. Gaitskell by March 1955 thought the party now needed a leader rather than a mere chairman.[192] From the early 1950s he followed the familiar pattern of cultivating sympathetic trade union leaders. His anti-Communist speech at Stalybridge in 1952 had impressed many of them, and demonstrated that he possessed a major attribute now much needed in the party's leader: courage. With the left-wing Frank Cousins as General Secretary of the TGWU from 1956, however, the old mode of controlling the party conference was at risk. During his first four years as Attlee's successor, Gaitskell did not take the combative view of the leader's role for which he was later remembered,[193] but Labour's electoral defeat in 1959 changed everything. He decided that the trade unions and Parliamentary Labour Party (PLP) would and should advocate Britain's remaining in NATO, with its concomitant of relying upon American nuclear weapons. On this issue, he thought, an internal battle might be worth fighting.[194]

At the party conference on 5 October 1960, after he had delivered one of the century's greatest political speeches, the unilateralists defeated the official motion by 3.3 million votes to 3.0. With passionate eloquence amidst boos and shouts from his enemies, Gaitskell had upheld the PLP's status against rival elements within the party, and had vowed to 'fight and fight and fight again to save the Party we love'.[195] That he now proceeded to achieve. A second small stage-army, this time on the right—the Gaitskellite 'Campaign for Democratic Socialism'—worsted the first small stage-army on the left, and got the decision reversed at the conference of 1961 by 4.5 million votes to 1.8 million. Gaitskell's hold on his party was now secure: he had demonstrated that he did not consider the PLP immediately bound by the party conference, but that the leader could survive only if he rapidly brought conference into line. The whole issue was defused after 1964 when Wilson retained the American submarine-based Polaris missile. The Gaitskellites held together thereafter, and by defying majority opinion within the party helped to shepherd Britain into the EEC in 1973, and in 1981 to weaken Labour seriously by prompting secession into the SDP.

Even before his defeat on unilateralism in 1960, Gaitskell took dramatic steps to show publicly how fully he recognized Labour's need to fend off the Liberal challenge by reaching out more widely; he feared a Labour split, a

[192] Crossman, *Backbench Diaries*, 410 (24 Mar. 1955); cf. Williams, *Gaitskell*, 345.

[193] Williams, *Gaitskell*, 404–5, 548.

[194] Benn, *Diaries 1940–62*, 344 (1 Oct. 1960).

[195] Quoted in Williams, *Gaitskell*, 612.

secession to the Liberals, and a fourth Labour defeat, which would be final. In such circumstances his metropolitan and even high-society connections were an asset. 'If one is to get power one may have to rely on non-Labour votes', he told Crossman in February 1958.[196] After the electoral defeat in 1959 Douglas Jay even suggested changing the Labour Party's name or appending the words 'reform' or 'radical';[197] he thought that the name 'Labour' deterred the better-off wage earners and the many salary earners who felt that this was not their class. 'We are in danger', he wrote, 'of fighting under the label of a class which no longer exists.'[198] Gaitskell, too, thought the name 'Labour' had been a hindrance at the election, especially on the new housing estates.[199] A change of name would perhaps have been too drastic, though a similar change preceded Labour's election victory in 1997, but the very discussion of such an idea shows the depth of the Labour leaders' concern. Gaitskell seized his opportunity, and when forced to fight for his position within the party he ended by consolidating his image in the country.

Gaitskell's handling of tax issues during the general election of 1959 had been clumsy, and in a party divided and demoralized by electoral defeat, its leader had been wise to choose his own ground for internal debate. More questionable was his decision to challenge the party's core beliefs. For Crossman two years earlier, the Labour Party's 'two most important emotions' were 'a doctrinaire faith in nationalization, without knowing what it means, and a doctrinaire faith in pacifism, without facing its consequences'.[200] This awareness somehow did not lead Crossman to back Gaitskell in courageously trying to get the party to confront both issues. There were several arguments for Gaitskell's questioning clause four of the party's constitution. Opinion polls showed that by 1960 nationalization was no vote-winner, and that three-fifths even of Labour supporters opposed it; Gaitskell told Benn in October 1959 that he was 'not prepared to lose another Election for the sake of nationalisation'.[201] The leader's battle to change it would, if successful, confirm his party in a less sectarian image and his own reputation for courage. Yet even Jenkins, Gaitskell's admirer, thought his assault on the party's emotions in 1959 too rationalistic and frontal. In the outcome, Gaitskell both failed to get his reform and for the first time drove his trade union centrist power base into the arms of the left; he later admitted that this had been a tactical error.[202] His party was not yet ready for the overt change of direction which social democrats in West

[196] Crossman, *Backbench Diaries*, 664 (18 Feb. 1958); cf. 789 (19 Oct. 1959) and Williams, *Gaitskell*, 544.

[197] Jay, *Change and Fortune*, 274.

[198] Crossman, *Backbench Diaries*, 791 nn. 2 and 4 (19 Oct. 1959); cf. 794 (21 Oct. 1959) for Mayhew's speech at a party meeting in Oct. 1959.

[199] As reported in Benn, *Diaries 1940–62*, 317 (11 Oct. 1959).

[200] *Backbench Diaries*, 615 (4 Oct. 1957).

[201] Benn, *Diaries 1940–62*, 317 (11 Oct. 1959). See also *Must Labour Lose?*, 31–7.

[202] Campbell, *Jenkins*, 64–5. Williams, *Gaitskell*, 549, 777. Benn, *Diaries 1940–62*, 344 (1 Oct. 1960).

Germany's SozialDemokratische Partei Deutschlands brought off at this time when expunging public ownership from their party's platform. Wilson and his successors defused the issue gradually and with less fuss, though slowly and with difficulty.

We have already seen how Gaitskell was more successful (though not easily) in his next two battles, over unilateral disarmament and over whether to back the government bid to join the EEC.[203] If the party was to equip itself with the policies and popular following necessary for power, Gaitskell's overall strategy was surely correct, and among the young people ready to follow his lead in the late 1950s was the future Liberal leader David Steel.[204] Facetiously and unabashed, Macmillan drew attention to Gaitskell's nagging governmental conscience, claiming that 'the whole point of being in opposition is that one can have fun and lend colour to what one says and does'.[205] Yet an effective radical party must continually ask itself Orwell's question: 'in such and such circumstances, what would you *do*?' The pursuit of honesty in politics, of championing in opposition only policies achievable in government, enabled Gaitskell to win public attention and respect, inspire his party, and generate intense loyalty from friends. He was, as Jenkins wrote, 'a man for raising the sights of politics'.[206] In rejecting a semi-religious commitment to nationalization Gaitskell's repudiation of clause 4 was successfully taken up in 1995 by Blair as Labour leader, but with the difference that Blair was then in his early forties with a long stretch in power before him, whereas Gaitskell died aged 56, still in opposition in 1963, of lupus erythematosus.

Taking office in 1964 with a tiny parliamentary majority did not immediately subject Labour's socialism to the test. The party won fewer votes than in 1959, and a lower share of the total vote (44.1%) than for any party with a parliamentary majority since 1922.[207] This was the first of many general elections centring on the theme of Britain's relative decline. For this Labour had a remedy not available to the Conservatives: planning and the restraint of incomes through a governmental partnership with the trade unions. Frank Cousins was only the most strident among the many trade union leaders who in the 1950s refused to collaborate with the Conservative governments' wages policies. When Macmillan indicated that he would welcome being invited to address the TUC as Chancellor of the Exchequer in 1956, Cousins was loudly applauded for his cheap question: 'what does he think it is—a Film Festival? We will welcome a Chancellor of the Exchequer, but . . . we will wait for a

[203] See above pp. 118, 451. [204] Williams, *Gaitskell*, 786.

[205] *Daily Mail* interview, quoted in Butler and Rose, *British General Election of 1959*, 33. See also Williams, *Gaitskell*, 296.

[206] Orwell, 'Rudyard Kipling' (1942) in his *Complete Works*, xiii (1998), 160. Jenkins, *T* (20 Jan. 1973), 14. [207] *BPF* (8th edn.), 234–7.

Labour Chancellor of the Exchequer.'[208] Cousins did not oppose Conservative wage planning on narrowly partisan grounds, but because he thought such a policy fair only if operated in conjunction with a planned economy which simultaneously reviewed the overall distribution of wealth. The Conservatives' centrism of the 1950s could not quite stretch to this, and they pursued a mildly deflationary policy instead. To this, Cousins's reply was forthright: 'in a period of freedom for all we are part of the all'.[209]

Whereas the employers' organizations were free-market in theory but in practice often corporatist, trade union theory was often socialist but in practice free-market. In wage bargaining they had collaborated with late-Victorian employers in gradually building up a voluntary system of 'free collective bargaining', a phrase often on trade union lips in the 1960s and 1970s. Beginning with negotiation about wages in a single locality, the system had cohered into national agreements involving many things besides wages. The idea that trade unions could bargain corporately with employers' organizations at the national level grew naturally out of this, and had worked well in wartime emergency conditions. At such times the moral authority of the state, itself a major employer, carried weight in what became a tripartite structure for mobilizing the economy to fullest effect. The TUC was at the centre of such activity, but unlike its constituent unions it could deploy little beyond moral force, and the employers' equivalent, the Confederation of British Industry, could hardly deploy even that. Although Labour's welfare and planning priorities led the party towards statism, its libertarian, trade union, social-class, and participatory aspects led it to fend off the state, especially when its supporters thought the state was in enemy hands. Trade unions' support for nationalization, welfare reforms, and redistributive taxation seemed socialist enough, but not their desire to keep the state out of industrial relations. For theirs was more a collectivism of groups than of the nation as a whole, a practical alliance between structures whose mutual protection aimed to enhance their members' bargaining position in unfettered negotiations with the employer: they had inherited the nineteenth-century Liberals' wariness of the state.

George Woodcock, TUC General Secretary from 1960 to 1969, believed strongly in eliminating unemployment through government planning, and was proud to have participated in the tripartite consensus and corporatist package of 1944. His outlook promised much to a Labour Party whose sails were filled from the early 1960s by the widespread desire for institutional and meritocratic reconstruction. If government planning was the aim, Labour could outclass the

[208] Quoted in Panitch, *Social Democracy and Industrial Militancy*, 272.

[209] G. Goodman, *The Awkward Warrior: Frank Cousins. His Life and Times* (1979), 134. See also W. H. Fishbein, *Wage Restraint by Consensus: Britain's Search for an Incomes Policy Agreement, 1965–79* (1984), 33, a valuable study of the whole subject.

Conservatives in providing the means, for its close trade union links would lend a Labour government more direct access to much of the workforce. Wilson, like many Labour leaders of his generation, had high hopes of 'physical' planning. He prefaced his account of his first two governments with a long quotation from Bevan about the difficulties involved in reconciling 'parliamentary popularity with sound economic planning'. Bevan said that 'the central problem falling upon representative government in the Western world' is 'how to persuade the people to forego immediate satisfactions in order to build up the economic resources of the country'.[210] In 1979 Wilson reprinted the quotation as an epigraph to his account of his last two governments, *Final Term*, claiming that it 'seems as apt now as it did then'. If the wartime consensus could be revived, if with a combination of renewed self-discipline and self-denial the trade unions could be harnessed behind the revived wartime union of science and planning, wealth might grow faster and be distributed more fairly. But an essential preliminary was to repair the long-standing alliance between Labour's parliamentary leadership and powerful trade union leaders, and Wilson in 1964 saw the need to bring Cousins on board. His courtship extended even to inviting the Cousins family in August 1964 for a stay at the Wilsons' holiday home in the Isles of Scilly, and Cousins agreed to run Wilson's new Ministry of Technology.

Discussing incomes planning in 1955, Barbara Wootton claimed that 'a deep reticence pervades the whole subject', especially in the higher income brackets. 'According to the prevailing code, a man's income is one of his private economic parts: reference to it is subject to a powerful social taboo.' She and others now wanted wage agreements to take account of the public interest: the whole subject should be opened up.[211] Social democrats felt that with planning incomes, as with nationalizing and rationalizing industry, success could come only through collaboration with and collecting ideas from those affected. The Attlee governments' disappointments had demonstrated that government could shape the economy in this way only by fully consulting the employers whose cooperation was needed.[212] This the Wilson government in the mid-1960s attempted in the most ambitious way, enlisting the TUC in vetting wage claims and in effect edging it towards becoming an arm of central government. With the election won in October 1964, the scene was set for the first Wilson government's massive publicity exercise entailed in the 'Joint Statement of Intent'. With a televised launch from Lancaster House on 16 December, it urged a combination of enhanced productivity and wage

210 Wilson, *Labour Government 1964–70*, p. xix.

211 B. Wootton, *The Social Foundations of Wage Policy. A Study of Contemporary British Wage and Salary Structure* (1955), 28. See also 35, 100, 102, 103, 160–1.

212 For a good discussion of this point see A. A. Rogow, *The Labour Government and British Industry 1945–51* (Oxford, 1955), 60–70.

restraint engineered through a partnership between employers and employees, and 50,000 copies were distributed to factories and offices.[213] Wilson aimed to divide control over economic policy between the Treasury and the newly created DEA, a strategy too central to his aims for the Department to have originated in a taxi on the back of an envelope, as was sometimes alleged; the plans for it had been worked out from autumn 1963 onwards in a series of study groups.[214] The DEA immediately set about drafting a 'national plan' which as we have seen was more a set of targets than a mechanism for attaining them, given that the control of market forces now seemed less feasible than in Attlee's time.[215]

Reinforcing these efforts was one of twentieth-century Britain's most ambitious and impressive exercises in state planning and public education: the Prices and Incomes Board. Its chairman was Aubrey Jones, a Conservative MP from 1950 to 1965 with extensive ministerial and business experience. He and his eight colleagues on the Board presided over a hard-working, publicity-conscious, self-critical, and efficient structure which accumulated much specialist expertise and gained wide respect for its impartiality. With extensive part-time advice from academics and experts, its sole weapons were publicity and persuasion, and it began its task in a non-legalistic way. Its reports covered 18 million people (three-quarters of the workforce) in what was in effect a huge and ongoing cumulative inquiry.[216] The Board's three prime objectives were educative (to persuade the public into wage restraint), advisory (to foster change in industry), and judicial (to adjudicate on the cases before it).[217] By December 1967 Crossman was pronouncing the incomes policy 'a fraud', for by then it was clear that the trade unions would not help to enforce it.[218] In its final two years the government paid lip service to it, but several leading ministers were privately sceptical: its purpose had become largely symbolic.[219] Yet Sweden exemplified how a more centralized, coordinated, and socialist trade union movement could successfully operate an incomes policy.[220] The Board's demise in 1970 did not stem from any fault of its own: it flowed from a change in political climate, and from the advent of a government more alert than Wilson's in 1964 to the difficulty of operating an incomes policy within a pluralist society.

[213] Panitch, *Social Democracy and Industrial Militancy*, 69.

[214] C. Clifford, 'The Rise and Fall of the Department of Economic Affairs 1964–69: British Government and Indicative Planning', *Contemporary British History* (Summer 1997), 96.

[215] See above, pp. 309–11.

[216] Fels, *Prices and Incomes Board*, 39. This paragraph owes much to Fels's excellent study, and to J. Mitchell, *The National Board for Prices and Incomes* (1972).

[217] Panitch, *Social Democracy and Industrial Militancy*, 98.

[218] *Cabinet Diaries*, ii. 611 (19 Dec. 1967).

[219] See e.g. Crossman, *Cabinet Diaries*, iii. 77 (26 May 1968), 700 (27 Oct. 1969).

[220] Fishbein, *Wage Restraint*, 230–3.

Wilson's difficulties with the trade unions on incomes made the idea of trade union reform, already attractive for other reasons, seem compelling. Just before the general election in 1964 Benn had privately included 'the terrible handicap of trade-union leadership' among the obstacles Labour faced.[221] With Hugh Scanlon elected President of the engineering union in 1967, and with Jack Jones succeeding Cousins in 1969, the Labour leadership's hold on the party conference was slipping. Wilson in his more depressed moments spoke privately of the need to imitate the American Democrats and separate the Labour Party from the trade unions.[222] The short-term impulse for their reform had begun in April 1965, when a powerful royal commission into trade unions and employers' associations was set up; it was chaired by the former Labour MP and judge Terence (now Lord) Donovan, with the TUC choosing its trade union representatives. It was captured by proponents of the Oxford 'school' of industrial relations. The school's strong practical purposes and its sympathy with both 'sides' in industry combined to lend its many publications considerable influence in the 1960s, and membership of the British Universities Industrial Relations Association rose steadily from eighteen in 1950 to 383 in 1986.[223] Impressive in the wealth and depth of its research, the Commission argued that there were now 'two systems of industrial relations' in parallel: the formal one which reached nationwide wage settlements between trade unions and employers, and the informal one which in negotiations between management and shop stewards at plant level settled local issues within the individual firm. Official strikes accounted for only 5 per cent of recent totals, and strikes would arguably best be curbed by drawing the informal and formal procedures together.[224]

The report's overall thrust was voluntarist and conservative, and its remedy was organizational: flexible but comprehensive company-wide collective agreements on pay, working practices, terms of employment, and negotiating procedures. These should be registered with the Department of Employment and Productivity, an Industrial Relations Commission should deal with any problems arising, the Secretary of State would ultimately have enforcement power through the courts, and (in a majority recommendation) an Industrial Law Committee would codify labour law. The Donovan Commission interpreted its brief rather narrowly, and did not address the concerns that by 1969 were urgent for Labour politicians. To them it seemed that the report focused unduly on the private sector and did not take a broad view of the trade unions' role in modern society, their relationship to the state, and their economic impact.

221 *Diaries 1963–7*, 147 (30 Sept. 1964). 222 Crossman, *Cabinet Diaries*, ii. 287 (22 Mar. 1967).

223 J. Berridge and J. Goodman, 'The British Universities Industrial Relations Association', *British Journal of Industrial Relations* (July 1988), 161.

224 Royal Commission on Trade Unions and Employers' Associations 1965–1968, *Report* (Chairman Lord Donovan, Cmnd. 3623, 1968), 12–13, 18–19, 28, 37, 97.

A minister as energetic as Castle, Secretary of State for Employment and Productivity from 1968 to 1970, was eager for her Department to be more active in improving industrial relations,[225] and wanted something bolder than the 'free collective bargaining' whose continuance the Commission endorsed. Its remedies seemed too careless of the need to enhance efficiency, too neglectful of the public interest, and insufficiently concerned for the weak and unorganized. So Castle and Wilson saw this as the moment for a new move. In the late 1960s, with a general election impending, Wilson saw possibilities in making a virtue of necessity: if he could curb trade union power through introducing the state into industrial relations, he could pre-empt the Conservatives with a bid for middle opinion, and make Labour seem the national party. By April 1969 *The Times* thought he was succeeding.[226]

Many years earlier the Fabians had made the socialist case for involving the state in industrial relations: a planned society could not leave industrial relations as its sole unplanned component. Addressing the TUC in 1949, Attlee had attacked preoccupation with wage differentials as 'bad economics and bad social morality', the latter 'because our Labour Movement has an ethical basis. We are trying to get away from the old scramble for competitive advantages.' The alliance between trade unionism and socialism in the Labour Party was in general close, but in this area fragile, yet 'industrial life is more complex now than it ever has been', wrote Benn in his diary for January 1969, urging the interdependence of modern social institutions.[227] The more difficult it proved after 1964 to get trade union backing for wage restraint, the easier it became to replace the distinction between left and right in the party with a new distinction between the trade unions' defenders on the one hand, and their (socialist and non-socialist) critics on the other. Castle argued for government intervention on socialist grounds, though even she recognized by 1970 that the government had no plans for complementing restraint of incomes by redistributing wealth.[228] Still, she saw this as the moment when socialism and the general interest must prevail over trade union individualism and special interests.

While preparing her white paper 'In Place of Strife', Castle bore in mind Nye Bevan's comment after Labour's defeat at the general election of 1959: 'the trade unionist votes at the polls against the consequences of his own anarchy', and she saw her remedy as being 'really . . . in line with Nye's philosophy'. The white paper's remedies were to appoint a Commission on Industrial Relations with legal powers of enforcement to encourage good practice in industrial relations, reduce inter-union disputes, press the trade unions to reform, and strengthen leaders' power over members. The Secretary of State would be empowered

[225] *HC Deb.* 2 May 1968 cc. 1308–17.
[226] *T* (17 Apr. 1969), 9 (editorial).
[227] Harris, *Attlee*, 436. Benn, *Diaries 1968–72*, 141 (3 Jan. 1969), cf. 186–7 (17 June 1969).
[228] *Diaries 1964–70*, 751 (19 Jan. 1970).

to introduce a 'conciliation pause' (enforced by fines) before unofficial strikes could be called, and to compel unions to ballot members on whether they really wanted a strike. Knowing that the unions would dislike these proposals, the white paper's compilers balanced them with more congenial proposals: the right to more information from management, for example, and protection against unfair dismissal. Castle was privately under no illusions: if she had misjudged reactions, she told her diary, 'I shall have mortally damaged my political career. I am gambling a lot on this.'[229]

Wilson, in giving full backing, was gambling less with opinion among the public than among his cabinet ministers. Given so dramatic a switch in government policy, so bold a breach with the party's past, it would have been wiser to carry colleagues with him from the outset, yet the cabinet was not consulted until after discussions with the TUC.[230] This combination of secrecy and haste was dangerous, and opposition within the cabinet ensured that only five white-paper proposals went into Castle's carefully balanced Bill, introduced in April 1969: imposed settlements of inter-union disputes enforced by fines; a compulsory twenty-eight-day conciliation pause, enforced by fines before an unofficial dispute could be called; a statutory right for every worker to join a trade union; employers compelled to recognize a trade union when the Commission on Industrial Relations so recommended; and no denial of unemployment benefit to workers laid off because of a strike in which they were taking no direct part.[231] Trade union leaders were not prepared to risk publicly backing the government. 'I get a little tired of hearing trade union leaders talk sense in private', Castle complained in her diary, 'while attacking us in public for doing the very things they know must be done.'[232]

Unsurprisingly Wilson, at a painful cabinet meeting in June, failed to get his policy through. Crossman describes him consuming three double brandies in the course of the argument, 'a terrible exhibition in which the P.M. was rasped, irritated and thoroughly demoralized, really shouting I won't, I can't, you can't do this to me'.[233] Wilson subsequently claimed that the voluntary agreement on reform later patched up with the TUC had reduced inter-union disputes, and that more would have been achieved if the Conservative victory of 1970 had not inflamed the situation.[234] Others felt that he had got the worst of both worlds—first seeking to appear tough, then backing down with little attained—and that trade union acquiescence and therefore success would have

[229] Quotations from Castle, *Diaries 1964–70*, 592 (18 Jan. 1969), 590 (15 Jan. 1969). See also 585 (7 Jan. 1969), 641 (29 Apr. 1969).

[230] Wilson, *Labour Government 1964–70*, 592.

[231] This discussion owes much to R. Taylor's valuable *The Trade Union Question in British Politics: Government and Unions since 1945* (Oxford, 1993), 147–73.

[232] Castle, *Diaries 1964–70*, 584 (7 Jan. 1969), cf. 636 (14 Apr. 1969).

[233] Crossman, *Cabinet Diaries*, iii. 524 (17 Jun. 1969).

[234] Wilson, *Labour Government 1964–70*, 662–3.

been more likely if he had legislated along Donovan lines.[235] So on this issue the conservatism of organized labour had held back the socialism of a radicalized Wilson and Castle. Hostility to Castle's scheme became so intense within the Labour Party and the trade union movement that further progress was impossible, and subsequent Conservative governments were freed to espouse legal intervention even more vigorously than Castle. The continuing need for action was clear enough in February 1970 when—to a packed annual general meeting of British Leyland, Britain's largest motor group—Lord Stokes (its chairman and managing director) complained that stoppages were imposing an intolerable strain on the factory management: 'I cannot believe that this state of anarchy is what the majority of our workers really want.' Summarizing discussion in cabinet in the previous October, Crossman ascribed the phrase 'complete anarchy', as describing the situation, to none other than the Secretary of State for Employment herself.[236]

Less public, yet troublesome, were Labour's strained relations with pressure groups of another type: the voluntary bodies promoting welfare and humanitarian causes already discussed.[237] The government's difficulties need to be appreciated: none of these groups had overall responsibility for apportioning scarce resources between competing good causes; nor were they confronted, as were Labour ministers in the late 1960s, with growing hostility to high taxation. Inflation had by then ensured that rises in income tax hit many of Labour's own supporters, and by 1967 Callaghan as Chancellor was already arguing that profits and incentives for managers were too low—'so Socialism isn't even about equality', Castle grumbled.[238] And whereas the beneficiaries of public welfare might be grateful enough, they were less likely to vote than their benefactors, who were becoming vocal about scroungers off the welfare state.[239] In an all-day discussion at Chequers on 5 September 1969 Jenkins, Callaghan's successor as Chancellor, claimed that the limits of taxation had now been reached.[240] For socialists, this was indeed a depressing conclusion.

6. PUBLIC OPINION ANATOMIZED

The most striking changes in the working of British political institutions between 1951 and 1970 owed little to the politicians, much to wider social developments, for in these years technical change enabled politicians to communicate with electors in an entirely new way. The Attlee years seem in

[235] This was Hugh Clegg's view in 1990. See his 'The Oxford School of Industrial Relations', *Warwick Papers in Industrial Relations*, 31 (Jan. 1990), 6.

[236] *T* (26 Feb. 1970), 21. Crossman, *Cabinet Diaries*, iii. 695 (23 Oct. 1969).

[237] See above, pp. 265–6, 271, 275.

[238] Castle, *Diaries 1964–70*, 240 (10 Apr. 1967).

[239] S. Fay, 'What Crossman Really Said about Scrounging on the Dole', *ST* (15 Sept. 1968), 2.

[240] Crossman, *Cabinet Diaries*, iii. 629 (5 Sept. 1969).

retrospect almost a dark age, with not even a fifty-year rule in operation, with psephology as yet struggling for acceptance, with politicians aloof from close questioning, party conferences untelevised, broad tracts of political discussion excluded from the media, and large areas of British government kept under wraps. Even within the more deferential society that prevailed before 1951, public opinion was thought to be like the weather: ultimately, in a democracy, beyond control. The diversifying media at first seemed to complicate matters still further. We have seen how Churchill's stroke was concealed in June 1953: Colville describes how Churchill's three press friends Lords Camrose, Beaverbrook, and Bracken came at once to Chartwell 'and paced the lawn in earnest conversation', agreeing in effect to gag Fleet Street, so that the stroke was not publicized until Churchill himself mentioned it in parliament a year later.[241] No such manipulation would have been possible a few years later, given a press that was by then less dependent on government, and with television in growing competition.

Television's political reticence in 1951 seems in retrospect remarkable. Politicians in the Second World War had banned the BBC from discussing any issue which parliament was likely to debate during the coming fourteen days in an agreement that was confirmed in 1947, yet the immediate success of the first regular televised current affairs programme *In the News*, which began in 1950, revealed the unexploited opportunities. In 1950 the parties turned down the opportunity to televise election messages, and at the general election of 1951 there were only three fifteen-minute televised party broadcasts, reaching less than a tenth of the electorate.[242] So eager was the BBC to remain neutral that apart from party broadcasts it excluded all reference to politics during election campaigns before 1959; even party broadcasts ceased five days before the poll. There was no question at this time of broadcasting parliament even on radio, and Labour in 1953 rejected a request to televise its party conference. Trade union leaders at the party's National Executive Committee did not want the public to see their block votes overturning overwhelming conference majorities: 'it was immensely funny', wrote Crossman, 'listening to the trade unionists showing their terror that anyone should see what really goes on'. In the following year the Conservatives allowed the cameras in, but not until 1955 were the cameras reluctantly admitted into both party conferences, and even then to only one morning of Labour's. Discussing British general elections in 1955, the Oxford psephologist David Butler repeatedly deplored such timidity. 'It is absurd', he wrote, 'that at the height of that most important of national political events, an election, the B.B.C. news bulletins should for all practical purposes ignore it.'[243]

241 Colville, *Fringes of Power*, ii. 329. 242 Butler, *British General Election of 1951*, 75.

243 Quotations from Crossman, *Backbench Diaries*, 257 (30 July 1953). Butler, *British General Election of 1955*, 64.

Here again Churchill was backward looking: when in 1955 he experimented with televising a three-minute broadcast announcing his retirement, he began by saying he was 'sorry to have to descend to this level, but there is no point in refusing to keep pace with the age'; appalled at the outcome, he rejected the project, and its failure remained secret for thirty years.[244] All this soon began to change. The Conservatives had an interest in frequent television appearances by their leaders, who by comparison with Labour's leaders were well-known and doing interesting things. Already by 1952 the party was learning from American presidential campaigns, and three years later it was the first British party to engage a 'media adviser' for his television expertise.[245] Eden, in the general election campaign of 1955, was the first prime minister to address the nation live in a fifteen-minute solo performance; and we have seen how few were Macmillan's media inhibitions.[246] Change accelerated with commercial television's advent in 1955. In February of that year Dingle Foot, chairman of the BBC discussion programme *In the News*, was debarred from allowing his panel to discuss the hydrogen bomb. This was because parliament would be debating it during the coming fortnight, and Foot described live the fourteen-day rule as a 'lunatic restriction'.[247] When challenged on the subject by the Liberal leader Jo Grimond, Churchill pronounced it 'shocking' to have parliament's debates forestalled 'by persons who had not the status or responsibility of Members of Parliament'.[248] The rule was suspended experimentally for six months after the Suez crisis, however, and in July 1957 the suspension was made permanent. Robin Day's interviews soon eroded undue deference towards politicians, Granada Television broke new ground in 1958 by broadcasting on the Rochdale by-election while it was in progress, and at the general election of 1959 the viewers of televised party broadcasts outnumbered the radio audience for the first time.[249]

Given the subsequent national integration of election campaigning, the campaigns of the early 1950s were curiously uncoordinated, but in 1959 it became clear that television was changing the shape of the entire general election campaign. By the late 1950s the party leaders had begun to time their speeches so as to meet television's requirements. In these media contests Labour had hitherto been at a severe disadvantage: it had no prime minister, its leader was wary of television, and the party was coy about selling its wares. Watching a Conservative Party broadcast in 1958, Benn almost despaired of a Labour party whose leaders owned no television set: 'they are totally unaware of these great developments that are going on which are influencing the minds and thought

[244] Gilbert, *'Never Despair'*, 1119. Cockerell, *Live from No. 10*, 22–4, ante-dates it by a year.
[245] Cockerell, *Live from No. 10*, 15, 29.
[246] Ibid. 36.
[247] Briggs, *BBC: First Fifty Years*, 292.
[248] *HC Deb.* 23 Feb. 1955, c. 1277.
[249] Butler and Rose, *British General Election of 1959*, 93.

of the voters'.[250] But during the election Labour took the initiative in capturing the headlines with a morning press conference, forcing the Conservatives to follow suit, and the psephologists detected 'a significant indication of a more analytical approach to the political process' in the widespread discussion of party 'images'—a preoccupation that by 1970 had captured all three parties.[251]

Wilson as Labour leader carried Macmillan's approachability much further. On the BBC's *Election Forum* in 1964 the three party leaders answered the questions raised in some 18,000 postcards from viewers and listeners.[252] Wilson exploited the media in a domestic rather than Olympian way, aiming to capitalize on his informality and ordinariness. His relations with journalists began well in 1964 when as prime minister he showed himself remarkably open, accessible, and understanding. But within two years the relationship had soured, nor could the party still rely on the *Daily Herald*, now revamped and renamed the *Sun*, which Benn pronounced a 'product of market research, without any inner strength and message';[253] from Labour's point of view the paper soon got even worse. Television could help to redress the imbalance: on 25 July 1969 Harold and Mary Wilson conducted an ITV audience on an unpretentious hour-long tour of 10 Downing Street, and on 18 April 1970 ITV was taken on a tour of Chequers. Familiarity did not preclude presidentialism, for in the election of that year both party leaders with their walkabouts, sound bites, and photo opportunities dominated the campaign, throwing both colleagues and sustained argument into the shade.[254] Television commercials from American presidential contests strongly influenced both sides' campaigning at this election: whereas Nixon's in 1968 had influenced the Conservatives, it was Johnson's of 1964 which influenced Wilson, happy now to perform as the seasoned old leader you know and love so well.[255]

From the 1940s to the 1960s political theory's virtual disappearance from public life has been seen as 'a strange death': with the defeat of philosophical idealism, the philosophers had become more abstract in their concerns, and British pragmatism seemed to have paid off. So in the classic period of the welfare state's growth the role of the state, and the citizen's defence against it, received little generalized discussion,[256] whereas information about political behaviour was becoming abundant. Before the advent of opinion polls, the politician had no systematic day-to-day guidance on opinion outside elections except what

[250] *Diaries 1940–62*, 276 (7 May 1958).

[251] Butler and Rose, *British General Election of 1959*, 1. Butler and Pinto-Duschinsky, *British General Election of 1970*, 225.

[252] Butler and King, *British General Election of 1964*, 161.

[253] *Diaries 1963–7*, 141 (15 Sept. 1964); see also 144, 159, and 'The Prime Minister and the Press', *O* (25 May 1969), 7.

[254] Butler and Pinto-Duschinsky, *British General Election of 1970*, 207. *T* (6 June 1970), 9 (leading article).

[255] Cockerell, *Live from No. 10*, 157–9.

[256] J. Harris, 'Political Thought and the State', in S. J. D. Green and R. C. Whiting (eds.), *The Boundaries of the State in Modern Britain* (Cambridge, 1996), 15, 17, 21, 24.

party activists and pressure groups could provide. 'I will tell you, young man, how to predict general-election results', the Chairman of the Conservative Party told Patrick Cosgrave in 1970. 'Once the prime minister . . . calls an election, go into a pub. Sit there for an hour or so and listen to what people are saying. Then saunter down a high street, still listening. Finally, count the number of posters in people's windows noting their affiliations. Once you put all this information together you know who is going to win.'[257] Opinion polls had been born in the United States and came to Britain through the British Institute of Public Opinion, founded in 1937; its Gallup polls were published in the *News Chronicle* exclusively till 1960. After 1951 several new agencies were founded—National Opinion Polls in 1957, Marplan in 1959, the Opinion Research Centre in 1965, MORI polls in 1969—and other newspapers took them up. But even when the pollsters' inquiries were sensible, and some early ones were not, the media had to overcome many prejudices and vested interests.

Where opinion was fluid and open to manipulation, the politician retained his insights into the art of the possible. As Wilson pointed out, 'he is a poor democratic leader, of any political party, in any country, who needs public opinion polls to tell him what is likely to be the popular reaction to particular policies'.[258] The polls subverted the alleged expertise of three groups: politicians, political activists, and journalists. The politician lost his claim to special expertise on the existing state of opinion, though he retained his power to shape it. The political activist lost influence because health and commitment no longer bestowed special influence: polls had to be representative. Furthermore, like the market surveys from which they had emerged, polls fostered the idea of the voter as consumer: the product (party strategy) must adjust to existing views rather than seek to change them [Fig. 5]. The journalist, too, was vulnerable: prodded by David Butler from his earliest days,[259] the journalist who wanted to be taken seriously needed numeracy to reinforce his skill at sniffing the wind. Here too it was 1959—with its conjuncture of opinion polls, television, and political advertising—which first exemplified the general election's new shape. By 1970 the polls had acquired an internal dynamic so formidable as even to threaten the prime minister's power to choose the election's timing.[260]

Less threatening to the politician was the party-political survey of opinion. Discussion in 1959 of topics such as electoral swing, marginal seats, opinion polls, and candidates' pulling power was far more sophisticated than before, yet when talking to the political organizers the psephologists were 'struck by their lack of knowledge about the nature of their market':[261] by the lack of

[257] Obituary of Oliver Poole, *Ind.* (29 Jan. 1993), 27.

[258] *O* (14 Mar. 1971), 29.

[259] See his comments in R. B. McCallum and A. Readman, *The British General Election of 1945* (1947), 290.

[260] *G* (19 May 1970), 10.

[261] Butler and Rose, *British General Election of 1959*, 3; see also 1, 17.

'If there is a general election tomorrow, which Party would you like Labour to resemble?'

Fig. 5. Gaitskell to housewife: Abu Abraham, *Observer* (12 Nov. 1961).

research into what the voters thought and wanted. A traditionalist suspicion of Americanized methods, combined with politicians' professional jealousy, no doubt explains such attitudes where they survived on the right. This had already begun to change: after 1956 the pollsters were increasingly active behind the scenes in advising the political parties on tactics,[262] and from 1957 to 1959 the Conservatives mounted a public-relations campaign on an unprecedented scale. The Labour Party was more suspicious of such developments because relatively distant from the world of advertising, a distance reinforced by its rationalistic distaste for preoccupation with 'images'. It did not see itself as catering for a 'market'. Gaitskell had, after all, begun his career in adult education, and Labour in the 1950s still saw itself as in effect part of that movement: if reason could receive its fair chance, and if the electors' higher

[262] Butler and King, *British General Election of 1964*, 206–7.

feelings could be enlisted, it had everything to gain. By the late 1950s, however, Mark Abrams was helping to induce a change. Rejecting the idea of changing the party's name in 1959, Benn argued half seriously 'that the prune had been resuscitated without a change of name by clever selling',[263] and Labour under Wilson became the new prune. In the run-up to the general election of 1964, it drew in from the fringes an informal group of public-relations experts, and outclassed the Conservatives in skilfully employing them;[264] hence the marked rise in real terms during the 1960s and 1970s in Labour's central spending on general elections.[265]

All these media developments simultaneously centralized and decentralized the election campaign, impoverishing the intermediate campaign at neighbourhood and community level, and undermining party branches. The agenda of London's somewhat introverted press conferences and media performances often diverged markedly from events in the constituencies, and the real election battle was increasingly fought by getting messages directly into the home through radio and television at the expense of public meeting and party branch. Doomed was the sort of constituency-branch 'social' whose dispiriting tail-end Crossman described in 1957: 'the usual dreary kind of affair, in which you enter a long school hall and see a few elderly ladies scattered around the edges of the empty dance floor, sitting chattering in low voices, while a woman plays the piano and the master of ceremonies fails to get anybody dancing'.[266]

What incentive could now be offered, then, to the 3 per cent of British electors who in 1964 participated in election campaigning, the 8 per cent who attended election meetings, the 14 per cent who subscribed to their local party, and the 25 per cent who were nominal party members?[267] A centralized campaign undermined the party activist's moral claim to influence over party policy, for knocking on doors and addressing leaflets now seemed still less important than what the party leader and his machine did at the centre. Working in the same direction were the psephologists' doubts by the 1960s on whether the election campaign did much to change voting intentions, given that these were formed over a much longer period.[268] 'Perhaps in retrospect it will be evident', wrote R. T. McKenzie, 'that the mass party saw its heyday during the period when the extension of the franchise had created a mass electorate, but there was as yet no effective means of reaching the voters in their own homes.'[269] Television's

[263] Benn, *Diaries 1940–62*, 317 (11 Oct. 1959).
[264] Pimlott, *Wilson*, 270, 309. Butler and King, *British General Election of 1964*, 70, 90–1.
[265] See the useful table in Pinto-Duschinsky, *British Political Finance 1830–1980*, 167.
[266] *Backbench Diaries*, 622 (24 Oct. 1957), at Upper Stoke, Coventry.
[267] Butler and Stokes, *Political Change* (2nd edn.), 21; (1st edn.), 421.
[268] D. E. Butler and A. King, *The British General Election of 1966* (1966), 95.
[269] McKenzie, *British Political Parties*, 648.

advent certainly played down the policy-forming role of the party conference and played it up as a media and publicity event. Academics increasingly flocked to them; their fringe meetings first grew in importance at Labour conferences, then with the Liberals, and finally with the Conservatives.[270] A double difficulty then faced the party leaders: receiving less deference from the party conference, they simultaneously had to pursue the ordinary voter whose views (as measured by polls and surveys) diverged from it.

Still the British people were far better informed in 1970 than in 1951 about how their political system worked. The wealth of information that became available in the 1950s fostered a shift towards behavioural rather than legal/constitutional or theoretical approaches to the study of politics. True, there was a continuing demand for the constitutional expert who travelled the world framing political structures for developing countries, but 'political scientists' of the modern type were more interested in understanding how the domestic political system worked. The contrast, for instance, between A. B. Keith's legalistic *British Cabinet System 1830–1938* (1939) and John Mackintosh's empirical/historical *British Cabinet* (1962) is striking, and encouraged Crossman, Gordon Walker, and others to publish on the realities of cabinet relationships in the 1960s. R. T. McKenzie's *British Political Parties* (1955) stripped away much mythology about the structure and working of the party system, and as the limits to reason's role in politics became increasingly apparent, Graham Wallas was retrospectively vindicated. In affecting the outcome of the election in any constituency, wrote Butler in 1952, 'it appears that the quality of the candidate and his organisation matter remarkably little'. A full-scale panel survey of voting behaviour was at last launched in the 1960s, a benchmark against which all subsequent shifts in political opinion could be measured. By 1972 the prominent Labour politician Shirley Williams was complaining about 'the quite extraordinary number of interviews we are expected to give these days, and questionnaires to fill in'.[271]

Some even began to fear that so close a preoccupation with the governed would devalue the study of government.[272] Yet at a time when the academic study of politics was growing so fast, there was no reason why the first should preclude the second, especially as the second gained so much from the growing openness of government. Democratic government could only benefit through closer knowledge of how voters think and behave, and we have seen how the psephologists encouraged important changes in election management. By illuminating the narrowness of the margin between the parties, and the potential

[270] A. Watkins, 'Rolling Conferences Gather No Media', *O* (17 Oct. 1982), 7. D. Leonard in *T* (1 Oct. 1969), 10.

[271] Butler, *British General Election of 1951*, 3–4. Williams, *TLS* (15 Dec. 1972), 1523.

[272] See M. Beloff's inaugural lecture (1958) in P. King (ed.), *The Study of Politics: A Collection of Inaugural Lectures* (1977), 175.

importance of quite small campaigning changes, psephologists encouraged the parties towards professionalizing their election campaigns.[273] By the 1950s the psephologists had also demonstrated the importance of national 'swing' and the national campaign, and the relative unimportance of candidate, party organization, and local issues as influences on the votes cast in any one constituency. This encouraged the parties' growing focus on winning marginal seats,[274] a trend already apparent in 1959 when party workers practised mutual aid.[275] By 1964 money and workers were being so extensively redeployed in this way as to render the campaign in the safe seats largely nominal.[276]

Enhanced information about politics does not necessarily bring political understanding or political wisdom, let alone willingness to participate. The media did not raise turnout beyond the threshold of 1950–1: in 1964 only 43 per cent of those eligible voted in contested local elections and only 77 per cent in general elections, though 92 per cent followed the general election campaign through the media or through conversation.[277] Even among those who voted, many were ill-informed. The majority of a sample interviewed for the *Sunday Times* in 1962 could not name any political figure in either major party other than the party leaders; according to a Gallup poll of 1963 several million electors thought Britain was then already in the EEC; and National Opinion Polls in the following year found that many electors favoured nationalizing the (already nationalized) mines and railways.[278] By the late 1960s serious people began to think more deeply about the wider political significance of these media developments, with Crossman and Benn to the fore. Though antedating the likely change, Benn in 1968 plausibly predicted that computers would enable governments both to make more information available and (through electronic referenda) to consult much more widely, as well as to integrate the taxation and benefit systems.[279] Both politicians worried about media trends. 'If it moves, film it', wrote the journalist Peter Jenkins in 1969, discussing television's editorial principle: 'if it doesn't move, spike it'.[280] This led the rationalist in Crossman to prefer radio: 'five minutes on The World at One can be far more valuable than five minutes even on a high peak evening television programme', he claimed in 1968, because it was easier on radio to 'get across quite a complicated idea'. Benn complained that 'almost all we see of trade union or business leaders are hurried little street interviews when they are pinned against a wall by a battery of accusing

[273] Butler and King, *British General Election of 1966*, 95. Butler and Stokes, *Political Change in Britain* (1st edn.), 419.

[274] D. E. Butler, *The Electoral System in Britain 1918–1951* (Oxford, 1953), 201; cf. Shirley Williams, 'The Relevance of Political Science', *TLS* (15 Dec. 1972), 1523.

[275] Butler and Rose, *British General Election of 1959*, 135.

[276] Butler and King, *British General Election of 1964*, 216.

[277] Butler and Stokes, *Political Change in Britain* (2nd edn.), 21.

[278] Ibid. 22–3.

[279] Speech at Llandudno to the Welsh Council of Labour, *G* (27 May 1968), 2.

[280] *G* (13 May 1969), 9.

microphones, wielded by interrogators who have just come from covering an air crash and are on their way to the hospital where some quins have been born'.[281]

Television's preoccupation with action and movement also risked encouraging violence, as Benn publicly warned. Broader channels of communication between people and government would, he thought, enable opinion to be expressed more spontaneously: 'if law and order were ever to break down, in part or in whole, in Britain', he claimed, 'the policy of restricted access and unrestricted coverage would have to bear a very considerable part of the responsibility'.[282] When ITN cameras filmed the second of two violent demonstrations against the Vietnam war in 1968, some thought that Benn's fears had been realized, though the Dutch precedent of ceasing to show film of Amsterdam riots was not followed.[283] Crossman felt that television's overrating of ratings put a premium on politics as fun, breaking up the speaker's material and giving the heckler more than his due. For Benn, politics was in itself trivialized,[284] and for similar reasons he complained that the media played down issues and played up personalities: there were 'columns and columns of personal tittle-tattle masquerading as serious political comment', and newsreaders who were becoming personalities in their own right.[285] R. T. McKenzie and Michael Foot complained that politicians were being treated like film stars seeking to boost their latest 'rating'.[286]

Particularly worrying was the growing cynicism about politics. In this, the media were merely echoing the mood of the time, nourished by the political satire of the early 1960s. Lunching with media people in September 1964, Benn sniffed a mood that 'was anti-political in a scornful and contemptuous way'. Five years later in a television programme on a by-election, Benn attacked the presenter Alastair Burnet for claiming that the candidates were looking worried perhaps because they had taken out a bet on the result: 'I just went for him and said this cheapened, vulgarised and denigrated politics', at which Burnet allegedly 'crumpled'.[287] The journalist Paul Johnson in June 1970 expressed disgust at 'the spectacle of TV professionals—not notorious for the gravity or sincerity of their opinions—attempting to corner politicians into admitting that they are liars, manipulators or even scoundrels', whereas in his experience the great majority were 'honest, with genuine convictions, trying to serve their country to the best of their ability'.[288] ITV set out to break with the BBC's undue deference and publicly to subject politicians to irreverence in House of

281 Crossman, Granada Lecture, *T* (22 Sept. 1968), 8. Benn speech at Bristol, *T* (19 Oct. 1968), 10.
282 Speech at Bristol, *T* (19 Oct. 1968), 10. See also his speech at Llandudno, *G* (27 May 1968), 2.
283 Potter, *Independent Television in Britain*, iv. 109.
284 Granada Guildhall Lecture, *T* (22 Oct. 1968), 8. Benn, Bristol speech, *T* (19 Oct. 1968), 10.
285 Speech at Llandudno, *G* (27 May 1968), 2. See also his Bristol speech, *T* (19 Oct. 1968), 10.
286 McKenzie, *O* (22 Oct. 1967), 10. For Foot see Crossman, *Cabinet Diaries*, iii. 327 (17 Jan. 1969).
287 Benn, *Diaries 1963–7*, 138 (8 Sept. 1964). Benn, *Diaries 1968–72*, 209 (30 Oct. 1969).
288 *NS* (19 June 1970), 858.

Commons style,[289] and the BBC followed suit. Indeed, in March 1963 the BBC broadcast a lampoon on itself when *That Was The Week That Was* included a sketch on Richard Dimbleby's coverage of the Queen's recent departure for Australia: it was directed less at the monarchy than at the BBC's sycophancy towards it.[290]

The BBC's decision in autumn 1968 to assign the party conferences no more than ordinary news coverage[291] was ominous: perhaps their enhanced political coverage in the early 1950s had reflected pursuit of novelty rather than respect for the political process, and perhaps in their pursuit of entertainment the media were now moving on. The general election of 1970 left the overall trend unclear. Audiences for almost all the political programmes were down on 1966, and yet as many as 8.5 million people saw even the least popular among the party political broadcasts, and some twenty million stayed up for the results.[292] Perhaps this reflected a media conversion of the election into a 'spectacle' which played down the intellectual content and fragmented such as remained by pursuing interesting camera shots.[293] Certainly politics could not compete with football: an ORC poll found that a fifth of those polled, most of them Labour supporters, said they were less interested in the general election than in the World Cup.[294]

This chapter has shown that British political institutions were not unchanging in the 1950s and 1960s, but that the change came primarily from without, not from within. It stemmed from technological innovation (most notably in the media), and from evolution in the social context: accelerating globalization, shifts in social-class relationships, speeded-up transport, new patterns of crime, and the like. So whereas monarchy, cabinet, parliament, civil service, and local government remained in externals largely the same, all had in practice evolved considerably between 1951 and 1970. Change in the political parties was obvious even in externals: lacking any fixed constitutional existence, and flourishing only through alertness to social trends, they were by 1970 less aloof, more resourceful in sounding out opinion, and better informed on what opinion most needed cultivating.

The fourth of the Introduction's eight motifs has already unobtrusively featured: much institutional reform in the 1950s and 1960s reflected attempts to grapple with the growing and paradoxical pressures on time created by so-called time-saving devices. There were mounting pressures on cabinet, parliament, and civil service for participation, representation, and legislation. Six more motifs are relevant. In these years the politician amply experienced

289 Cockerell, *Live from No. 10*, 43–4.
290 Pimlott, *The Queen*, 321.
291 *T* (26 Sept. 1968), 10.
292 Butler and Pinto-Duschinsky, *British General Election of 1970*, 227–8, 337 n. 1.
293 As argued in *T* (6 June 1970), 9 (leader).
294 Butler and Pinto-Duschinsky, *British General Election of 1970*, 154 n. 1.

the second: the tension between hermetic and receptive responses to worldwide developments. Even parliament and the judiciary by the 1960s thought they had much to learn from the USA and also from Sweden, and the civil service had become much more respectful towards France, as well as receptive to Scandinavia. As for the political parties, they were eager for any ideas on how to enhance their impact, and this despatched them quickly to the USA for guidance. In so far as they were becoming unashamed in espousing a materialist agenda and repudiating austerity, party change also picks up the fifth motif of Christian structures undermined by more earthbound values. The motif most prominent in this chapter, however, is the sixth; the persisting apparent stability in political institutions amidst substantial change within their social context. Also apparent is the seventh, given the institutional and cultural limits to the British politician's power. Not only had he to operate within pluralistic but centralizing structures: he was now exposed to the added force that the pollsters lent to opinion. British primacy in the continuity of its institutions might still be incorporated into a distinctive world role (the eighth motif), but the UK was less confident of institutional superiority. As for the first motif, the Second World War's initial impact had been to reinforce conservatism in all British political institutions, with monarchy now secure and parliament's prestige enhanced. The 1960s, however, saw much less complacency, and also an easing in the war's contraints on nationalism within Scotland and Wales. Northern Ireland was, as usual, special. Its wartime memories of resisting Hitler were integral to Ulster Unionism, and were long treasured, whereas Irish nationalist memories about both world wars were selective indeed.

CHAPTER 9

'The Sixties'

Apart from Chapter 1, on the late 1940s, the chapters in this book so far have each followed through the entire period 1951–70. All have been concerned with selected fields of inquiry concerning actualities as much as attitudes. This chapter is different: it moves towards rounding off the book by taking only one decade as its main concern, not with the aim of narrating events within it, but in order to clarify the decade's reputation and impact. The phrase 'the sixties' conjures up at least four images: of youth in revolt, relaxed manners, political radicalism, and puritanism repudiated—though intimately linked with the latter was a 'new puritanism' that was in some ways at least as austere as what it replaced. The first section will show that 'sixties' attitudes and values began rather earlier. The four middle sections will be assigned to each of these images in turn. The sixth, concluding, section will ask how far, if at all, the sixties ended in 1970.

1. THE SIXTIES BEGIN

'The sixties' was a phrase which in Britain came to signify rather more than the events of a decade. In denoting distinctive attitudes and experiences, it resembled the 1840s, the 1890s, the 1920s, the 1930s, and the 1980s in British history. Each of these decades acquired a distinctive cultural resonance: the first and fourth came to symbolize scarcity and poverty, whereas the other three symbolized rejection of hitherto prevailing convention. The 1980s discarded a constricting set of economic attitudes, whereas the 1890s and 1920s repudiated constricting conventions on morals and manners. Most other decades since the 1850s have lacked distinctiveness because fractured by war, political overturn, or both. In 1964 the sixties too experienced political overturn, but less in substantive policy than in the government's party label. As so often after 1951, social was more important than political change, and such distinctiveness as the decade possessed concerned rebellion in manners and morals, aligning it with the 1890s and the 1920s. And yet there are drawbacks in playing parlour games of this kind. To begin with, some of these fluctuations have an international dimension: the 1920s and 1960s, for example, acquired a 'permissive' image in America as well as in Britain. Furthermore, social change is neither sudden, not does it coincide precisely with arbitrary ways of dividing up time: in both Britain and America the twentieth-century permissive trend was continuous, and in these two decades did no more than accelerate or gain more publicity.[1] Furthermore, social changes in any one society are not uniform or unanimous, if only because any major social change will be controversial, and will evoke an opposite (if not equal) reaction; and in so far as such changes catch on, they will diffuse gradually through the regions. London set much of the permissire pace in the 1960s, for instance, and sixties trends moved only slowly across the country in a shift that was certainly not confined to one decade.

Yet labelling decades is useful for comprehending events within them that might otherwise seem random; the labels help later decades to locate themselves. Most people who lived through the 1960s did not feel that they were collectively experiencing an outlook special to a decade, nor in the decade's early years would it have been possible to view events in that way. But once the decade could be viewed complete, the phrase 'the sixties' became identified with throwing off old inhibitions, conventions, and restraints. All four of the 'sixties' images outlined appeared during the previous decade, each coming from different directions with their separate chronologies, but drawing closer together towards the end of the fifties. The first, youth in revolt, was far from new. In 1778 Samuel Johnson complained that 'subordination is sadly broken down in this age', and grumbled about 'a general relaxation of reverence', whereby 'no son now depends upon his father as in former times'.[2] Indiscipline among the young was one reason adduced in the 1880s to explain Britain's declining industrial competitiveness,[3] and for many Edwardians the vitality of the suffragette and socialist movements betokened a dangerous social indiscipline. 'There's one thing about freedom . . . ', says Rome in Rose Macaulay's *Told by an Idiot* (1923), 'each generation of people begins by thinking they've got it for the first time in history, and ends by being sure the generation younger than themselves have too much of it.'[4].

None the less, it is from the mid-1950s that the widening cultural divide between youth and age conventionally dates, with James Dean as deceased icon and Elvis Presley as ongoing performer. 'Consciousness raising' is less feasible for age groups than for a social class, a religious group, or a sex. Aids to self-awareness—concentrated patterns of residence or work, key self-written inspirational texts, integrating and exclusive institutions—were almost by

[1] As pointed out in C. Davies, *Permissive Britain* (1975), 9, 11. Difficulties in interpreting the sixties are more fully discussed in B. Harrison, 'Historiographical Hazards of Sixties Britain' in W. R. Louis (ed.) *Ultimate Adventures with Brittania* (2009).

[2] J. Boswell, *Life of Johnson,* ed. R. W. Chapman (World's Classics edn. 1980), 924.

[3] Royal Commission . . . into the Depression of Trade and Industry, *Final Report*, PP 1886 (C.4797), xxiii, 569.

[4] R. Macaulay, *Told by an Idiot* (1st publ. 1923, Leipzig: Tauchnitz edn., 1924), 46.

definition denied to British youth even in the sixties, let alone earlier. Dispersed within their homes, the young had no shared institutions of their own. Besides, youth is a relatively ephemeral, transitional state. Even popular culture could draw together only rapidly successive cohorts among the young, each new cohort discrediting its precursor by espousing the latest fashion. Furthermore, the young are at all times fragmented by small age gradations, and these are often reinforced by educational rites of passage. 'For most of us education is an instrument of war', Edmund Leach complained in 1967, 'a weapon by which the individual beats down his competitors and defends himself against adversity.'[5] The young were also divided by sex, in a segregation that was encouraged at least until the 1950s by parental prudence, and co-education had not yet become the norm. Yet during the 1950s four new influences had begun to render young people more self-aware: earlier physical maturity without concomitant social adjustment, the cultivation of the young as a commercial category, extended education, and growing international contact with their own kind. The concept of the 'teenager' originates in the steady long-term fall in the age of reproductive maturity,[6] to which social institutions adapted only too slowly. We have already seen how the 'two cultures' of C. P. Snow were complemented in the 1950s by the far more pervasive 'two cultures' of teenager and adult.[7] By 1967 the phrase 'generation gap' was being used in the USA, and later in the decade it came into regular use in the UK.[8] Young people from the mid-1950s were being drawn together as never before by shared grievances (against adults, with their institutions, rules, and regulations) and by shared tastes (in recreation, clothes, and other goods readily provided by the many industries feeding off their relatively uncommitted wealth).

Political radicalism, the second of the sixties themes, was also present in the 1950s, though in a decade which saw the Conservatives continuously in power from 1951, it can hardly be said to have been dominant. This mood, in so far as it was associated with meritocratic ideas, stemmed from the social radicalism of the Second World War.[9] From the late 1940s that radical impetus had temporarily run down, and Churchill's last years as prime minister witnessed a cautious return to traditionalist colour and ceremonial. After 1956, however, the left resumed its cultural advance, more radical than socialist in flavour, reinforced by a new and often provincial realism in fiction, stage, and film, and a provincial rejection of privilege and tradition was integral to the mood of the Labour Party which took office in 1964. This renewal on the left owed much to the Suez landings in November 1956: 'Suez, that was when we lost

[5] E. Leach, *A Runaway World?* (1969), 67.

[6] For a full discussion of this see R. V. Short, 'Man, the Changing Animal', in E. M. Coutinho and F. Fuchs (eds.), *Physiology and Genetics of Reproduction* (New York, 1974), A. 5–8.

[7] See above, pp. 260–3.

[8] COPAC search.

[9] See above, pp. 64–5, 301–2.

the intellectual vote', Iain Macleod recalled.[10] True, the Conservatives won their third successive election victory handsomely in 1959, but that was partly because the episode's full significance had not yet become public; delayed in its impact, it was ultimately significant, politically and culturally.[11]

John Wain and Kingsley Amis fashioned a new type of self-dependent hero who rejected modernism and elite culture: Wain's Charles Lumley in *Hurry on Down* (1953) and Amis's Jim Dixon in *Lucky Jim* (1954). In this they were influenced by their experience of service life, by logical positivism, by their rejection of fashionable literary London, and by the attitudes of Orwell and Leavis.[12] In his powerful novel *Room at the Top* John Braine, who later published a critical study of Priestley, assimilated this provincial and meritocratic mood to the increasingly relaxed moral conventions of the time by portraying the career of Joe Lampton, a northern working-class lad immediately after the war. Almost parodying the nineteenth-century self-help story, Joe forces himself into the world of privilege through merit, but his merit is sexual, with no hint of self-denial. He squares off against his more polished rival for the daughter of the rich factory-owner in the northern industrial town of Warley, later recalling that 'I was going to enjoy all the luxuries which that young man enjoyed . . . It was as clear and compelling as the sense of vocation which doctors and missionaries are supposed to experience, though in my instance, of course, the call ordered me to do good to myself not others.'[13] In his approach to the establishment, Alan Sillitoe's challenge in *The Loneliness of the Long-Distance Runner* (1959, film 1962) was more frontal, for whereas Joe aimed ultimately to join it, Sillitoe's Borstal-boy anti-hero Colin Smith outwitted it by making only an initial and deceptive pretence of cooperating with it. Sillitoe (like Stan Barstow, Barry Hines, and David Storey) made all the more impact from the late 1950s, when the working-class author was in vogue, because drawn from a lower social level than the decade's earlier literary rebels. It was this mood which prompted what in retrospect seemed the wholly unjustified enthusiasm for Colin Wilson's *Outsider* in 1956: fashionable opinion's head had been turned by Wilson's self-educated background and French cultural enthusiasms.

The third sixties theme, the challenge to the rigidities and formalities of the adult world, was in some respects a social equivalent of political radicalism. The relaxation of manners had long been building up. Sixties culture was the latest among the many offspring of the eighteenth-century Enlightenment project: rationalistic in readily brushing aside tradition in its pursuit of the modern; optimistic in releasing human nature from its constraints. In remodelling social

[10] R. Blake quotes this remark made to him in his 'Anthony Eden', in J. P. Mackintosh (ed.), *British Prime Ministers in the Twentieth Century*, ii. *Churchill to Callaghan* (1978), 115.

[11] See above, pp. 104–7, 439–40.

[12] R. Hewison, *In Anger: Culture in the Cold War 1945–60* (1981), 116–17.

[13] Braine, *Room at the Top*, 29.

and political institutions it hoped to improve human nature. In repudiating hypocrisy and convention it relished spontaneity and informality, and readily strayed into humour, satire, and sarcasm. The 1950s saw the high point of the progressive educational methods that had been advancing in Britain at least since the 1920s. The child-centred approach, designed to make learning enjoyable and to reveal new talent, was now by no means confined to the so-called 'progressive schools'. As an influence upon curriculum and teaching methods, it was reinforced by a political concern for equal opportunity that involved a daily confrontation in school with formality and hierarchy, undermining the earlier emphasis on rote learning, and on the importance of grammar, spelling, punctuation, right-handedness, legible handwriting, correct spelling, and correct pronunciation. Well before the 1960s, school hierarchies were being humanized, curricular compulsions were relaxing, consultation with parents and pupils was extending, discipline was becoming less harsh, uniforms were in retreat.

Formality in personal relations had been relaxing for decades before the 1960s. Many early-Victorian sons addressed their fathers as 'Sir' and their schoolfriends by surname, and few wives addressed their husbands by first name in public, yet by the end of the nineteenth century all this was changing.[14] American and democratic influences, together with the intimacy of the radio which could readily be turned off, carried the process further between the wars. In 1944 E. M. Forster could refer to the interwar transition from the stranger's 'Dear Sir' to 'Dear Mr Forster' as a way of addressing him: a 'more friendly' convention which 'I expect . . . came in, like other speakeasies, from America'. Radio's interwar influence had also rendered politicians' speeches less pompous.[15] By the 1960s the situation had so reversed that addressing John Smith with the once-familiar 'Smith' risked giving offence, and men were almost indiscriminately using first names; the signifiers of genuine intimacy between men were lost in the process.[16] Writers and artists too in the 1950s were relaxing attitudes to hierarchy and traditional forms. Cultural innovation was reinforced by the vogue for science fiction and jazz; like radio and television, though unlike many earlier cultural fashions, they travelled upwards from below. Wain, Amis, and Larkin all developed a sideline as jazz critics, at the same time as artists' interest in science fiction was preparing the ground for the pop art of the 1960s.[17] The 'movement' in literature[18] prepared the ground well for John Osborne and the so-called 'angry young man', a phrase only just

[14] A. West, 'Some Changes in Social Life during the Queen's Reign', *Nineteenth Century* (Apr. 1897), 649.

[15] E. M. Forster, 'English Prose between 1918 and 1939' (1944) in his *Two Cheers for Democracy* (1st publ. 1951, paperback edn. Harmondsworth, 1965), 282.

[16] A. S. C. Ross with R. Brackenbury, 'U and Non-U Today: 1. Language', *New Society* (22 Aug. 1968), 265.

[17] Hewison, *In Anger*, 114–15.

[18] See above, p. 170.

catching on when used in this context by J. B. Priestley in the *New Statesman*, then still an important literary medium.[19]

These cultural protests should not be reified into a coherent campaign, not least because the rather rugged pipe-smoking Englishness of 'the movement' differed markedly from Colin Wilson's European cultural enthusiasms and existentialist angst. The stage embodiment of the 'angry young man', a concept much discussed at the time, was Jimmy Porter, who plays out in a Midlands attic flat his resentful and self-pitying story in *Look Back in Anger* (1956, film 1958). The play's 'freewheeling . . . and blazingly intemperate language'[20] burst the bounds of conventional West End drawing-room theatre, and helped to establish the Royal Court Theatre in Sloane Square as London's theatrical pacesetter: Tynan announced doubts 'if I could love anyone who did not wish to see' the play. The targets of the angry young men were diverse enough and their approach sufficiently anti-political and self-advertising to catch many a young intellectual eye, but without practical outcome. Their anger often reflected an impatient desire to arrive which moderated on reaching the desired destination. Commenting on the play in 1957, a stage meritocrat from an earlier generation whose mode of arrival had been very different was puzzled: 'I wish I knew why the hero is so dreadfully cross and what about', wrote Noel Coward privately in his diary—'I . . . cannot understand why the younger generation, instead of knocking at the door, should bash the fuck out of it.'[21]

The meritocratic and radical mood so widespread by the mid-1950s was not confined to the grammar schools; an undercurrent of subversive humour in press and radio had for some time been ridiculing conservatives of the more backward-looking variety,[22] and a similar mood now emerged within the training grounds of the young elite. Retaining throughout an English amateurism and taste for national self-depreciation, the amateur dramatics and smoking concerts of public school and Oxbridge gave birth to the very English *At the Drop of a Hat* (1956) of Michael Flanders and Donald Swann, an unusual partnership that had originated before 1939 at Westminster School. Given the long run this revue enjoyed in its various guises, the vein of national self-mockery, highly developed in Noel Coward's cabaret acts of the 1950s, was carried forward into the 1960s, not least because it combined Coward's traits with a gentle variation on the national theme of eccentricity and understatement. Culturally more significant were the somewhat more abrasive magazine *Private Eye* and the stage revue *Beyond the Fringe* (1960), both of which interacted, and both only half-subversive in mood. They owed much to prior public-school and university friendships, and half-affectionately ridiculed the culture of the

[19] Hewison, *In Anger*, 130. [20] Billington, *State of the Nation*, 102.
[21] Tynan, *View of the English Stage*, 178. *Noel Coward Diaries*, 349 (17 Feb. 1957).
[22] See above, pp. 399–401.

stiff upper lip which had upheld an empire that could provide employment no longer.

The key partnership behind *Private Eye*, between Richard Ingrams and Paul Foot, originated in their schoolboy journalism at Shrewsbury School. With the friendship resumed after national service at University College Oxford, they helped to run a student magazine, and this foreshadowed *Private Eye*, launched in November 1961. We have seen how Ingrams's failure to get a national-service commission had enabled him to view the officer class sceptically from below;[23] another of the *Eye*'s founders William Rushton (cartoonist and satirist), also at Shrewsbury, refused during national service to apply for a commission, and in later life declined invitations to speak at public-school functions.[24] The paper's tone was left-liberal, owing much to the Liberal journalistic tradition whereby members of the elite knowingly exposed scandal and humbug in high places; it often drew upon volunteered inside information. Neither Ingrams nor the paper were politically partisan. Evidence that *Private Eye* criticized whichever party was in power comes from its two long-lived humorous serialized spoof documents written by Ingrams with another Oxford contact, the actor and author John Wells: 'Mrs Wilson's Diary' (from the mid-1960s) and 'Dear Bill' (satirizing Denis Thatcher, and subsequently made into the successful musical, *Anyone for Denis?*). Mildly conservative by temperament and intuitive in his journalism, Ingrams complemented his assiduous and fiercely left-wing colleague Foot: whereas Ingrams 'wanted to stop the world changing for the worse, Foot wanted to change it for the better'.[25]

Their link with the stage came through Peter Cook, who in political outlook resembled Ingrams in some respects. With a grandfather and father pursuing careers in the empire, Cook as a schoolboy at Radley also criticized the system from within. A brilliant mimic, he quietly detested arrogance and hypocrisy, but not in such a way as to become strongly politicized, let alone to identify with the left. His surreal humour owed much to the Goons, and he took a delight in parodying the type of wartime patriotic film on which his generation had been brought up. It was his surreal send-up of the heroic Antarctic story through a spoof interview with the polar adventurer 'Scribble' Gibbons that gained him acceptance with the Cambridge Footlights, and his burlesque of Macmillan's television style in *Beyond the Fringe* instantly rendered political oratory in that vein impossible, just as Alan Bennett's hilarious parsonical performance pulverized the pulpit's precious affectation. Cook in devising his sketch had felt no personal hostility to Macmillan, nor was *Beyond the Fringe* (with Jonathan Miller and Dudley Moore) forcing itself on the Edinburgh Festival from outside; on the contrary, it was encouraged by its artistic director as an official

[23] See above, pp. 91–2. [24] Obituary, *DT* (12 Dec. 1996), 21.

[25] H. Thompson, *Richard Ingrams: Lord of the Gnomes* (1st publ. 1994, paperback edn. 1995), 201.

rival to compete with the growing number of late-night unofficial fringe events, and its four performers were drawn from the two leading universities. The wartime theme reappeared in the revue's sketch on 'The aftermyth of war', but although its four performers opposed reactionary views, their outlook was non-party, not politically progressive.[26] Tynan saw *Beyond the Fringe* as a major breakthrough in British comedy, though less radical than he would have liked.[27] It ran on the London stage from 1961 to 1966, and interacted with the satirical television programme *That Was The Week That Was*, to which much of the *Eye*'s early talent deserted. The programme's weekly exposure of the corrupt, the pompous, and the self-serving exposed politics and government to commentary less reverential than at any time since Gillray and Rowlandson,[28] and what was later seen as an important aspect of sixties culture was now fully launched.

The fourth sixties theme, too—the reaction against wartime austerity and puritanism—was gestating well before 1960. Fluctuations in personal conduct are at least as central as economic fluctuations to a nation's daily experience, but they are more difficult to measure; if personal conduct could be assessed as precisely as economic behaviour, it would probably be revealed as more stable than public attitudes to it. From 1600 to 1660 puritanism was advancing, and the term was eventually extended to denote 'a member of any religious sect or party that advocates or aspires to special purity of doctrine or practice'. After 1660 the national outlook on personal conduct relaxed till the late eighteenth century. Then puritanism, in the sense of the public pursuit of purity in personal conduct, reappeared in force during the evangelical revival, only to be sent into reverse a century later. The First World War revived the ancient association between national self-defence and a puritan appeasement of the Almighty, which after the hedonism of the 1920s revived again during the Second World War. It was during the 1950s that the hedonistic and materialistic reaction in Britain against wartime puritanism began. It owed much to an American influence which had begun in wartime, when jitterbugging and jiving Americans advertised in Britain the less formal approaches to dancing already familiar in American films. Here the fashions were being set from below, and the partners were acting less as a pair than as individuals—a move towards informality that was extended later to rock and roll and the twist. British pop singers from the mid-1950s often assumed a mid-Atlantic accent and vocabulary, much of which they and their followers carried over into ordinary speech—though this tendency was moderated by the Beatles' distinctively British contribution to pop music in the 1960s, and (still more) by punk groups in the 1970s.

[26] This paragraph owes much to H. Thompson's admirable *Peter Cook: A Biography* (1997).

[27] Tynan, *View of the English Stage*, 311.

[28] *T* (12 Dec. 1996), 23.

In discussing American films in 1951, Rowntree and Lavers implicitly acknowledged their threat to the socialist ideal, complaining that 'wealth and luxury are constantly held out to be desirable ends in themselves'. The novel of violence, luxury, and lust was pioneered by Ian Fleming's James Bond story *Goldfinger* (1959); Harold Nicolson thought it 'an obscene book, "liable to corrupt"'. Fleming was unashamed in saying that his motive in writing was primarily financial, and that his James Bond novels were 'written for warm-blooded heterosexuals in railway trains, airplanes or beds';[29] he had many successors, and Nicolson's reaction soon became rare. By later standards the 1950s found violence within British society un-English and peculiarly distasteful. Such feelings were strong enough to procure legislation in 1955 against importing violent American comics for children,[30] but not strong enough by 1965 to drive Edward Bond's *Saved* (1965), with its brutal and motiveless torture and murder of a baby in a pram, from the Royal Court Theatre—despite the fact that polls in 1965 and 1967 about televised violence revealed respondents declaring by a large margin that there was too much of it.[31]

Capitalist accumulation was not necessarily associated with freedom in personal conduct: Conservative governments had often tightened moral controls while championing economic freedom, and in the 1950s important Conservative and Labour groups wanted moralistic interference curbed. However, Macmillan privately told ministers in 1959 that many restrictions reflected a primitive distrust of the people, whereas 'like children growing up we can all now be trusted to do more of what is right'. With Conservative help, Anglo-American contrasts in attitudes to gambling began to fade. In 1956 Macmillan as Chancellor introduced premium bonds, which the Archbishop of Canterbury pronounced as promoting 'private gain without responsibility',[32] and between then and the 1960s the Conservative government helped to take betting off the streets by greatly liberalizing gambling law through the Betting and Gaming Act (1960). The Act prompted changes that surpassed what had been intended: betting shops, initially uninviting and uncomfortable, gradually moved into the high street and became more public and less spartan. By the end of the 1960s there were nearly 16,000, increasingly being mopped up by William Hill,

[29] *English Life and Leisure*, 249. Nicolson, *Diaries 1945–62*, 371 (22 Nov. 1959). I. Fleming, 'How to Write a Thriller', *Books and Bookmen* (May 1963), 14.

[30] See M. Barker, *A Haunt of Fears: The Strange History of the British Horror Comics Campaign* (1984), and the discussion of the Bentley case above, pp. 292–3.

[31] *Gallup Polls*, 844 (Dec. 1965), 934 (June 1967). See also B. Ford (ed.), *The New Pelican Guide to English Literature*, viii. *From Orwell to Naipaul* (1st publ. 1983, rev. edn. 1995), 264.

[32] Macmillan quoted in Jarvis, *Conservative Governments, Morality and Social Change*, 1, to the 12th meeting of the 'steering committee' on 26 June 1959. Archbishop quoted in E. R. Norman, *Church and Society in England 1770–1970: A Historical Study* (Oxford, 1976), 390.

Ladbrokes, Coral, and Mecca[33]—firms which soon diversified into casinos and bingo halls. The Act prompted the opening of the UK's first commercial bingo hall in 1961. Imported from the USA, the game moved into many vacant old cinemas, and in its peak year (1974) there were 1,820 halls in Great Britain, especially attractive to women, less attractive to the young.[34] The Conservatives' Licensing Act (1961) relaxed pub opening hours, but—in a combination of restriction and liberation that recurred in the sixties—raised the penalties for drunkenness. Opinion polls from April 1958 to January 1968 showed increasing support for Sunday theatres, cinemas, and professional sport,[35] and in fiction materialist values were noticeably advancing.

The sexual dimension of the anti-puritan reaction goes back not only before the 1960s, but far back into the nineteenth century. 'Sexual intercourse began in nineteen sixty-three', Larkin famously wrote in 1967, '(Which was rather late for me)'. For Larkin it had in truth been launched, in the sense of sexual intercourse outside marriage, with Ruth Bowman in October 1945, and much earlier than that for many others still alive.[36] In the 1940s Larkin's correspondence with Amis on such matters had been forthright, to say the least, and in the 1950s his interest in pornography was lively. The 1960s merely rendered public much of what had long been going on privately among ever-widening circles. Reading H. G. Wells for a review in 1984, Larkin was surprised to find that 'sexual intercourse began in 1895, before I was alive'.[37] He could have gone back further than that, for on sexual behaviour Bentham had decades earlier envisaged a purely utilitarian approach.[38] The very survival of the 'arranged marriage', integral to aristocratic life before the twentieth century, had demanded a mutual and preferably discreet tolerance of sexual infidelity, and its persistence in elite circles into the 1950s and 1960s was advertised by the very public scandals involving the Duchess of Argyll and John Profumo. In some fashionable interwar intellectual circles, sexual liberation had been preached with an almost missionary zeal. Bloomsbury's language and manners were not so dissimilar to those of the permissive generation of the 1970s.[39] Prominent feminists noted in the mid-1930s that among some young unmarried middle-class women virginity evoked more shame than sexual experience would have evoked from their predecessors;

[33] P. Jones *et al.*, 'Back Street to Side Street to High Street: The Changing Geography of Betting Shops', *Geography*, 79/2 (1994), 122.

[34] J. A. Patmore, *Recreation and Resources: Leisure Patterns and Leisure Places* (Oxford, 1983), 26. 'British Bingo History', at <www.74simon.co.uk/bingomaniacs/bingohistory.html>, consulted 18 Mar. 2007.

[35] Jarvis, *Conservative Governments, Morality and Social Change*, 79 (licensing). P. G. Richards, *Parliament and Conscience* (1970), 175 (polls).

[36] Motion, *Larkin*, 338.

[37] To Anthony Thwaite, 3 Sept. 1984, in Larkin, *Letters*, 718.

[38] V. Le R. Bullough, *Homosexuality: A History* (New York, 1979), 38–9.

[39] See e.g. Q. Bell, 'Introduction', to *The Diary of Virginia Woolf*, i. *1915–19* (1st publ. 1977, paperback edn. 1979), p. xxii; Q. Bell, *Virginia Woolf: A Biography*, i. *Virginia Stephen 1882–1912* (1st publ. 1972, paperback edn. 1976), 99, 124.

'there is fashion in these things', wrote Mary Agnes Hamilton.[40] By the 1960s it was becoming clear from Waugh's diaries and other sources that fifty years earlier a decided permissiveness had influenced prominent Oxbridge contemporaries of Lord Longford and Malcolm Muggeridge, those two vigorous critics of the permissive society. Lower down in society, the complexities of interwar family relationships, and their numerous cover-ups, were strikingly revealed when biographies discussed the family background of the prime ministers John Major and Tony Blair.[41] More open, though perhaps more self-advertising, were interwar rationalists like H. G. Wells and Bertrand Russell, who publicly predicted that contraception, in separating sexual relations from procreation, would produce a social transformation. Russell's *Marriage and Morals* (1929) had boldly brought reason, common sense, and imagination publicly to bear on problems that were still causing disquiet half a century later.

Many relationships inside and outside the elite in the 1950s were moulded by conduct that after the 1960s might have been labelled 'permissive', and for their prevalence (at least in the USA) the Kinsey reports had already provided ample empirical backing. Peter Tynan, shopkeeper father of Kenneth, led a double life, and when in Warrington was Sir Peter Peacock, a wealthy draper and six times mayor; though Peter Tynan had left his 'official' wife, he had not married Kenneth's mother.[42] Crossman's second wife Zita had undergone an illegal abortion for fear of compromising his career, and the pregnancy of Macmillan's daughter Sarah (perhaps really Robert Boothby's) before her marriage in 1953 was terminated (leaving her sterile) because to continue with it would, in her mother's words, 'ruin your father's career'.[43] Gaitskell, sometimes with Crosland's consent, used his flat in the Boltons for pursuing his relationship with Ann Fleming, the society hostess,[44] and it would have been surprising if these leading revisionists had not carried at least some liberal ideas on personal conduct from their private into their public lives—though their party's nonconformist affinities, Fabian traditions, and socialist convictions complicated matters. Crosland championed a more libertarian outlook which would be compatible with 'open-air cafés, brighter and gayer streets at night, later closing-hours for public houses, more local repertory theatres'.[45] Gaitskell induced his party to accept liberalization of the licensing laws, and his ally Jenkins in 1959 secured a reform of the law on obscene publications in a personal campaign against puritanism which he carried much further when Home Secretary in 1965–7.[46]

[40] In R. Strachey (ed.), *Our Freedom and its Results* (1936), 269; cf. 252–3 and Winifred Holtby in *Time and Tide* (4 May 1935), 647.

[41] J. Major, *The Autobiography* (1999), 6. A. Seldon, *Blair* (2004), 18–19.

[42] K. Tynan, *The Life of Kenneth Tynan* (1987), 17.

[43] A. Howard, *Crossman: The Pursuit of Power* (1990), 62. Horne, *Macmillan 1894–1956*, 341–2.

[44] K. Jefferys, *Anthony Crosland* (1999), 69.

[45] *Future of Socialism*, 521–2; see also 288.

[46] Jenkins, *Life at the Centre*, 176. Williams, *Gaitskell*, 390.

One further 'sixties' theme, not clearly distinct from the fourth, draws all the themes together: the new puritanism which replaced the old. It is foreshadowed in that remarkable movement, CND, which drew together youthful revolt, informality, and political radicalism, together with sharpness of personal commitment [Plate 10]. It is important to distinguish between two polarities: between hedonism and puritanism old-style, but also between hedonism and a 'new' puritanism which is concerned more with purity of public commitment than of personal conduct. While not puritan in the sense of promoting personal abstinence, the 'new' puritans in their stringent rethinking of personal priorities could nourish a reproachful, sectarian, and intense rejection of convention. As we have seen, the new mood was first struck in the theatre in the mid-1950s, but the areas of protest remained as yet distinct: British novelists were not greatly concerned about Suez, for example.[47] What CND achieved was to weave them together; its heady mixture of youth protest, left-wing views, cultural revolt, and informal dress and manners was launched in 1958. Its attraction for teenagers rebelling against their parents helps to explain why two-fifths of those on the Aldermaston march in 1959 were under 21.[48] Its mood chimed in with erosion of the self-disciplined hierarchies of war and empire, whose structured ideals now retreated before a new romanticism that was more egalitarian and participatory in nature. With shams torn aside, a painful honesty became the vogue, generating a fierceness of commitment that confronted consciences with sudden crises and imperilled careers. CND took the middle-class young into unfamiliar territory where they felt the need to band together in self-defence. The parallels with the militant suffragettes were close, and were often drawn. Indeed, between these two great twentieth-century protest movements there was not only direct influence but also a thin but direct line of personal linkage. This new idealism sometimes mistook rudeness for integrity and intolerance for commitment, but in 1961 Crossman looked wistfully at the young people on an anti-apartheid vigil and wished that the Labour Party could harness such youthful dedication. Within CND the earlier Bohemian fashion for European coffee bars, casual clothing, and polo necks acquired a practical justification, for—to quote Ibsen's reformer-hero in *An Enemy of the People*—'you should never have your best trousers on when you turn out to fight for freedom and truth'.[49]

Shelagh Delaney's *A Taste of Honey* (directed by the bisexual Tony Richardson) also drew together the five sixties themes, despite the fact that it was first performed in 1958, published in 1959, and not filmed till 1961. The film centred upon Jo (Rita Tushingham), illegitimate teenage daughter of a fun-loving but

[47] As noted by Taylor, *After the War*, 81. [48] Driver, *Disarmers*, 60 (10% random sample).

[49] H. Ibsen, *An Enemy of the People* (Oxford World's Classics edn., publ. with *The Wild Duck*, and *Rosmersholm*, tr. J. W. McFarlane, 1999), 87. See also Crossman, *Backbench Diaries*, 940 (8 Mar. 1961).

tough mother. When a young black sailor makes Jo pregnant and then deserts her, she is joined by Geoff (Murray Melvin), who has been thrown out of his digs for homosexuality. At first Jo and Geoff seem likely to make a successful family unit, given that Geoff enjoys housekeeping and caring for the baby, but Jo's mother then re-enters her life, leaving no room for Geoff, who walks quietly out of it. This poignant plot puzzled a homosexual from an earlier generation, Noel Coward, in 1959: 'a squalid little piece about squalid and unattractive people . . . written by an angry young lady of nineteen'.[50] This was a major misjudgement, as later emerged from the impact of its highly evocative film version. From the mid-1950s censorship gradually relaxed during continuous negotiation between censors, scriptwriters, and film-makers. The ban on homosexuality as an issue in films was lifted in 1957, soon after the Wolfenden report was published. Censorship readily finds new outlets, however, and while the media were securing freer treatment of sexuality, librarians were responding to W. E. Johns's racial views by removing Biggles books from their shelves.[51] In Bradbury's *The History Man* (1975, serialized on television 1981), the right-wing student George Carmody at Watermouth University asks his sociology tutor Howard Kirk if he must share Kirk's views in order to pass his course. 'It's not required, George', is the reply. 'But it might help you see some of the problems inside this society you keep sentimentalizing about.'[52]

2. YOUTH IN VOGUE

If none of the five aspects of 'the sixties' sprang fully armed into existence in 1960, each was prominent during that decade. Growing youth-consciousness owed much to prolonged education and enhanced articulateness, but much also to the relative ease and cheapness of international travel. 'Virtual' travel was easier, too: the mass media gathered the young into pop festivals, and provided underground newspapers such as *Friends*, *Time Out*, *Oz*, *Rolling Stone*, and *It*—ephemeral, scurrilous, unpompous, intimate, subversive, and mildly pornographic. There were mutual support groups, too—formal (Release, Street Aid) and informal—and a highly informal lifestyle involving relaxed relations between friends of either sex, often without need for surnames. Radical adults fomented youthful protest-mindedness. Examinations came under closer scrutiny from commentators like Leach who preferred variety and creativity to conformity: 'we must try to get rid of competitive examinations altogether', he wrote.[53] The American author Ivan Illich, in his *Deschooling Society* (1971),

[50] *Noel Coward Diaries*, 408 (5 May 1959).
[51] P. B. Ellis and P. Williams, *By Jove, Biggles!* (1981), 230–1.
[52] M. Bradbury, *The History Man* (1st publ. 1975, paperback edn. 1985), 134.
[53] Leach, *Runaway World?*, 70.

then widely discussed, went so far as to attack the very concept of school. Through their fetish of certification, he claimed, teachers rendered their skills scarce, and substituted conformity for true learning. Self-education within the community was his alternative: education should not be confined to specialized buildings housing people between the ages of 4 and (say) 14, if only because education should be a lifelong process, and because 'schools' created the distorting construct of 'childhood'.[54]

Many educationally progressive ideas were gathered into the controversial *Little Red School-Book*. First published in 1969 in Denmark, it was translated into English and republished in Britain in 1971. Optimistic and rationalistic in mood, yet profoundly gloomy about society as at present organized, this little manual collected ample practical information in simple language on matters that concerned schoolchildren. It tried to set schools into their social and economic context and, because 'democracy is built on action', urged readers to participate and seek to understand: they should set up schools councils and question their teachers closely. Pupils and teachers should be allies, it argued, but teaching methods should be flexible, and desks should not always be arranged in rows: classrooms 'should be workshops' with 'work-tables, notice boards, shelves and tools for everybody', and with the furniture moved around 'as needed'.[55] Distinguishing clearly between education and passing examinations, it edged the reader towards self-realization rather than passivity. For a brief moment it seemed as though schoolchildren might join the many minority groups that by the late 1960s were mobilizing in protest. 'Street Aid', founded in 1970, was one of several self-help organizations created by young people for young people which grew out of sixties squats and communes wary of parents and police.[56] In 1970 the National Council for Civil Liberties launched a campaign to end compulsory religious education and corporal punishment in schools, and to give children more say in decision-making. It inspired some pressure in the early 1970s from the Schools Action Union, especially in the London area.[57] Its leaflet urged Paddington schoolchildren in May 1972 to get uniforms, caning, and other punishments abolished and to 'smash the dictatorship of the head'.[58] Little came of it, and for Home Secretary Reginald Maudling the Union's strike was 'the ultimate in absurd demonstrations'.[59]

It was no soft option to be headmaster of a single-sex boys' independent school in the sixties in such circumstances. Lindsay Anderson's film *If . . .*

[54] I. D. Illich, *Deschooling Society* (1971), 1, 27–8, 76, 81, 84, 88–9.

[55] S. Hansen and J. Jensen, *The Little Red School-Book* (1st publ. 1969, tr. B. Thornberry, 1971), 197, 156–7.

[56] *T* (16 Dec. 1970), 2, has a useful discussion of these.

[57] *T* (11 Dec. 1970), 2 (NCCL). *G* (9 Feb. 1970), 9 (SAU).

[58] Cyclostyled leaflet in author's possession. For more on the Union see *ST* (14 May 1972), 4.

[59] *G* (18 May 1972), 9.

was shot on location at his old school, Cheltenham College, in spring 1968, just before the student revolt of that year, and did not help matters. The film's central figure, Michael Travis, his study adorned by posters of revolutionary heroes, marshals a trio of disaffected teenagers against the traditionalism, militarism, hypocrisy, bogus liberalism, and religiosity of a sexually repressed public school. A brutal beating scene, where the prefects exercise their power, is complemented by the film's savage denouement: Travis, who claims that 'one man can change the world with a bullet in the right place', literally directs his fire at the entire system. When released later in the year, the film's likely impact worried many headmasters. The independent schools rapidly made concessions: a wider choice in sport, more relaxed relations with masters, an end to corporal punishment, closer interaction with the local community, and more parental involvement. John Rae recalled that 'during these years there were few headmasters who did not have to face some sort of protest in chapel', given that compulsory chapel in a secularizing age was not easily defended.[60] For boarding schools the ultimate concession was the admission of girls, which John Dancy pioneered at Marlborough in 1968, partly in the hope of safeguarding liberal reforms already made.[61]

Voluntary organizations for young people also had to adjust, and here the experience of the most prominent among them, the Boy Scouts, must stand for the rest. We have seen that the movement's postwar recovery was not sustained after the 1950s.[62] Numbers were still large—Cubs, Brownies, Scouts, and Guides totalled 539,340 in 1970, and in the previous quarter-century had grown by 14 per cent, but in the years 1962–5 the Scouts' share of the age group was found to decline markedly from 12-year-olds onwards.[63] The movement was falling out of fashion with teenagers, as well as upsetting self-consciously progressive opinion with its residual echoes of empire and of the founder's personal quirks, with its stress on the need for unquestioning obedience, and even with its valuation of childhood for its own sake. Facetiously discussing its outlook on adolescent sexuality, Norman Mackenzie announced in 1965 that 'something had gone badly wrong when we were urged to douse the racial organ in cold water to inhibit the promptings of Nature'.[64] Most organizations would be tempted to ignore such critics, yet the movement's reaction was to commission from twenty-four scout leaders under 45 the Chief Scout's unanimous *Advance Party Report* (1966), and to respond constructively to its recommendations. The report was wide-ranging, self-critical, and recognized

[60] Quoted from Rae, *Public School Revolution*, 102. The book contains many shrewd insights into the situation; see esp. 111, 119, 144, 177–8.
[61] Ibid. 132.
[62] See above, pp. 261–2.
[63] Sandbrook, *Never Had It So Good*, 393. Chief Scout's Advance Party, *Report*, 149.
[64] N. Mackenzie, 'Sweating it out with B-P', *NS* (15 Oct. 1965), 555. See also M. Archard, 'Cold Showers and Unfurling the Flag', *Evening Standard* (20 July 1967), 8.

the need for better publicity. It also saw the need to adjust names and uniforms: members' wearing of shorts was, for instance, 'one of the most damaging aspects of our present public image'. Much debate within the movement followed, with an eventual secession of the traditionalist 'B-P Scouts' in 1979, but major changes were made: the prefix 'boy' was dropped, hierarchical titles were muted, short trousers and wide-brimmed hats were jettisoned, standards of accommodation and equipment were improved to reflect growing affluence, and the earlier emphasis on thrift was played down. Less easily tackled was the growing shortage of adult volunteer leaders, who were emerging from the universities less readily than the founder had hoped.[65] Yet the Boy Scouts understood boys' mentality, and recognized the need to cater for their spirit of adventure: anyone who flippantly criticized them and who later complained about rising juvenile delinquency had much to answer for.

In chasing fashion for its own sake, the youth of the 1960s did not diverge from their parents, but the fashions were different and the pressures to conform were more intense. Technological advance in a peaceful context seemed at last about to subordinate the work ethic and render leisure, if fairly distributed, a luxury available to the masses, provided that they ceased to pursue consumption for its own sake. Following Keynes, Crosland hoped in 1956 that Britain would follow the trend among European intellectuals for conspicuously underconsuming,[66] but the young were not obviously espousing this cause. The fashion and entertainment industries had much to gain from exploiting the 'generation gap' and from promoting instant obsolescence. It seemed in the mid-1960s as though Keynes's leisured ideal of the 1930s was about to come about: the anti-puritan, hedonistic, materialist, and consumerist reaction against economy and austerity was encapsulated in the phrase 'swinging London'. This affluence was nourished by a hope of East/West détente which was delayed for longer than at first expected.

While teenagers were by their parents' standards beginning to dress down, this merely entailed substituting one set of ephemeral styles for another. With James Dean, Marlon Brando, and Elvis Presley as trendsetters, denim jeans were becoming almost universal among young males by the early 1960s. By ousting flannel, corduroy, and tweed—jeans and sweaters dissolved any clear distinction between clothes for work and for leisure. Yet subtle status gradations were not eliminated, and soon enabled the new fashions to gravitate upwards by social status and age. The sixties did, however, greatly diversify fabrics, styles, and colours: leather jackets with the rockers; flowered shirts and faded second-hand uniforms with the Rolling Stones; smart jackets and then oriental caftans and peaked caps with the Beatles. Young people could now select the clothes they thought suited them best, rather than defer (albeit

[65] Quotation from Advance Party, *Report*, 303; see also 241.

[66] *Future of Socialism*, 284.

at several removes) to the Paris fashion houses. The distinction between the designs and colours thought suitable for men and women became less clear. Long hair, earrings, and necklaces became increasingly acceptable for men, and with women's encouragement men began to spruce themselves up with Old Spice aftershave, the first male cosmetic to erode traditional male attitudes to masculinity; first marketed in Britain in 1957, it was by 1969 being used by over half the male population.[67] Amidst this freedom of choice, homosexuals, who took a special interest in clothes, could merge still more completely into the background if they so wished,[68] and Jan Morris in mid-transition from male to female was able to wear the same clothes when assuming either identity.[69]

The body's fashion potential was also being explored. By 1969 the tattoo had become prevalent enough among the young to merit debate in the House of Lords on the need to protect under-18s from being pressured into 'permanent disfigurement'. It was noted that 40 per cent of those in borstals and detention centres were tattooed, and that 'among young people generally it has become a "trendy" thing to do',[70] and yet during the debate three peers revealed that they too bore a tattoo. Hair fashions had been important since the covered car had sent the hat into long-term gradual decline, but in the 1960s they occasioned strong feeling. In 1970 Crossman noted in his diary the scale of the change that had taken place since 1965: 'even hair-cuts are politically significant—there's been a whole revolution in men's appearance', and men 'can now have their hair designed in a way which five years ago would have been thought kinky or unnatural'.[71] Hair length became an emotive issue in schools for boys, some of whom felt that lock-shearing infringed their personality and integrity. Older university teachers could do no more than complain about their students and be rebuffed,[72] but in schools the conflicts were sometimes bitter, and caused many sixth-formers to migrate to further education colleges: in less than a decade the number of their full-time students working for A levels had trebled.[73] For many adults, however, wartime and national service were too recent to erode the alleged link between discipline, morality, and 'short back and sides', and when Gallup in October 1965 asked whether schools should require boys to keep their hair cut short, 79 per cent said yes and only 15 per cent no.[74] Roz Balcombe was among the 15 per cent: she told the *Guardian* in 1970 of the

[67] Obelkevich and Catterall (eds.), *Understanding Post-War British Society*, 148.

[68] 'G.Westwood', *A Minority*, 63; *Society and the Homosexual*, 124.

[69] J. Morris, *Conundrum* (1st publ. 1974, paperback edn. 2002), 102.

[70] Quotations from Lord Stonham, *HL Deb.* 28 Apr. 1969, c. 655. Lord Robertson of Oakridge, *HL Deb.* 28 Apr. 1969, c. 643. By 2005 there were 2 million tattooed Britons, *Ind.* (19 Jan. 2005), 9.

[71] *Cabinet Diaries*, iii. 877 (2 Apr. 1970).

[72] As was John Sparrow, Warden of All Souls College Oxford, by Sally Beauchamp in *ST* (6 Sept. 1970), 10: 'his code is relative to him, just as mine is relative to me'.

[73] The percentage of university students arriving from further education colleges doubled in four years, *T* (23 Jan. 1973), 4.

[74] *Gallup Polls*, 833 (Oct. 1965).

conflict in the life of her son Jeremiah between home where 'ideas fly' and the highly undemocratic Kingsdale School, where opportunities for democratic self-expression were lacking. Jeremiah, she reported—reared in a world of CND and protests about arms sales to Nigeria—'wears long hair as a matter of principle'. The headmaster of Bede School Sunderland banned a pupil from future attendance till he got his hair cut, but the well-known actor Bernard Miles disconcertingly informed *The Times* that when the most distinguished European painters portrayed Jesus, his hair was usually shoulder-length.[75] To judge from long-term trends in facial hair, as revealed in the *Illustrated London News*, there had been a marked and continuous overall decline in male hairiness after its peak in the 1880s: sideburns declined after 1853 to nil in the Edwardian period and did not revive, beards plunged after 1892 and were beginning to revive only in the 1960s, and moustaches withered after the First World War without resprouting.[76] Yet these long-term trends were by the 1960s going into reverse, though the change would have been slow to impinge on such a paper, given that it was among the young, and especially within CND, that beards made an above-average appearance.[77]

Fashions emblematic of the sixties emerged from outside the fashion establishment, and combined commercialism with celebrity, a meritocratic thrust with youthful appeal. They did not suddenly change in 1960, but by the late 1960s London's fashion world, centring on Carnaby Street and Chelsea's King's Road, was outpacing Paris as a centre for experiment in design and fashion, as in other areas of change.[78] This was the decade of the 'boutique', in the sense of 'a small shop selling "trend-setting" clothes or other articles, especially for young or fashionable people'.[79] Used in this sense, the term originated in the USA in the 1950s but transferred to the UK in the 1960s, and in such places youth and merit edged out age and privilege. John Stephen, 'King of Carnaby Street', was a Glaswegian; sixth of nine children, he worked for four years in Moss Bros. After opening his own modest shop in his early twenties in 1956, moving to Carnaby Street in the following year, he attracted pop stars as customers. Through rescuing British men from their postwar grey austerity with his daring colours, low-slung trousers, and flared jackets—he was soon able to acquire his first Rolls Royce.[80] It was the son of a storesman in his late twenties, Ossie Clark, who as a fashion designer produced his famed floaty gowns and plunging necklines. The tailor Dougie

[75] *G* (9 Feb. 1970), 9. *T* (10 Feb. 1971), 13.

[76] See D. E. Robinson's trail-blazing 'Fashions in Shaving and Trimming of the Beard: The Men of the *Illustrated London News* 1842–1972', *American Journal of Sociology* (Mar. 1976), 1135–6.

[77] F. Parkin, *Middle Class Radicalism: The Social Bases of the British Campaign for Nuclear Disarmament* (Manchester, 1968), 52.

[78] See Jenkins's speech at Abingdon reported in *ST* (20 July 1969), 1.

[79] *OED* definition. For a useful discussion see Sandbrook, *White Heat*, 233–7.

[80] Obituary, *Scotsman* (9 Feb. 2004), 16.

Millings, who set up on his own in 1958, was rather older, but (like Stephen) mixed with pop singers, and in 1962 produced the first collarless suits for the Beatles.[81] Mary Quant, from a Welsh working-class background, was in her early twenties when she and her publicity-conscious husband (whom she met at art school) opened Bazaar in 1955. Her mini-skirts, high lace-up boots, and hot pants were not popular till about 1967, but their bold colours and designs became emblematic of the sixties, and helped to orient the fashion world round London rather than Paris. Barbara Hulanicki was in her mid-twenties when she set up the BIBA fashion boutique in Kensington whose interior was as dark as her fabrics and vibrated with rock music. Like Quant she aimed at the younger woman, but her speciality was affordable fashion: 'cut-price glamour and disposable glitz'[82] with suitable accessories provided; high shoulders, tight-fitting long sleeves, long and flowing skirts in velvet and satin were modelled by skinny girls with big eyes. Janet Reger was in her early thirties in 1967 when Janet Reger Creations Ltd ruffled the utilitarian world of women's underwear; her end-of-decade flighty shapes and daring colours were shedding inhibitions, like those who wore them, and her business boomed.[83]

The sixties also shifted the social background of fashion models and their promoters. Several famous models—Jean Shrimpton, Sandra Paul, Celia Hammond, Joanna Lumley—emerged from the top model agency, the Lucie Clayton Model and Charm School, which also offered deportment and art appreciation, but the lifestyle for which it catered soon fell out of fashion. Beauty at any social level could force its way through the class barriers, and the world of Cecil Beaton and the royal photographers succumbed to glottal stops and dropped H's. Photographers like the self-taught East Ender David Bailey, in *Vogue* from 1959, and Terence Donovan (only child of a lorry driver) in *Vogue* from 1963, were more raffish than their predecessors. 'Before 1960,' said their colleague Brian Duffy, 'a fashion photographer was somebody tall, thin and camp. But we three are different: short, fat and heterosexual.' The master-carpenter's daughter and fashion model Lesley Hornby ('Twiggy') and her manager/boyfriend who assumed the name Justin de Villeneuve, promoted one another out of lower-middle-class suburban Neasden. With no O-levels, and with her artless manner and marked cockney accent, Twiggy was a novelty in the fashion world, and her waif-like figure, boyish haircut, and large heavily made-up eyelashes made her in 1966 at 16 a world-famous fashion icon, enabling her to meet her teenage heroes the Beatles and go abroad for the first time. 'The phone never stopped. People wanted to interview me all the time. And I'd done

[81] Obituary, *Ind.* (22 Oct. 2001), review section, 6.
[82] Obituary of Stephen Fitz-Simon, *T* (14 Feb. 1997), 23.
[83] L. Armstrong, 'Memories of a Basque Revolutionary', *T* (16 Mar. 2005), ii. 6.

nothing! I was an instant celebrity.'[84] Well might she pronounce the sixties 'a time when ordinary people could do extraordinary things'.[85]

The considerable cultural achievement of the sixties owed much to art schools. Their classless tone encouraged art, music, the media, and design to interact, as well as to absorb radical ideas in an experimental, international, and creative environment. There the Beatles naturally encountered pop art, which unlike its modernist precursors was youthfully populist in tone: subversively witty, hedonistic in its unashamed alignment with Americanized consumerism, unsnobbishly adventurous in its working materials, and seeking immediate impact rather than a timeless and universal permanence.[86] Terence Conran opened his first Habitat store in Fulham Road, London, in spring 1964 and carried into middle-class households the simplicity of French peasant kitchenware and pottery. It was a turning point in middle-class lifestyles, and an important moment in the history of British design. A rural traditionalism also pervaded the designs of Laura Ashley, whose first shop opened in 1967. The flowing lines, traditional prints, and natural fabrics of her dresses were the equivalent in women's clothing of the healthy, wholefood eating promoted in her firm's canteens, and in the successful Cranks self-service vegetarian restaurants. Her successes illustrate the sheer abundance of sixties creativity, given that her styles in some respects involved a romantic reaction against the prevailing emphasis on youth and modernity.

3. A DISCONCERTING SINCERITY

Among a minority of young people after the mid-1960s the reaction against conventional manners was moving on apace, for by then the teenagers of the world (or at least a teenage minority within the Anglo-American world) felt they had nothing to lose but their inhibitions. Elvis Presley and Lonnie Donegan in the late 1950s were in more than one respect the natural precursors of Che Guevara and Herbert Marcuse in the late 1960s. When confronted by uncomprehending adults and constraining institutions, and still more by wars enlisting them (in the USA) against their will, teenagers felt that there were things more important than good manners, and that they had more in common with one another than with their parents. What was peculiar to the sixties was the fierceness of the radical students' commitment—so fierce as often to lead them to deny a hearing to their critics, whom they somewhat indiscriminately labelled 'Fascist', thereby depreciating the coinage. Their critics wryly noted

[84] For Duffy see F. Wyndham, 'The Modelmakers', *Sunday Times Magazine* (10 May 1964), 17. *Twiggy: An Autobiography*, 41.

[85] As quoted in website www.twiggylawson.co.uk/fashion.html#story, consulted 6 Apr. 2005.

[86] For a good discussion see Whiteley, *Pop Design*, 33, 44, 219, 224–5, 229.

that Fascism had not been unrelated to the left, and that the student militancy exemplified some of its traits.[87] Though youth protest in the universities tended to focus upon such local grievances as it could find, its impulse was partly political, international, and generational. Sincerity, spontaneity, participation, and debate were all central to its mood. Its radical preoccupation with 'relevance' and practical impact was not peculiar to the student movement at that time: it informed the outlook and recommendations of the Fulton report on the civil service. Nor was suspicion of manufacture and commerce unknown in British intellectual life. Protest was at its most dramatic at two universities. In the controversy over student files at the new University of Warwick in 1969, distaste for academic links with local industry was central. At Cambridge, protest focused on international and race issues. There, Powell was forced to cancel a lecture on the medieval House of Lords in 1968,[88] and protests in 1970 against the Greek colonels' regime prompted the violent disruption of a dinner/dance held in connection with the local promotion of holidays in Greece. The resultant sentences—which included prison, borstal, and recommendations for deportation—provoked a controversy whose intensity overflowed on to the pages of *The Times*.[89] When interruptions prevented the Foreign Secretary from being heard at the Oxford Union in 1969, *The Times* described 'the extreme student left' as 'at its worst one of the nastiest political phenomena that Britain has experienced in this century'.[90]

With radical opinions and informality in dress came informality in personal relations. First names were not only being used more freely: they also often took a shorter and more familiar format, with Anthony Wedgwood Benn in the van. His friends had always called him 'Tony Benn', but the media made much of his publicly espousing that designation, though he failed to persuade Wilson in his 1964–70 governments to get cabinet colleagues to address one another in first-name terms.[91] The media encouraged this trend. By 1953 Evelyn Waugh's distaste for the informality of television interviews was beginning to seem antique. 'I do not think I have the necessary talents to give the impression that I am taking part in a three-cornered intimate chat with personal friends', he wrote, 'with the bandying about of Christian names and so forth, of the kind which deeply shocks me in some of the performances I have sometimes begun to hear.' Marghanita Laski felt that the coinage of friendship was devalued when the media encouraged in broadcasters expressions of affection and first-name familiarity so indiscriminately.[92] It was not friendship as such that the media encouraged, but a deliberately informal spontaneity. Nastiness was as good as

[87] See e.g. H. R. Trevor-Roper, 'The Past and the Present: History and Sociology', *Past and Present* (Feb. 1969), 12.
[88] *T* (8 May 1968), 11 (leader).
[89] *T* (4 July 1970), 2; (7 July 1970), 11.
[90] *T* (12 May 1969), 9.
[91] Author's collection: letter from Tony Benn postmarked 25 Apr. 2005.
[92] Waugh, *Letters*, 409. M. Laski, 'I was a TV Personality', *Twentieth Century* (Nov. 1959), 380.

niceness from this point of view: indeed, nastiness added a touch of drama, and several media personalities profited from their displays of bad manners.

Informality of speech and gesture accompanied these changes. The decline in the notion of 'correct' speech has already been discussed.[93] Bevan complained that Macmillan's speeches were too carefully prepared, but this evoked from Macmillan's diary the complaint that 'anything properly done is out of date today—like hand-made clothes or furniture, it is "reactionary". To finish your sentences; to put in verbs; to worry about neat turns of phrase or apt and appropriate adjectives—all this is "undemocratic" and "Victorian".'[94] As for gesture, British upper lips once conventionally stiff had begun to relax in the 1960s, partly under the influence of Caribbean immigrants less inhibited,[95] as exemplified in jollifications such as the Notting Hill carnival. In roles where discipline was seen as central, informality could not be taken very far, but the sixties discovered that in several such roles the discipline could be significantly relaxed, most notably in education and religion. Informal relations between children and adults lay at the heart of the interwar progressive school movement. Its ideals were by the 1960s being diffused throughout the community. In Bradbury's Watermouth University, teaching methods were constantly evolving through continuous introspection: 'Watermouth does not only educate its students; it teaches its teachers'.[96]

The sixties saw all churches in Britain vulnerable in their liturgy to pressures for spontaneity, threatened in their traditional structures as they were by ecumenical and evangelical priorities. Spreading out from California, neo-pentecostalist singing and dancing penetrated widely, even into Catholic churches, and was welcome within a Church of England whose evangelical tendency had for some time been gaining ground among the middle-class suburban young in the south of England.[97] Authority was most notably undermined within the most authoritarian church of all when Britain's leading Catholic theologian, Charles Davis, inspired by sixties attitudes simultaneously on the religious and sexual front, resigned from the priesthood and left the church as 'a pseudo-political structure from the past' which no longer represented its founder's intentions.[98] There was much restiveness among intellectuals in both the Catholic and Anglican churches during the late 1960s, with the Vatican Council and with Bishop Robinson spilling so many beans. In 1964 he viewed 'with horror the prospect of spending the rest of my life as the maintenance-man or manager of a religious club', and felt that faith was actually endangered by an all-consuming preoccupation with buildings; on the day he retired as

[93] See above, pp. 168–9. [94] Macmillan, *Diary*, ed. Catterall, 294 (22 Feb. 1954).

[95] K. Fitzherbert, 'West Indian Children in London', *Occasional Papers in Social Administration*, 19 (1967), 50. [96] Bradbury, *History Man*, 127.

[97] D. W. Bebbington, *Evangelicalism in Modern Britain: A History from the 1730s to the 1980s* (1989), 245–6. [98] N. K. Watson, 'Charles Alfred Davis', *ODNB*.

bishop in 1969 he said he regretted nothing about the permissive stand he had taken up.[99]

Without significant public discussion, but with a significant practical outcome, the sixties' pursuit of sincerity encouraged a new approach to manners. Hitherto a set of formulae integral to a middle-class upbringing, reflecting a blend of Christian and chivalric traditions, good manners had been almost routinely passed down from parent to child without much reflection. But now they came under challenge. Adult complaints about the manners of the young are probably perennial, but they reached a new intensity in the 1950s. Earl Waldegrave in a Lords debate of 1958 referred to the 'terrible habit growing up among some of the young' of greeting adult requests with pert phrases such as 'so what?'[100] The phrase 'couldn't care less' became a stock rejoinder, and *I'm All Right, Jack* became the title of a film about trade union attitudes in 1959. Television interviewers were by then becoming more aggressive, and the radio personality Gilbert Harding had for some years been notorious for his rudeness. Correspondence in *The Times* during August 1992[101] was premised on the assumption that manners had declined markedly since 1951, and forty years later television interviews from the 1950s certainly seemed stylized, affected, and bland. On the death of Anthony Eden in 1977, *The Times* referred to him as 'a man of obvious and now unfashionable virtues—honour, probity, patriotism—and of a debonair style that may now be outdated'.[102]

Associated with these developments were changes in attitudes to the uniform. It remained fashionable only if worn as parody and not as indicating the wearer's conformity; wearing it must proceed from the wearer's unconstrained choice. Behind all this lay a complex trend which joined anonymity to intimacy, and strangely blended consensus statism with an atomized view of the individual. The state's benevolent welfare and planning role was taken for granted, but the individual was now viewed as standing alone, assessed on a personality divorced from parentage, schooling, locality, personal achievement, marital status, and even nationality. Medals and ribbons were out, and badges became mere adornments. To wear a medal was to risk being dismissed as a member of the 'bowler-hat brigade' whose numbers, given war's scarcity after 1945, were dwindling. The old-school and club ties once so widely worn among middle-class teenagers and male adults, prevalent enough even to support specialist shops in big cities, were now less often seen. To that extent, sanctions on conduct were scaled down, with 'character' and family reputation devalued. On the other hand, the pursuit of celebrity was mounting,

[99] James, *Bishop Robinson*, 145. See also above, pp. 345–7. 'Farewell to the Sixties', *O* (28 Sept. 1969), 10.

[100] *HL Deb.* 15 May 1958, c. 384.

[101] Correspondence in *T* (7 Aug. 1992), 11, in response to Nicholas Ridley's 'Snobbery and Yobbery', *T* ('Life and Times' section), 3 Aug. 1992, 1. For current practice on manners as at 1991, see *T* (17 Sept. 1991), 2.

[102] *T* (15 Jan. 1977), 15 (leader).

with diminished attention to significant achievement or past record. And with enhanced anonymity came more overt gestures of warmth in personal relations that transcended barriers of status, race, or nationality.

It was at about this time that people ceased addressing a young man as 'master'; when the American feminist term 'Ms' for women, whether married or not, gained some currency; and when male chivalry ceased to govern good manners. This was not the only shift in modes of address at about this time. The substitution of 'Mr John Smith' for 'John Smith Esq.' in his correspondence was among Benn's symbolic reforms as postmaster general;[103] the change gained gradual acceptance thereafter, and once that point had been reached it was but a short journey to drop the 'Mr', and to leave 'John Smith' unadorned. The revival of British feminism by the mid-1960s launched the idea that chivalry to women was patronizing and even anti-feminist in motive. Mary Stott had created the *Guardian* women's page in 1957, and the phrase 'Guardian woman' entered the language to denote a woman who seemed tiresomely liberal. *The Times* followed suit with its own women's page on the same day that news supplanted advertisements on its front page—3 May 1966. In November 1970 the 'Miss World' contest, devoted to displaying women wearing rather few clothes, was disrupted with a bomb from the Angry Brigade in the BBC's van and with bags of flour hurled by the supporters of women's liberation. In later years the contest slowly lost much of its following.

If apparently lacking in manners, the young could point to their enhanced preoccupation with humane values far more significant: to their growing involvement with environmentalist, internationalist, and welfare causes, and to their diminished preoccupation with social class. From the 1960s there was a growing tendency among the middle-class young to seek their exemplars lower down rather than higher up. Among the reasons for the shift was the powerful influence upon them of pop singers and sportsmen, the growth of solidarity among teenagers of all classes, with perhaps a middle-class hunch about where power in British society increasingly now lay. In the 1960s university students frequently adopted what they thought was a working-class accent and vocabulary, and in 1969 the Headmaster of Charterhouse School referred to his pupils' feelings of guilt about their privilege, which they assuaged whenever possible by embracing long hair, untidy clothes, and guitars.[104]

This revolution in manners interacted with major changes in the theatre that had already occurred in the mid-1950s.[105] A preliminary skirmish between old and new styles occurred in 1957, when Rattigan bridled at Tynan's 'constant

[103] Benn, *Diaries 1963–7*, 243–4 (8 Apr. 1965).

[104] At the Headmasters' Conference, York, quoted in *T* (26 Sept. 1969), 4. For similar attitudes in Oxford rather earlier, see J. Dawson, 'Blue Jeans and Brotherhood: A Memo for the Left Wing', *Isis* (20 Jan. 1960), 24–5.

[105] See above, pp. 374–6, 477.

denigration' of the British theatre as parochial. Of the six well-received serious or semi-serious plays in the current New York season, Rattigan noted that five (which incidentally included his own *Separate Tables*) were in some sense British in origin. Tynan's riposte was to note that of the six new British plays in London that season, three were murder mysteries and three drawing-room comedies.[106] Rattigan was rightly alert to the playwright's need for an audience: 'no audience means no performance, and no performance means no play'. But the argument was about how far playwrights should defer to audiences of a particular type. Unfortunately for his own reputation, Rattigan had earlier rather innocently confessed the need to attract the invented lowbrow playgoer Aunt Edna, 'a nice, respectable, middle-class, middle-aged, maiden lady with time on her hands and the money to help her pass it'; he had claimed that her opinions expressed in the lounge of her West Kensington hotel could prove damaging.[107]

Noel Coward, too, was concerned about Aunt Edna. He did his best to understand Pinter in 1960, modifying his initial view that Pinter's was 'the surrealist school of non-playwriting', and forcing himself to admit that 'he is at least a genuine original'. But by then Coward's plays were receiving hostile reviews,[108] and he had little to lose, so in January 1961 he felt it was time to state the counter-case. Far more forcibly than Rattigan, he let rip with relish in three highly entertaining and uncompromising articles, somewhat world-weary in tone, in the *Sunday Times*. The furious response evoked in the correspondence columns did not begin to match the stylish vigour of Coward's first two articles, and he revelled at the sight of the London press 'squealing like stuck pigs'.[109] He pronounced anyone who dwelt 'exclusively on the limited and monotonous problems of a fast diminishing proletariat' as 'very definitely old-fashioned': playwrights should avoid the 'inverse snobbery' involved in focusing so exclusively on the workers. Political propaganda in the theatre was usually 'a cracking bore'. The new fashions jeopardized the theatre's magic, the need for professionalism in the actor, and respect for the audience and its needs. Among the progressive playwrights' 'principal faults' was 'their supercilious attitude to the requirements of an average audience',[110] whereas the list of London's currently successful plays showed that 'the public, on the whole, prefer to see extraordinary people on the stage rather than ordinary ones; fantastic situations rather than familiar, commonplace ones, and actors of outsize personality and talent rather than accurately competent mediocrities'.

106 *O* (3 Feb. 1957), 11; (3 Mar. 1957), 8.

107 T. Rattigan, 'Preface', to his *Collected Plays*, ii (1953), p. xi.

108 Quotations from *Noel Coward Diaries*, 431 (27 Mar. 1960); 436 (2 May 1960). See also 413 (19 July 1959); 462 (7 Jan. 1961).

109 Ibid. 464 (5 Feb. 1961).

110 All quotations up to this point from Coward's 'These Old-Fashioned Revolutionaries', *ST* (15 Jan. 1961), 23.

Coward was impatient with the fad for 'Method acting', whose emphasis on the need for the actor actually to live the interior truth of a character was in practice what every experienced actor did; where 'Method' went wrong was to place 'too much emphasis on actual realism and too little on simulated realism'. A good actor must learn to speak audibly and acquire 'technique'—'a much despised word nowadays'—for if success at performing a role lay merely through 'being' the character, 'anybody playing a heavy dramatic role in a smash success would be in a mental home after a few weeks'.[111] The sixties failed to see that abundant sincerity is as intolerable for actors onstage as it is disruptive for human relations offstage.

In the 1950s the national anthem was normally played at the end of the performance in cinemas and theatres, but sincerity was hardly compatible with preserving it on such occasions if, as in the late 1960s, the audience tried to beat a retreat beforehand in order to be first out of the car park. So at the end of the 1960s, in one of those major historical transitions with no precise date or single impulse, the national anthem faded out on such occasions.[112] Britain's growing tendency in the 1960s to harp upon its relative economic decline fostered a new facetiousness about patriotic symbols. Carnaby Street lent a new lightness of touch to the British taste for national self-deprecation by selling shopping bags, umbrellas, humorous hats, and men's shorts decked out in Union Jack patterns. In its more serious variant, too, patriotism was in transition—from the rather earnest and high-minded outlook closely associated with Germany's defeat in two world wars to a narrower and chauvinistic trumpeting of sporting and ethnic loyalties.

In a climate so challenging to authority and tradition, sociology flourished. The weekly sociological periodical *New Society*, launched in 1962, drew together and popularized much of what was being done in sociology and social work, and by the mid-1960s its circulation rose to the upper 20,000s—soon to rise much higher.[113] A levels in sociology were launched in 1964, and sociology expanded fast within university life, breaking out into Oxbridge from its LSE redoubt. By 1976 in their summer examination 36,700 schoolchildren were attempting sociology papers at O level, and 14,600 at A level.[114] We have seen how well-developed was the British empirical tradition in the subject,[115] but the 1960s infused it powerfully with theory imported from the USA. This was reinforced by French and German influences that caused Marxism to reappear as an articulated influence on the left, with the publishers Lawrence & Wishart

[111] 'The Scratch-and-Mumble School', *ST* (22 Jan. 1961), 23.

[112] See Ernest Dewhurst, 'When Anthem and Audience are Not in Harmony', *G* (1 Feb. 1969), 5.

[113] For an assessment after ten years see G. Wansell, 'The Parish Magazine of the Sociology Set', *T* (4 Oct. 1972), 14. For circulation see P. Barker 'Painting the Portrait of "The Other Britain": *New Society* 1962–88', *Contemporary Record* (Summer 1991), 49.

[114] DES, *Statistics of Education 1976*, 44–7.

[115] See above, pp. 176–7.

and the *New Left Review* as megaphones. Sociologists had not yet retreated as an influence on policy: in education they provided the intellectual backbone for comprehensivization, in public policy they fuelled the welfare state's further advance, and in industrial relations they lubricated corporatist machinery. Together with Treasury economists, sociologists from all three groups were regularly seen in Whitehall after 1964. Social anthropology, too, was a major influence. Its relativist outlook could prove very controversial when applied to contemporary British society, as in Edmund Leach's lectures of 1967, where he claimed to be more alarmed by order than by chaos: 'in the context of a technological revolution orderliness is simply a marker of how far the members of society have got out of touch with what is really going on'.[116] With such ideas in currency, the radical young found allies and even role models among older people who were open-minded, young in mind, or yearning once more to be young: the philosophers Herbert Marcuse and Bertrand Russell, for example; the historians E. P. Thompson and Christopher Hill; and the Reith lecturers Leach and the distinguished psychiatrist G. M. Carstairs.

Radical sociology subjected existing institutions to close and irreverent scrutiny. It sharpened the rejection of flummery, and pursued instead an uncomplicated sincerity nourished in the early 1960s by scandals and splits within the Conservative government. After 1964 such irreverence was present in a milder form at the Labour government's highest levels. Benn after a Privy Council rehearsal in 1964 'left the Palace boiling with indignation' at the formality of it all. 'This is what I have been dreading', he wrote in his diary on receiving an invitation to a sherry party at the Palace, and declined.[117] 'Why aren't you properly dressed?', asked 'some City bigwig' at the Lord Mayor's Dinner when Benn (alone with George Brown among ministers) wore a black tie instead of white tie and tails.[118] As Postmaster General, Benn made a point of taking a taxi rather than using his ministerial car, of lunching in the staff canteen, and of substituting for a sherry party with the staff a working conference with tea and biscuits.[119] The issue generated crises of conscience in Crossman, too, and in 1967 he 'really was dreading' having to hire morning dress for the first time in his life for the state opening of parliament.[120]

4. POLITICIANS UNDER FIRE

Aiming to become prime minister at the relatively young age of 48, Wilson launched his election campaign in 1964 with a rally that included Humphrey

[116] Leach, *Runaway World?*, 9.
[117] *Diaries 1963–7*, 169 (21 Oct. 1964), 187 (16 Nov. 1964), 191 (20 Nov. 1964).
[118] Ibid. 189 (16 Nov. 1964); cf. 320 (16 Sep. 1965).
[119] Ibid. 243–4 (8 Apr. 1965); see also 167 (20 Oct. 1964), 178 (4 Nov. 1964).
[120] Crossman, *Cabinet Diaries*, ii. 125 (14 Nov. 1966), 534 (24 Oct. 1967); cf. 544 (31 Oct. 1967).

Lyttelton's jazz band, and joked on television with the Beatles.[121] Towards the Treasury, the Bank of England, and some of the stuffier conventions Wilson showed an almost cocksure anti-establishment irreverence reminiscent of Lloyd George. In Britain as in several other countries, the sixties in retrospect added little lustre to parliamentary government, and came to be identified with a new style of anti-system, direct-action, politics. The politicians had embarked on the decade hopefully enough. The two-party system seemed to be working smoothly, with the Liberals containable and with sufficient consensus on policy between the Labour and Conservative parties to make parliamentarism seem firmly established within both. The fire behind CND was apparently dying down, and the two parties felt there was a good chance of drawing the trade unions further into the planning process as part of an agreed aim to curb inflation and unemployment. We have seen how the Conservative government in the early 1960s favoured involving the state more fully in economic planning,[122] and Labour's hopes for a better economic future rested on meritocratic and modernizing approaches without radically restructuring leading political institutions. The scale of Britain's relative economic decline, or even of her diminished world role, was not yet apparent.

Wilson did not immediately disappoint his idealistic followers. Many of his government's immediate difficulties in 1964 could be blamed on its Conservative precursor, or on Labour's small parliamentary majority. But the first of these scapegoats was a steadily waning resource, and the second was removed at the general election in March 1966 when Wilson won an overall majority of 96. Henceforth there could be no excuses. Meanwhile, trouble was accumulating on several fronts. Policy did not significantly shift after 1964 on nuclear weapons, the National Plan was getting nowhere, the trade unions increasingly realized that moving from Trafalgar Square to Whitehall seriously threatened their freedom of manœuvre, Wilson's relations with the media were deteriorating, and splits were opening up at the highest levels of government. What alienated the idealists still further was the uninspiringly tactical style of leadership that was increasingly observed in Wilson, a feature much discussed in the diaries of cabinet ministers published later. The collapse in 1967 of the government's economic policy, which was not only reversed but was apparently mishandled, produced widespread disillusion. Already by February 1965 Bertrand Russell was telling students at the LSE about the 'ironic fun' to be derived from quoting the party's manifesto of only a year before.[123]

In the late 1960s a wide gulf between university students and the political system, unfamiliar in modern British history, began to open up: Labour's cabinet ministers in their parliamentarism had nothing in common with their

[121] Cockerell, *Live from No. 10*, 102–3.
[122] See above, pp. 308–9, 441, 453–4.
[123] Quoted in Russell, *Autobiography*, iii. 209.

radical student critics' apolitical or anti-political stance.[124] Student unrest did not coincide precisely with the 1960s. Owing much to international influences, it became serious only towards the end of the decade and continued until the mid-1980s. It was a rather intense and humourless world of principled stands and non-negotiable demands. Protestors adduced big issues to justify 'direct action'—that is, breaking hitherto accepted but now despised liberal procedures—yet quickly invoked those procedures if there was any question of punishment.[125] It was all very wearing for vice-chancellors and for anyone in authority, and was but one small instance of a longer term and wider trend whereby those in authority were losing both the glamour and the relative financial reward hitherto attending willingness to accept responsibility. At the same time, the doctors were emphasizing how health was threatened by the 'type-A personality' (a designation emerging from research by the American cardiologist Meyer Friedman in 1943), while media people and pressure groups were readier than ever to probe the reticences inevitable in the exercise of power. Given the satirical trend already discussed,[126] interviewers and journalists were subjecting politicians to mounting irreverence: 'it is not easy nowadays', Michael Palin recalled in 1995, 'to convey the sensational audacity, the explosively liberating effect of hearing the prime minister of the day impersonated or judges, bishops, police chiefs and army officers mocked. It was shocking and thrilling.'[127] During the 1960s—as in the 1830s, the 1880s, and the Edwardian period—familiar landmarks seemed to be disappearing, and a growing crisis of authority seemed to be changing the relations between pupil and teacher, employer and employee, parent and child, government and citizen.

Both Conservative and Labour were equipped in their different ways to contain student unrest. Conservatives were instinctively unembarrassed by the need to uphold order, whereas Labour (especially when led by Wilson) had inherited much of the nineteenth-century Whig/Liberal tactical subtlety in the face of unrest, reinforced by trade union pragmatic anti-intellectualism. Wilson was stripped of his honorific title as president of Cambridge University's Labour Club late in 1966 and in the following October was badly jostled by radical students at a regional Labour Party meeting there.[128] When George Brown visited Essex University in June 1970, punches were thrown.[129] Crossman repeatedly grumbled in his diary in 1968–9 at the absence of any fruitful dialogue in a non-revolutionary situation between the politicians and

[124] For some examples see B. Harrison, 'Oxford and the Labour Movement', *TCBH* 2/3 (1991), 256–7.

[125] See Ernest Gellner's important 'Myth, Ideology and Revolution', in B. Crick and W. A. Robson (eds.), *Protest and Discontent* (Harmondsworth, 1970) 206–7.

[126] See above, pp. 477–9.

[127] *O* (15 Jan. 1995), review section, 5.

[128] Pimlott, *Wilson*, 459, 473.

[129] *T* (3 June 1970), 1.

revolutionaries who were 'sentimentalists with no understanding of power';[130] the radical attacks on parliamentarism constituted 'a volcanic eruption' which rendered his 'main philosophy of life appallingly out of date'.[131] Seeking always to position himself for a mediating role, and reluctant to weaken the economy further by risking American disapproval, Wilson none the less refused to give moral and material backing to the USA in the Vietnam war, and in the short term got the worst of both worlds. He was unloved—or, worse, ignored—by American governments; yet he was also detested by radical students. They identified with their American contemporaries, who were being conscripted into what seemed an unjust war. In supporting the USA on the war Alastair Hetherington as editor of the *Guardian* found it difficult to hold the line.[132]

When French students in 1968 displayed their power during the 'days of May', a heady concoction of revolutionary fervour, Marxist rhetoric, and romantic histrionics generated in British universities a mood that was entirely unfamiliar, and owed little to genuine domestic grievance. Vietnam made things worse, especially as Herbert Marcuse, influential with students, portrayed the young as potential allies of the poor and the excluded. If only the latter could be brought to see liberal democracy as a confidence trick which traded affluence for freedom and justice, their forcible protests would expose the violence lurking behind democracy's bland façade. 'Direct action' as a tactic in Britain had grown out of CND as a route to publicity, but it now reflected genuine if misplaced indignation. In October 1968, before the second of two alarming anti-American demonstrations outside the American embassy in London, Benn predicted extensive television coverage of the violence, 'but the one thing we shan't get, either before, during, or after, is any opportunity to hear first-hand at length and in peace, the views of those who are organizing these demonstrations'.[133] After the Grosvenor Square demonstrations the Metropolitan Police set up a 'special demonstration squad', known as 'hairies' because of how they looked and lived [Fig. 6], to infiltrate other left-wing direct-action groups and interact with MI5.[134] The government was the more confident in its stance for being able to rely on the chauvinist anti-intellectualism widespread in the labour movement, let alone elsewhere. By January 1969 the minister of education, Edward Short, once head of a secondary school, felt embattled against a minority of overseas students at the LSE who were, he said, 'the thugs of the academic world'; he hoped that parents and local authorities would help 'to stop this squalid nonsense'.[135]

[130] *Cabinet Diaries*, iii. 385 (25 Feb. 1969); cf. his 'Role of the Volunteer', 267.
[131] *Cabinet Diaries*, ii. 779–80 (14 Apr. 1968).
[132] Obituary, *G* (4 Oct. 1999), 16
[133] Bristol speech, *T* (19 Oct. 1968), 10, referring to the impending demonstration on 27 Oct.
[134] *G* (23 Oct. 2002), 11; supplement, 3.
[135] *HC Deb.* 29 Jan. 1969, cc. 1372–3.

" I'm afraid Sydney won't be coming—he swallowed his Molotov cocktail."

Fig. 6. Jak, *Evening Standard* (26 Oct. 1968)

The advance of school and university examinations as ways of assigning people to jobs, the decline of aristocracy, the mounting importance of professions requiring scientific or technical knowledge, and the pressure for Britain fully to exploit its intellectual capital—all worked against rigid class distinctions after 1945.[136] In such a situation it is at first sight highly paradoxical that the left in the sixties was so preoccupied with Marxian class categories. The explanation lies partly in the international currency given to such ideas, especially in French and American sociological hothouses of theory; their inspiration was 'the early Marx' whose recent reinterpretation by political theorists made such discussions seem intellectually more respectable. A purely British impulse lay in the New Left's secession in 1956 from the CPGB, which had made Marxian insights more accessible. Revolutionary or utopian variants of socialism lay behind many of the experiments in communal living that were much discussed at the time, and the New Left was more interested than the CPGB in anarchist ideas. At the same time British anarchists were becoming more pragmatic,

[136] For more on this see above, pp. 195, 200–4, 210–13, 216–17.

readier to impinge directly on present-day society, evoking from *The Times* on 3 June 1968 what was probably the first leader on the subject since Kropotkin had worked on its staff.[137]

The late 1960s witnessed a ferment of new ideas, whether operating on the right, the left or on a different plane from either. Their very novelty made them difficult to gear into the party system, so suspicious were such movements of the state and its police and military outcrops. If the Liberals were more accessible to such groups than the two mainstream parties, this was partly because the party was then at risk of declining into a protest or pressure group; the 'Young Liberals' were then seeking to convert it into a street-based crusade for community action. By the mid-1960s community-action groups were pioneering conservation movements which in some ways anticipated the 'green' movement: helping to improve housing and amenities in areas like London's Notting Hill under the former CND activist George Clark,[138] creating adventure playgrounds for inner-city children, and mobilizing the unemployed to defend themselves through the so-called Claimants' Union founded in 1970, with more than a hundred branches two years later.[139] 'Squats' in unoccupied buildings escalated into a movement from 1968, inspired by the contrast between widespread homelessness and empty urban buildings, especially in selected parts of London. The squatters' selectiveness reflected the distribution of actual or planned redevelopment, and their need for shared information, self-defence, and mutual reassurance. They tended to choose local-authority rather than private property because councillors could more easily be embarrassed by bad publicity[140]—so much so, that by 1972 almost half the London boroughs had made short-term licensing agreements with squatters' groups. In January 1974 there was a symbolic and much-publicized two-day occupation of Centre Point, empty since its completion in 1963; by mid-1975, however, the movement had reached its peak, with 40,000–50,000 squatters, mostly in inner London,[141] and legislation in 1977 produced a downturn.

Out of North London communes of young people with European revolutionary (especially 'situationist') connections in the late 1960s,[142] a more startling movement emerged: the Angry Brigade, Britain's short-lived pale imitation of West Germany's Baader Meinhof terrorist gang. It planted twenty-five

[137] D. Stafford, 'Anarchists in Britain Today', in D. E. Apter and J. Joll (eds.), *Anarchism Today* (London and Basingstoke, 1971), 90–5.

[138] See Des Wilson in *Observer Colour Supplement* (26 Aug. 1973), 17.

[139] *T* (7 Dec. 1972), 18. *O* (3 Aug. 1975), 2.

[140] Anon, 'Myth and Reality', in N. Anning *et al.*, *Squatting: The Real Story* (1980), 231.

[141] S. Platt, 'A Decade of Squatting', in Anning *et al.*, *Squatting*, 32, 40.

[142] G. Carr, *The Angry Brigade: The Cause and the Case* (1975), 17–24. The Situationist International, consisting mainly of artists and intellectuals, had been formed in 1957 round Guy Debord's theory of the Spectacle: the world we see is not real but what we are conditioned to see.

bombs in all, including bombs at the houses of two cabinet ministers; nineteen of them exploded. Its convicted leaders were drawn from radical students disillusioned with the Wilson government who had dropped out from university into welfare and protest movements and who felt completely alienated from established institutions.[143] Giving judgement in 1972, Mr Justice James declared that 'undoubtedly a warped understanding of sociology has brought you to the state in which you are'.[144] A longer lasting and more tragic outcrop of the 'direct action' movements of the 1960s, drawing on a very different situation and somewhat different ideas, was the IRA's revival in Northern Ireland.

Disillusionment with a Labour government, in addition to prompting movements further left, sometimes off the parliamentary plane altogether, might have been expected to shift voters further right. What is surprising about the late 1960s is that its rightward shift was so modest. The violence had certainly alarmed *The Times* by July 1969,[145] but the failure of left-wing disillusionment to generate support for the Conservative Party partly reflected the fact that Heath (its leader) was too pragmatic in style and too wooden in personality to inspire any mass following. Furthermore, Powell's attempts to exploit fears of disorder[146] were themselves seen as inflammatory, given the reactions to his Birmingham 'rivers of blood' speech. Branded by students as a Fascist, his meetings repeatedly disrupted, Powell was consigned by his critics to the margins of politics in an entirely misleading analogy with Mosley between the wars, whereas Powell's model was Churchill in the late 1930s. More importantly, Wilson was still occupying the political middle ground. Quintin Hogg might try to aggregate strikers, radical students, pornographers, and drug peddlers into an imaginary coordinated threat to the social order,[147] but with Wilson's Baldwinesque pipe-smoking image of stability and Callaghan's easy-going populist traditionalism at the Home Office, the Conservatives found that their clothes had been stolen. Though Heath won the general election in 1970, it was not through repudiating all that the sixties stood for, but through pursuing a programme that aimed more effectively to achieve Wilson's objectives of 1964. For however much they disliked one another, Heath and Wilson shared a meritocratic and modernizing programme; indeed, Heath had been chosen as Conservative leader in 1965 largely because he was seen as the Conservative riposte to Wilson. Both were also quietly determined to frustrate the anti-parliamentarism and anti-politics that became so fashionable during the decade.

[143] For good accounts of their lifestyle see *T* (7 Dec. 1972), 18; *G* (7 Dec. 1972), 12.

[144] *T* (7 Dec. 1972), 2.

[145] e.g. the leader 'Reform and Restraint' in *T* (26 July 1969), 9.

[146] e.g. when addressing Conservative students at York, *T* (9 Mar. 1970), 4.

[147] *T* (5 May 1969), 1.

Given this situation, British government applied its time-honoured device of dividing its critics by fostering and co-opting responsible members of the potentially alienated group. On three occasions Gallup polls revealed a large majority hostile to lowering the voting age to 18,[148] but the politicians thought otherwise. Already in February 1964 the Beatles had been invited (in vain) to dinner by the wife of the British ambassador in Paris; they now found themselves invited to the Washington embassy on their first American tour. 'We always tried to get out of those crap things', George Harrison recalled. 'But that time we got caught. They were always full of snobby people who really loathe our type, but want to see us because we're rich and famous';[149] subsequent such invitations were declined. Yet the element of political protest lying behind such refusals should not be exaggerated. Even the more rakish Mick Jagger of the Rolling Stones was less hostile to 'the system' than his stage performances might imply. There were passing suggestions in the late 1960s that he might become a Labour candidate, and given the element of performance in the politician's career, the suggestions were not wholly absurd. Jagger was intelligent, distant from the establishment, and espoused various causes congenial to Labour; a Labour allegiance for him seems the more plausible in the light of late-century developments in the party. On the other hand, his lifestyle was too reminiscent of J. S. Mill's 'experiments in living' to please the more austere variant of Labour supporter, and Jagger's libertarian informality would perhaps have fitted better with the Liberals. Other aspects of his career fit more readily into a Conservative mould, given the highly competitive, free-market, and shrewdly money-making context within which his career was pursued. Yet the anti-political or even politically indifferent dimensions to youth culture eventually prevailed, and it was to curb these that the government's avoiding actions were taken. Although the Liberals voted out the idea of enfranchising 18 year olds at their conference as late as 1963, Labour when in power followed up its earlier commitment. When the Lord Chancellor appointed the Latey committee on the age of majority in July 1965 the vote was excluded from its brief, but the government fully endorsed the committee's liberal approach. Although the committee opposed early marriage, it did not feel that the law should endorse any continued withholding of parental consent as a remedy, and reluctantly opted for 'free marriage'.[150] The Speaker's conference by a majority favoured reducing the voting age to 20, but the government proposed 18 instead, and the Representation of the People Bill went through parliament in 1968–9.

The outcome was of no trivial significance, given that *Fix* v *Stirk* (1970) enabled university student voters to register both at home and at university,

[148] *Gallup Polls*, ii. 805, 944, 1041. [149] Quoted in Davies, *Beatles*, 275.
[150] See above, p. 263.

and to decide for themselves on where to cast their single ballot. Voters between 18 and 21, often strategically located in university towns, probably halved the Conservative majority at the general election of 1970, and made a decisive difference in the two general elections of 1974.[151] As for university protest, its more violent and distasteful aspects could be left to discredit themselves, but those who favoured indiscriminately resisting student demands received little comfort, for the government and the CVCP sought to control the student movement through establishing closer relations with the NUS. In 1968 a joint report welcomed student participation in student welfare matters, and the NUS President, Jack Straw, dined at 10 Downing Street in 1970.[152] Though Powell likened Straw, in his relations with the Vice-Chancellor of Warwick University, to 'a baron standing over King John',[153] Straw showed some skill in steering the student movement away from extremist protest and into collaborating with a sympathetic government.[154]

5. PURITANISM REPUDIATED?

Penguin Books sounded the trumpet for retreat from old-style puritanism in 1960 when they challenged the Lord Chamberlain in court over their right to publish D. H. Lawrence's *Lady Chatterley's Lover*. Nabokov's *Lolita*, with its paedophile narrator-hero, had been published in Paris in 1955, and escaped prosecution when published in London in 1959 because priced high; but during the 1950s books such as *The Naked and the Dead* and *Catch 22*, which libraries would have excluded, were made readily available as paperbacks, and *Lady Chatterley* did well, selling two million copies in two years.[155] Among the distinguished authors testifying to its literary merits at the trial was E. M. Forster, who claimed that if the novel were condemned, 'our country will certainly make itself look ridiculous in America and elsewhere'.[156]

It is almost necessary to have been an adult at the time to appreciate why such an impact was made by the trial, whose context is the remarkable public silence then prevailing on all sexual matters. The boundary between public and private was now being repositioned by progressives aiming simultaneously to demystify and purify: to enhance human happiness by ensuring that in sexual matters honesty and knowledge replaced guilt and ignorance. Prominent Christians, probably ahead of their congregations, were not shy in supporting these liberal moves. 'Our first duty', said the British Council of Churches, '. . . is not to

[151] Butler, *British Elections since 1945*, 63. [152] *T* (9 Apr. 1970), 12.
[153] Address to Conservative students at York, *T* (9 Mar. 1970), 4.
[154] See esp. his speech to union presidents at Durham, *T* (17 Mar. 1970), 1, and praise from Brian Macarthur in *T* (17 Feb. 1971), 14.
[155] Sutherland, *Reading the Decades*, 49, 51; *Fiction and the Fiction Industry*, 20–1.
[156] Hare (ed.), *Penguin Portrait*, 242.

condemn, but to try to understand what is happening.'[157] Bishop Robinson spoke up for *Lady Chatterley* in 1960, and three years later his *Honest to God* dismissed simplistic views of right and wrong in personal morality: 'chastity is the expression of charity—of caring, enough', he wrote, 'and this is the criterion for every form of behaviour . . . in sexual ethics or in any other field'. On the day he retired as Bishop of Woolwich he said he was proud to have been associated with three best-sellers of the 1960s: *Lady Chatterley's Lover*, the *New English Bible*, and *Honest to God*.[158] The sixties crusade for honesty also enlisted the philosopher-enthusiast for open and rational debate, the social anthropologist with his relativist perspective, the psychologist eating away at the roots of superstition, and the agony aunt whose profession daily alerted her to the hidden miseries then stemming from the prevailing reticence. 'Marje' Proops, whose own personal life was later revealed as far from orthodox, for decades ran her 'Dear Marje' weekly advice column for the *Daily Mirror*, backed by a team of medical and psychiatric experts. She seems to have been the first journalist to use the word 'masturbation' in a national paper: 'I have never believed in messing around', she said; 'I've always believed in being straight with people and using the words.'[159] *The Little Red School-Book* thought likewise, though under judicial pressure its advice to children on sex had to be rewritten. But even the revised version retained its four-letter words, and supplied sensible, precise, clear, and practical advice of a sociological as well as physiological kind on such subjects as venereal disease, homosexuality, abortion, menstruation, and masturbation.

From the early 1960s censorship relaxed at several levels, as a result of legislation, a more permissive outlook in the courts, juries' growing reluctance to convict, a consequent reluctance to prosecute, and a decline in self-censorship within the literary world.[160] The journey of the word 'fuck' towards acceptability with the media provided milestones along the high road to sixties culture: in the *Observer* in 1960 Tynan first thrust it into the Sunday papers in the context of the *Lady Chatterley* trial, and in 1965 provoked a national furore when he was the first to utter it in a BBC programme on 13 November late at night; the much less flamboyant Alastair Hetherington, editor of the *Guardian*, was the first editor to allow the word into his paper.[161] Public nudity provided a further set of milestones. Jenkins as Home Secretary used a threat of resignation to force abolition of the Lord Chamberlain's powers of censorship over the live theatre, a reform which became law on 26 September 1968. On the following day the American musical *Hair* received its first performance, complete with its

[157] British Council of Churches, *Sex and Morality. A Report . . . October 1966* (1966), 7.
[158] Robinson, *Honest to God*, 119. 'Farewell to the Sixties', *O* (28 Sept. 1969), 10.
[159] *Tickle the Public* (BBC Radio 4 programme on the *Mirror*, 4 Mar. 1996).
[160] Davies, *Permissive Britain*, 46.
[161] Tynan, *Tynan*, 178, 236. Obituary of Hetherington, *G* (4 Oct. 1999), 16.

controversial nude scene, on the London stage. There was nudity and much else onstage in Kenneth Tynan's revue *Oh! Calcutta*, which transferred from New York to London in June 1970. 'I cannot remember a more tedious evening', said Bishop Stockwood after seeing it in August, despite having earlier found *Hair* 'challenging and full of good things'.[162] Tynan's pocket benefited from the production. Not so Keele University's budget when about twenty of its anarchist students decided to sunbathe in the nude on 19 June; Staffordshire's education committee withdrew its annual grant.[163] On 17 March 1971 nudity even reached *The Times*, in an advertisement which unleashed a shower of shocked letters.[164]

In the sixties, areas of change and protest tended to flow into one another, and Anglo-American radicals were gradually transferring the term 'obscene' from personal conduct to contexts of political power involving war and exploitation. It was itself a radical act to reshape the language. 'Obscene is not the picture of a naked woman who exposes her pubic hair', wrote Marcuse, 'but that of a fully clad general who exposes his medals rewarded in a war of aggression.'[165] Two of the BBC's Reith Lecture series were important for crystallizing the progressive outlook of the time. Carstairs revealed in his lectures his strong interest in social anthropology, and in 1962 described the prevailing popular morality as 'a wasteland, littered with the debris of broken convictions'. He questioned whether chastity really was 'the supreme moral virtue', and claimed that premarital sexual experience with due precautions had become 'a sensible preliminary to marriage' and likely to enhance its quality.[166] For Leach, lecturing in 1967, the family 'with its narrow privacy and tawdry secrets' was 'the source of all our discontents', and he welcomed the revolt of the young against it. He was well qualified to point out that different situations create different types of family, and to predict that a century hence 'the general pattern of domestic life in Britain will be altogether different from what it is now'.[167]

Eager to spread the new gospel were the sex educators, but only within limits. *Towards a Quaker View of Sex* (1963) was a key document in getting the schoolteacher to supplement the parent. The early sixties inherited from the 1950s the social hygiene approach to sex education: heterosexuality, the nuclear family, and premarital chastity were seen as the norm, and healthy reproduction the aim. Later in the decade, psychological perspectives and 'relationships'

[162] 'The Bishop at the Round House', *G* (19 Aug. 1970), 8.

[163] *T* (23 June 1970), 2. *ST* (28 June 1970), 3.

[164] e.g. from Trevor Abbott, *T* (19 Mar. 1971), 21. For a more sustained discussion of changing attitudes to nudity see B. Harrison, 'The Public and the Private in Modern Britain' in P. Burke *et al.* (eds.), *Civil Histories: Essays Presented to Sir Keith Thomas* (Oxford, 2000), 338–9.

[165] H. Marcuse, *An Essay on Liberation* (1st publ. 1969, paperback edn. Harmondsworth, 1972), 18; cf. 41–2.

[166] Quotations from G. M. Carstairs, *This Island Now* (1st publ. 1963, paperback edn. Harmondsworth, 1964), 54, 49.

[167] Leach, *Runaway World?*, 44–5.

received increasing attention, and guidance for the young became more practical and explicit. But because they advocated sexual enjoyment only within, or with the aim of, a 'responsible' and lasting heterosexual relationship, the manuals put severe limits on what could be done and in what circumstances.[168] So much so, that Alex Comfort, a medically trained psychologist, declared that before his influential *The Joy of Sex* (1973), 'writing about sex gave the impression of being written by non-playing coaches'.[169] Practice was continually edging ahead of prescription, and the sex-education manuals needed to move ever faster in order to keep up. Now that sexual enjoyment was becoming accepted for its own sake, commentators felt free to recite the full sexual menu, and could now apply the concept of 'responsible' sexual conduct to same-sex relations.[170] During the sixties a consumerist attitude to sexuality grew apace, nourished by the appearance of hedonistic sex shops, magazines, and London policemen who (for a consideration) refrained from enforcing the law. Given that Britain was more restrictive than any EEC country, a genuinely international trade in pornography ensured that Britain became a net importer: 'Mr Heath could have found few better Europeans than the pornographers in 1971.'[171] Taboos—on male and female masturbation, abortion, venereal disease, and homosexuality, to mention only four—now began to tumble like ninepins, with much American help. Two writers of fiction gave special attention to masturbation at the end of the decade. Anthony Burgess claimed that the American author Philip Roth's *Portnoy's Complaint* (1969), 'the first great novel of masturbation', liberated the whole subject through laughter.[172] Brian Aldiss's autobiographical novel *The Hand-Reared Boy* (1970) was entirely self-conscious in breaking down the taboo on a boyhood experience far more widespread than might have been guessed from the public silence then prevailing on the subject.

The move towards discussing abortion more openly in the early 1960s has already been discussed,[173] but by the end of the decade abortion's incidence was for several reasons causing growing concern. To begin with, the Abortion Act (1967) at last laced public discussion with precise statistics: by 1970 the growing number of abortions conducted in private practice and under the NHS had reached a tenth of live births to women resident in England and Wales.[174] Abortion was at risk of becoming a routine method of contraception. The Family Planning Act (1967) removed restrictions of medical or marital status on women's access to local-authority birth-control services in England

[168] J. Newman, 'Sex Education and Social Change: Perspectives on the 1960s' (Open University Ph.D. thesis, 1990), 48, 125, 178, 180, 184, 194, 211.

[169] Obituary, *DT* (28 Mar. 2000), 33.

[170] Newman, *Sex Education*, 212, 250, 263, 266.

[171] J. Sutherland, *Offensive Literature. Decensorship in Britain 1960–1982* (1982), 167; see also 4–6.

[172] *ST* (20 Apr. 1969), 61.

[173] See above, pp. 247–9.

[174] *BST* 60.

and Wales, but horses were already bolting fast from the politicians' stables. The phrase 'to make love' was becoming a euphemism for 'to have sexual intercourse', and the number of births premaritally conceived rose by a tenth between 1964 and 1968—to more than a tenth of legitimate births.[175] The Divorce Reform Act (1969) had the effect of acknowledging, as in many other West European countries at that time, the absence of marital bliss from many conventional marriages. It changed the grounds for divorce, replacing matrimonial offence by marital breakdown, and for the first time allowed marriages to be dissolved by mutual consent after two years' separation, and without consent after five; legislation in 1984 cut the two-year waiting period to a year. The clarity of the moral distinction between the married and the unmarried state was being blurred. A further sign of relaxing restraints was the incidence of venereal disease: after reaching an all-time low in the 1950s, it more than doubled between 1960 and 1973, in which year it reached a new record level.[176]

Every generation finds something different to worry about, and a waning British concern after 1945 was the idea that the nation's virility and stature required a rising birth rate. The decline of empire made it no longer seem urgent to generate a steady supply of soldiers and white settlers, and given that contraception had now decoupled sexual activity from procreation, there seemed much less reason to frown upon the unmarried state, on childlessness, or even on homosexuality. The Wolfenden report had opened up discussion of homosexuality in the mid-1950s, and in 1966 the British Council of Churches claimed that 'immense mischief has been done by grossly over-emphasizing the harm done by masturbation', that 'homosexuality and other abnormalities are far commoner than used to be thought', and that they could no longer be seen 'simply as wicked perversions'.[177] The way was now open to substituting 'gay liberation' for 'homosexual law reform'. To carry opinion with them on the main front, the reformers had to tighten up elsewhere. The Sexual Offences Act (1967) liberated only those homosexuals who in pursuing their sexual relations in private resembled respectable heterosexual couples. If anything, it worsened the situation of the homosexual who operated in public space: against him the law was if anything even more tightly enforced after 1967. The Act's definition of 'private' was stringent: in 1967–77 the recorded incidence of indecency between males in Britain approximately doubled, and the number prosecuted trebled.[178] Furthermore, the Act strengthened the law against male importuning and child abuse. 'Well, you're legal now', Joe Orton's agent Peggy

[175] Coleman and Salt, *British Population*, 154. [176] Ibid. 249.

[177] Quotations from *Sex and Morality*, 61, 13.

[178] T. Newburn, *Permission and Regulation: Law and Morals in Post-War Britain* (1992), 62; see also 53, 59, 63–4, and the argument conducted in M. Houlbrook, *Queer London: Perils and Pleasures in the Sexual Metropolis, 1918–1957* (Chicago, 2005), 243, 252, 256–7, 260, 263.

Ramsay told him on 4 July 1967, the day when the Act became law. 'It's only legal over twenty-one', he replied; 'I like boys of fifteen.'[179] His partner Kenneth Halliwell killed him with a hammer on 9 August, only a few days after Orton had recorded in his diary his hopes of once more visiting North Africa in search of Arab youths unavailable in England. The Act did not legalize homosexuality or even aim significantly to change attitudes towards it: like the Wolfenden report it merely shifted the balance of regulation from public control towards self-control. It did not apply in Scotland, Northern Ireland, the armed forces, or the merchant navy. For the history of British lesbians, 1967 is an even less significant date, if only because they were still less salient than male homosexuals in British society. Their relationships had not been illegal before 1967; indeed, the Gateways Club in Chelsea had already begun to pioneer the same-sex bar for women in London.[180]

Education, secularization, and contraception were removing such influence as political and religious leaders had ever enjoyed over personal relationships, and a genuine democratization of decision-making in the area was in progress. But the politicians' impulse to sexual liberation in 1967 promised little for the future. Both political parties had their own reasons for evading direct involvement in moral-reform issues. Crossman in his diaries worried about the working-class reaction to the Sexual Offences Bill: 'working-class people in the north jeer at their Members at the weekend', he wrote, 'and ask them why they're looking after the buggers at Westminster instead of looking after the unemployed at home'.[181] Given its many Roman Catholic supporters inside and outside the cabinet, the Labour government was also keen to distance itself from divorce-law reform. Crossman as Leader of the House admitted privately that the government was 'really giving a great deal of help' to the divorce reform legislation, but said this could not be openly admitted.[182] Whereas as Home Secretary (1965–7) Jenkins had been a liberal influence on moral issues, his successor Callaghan (1967–70) applied the brake. But even if the politicians had been more whole-hearted in their commitment, their influence on sexual conduct could be only very limited—at most retrospectively legalizing conduct hitherto covert. No single piece of legislation could transform attitudes in so private a sphere. More important for liberation than any legislation were non-political influences such as the growing affluence since the 1950s, which lifted homosexual relations out of the public convenience and into the private bedroom; and more central to persecution was the non-political harassment of homosexuals through bullying in schools, street violence, and social disapproval. Such prejudice long outlasted 1967.

[179] *Orton Diaries*, 233 (4 July 1967). [180] Obituary of Gina Ware, *T* (22 Aug. 2001), 15.
[181] Crossman, *Cabinet Diaries*, ii. 407 (2 July 1967), cf. ii. 171–2 (19 Dec. 1966).
[182] Ibid. ii. 610 (19 Dec. 1967).

Yet the defence of puritanism in personal conduct was by no means dead, as became clear in 1971, which witnessed the longest obscenity trial in British history. The three editors of the periodical *Oz* were found guilty (reversed on appeal) on four obscenity charges relating to its 'school kids issue', and the same concern about distributing corrupting material to the young inspired the summons served in the same year on Richard Handyside, publisher of *The Little Red School-Book*. The customs authorities had been seizing Denmark's pornographic exports to Britain in escalating quantity during the 1960s,[183] and the book's hedonistic approach and failure to stress the need for self-control were criticized during the trial. Active behind the scenes in both these cases was Mary Whitehouse. This courageous, energetic, and commonsensical, yet simplistic and populist schoolteacher, housewife, and mother had been influenced at a crucial moment by Moral Rearmament. With an aptitude for publicity, she embarked on her campaign to clean up the media when three of her 14-year-old pupils in 1963 decided to experiment with prostitution after watching televised coverage of the Profumo affair. Her National Viewers' and Listeners' Association tapped a vein of spontaneous hostility to the new permissiveness, and her apparently artless and provincial simplicity shocked the sophisticated. Conservative in her outlook, she appropriated ways of speaking and communicating more widely used on the left, whose preoccupation with media conspiracy she shared; she also shared Marcuse's inflated and conspiratorial view of media power, but for her it was biased against traditional moral values, and not against the left.[184] To her critics she seemed a blinkered, narrow, and determined busybody, impervious to ridicule, but her movement indicates that the decade never universally endorsed sixties attitudes, which generated their own antidote.

How far, then, did the sixties repudiate puritanism? The puritanism involved in overtly monitoring personal morality (in the use of time and money, and in personal relationships) was, as we have seen, on the retreat. Puritanism, however, is not a specific area of concern but an attitude. Protean and elusive, it ranges over the whole of human conduct, alighting unpredictably upon its changing preoccupations: when banished from one area it tends unobtrusively, unexpectedly, and often incongruously to reappear in another. For Rosie Boycott, co-founder of the feminist journal *Spare Rib*, the paper seemed to be selling 'unremitting gloom' to a fourth-phase British feminist movement that was shaped by a 'kind of censorship against happiness', and she eventually felt she must escape.[185] The new puritanism involved self-denial, and could prompt self-sacrifice and even self-sabotage or 'dropping

[183] For these exports, see *O* (15 Aug. 1971), 9.
[184] *Essay on Liberation*, 69.
[185] J. Green (ed.), *Days in the Life: Voices from the English Underground 1961–1971* (1st publ. 1988, paperback edn. 1989), 417.

out'; but it was less concerned with mortifying the flesh than with exploring new lifestyles and repudiating Western values. It was espoused by only a small and 'underground' minority, but its outlook was much discussed, it became a prominent theme in influential plays,[186] and in retrospect it influenced the concept of the sixties more profoundly than its few adherents would lead one to expect.

The new puritanism took two forms. There was first a repudiation of the affluent lifestyle in Western industrial societies. Keynes had envisaged that with wealth accumulated, 'some of the most distasteful of human qualities' would no longer need to be 'exalted . . . into the position of the highest virtues', and that love of money would 'be recognised for what it is, a somewhat disgusting morbidity'.[187] His (probably unconscious) disciples in this assumed an unexpected guise in the 1960s—in expecting the new society to arrive more quickly if people deliberately opted to reduce their pretensions and their requirements of life. Marcuse thought it more important to be morally than physically clean: 'the aesthetic morality is the opposite of puritanism. It does not insist on a daily bath or shower for people whose cleaning practices involve systematic torture, slaughtering, poisoning; nor does it insist on clean clothes for men who are professionally engaged in dirty deals.'[188] The new alternative lifestyle seemed encapsulated in the groups of 'travellers' (formerly known as 'gypsies') who moved around the country or even between countries, for the internationalism of sixties teenage culture reached the remotest parts. The British embassy in Kabul between March and October 1970 found itself issuing an average of two one-way tickets to London every week to British pilgrims unable to fund their homeward return from the paradise they had sought.[189]

In 1951 it had been assumed that all justification for begging had now ceased: the welfare state would cater for all in need, and street begging allegedly deserved no sympathy. But in the 1960s young people dropping out reinforced the dwindling number of placarded and often bemedalled beggars from the wartime generation, and with their guitars, mouth organs, and dogs they appeared in the passages of London's underground network. In the 1980s an even later generation joined them for rather different reasons: benefits for young people not pursuing work were being cut. Owing much to American exemplars, Britain's underground culture in the 1960s 'was ultimately opposed to the materialism which had created the opportunity for it to flourish'.[190] There were parallels between the improvident and hedonistic lifestyle adopted by

[186] Billington, *State of the Nation*, 151.

[187] J. M. Keynes, 'Economic Possibilities for Our Grandchildren' (1930), in Keynes, *Essays in Persuasion* (1931), 369.

[188] *Essay on Liberation*, 35.

[189] *O* (15 Aug. 1971), 2.

[190] R. Hewison, *Too Much: Art and Society in the Sixties, 1960–75* (1988), p. xiii.

progressive intellectuals in their communes and some aspects of working-class upbringing and behaviour. But such attitudes had prevailed among working people more by necessity than choice, as an outcrop of the sense of community stemming from enforced poverty rather than from any deliberate rejection of affluence. Little sympathy was felt when this lifestyle was voluntarily assumed by people from affluent backgrounds under subsidy from taxpayers who were themselves far from rich. Besides, the entire hippy lifestyle offended another major strain within the British working class: respectability. The allegedly middle-class values of ambition, family-centredness, patriotism, cleanliness, and respectability were far from absent lower down in society, and were well represented among the working-class supporters of Powell. When about 300 dockers lobbied their MPs in support of Powell's attitudes to race in April 1968, three long-haired youths baited them by holding up a picture of a uniformed Nazi.[191] When hippies were being expelled from a squat in Piccadilly in September 1969, there were shouts of 'here they come', or 'you will get a good wash', and 'look at this one'. When a long-haired youth accused the bystanders of being Fascists, he was told to 'get your hair cut and get to Vietnam'.[192] In 1971 when demonstrators showed sympathy for the accused in the *Oz* trial, building workers perched on scaffolding shouted 'Go and get a bath' and a postal worker weighed in with 'Why don't you go and find some work?'[193]

The 'new puritanism' of the sixties took a second form: the retreat from reason. This occurred from two directions: first, from an unexpected quarter—universities. Though highly tolerant of contrasting lifestyles, the student protest movement valued 'commitment' too strongly to extend such tolerance to ideas. Commitment on this scale could in theory have prompted an intellectually invigorating fight to the finish within the student community between rival belief systems, but the outcome was rather to opt for the relative harmony of intellectual pluralism, and 'if almost everything is true in its own fashion, truth cannot matter very much'.[194] The drug culture, not absent from universities but not centred there, was prominent from the mid-1960s, and carried the retreat from reason to an extreme. Rejecting Western materialism and the work ethic, it took no thought for the morrow, yet simultaneously embraced the dominant hedonistic values in an unorthodox form. Its participants were relatively unconcerned about social status, but they shared with hedonistic consumerism an irrational pursuit of short-term enjoyment for

[191] *T* (2 May 1968), 1.

[192] *G* (22 Sept. 1969), 1. For comment sympathetic to the hippies see *NS* (26 Sept. 1969), 397, and *T* (26 Sept. 1969), 11; cf. the confrontation with Covent Garden porters, *G* (26 Sept. 1969), 5.

[193] *O* (8 Aug. 1971), 28. For similar confrontations, see *ST* (5 July 1970), 3 (Cambridge); *T* (9 July 1973), 1 (St Ives).

[194] Gellner in Crick and Robson (eds.), *Protest and Discontent*, 215; see also 204, 212, 219.

its own sake, together with what was sometimes an urgent need for money. The white population had hitherto taken its drugs mainly through smoking cigarettes and consuming alcoholic drinks, whereas cannabis reached Britain from Indian and African ports for consumption in London dockside clubs and pubs. During the 1950s drug use spread from there to non-white communities elsewhere in Britain, and through jazz clubs and other recreation places to the white population. The number of convictions for cannabis offences rose slowly in the 1950s, quadrupled in 1960–4, and doubled between 1966 and 1967; 1964 was the first year when white people constituted the majority of cannabis offenders.[195] By the early 1960s the number of known opiate and heroin addicts in the UK was rising fast; this was because younger and highly evangelical self-addicts were supplementing the 454 heroin addicts, largely middle-aged victims of medical prescription, who were known to exist in Britain in 1959.[196] Alarmist interpretations of such escalating statistics failed to acknowledge that they partly reflected growing awareness of a long-hidden problem—a problem which by the mid-1960s seemed to be worsening. High-profile prosecutions indicated interaction between 'the drug scene' and musicians influential with the young, and between 1964 and 1968 the known numbers under 20 who were addicted to heroin rose from 40 to 785.[197]

Among the many teenage routes to self-assertion and rebellion, the drug scene mixed inquisitiveness and pleasure with danger: its rejection of accepted adult values was uncompromising, and was captured in the student slogan 'do not adjust your mind, there is a fault in reality'.[198] It offered an alternative and classless community, and a source of emotional support. It was a private world where spontaneity was valued, and where constraints and boredom could be forsaken for freedom, excitement, and even creativity of a kind. It was in some ways appropriate that such ideas should be propagated by the most affluent society of all: the term hippie, 'a hipster; a person, usually exotically dressed, who is, or is taken to be, given to the use of hallucinogenic drugs; a beatnik' originated in USA in the 1950s and crossed the Atlantic in the mid-1960s, initially to describe people not seen as British. Drugtaking was seldom solitary, but involved choosing a lifestyle, espousing a subculture, and joining a circle of friends united by a shared esoteric experience. Police powers of arrest and search on suspicion, without a warrant, drew that circle more tightly together and distanced it still further from the wider society.

195 B. Wootton (chairman), *Cannabis: Report by the Advisory Committee on Drug Dependence* (1968), 8.

196 R. Davenport-Hines, *The Pursuit of Oblivion: A Global History of Narcotics 1500–2000* (2001), 311. M. A. Plant, *Drugtakers in an English Town* (1975), 36.

197 As cited by Callaghan in *HC Deb.* 27 Jan. 1969, c. 963.

198 Slogan chalked on Broad Street wall of Balliol College, Oxford, as observed by the author in the late 1960s.

Within this context, Baroness Wootton chaired the Advisory Committee on Drug Dependence in preparing its intelligent, careful, and courageous report to the Home Secretary in 1968. Like *The Little Red School-Book*, the report sought to reconcile the tension between the rationalistic and the hedonistic components of sixties radicalism by distinguishing between drugs. 'Drugs won't solve your problems', said the *School-Book*; the important thing, then, for both was to treat the less harmful drugs such as cannabis (with its variants, hashish and marijuana or 'pot') in the same way as tobacco or alcohol. With all these, police powers and legal penalties should be curbed so as to avoid unnecessarily accentuating the social isolation of their users and driving them into bad company.

Wootton's report therefore wanted the law to distinguish between cannabis, which it thought less harmful than smoking cigarettes, and addictive harder drugs such as heroin and the other opiates that doctors often prescribed. 'Possession of a small amount of cannabis should not normally be regarded as a serious crime to be punished by imprisonment';[199] such a response merely drove cannabis users into all the dangers of buying it from people who also dealt in harder drugs. With approving references to the libertarian ideas of John Stuart Mill, the committee felt that so long as cannabis could not be shown to harm anyone beyond the user, the presumption should—here as with homosexual conduct in private—favour encouraging individuals to make their own choices. From the publicity point of view, the committee when phrasing its recommendations did not perhaps take sufficient care to ward off populist attack. In responding to it, Callaghan as Home Secretary played to the gallery: almost deliberately missing the committee's point, he resoundingly declared (to Conservative applause and much trade union approval) the need 'to call a halt in the advancing tide of so-called permissiveness', a word which he pronounced 'one of the most unlikeable . . . invented in recent years'. Wootton's rejoinder was also resounding, though less influential: 'I should like to . . . protest against the current habit of using the term "permissive society" with sinister undertones. I should have thought that any society which valued personal liberty would feel that the onus of proof was upon those who wished to restrict liberties rather than upon those who wished to preserve or extend them.'[200]

The outcome was to leave the police with their powers and penalties and to ensure prosperity for 'Release', the London-based voluntary and relatively informal body founded in 1967 with a free helpline for young people charged with drug offences. 'If pot was legalised', said *The Little Red School-Book*, 'it would eliminate most of the artificial glamour and mystery that are sometimes

[199] *Cannabis Report*, 33.

[200] Callaghan, *HC Deb.* 27 Jan. 1969, c. 959. Wootton, *HL Deb.* 26 Mar. 1969, c. 1308.

associated with it.'[201] The drug culture, promoted through a network of personal contacts, media events, and underground newspapers, acquired a certain glamour from the police raids which aimed to curb it. These encounters help to explain the bad relations that developed in some urban areas between young people and blacks on the one hand and the police on the other. For the drug culture simultaneously offended and fascinated the conformist, respectable, and anti-intellectual elements of the working class from which the police were recruited, and with which Callaghan as Home Secretary identified. The drug trade focused on the pop festivals organized from the late 1960s, not just because it was part of the counter-culture, but because the sheer number of potential customers at such functions precluded law enforcement. At the pop festival in Windsor Great Park during August 1974, 600 police took action against 2,000 fans; 220 fans were arrested, and 51 people were injured, 22 of them police officers.[202] The contrasting reactions to the Isle of Wight pop festival in 1970 drew together neatly the features we now associate with the disconcerting sincerity of the sixties. For Mark Woodnutt, Conservative MP for the Isle of Wight, there was much to deplore: 'I am not a prude and I do not mind nude bathing at the right place at the right time, but I do not like fornicating on the beach, which is what we have been seeing. There has been very little trouble because the police have exercised their discretion and not enforced the law.' But this drew Sue Whittles into the lists. She welcomed the fact 'that for five days all barriers of class, creed and nationality were totally ignored. People shared their food, money and possessions with complete strangers and the "natural reserve" of the British was entirely forgotten. This strange and wonderful state of affairs was not only due to the hippies, but to the vast majority, who were students and ordinary working tax-payers.'[203]

6. THE SIXTIES END?

The search for the end of the sixties must range forward far beyond 1970. Sixties values might have been expected soon to succumb to the hostile moralistic reaction that had so often been predicted. Many sixties people did not even perceive, let alone accept, sixties values. In 1970 Larkin enjoyed reading *The Neophiliacs*, Christopher Booker's account of cultural change in the 1950s and 1960s, but then felt rather out of touch: 'I don't think I have ever read a copy of *Private Eye*, seen a performance of *Beyond the Fringe*, "That Was The Week That Was", or whatever David Frost does. I have registered the Beatles and the mini-skirt, but that's about all.'[204] Enough people between 1964 and

201 *Little Red School-Book*, 139.
202 *G* (30 Aug. 1974), 1; cf. Professor P. B. Fellgett's letter in *T* (30 June 1971), 15.
203 *T* (1 Sept. 1970), 1 (Woodnutt); (4 Sept. 1970), 9 (Whittles).
204 P. Larkin to C. B. Cox in Larkin, *Letters*, 426.

1970 were sufficiently remote from sixties values for Ian Fleming's novels to remain best-sellers and for even Charlotte Yonge's *The Heir of Redclyffe* to sell an average of 235 copies through Duckworth in each of those years, more than half of them to libraries.[205] Given such minorities, there was some hope of an ongoing following for the 'Victorian values' which Thatcher championed in the early 1980s.

Furthermore sixties values, almost by definition and design, lacked staying power: they were never crystallized into a memorable manifesto, nor did they generate the classic texts that secure long-term influence. Given the classless outlook of pop art and pop music, deliberately repudiating reason and tradition, this is hardly surprising; structure-free spontaneity, informal vocabulary, and an emphasis on shared experience do not encourage the sustained effort that makes for lasting achievement. Sixties trendsetters were preoccupied with fashion, which is at permanent risk of becoming respectable and therefore obsolescent. Well-tailored denim suits soon appeared and long hair ceased to seem radical. An unreflecting pursuit of the up-to-date lacks roots, and age consciousness lacks the staying power of class loyalty. Media sights and sounds may make an immediate show, but 'the written word . . . represents permanence of a sort. Thought is trapped there.'[206] With greater responsibilities and advancing years, the young whose formative period was the sixties moved on in their ideas, if only because a lifelong attachment to once-youthful fashions invites ridicule; Peter Cook was not the only sixties talent whose failure to move on ensured ultimate and tragic anti-climax. A rather similar impermanence inevitably attached to the unstructured approach of sixties trends in religion. Buildings, hierarchies, and liturgical practice make for continuity and loyalty: unguided mysticism and self-fashioned beliefs die with the individual.

The sixties made enemies from the outset. The allegedly 'permissive' decade was also the decade of Mary Whitehouse. Provincial England lagged behind the sophisticated metropolitan reign of Hugh Carleton Greene at the BBC, and Lord Reith was unhappy that its concern for recreation and ratings was ousting his high-minded educational and cultural agenda.[207] Liberal progressive rationalists in the universities soon gravitated rightwards when pupils in their passionate push for participation shed deference to intellectual authority. Positions rapidly polarized and feelings ran high. Meritocratic intellectuals who had earlier seen themselves as open-minded in the face of new ideas from the young were soon alarmed by what they had initially encouraged when they found that the young were on many issues far from open-minded, let alone rational: in the mysticism of their Eastern cults, for example, in their drug culture, and in rejecting long-term cumulative self-improvement. The

[205] Author's collection: information provided by Duckworth in letter dated 3 Nov. 1971.
[206] Melly, *Revolt into Style*, 205. [207] *T* (14 Feb. 1970), 1, 9; (16 Feb. 1970), 9.

students seemed to be threatening not only serious research but also the very finances of those one-time temples of the Enlightenment: the universities. A leader in the *Daily Telegraph* on 2 November 1963 expressed alarm at the empty-headedness of Beatlemania, and still more at the intellectuals who deferred to it. What would fill the empty heads next? Hitler would have come forward with something: 'Is there not something a bit frightening in whole masses of young people, all apparently so suggestible, so volatile and rudderless?' One irrationality begat another, and in the bald and bespectacled Alf Garnett the right-wing reaction found a televised fictional embodiment; from 1966 to 1974 he appeared in the influential sitcom *Till Death Us Do Part*. So accurately did the playwright Johnny Speight capture a national mood that seven out of ten people polled by a newspaper thought Garnett was real. 'I didn't create Alf Garnett', said Speight; 'Society did. I just grassed on him.'[208]

Sixties moral reforms had too many enemies from the outset for leading politicians to risk embracing sixties values, so backbenchers stood in for them. In her *On Iniquity* (1967) Pamela Hansford-Johnson suggested that the child-killers Brady and Hindley had been the products of a 'permissive society'. By July 1969 *The Times* feared that the reforms' cumulative effect 'has been to weaken the sense of social discipline'.[209] When in 1971 the so-called 'Festival of Light', evangelical in origin and united by concern about pornography, held a meeting in Trafalgar Square, it clashed with the Gay Liberation Front, after which the Festival gradually faded away.[210] In May 1973 *The Times*, discussing deteriorating standards in British public life, described the Protestant ethic as 'not crumbling by sectors: it is the whole line of cliffs that is being eroded by the sea'. By November 1975 it thought that 'people have come to believe that the permissive society . . . depends for its fragile stability on spending the capital of the discipline of the past'.[211] By then, campaigners for family values and opponents of pornography were mobilized in several organizations approaching the situation from different starting points, but usually operating independently of political party.[212] It cannot be assumed that people were indelibly puritan or permissive: some sixties progressives, once they saw the world they were creating, did not like it, and joined the restrictive camp. The more open discussion of sexuality, for example, did not necessarily produce a feminist outcome, nor did it realize Michael Schofield's dream of 1952 that 'if the subject were brought

[208] *DT* (2 Nov. 1963), 8. *G* (6 July 1998), 15 (Speight). [209] *T* (26 July 1969), 9 (leader).

[210] For the Festival's origins see *T* (9 July 1973), 14. For Trafalgar Square, *ST* (26 Sept. 1971), 7.

[211] See its leaders 'The Changing British Ethic' (25 May 1973), 19; 'The Cycle of Discipline' (29 Nov. 1975), 15.

[212] See 'The Protectorate', *O* 4 Feb. 1973, 44 for a useful discussion. Compare the structures listed in *T* (5 Jan. 1987), 14.

out into the clear light of day, it would hold little interest as a subject of conversation'.[213]

There was a literary dimension to the reaction against the sixties. Larkin's reinstatement of the novelist Barbara Pym was one aspect of it. 'Why should I have to choose between spy rubbish, science fiction rubbish, Negro-homosexual rubbish, or dope-taking nervous-breakdown rubbish?' he grumbled in 1965. It took until the early 1980s for Pym's reputation to recover from the devastating impact of the sixties on fiction concerned with what Larkin called 'people . . . who try to behave well in the limited field of activity they command'.[214] From about 1968 'a definable literary genre', the anti-1960s novel, had emerged, and most novelists in the 1970s and early 1980s who wrote about the sixties did not like them.[215] Bradbury had initially found sixties radicalism liberating, but he recalled that his sympathies with it became 'more and more qualified', and he wrote *The History Man*, 'certainly my bleakest book', in a depressed mood.[216] In the theatre, we have already seen how Coward's public reaction against the sixties (really against the mid-fifties) had begun as early as 1961. His renaissance began in 1963 with a revival of *Private Lives*, and culminated with his seventieth birthday in 1969.[217] The reaction against the sixties was linguistic as well as sartorial. The Prince of Wales complained in 1989 that 'we have arrived at a wasteland of banality, cliché and casual obscenity', and by 1993 his aim had grown into a desire to 'roll back some of the more ludicrous frontiers of the 60s in terms of education, architecture, art, music, and literature, not to mention agriculture!'[218] Of all the fine arts, architecture suffered most from the reaction against the sixties: we have seen how the practical drawbacks of the modern style had already by 1970 forced themselves on their patrons' attention.[219] Cost overruns at Sussex University tagged Basil Spence with the label 'Sir Basil-Expense', and clients often complained about architects more visual than technical in their preoccupations, more concerned with a building's visual impact than with its practicalities. Bradbury describes how the buildings stemming from the 'Edifice Complex' of Watermouth University's vice-chancellor soon acquired 'the worn, public look of a place that has seen much, and is used by everybody, and belongs to nobody', with stained concrete, dirty glass, and graffiti. It was a sad end to the sixties' high hopes for a futuristic campus.[220]

None the less, the enemies of the sixties did not prevent all five of the sixties traits (the cult of youth and modernity, the pursuit of informality, political

[213] 'G.Westwood', *Society and the Homosexual*, 173.

[214] To Charles Monteith, quoted in Motion, *Larkin*, 332.

[215] Taylor, *After the War*, 198.

[216] Haffenden (ed.), *Novelists in Interview*, 35, 26.

[217] *Noel Coward Diaries*, 572 (16 Aug. 1964), 673.

[218] Dimbleby, *Prince of Wales*, 453, 494.

[219] See above, pp. 153–60.

[220] Bradbury, *History Man*, 47, 66, 221. See also Brian Edwards's article on Spence in *ODNB*.

radicalism, the attack on old-style puritanism, and the emergence of the new) from long outlasting the decade. With their armoury of anti-ageing creams, facelifts, exercise bicycles, slimming courses, toupees, and dyes, a surprising number of British middle-aged men and women struggled after the sixties to display themselves as younger than they really were, though they were probably less likely than Americans to resort to cosmetic surgery. The major political parties continued to pursue youth and modernity for the rest of the century and beyond. In the arts, a youthful taste for the modern remained central to creativity in later decades, as in the sixties. Fashionable styles in the theatre might become more eclectic, and less might be heard of Osborne, Braine, Wesker, and Delaney—but on the London stage, drawing-room comedy never resumed its supremacy of the early 1950s. Pop art was a major inspiration for the printmaking of Eduardo Paolozzi, whose sculpture took new and fruitful directions,[221] and Pinter's late twentieth-century acquisition of classic status illustrated the tenacity of genuine sixties talent.

The sixties pursuit of informality and spontaneity continued apace after 1970 at several levels. The shock the young sixties designers delivered to the fashion trade was powerful enough permanently to loosen its constraints. Rule by Paris fashion houses gave way to a multiplicity of styles or to no style at all, and between 1961 and 1975 the circulation of women's fashion periodicals declined.[222] In the 1990s it was still possible for a man to wear a pin-stripe suit or white tie and tails, but his decision to do so was personal. The sixties had launched a major diversification of lifestyles and fashions. Hair could henceforth be long or short, according to taste. As for the tie, by 13 April 2005 so many men had discarded it as to inspire a leading article in the *Guardian*. After 1970 there was far freer movement for both sexes: ties were loosened, heels were lowered, braces were exposed and then discarded, hats were cast aside. *Debrett's Etiquette* pointed out in 1981 that in clothing 'individuality is welcomed rather than frowned upon in fashionable circles. Errors of judgement, unless very obviously so, are merely regarded as evidence of character or a novel variant on current fashion, rather than serious blunders.'[223] Benn in 1996 claimed to have pioneered the shirt-sleeve look that was later adopted by leaders of both Labour and Conservative parties at their annual conferences. 'I would never have done it', Callaghan commented. 'I always wore my jacket. It never occurred to me to take it off. It would have been ill-mannered to have done so.'[224] None the less, the City's bowler hat and black jacket, widely shed by the early 1960s, did not return, and soft collars and striped shirts were henceforth acceptable.[225] By the

[221] Obituary, *G* (23 Apr. 2005), 25.
[222] There are good figures in White, *Women's Periodical Press*, 36–7.
[223] E. B. Donald (ed.), *Debrett's Etiquette and Modern Manners* (1981), 380, repeated in 1990 edn., 371.
[224] *T* (10 Oct. 1996), 1; cf. Benn, *Diaries 1963–7*, 167 (20 Oct. 1964).
[225] Kynaston, *Club No More*, 147.

1980s morning and evening dress were in decline, and court dress had almost disappeared; hats were by then ceasing to be part of the uniform for either sex on social occasions,[226] and among men the bowler was regularly worn only by off-duty army officers, by huntsmen for utilitarian reasons, and by Orangemen as an identifier.[227]

The freedom to wear what seemed suited to oneself was in itself a major and lasting liberation. It was not so much that uniforms were abandoned as that a single uniform was no longer universally required: beneath the superficial sartorial variety which the sixties had encouraged, conformity within the subgroup persisted. The diversity of the clothes worn at the Kirks' party in Watermouth University in the 1970s in itself constituted a uniform. 'There are students in quantities; bearded Jesus youths in combat-wear, wet-look plastic, loon-pants, flared jeans, Afghan yak; girls, in caftans and big boots, with plum-coloured mouths. There are young faculty, serious, solemn examiners of matrimony and its radical alternatives.'[228] All this damaged the British reputation for being well dressed. *British Style*'s editor complained in 1989 of the trend youth had been setting for the last twenty years: the 'sordid syndrome of dirty denim, shapeless blouson, uncleaned trainers, and the curious self-degradation of designer stubble'.[229] The option of fine tailoring survived in Britain, but colour and imagination could now spread their wings. In women's fashions, designers such as Zandra Rhodes whose careers were launched in the sixties went from strength to strength, and the career of Vivienne Westwood in the 1970s showed how pop music and fashion could still fruitfully interact.

In 1990 *Debrett* noted how during the 1980s modes of address had become less formal: 'first names are becoming established practice everywhere and today almost no one needs be offended by what used to be thought a step over the boundary between friendliness and familiarity'.[230] Not only did the Labour cabinet decide, on 5 March 1974, to address one another by first name;[231] its members often publicly referred to one another in that way. The public release of emotion and the free-flowing gesture so evident at the death of Princess Diana in September 1997 were an echo of the sixties, reinforced perhaps by the less inhibited style among some immigrant groups. In late twentieth-century Britain, upper lips were growing less stiff, and spontaneity even began to pervade church services. The growing informality after 1970 in ways of speaking had more than one cause. By the mid-1970s a 'throwaway, mumbling, stumbling' style of speech, involving 'a reluctance to open one's mouth, to

[226] Donald (ed.) *Debrett's Etiquette* (1981), 384, 385, 386, 391. See also the 1990 edn. (Exeter, 1990), 375, 377, 382.

[227] *T* (23 Aug. 1986), 7 (leader).

[228] Bradbury, *History Man*, 222.

[229] John Taylor, letter to *T* (22 Mar. 1989), 15.

[230] *Debrett's Etiquette* (Exeter, 1990), 13.

[231] Benn, *Diaries 1973–6*, 114 (5 Mar. 1974). Castle, *Diaries 1974–6*, 36 (5 Mar. 1974).

move one's lips, and to raise one's voice' was allegedly moving upwards from students to university lecturers,[232] together with 'a defiant "manual worker" image'[233] not always accompanied by the prime working-class characteristic of willingness to work. This 'strange, inward-looking proletarianism' was widespread even at the top of the Labour Party in the 1970s,[234] at a time when much deference was being paid to the trade unions. In his later career the decidedly Oxford-accented Crosland affected something of a proletarian style, together with alleged footballing enthusiasms and frequent references to his Grimsby constituents. Proletarian pretensions combined with the influence by the 1980s of American youth culture to lace conversation with meaningless (because redundant and misapplied) scatological and sexual expletives, though the BBC presenter Anna Ford could still in 1997 run into trouble when she described a fictional character in *The Archers* as 'a shit'.[235] Informality was encouraged by the media, given the approachable manner required on television, and the unstructured formulations encouraged by the relative impermanence and haste of email, text-messaging, and mobile telephone. By 2001 it could become a matter of dispute whether a 43-year-old was insulting the police by telling them to 'fuck off' when they asked him to wait while they checked whether a warrant was out for his arrest. His conviction was overturned with help from a professor of English language at Edinburgh University, who pronounced the words 'endemic', and thought it possible 'that no offense [*sic*] was intended'.[236]

Formal 'manners' of the traditional kind were vulnerable from both left and right. The good manners associated with working-class respectability were not uppermost in the labour movement during the 1970s, a time of trade union militancy and middle-class Marxism; many would then have dismissed them as class identifiers lacking in the spontaneity and sincere concern that could be found lower down in society—or, for that matter, among the young, for progressive people had long discarded the notion that children should be seen and not heard. Others on the left would have reserved their fire for allegedly patronizing male 'chivalry' towards women. After 1970 good manners also came under threat from the right. The revived entrepreneurship of the 1980s did not make for comfort in society at large: imported Americanized business and publicity techniques gave short shrift to the reticence and privacy that had earlier been integral to good manners, and if it increasingly substituted formal training in handling customers, it did so through a formulaic and schooled

[232] Dr Alice Heim in *G* (7 June 1976), 1.

[233] As John Taylor, editor of *British Style*, complained in his letter to *T* (22 Mar. 1989), 15.

[234] David Marquand, 'Inquest on a Movement: Labour's Defeat and its Consequences', *Encounter* (July 1979), 13.

[235] *DT* (2 Apr. 1997), 6. See also the survey of manners cited in *T* (17 Sept. 1991), 2.

[236] *Ind.* (26 Apr. 2001), 13.

routine that lacked all sincerity. While publicly scrupulous in her manners, thoroughly conventional in her belief in the customary courtesies from men to women, and notably courteous to people who worked for her, Thatcher was forthright in public, and as Conservative leader in 1975–90 shocked colleagues by revealing herself as anything but ladylike in private cabinet debate. To British women she offered a new model of female assertiveness, and social relations once thought considerate and chivalrous she dismissed in the 1980s as 'wet' and as lacking the necessary 'go-getting' impulse.

The media were partly responsible for shifts in manners. Mateyness and familiarity became their dominant tone, together with a readiness to interrupt informants that would once have been thought to set a bad example. Nicholas Ridley complained in 1992 that 'respect for the senior and—dare I say it—the successful has evaporated into a general mateyness irrespective of age, experience or achievement'.[237] New types of hero—footballers, entertainers, even tennis stars—lacked the training or even the inclination to act as exemplars. Public figures were expected to be accessible and approachable, and even monarchy now had to stage its walkabouts. Stephen Spender in 1990 drew an astonished contrast between how freely people now approached the famous (often by telephone), and his own interwar reticence in contacting famous writers.[238] For some, this decline in 'manners' seemed democratizing and liberating. Certainly it moderated the fear of losing caste by transgressing unknown rules on what to say, what to wear, what to do—whether on social occasions, or in relation to the opposite sex. For others, however, these changes betokened indiscipline and assertiveness in the young and energetic, and evoked nostalgia for the traditional British art of understatement. A 'Polite Society' even sprang up in the 1990s to revive the good manners that the sixties had allegedly undermined.[239]

As for student radicalism, some of the most notorious instances of radical student unrest occurred after the 1960s: with Cambridge's 'Garden House' affair in 1970; when Stirling University students insulted the Queen in 1972;[240] and when Sussex students prevented Professor Samuel Huntington from lecturing on the role of the military in American foreign policy. Oxford students occupied the University's examination buildings in 1973, and about fifty intruders were forcibly expelled from the University's administrative premises in 1974.[241] Not till Thatcherism in the mid-1980s showed signs of effecting permanent change did protests of this type die down. As the young

[237] 'Snobbery and Yobbery', 1.

[238] Interview in F. du Sorbier (director), *Oxford 1919–1939* (Paris, 1991), 50.

[239] See the controversy evoked by Nicholas Ridley's 'Snobbery and Yobbery' in *T* (7 Aug. 1992), 11.

[240] *T* (4 July 1970), 2. *G* (13 Oct. 1972), 1.

[241] *G* (6 June 1973), 1. Harrison (ed.), *The History of the University of Oxford*, viii. *The Twentieth Century*, 745–6.

Tony Blair (at Oxford from 1972 to 1975) told Michael Foot in 1982, 'it is impossible to understand the 30–40 age group in today's Labour Party without understanding the pervasiveness of Marxist teaching. For me, at university, left-wing politics was Marx and the liberal tradition was either scorned or analysed only in terms of its influence on Marx.'[242] The reaction after 1970 against the radical politics of the 1960s was surprisingly muted. Standing at Epping for selection as a Conservative candidate in 1969, Norman Tebbit uncompromisingly condemned the permissive society, and later felt proud to have done so, but his party at that time showed no sign of taking up the cause. A brief experiment with such an assault came in 1974 when Keith Joseph, after singling out Mary Whitehouse for special praise, said that 'the worship of instinct, of spontaneity, the rejection of self-discipline' entailed 'degeneration' rather than progress,[243] but he took the experiment no further.

Conservatives after 1970 did, however, gradually realize that it could be politically useful to attack the sixties. Parents in the 1970s began to mobilize against 'progressive' methods in education, and Whitehouse's claim in 1979 that if the decade's educational reforms were measured against the outcome, the permissive society 'is now seen as a total illusion' seemed less ridiculous than it would have done ten years earlier. 'The time for counter-attack is long overdue', said Thatcher in March 1982: 'we are reaping what was sown in the Sixties'. The attack on 'the fashionable theories and permissive claptrap' allegedly fostering crime now quite often featured in Conservative rhetoric, together with repudiation of progressive methods in education and 'loony left' local authorities.[244] In 1985 Tebbit blamed the sixties for recent riots, and later referred to 'the era and attitudes of postwar funk which gave birth to the permissive society which in turn generated today's violent society'.[245] In the late 1980s Thatcher edged the attack on the sixties further forward with her populist championing of politeness, tidiness, and neighbourliness. 'This business of breaking the rules began in universities', she pointed out, 'where most of these theoretical philosophies always start. They never start with ordinary people.'[246]. There was even a brief reactionary fashion in the mid-1980s, identified with the so-called 'Young Fogeys', for wearing clothes more suited to older people.

[242] Blair to Foot, 18 July 1982, published in *DT* (16 June 2006), 11.

[243] N. Tebbit, *Upwardly Mobile* (1988), 80. Joseph, speech at Birmingham, *T* (21 Oct. 1974), 3.

[244] Whitehouse interview with David Dimbleby in *Listener* (5 July 1979), 10. Thatcher speech at Harrogate, *O* (28 Mar. 1982), 1. See also K. Baker, *The Turbulent Years: My Life in Politics* (1993), 200–1; *DT* (8 Oct. 1992), 10 (J. Patten). For Major see his conference speeches of 1991 and 1993 in *DT* (12 Oct. 1991), 9; (9 Oct. 1993), 10.

[245] Quotations from *T* (8 Oct. 1985), 1.*G* (14 Nov. 1985), 30 (first Disraeli lecture to St Stephen's Constitutional Club). Compare James Wellbeloved, *HC Deb.* 14 July 1981, c. 976.

[246] Interview in *Daily Mail* (29 Apr. 1988), 7.

None the less, British Conservatives did not mobilize a UK equivalent of the American 'moral majority'. Even the reaction against Marxism and radical sociology was slow in coming. It did not attain its full force till Thatcherism had proved durable in the 1980s, and even then it owed much to overseas events, most notably to the worldwide collapse of Communism. British Conservative politicians were cautious by American standards, and any moves towards a full-blown anti-permissive crusade tended quietly to fade away or even (as with Major's misunderstood 'back to basics' initiative of 1993[247]) ended in ridicule. Conservative caution partly reflects the British parliamentary convention for keeping moral issues out of party politics; Labour had after all carefully distanced itself in the 1960s from the decade's moral reforms. Besides, the wider society did not provide anti-sixties Conservatives with any ground to stand upon: the old-style puritan reaction against sixties values, though often predicted, never materialized. Conservative politicians were reluctant to mobilize the 'moral majority' because they suspected that it did not exist, so secularized was the UK by comparison with the USA. Politicians also probably sensed that more and more electors felt a vested interest in consolidating sixties values: not just homosexuals, feminists, or co-residing unmarried couples, but the many others whose lives had been unnecessarily cramped under the old regime. The austere values widespread before the 1950s had owed more to scarcity than choice, whereas affluence had now arrived. After the 1960s consumerism might go temporarily into eclipse during economic downswings, but overall it continued to grow apace, together with reliance on credit and a growing acceptance of gambling.

As for the anti-puritan shift in personal relationships during the sixties, there were too many inhibitions yet to be shed for liberation to go into reverse; in retrospect even the sexual component of sixties values seems somewhat inhibited. This is partly because so much of the sixties' emancipatory legislation combined liberation with constraint. We have already seen[248] how homosexual law reform occurred in this way in 1967, but a similar marriage occurred elsewhere. For the homosexual law reformer Antony Grey, the term 'permissiveness', which together with 'permissive society' was a term in regular use by the late 1960s, was 'a silly and misleading term because it wrongly implies that there are some people in society who are entitled to permit, or withhold permission from, the moral choices of others'.[249] The Abortion Act (1967) combined emancipation with enhanced control, if only because it aimed to destroy the unqualified backstreet abortionist.[250] And while those who framed

[247] On this see *DT* (19 Sept. 1996), 4. *STel.* (20 Oct. 1996), 1.

[248] See above, pp. 510–11.

[249] A. Grey, *Quest for Justice: Towards Homosexual Emancipation* (1992), 207.

[250] For good discussions of this aspect see J. Keown, *Abortion, Doctors and the Law: Some Aspects of the Legal Regulation of Abortion in England from 1803 to 1982* (Cambridge, 1988), 159, 164–6. Newburn, *Permission and Regulation*, 147, 154–7.

the Obscene Publications Act (1959) aimed to protect literary freedom, they simultaneously tried to curb the pornography then arriving in large quantities from abroad (most notably from Scandinavia and the USA). The Act's powers to search, seize, and destroy without first obtaining evidence of sale made it at first easier to prosecute pornographers, and we have seen[251] how it took several subsequent court cases, their outcome by no means certain, before the law could reach its present state; even the abolition of censorship in the theatre (1968) needed legal clarification. But with this achieved, it was not long before the tampons which for ten years Virginia Woolf had manufactured for herself rather than embarrassingly buy in the shops were being advertised nightly during prime time on national television.[252] The internet from the late 1990s displayed cornucopias still more abundant, with what had hitherto been seen as pornography readily accessible on every screen: computers had indeed made the world a 'global village', if not a 'global cottage'.

Such dramatic changes in daily life seemed at first alarming. Social and political structures, let alone expectations, had by no means yet adjusted to them. These changes left many casualties and unsolved problems in their wake. Nobody knew where the changes would stop, and even their advocates did not recognize their full implications. To its critics, both at the time and later, the sixties mood seemed dangerously negative. Enthusiasts for breaking down institutions and taboos rarely explained how—in the absence of the existing religious, political, family, and social-class structures—society would cohere. Only in retrospect could it be known that the tough resilience of social groups and the common sense of those who operate them would make it possible to cope. In such circumstances, widespread protest is hardly surprising. 'I hope that we shall not introduce a Scandinavian society here', said one MP in a debate on maintenance orders in 1967.[253] In vain: the genie could not now be put back into the bottle. The sixties had launched a progressively unfolding national striptease in sexual awareness, whereby more and more layers of conduct hitherto concealed were gradually revealed. Much was liberating about the spread of what John Stuart Mill would have called 'experiments in living', and to foreigners more worldly wise, this shift in British life must have seemed strange. Fornication, abortion, and homosexuality emerged from the closet in the late 1960s, with lesbianism a relatively slow starter. In her book on the menstrual cycle published in 1969, Katharina Dalton said of menstruation that 'only recently has the subject been considered to be respectable enough to mention in the press or radio', and in the early 1970s the menopause had still 'received relatively little attention in the medical

[251] See above, pp. 484, 506–7.

[252] V. Woolf, *Letters*, vi, ed. N. Nicolson and J. Trautmann (1980), 505 (letter dated 15 Feb. 1924).

[253] Ronald Bell, *HC Deb.* 8 Dec. 1967, cc. 1877–8.

literature'.[254] In the 1980s the press opened up on the rape of women, and in the early 1990s on the 'last taboo': male rape. Attention then turned to masturbation and child abuse, culminating in reports about how the MP Stephen Milligan died in 1994 and in numerous revelations of tragic events that had occurred many years before in children's homes.

Heterosexual relationships changed too. The Family Law Reform Act (1969) freed young people to marry without parental consent at 18 instead of 21, but this did not prevent premarital intercourse from soaring in the 1970s. By the late 1990s cohabitation preceded about three-fifths of first marriages and over three-quarters of remarriages.[255] The rush to earlier marriage which had peaked in the 1950s came to seem a mere quirk of social history. The subsequent trend towards deferring marriage did not signify postponed gratification: by the early 1990s nearly half the conceptions were taking place outside marriage.[256] The proportion of live births out of wedlock doubled in England and Wales between 1970 and 1985, and in the same period the ratio of legal abortions to live births more than doubled.[257] By the end of the 1980s the term 'partner' was beginning to oust 'husband' and 'wife', and to use the word 'illegitimate' of a child by 1990 had become 'in a gathering of academics . . . a *faux pas*, causing pained silence'.[258] Traditionalists had to make compromises: in 1974 the Mothers' Union decided to admit divorced women as members, and in 1995 a Church of England report argued that couples living together without marrying should no longer be seen as living in sin.[259] For conservatives it was a slippery slope: one concession merely set a precedent for more. What, then, was the alternative? Such power as the churches had ever possessed for moulding personal conduct had been eroded through a secularization process that had been gathering pace since at least the mid-nineteenth century. By calling a halt, their weakness would have been advertised, contracting their potential support still further: the simplicities involved in enforcing the old standards clashed too frontally with the complexities of real-life situations for the churches' waning influence to be conserved on any terms other than compromise.

The tenacity of pre-sixties puritanism emerges from the fact that almost to the end of the century higher standards of sexual morality were expected from public figures than from their constituents. Yet the barriers could not hold: the speed of change in public attitudes to sexuality emerges from evolving responses to a sequence of sexual scandals. The objections raised in the 1950s

[254] K. Dalton, *The Menstrual Cycle* (1969), 12. S. M. and J. B. McKinlay, 'Selected Studies of the Menopause', *Journal of Biosocial Science*, 5 (1973), 534.

[255] *TCBST* 60.

[256] *Ind.* (23 Sept. 1993), 1. See also Coleman and Salt, *British Population*, 181, 186–7.

[257] *BST* 60 (abortion), 63 (illegitimacy).

[258] C. Murray, *The Emerging British Underclass* (1990), 4.

[259] *T* (13 Sept. 1974), 18. *DT* (7 June 1995), 1.

to Peter Townsend as a potential spouse for Princess Margaret would have seemed staid later, and by the 1980s royal divorces were becoming all too familiar. Permanent resignation from political office was required in 1963 from John Profumo and from Lords Lambton and Jellicoe in 1973 for endangering national security by consorting with prostitutes, but the air of moral disapproval had grown far less intense during those ten years, even though Jellicoe was in the cabinet.[260] Cecil Parkinson had to resign from the cabinet in 1983 when exposed as having fathered the child of his secretary Sarah Keays, but 16,000 of his correspondents on the subject supported him, and fewer than fifty were hostile; many felt that he should have endorsed the new morality (the secretary) rather than the old (the wife), and within four years he was back in office. His chances of succeeding Thatcher as prime minister were destroyed less because of the pregnancy than because he had handled it so indecisively. When Paddy Ashdown as Liberal leader confessed publicly in 1992 to a brief affair with his secretary several years before, his personal popularity ratings surged,[261] and he remained in post. In the following year the Conservative MP Alan Clark could confess to extensive sexual adventurism in his published diaries without apparently endangering his career, nor did Major as prime minister suffer anything more than personal embarrassment in 1995 when a youthful extra-marital liaison came to light.

Sixties moral changes removed much hypocrisy, much concealed suffering and many obstacles to self-realization—though even liberty carried a price, for with it came decisions, and personal responsibility for them. We saw earlier[262] that nowhere were changes in attitudes to conduct more striking than when challenges confronted the attempt to sort the entire population neatly into polarized male and female camps. One dimension of this, affecting only a small section of the population, had begun well before the 1960s, but made important advances after 1970. Roberta Cowell had revealed the possibility of changing sex,[263] Kinsey and homosexual liberation had exposed the rich variety of human sexual tendencies, and feminists had challenged any sex-based delimitation of roles. All these threw into question the standardized family structure hitherto regarded as normal, and the fashion industry was quick to draw the implications. Looking back in 2002 at the reception for her published account in 1974 of her sex-change two years earlier, Jan Morris thought she had been 'lucky that it all came to light in what is now disparagingly called the Permissive Age, but which still seems to me, for all its excesses, a time of joyous liberation throughout the western world'. Physiological causes of transsexualism might subsequently have been discovered, but 'for myself,

260 See B. Levin, 'Time to Belt up about Falling Trousers', *T* (29 May 1973), 12.

261 C. Parkinson, *Right at the Centre: An Autobiography* (1992), 40. P. Ashdown, *The Ashdown Diaries*, i. *1988–1997* (2000), 144 n. 1.

262 See above, pp. 29, 235–44.

263 See above, pp. 243–4.

I am past caring . . . What matters is the liberty of us all to live as we wish to live.'[264]

If the old puritanism had retreated, what of the new? The puritanism involved in repudiating Western culture and leading a life of self-denial was not sufficiently attractive, especially in British weather, to attract a large following, though a continuous and ill-coordinated undercurrent of protest survived the century, with an influence reaching its peak during the violent protests of 1990 against the polltax. More weighty was the new and wholly unexpected direction taken by the new puritanism in endorsing the new morality. In a remarkable reversal of values, moralistic indignation now embarrassed adherents of the old morality, not of the new. Keith Joseph created a storm when one passage in his notorious and somewhat shrill speech of 19 October 1974 at Edgbaston was almost wilfully misunderstood. He stressed the need for birth-control facilities to allow for the fact that 'a high and rising proportion of children are being born to mothers least fitted to bring children into the world', but seriously damaged his career thereby. And in 1993, when modestly asserting the role which personal responsibility should play in tackling social problems, John Redwood as a cabinet minister made considerable trouble for himself.[265]

In all four 'sixties' characteristics, then, 1969 no more marked the end than 1960 had marked the beginning. For the fifties, too, had witnessed the cult of youth and modernity, the pursuit of informality, political radicalism, the attack on old-style puritanism and the emergence of the new, and we have seen how these were drawn together towards the end of the decade. All but one of the Introduction's eight motifs have featured in this chapter, most notably the UK's ongoing tension between hermetic and receptive tendencies: in educational fashions the USA was drawn upon, in sexual liberation both the USA and Scandinavia, in political radicalism the USA and France. Integral to the sixties was the rejection of Second World War myth-making, most powerfully through humour, though at the same time the decade's political protest involved reviving wartime radicalism, and even (through incomes policies) refurbishing its corporatist mechanisms. Once more in the sixties the UK witnessed the contrast between public anxiety about the economy and the individual's experience of affluence, flamboyantly celebrated as it was in sixties fashions and culture. There was even, with the Beatles and Carnaby Street, a brief glimmering of a new role for Britain as worldwide trendsetter. The associated hedonistic lifestyles and this-worldly priorities enhanced the challenge to conventional religious values

[264] J. Morris, introductions (dated 2001 and 1997) to her *Conundrum* (Faber, 2002 edn.), p. x, and Penguin edn. 1997, 8.

[265] A. Denham and M. Garnett, *Keith Joseph* (1st publ. 2001, paperback edn. 2002), 267. Redwood, *ST* (11 July 1993), 4.

and priorities. And although the more utopian dreams of the sixties could not survive contact with reality, especially after the oil crisis of the early 1970s, politicians in the sixties had once more found themselves responding to events which they could neither control nor sometimes even comprehend. Yet amidst all these changes the UK's political structure remained intact, though now more readily criticized and in some quarters threatened. 'The Sixties did not really begin until about 1963', it has been claimed, 'and . . . they do not fade away until 1975'.[266] Such a comment usefully discards the decade as a significant cultural unit, though the myth of the sixties was real enough, but it does not allow sufficiently for the raggedness of the edges; for the fact that in any decade society does not move forward uniformly, and that in any society at any one time there are conflicting tendencies. Nor does it recognize that in all their significant aspects 'the sixties' long outlasted 1975. Indeed, the sixties are with us still.

[266] Hewison, *Too Much*, p. xiii (foreword).

CHAPTER 10

Retrospect

Chapter 9 has drawn this book ineluctably towards events beyond 1970, but to understand the 1950s and 1960s it is also important to range backwards—even further back than the 1940s. The British people in 1951, for all their economic and other anxieties, felt secure in their national traditions, internal cohesion, recent wartime achievement, and sense of world stature. Yet change soon became so rapid that for the journalist Anne Scott-James by 1973 it resembled a disorienting torture. Serious anxiety about the environment was beginning, and stability was lacking in working practices, family patterns, ethnic composition, and even (given Britain's two failed applications to the EEC) in the nation's international alignments—not to mention decimalization, postcodes, and the built-in obsolescence of consumer goods: 'the total is stupefying', she wrote.[1] To her list she might have added the long-term decline in Britain's diplomatic standing and economic status, and her loss of empire. By the late 1960s the very symbols of stability seemed fragile: public ceremonial, social hierarchy, the conventions of religious worship, even the national anthem.

The smoothness of Britain's transition from white world-imperial power to multi-racial middle-ranking European state was something of an achievement, and was never inevitable. How, then, was it possible in such circumstances for British society to cohere? The nature of the changes under discussion helps to explain it. Most were so continuous and gradual that people rarely felt the need to look back over how far they had travelled. In several areas where change was most dramatic (demographic, environmental, cultural), relative decline did not exist, or was not perceived, or was seen as only temporary, or was not blamed on the government. The UK's remarkable growth in economic prosperity during the 1950s and 1960s also helped—though as we have often seen, this was not matched by the climate of public economic debate. One further stabilizing factor deserves attention, however. Nations, like communities and even families, treasure the idea that they are in some sense special, and build up a national myth or personality. Such myths or even self-deceptions enable countries in the medium term to turn dangerous corners. The myths change over time to reflect changes

[1] A. Scott-James, 'When a Change is as Good as a Nightmare', *T* (9 Jan. 1973), 12.

in the society itself, and are rarely defined precisely. Sometimes different myths coexist in the same society for subgroup purposes. In the UK after 1945 there was ample room for self-deception and wishful thinking. It is rarely the politician's function, and still more rarely in his interest, to alert voters to unpleasant truths. The Attlee governments could not avoid confronting voters with the serious state of the economy, but the complex mid-century enterprises of steering a corporatist economy, smoothing Britain's way into the EEC, and fostering a multicultural society involved balancing many considerations. In collective diplomacy, as in personal relations, telling the whole truth can be not only uncomfortable but also counterproductive, and only political bystanders felt free in the 1950s and 1960s to emphasize the UK's stark choices and ominous possibilities.

There was no decline after 1945 in selective amnesia, whereby awkward facts were glozed over with a reassuring national myth. Amnesia about Britain's seventeenth-century republican moment had for centuries been the most striking among such attempts, and a postwar amnesia about the abdication of 1936 helped further to shore up the monarchy. This myth, one among many instances of the motif whereby apparent political stability persists amidst social change, reflected the convenience of forgetting that the British monarchy, so securely respected and dignified amidst the wartime ruination of so many European royal houses, had itself averted disaster only narrowly a few years before. The abdication was presented as a mere aberration in a continuous and dignified family history. Magazine photographs portrayed the once debonair and popular but now shrunken and wrinkled socialite Duke of Windsor drifting in the 1950s and 1960s with his heavily made-up wife through pointless European social functions. There was an implied but striking contrast here with the relatively purposeful and patriotic lives being led by George VI and his family. Yet while Britain had indeed stood alone in 1940, and had found herself on the winning side thereafter, it was seldom emphasized how much her unique role stemmed from her island location and from the lack of any alternative course. If geography had not prevented it, the Quislings who appeared in other countries would doubtless also have appeared in mainland Britain, as in the Channel Isles. The Duke of Windsor was in many ways suited for the role, and it would not necessarily have been unpatriotic in different circumstances for him to take it on; hence the British government's wartime eagerness to place him well beyond the enemy's reach.

Myths about interwar Britain were cultivated on right and left. Labour's internal power struggles in the 1960s and 1970s, for instance, were widely interpreted in the context of Ramsay MacDonald's alleged betrayal of the labour movement by seceding into the National Government coalition in 1931, and in 1984–5 the miners' strike was still being seen through the rear-view mirror of 1926.[2] As for the depression of the 1930s, a reproachful attitude to the National

[2] John Lloyd in *FT* (31 Oct. 1984), 14.

Government's role helped to fuel the postwar case for a more interventionist approach to the economy. On the left, the depression had been a formative moment in Frank Cousins's left-wing commitment when he saw a young couple walking from Shields to London during the slump with their baby, fed with water from a bottle and with newspapers doing duty for nappies.[3] On the right, Macmillan's memories of unemployment in his Stockton constituency fuelled his 'One Nation' variant of Conservatism, just as the free-market rejection of his outlook entailed setting those memories into a new context. For Heath after 1975, 'Thatcherism' was so repugnant partly because it seemed to threaten his generation's achievement in distancing Conservatism from unemployment.[4] A more nuanced view of the depression's causes, however, had always existed, and was quietly gaining ground in the 1960s.

Popular historiography of the 1930s often wrapped up the depression with 'appeasement' in a distasteful package. The motif of the Second World War's equivocal legacy has often recurred, and is particularly apposite here. Appeasement carried such resonance partly because a reputation for having resisted it advanced so many influential political careers during the next half century—most notably Churchill's, Eden's, Macmillan's, and Heath's. Neither side at the general election of 1945 had an interest in viewing the 1930s objectively, or in disentangling the many strands within 'appeasement', or in noting that 'appeasement' strategies had persisted under Churchill as prime minister;[5] neither side had any interest in emphasizing that Churchill had been acceptable as prime minister in 1940 only because he had not fully assimilated the 'appeasers'' realistic view of Britain's plight, and because Hitler had left the country with no alternative. In the outcome, however, the 'finest hour' of 1940 was incorporated into the nation's Elizabethan and Cromwellian traditions. The so-called 'Dunkirk spirit' came to epitomize an alleged national aptitude for uniting in the face of disaster,[6] with the image of Britain standing alone, aloof from Europe, superior to it, and as ultimately triumphing through its own effort, character, and traditions. Churchill's war memoirs did everything to confirm that picture, fostering a simplistic view of appeasement, and playing down how much victory owed to the Russian winter, to American wealth, and to Commonwealth backing.[7]

There was self-deception, too, in our empire's story. There was justified emphasis upon the high-minded missionary motives that had so often complemented the commercial, and on the high-toned idealism that had shaped

[3] G. Goodman, *The Awkward Warrior: Frank Cousins: His Life and Times* (1979), 37.
[4] *HC Deb.* 27 Nov. 1980, cc. 917–18.
[5] D. Reynolds, *In Command of History: Churchill Fighting and Writing the Second World War* (2004), 169, 195.
[6] P. Foot, *The Politics of Harold Wilson* (Harmondsworth, 1968), 155.
[7] Reynolds, *In Command of History*, 228, 246, 310–12.

so much colonial administration. Noting in 1953 how Labour had welcomed Britain's departure from the Sudan, Harold Nicolson admitted that 'true democratic principles render imperialism illogical', yet felt 'sad . . . to see the fruit of that great work picked before it is even half ripe', adding that 'nobody will persuade me that our work in the Sudan was anything but a real civilising and selfless mission'.[8] Noel Coward, looking back in February 1957 over the Suez venture, insisted to himself that 'the British Empire was a great and wonderful social, economic and even spiritual experiment'; there was, he thought, 'much to be deplored in the British character but . . . also much, very much, to be admired and respected. We have done a great deal of good to a great many million people'.[9] Yet the liberal theory of empire, with self-government the planned long-term aim, and with freedom willingly conceded, presents too many anomalies to carry conviction, least of all in Kenya during the 1950s.[10]

Britain's interwar world standing had been artificially prolonged by the retreat into isolation of the two great anti-colonial powers, USA and USSR. Immediately after 1945 we have seen how it suited the Americans, who needed allies against the USSR's growing ambitions, to prolong the appearance of British world-power status,[11] and surveys even half a century later found that former wartime allies viewed one another more favourably than former enemies.[12] The postwar Atlantic alliance had the effect of prolonging Britain's economic weakness by diverting resources from productive peacetime purposes. Britain was thus placed at an economic disadvantage by comparison with her relatively lean leading industrial rivals, Japan and Germany, both of which within a generation turned military defeat into economic success. Indeed, military victory in 1945 brought with it the penalty for Britain in both overseas and domestic spheres which pervades this book: it fostered national complacency in the economic sphere and an inflated self-image in international relations. Churchill's illusions persisted somewhat precariously to the end of his second premiership, with its notion that a 'New Elizabethan age' could then be launched,[13] and with his grandiose concept of Britain as mediator between the super-powers, harnessing the Commonwealth to his quest for a 'third way' in world affairs. Even the Wilson governments in 1964–70 grasped international realities only slowly. The appeasement story was doubly harmful, given that it was also deployed after 1945 as an emotive reach-me-down self-justificatory device in overseas or domestic situations which seemed to demand resolute action. The resolute action may have been needed, but the parallel was misleading—whether in Eden's handling of Nasser in 1956, Heath's handling of the miners in 1973–4, or Thatcher's of Galtieri in 1982. Yet there were cheers

[8] Nicolson, *Diaries and Letters, 1945–62*, 237 (12 Feb. 1953).
[9] Coward, *Diaries*, 348 (3 Feb. 1957). [10] For more on this see above, pp. 109–10.
[11] For more on this see above, pp. 10–11, 90, 100, 102–3. [12] *DT* (25 Aug. 1989), 3.
[13] For more on this see above, pp. 101–2, 115.

in the House of Commons when the Foreign Secretary announced during the Falklands debate of February 1982 that 'Britain does not appease dictators'.[14]

The memory of both world wars, deeply imprinted, ramified in its effects in many directions, especially as Britain felt no need for the reticence on the subject shown by the defeated, occupied, or even neutral countries. There was initial indecision about the day when the Second World War's ending should be commemorated, but it was eventually attached to the well-established armistice ceremony commemorating its precursor.[15] A sensible civil service suggestion in 1975 that the armistice celebration might be modified or discontinued 'as the wars become increasingly distant' predictably got nowhere at the time, though it was followed up later.[16] Too many war pensioners survived in Britain—725,000 disabled and 323,000 widows and dependants in 1950, a quarter of them still alive in 1990—for memories quickly to fade, nor had expenditure upon them fallen significantly in real terms by that date.[17] Not till 29 January 2006 were the wartime loans of 1945–6 from the USA and Canada paid off, when the last of the fifty repayments was made. Long afterwards, wartime memories could evoke fierce disputes even between friends: in 1992, for instance, rival interpretations of Britain's priorities half a century earlier were held strongly enough to sour Anglo-Australian relations.[18] Visible evidence of the Second World War's destructiveness hung oppressively over the UK in the 1950s and 1960s. Lord Robbins in the House of Lords pronounced it in 1967 'a national disgrace' that the British Museum's bomb damage had still not been fully repaired.[19] Heath's war service spiced his indignation two years later when Wilson accused Conservatives of being unpatriotic for expressing concern about the state of the economy.[20] Given these lasting reminders, a Second World War gestated in power politics and launched in a desperate bid for national survival, retrospectively and reassuringly became a 'just' war which nursed wounded national pride. It seemed overwhelmingly vindicated by the truckloads of corpses photographed in the Nazi concentration camps that were later exposed to view—a horrible image which for decades sullied Germany's reputation and self-respect.

The Second World War's long-term impact was politically and in other ways deeply conservative. Together with its continuation into national service, it reinforced hierarchical attitudes more than it subverted them. By the early 1950s, distaste for Nazism fuelled the male-action war books which by then had become so popular. Films were made of Paul Brickhill's best-selling *Dambusters*

[14] *HC Deb.* 7 Apr. 1982, c. 960. See also Young, *One of Us*, 272.

[15] See K. Robbins, 'Commemorating the Second World War in Britain: Problems of Definition', *History Teacher*, 29/2 (Feb. 1996), 155–8.

[16] *DT* (29 Dec. 2005), 5.

[17] See the useful table in *TCBST* 562.

[18] *FT* (28 Feb. 1992), 18.

[19] *HL Deb.* 19 Apr. 1967, c. 263.

[20] Party conference speech, *G* (13 Oct. 1969), 6.

(1951), Nicholas Montserrat's *The Cruel Sea* (1951), P. H. Reid's *The Colditz Story* (1952), Douglas Bader's *Reach for the Sky* (1954), and Dudley Pope's *The Battle of the River Plate* (1956).[21] Jack Hawkins and Kenneth More were thought to exemplify an alleged British military and naval prowess and basic decency. Up to 1960 eighty-three feature films had been produced to which the war was central, none questioning its justice.[22] War-induced conservatism influenced both major parties. The Labour Party's status rose considerably as a result of the labour movement's role in the war, and the welfare state owed much to it. Anti-German feeling fuelled much Labour hostility to German rearmament in the 1950s, and Healey noted how, as Labour's Minister of Defence in 1964–70, his task was eased by finding himself working with several generals who had been wartime friends.[23]

By fostering hierarchical attitudes, however, and by highlighting Churchill's remarkable personality, the war built national mythology and national self-deception lastingly into one of the two great political parties. The limited long-term cultural significance of anti-war humour emerges from the seriousness which greeted Churchill's funeral ceremony in 1965. Wartime loyalties enhanced the postwar claims of right-wing causes not always convenient even for Conservative governments. Ulster Unionists did not forget that five of the nine British field marshals active in the Second World War came from Northern Ireland. Lord Brookeborough, prime minister of Northern Ireland from 1943 to 1963, won his Military Cross at Ypres in 1916; when interviewed in 1971 he vividly recalled how the Irish Republic's bright lights had helped to guide German bombers in the Second World War towards Belfast; his wife chipped in with an ironic misquotation from Clough: 'westward, look, the land was bright'.[24] Given such memories, the indiscriminate slaughter by the Provisional Irish Republican Army on remembrance day at Enniskillen in 1987 seemed particularly callous.[25] The Irish Republic long remained coy about southern Ireland's role in the two world wars. Symbolic of its belated change in outlook was the ceremony on 11 November 1998, when the Queen and the Irish President both laid wreaths before the Messines peace tower, built to acknowledge the role of all the Irish people; it was the first public event since partition to be undertaken jointly by a British monarch and an Irish head of state.[26] White Rhodesia, too, embarrassed Conservatives, especially when its

[21] Sutherland, *Reading the Decades*, 27–8.

[22] N. Pronay, 'The British Post-Bellum Cinema: A Survey of the Films Relating to World War II made in Britain between 1945 and 1960', *Historical Journal of Film, Radio and Television*, 8/1 (1988), 39.

[23] Healey, *Time of My Life*, 252.

[24] Interview in Nov. 1971, in T. Coleman, *The Scented Brawl: Selected Articles and Interviews* (1978), 105.

[25] For Northern Ireland's contribution to the war against Hitler see Lyons, *Ireland since the Famine*, 718, 721, 723.

[26] *DT* (12 Nov. 1998), 12.

declaration of independence—issued in 1965 on the anniversary of the 1918 armistice—noted how Rhodesians had 'demonstrated their loyalty to the crown and to their kith and kin . . . throughout the two world wars'.[27]

The selective national memory of the Second World War helps to explain the prominence of a further motif in this book: the recurrent tension between receptive and hermetic tendencies in the UK's world view. The war fuelled both sides of the controversy from the 1950s onwards about Britain's relations with Europe. Whereas some saw 1940 as signalling Britain's distinctness from Europe, Heath was among those who drew the opposite conclusion, urging the need simultaneously to reinforce European democratic traditions and strike out in more promising foreign-policy directions by engaging ever more closely with the EEC. In the late 1980s, however, at the highest political levels, there still lurked a coarse anti-Germanism that too readily ignored the scale of West Germany's postwar democratic achievement, together with the EEC's role in consolidating it.[28] For decades afterwards Germans remained the villains, or their accents seemed villainous, in children's comics and in television programmes.[29] The Queen's visit to West Germany in 1965 was a gesture of reconciliation successful at the time, but it failed to scotch British anti-German feeling. The tension between Britain's wartime memories and her current self-interest caused much heart-searching at the highest level when it came to deciding in 1985 on whether to celebrate the thirty-year anniversary of Germany's defeat in 1945.[30] The German culture minister in 1999 claimed that Britain, alone among nations, had converted the Second World War into 'a sort of spiritual core of its national self-understanding and pride'. Six years later the German ambassador thought Britain still 'obsessed with the Nazi period' and 'ignorant' about German history thereafter—an outlook frequently influencing the media and moulding classroom teaching.[31] Despite Japan's brutality to British prisoners of war, Germany was far more central than Japan in the British wartime memory, though when the Queen processed down the Mall with the Emperor and Empress of Japan during their state visit in May 1998, hundreds of former prisoners of war visibly and audibly displayed their hostility.[32]

None the less, in the short and medium terms, wartime memories edged the Conservative Party leftwards, if only because the mere fact of having seen war

[27] Madden (ed.), *Imperial Constitutional Documents*, 112–13.

[28] Lawson, *View from No. 11*, 656, 900. M. Thatcher, *The Downing Street Years* (1993), 791.

[29] *T* (9 Dec. 1976), 15 (leading article), commenting on the lively correspondence evoked by Mrs Von Zugbach de Sugg's indignant letter in *T* (20 Nov. 1976), 13, about anti-German attitudes in the British media.

[30] I. Davidson, 'Let's Be Firm, But Generous', *FT* (21 Jan. 1985), 13.

[31] German culture minister quoted in H. Young, 'Germano-phobia Still Grips Us as the British Refuse to Forget the War', *G* (16 Feb. 1999), 16. Thomas Matussek, *STel.* (8 May 2005), 1.

[32] *DT* (27 May 1998), 1.

service created bonds across the social classes. Young soldier survivors of the First World War were, said Macmillan, 'haunted' by the memory of deceased contemporaries.[33] A combination of social obligation and guilt at surviving inspired Macmillan's pursuit of the 'middle way', and often induced a hush in his audiences when eloquently recalled in later life. 'It breaks my heart to see what is happening in our country today', he told the House of Lords in his maiden speech there in November 1984, referring (with implied criticism of the Thatcher government) to the miners' strike of that year: 'a terrible strike is being carried on by the best men in the world, who beat the Kaiser's and they beat Hitler's army. They never gave in.'[34] Whitelaw's centrist Conservative outlook owed much to the solidarity between officers and men which he had experienced in the Second World War when commanding tanks in France after D-day. This had sent him into politics: 'you become deeply attached to people', he said, 'and that never leaves you'.[35] On the left, the war's radicalizing effect took the form of a corroded respect for authority. The First World War was increasingly viewed in terms of stupid or even heartless generals and politicians sacrificing helpless subordinates in their tens of thousands; the sufferings of the other ranks were captured through the poignant renderings of their songs in shows as memorable as Joan Littlewood's *Oh! What a Lovely War!* (1963). Nazism carried the postwar questioning of authority to further lengths by advertising how dangerous it was to obey orders uncritically. The war's impact on British fiction was longer delayed, but its anti-hierarchical impact on humour was almost immediate[36] as well as long-lived: the television serial *Dad's Army* ran through eighty episodes between 1968 and 1977.[37]

Such humour light-heartedly echoed the highly emotive way in which accusations of Fascism were deployed in British life after 1945. Those who held a simplistic view of how and where Fascism originated sometimes applied the label to people who lacked the slightest sympathy with it. The anti-semitic impulse to Nazi genocide was acknowledged more slowly in Britain than in Western Europe, but was accelerated in the mid-1950s when Anne Frank's diary appeared and Lord Russell of Liverpool published his *Scourge of the Swastika*.[38] The phrase 'the holocaust' was increasingly used to distinguish this particular holocaust from the many others, past and future. This brought two dangers. First, it located genocide safely in the past, as though it would not recur. But, second, it masked the sheer scale of Nazi irrationalism, militarism, and pessimism: 'it wasn't only the Holocaust that made Nazism evil. Rather the opposite: it was the intrinsic evil of Nazi doctrine that made the Holocaust

[33] Macmillan, *Winds of Change*, 98.
[34] *HL Deb.* 13 Nov. 1984, c. 240.
[35] Interview in *T* (5 May 1989), 10.
[36] See above, pp. 399–400.
[37] B. Pertwee, *Dad's Army: The Making of a Television Legend* (Newton Abbot, 1989), 7.
[38] T. Kushner, 'The Impact of the Holocaust on British Society and Culture', *Contemporary Record* (Autumn 1991), 349, 362.

possible.'[39] Eventually the fear of being thought in any way to condone Fascist ideas discouraged rational research into contrasts between the races and the sexes, as scholars such as Eysenck became painfully aware, and concentration-camp memories ensured that even the most cautious proposals for euthanasia or for research into embryos encountered a special wariness.[40] We have seen how at the political level, racist ideas encountered two rival democratic strategies in the 1960s: party leaders such as Wilson and Heath tried simultaneously to exclude racist policy from public discussion and stifle it with welfare payments, whereas others thought democratic values better protected through dividing and eroding racist ranks by demonstrating that a democratic system can discuss and tackle rational grievances head-on.

The outcome of Britain's being on the winning side in the Second World War was therefore a long period of self-deception about Britain's world status, about the permanence and continued significance of the Commonwealth, about Britain's 'special relationship' with the United States, and about her distinctness from Europe. This delayed Britain's entry to the EEC, and full participation in it, until long after others had launched and shaped it, and it lost Britain many of her European admirers. So for the next half-century 'Britain struggled to reconcile the past she could not forget with the future she could not avoid'.[41] Jean Monnet, enthusiastic for British influence in Europe, ascribed British reluctance to bid for leadership in Europe as '*the price of victory*—the illusion that you could maintain what you had, without change'.[42] Postwar membership of the United Nations Security Council inflated British illusions of world influence, and at least until 1956 the British people thought of themselves as a small superpower rather than as a strong middle-ranking power. Thereafter the UK maintained the independent nuclear deterrent as a substitute for the military strength she could no longer afford.[43] When asked in the early 1960s whether Britain should try to be a leading world power or become more like Sweden and Switzerland, nearly half Gallup's sample favoured the former, though in the late 1960s this declined to a third.[44] Wishful thinking about national status was by no means absent from the House of Commons in the 1960s, and if the Wilson governments eventually retreated from over-extension abroad, this was less from intent than from economic weakness; 'we have never done things in time', wrote Crossman in December 1968: 'every decision has visibly been extracted from us'.[45] Even the British advocates of European union included many who saw it less as a collaborative exercise than as an arena for the continued or

[39] David Wedgwood Benn, *FT* (6 Jan. 2001), weekend supplement, viii.

[40] See Coggan on euthanasia in *G* (14 Dec. 1976), 30.

[41] Young, *Blessed Plot*, 1. See above, pp. 115–16.

[42] Quoted in Charlton, *Price of Victory*, 307.

[43] For a good discussion see Pierre, *Nuclear Politics*, 303.

[44] *Gallup Polls*, i. 665, 684, 761; ii. 790, 869, 940, 968, 1156, 1370, 1421.

[45] See e.g. Crossman, *Cabinet Diaries*, ii. 381 (13 June 1967), 564 (9 Nov. 1967); iii. 278 (1 Dec. 1968).

recovered deployment of British power. All in all, British attitudes to the war, while never regretful at the role played, followed an undulating pattern. Up to the mid-1950s the mood was one of pride and even celebration. Military values and national self-confidence then went into decline, only to recover unexpectedly during the Falklands War of 1982; they were preserved during Thatcher's extraordinary international balancing act of the 1980s, only then once more to decline and rise in the 1990s in response to politicians' pretensions.

Viewing the recent past self-indulgently was one way to ward off reality: sheer escapism was another—geographically, through joining expatriate communities in Mediterranean islands or old colonies; psychologically, through a bucolicism as central to British culture as to Australian. It was no accident that neo-romanticism in British art flourished in the 1940s, or that so many mid-century British novels concerned lost innocence, whether in childhood, or in a country-house arcadia, or (with *The Go-Between*) in both simultaneously. Servants, high-ceilinged rooms, large windows opening on to distant views and a leisured and elegant lifestyle were beyond most people's pockets, but they could at least be briefly glimpsed and visited. Brideshead, Miss Marple, and a certain yearning for Anglo-India ministered to such needs.[46] So did the patriotic and only half-facetious 'Last Night' of London's Promenade Concerts; its mould was set by the mid-1950s, and survived the BBC's two attempts to crack it, in 1969 and 2001.[47] The nostalgic magazine *This England*, founded in 1967 with a title drawn from the dying John of Gaunt's speech in *Richard II*, was a success, and thirty years later each issue sold more than the combined weekly sales of the *Spectator*, the *New Statesman, Country Life,* and the *Tatler.*[48] From the 1950s the Post Office began responding to the taste for commemorative stamp issues, of which there had been only ten between 1924 and 1951; in the following decade there were fewer than ten, but in the five years from 1962 to 1966 there were twenty-six.[49]

Growing leisure, burgeoning media, and mounting car ownership eased the way to such nostalgia, for (in another recurring motif) politicians' worries about the economy jarred with people's more favourable experience. In their thousands they drove out from city and suburb to visit the real or refurbished thing, and carried off imitations of it from the tourist shop to adorn their homes: pots pourris, country crafts, and facsimiles of Victorian books. And for those of more scientific bent, there was the growing taste for industrial archaeology—to some extent the product of Britain's industrial decline, but deployed for new purposes by the Association for Industrial Archaeology founded in 1973.

[46] For ongoing Commonwealth cultural links, see above, pp. 7–8, 111–12, 374.

[47] D. Cannadine, 'Last Night Fever', *London Review of Books* (6 Sept. 2007), 21–4.

[48] Paxman, *The English*, 77–80.

[49] L. N. and M. Williams, *Commemorative Postage Stamps of Great Britain 1890–1966* (n.pl., 1967), 9–10; see also 163 and ff.

During the 1980s all this built up into something like a movement, identified by that vogue but elusive word of the 1980s: heritage. The Museums Action Group adopted the name 'National Heritage' in 1971, and the American New Right appropriated the term when the Heritage Foundation, launched in 1973, funded a think tank promoting conservative political philosophy. Then 1975 was designated 'European Architectural Heritage Year', and National Heritage Acts were passed in 1980 and 1983.[50] The heritage trail was not entirely backward-looking, for mass recreation was a twentieth-century growth industry. Britain was at its forefront, and despite hindrance from the British weather, Britain's 'heritage' had assets to deploy that had worldwide appeal. The conservation, collection, cataloguing, and renovation of antique objects fostered new trades and skills. The leisure which other new industries increasingly made possible ensured a large domestic 'heritage' market, and a substantial overseas market was nourished by the traditions of empire, English as a world language, and the memory of Britain's overseas cultural, economic, and political achievements. With the modern style in retreat,[51] nostalgia had become profitable.

The Georgian, Victorian, and Edwardian achievement was increasingly thrown into relief, and not only in its architectural dimension. The eighteenth century—whose unattractive monarchs, political corruption, urban squalor, and rural repression had long sent it out of fashion except with J. R. Seeley—was already by the 1930s being seen as the century which laid the foundations of empire, consolidated the UK's merging of nations, brought the country house to its peak of perfection, and established the constitutional structure whose essentials were not seriously challenged until the 1990s. As for the Victorians, they had been undergoing revaluation at least since G. M. Young's *Portrait of an Age* (1936), in a process that was ongoing for the rest of the century. The image of the Edwardians had suffered much from the advance of the Labour Party, which deplored their extremes of wealth and poverty. But in the 1980s and 1990s the growing respect on the left for the Edwardian Liberal Party's wide-ranging appeal and intellectual vigour prepared the way for Labour's slow transformation into a Liberal Party in all but name. As for the right, the growing recognition in the 1960s and 1970s that poverty could not easily be eliminated through state action brought a renewed faith in widened income differentials as a spur to achievement.

With props and aids such as these, the UK reached 1970 united, with a stable political structure and a population far more affluent than in 1951. What, then, of Dean Acheson's much-discussed comment on Britain's changing role?[52]

[50] Hewison, *Heritage Industry*, 89, 91, 31. [51] On which see above, pp. 153–8, 520.

[52] P. Catterall's 'Roles and Relationships: Dean Acheson, "British Decline" and Post-War Anglo-American Relations', in A. Capet and S.-W. Aissatou (eds.), *The 'Special Relationship'* (Rouen, 2003), 109–26, sets the remark into broad context; Dr Catterall kindly made his article available to me.

Controversy about the idea in 1962 that Britain could or should pursue a distinct national role in the world indicates how tightly knit, culturally and ethnically, the UK still then seemed. Seeking later to explain the indignation Acheson evoked, Maudling said that 'British opinion was angry with him precisely because what he said was fundamentally true'—a line also taken at the time by *That Was The Week That Was*.[53] Yet Acheson's claim cannot be uncritically accepted. Was it true in 1962 that the empire had been lost? The subsequent controversy indicates that many British people did not think so, and still fewer among the leading politicians from either major party thought it prudent to say so. We have seen how slow and sometimes imperceptible was Britain's withdrawal, how highly the Anglo-American connection was valued as a boost to Britain's world status, and how prolonged was the empire's postcolonial cultural aftermath. We have also seen how some saw Britain's new European role as merely extending or substituting for the UK's earlier worldwide role.[54] Even the loss of empire could be geared into the national myth to the extent that all-party pride could be taken in the manner of its ending: 'empires have often fallen', Maudling recalled, 'but usually in bloodshed and chaos, and against the background of defeat for the former Imperial power. We were not defeated; we withdrew of our own volition.' John Strachey referred in 1959 to 'the unique British achievement of acquiescing in the dissolution of her empire by a process far less violent and more voluntary than any comparable process hitherto known to history'.[55]

Acheson's remark did not capture the fact that Britain's imperial role was only the first among at least six roles competing for attention after 1945, all of which have already been foreshadowed. The second—different from the imperial role, though not entirely distinct from it—was the UK's role in courageously 'standing alone' against tyranny, exemplifying parliamentary and perhaps also democratic government, and championing both worldwide. Britain's parliament was indeed old, but Britain had been slow to democratize, so aspects of this second national self-image were quite new. The image was rendered particularly powerful for Britain in 1951 by memories of 1940 that were so vivid and so recent. Hence the indignation when the BBC in September 1960 proposed to launch its evening news programme with only one of Big Ben's chimes.[56] Linked to this myth was a third: the idea that Britain's long experience lent it some special skill in government and diplomacy. Macmillan in his dealings with the USA continued to hold such a notion even after the Suez crisis,[57] and it was Bevan who, when denying in 1956 that Britain had become

[53] R. Maudling, *Memoirs* (1978), 233. See also S. Ward (ed.), *British Culture and the End of Empire* (Manchester, 2001), 101–2.

[54] See above, p. 114.

[55] Maudling, *Memoirs*, 231. J. Strachey, *The End of Empire* (1959), 239.

[56] Briggs, *Competition*, 329–30.

[57] See above, pp. 11, 109.

a second-class power, saw it as 'a depository of probably more concentrated experience and skill than any other country in the world'.[58] A fourth national role, less salient than the second but influential from the 1940s to the 1970s, was the idea of Britain as exemplifying the potential 'middle way' between Communism and capitalism, gearing in well with the alleged national aptitude for pragmatic compromise, and combining the state planning and social justice allegedly present in the former with the liberty and enterprise claimed by the latter.[59] John Strachey, dismissing in 1959 any Americanized money-making substitute for empire as a national ideal, claimed that 'nations which have known empire may simply break their hearts if they do not find a higher ideal than personal enrichment by which to live'; instead he recommended collective enrichment, the 'welfare ideal'.[60] This easily elided into the related notion that Britain had some special diplomatic role as mediator between the Russians and the Americans. It was a useful national myth at the height of the cold war, when the ideology behind public welfare was powerful, but it was fading by the 1970s, and with the fall of the Berlin wall in 1989 both its variants almost vanished, though hints of them pervaded the Blair governments' notion of a 'third way'. Often recurring, and easily reconciled with the third role, was a fifth: the UK's alleged potential or actual role as cultural exemplar. Michael Young in 1960, for instance, emphasized the lack of any 'necessary connection between power and greatness', and recommended in place of the imperial ideal that the nation compete in such areas as art, intellect, and social concern.[61] The sporting extension of the UK's alleged cultural role would have been widely endorsed, and was all the more powerful for being linked to the UK's undeniable worldwide formative influence on many sports. It was buttressed by claims to an allegedly British ideal of personality, centring on the referee's impartiality—on the ideal of fair play, and of quietly accepting both success and failure with equanimity. Unlike the first five roles, the sixth—moral leadership for the UK—had once been integral to British self-respect, especially during the evangelical revival and in times of war. A pale reflection of it was the notion prevalent in CND that Britain could provide the world with moral leadership in peace rather than in war: that is, by unilaterally giving up nuclear weapons.

By 1970 none of these six roles carried conviction even within the UK, let alone elsewhere. It was clear by then that the empire was fading away, and that Britain could not now even get its way within the Commonwealth. After the Notting Hill riots even the appendage to this role—that of exemplar in operating a multi-racial society—could not persist. No substitute potential role for Britain in the EEC had yet materialized by 1970: only two rejected

[58] *HC Deb.* 19 Dec. 1956, c. 1404.
[59] See above, pp. 9, 38.
[60] Strachey, *End of Empire*, 229.
[61] Young, *Chipped White Cups of Dover*, 5.

applications for entry. The second role, of Britain as exemplar of parliamentary government was more convincing than its related claim to be exemplar of democracy, but since the British parliament was coming under fire by the 1960s, with critics keen to learn from other legislatures, that role too went into decline. Britain's third role, as possessing special experience which could guide the more powerful, had never been very credible, and suffered seriously from the Suez crisis (1956) and from the low profile the UK felt bound to take during the Vietnam war. Britain's fourth, 'middle way', role seemed less significant after the 1950s, when Soviet Communism's defects were more widely perceived. Besides, Britain was by then far from alone in possessing public-welfare facilities, and there was even a debate about how far the UK had chosen the right welfare model.

The UK's alleged fifth role, as cultural exemplar, was certainly an aspiration in 1951, and helps to explain why the South Bank in that year so completely outclassed the Millennium Dome in 2000. In architecture, however, it was never clear what twentieth-century Britain could offer which could compare with Fountains Abbey, Salisbury Cathedral, Petworth, and Blenheim—or, for that matter, which twentieth-century British painter could rival Gainsborough, Reynolds, or even Raeburn. Besides, the UK still had much ground to make up if it was to compete on the aesthetic front with European nations whose artistic traditions went back far further. As for sporting primacy, there was much English distress at defeats by Hungary in 1953, and by Germany in the World Cup match of 1970, the latter bringing decades of English triumphs over German teams to an end. Furthermore, the UK ideal of individual and national personality on the sports field could not survive the professionalism and internationalism pervading mass spectator sport from the 1960s.[62] The UK's claims to worldwide moral leadership might have profited from the manner of its departure from empire if withdrawal had not so often been so hasty, and so obviously proceeding from pressures other than free choice. The tenacity of such claims helps to explain the close links between CND, anti-colonialism, and anti-racism, and why serious people were so shocked by the Suez expedition. Lady Violet Bonham Carter, for one, was appalled in November 1956 when the Soviet invasion of Hungary coincided with government action destroying 'our moral authority and leadership' when it was 'most direly needed'; she went on to claim that 'never have we stood so ingloriously alone' with 'our proud tradition . . . tragically tarnished'.[63]

All in all, none of the six candidates for a distinctive national role really fits. None the less, Britain's worst fears had not been realized by 1970: the cold

[62] See above, pp. 387, 389–90.
[63] Letter to *T* (6 Nov. 1956), quoted in Bonham Carter, *Daring to Hope*, 174–5.

war had not grown hot, the empire had been dismantled with surprisingly little difficulty, corporatist approaches to the economy still seemed viable enough to predominate, high hopes of the EEC's likely benefits were widely held, and entry at the third attempt at least seemed possible. There were as yet few signs of the gloom that was shortly to descend.

The United Kingdom: Chronology of Events: 1951–1970

Date	Political/International	Economic/Social	Cultural/Religious
1951	9 Mar. Bevin resigns as Foreign Secretary (died 14 Apr.), Morrison succeeds him 21 Apr. Bevan resigns as Minister of Labour in protest at prescription charges 7 Jun. Diplomats Guy Burgess and Donald Maclean flee to USSR 25 Oct. GENERAL ELECTION; Conservatives 321, Labour 295, Liberals 6	Dec. London reopens as an international market for dealing in foreign exchange *Good Food Guide* launched (Good Food Club founded May 1950) Zebra crossing first introduced in Slough Robert Cowell legally becomes Roberta on 15 May, but the sex-change operation 1951–2, not publicized till 1954 Railway Development Association grows out of the movement to restore the Talyllyn Railway	1 Jan. First national broadcast of *The Archers* (first broadcast on Midland region, Whitsun 1950) 4 May South Bank exhibition in Festival of Britain opens with visit by royal family, closes 30 Sep.(Battersea Park funfair opens 11 May, Festival Gardens open 29 May, both closed 3 Nov) 28 May First broadcast of *The Goon Show* (last broadcast Jan.1960) Jly. Pevsner's first volumes in 'The Buildings of England' series published (on Cornwall and Nottinghamshire) Dec. First performance (at Covent Garden) of Britten's *Billy Budd* C.P.Snow's *The Masters* E.R.Dodds's *The Greeks and the Irrational* Paul Brickhill's best-selling *Dambusters* published Nicholas Montserrat's *The Cruel Sea* published

Date	Political/International	Economic/Social	Cultural/Religious
1951			Philip Jones Brass Ensemble founded by Philip Jones (1928–2000) O and A levels introduced, replacing School and Higher School Certificate
1952	6 Feb. Death of George VI. Elizabeth II succeeds 21 Feb. Government announces identity cards abolished 25 Jly. Treaty establishing the European Steel and Coal Community comes into force 3 Oct. First British atomic bomb tested at Monte Bello islands, off Australia 5 Oct Gaitskell's strongly anti-Communist speech at Stalybridge 20/21 Oct. Mau Mau killings prompt Kenya's Governor to declare state of emergency Pass laws introduced in South Africa	29 Feb. Cabinet decides to drop the ROBOT scheme for floating the pound 2 May BOAC's first passenger service jet airliner, the Comet1, launched, but high accident rate caused government to ground all seven BOAC Comet1s in 1954 Aug. Lynmouth flood disaster kills 34 and destroys 90 houses 5 Oct. Tea, gammon and ham derationed Nov. The great London 4-day 'smog' Morris and Austin Motors amalgamate to form the British Motor Corporation, then the largest builders of private cars in Europe Lord Montagu sets about rescuing Beaulieu's finances by opening it to the public	Oct. House church communion begins at Halton, Leeds 15 Nov. *New Musical Express* launches top twelve pop music chart based on sales in leading shops, extended to 'Top Twenty' in 1954 Southampton University gets its charter Science fiction first televised with *The Quatermass Experiment* (*Quatermass* II 1955; *Quatermass and the Pit* 1958) P.H.Reid's *The Colditz Story* published First James Bond novel, *Casino Royale*, published (29 million Bond books were sold in 1965) *Manchester Guardian* puts news on its front page, leaving only the *Times* without it

Date	Political/International	Economic/Social	Cultural/Religious
1952		College of General Practitioners founded (royal charter 1972) Spastics Society (from 1994 Scope) founded Egon Ronay opens his first restaurant, 'The Marquee' in London Charges for prescriptions and dental treatment introduced	
1953	25 Mar. Queen Mary, George V's widow, dies 6 May Transport Act, denationalizing British Road Services, receives royal assent 14 May Iron and Steel Act, denationalizing iron and steel, receives royal assent 2 Jun. Queen Elizabeth II crowned 23 Jun. Churchill suffers major stroke; cover-up ensues	27 Jan. Derek Bentley hanged as accomplice to the shooting of a policeman; fuels case against capital punishment (guilty verdict quashed 1998) 31 Jan.–1 Feb. North Sea storm tide causes serious flooding on the East coast May volunteer regular soldier Ronald Maddison for Porton Down medical tests dies from lethal dose of sarin	May The first two volumes in the 'Pelican History of Art' published L.P.Hartley's *The Go-Between* The Leavises' critical periodical *Scrutiny* (founded 1932) discontinued Watson and Crick propose double-helix structure for DNA

Date	Political/International	Economic/Social	Cultural/Religious
1953	Dec. During this month Macmillan achieves his target of 300,000 new houses a year	29 May Hillary climbs Everest 15 Jly. John Christie, chief prosecution witness at the trial of Timothy Evans (executed in 1949 for murder) hanged as a mass murderer 26 Sep. Sugar rationing ends 16 Nov. London Stock Exchange visitors' gallery opens 25 Nov. England's footballers lose their first ever game at home to a continental country: 6–3 to Hungary Myxomatosis outbreak begins in Kent, and by 1955 had reached every county in England and Wales and some counties in Scotland First Graham Lyon motel opened at Hythe College of General Practitioners instituted Institute of Community Studies founded	
1954	Jan. Queen and Duke tour New Zealand, Queen opens New Zealand Parliament Feb. Queen and Duke tour Australia, Queen opens Federal Parliament	Mar. Prison sentences for Lord Montagu of Beaulieu, Peter Wildeblood and Michael Pitt-Rivers for homosexual offences	1 Mar. Billy Graham launches his revivalist 'Greater London Crusade' at Harringay 30 Jly. Royal assent for Television Act, establishing Independent Television

Date	Political/International	Economic/Social	Cultural/Religious
1954	13 Feb. *Economist* coins the term 'Butskellism' Jun. King Gustaf VI of Sweden pays state visit to London 14 Jun. Winston Churchill installed Knight of the Garter 16 Jun. Churchill and his defence ministers secretly agree to produce a British hydrogen bomb, cabinet on 26 July approves decision 7–9 Oct. Parts of the Conservative Party conference televised for the first time. Labour Party refuses access till 1955, when both conferences are televised	2 Apr. First TV soap programme aimed at adults, *The Grove Family* (1954–7), launched 6 May Roger Bannister runs 4-minute mile 8 May Butter, cheese, margarine and cooking fats derationed 3 Jly. Bacon and meat derationed 24 Aug. Wolfenden Committee appointed to consider the law on homosexual offences (reported 4 Sept. 1957) 18 Oct. Rationing formally ends. Ministry of Food integrated into Ministry of Agriculture and Food First live TV weather forecasts England suffered its heaviest defeat in an international match: 7–1 to Hungary in Budapest Spring BBC launches its first regular TV sports magazine programme, the long-running *Sportsview*, later re-named *Sportsnight*	14 Sep. Kidbrooke, the first purpose-built comprehensive school, opened 12 Dec. TV version of Orwell's *1984* makes major impact Kingsley Amis's *Lucky Jim* published William Golding's *Lord of the Flies* published Douglas Bader's *Reach for the Sky* published Iris Murdoch's *Under the Net* published Hull University gets its charter John Betjeman's *A Few Late Chrysanthemums* published

Date	Political/International	Economic/Social	Cultural/Religious
1955	5 Apr. Churchill retires as prime minister, Eden succeeds him on 6 Apr 26 May GENERAL ELECTION: Conservatives 344, Labour 277, Liberals 6 Jun. Messina conference of the EEC Six 27 Jly. Postmaster General imposes '14-day rule' preventing BBC from discussing controversial matters in the fortnight before parliament debates them (experimentally suspended 18 Dec. 1956) 28 Jly. From this date, RAF has capacity to drop an atomic bomb 21 Sep. Rockall annexed to Crown dominions (fully incorporated into UK 10 Feb. 1972) Oct. President Lopes of Portugal pays state visit to London Oct. Princess Margaret announces she will not marry Group-Captain Peter Townsend 5 Oct. H.Wilson's 'penny farthing' report on Labour Party organization	25 Jan. R.A.Butler announces phased introduction of equal pay for women in civil service May ASLEF strike, the first national strike for 20 years seriously to inconvenience the public 13 Jly. Ruth Ellis the last woman hanged in UK Sep. Commercial television begins, first advertisement (for Gibbs SR toothpaste) 22 Sep. City of London becomes smokeless zone Duncan Sandys extends green-belt idea to areas outside London (it covers 9% of England and Wales by 1960) First hovercraft crossing of the English Channel (first Channel commercial hovercraft service Jly. 1968) Sainsburys opens its first supermarket The Westbury, first new large postwar London hotel, opened Duke of Bedford opens Woburn Abbey to the public	Jan. Margaret Knight, Aberdeen psychology lecturer, gives 3 controversial programmes on the Home Service 'from a Humanist point of view' Jan. London release of Orwell's *Animal Farm* as film 3 Aug. First performance in English of *Waiting for Godot* (first published in French, 1952) at the Arts Theatre, London 22 Sep. Second (commercial) channel television begins broadcasting. 22 Sep. Widespread shock when BBC radio kills off Grace Archer in the serial *The Archers* Duke of Edinburgh award scheme launched Exeter University gets its charter Industrial Fund for the Advancement of Scientific Education established to help fund science at independent schools Bill Haley's 'Rock around the Clock' makes an impact when used as theme song of the film *Blackboard Jungle*

Date	Political/International	Economic/Social	Cultural/Religious
1955	Nov. B.Castle visits Kenya and publicizes torture of Mau Mau suspects 7 Dec. Attlee retires as Labour leader, Gaitskell is elected his successor on 14 Dec 20 Dec. R.A.Butler transferred to Home Office, Macmillan becomes Chancellor of Exchequer	Women's Institute resolution of 1954 causes Keep Britain Tidy Group to be formed Duke of Edinburgh becomes President of the Football Association Devonshire family decide to move back into Chatsworth, which they'd last occupied in 1938 First FA Cup tie to be played under floodlights: a replay between Kidderminster Harriers and Brierley Hill Alliance (used on several other occasions later that year)	Ealing Studios *The Ladykillers* released, last of the Ealing comedies (Ealing studios closed 1958) Michael Tippett's first opera, *The Midsummer Marriage*, first produced BBC TV first broadcasts *This is Your Life* (discontinued 1964, resumed by ITV 1969–93, resumed by BBC 1994–2003)
1956	1 Jan. Sudan independent from Britain 18 Apr. Bulganin and Khrushchev arrive on visit to Britain 10 May Frank Cousins becomes General Secretary of the TGWU (till 1964, resumes 1966–9) Jun. Queen pays state visit to Sweden 13 Jun. Last British troops leave the Suez Canal zone	17 Apr. Macmillan's budget introduces premium bonds 22 May Calder Hall, world's first civil nuclear power station, goes into operation Kennet and Avon Canal Trust's precursor formed to promote repairs, reopened to navigation 1990, project complete Dec.2002	May Lonnie Donegan's *Rock Island Line* first reaches No.1 in the charts May Elvis Presley's *Heartbreak Hotel* top of the charts in 14 different countries 6 Jly. First broadcast of *Hancock's Half Hour* (63 episodes to 1961) John Osborne's *Look Back in Anger* first performed Colin Wilson's *The Outsider* published

Date	Political/International	Economic/Social	Cultural/Religious
1956	Jly. King Feisal of Iraq pays state visit to London 26 Jly. Egypt nationalizes Suez Canal 31 Oct. British bombing of Egyptian airfields 5 Nov. British paratroops land at Port Said, Egypt, and capture it on 6 Nov 23 Nov. Eden leaves for Jamaica, Butler acting prime minister 3 Dec. Suez invasion ends with Anglo-French acceptance of UN resolutions for their forces' withdrawal 5 Dec. Anglo-French forces begin withdrawing from Suez C.A.R.Crosland's *The Future of Socialism* published IRA launches border campaign of arms raids and explosions in Northern Ireland (called off 1962)	Tesco opens first supermarket (first self-service store opened at St Albans 1949) Duke of Edinburgh's Award for Boys launched (extended to girls 1958) Restrictive Practices Act frees shops to engage in price-cutting John Stephen, fashion designer, opens his first shop, moving it to Carnaby Street in 1957	Dudley Pope's *The Battle of the River Plate* published Trevelyan scholarships launched *New Scientist* first published Statutory newsprint rationing ends Society for Medieval Archaeology founded Government allows television broadcasting between 6 p.m. and 7 p.m., an hour hitherto reserved for children's homework or preparation for bed Lord Montagu's first jazz festival at Beaulieu (last one held 1961)
1957	9 Jan. Eden resigns as prime minister, Macmillan succeeds him on 10 Jan. Feb. Queen's state visit to Portugal	12 Aug. Council on Prices, Productivity and Incomes appointed	25 Jan. Walton's Cello Concerto first performed 28 Oct. First broadcast of the *Today* radio programme

Date	Political/International	Economic/Social	Cultural/Religious
1957	6 Mar. Gold Coast becomes independent (as 'Ghana') within the Commonwealth 25 Mar. Treaty of Rome signed, establishes EEC Apr. Queen's state visit to France 4 Apr. Protest march from London to Aldermaston atomic research establishment 4 Apr. Sandys's defence white paper backs reliance on nuclear deterrence, and envisages an end to national service 15 May First British hydrogen bomb exploded at Christmas Island Jun. Human rights organization 'Justice' founded 6 Jun. Rent Act passed (comes into operation 6 Oct. 1958, and removes or loosens control of rents on over 5 million houses) 19–26 Jly. National bus strike 20 Jly. Macmillan's 'never had it so good' speech at Bedford	11 Oct. Windscale nuclear reactor overheats in Britain's worst nuclear accident Consumers' Association founded and *Which?* launched Pilkington Brothers begin pilot-scheme for manufacturing float glass Work on Birmingham's inner ring-road begins (first section opened 1960, completed 1971) Government anti-smoking campaign launched, now that the link with cancer demonstrated; cigarette advertising banned 2003 Michael Young and Peter Willmott's *Family and Kinship in East London* published Flogging in the navy ends Homicide Act distinguishes between capital and non-capital categories of murder Mary Stott becomes editor of the *Guardian* women's pages (till 1971)	Civic Trust founded Leicester University gets its charter BBC natural history unit founded John Osborne's *The Entertainer* first performed John Braine's *Room at the Top* (film 1958) Richard Hoggart's *The Uses of Literacy* published

Date	Political/International	Economic/Social	Cultural/Religious
1957	31 Aug. Malayan Federation becomes independent from Britain Oct. Queen and Duke visit Canada 4 Oct. First earth satellite: Sputnik	Home Office Research Unit established, with statistician T.S.Lodge as its first head	
1958	6 Jan. Thorneycroft (Chancellor of Exchequer), Powell and Birch resign from government over failure to cut government expenditure Jan.-Mar. Queen Mother's world tour, visiting Australia and New Zealand 17 Feb. Campaign for Nuclear Disarmament (CND) holds its first meeting (Central Hall, Westminster) Mar. Queen's state visit to Netherlands 27 Mar. Liberal gain in Torrington by-election overturns large Conservative majority 4 Apr. CND march leaves London for Aldermaston (arrives 7 Apr) 30 Apr. Life Peerages Act receives royal assent, first women admitted 21 Oct.1958	5 Feb. Munich air crash kills eight of Manchester United's players, plus the Club secretary, two trainers and eight journalists 21 Mar. Last presentation of debutantes 12 May Homosexual Law Reform Society and Albany Trust founded Jun. Clean Air Act comes into force Dec. In the 'aluminium war', the USA's Reynolds Metals with Tube Investments defeats the old banks in buying UK's sole aluminium company: British Aluminium Company Dec H. Macmillan opens Britain's first motorway, the Preston by-pass, later part of the M6 Parking meters first appear in London streets	28 Feb. Victorian Society founded 2 Apr. Vaughan Williams's ninth and last symphony first performed (he died on 26 Aug) Oct. Jodrell Bank radio telescope comes into operation Dec. John Betjeman's *Collected Poems* published Government approves establishment of the University of Sussex Harold Pinter's *The Birthday Party* (1957) first performed BBC's Radiophonic Workshop founded Shelagh Delaney's *A Taste of Honey* first performed on stage (film 1961) Alan Sillitoe's *Saturday Night and Sunday Morning* (released as film 1960)

Date	Political/International	Economic/Social	Cultural/Religious
1958	May London bus strike May President Gronchi of Italy pays state visit to London Jly. Prince Charles created Prince of Wales 30 Aug.–7 Sep. Race riots in Notting Hill, London Oct. President Heuss of West Germany pays state visit to London Oct. Opening of parliament televised for first time 6 Nov. Vicky's first 'Supermac' cartoon on Macmillan Dec. Empire Day becomes Commonwealth Day	Convertibility of sterling restored for non-residents Everton the first British club to use an electrified pitch to defeat frost John Koon founds the Lotus House chain of upmarket Chinese restaurants in London Scunthorpe builds Britain's first cantilevered football stadium	
1959	3 Mar. 11 detainees murdered at Hola Camp, Kenya (House of Commons debate 27 July) May Shah of Iran's state visit to London 3 Jun. Singapore independent 31 Aug. Eisenhower and Macmillan make pre-dinner TV broadcast from 10 Downing Street	Apr. First 'Drinka pinta milka day' poster 18 Aug. British Motor Corporation launches the Mini 2 Nov. Ernest Marples opens first section of M1 motorway, from Watford to Rugby (reached Leeds 1977) Serious drought raises doubts whether the rapidly growing demand for water can be met	29 Jly. Obscene Publications Act relaxes law on censorship of published material on grounds of obscenity Apr. Chris Barber's first jazz success: *Petite Fleur* Aug. Cliff Richard reaches No.1 in record charts with *Living Doll* 24 Aug. *Manchester Guardian* changes title to *Guardian*, henceforth London-based

Date	Political/International	Economic/Social	Cultural/Religious
1959	8 Oct. GENERAL ELECTION; Conservatives 365, Labour 258, Liberals 6, other 1 20 Nov. EFTA agreement signed 28–9 Nov. Labour Party conference: Gaitskell fails to remove clause 4 from Party constitution	Boulting Brothers release their successful film *I'm All Right Jack*, worsening the trade unions' deteriorating image Double white lines introduced to limit overtaking on roads London Weather Centre opened Mental Health Act introduces major reforms in treatment of the mentally ill Marie Stopes Clinic holds its first evening birth-control session for unmarried women	Lord Hailsham appointed Britain's first Minister for Science Muriel Spark's *Memento Mori* Sillitoe's *The Loneliness of the Long Distance Runner* Nobel-prizewinning biologist Peter Medawar rejects pessimistic views about science's impact on daily life in his Reith Lectures, published as *The Future of Man* (1960)
1960	12 Jan. Kenya state of emergency ends 3 Feb. Macmillan's 'wind of change' speech in South African parliament 19 Feb. Prince Andrew born Apr. Blue Streak missile abandoned Apr. General de Gaulle pays state visit to London 25 Apr. Last batch of republican prisoners from the IRA's border campaign released 6 May Princess Margaret marries Antony Armstrong-Jones (Lord Snowdon) in Westminster Abbey	20 Oct. Michael Woodruff's kidney transplant the UK's first successful organ transplant First motorway service station opens, at Newport Pagnell on the M1 Traffic wardens introduced MOT test introduced for vehicles over 10 years old (3 years w.e.f. 1967) First self-service petrol stations open Contraceptive pill invented, and by 1963 in widespread use Age Concern founded	9 Dec. First episode of the TV serial *Coronation Street* 17 Dec. Beatles' first booking at Liverpool's Cavern club Pinter's *The Caretaker* (1959) first performed Amis's *Take a Girl like You* Lynne Reid Banks's *The L-shaped Room* Stan Barstow's *A Kind of Loving* David Storey's *This Sporting Life* (film, directed by Lindsay Anderson, 1963) John Betjeman's *Summoned by Bells*

Date	Political/International	Economic/Social	Cultural/Religious
1960	26 Jun. British Somaliland independent 6 Jly. Aneurin Bevan dies 16 Aug. Cyprus independent Sep. CND's Committee of 100 formed to promote 'direct action' 1 Oct. Nigeria independent 5 Oct. Labour Party conference defeats Gaitskell through backing unilateralism by 3.3 m to 3.0 m votes 23 Nov. Campaign to reverse the unilateralist vote takes the name 'Campaign for Democratic Socialism' Conscription for national service ends (last national serviceman demobbed 1963)	First stretch of 'Bluebell Railway' (Sussex) re-opened, showing that a standard-gauge line could be operated by voluntary effort Peter Willmott and Michael Young's *Family and Class in a London Suburb* published Much hostility evoked when BBC ceases broadcasting all Big Ben's chimes before the evening news	Obscenity prosecution for D.H.Lawrence's *Lady Chatterley's Lover* Michael Powell's chilling thriller *Peeping Tom* withdrawn 5 days after release *Beyond the Fringe* opens at Edinburgh Festival Walton's Second Symphony first performed Geoffrey Fisher, Archbishop of Canterbury, visits Pope John in Rome, the first such event since the fourteenth century Risinghill comprehensive school opened, using progressive teaching methods (closed 1965) William Glock's first Prom season (last, 1973)
1961	Mar. Queen's state visits to Iran and Nepal 27 Apr. Sierra Leone independent May Queen's state visit to Italy 31 May South Africa leaves Commonwealth	Apr. BBC drops the name *Children's Hour* for its programmes aimed at the young May First betting shops opened in response to Betting and Gambling Act (1960)	5 Feb. *Sunday Telegraph* first published Mar. New Testament of *New English Bible* published

Date	Political/International	Economic/Social	Cultural/Religious
1961	Jun. Queen and Duke entertain President Kennedy at Buckingham Palace 28 Jun. Frank Haxell and 4 other Communists found guilty of rigging ETU presidential election Jly. Britain applies to join EEC Sep. Large CND demonstration in Trafalgar Square 2–6 Oct. In Labour Party conference, Gaitskell reverses the unilateralist vote of 1960 by 3.7 m to 2.4 m votes 9 Dec. Tanganyika independent (republic within Commonwealth 1962) Amnesty International founded	Jun. David Cantor opens first branch of Cranks vegetarian restaurant in Marshall St, London Aug. First National Jazz Festival held at Richmond Athletic Ground (moved to Reading 1971, organized from 1989 by the commercial firm Mean Fiddler) 8 Aug. Government invites TUC and employers to help coordinate economic policy Relocation of London's Covent Garden market planned Carlton Tower, first London skyscraper hotel, opened Peter Scott founds World Wildlife Fund-UK Much conservationist criticism of the Duke of Edinburgh for his tiger-shooting on state visit to India Donald Shepherd invents the 'Portakabin' self-contained building unit Suicide Act abolishes the crimes of suicide and attempted suicide	May first performance of *Beyond the Fringe*, at London's Fortune Theatre (continues till 1966) 30 Nov. First number of *Private Eye* Crick and Brenner claim to determine DNA's structure, thus breaking the genetic code 5th Duke of Westminster begins demolishing Alfred Waterhouse's Eaton Hall (modern-style house replaces it 1971–3) W.H.Smith terminates its lending library services Work begins on erecting Post Office Tower (complete 1964, bomb damage 1971, restaurant closes 1980) Roald Dahl's first children's book, *James and the Giant Peach*

Date	Political/International	Economic/Social	Cultural/Religious
1961		Birth-control pill becomes generally available in Britain (1.8 million using it by 1971) Recognition that thalidomide given in early pregnancy could produce gross deformities Brook Street Bureau founded to promote birth-control advice for unmarried women (first admits girls under 16 in 1967) Release of the film *Victim*, important for its pioneering and sympathetically portrayed homosexual theme Football Association, after a strike threat, abolishes maximum wage; henceforth players can become stars First commercial bingo hall opens, in Maida Vale (1,820 bingo clubs by the peak year, 1974)	
1962	25 Feb. IRA communiqué calls off its "campaign of resistance to British Occupation"	2 Feb. 2.0–2.5% 'guiding light' for incomes announced	4 Feb. *Sunday Times* magazine launched as *Sunday Times Colour Section*

Date	Political/International	Economic/Social	Cultural/Religious
1962	14 Mar. Liberals capture Orpington in by-election (Conservatives had won in 1959 by majority of 14,760) Jly. Commonwealth Immigrants Act (first government restriction on entry from the Commonwealth) 13 Jly. Macmillan's 'night of the long knives' purge of a third of his cabinet Aug. Queen entertains the Eisenhowers at Buckingham Palace 6 Aug. Jamaica independent within Commonwealth 14 Aug. Kenyatta released from detention in Kenya 16 Aug. Aden enters Federation of South Arabia 31 Aug. Trinidad independent 3 Oct. Gaitskell at Labour's Brighton conference declares against EEC membership 9 Oct. Uganda independent	8 Feb. National Economic Development Council [NEDC] established to promote indicative planning 26 Jly. Government sets up National Incomes Commission 26 Nov. Separate status of amateur and professional abolished in cricket in favour of the single category: player Grand Metropolitan Hotels formed under chairman Maxwell Joseph American Rachel Carson's *Silent Spring* published in USA and exposes the ecological damage done by insecticides National Autistic Society founded	1 Apr. *Steptoe and Son* first broadcast on TV (till 1974) May Last performance by the Crazy Gang a landmark in music hall's decline Jly. Buckingham Palace's rebuilt chapel opened to the public as an art gallery 4 Oct. Beatles' *Love Me Do* first released 11 Oct. Pope John XXIII opens the Second Vatican Council; John Moorman, Bishop of Ripon, heads the Anglican delegation of observers 24 Nov. *That Was the Week that Was* launched (12 million viewers by Feb.1963, continues till early 1964) Protests fail to prevent Euston Arch from being demolished in November Keele (founded as a university college 1949) gains university status Basil Spence's new Coventry Cathedral consecrated, with Britten's *War Requiem* performed The periodical *New Society* launched

Date	Political/International	Economic/Social	Cultural/Religious
1962	22 Oct. Admiralty clerk William Vassall imprisoned for spying after the Russians blackmail him over homosexual activities 22–28 Oct. Cuban missile crisis Nov. Anglo-French agreement to develop Concorde airliner		
1963	14 Jan. De Gaulle's veto on British entry to EEC 18 Jan. Gaitskell dies (Wilson succeeds as Labour leader, 14 Feb) Feb. Queen and Duke visit Fiji, New Zealand and Australia Mar. *That Was the Week that Was* lampoons BBC treatment of royal occasions 22 Mar. Profumo makes Commons statement denying improper association with Christine Keeler (resigns as War Minister 4 Jun) 25 Mar. Lord Brookeborough retires as prime minister of Northern Ireland, Terence O'Neill succeeds him	27 Mar. Beeching report argues for drastic cuts in British railway services 29/30 Mar. 100 arrested in first Mods/Rocker clash at Clacton 3 Apr. Maudling's budget speech launches expansionary 'dash for growth' 8 Aug. Great train robbery Location of Offices Bureau established (abolished by Conservative government 1979) London Hilton opened Buchanan report on traffic in towns Birmingham's Bull Ring shopping complex redevelopment complete McCarthy and Stone, builders of retirement homes, founded	Jan. Beatles' first LP released Nov. Geoffrey Rippon announces the decision to demolish Gilbert Scott's Foreign Office 4 Nov. Beatles at Royal Variety Performance with Queen Mother present 23 Nov. *Doctor Who* series first broadcast on BBC television, continuing till 1989 Robbins report on higher education Joan Littlewood's musical *Oh! What a Lovely War!* first performed J.A.T.Robinson's *Honest to God* John Le Carré's *The Spy Who Came in from the Cold* published

Date	Political/International	Economic/Social	Cultural/Religious
1963	May. King Baudouin of the Belgians pays state visit to London 1 Jun. Jomo Kenyatta invested as Kenya's first prime minister Jly. Protests greet the state visit to UK of King and Queen of Greece Jly. Peerage Act permits disclaimers 8 Jly. Rachman scandal on property rental in London 25 Jly. USSR, UK and USA initial Test Ban Treaty banning above-ground nuclear tests 1 Oct. H. Wilson's 'white heat' speech at Labour Party conference 18 Oct. Macmillan resigns. Alec Douglas-Home succeeds him as Conservative prime minister 10 Dec. Zanzibar independent (merges with Tanganyika 1964) 12 Dec. Kenya independent, with Kenyatta as President 31 Dec. Central African Federation ends London Government Act passed (implemented 1965)	*Eastham* v *Newcastle United Football Club* case, heard in the High Court, ends the retain-and-transfer system Outside sponsorship in first-class cricket first introduced in the form of the Gillette Cup Blundeston prison opened, the first purpose-built prison built since the 19th century	Stirling and Gowan's engineering building at Leicester University (begun 1959) completed

Date	Political/International	Economic/Social	Cultural/Religious
1964	Jan. Queen encounters signs of hostility to the monarchy during her tour of Canada 10 Mar. Prince Edward born Spring Queen twice visits Duke of Windsor at the London Clinic, so twice meets Duchess 6 Jly. Nyasaland (Malawi) independent 21 Sep. Malta independent 15 Oct. GENERAL ELECTION Labour 317, Conservatives 304, Liberals 9 16 Oct. Harold Wilson becomes Labour prime minister Queen's state visit to Germany the first since the War, and evokes much enthusiasm	Easter Mods vs Rockers disturbances at seaside resorts 11 May Terence Conran's Habitat furniture store opened (second store, in Tottenham Court Road, opened 11 Oct.1966) 16 Jly. Resale Price Maintenance Act comes into force, abolishing resale price maintenance 13 Aug. Last judicial hangings in the UK 7 Sep. First BIBA clothes shop opens in Abingdon Road, Kensington First commercial hovercraft produced (British Hovercraft Corporation's SRN.5) Clearance begins for building (1966–70) the Westway elevated motorway in Paddington, opened in Jly.1970 as the only section of the 'motorway box' to be erected First professor of geriatrics in Britain, W.Ferguson Anderson, appointed in Glasgow	Mar. Pirate radio station Radio Caroline begins broadcasting (Radio Atlanta in May) May Orton's *Entertaining Mr Sloane* (written 1963) first produced, reaching West End in Jun 6 Sep. *Observer Colour Supplement* launched 15 Sep. *Daily Herald* becomes the *Sun*, re-launched by Murdoch as a tabloid 17 Nov.69 25 Sep. *Daily Telegraph Magazine* launched BBC2, second public TV channel, begins transmitting Richard Seifert's high-rise Centrepoint (Charing Cross Road, London) offices completed; not occupied till 1979 Manchester University establishes its Department of Computer Science, the first UK department to offer undergraduate degrees in the subject Pinter's *The Homecoming*

Date	Political/International	Economic/Social	Cultural/Religious
1964		Victim Support, founded in Bristol (by 2004 was helping 1.7 m victims p.a., with 1,000 members of staff) Manchester United introduce Europe's first private box for spectators at a football ground BBC launches its TV magazine programme *Match of the Day* Police Act institutes reformed system for dealing with complaints against the police	
1965	Jan. Foreign and Commonwealth services merge as Diplomatic Service 14 Jan. Northern Ireland's Prime Minister O'Neill receives the Irish Premier Sean Lemass at Stormont in gesture of reconciliation 30 Jan. State funeral of Winston Churchill (died 24 Jan.) 31 Jan. R.A.Butler retires from politics to become Master of Trinity College, Cambridge	11 Feb. Prices and Incomes Board set up (Aubrey Jones accepts chairmanship 17 Mar) 2 Mar. Government announces ban on TV cigarette advertising, effective 5 months later Mar.-Apr. Launch of what became the Child Poverty Action Group 11 May Duke of Edinburgh launches Enterprise Neptune (sea-coast conservation appeal)	5 May Mary Whitehouse's 'Clean up TV' campaign culminates in Birmingham Town Hall meeting 12 Jly. Ministry of Education circular 10/65 asks local authorities to submit plans for comprehensive schools Oct. The radio news magazine programme *The World at One* first broadcast 29 Nov. Fleet Street press conference launches Mary Whitehouse's National Viewers' and Listeners' Association

Date	Political/International	Economic/Social	Cultural/Religious
1965	17 Feb. Gambia independent 8 Apr. Donovan Commission on trade unions and employers' associations appointed (report published May 1968) 27 Jly. Conservative leadership first ballot (Heath 150, Maudling 133, Powell 15). Heath's rivals withdraw from the second ballot in his favour 24 Oct. Northern Rhodesia becomes the independent republic of Zambia 8 Nov. Race Relations Act establishes Race Relations Board to monitor discrimination 11 Nov. Smith regime in Rhodesia declares UDI, British sanctions subsequently imposed	24 May Metric system announced 20 Jly. Owen Maclaren, retired aeronautical designer, patents the baby buggy, first easy-to-use push-chair or stroller Sep. BP reports its first gas strike in North Sea 16 Sep. National Plan published 9 Nov. Abolition of Capital Punishment Act suspends execution for murder for 5 years (abolished 1969) 13 Nov. TV viewers first hear the word 'fuck' (uttered by Ken Tynan) 27 Dec. BP's drilling rig Sea Gem capsizes and sinks, 13 men die 70 m.p.h. speed limit introduced experimentally on motorways, permanent from 1967 Continental traffic signs introduced In the New Year honours, Stanley Matthews the first footballer ever to be knighted Notting Hill, London, carnival first held	Education Minister Crosland announces establishment of the binary divide between universities (autonomous and relatively academic) and polytechnics (LEA-controlled, relatively vocational and regional in recruitment and role) Government science funding redistributed from the DSIR and other bodies to three new research councils: Science, Natural Environment and Social Science Research Councils A.J.P.Taylor's concluding volume on 1914–45 completes the 15-volume 'Oxford history of England' Times Book Club closes Dainton report recommends broadening the appeal of science through widening school curriculum Labour government organizes first national census of gypsies The Beatles receive their MBEs Certificate of Secondary Education introduced

Date	Political/International	Economic/Social	Cultural/Religious
1965		First Pizza Express restaurant opened in Soho (second in 1967) The Pennine Way, Britain's first long-distance footpath, opens Special Patrol Group formed in London to help local forces deal with rising urban crime	
1966	Jan. Prince of Wales leaves for Geelong Grammar School, Australia Feb. Queen and Duke on a month's Caribbean tour Mar. Queen Mother tours Australia, Fiji and New Zealand 31 Mar. GENERAL ELECTION: Labour 363, Conservatives 253, Liberals 12, Others 2 May Queen's state visit to Belgium May President Jonas of Austria's state visit to London 23 May State of Emergency declared when National Union of Seamen strike affects trade	1 Mar. Decimal currency announced (introduced 15 Feb. 1971) Easter Safari park opens at Longleat 6 May Myra Hindley and Ian Brady found guilty of the moors murders and imprisoned for life 29 Jun. The first credit cards (Barclaycard) launched (over 9 m in use in 1996) 20 Jly. Statutory wage-freeze imposed for 6 months, 'severe restraint' w.e.f. 20 Jan. 1967 Jly. British and French prime ministers jointly announce approval for building a Channel tunnel 30 Jly. England win football's World Cup Final at Wembley	Jan. Boots Book Lovers' Library terminates its 121 remaining lending library branches 25 Feb. White paper proposes university of the air Mar. Archbishop Ramsey the first Archbishop of Canterbury officially to meet the Pope (Paul VI in Rome) since the Reformation, with shared ecumenical service 3 May *The Times* first supplants classified adverts by news on its front page 6 June *Till Death Us Do Part*, starring Warren Mitchell as Alf Garnett, first broadcast (series lasts till 1974)

Date	Political/International	Economic/Social	Cultural/Religious
1966	26 May British Guiana independent as 'Guyana' Jly. King Husain of Jordan's state visit to London 3 Jly. Frank Cousins resigns as Minister of Technology because opposes regulation of wages; Benn replaces him 14 Jly. Gwynfor Evans wins Carmarthen by-election for Plaid Cymru 31 Jly. Colonial Office dissolved and merged with Commonwealth Relations Office 3 Sep. Botswana independent 4 Oct. Lesotho independent 11 Nov. Barbados independent 2 Dec. Wilson-Smith Rhodesia talks on HMS *Tiger* 25 Dec. 1-hour TV film *The Royal Palaces of Britain* is precursor to *Royal Family* film (1969) first terrorist actions against the IRA by the revived Ulster Volunteer Force (UVF)	Sep. Severn road bridge opened 21 Oct. Aberfan coal tip collapses and kills 116 children and 28 adults Correspondence in *Observer* prompts foundation of the Anti-Concorde Project BMC merges with Jaguar into British Motor Holdings Archbishop of Canterbury's committee report *Putting Asunder* advocates divorce reform that dispenses with the concept of blame Boy Scouts Association's influential *Advance Party Report* (launched 1963) urges an updated image Jeremy Sandford's television play on homelessness: *Cathy Come Home* Family Doctors' Charter fosters the revival of the GP, who annexes the earlier concept of 'health centre' to the practice	20 Dec. Respected Catholic theologian Charles Davis announces he's leaving the Church forthwith Quinlan Terry becomes partner with Raymond Erith in firm reviving the classical style in architecture

Date	Political/International	Economic/Social	Cultural/Religious
1967	16 Jan. Wilson and George Brown tour Europe discussing EEC entry Feb. Queen and Duke entertain Kosygin (from USSR) in London 1 Feb. Non-party Northern Ireland Civil Rights Association founded 7 Feb. National Front founded from merger of several Fascist and racist groups 22 Mar. Iron and Steel Act renationalizes steel and road transport 22 Mar. Parliamentary Commissioner (Ombudsman) set up on Scandinavian model to investigate administrative abuses (takes up post 1 Apr.) May King Faisal of Saudi Arabia pays state visit to London	6 Mar. First landing at Easington of North Sea gas from West Sole 22 Mar. Iron and Steel (nationalization) Bill enacts renationalization 27 Jun. Barclays Bank installs its first high-street cash dispenser at Enfield 9 Jly. First flight in UK of a recreational balloon, the *Bristol Belle*, from Weston-on-the-Green to Bicester, thus launching its Bristol-based manufacture 27 Jly. Sexual Offences Act permits homosexual acts between consenting adults in private 27 Oct. Abortion Act legalizes abortion in certain circumstances 18 Nov. Sterling devalued from $2.80 to $2.40	7 Jan. BBC2's immensely successful *Forsyte Saga* serial begins 11 Apr. *The Times* launches its 'Business news' as a separate section, but it becomes part of the main paper on 23 Dec. 1970 Jly. Colour TV begins on BBC2 (on BBC1 and ITV in Nov) 3 Jly. *News at Ten* first transmitted on ITV Sep. Theatres Act abolishes censorship 17 Sep. First broadcast of the news magazine programme *The World this Week-End* 8 Nov. eight BBC local radio stations launched experimentally for 2 years, renewed 1969

Date	Political/International	Economic/Social	Cultural/Religious
1967	10 May House of Commons agrees by 488 to 62 votes to seek EEC entry Jun. Duke and Duchess of Windsor attend when Queen unveils plaque to Queen Mary 5 Jun. Arab-Israeli war 10 Aug. Public Records Act makes most government documents available 30 years after their creation (implemented w.e.f. 1 Jan. 1968) 2 Nov. Winifred Ewing wins Hamilton by-election for Scottish nationalists 7 Nov. Hugh Scanlon elected President of Amalgamated Engineering Federation 27 Nov. De Gaulle vetoes British entry to EEC for the second time 30 Nov. Aden independent	21 Nov. Herman Bondi reports in favour of a retractable Thames barrier (approved by parliament 1972) Claus Moser becomes head of Government Statistical Service Annual MOT tests for all cars over 3 years old introduced Seat belts compulsory in new cars registered after 1 April Breathalyser test introduced Oil tanker *Torrey Canyon* wrecked off Land's End, environmental disaster results First London dock closure (East India) General Electrical Company (GEC) takes over Associated Electrical Industries (AEI), absorbing English Electric in 1968 London Street, Norwich, the first pedestrianized street closed to traffic Cicely Saunders founds the first postwar hospice	Civic Amenities Act introduces the concept of the conservation area Gilbert Scott's St.Pancras station gains Grade 1 listed status Pressure from pirate radio stations leads BBC Radio to divide into Radio 1, 2, 3, 4 Marine Broadcasting Offences Act kills off pirate radio by making it an offence to supply/buy advertising time on the pirate radio stations Roy Strong becomes Director of the National Portrait Gallery National Evangelical Anglican Congress at Keele University a landmark in postwar evangelical renaissance Naval divers seriously damage Sir Cloudesley Shovell's flagship *The Association* off the Scillies, leading to pressure for protective legislation Michael Holroyd's *Lytton Strachey*

Date	Political/International	Economic/Social	Cultural/Religious
1967		Society for the Protection of Unborn Children founded to resist extended abortion Court Lees approved school closed Corporal punishment in prisons and borstals ends Boy Scouts shed their short trousers Family Planning Act makes local-authority services available to all women regardless of medical criteria or marital status	
1968	16 Jan. Major deflationary package involves withdrawing British military forces from east of Suez by 1971, defence cancellations, and cuts in welfare benefits 1 Mar. Commonwealth Immigrants Act enacted: restricts entry of unskilled blacks and Asians. 15 Mar. George Brown resigns, condemning H.Wilson's handling of the cabinet 20 Apr. E.Powell's 'rivers of blood' immigration speech (sacked from shadow cabinet 21 Apr)	18 Feb. British Standard Time (one hour ahead of Greenwich mean time) introduced, but abandoned after two years 16 Sep. Post Office introduces two-tier postal delivery system BMH joins Leyland Motor Corporation and becomes British Leyland Motor Corporation (BLMC, re-named British Leyland when nationalized in 1975) Last steam-hauled passenger train ceased operating	16 May Ronan Point tower block reveals defects of high-rise residential building 1 Jun. Open University chartered 31 Jly. First performance of the BBC TV programme *Dad's Army*, continued in 80 episodes till 13 Nov. 1977 21 Aug. London Coliseum, earlier in the year closed as a cinema, reopens as permanent home of Sadlers Wells Opera (re-named English National Opera 1974) 26 Sep. Lord Chamberlain's censorship power over the live theatre ends

Date	Political/International	Economic/Social	Cultural/Religious
1968	13 May Donovan Commission recommends decentralizing wage bargaining. Commission on Industrial Relations to investigate labour disputes 26 Jun. Fulton Committee report on civil service 30 Jun. Ray Gunter resigns as Minister of Employment Aug. Duke of Windsor's last visit to Britain, for Princess Marina's funeral 24 Aug. First Northern Ireland civil rights march (from Coalisland to Dungannon) 6 Sep. Swaziland independent 5 Oct. Second civil rights march in Londonderry ends in violence 9 Oct. Wilson/Smith Rhodesia talks on HMS *Fearless* 16 Oct. Commonwealth Relations Office merged into Foreign Office	Society of Teachers Opposed to Physical Punishment [STOPP] founded	27 Sep. The American musical *Hair* receives its first performance, complete with its controversial nude scene, on the London stage Marlborough College admits 15 girls, the first male public school to do so The papal encyclical *Humanae Vitae*, rejecting artificial contraception, provokes fierce controversy among English Catholics Launch of Booker prize for a work of fiction by a British author published in Britain within a specified period (first awarded 1969) Lindsay Anderson's film *If. . .* set in Cheltenham College

Date	Political/International	Economic/Social	Cultural/Religious
1968	25 Oct. Race Relations Act enables Race Relations Board to investigate complaints and initiate proceedings, brings housing and employment within its scope, and establishes Community Relations Commission 3 Nov. Mauritius independent		
1969	8 Jan. Ulster Defence Force (UDF) founded to defend Protestant lives and property 17 Jan. B.Castle introduces white paper 'In Place of Strife' to parliament, with penal measures enforcing strike ballots and compulsory 'cooling off' periods in strikes Feb. Queen entertains President Nixon to lunch 24 Feb. General election called in Northern Ireland to resolve Unionist differences 17 Apr. Representation of the People Act lowers voting age-limit to 18	9 Apr. First flight of the British prototype of Concorde (002) at Filton (last commercial flight lands in UK on 24 Oct.2003) 5 Oct. Department of Economic Affairs abolished 22 Oct. Enactment of Divorce Reform Act makes irretrievable marriage breakdown the sole ground required Post Office moves from status of government department to public corporation Friends of the Earth founded Laker Airways first appears on the transatlantic route as a charter airline	2 Jan. R.Murdoch buys *News of the World* 24 Jan. Student violence causes London School of Economics to be closed down for a month 25 Apr. Much protest when BBC ends its radio serial *The Dales* (launched 1948) 20 Jly 600 m people world-wide watch the moon landing, including 14.5 m on ITV and 12 m on BBC 17 Sep. *The Sun* goes compact from broadsheet (*Daily Mail* likewise in 1971, *News of the World* in 1984, *Independent* partially in 2003)

Date	Political/International	Economic/Social	Cultural/Religious
1969	17 Apr. Parliament Bill for House of Lords reform abandoned due to all-party backbench opposition 25 Apr. 500 British troops arrive in Northern Ireland 28 Apr. James Chichester-Clark replaces T.O'Neill as prime minister of Northern Ireland 11 Jun. Redcliffe-Maud Commission recommends extensive local-government boundary changes Jly. Prince Charles invested Prince of Wales at Caernarvon Castle 14 Aug. Bogside (Londonderry) violence; government sends more troops to Northern Ireland 8 Sep. Jack Jones succeeds Cousins as TGWU General Secretary, working closely thereafter in a left-wing alliance with Hugh Scanlon (Amalgamated Engineering Federation) Three USA republicans set up Noraid to fund IRA armaments	Family Law Reform Act lowers age of majority from 21 to 18, after which young people free to marry without consent Committee for Homosexual Equality founded Heart transplants discontinued (resumed 1979) Centrepoint (charity for homeless young in London) launched in Soho in disused basement British Fluoridation Society founded	26 Sep. Rupert Murdoch buys the *Sun* 5 Oct. Television first broadcasts *Monty Python's Flying Circus* (ends Dec. 1974) Kenneth Clark's BBC TV programmes on *Civilisation*

Date	Political/International	Economic/Social	Cultural/Religious
1970	11 Jan. IRA splits: Provisional IRA breaks off 30 Jan. Conservative leadership conference at Croydon's Selsdon Park Hotel acquires subsequent unjustified reactionary image Feb. Prince of Wales takes seat in House of Lords Mar. Queen, Duke, Prince of Wales and Princess Anne visit Fiji, Tonga, New Zealand and Australia Mar. Queen's first 'walkabout' in New Zealand, followed by her first 'walkabout' in the UK, in Coventry in Jun. Apr. B Specials (police auxiliary force) disbanded; Ulster Defence Regiment replaces it May South African cricket tour of England cancelled 4 Jun. Tonga independent 18 Jun. GENERAL ELECTION: Conservatives 330, Labour 287, Liberals 6, Others 7	Jan. Protests at cricket grounds get the South African cricket tour cancelled Apr. ILEA commits itself to implementing the Plowden recommendation against corporal punishment (on 26 Nov. 1971 ILEA announces that the cane will be banned from London maintained primary schools from Jan. 1973) 29 May Equal Pay Act, promoting equal pay for work of equal value, to be implemented on a voluntary basis till 1975 13 Oct. London Gay Liberation Front founded 2 Nov. Prices and Incomes Board wound up Trust Houses and Forte merge First Gay Pride Festival in London The pressure group LIFE founded to curb abortion Robin Day presents the first national phone-in programme, *It's Your Line*	4 Apr. 'The Third Programme' becomes 'Radio 3' Jun. *Oh, Calcutta!* first opens in London at the Roundhouse; transferred to West End on 3 Oct. 30 Jun. Ministry of Education circular 10/70 reverses the 1965 policy on comprehensivizing secondary education 19 Sep. 1,500 attend the first Glastonbury festival, then named the 'Pilton festival' Nov. Queen opens first session of the Church of England's new General Synod E.P. Thompson's *Warwick University Ltd* exposes industrialists' influence over the newly-founded university University of East Anglia launches its course in creative writing Penguin Books sold to the Longman Pearson Group, a commercialized conglomerate Pinter's *Old Times*

Date	Political/International	Economic/Social	Cultural/Religious
1970	19 Jun. Heath becomes Conservative prime minister 30 Jun. EEC entry negotiations start (concluded 23 Jun.) Jly. Queen, Duke, Prince of Wales and Princess Anne visit Canada 16 Jly. State of Emergency declared as dockers' strike begins to affect trade 20 Jly. Chancellor of Exchequer Iain Macleod dies, Anthony Barber succeeds him 23 Jly. two CS gas bombs thrown into House of Commons to remind MPs of conditions in Northern Ireland 21 Aug. Social Democratic and Labour Party founded in Northern Ireland 29 Oct. Lord Rothschild becomes head of the Central Policy Review Staff to advise the cabinet 1 Nov. Ministries of Health and Social Security merge into Department of Health and Social Security (DHSS) 15 Dec. Industrial Relations Bill passes second reading debate by 324 votes to 280	Standing Conference for the Advancement of Counselling established, later re-named British Association for Counselling and Psychotherapy	

Bibliography

1. GENERAL

For British history between 1951 and 1970 the secondary literature is already large, and the primary sources still larger. A comprehensive bibliography would be pointless for two reasons: it would be huge, and it would date rapidly. A short bibliographical introduction must suffice, complemented by the footnotes. Books are published in London unless otherwise stated.

Secondary studies of the period are becoming abundant. K. O. Morgan, *The People's Peace: British History 1945–1990* (2nd edn. 1999) is the best single-volume study. P. Hennessy's *Having it So Good: Britain in the Fifties* (2006) is the second in a multi-volume sequence and draws heavily on unpublished documents. D. Sandbrook covers a wide span in his two synoptic volumes, *Never Had it So Good: A History of Britain from Suez to the Beatles* (2005) and *White Heat: A History of Britain in the Swinging Sixties* (2006). V. Bogdanor and R. Skidelsky gathered useful essays in their *The Age of Affluence* (1970), followed by T. Gourvish and A. O'Day's *Britain since 1945* (1991). See also K. Burk (ed.), *The British Isles since 1945* (Oxford, 2003). Successive snapshots of the period were taken by the shrewd and well-informed journalist Anthony Sampson: they include *The Anatomy of Britain* (1962), *The Anatomy of Britain Today* (1965), and *The New Anatomy of Britain* (1971).

Reference works are increasingly best consulted on the internet, most notably the ongoing *Oxford English Dictionary* and *Oxford Dictionary of National Biography*, but P. Catterall's remarkably detailed *Bibliography of British History 1945–1987: An Annotated Bibliography* (Oxford, 1991) in book form was early in the field, and formidable is K. Robbins, *A Bibliography of British History 1914–1989* (Oxford, 1996). B. Brivati, J. Buxton, and A. Seldon (eds.), *The Contemporary History Handbook* (Manchester, 1996) offers a wealth of guidance, stimulus, and information. G. Foote's *A Chronology of Post War British Politics* (1988) is useful. The essential *British Political Facts*, edited by D. E. Butler and others, went through eight editions between 1963 and 2000. See also I. Crewe, A. Fox, and N. Day, *The British Electorate 1963–1992: A Compendium of Data from the British Election Studies* (Cambridge, 1995); and F. W. S. Craig's constituency-by-constituency compendium *British Parliamentary Election Results 1950–1970* (Chichester, 1971), supplemented by S. Elliott's *Northern Ireland Parliamentary Election Results 1921–1972* (Chichester, 1973). There have been three editions, all still valuable, of the statistics-based collaborative study edited by A. H. Halsey: *Trends in British Society since 1900: A Guide to the Changing Social Structure of Britain* (London and Basingstoke, 1972); *British Social Trends since 1900* (London and Basingstoke, 1988); and *Twentieth-Century British Social Trends* (London and Basingstoke, 2000). For census history see I. Mills's useful 'Developments in Census-Taking since 1841', *Population Trends* (Summer 1987). The Department of Employment and Productivity's valuable *British Labour Statistics.*

Historical Abstract 1886–1967 (1971) is valuable, but should be updated. B. R. Mitchell's *European Historical Statistics 1750–1975* (2nd edn. 1981) provides valuable comparative perspective.

Valuable **sources on opinion** include G. Gallup, *The Gallup International Public Opinion Polls: Great Britain 1937–1975* (2 vols., New York, n.d.); A. King (ed.), *British Political Opinion 1937–2000: The Gallup Polls* (2001); and R. J. Wybrow, *Britain Speaks Out, 1937–87: A Social History as Seen through the Gallup Data* (Basingstoke and London, 1989). The back numbers of more and more newspapers, including *The Times, Times Literary Supplement, Observer,* and *Guardian* are available on the internet; so are parliamentary and governmental documents, including Hansard's *Parliamentary Debates.* This facility will eventually transform research possibilities. Parliament remains the focus of opinion, and House of Lords debates are in some respects superior to House of Commons debates as a historical source: wider ranging, more expert, and less preoccupied with scoring party points.

Several **periodicals** are valuable. For a rich collection of government statistics see the *Annual Abstract of Statistics* published by the Central Statistical Office and its successors. For specialist aspects see the National Institution of Adult Education's yearbook: *Adult Education in 1934–*, with an annual bibliography; the Ministry of Agriculture and Food's *Agricultural Statistics, United Kingdom* (1867–), continued from 1991 as *Digest of Agricultural Census Statistics. UK*; *Economic Trends* (1953–); *Abstract of Regional Statistics* (1965–); *Local Government Trends* (1973–); *Local Government Financial Statistics* (1953–; from 1981 *Local Government Comparative Statistics*); *Trends in Education* (1966–); and *Social Trends* (1970–). For London see the London County Council's *Statistical Abstract* (1897–), succeeded in 1966 by the *Annual Abstract of Greater London Statistics.* For Scotland see the *Digest of Scottish Statistics* (1953–71), continued as *Scottish Abstract of Statistics.* For secondary writing see the journals *Twentieth Century British History* (1990–), and the Institute of Contemporary British History's *Contemporary Record* (9 vols., 1987–95), continued from volume 10 as *Contemporary British History* (1996–).

Diaries invaluably provide contemporary flavour. See especially H. Nicolson's *Diaries and Letters 1945–1962,* ed. N. Nicolson (1968), and the relevant, highly prejudiced, and eminently readable volume of James Lees-Milne, strong on architectural and aristocratic aspects: *A Mingled Measure: Diaries 1953–1972* (1994). A very different angle comes from *The Noel Coward Diaries,* ed. G. Payn and S. Morley (1982), covering the period 1941–69. Also from an actor, but moving at different social levels, is K. C. Williams, *The Kenneth Williams Diaries,* ed. Russell Davies (1993), covering the years 1942–88; it can be supplemented by Williams's *Letters* (ed. Davies, 1994) from 1947 to 1988. Different again is the perspective in *The Robert Hall Diaries 1947–53,* ed. A. Cairncross (1989); as Director of the Cabinet Office's Economic Section 1947–53, Hall could portray economic policy formation from the inside. Collections of correspondence resemble diaries in their bird's-eye-view usefulness. J. Betjeman, *Letters,* ed. C. Lycett-Green, ii (1995), for example, covers the years 1951–84; see also *The Selected Letters of Philip Larkin, 1940–1985,* ed. A. Thwaite (1992).

2. THE UNITED KINGDOM IN 1951

K. O. Morgan, *Labour in Power 1945–51* (Oxford, 1984) provides the political background. B. de Jouvenel, *Problems of Socialist England* (tr. J. F. Huntington, 1949) intelligently discusses important political issues arising in the late 1940s. Hulton Press, *Patterns of British Life* (1950) quantitatively analyses social conduct and attitudes. For the viewpoint of a reflective yet down-to-earth housewife, see *Nella Last's Peace, The Post-War Diavies of Housewife, 49* (eds. P. and R. Malcolmson, 2008). The rest of this section lists, roughly in the order of the chapter's discussion, contextual material essential for what was to follow.

On **defence**, D. Reynolds, *In Command of History: Churchill Fighting and Writing the Second World War* (2004) brilliantly records the gestation of mythology about the UK's wartime role. On nuclear weapons see M. Gowing with L. Arnold, *Independence and Deterrence: Britain and Atomic Energy, 1945–1952* (2 vols., 1974), and S. R. Twigge's very detailed *The Early Development of Guided Weapons in the United Kingdom, 1940–1960* (Reading, 1993). For a concise and efficient account of the Korean war see C. A. MacDonald, *Britain and the Korean War* (Oxford, 1990); the official history is A. Farrar-Hockley, *The British Part in the Korean War* (2 vols., 1990 and 1995), a massive and somewhat unfocused work which is in effect a history of the entire war.

For the **empire/Commonwealth** see two magisterial works: J. M. Brown and W. R. Louis (eds.), *The Oxford History of the British Empire*, iv. *The Twentieth Century* (Oxford, 1999), and P. J. Cain and A. G. Hopkins, *British Imperialism: Crisis and Deconstruction 1914–1990* (1993). R.Holland's 'The Imperial Factor in British Strategies from Attlee to Macmillan, 1945–63', *Journal of Imperial and Commonwealth History* (Jan. 1984) links empire with foreign policy in an impressive synoptic sweep which has stood up well. See also J. Gallagher's *The Decline, Revival and Fall of the British Empire: The Ford Lectures and Other Essays* (Cambridge, 1982), R. Hyam's scholarly yet sprightly *Britain's Declining Empire: The Road to Decolonisation, 1918–1968* (Cambridge, 2007), and J. Darwin's *Britain and Decolonisation* (1988).

For **immigration** see S. Glynn, 'Irish Immigration to Britain, 1911–1951: Patterns and Policy', *Irish Economic and Social History*, 8 (1981); and E. Stadulis, 'The Resettlement of Displaced Persons [from Europe] in the United Kingdom', *Population Studies* (Mar. 1952).

For long-term context on the **environment** see B. W. Clapp, *An Environmental History of Britain since the Industrial Revolution* (1994). For **regional contrasts** see D. C. D. Pocock's valuable 'The Novelist's Image of the North', *Transactions of the Institute of British Geographers* (1979). On **housing** history J. Burnett, *A Social History of Housing 1815–1970* (1978) provides a good introduction.

For the **family** see, especially on birth control, Royal Commission on Population, *Report* (1949, Cmd.7695), and E. M. Hubback, *The Population of Britain* (West Drayton, 1947). On feminist history, M. Pugh, *Women and Women's Movement 1914–1959* (1992) provides essential background. For **sexuality** see P. Robinson's fine cross-cultural study of sex research: *The Modernization of Sex: Havelock Ellis, Alfred Kinsey, William Masters and Virginia Johnson* (1976); M. Dillon's remarkable and pioneering *Self: A Study in*

Ethics and Endocrinology (1946) on transsexuals; and L. Hodgkinson, *Michael [Dillon], nee Laura* (1989). On **old age** see L. Hannah, *Inventing Retirement: The Development of Occupational Pensions in Britain* (Cambridge, 1986). M. R. Miller's valuable Kent Ph.D. thesis: 'The Development of Retirement Pensions Policy in Britain from 1945 to 1986: A Case of State and Occupational Welfare' (1987) covers neglected territory, as does P. Johnson's 'The Employment and Retirement of Older Men in England and Wales, 1881–1981', *Economic History Review* (Feb. 1994), important on employment aspects.

For the **economy** P. Deane and W. A. Cole, *British Economic Growth 1688–1959: Trends and Structure* (2nd edn., Cambridge, 1969) and L. Hannah, *The Rise of the Corporate Economy: The British Experience* (2nd edn. 1983) provide a broad-ranging run-in. J. Jewkes interestingly dissented from contemporary orthodoxies in his *Ordeal by Planning* (1948; see also its 2nd edn. 1968). A. A. Rogow's *The Labour Government and British Industry 1945–1951* (Oxford, 1955) is penetrating. See also L. Hannah, 'A Failed Experiment: The State Ownership of Industry', in R. Floud and P. Johnson, *The Cambridge Economic History of Modern Britain*, iii. *Structural Change and Growth, 1939–2000* (Cambridge, 2004), 84–111.

For **religion** see, on statistical aspects, R. Currie, A. Gilbert, and L. Horsley, *Churches and Churchgoers: Patterns of Church Growth in the British Isles since 1700* (Oxford, 1977); P. Brierley, *A Century of British Christianity: Historical Statistics 1900–1985 with Projections to 2000* (1985). M. Freeman's article 'Britain's Spiritual life: How can it be Deepened? Seebohm Rowntree, Russell Lavers, and the "Crisis of Belief" c.1946–54', *Journal of Religious History* (Feb. 2005) is important. A. Hastings, *A History of English Christianity 1920–1985* (1986) is fair-minded and wide-ranging, strongest on the Catholic tradition. G. Davie, *Religion in Britain since 1945: Believing without Belonging* (Oxford, 1994) provides an overview, and her article, '"An Ordinary God": The Paradox of Religion in Contemporary Britain', *British Journal of Sociology* (Sept. 1990) concisely gathers valuable statistics. See also P. Badham (ed.), *Religion, State and Society in Modern Britain* (1989). For a significant Catholic who abandoned the priesthood see C. A. Davis's autobiographical *A Question of Conscience* (1968).

On **education** D. Wardle, *English Popular Education 1780–1975* (Cambridge, 1976) and the Ministry of Education's *Education 1900–1950* (1951) provide useful background. For school architecture see M. Seaborne and R. Lowe's lavish *The English School: Its Architecture and Organization*, ii. *1870–1970* (1977). S. L. Hunter outlines *The Scottish Educational System* (2nd edn., Oxford, 1971) in businesslike fashion.

For **recreation** see B. S. Rowntree and G. R. Lavers, *English Life and Leisure: A Social Study* (1951). For an excellent article on the growth of punctuality see D. Parkes and N. Thrift, 'Time Spacemakers and Entrainment', *Transactions of the Institute of British Geographers* (1979).

For **political institutions**, B. Harrison's *The Transformation of British Politics 1860–1995* (Oxford, 1996) provides an overall historical introduction. See also J. P. Mackintosh's essential *The British Cabinet* (3rd edn. 1977); G. C. Baugh, 'Government Grants in Aid of the Rates in England and Wales, 1889–1990', *Historical Research* (1992); D. E. Butler, *British General Elections since 1945* (Oxford, 1989).

3. THE UNITED KINGDOM AND THE WORLD

For an especially penetrating overall perspective see D. Sanders, *Losing an Empire, Finding a Role: British Foreign Policy since 1945* (London and Basingstoke, 1990). M. Charlton's *The Price of Victory* (1983) is also valuable.

Internationalism in its cultural dimension has not been well served: there is no good book on the UK's relations with the United Nations, for instance. On the cultural dimension see B. King (ed.), *The Oxford English Literary History*. xiii. *1948–2000: The Internationalization of English Literature* (Oxford, 2004), and B. Brothers and J. M. Gergits (eds.), *British Travel Writers, 1940–1997* ('Dictionary of Literary Biography', 204; Detroit, 1999).

On **defence and warfare** see E. Grove, *Vanguard to Trident: British Naval Policy since World War Two* (Annapolis, Md., 1987); see also A. J. Pierre, *Nuclear Politics: The British Experience with an Independent Strategic Force 1939–1970* (1972). Visually striking is W. D. Cocroft and R. J. C. Thomas, *Cold War: Building for Nuclear Confrontation 1946–1989*, ed. P. S. Barnwell (Swindon, 2003). There is no really good book on national service, but see D. Baxter's evocative *Two Years to Do* (1959), and R. I. Raitt, 'National Service 1945–1961', *Army Quarterly* (Oct. 1961). For the Sandys defence cutback see *Defence: Outline of Future Policy. Presented by the Minister of Defence to Parliament . . . April 1957* (*Parl. Papers* 1956–7 xxiii, Cmnd. 124); and L. Martin's penetrating 'The Market for Strategic Ideas in Britain: The "Sandys" Era', *American Political Science Review* (Jan. 1962). P. M. Hammond and G. Carter, *From Biological Warfare to Healthcare: Porton Down, 1940–2000* (Basingstoke, 2001) is important.

The **Campaign for Nuclear Disarmament** has been well covered. See F. Parkin, *Middle Class Radicalism: The Social Bases of the British Campaign for Nuclear Disarmament* (Manchester, 1968); C. Pritchard and R. Taylor, *The Protest Makers: The British Nuclear Disarmament Movement of 1958–1965. Twenty Years On* (Oxford, 1980); C. Driver, *The Disarmers: A Study in Protest* (1964); and P. Byrne, *The Campaign for Nuclear Disarmament* (1988).

For the **Suez crisis (1956)** see L. D. Epstein, *British Politics in the Suez Crisis* (1964) and H. Thomas, *The Suez Affair* (rev. edn., Harmondsworth, 1970). On the **Anglo-American relationship** see D. C. Watt, *Succeeding John Bull: America in Britain's Place 1900–1975* (Cambridge, 1984); W. R. Louis and H. Bull (eds.), *The 'Special Relationship': Anglo-American Relations since 1945* (Oxford, 1986); J. Dickie, *'Special' No More: Anglo-American Relations. Rhetoric and Reality* (1994). See also *The Churchill–Eisenhower Correspondence 1953–1955* (Chapel Hill, NC, 1990), and P. Boyle (ed.), *The Eden–Eisenhower Correspondence, 1955–57* (Chapel Hill, NC, 2005).

On the **European Economic Community** H. Young's *This Blessed Plot: Britain and Europe from Churchill to Blair* (1998) comes from an enthusiast, but is splendidly clear and synoptic. An admirable reference work is T. Bainbridge with A. Teasdale, *The Penguin Companion to European Union* (corrected edn. 1996). See also N. E. A. Moore's lucid and well-informed *The Decimalisation of Britain's Currency* (1973) and O. J. Daddow (ed.), *Harold Wilson and European Integration. Britain's Second Application to Join the EEC* (2003), especially chapters by Parr, Ludlow and Toomey.

On **empire and Commonwealth** see J. Strachey, *The End of Empire* (1959); J. Darwin, *Britain and Decolonisation* (1988); R. Hyam, *Britain's Declining Empire: The*

Road to Decolonisation, 1918–1968 (Cambridge, 2007); and S. Ward (ed.), *British Culture and the End of Empire* (Manchester, 2001), a wide-ranging collection. The editors' first chapter, 'An Orderly Retreat? Policing the End of Empire', in D. M. Anderson and D. Killingray (eds.), *Policing and Decolonisation: Politics, Nationalism and the Police, 1917–1965* (Manchester, 1992) provides a valuable overview; the detailed area studies in chapters 5–9 have the great advantage of drawing heavily upon unpublished British government material. Two books published in 2005 portray the less acceptable face of colonialism: David Anderson's *Histories of the Hanged: Britain's Dirty War in Kenya and the End of the Empire* and Caroline Elkins's *Britain's Gulag: The Brutal End of Empire in Kenya*. On race in South Africa see R. Fieldhouse, *Anti-Apartheid: A History of the Movement in Britain. A Study in Pressure Group Politics* (2005). For **overseas aid** see M. Black, *A Cause for Our Times: OXFAM. The First Fifty Years* (Oxford, 1992).

4. THE FACE OF THE COUNTRY

On **agriculture** see J. K. Bowers, 'British Agricultural Policy since the Second World War', *Agricultural History Review*, 33 (1985). D. K. Britton and K. Ingersent, 'Trends in Concentration in British Agriculture', *Journal of Agricultural Economics*, 16 (1964); A. D. Grigg, *English Agriculture: An Historical Perspective* (Oxford, 1989); T. Beresford, *We Plough the Fields: Agriculture in Britain* (Harmondsworth, 1975); J. G. S. and F. Donaldson with D. Barber, *Farming in Britain Today* (1969); J.Hutchinson, *Farming and Food Supply: The Interdependence of Countryside and Town* (Cambridge, 1972).

For **archaeology** see the informative I. Longworth and J. Cherry, *Archaeology in Britain since 1945: New Directions* (1986); T. Gregory's influential article 'Metal-Detecting in Archaeological Excavation', *Antiquity*, 58 (1984); and C. Dobinson and S. Denison's informative *Metal Detecting and Archaeology in England* (London and York, 1995).

On **the environment** L. Gardiner's *The Changing Face of Britain from the Air* (1989) includes aerial photographs of the UK taken in the 1930s and 1980s whose contrasts illuminate change in, for example, urban sprawl and coastline erosion. See also A. W. Gilg, *Countryside Planning: The First Three Decades 1945–76* (1979), and the Countryside Commission's informative *The Planning of the Coastline: A Report on a Study of Coastal Preservation and Development in England and Wales* (1970). G. F. Peterken's *Woodland Conservation and Management* (2nd edn., 1993) is historically aware and valuable. O. Rackham's *Trees and Woodland in the British Landscape* (rev. edn. 1996) is wide-ranging and very well informed. Path-breaking was the committee chaired by Sir A. Wilson on the problem of noise; see its admirable *Final Report* (1963, Cmnd. 2056). See also the Department of the Environment's *This Common Inheritance: Britain's Environmental Strategy* (1990). J. Hassan introduces a neglected historical topic with his *A History of Water in Modern England and Wales* (Manchester, 1998). H. T. Bernstein, 'The Mysterious Disappearance of Edwardian London Fog', *London Journal*, 1/2 (Nov. 1975) is valuable. For floods see D. Barker, *Harvest Home: The Official Story of the Great Floods of 1947 and their Sequel* (1948); H. E. P. Grieve, *The Great Tide: The Story of the 1953 Flood Disaster in Essex*

(Chelmsford, 1959); D. Summers, *The East Coast Floods* (Newton Abbot, 1978); and the detailed and well-informed S. K. Gilbert and R. Horner, *The Thames Barrier* (1984). For oil pollution see R. Petrow's detailed *The Black Tide: In the Wake of the Torrey Canyon* (1968).

On **transport** the Ministry of Transport's periodic compendia *Transport Statistics* are valuable, and see M. A. Cundill and B. A. Shane, *Trends in Road Goods Traffic 1962–77* (1980). Good secondary works on the history of canals, air travel, motorways, and commercial seafaring are much needed, and a good history of the telephone in the UK since 1945 has become urgent. One of the few authors to transcend transport antiquarianism is C. Loft, with his excellent *Government, the Railways and the Modernization of Britain: Beeching's Last Trains* (2006). T. R. Gourvish has published a huge two-volume history of British Rail; its first volume is *British Railways 1948–73: A Business History* (Cambridge, 1986). For canals see R. W. Squires, *Canals Revived: The Story of the Waterway Restoration Movement* (Bradford-on-Avon, 1979), but more is needed. D. Starkie's *The Motorway Age: Road and Traffic Policies in Post-War Britain* (Oxford, 1982) makes a good start on an important subject; G. Charlesworth's *A History of British Motorways* (1984) and his *A History of the Transport and Road Research Laboratory 1933–1983* (Aldershot, 1987) are also valuable, but historians have yet to give the motorway system's full impact due attention. W. Glanville's 'Roads and Road Usage: The Application of Science', *Proceedings of the Institution of Civil Engineers* (July 1959) is important. Valuable raw material has been collected by the Motorway Archive; see especially its first two volumes, generously illustrated: Sir P. and R. Baldwin (eds.), *The Motorway Achievement*, i. *The British Motorway System: Visualisation, Policy and Administration* (2004); and R. Bridle and J. Porter (eds.), *The Motorway Achievement*, ii. *Frontiers of Knowledge and Practice* (2002). From the opposite side see J. Tyme's trenchant *Motorways versus Democracy: Public Inquiries into Road Proposals and their Political Significance* (1978) and P. Hall, 'London's Motorways', in his *Great Planning Disasters* (1980), whose other topics include Concorde, and London's third airport. See also D. A. Hart, *Strategic Planning in London: The Rise and Fall of the Primary Road Network* (Oxford, 1976).

On **towns and cities** B. White's *The Literature and Study of Urban and Regional Planning* (1974) is a splendid work of reference. See also F. Schaffer's excellent *The New Town Story* (1970). On **housing** R. H. Duclaud-Williams, *The Politics of Housing in Britain and France* (1978) is illuminating on the period 1965–72; A. A. Nevett's *Housing Taxation and Subsidies: A Study of Housing in the United Kingdom* (1966) explains thoroughly how the system then worked. See also the Building Societies Association's *Compendium of Building Society Statistics* (6th edn. 1986); the Association also published *Facts and Figures*, a *Bulletin*, and a *Yearbook*. An important theme is treated in C. L. Bielckus *et al.*, *Second Homes in England and Wales* (Wye College Studies in Rural Land Use, Report 11, Dec. 1972). On architectural style see S. Games (ed.), *Pevsner on Art and Architecture: The Radio Talks* (2002).

For **non-English nationality and culture** see R. F. Foster, *Modern Ireland 1600–1972* (1988); R. Coupland's still valuable *Welsh and Scottish Nationalism: A Study* (1954); and J. G. Kellas, *Modern Scotland: The Nation since 1870* (1968).

M. Watson discusses the important subject of *Being English in Scotland* (Edinburgh, 2003). For Wales see K. O. Morgan, *Rebirth of a Nation: Wales 1880–1980* (Oxford, 1982); J. Williams, *Digest of Welsh Historical Statistics* (2 vols., Aberystwyth, 1985); and A. Butt Philip, *The Welsh Question: Nationalism in Welsh Politics 1945–1970* (Cardiff, 1975). The Central Advisory Council of Education for Wales's *Report on the Place of Welsh and English in the Schools of Wales* (1953) is valuable, and see J. Aitchison and H. Carter's well-informed *A Geography of the Welsh Language 1961–1991* (Cardiff, 1994).

5. THE SOCIAL STRUCTURE

For **monarchy** see D. Cannadine, 'The Context, Performance and Meaning of Ritual: The British Monarchy and the "Invention of Tradition", c.1820–1977', in E. Hobsbawm and T. Ranger (eds.), *The Invention of Tradition* (Cambridge, 1984). The best of several biographies of George VI is by Sarah Bradford (1989). B. Pimlott's *The Queen* (1996) is the best of several on Elizabeth II. Valuable, too, is J. Dimbleby, *The Prince of Wales* (1994). See also J. Pope-Hennessy, *Queen Mary 1867–1953* (1959); P. Ziegler, *Mountbatten: The Official Biography* (1985); J. Walker, *The Queen has been Pleased: The British Honours System at Work* (1986); and S. Martin, *The Order of Merit: One Hundred Years of Matchless Honour* (2007).

For the **upper classes** F. M. L. Thompson's four excellent essays on 'English Landed Society in the Twentieth Century' in successive volumes of the *TRHS*, should have appeared in book form: 'Property: Collapse and Survival' (1990); 'New Poor and New Rich' (1991), 'Self-Help and Outdoor Relief' (1992); 'Prestige without Power?' (1993). On the distribution of wealth see, as a general introduction, W. D. Rubinstein, *Wealth and Inequality in Britain* (1986); C. H. Feinstein, 'The Equalizing of Wealth in Britain Since the Second World War', *Oxford Review of Economic Policy*, 12/1 (1996); J. Revell, 'Changes in the Social Distribution of Property in Britain during the Twentieth Century', in *Third International Conference of Economic History, Munich 1965*, i (1968); and Royal Commission on the Distribution of Income and Wealth, *Report No. 1* (Cmnd. 6171, 1975). On lifestyle see M. Cornforth, *The Country Houses of England: 1948–1998* (1998); J. M. Robinson, *The Latest Country Houses 1945–83* (1983). F. MacCarthy, *Last Curtsey: The End of the Debutantes* (2006) does not quite live up to its bravura beginning, but is the best that there is on an important subject, which is also well treated in M.Pringle's *Dance Little Ladies: The Days of the Debutante* (1977), amply illustrated, with richly evocative interviews.

The middle classes remain relatively neglected, but see G. Millerson, *The Qualifying Associations: A Study in Professionalization* (1964); D. Lockwood, *The Blackcoated Worker: A Study in Class Consciousness* (1958). For the counselling professions see Paul Halmos's interesting and somewhat neglected *The Faith of the Counsellors* (2nd edn. 1978). For service-sector growth see R. F. Elliott, 'The Growth of White Collar Employment in Great Britain 1951–1971', *British Journal of Industrial Relations*, 15 (1977).

For **the working class** in the 1950s, the studies by Ferdynand Zweig cited in the footnotes are evocative. See also N. Dennis, F. Henriques, and C. Slaughter,

Coal is Our Life: An Analysis of a Yorkshire Mining Community (1956); M. Kerr, *The People of Ship Street* (1958); and the influential works of the Institute for Community Studies: P. Willmott and M. Young, *Family and Class in a London Suburb* (1960), and M. Young and P. Willmott, *The Symmetrical Family: A Study of Work and Leisure in the London Region* (1973). The many studies of communities outside London published by empirical sociologists in these years are discussed in R. Frankenberg's *Communities in Britain: Social Life in Town and Country* (1965). For the 1960s J. H. Goldthorpe's three volumes on *The Affluent Worker* (Cambridge, 1968–9) are of central importance. R. Hoggart's *The Uses of Literacy: Aspects of Working Class Life with Special Reference to Publications and Entertainments* (1957) influentially worried about cultural changes within the working class.

For **trade unions** the overall statistical picture appears in P. A. J. Waddington, 'Trade Union Membership Concentration, 1892–1987: Development and Causation', *British Journal of Industrial Relations* (Sept. 1993); see also the important work by G. S. Bain, *Trade Union Growth and Recognition* (Royal Commission on Trade Unions and Employers' Associations, Research Papers, 6, 1967); R. Price and G. Bain, 'Union Growth Revisited: 1948–1974', *British Journal of Industrial Relations* (1976). R. Taylor provides a valuable synthesis in his *The Trade Union Question in British Politics: Government and Unions since 1945* (Oxford, 1993), and R. Currie's *Industrial Politics* (Oxford, 1979) is penetrating. The Royal Commission on Trade Unions and Employers' Associations 1965–1968, *Report* (Chairman Lord Donovan, Cmnd. 3623, 1968) is essential. For biographies see G. Goodman, *The Awkward Warrior: Frank Cousins. His Life and Times* (1979) on the TGWU's General Secretary 1956–69; E. Silver, *Victor Feather, T.U.C.* (1973), on the TUC's General Secretary 1969–73. See also A. Horner, *Incorrigible Rebel* (1960), by the NUM's National Secretary 1946–59; and Jack Jones's *Union Man* (1986), on the TGWU's General Secretary 1969–78.

On **poverty** see P. Townsend's massive *Poverty in the United Kingdom: A Survey of Household Resources and Standards of Living* (1979); and Frank Field's very detailed *Losing Out: The Emergence of Britain's Underclass* (Oxford, 1989).

For **immigrant/minority groups** S. Castles, *Here for Good: Western Europe's New Ethnic Minorities* (1984) provides a good introduction. R. Hansen's *Citizenship and Immigration in Post-War Britain: The Institutional Origins of a Multicultural Nation* (Oxford, 2000) is important on the legislative side. On particular minorities, R. E. Oakley, 'Cypriot Migration and Settlement in Britain' (Oxford D.Phil. thesis, 1971) and C. Peach's 'The Force of West Indian Island Identity in Britain', in C. G. Clarke, D. Ley, C. Peach, and P. Paget (eds.), *Geography and Ethnic Pluralism* (1984) are excellent. E. Pilkington's *Beyond the Mother Country: West Indians and the Notting Hill White Riots* (1988) gains much in context and perspective from local knowledge and black reminiscence. For the Irish see D. Garvey, 'The History of Migration Flows in the Republic of Ireland', *Population Trends* (Spring 1985). For Poles see K. Sword's excellent *Identity in Flux: The Polish Community in Britain* (1996), which takes the story up to the 1990s; also P. D. Stachura (ed.), *The Poles in Britain, 1940–2000: From Betrayal to Assimilation* (2004). For the Italians see T. Colpi, *The Italian Factor. The Italian Community in Great Britain* (Edinburgh, 1991), and

R. King's two articles: 'Italian Migration to Great Britain', *Geography* (July 1977); and 'Italians in Britain: An Idiosyncratic Immigration', *ATI: Association of Teachers of Italian Journal* (Autumn 1979). For travellers see J. Okely, *The Traveller-Gypsies* (Cambridge, 1983).

6. FAMILY AND WELFARE

D. A. Coleman and J. Salt's fine *The British Population: Patterns, Trends, and Processes* (Oxford, 1992) is essential for all demographic aspects. Articles by J. Haskey in *Population Trends*, cited in numerous footnotes, shed a flood of light on demographic issues. See also M. Britton and N. Edison, 'The Changing Balance of the Sexes in England and Wales, 1851–2001', *Population Trends* (Winter 1986).

On **the family** see M. Anderson's classic article, 'The Emergence of the Modern Life Cycle in Britain', *Social History* (Jan. 1985), admirably and concisely informative on major issues. See also B. J. Elliott, 'Demographic Trends in Domestic Life, 1945–87', in D. Clark (ed.), *Marriage, Domestic Life and Social Change: Writings for Jacqueline Burgoyne (1944–88)* (1991). On legal aspects the essential work is S. Cretney, *Family Law in the Twentieth Century: A History* (Oxford, 2003). M. Young and P. Willmott's *Family and Kinship in East London* (1957) illuminates working-class family life. See also Department of Health and Social Security, *Report of the [Finer] Committee on One-Parent Families* (1974, Cmnd. 5629).

On **sexuality** see, for young people, M. Schofield, *The Sexual Behaviour of Young People* (2nd edn. 1968). For abortion, see P. Ferris, *The Nameless: Abortion in Britain Today* (1966); K. Hindell and M. Simms, *Abortion Law Reformed* (1971); J. Keown, *Abortion, Doctors and the Law: Some Aspects of the Legal Regulation of Abortion in England from 1803 to 1982* (Cambridge, 1988). For homosexuality see J. Weeks's pioneering *Coming Out: Homosexual Politics in Britain from the Nineteenth Century to the Present* (rev. edn. 1990), and the even more pioneering 'G. Westwood' [pseud. for M. Schofield], *Society and the Homosexual* (1952) and *A Minority: A Report on the Life of the Male Homosexual in Great Britain* (1960). See also M. Houlbrook's 'The Private World of Public Urinals: London 1918–57', *London Journal*, 25/1 (2000) and his *Queer London: Perils and Pleasures in the Sexual Metropolis, 1918–1957* (Chicago, 2005). There are several studies of individual homosexuals, of which the most important is A. Grey, *Quest for Justice: Towards Homosexual Emancipation* (1992); see also P. Wildeblood, *Against the Law* (1955), J. Lahr's remarkable *Prick up your Ears: The Biography of Joe Orton* (1978), and Lahr's edition of Orton's even more remarkable *The Orton Diaries* (1986). Simon Raven is informative and unmoralistic on 'The Male Prostitute in London' in his *Boys will be Boys* (1963). For lesbians see R. Jennings, *A Lesbian History of Britain: Love and Sex between Women since 1500* (Oxford, 2007); and for transsexuals see R. Cowell, *Roberta Cowell's Story* (1954).

For **women** see E. James, 'Women at Work in Twentieth Century Britain: The Changing Structure of Female Employment', *Manchester School*, 30 (Sept. 1962); Political and Economic Planning, *Sex, Career and Family* (1971); A. Hunt, *A Survey of Women's Employment* (2 vols., 1968). For domestic violence see E. Pizzey, *Scream Quietly or the Neighbours will Hear* (Harmondsworth, 1974).

On the rearing of **children** see C. Hardyment's *Dream Babies: Childcare Advice from John Locke to Gina Ford* (2nd edn. 2007), broad-ranging in time and space; it tackles neglected territory, but lacks adequate context, and is more concerned with attitudes than with conduct. J. M. Tanner, 'The Trend towards Earlier Physical Maturation', in J. E. Meade and A. S. Parkes (eds.), *Biological Aspects of Social Problems: A Symposium Held by the Eugenics Society in October 1964* (1965) is valuable. N. Parton, *The Politics of Child Abuse* (1985) covers an area of growing concern in this period. On the naming of children see S. Wilson, *The Means of Naming: A Social and Cultural History of Personal Naming in Western Europe* (1998); L. A. Dunkling, *First Names First* (1977); and E. Merry, *First Names: The Definitive Guide to Popular Names in England and Wales 1944–1994* (1995). On literature written for children see two 'Dictionary of Literary Biography' volumes: D. R. Hettinga and G. D. Schmidt (eds.), *British Children's Writers, 1914–1960* (160, Detroit, 1996); and C. C. Hunt (ed.), *British Children's Writers since 1960* (161, Detroit, 1996).

For the factual aspects of **public welfare** the DHSS published *A Guide to Health and Social Service Statistics* (1974); see also *Social Services Yearbook* (1983–); and the Chartered Institute of Public Finance and Accountancy's annual *Personal Social Services Statistics* (1974–). For interpretation see J. F. Sleeman, *The Welfare State: Its Aims, Benefits and Costs* (1973); J. Hills, *The State of Welfare: The Welfare State in Britain since 1974* (Oxford, 1990). For a comparative perspective see H. L. Wilensky's important *The Welfare State and Equality. Structural and Ideological Roots of Public Expenditures* (Berkeley, Calif., 1975).

On **health and disability** For an excellent general introduction see V. Berridge, *Health and Society in Britain since 1939* (Cambridge, 1999). For a short introduction to political aspects see C. Webster, *The National Health Service: A Political History* (Oxford, 1998); his two-volume *The Health Services since the War*, i (1988) covers the period up to 1957, ii (1996), 1958–79, and treats the subject more fully. I. Loudon, J. Horder, and C. Webster (eds.), *General Practice under the National Health Service 1948–1997: The First Fifty Years* (Oxford, 1998) tackles important territory not covered elsewhere. For an excellent portrait of how it all worked in the early 1950s see S. Taylor, *Good General Practice: A Report of a Survey* (1954). The Department of Education and Science's *The School Health Service, 1908–1974: Report of the Chief Medical Officer of the Department* (1975) is informative. On the incidence of disease/disability see Sir R. Doll, 'Major Epidemics of the Twentieth Century', *Journal of the Royal Statistical Society*, series A, 105 (1987); P. E. H. Hair, 'Deaths from Violence in Britain: A Tentative Secular Survey', *Population Studies* (Mar. 1971), 9; and Office of Population Censuses and Surveys, *Trends in Mortality 1951–1975* (1978). D. Tyrell and M. Fielder, *Cold Wars: The Fight against the Common Cold* (Oxford, 2002) readably chronicles the Common Cold Unit's failure to find a cure in 1946–89. For the Labour MP who campaigned on behalf of the deaf see J. Ashley's autobiographical *Journey into Silence* (1973) and *Acts of Defiance* (1992).

On **old age** generally see P. Thane, *Old Age in English History: Past Experiences, Present Issues* (Oxford, 2000). Other important dimensions are covered in M. R. Miller's valuable Kent Ph.D. thesis 'The Development of Retirement Pensions Policy in Britain from 1945 to 1986: A Case of State and Occupational Welfare' (1987), which cultivates difficult and neglected territory, though see also L. Hannah, *Inventing Retirement: The Development of Occupational Pensions in Britain* (Cambridge, 1986). P. Townsend's *The Family Life of Old People: An Inquiry in East London* (1957) is evocative.

On **attitudes to death** see G. Williams's trail-blazing *The Sanctity of Life and the Criminal Law* (1958). See also L. Bulusu and M. Alderson, 'Suicides 1950–82', *Population Trends*, 35 (Spring 1984). For hospices see H. L. G. Hughes, '*...Peace at the Last': A Survey of Terminal Care in the United Kingdom. A Report to the Calouste Gulbenkian Foundation* (1960); S. Du Boulay, *Cicely Saunders: Founder of the Modern Hospice Movement* (1984); and C. Saunders, *Selected Letters 1959–1999* (Oxford, 2002). The only serious historical study of euthanasia is N. D. A. Kemp, *'Merciful Release': The History of the British Euthanasia Movement* (Manchester, 2002).

7. INDUSTRY AND COMMERCE

A. Cairncross, *The British Economy since 1945* (Oxford, 1992) provides a lucid introduction; J. F. Wright, *Britain in the Age of Economic Management* (Oxford, 1973) is clear and unjustly neglected. R. Floud and D. McCloskey (eds.), *Economic History of Britain since 1700* (2nd edn. 1994), iii, contains important essays on many aspects of economic history, most notably those by C. H. Feinstein, A. K. Cairncross, and S. N. Broadberry. Likewise R. Floud and P. Johnson (eds.), *The Cambridge Economic History of Modern Britain*, iii. *Structural Change and Growth, 1939–2000* (Cambridge, 2004)—see especially the contributions from Broadberry, Hannah, Tomlinson, Johnson, and Millward. An essential reference work is D. J. Jeremy (ed.), *Dictionary of Business Biography: A Biographical Dictionary of Business Leaders Active in Britain in the Period 1860–1980* (5 vols., and supplement, 1984–6). R. C. O. Matthews's 'Why has Britain had Full Employment since the War?', *Economic Journal* (Sept. 1968) is important. W. D. Rubinstein, *Capitalism, Culture, and Decline in Britain 1750–1990* (1993) is wide-ranging and provocative. A. Cairncross and N. Watts in *The Economic Section 1939–1961: A Study in Economic Advising* (1989) view economic policy-making from within. See also S. N. Broadberry 'The Impact of the World Wars on the Long Run Performance of the British Economy', *Oxford Review of Economic Policy*, 4/1 (1988). J. Tomlinson's *The Politics of Decline: Understanding Post-War Britain* (Harlow, 2000) and 'Inventing "Decline": The Falling Behind of the British Economy in the Postwar Years', *Economic History Review* (Nov. 1996) tackle the important and interesting subject of changing attitudes to the economy.

For **incomes policies** see W. H. Fishbein's neglected but valuable *Wage Restraint by Consensus: Britain's Search for an Incomes Policy Agreement, 1965–79* (1984); S. Brittan and P. Lilley, *The Delusion of Incomes Policy* (1977); B. Harrison, 'Incomes Policies in Britain since 1940: A Study in Political Economy', in K. Bruland and P. O'Brien (eds.), *From Family Firms to Corporate Capitalism: Essays in Business and Industrial History in Honour of Peter Mathias* (Oxford, 1998). For two good studies of the Prices and Incomes Board see A. Fels, *The British Prices and Incomes Board* (Cambridge, 1972) and J. Mitchell, *The National Board for Prices and Incomes* (1972).

For the practical outcome of policy see G. Owen's readable and wide-ranging *From Empire to Europe: The Decline and Revival of British Industry since the Second World War* (1999). USA investment in the UK is exhaustively covered in J. H. Dunning's *American Investment in British Manufacturing Industry* (1958). For particular industries see (on cars) G. Bardsley, *Issigonis: The Official Biography* (Thriplow, 2005); B. M. D. Smith's informative *The History of the British Motorcycle Industry 1945–1975* (Birmingham, 1981); L. Hannah, *Engineers, Managers and Politicians: The First Fifteen Years of Nationalised Electricity Supply in Britain* (1982); and R. Williams, *The Nuclear Power Decisions: British Policies 1953–78* (1980).

For **regional economic contrasts** see B. E. Coates and E. M. Rawstron, *Regional Variations in Britain: Studies in Economic and Social Geography* (1971); its section on employment is particularly useful. See also G. Manners and D. Morris, *Office Policy in Britain: A Review* (Norwich, 1986); R. Martin, 'The Political Economy of Britain's North–South Divide', *Transactions of the Institute of British Geographers* (1988); and R. Saville (ed.), *The Economic Development of Modern Scotland 1950–1980* (Edinburgh, 1985). On the changing composition and experience of **the workforce** see I. S. Greeves, *London Docks 1800–1980: A Civil Engineering History* (1980). For training of the workforce see J. Sheldrake and S. A. Vickerstaff's concise and well-informed *History of Industrial Training in Britain* (Aldershot, 1987) and P. E. Willis's remarkable and uninhibited *Learning to Labour: How Working Class Kids Get Working Class Jobs* (Aldershot, 1977). On the accountancy aspect, two articles are helpful: D. Matthews, M. Anderson, and J. R. Edwards, 'The Rise of the Professional Accountant in British Management', *Economic History Review* (Aug. 1997), and D. Matthews, 'The Business Doctors: Accountants in British Management from the Nineteenth Century to the Present Day', *Business History* (July 1998). See also E. Jones, *True and Fair: A History of Price Waterhouse* (1995).

For **banking and finance** R. C. Michie's *The City of London: Continuity and Change, 1850–1990* (London and Basingstoke, 1992) is concise and excellent. Also valuable are J. S. Fforde, *The Bank of England and Public Policy 1941–1958* (Cambridge, 1992); R. Roberts and D. Kynaston (eds.), *The Bank of England: Money, Power and Influence 1694–1994* (Oxford, 1995); D. Kynaston, *The City of London*, iv. *A Club No More 1945–2000* (2001). J. R. H. Pringle's *A Guide to Banking in Britain* (1973) is informative and lucid.

Few historians have focused on **advertising**, but see T. R. Nevett, *Advertising in Britain: A History* (1982); D. West, 'Multinational Competition in the British Advertising Agency Business, 1936–1987', *Business History Review* (Autumn 1988); and J. Tunstall, *The Advertising Man in London Advertising Agencies* (1964).

For **consumerism** see J. Obelkevich's 'Consumption' in J. Obelkevich and P. Catterall (eds.), *Understanding Post-War British Society* (1994), and S. Bowden and A. Offer, 'Household Appliances and the Use of Time: The United States and Britain since the 1920s', *Economic History Review*, 47 (1994). See also T. A. B. Corley, *Domestic Electrical Appliances* (1966). J. Benson and G. Shaw (eds.), *The Retailing Industry*, iii (1999) is edited too lightly, but it usefully collects informative essays on many aspects of retailing, including good studies of the early supermarkets, the co-op movement, and the impact of urban geography and planning. R. Coopey, S. O'Connell, and

D. Porter's *Mail Order Retailing in Britain: A Business and Social History* (Oxford, 2005) is excellent. For a shopkeeping entrepreneur see M. Corina, *Pile it High, Sell it Cheap: The Authorised Biography of Sir John Cohen* (1971). On diet C. Driver's *The British at Table 1940–1980* (1983) was a pioneering work. See also D. H. Buss, 'The British Diet since the End of Food Rationing', in C. Geissler and D. J. Oddy (eds.), *Food, Diet and Economic Change Past and Present* (Leicester, 1993); and Ministry of Agriculture, Fisheries and Food, *Fifty Years of the National Food Survey 1940–1990* (1991), which has ample statistics on dietary change. For mass catering see Charles Forte, *Forte* (rev. edn. 1997). There is no good book on vegetarianism. On drink, J. A. Spring and D. H. Buss, 'British Drinking Patterns for the Last 300 Years', *Nature* (1977) provides a wide perspective. See also T. R. Gourvish and R. G. Wilson, *The Brewing Industry 1830–1980* (Cambridge, 1994).

8. INTELLECT AND CULTURE

On **religion**, for statistical aspects see R. Currie, A. Gilbert, and L. Horsley, *Churches and Churchgoers: Patterns of Church Growth in the British Isles since 1700* (Oxford, 1977); P. Brierley, *A Century of British Christianity: Historical Statistics 1900–1985 with Projections to 2000* (1985); and Statistical Unit of the Central Board of Finance, *Facts and Figures about the Church of England* (1962). G. Davie, *Religion in Britain since 1945: Believing without Belonging* (Oxford, 1994) provides an overview. A. Hastings, *A History of English Christianity 1920–1985* (1986) is fair-minded and wide-ranging, strongest on the Catholic tradition. See also P. Badham (ed.), *Religion, State and Society in Modern Britain* (1989); D. J. Jeremy, *Capitalists and Christians. Business Leaders and the Churches in Britain 1900–1960* (Oxford, 1990), and H. McLeod's valuably comparative *Religion and the People of Western Europe 1789–1970* (Oxford, 1981).

Important documents on **schools** appear in J. S. Maclure (ed.), *Educational Documents: England and Wales. 1816 to the Present Day* (3rd edn. 1973). The Department of Education's regular publications of examination results represent a rich resource that historians have scarcely exploited: *Education in 1951*, *Education in 1961*, etc. Education history tends to be stronger on administration than on the classroom, but for three memoirs by resilient teachers in state schools see M. Croft, *Spare the Rod* (1954); E. Blishen, *Roaring Boys: A Schoolmaster's Agony* (1955); and E. R. Braithwaite, *To Sir, With Love* (1959). P. L. Masters, *Preparatory Schools Today: Some Facts and Inferences* (1966) usefully discusses this neglected area. On the 'public' (later 'independent') schools, J. Rae, *The Public School Revolution: Britain's Independent Schools. 1964–1979* (1981) is illuminating.

The report of the Committee on Higher Education, chaired by L. Robbins (1961–3, Cmd. 2154) threw a flood of light on **universities**. For a short introduction on UK university history see R. Anderson, *British Universities Past and Present* (2006). There are many histories of individual universities, most notably C. N. L. Brooke, *A History of the University of Cambridge*, iv. *1870–1990* (Cambridge, 1993); T. W. Bamford, *The University of Hull: The First Fifty Years* (Oxford, 1978); M. Moss, J. F. Munro, and R. H. Trainor (eds.), *University, City and State: The University of Glasgow since 1870* (Edinburgh, 2000); R. Dahrendorf, *LSE: A History of the London School of Economics* *and Political Science 1895–1995* (Oxford, 1995); and the collaborative *The History of the University of Oxford,* viii. *The Twentieth Century,* ed. B. Harrison (Oxford, 1994). Keele University's experimental origins are captured in W. B. Gallie, *A New University: A. D. Lindsay and the Keele Experiment* (1960). A. H. Halsey and M. A. Trow, *The British Academics* (1971) marshals ample information on university teachers, and J. Carswell, *Government and the Universities in Britain: Programme and Performance, 1960–1980* (Cambridge, 1986) is invaluable on governmental aspects. M. Sanderson, *The Universities and British Industry 1850–1970* (1972) pursues an important overall theme. For two iconic intellectuals, both philosophers, see M. Ignatieff, *Isaiah Berlin* (1998), and R. W. Clark, *The Life of Bertrand Russell* (1975), together with the third volume of Russell's *Autobiography* (1968), covering the years 1944–67. Russell's *Selected Letters,* ii, ed. N. Griffin (2001) are primarily concerned with his efforts for peace, but are illuminating on CND's internal workings. On overall intellectual trends see B. Harrison, 'Professionalism and Populism in British Intellectual Life since 1945', in J. E. Myhre (ed.), *Intellectuals in the Public Sphere in Britain and Norway after World War II* (Oslo, 2008). See also P. B. Dematteis, P. S. Fosl, and L. B. McHenry (eds.), *British Philosophers, 1800–2000* ('Dictionary of Literary Biography', 262, Farmington Hills, Mich., 2002).

For university research see R. Simpson, *How the Ph.D. Came to Britain: A Century of Struggle for Postgraduate Education* (Guildford, 1983), which collects important information on postgraduate study. For **research in the natural sciences** see P. Gummett, *Scientists in Whitehall* (Manchester, 1980). Excellent on the organization of scientific research is B. Trend (chairman), *Report of the Committee of Enquiry into the Organisation of Civil Science* (Cmnd. 2171, 1963). D. Edgerton opens wide perspectives in his *Warfare State: Britain, 1920–1970* (Cambridge, 2006). See also A. Brown, *J. D. Bernal: The Sage of Science* (Oxford, 2005); F. S. Dainton, *Doubts and Certainties* (Sheffield, 2001); J. D. Watson, *The Double Helix: A Personal Account of the Discovery of the Structure of DNA* (1968). For **research in the arts and humanities** see R. J. Johnston's informative *Geography and Geographers: Anglo-American Human Geography since 1945* (1997). The contributors to R. Finnegan (ed.), *Participating in the Knowledge Society: Researchers Beyond the University Walls* (Basingstoke, 2005)—especially A. J. Hunt, J. J. D. Greenwood, D. Cummings, F. Webster, and Finnegan herself—provide a salutary reminder that much valuable research occurs outside universities.

To **literary history** the best short guide is R. Stevenson's *The British Novel since the Thirties: An Introduction* (1986). Valuable introductions are the two compendia edited by B. Ford, *The Pelican Guide to English Literature,* vii. *The Modern Age* (1971) and *The New Pelican Guide to English Literature,* viii. *From Orwell to Naipaul* (first published 1983, rev. edn. 1995). In the 'Dictionary of Literary Biography' series there are B. Oldsey (ed.), *British Novelists, 1930–1959* (15, 2 parts, Detroit, 1983); M. Mosely's three volumes on *British Novelists since 1960* (194, 207, 231, Detroit, 2nd–4th ser., 1998, 1999, 2001, respectively) and his *British and Irish Novelists since 1960* (271, Farmington Hills, Mich., 2003); see also D. Baldwin (ed.), *British Short-Fiction Writers* (139, Detroit, 1994); C. A. and D. Malcolm (eds.), *British and Irish Short-Fiction Writers, 1945–2000* (319, Farmington Hills, Mich., 2006); B. Benstock and T. F. Staley (eds.), *Mystery and Thriller Writers since 1940* (1st ser. 87, Detroit, 1989); and G. Macdonald (ed.), *British Mystery and Thriller Writers since 1960* (276, Farmington Hills, Mich., 2003), D. Harris-Fain (ed.), *British Fantasy and Science-Fiction Writers, 1918–1960* (255, Detroit, 2002) and *British Fantasy and Science-Fiction Writers since 1960* (261, Farmington Hills, Mich., 2002). For poetry see V. B. Sherry's three volumes: *Poets of Great Britain and Ireland, 1945–1960* (27, Detroit, 1984); and *Poets of Great Britain and Ireland since 1960* (40, 2 parts, Detroit, 1985). For women's popular fiction see J. McAleer, *Passion's Fortune: The Story of Mills and Boon* (Oxford, 1999).

There is much critical comment. Perceptive on many aspects are B. Bergonzi, *Wartime and Aftermath: English Literature and its Background 1939–60* (Oxford, 1993), and D. J. Taylor, *After the War: The Novel and England since 1945* (1993). Valuable biographies include A. Motion, *Philip Larkin: A Writer's Life* (1993), complemented by *The Selected Letters of Philip Larkin, 1940–1985*, ed. A. Thwaite (1992); and M. Drabble, *Angus Wilson: A Biography* (1995). See also S. Serafin (ed.), *Twentieth-Century British Literary Biographers* ('Dictionary of Literary Biography', 155, Detroit, 1995).

For **publishing**, see the statistical and comparative approaches adopted in R. E. Barker, *Books for All: A Study of International Book Trade* (Paris, 1956) and R. Escarpit, *The Book Revolution* (London and Paris, 1966). See also J. Rose and P. J. Anderson (eds.), *British Literary Publishing Houses, 1881–1965* ('Dictionary of Literary Biography', 112, Detroit, 1991).

On **cultural history** Robert Hewison presides with assurance over a wide range, especially with his *In Anger: Culture in the Cold War 1945–60* (1981); *Too Much: Art and Society in the Sixties, 1960–75* (1988); and *The Heritage Industry: Britain in a Climate of Decline* (1987). For sculpture see R. Berthoud, *The Life of Henry Moore* (1987); S. Festing, *Barbara Hepworth: A Life of Forms* (1995). Serious historical books are lacking on the recent history of ballet and painting, but for **design** see N. Whiteley, *Pop Design: Modernism to Mod* (1987); A. Forty, *Objects of Desire: Design and Society 1750–1980* (1986); and M. Farr's exhaustive and pioneering *Design in British Industry: A Mid-Century Survey* (Cambridge, 1955).

On **the theatre**, M. Billington's informative synopsis, the unfootnoted and oddly titled *State of the Nation: British Theatre since 1945* (2007), is self-confessedly partisan, at times autobiographical, and racily readable. Its laudable aim of relating theatre history to contemporary socio-political events, however, could succeed only if tied to something more than the analysis of plays and plots: to the sociology and even the business history of the theatre which he does not supply. Also valuable is Billington's *Life and Work of Harold Pinter* (1996). See also J. Bull, *Who Was Who in the Theatre, 1912–1976* (4 vols., 1976). In the 'Dictionary of Literary Biography' see S. Weintraub's four volumes: *Modern British Dramatists* (10, 2 parts, Detroit, 1982), *British Dramatists since World War II* (13, 2 parts, Detroit, 1982); and J. Bull's two volumes: *British and Irish Dramatists since World War II* (3rd ser. 245, Detroit, 2001; 4th ser. 310, Farmington Hills, Mich., 2005). See also J. Elsom, *Post-War British Theatre* (rev. edn. 1979); J. Croall, *Gielgud: A Theatrical Life 1904–2000* (2001); A. Holden's *Olivier* (1988); and J. C. Trewin's informative *Drama in Britain 1951–1964* (1965).

For an overview of **the press** see J. Cunningham, 'National Daily Newspapers and their Circulations in the UK, 1908–1978', *Journal of Advertising History* (Feb. 1981).

There are several histories of individual newspapers and periodicals, including *The History of 'The Times'*, v (1939–66, by I. McDonald, 1984), and vi (1966–81, by J. Grigg, 1993); D. Kynaston's *The 'Financial Times': A Centenary History* (1988); D. Cockett, *David Astor and the 'Observer'* (1991); H. Hobson, P. Knightley, and L. Russell's *The Pearl of Days: An Intimate Memoir of the 'Sunday Times' 1822–1972* (1972), half of the volume extending into this period; and R. Dudley Edwards, *The Pursuit of Reason: The 'Economist' 1843–1993* (1993).

Essential for **the electronic media** are the fourth and fifth volumes of A. Briggs's five-volume history of UK broadcasting, centring on the BBC: *Sound and Vision* (Oxford, 1979) covers 1945–55 and *Competition* (Oxford, 1995) covers 1955–74. Briggs's *The BBC: The First Fifty Years* (Oxford, 1985) is valuably synoptic over a longer period. See also G. Higgens's wide-ranging and well-annotated *British Broadcasting 1922–1982: A Selected and Annotated Bibliography* (1983). H. Carpenter's *The Envy of the World* (1996) covers the first fifty years of the Third Programme/Radio 3. See also P. Harris's excellent survey of pirate radio in *When Pirates Ruled the Waves* (1968). H. H. Wilson's *Pressure Group: The Campaign for Commercial Television* (1961) describes how the BBC's monopoly was broken. The series *Independent Television in Britain* is heavily administrative in emphasis: B. Sendall's two volumes are chronologically divided: 1946–62 (1982) and 1958–68 (1983); J. Potter's two volumes on 1968–80 are thematically divided into *Politics and Control* (1989) and *Companies and Programmes* (1990). M. Cockerell, *Live from Number 10: The Inside Story of Prime Ministers and Television* (1988) takes a broad sweep from Churchill to Thatcher and is invaluable on the political side.

Sport history received a welcome injection of reflectiveness in A.Guttmann's *From Ritual to Record: The Nature of Modern Sports* (New York, 1978). In the UK, sports history has in recent years begun to transcend antiquarianism, and has been advanced through the *British Journal of Sports History* (1984–6), continued from 1987 as the *International Journal of the History of Sport*; see also R. W. Cox, *A Bibliography of British Sports History, 1800–2000* (3 vols., 1991). R. Holt and T. Mason, *Sport in Britain 1945–2000* (Oxford, 2000) maps out the territory. Also valuable are G. Green, *Soccer in the Fifties* (Shepperton, 1974); G. W. Keeton, *The Football Revolution: A Study of the Changing Pattern of Association Football* (Newton Abbot, 1972); H. Richards, *A Game for Hooligans: The History of Rugby Union* (updated edn., Edinburgh, 2007). K. F. Dyer, *Catching up the Men: Women in Sport* (1982), and E. Cashmore, 'Women's Greatest Handicaps: Sex, Medicine and Men', *British Journal of Sports Medicine*, 33/2 (Apr. 1999) open up an important dimension.

On the history of **recreation** see the Home Office's informative and judicious *Review of British Standard Time* (1970). M. Smith, S. Parker, and C. S. Smith (eds.), *Leisure and Society* (1973) contains useful essays. The British Travel Association's *Patterns in British Holidaymaking 1951–68* (1968) has useful statistics. Other valuable items are M. Featherstone's interesting 'Leisure, Symbolic Power and the Life Course', in J. Horne, D. Jary, and A. Tomlinson (eds.), *Sport, Leisure and Social Relations* (1987); and J. Chapman, *Licence to Thrill: A Cultural History of the James Bond Films* (1999). J. Walsh's *Are You Talking to Me? A Life through the Movies* (2003) brilliantly evokes the cinema's impact on a suburban London teenage boy in the 1960s. L. G. Wood's 'The

Growth and Development of the Recording Industry', *The Gramophone* (Nov. 1971) is informative. For non-classical music see J. Street, 'Youth Culture and the Emergence of Popular Music', in Gourvish and O'Day (eds.), *Britain since 1945* (1991), and S. Frith, *Sound Effects: Youth, Leisure and the Politics of Rock* (1983). For the managerial side see D. Geller, *The Brian Epstein Story* (2000).

9. POLITICS AND GOVERNMENT

For the governmental system as a whole H. Morrison, *Government and Parliament: A Survey from the Inside* (3rd edn. 1964) is important for both its author and its content. V. Bogdanor's 'Britain: The Political Constitution', in V. Bogdanor (ed.), *Constitutions in Democratic Politics* (Aldershot, 1988) is excellent.

For **parliament**, S. A. Walkland (ed.), *The House of Commons in the Twentieth Century: Essays by Members of the Study of Parliament Group* (Oxford, 1979) collects abundant material. A. King, 'The Rise of the Career Politician in Britain—and its Consequences', *British Journal of Political Science* (1981) is important, and is reprinted with contributions from S. Brittan, J. Mackintosh, and others in King's compendium *Why is Britain Becoming Harder to Govern?* (1976). See also A. H. Hanson and B. Crick (eds.), *The Commons in Transition: By Members of the Study of Parliament Group* (1970). There is no study of the House of Lords since 1945 to compare with A. Adonis's study of 1884–1914, *Making Aristocracy Work* (Oxford, 1993).

For the **executive** see J. P. Mackintosh's essential *The British Cabinet* (3rd edn. 1977); P. Gordon Walker, *The Cabinet* (rev. edn. 1972); and A. King (ed.), *The British Prime Minister* (1st edn., 1969). For the **civil service** see the two editions of F. M. G. Willson, *The Organization of British Central Government 1914–1964* (first published 1957, 2nd edn. 1964), both still valuable. The *Report* of the Committee on the Civil Service (1966–8) chaired by John Fulton (5 vols. Cmnd. 3638) is essential for grasping the reforming agenda of the 1960s. See also G. K. Fry, *The Changing Civil Service* (1985); P. Hennessy, *Whitehall* (1989) is compendious and informative. There are many books on individual ministries, among which J. Garner's *The Commonwealth Office, 1925–1968* (1978) is especially useful.

Much of the writing on the **legal and penal system** is written only for lawyers, and there is a serious lack of historical analysis. See R. F. V. Heuston, *Lives of the Lord Chancellors 1940–1970* (Oxford, 1987). For the reforming agenda of the 1960s see G. Gardiner and A. Martin, *Law Reform Now* (1963); Gardiner became Lord Chancellor a year later. See also J. A. G. Griffith, *The Politics of the Judiciary* (2nd edn. 1981). For crime see T. Morris, *Crime and Criminal Justice since 1945* (Oxford, 1989); E. Gibson and S. Klein, *Murder: A Home Office Research Unit Report* (1961), and their *Murder 1957 to 1968: A Home Office Statistical Division Report on Murder in England and Wales*; also E. Gibson, *Homicide in England and Wales 1967–1971* (1975). J. B. Christoph, *Capital Punishment and British Politics: The British Movement to Abolish the Death Penalty 1945–57* (1962), a study of the Howard League, is valuable. There is no good overall study of prisons, but T. and P. Morris, *Pentonville: A Sociological Study of an English Prison* (1963) is critical and thorough. Few biographies are useful, but see B. Brivati, *Lord Goodman* (1999). For prisoner memoirs see P. Baker, *Time out* *of Life* (1961), and R. Croft-Cooke, *The Verdict of You All* (1955). See also J. P. Martin, 'The Development of Criminology in Britain, 1948–60', *British Journal of Criminology*, 1988. Legal aid has yet to find its historian.

Local government is best approached through K. Young and N. Rao, *Local Government since 1945* (Oxford, 1997), supplemented by T. Byrne's admirable reference work, *Local Government in Britain: Everyone's Guide to How it All Works* (5th edn. 1990). See also M. Loughlin *et al.* (eds.), *Half a Century of Municipal Decline 1935–1985* (1985); the Royal Commission on Local Government in England 1966–1969 *Report* (Chairman Lord Redcliffe-Maud, Cmd. 4040, n.d.); and G. C. Baugh, 'Government Grants in Aid of the Rates in England and Wales, 1889–1990', *Historical Research* (1992).

The most sustained and comparative study of **pressure groups** is K. Middlemas's three-volume *Power, Competition and the State* (1986–91), which covers analytically the period from 1940 to the 1980s; the second volume takes the analysis up to 1974. For **political parties** R. T. McKenzie, *British Political Parties* (2nd edn. 1963) is a classic. Also important are M. Pinto-Duschinsky, *British Political Finance 1830–1980* (Washington, DC, and London, 1981); S. E. Finer, *The Changing British Party System 1945–1979* (Washington, DC, 1980); and S. E. Finer (ed.), *Adversary Politics and Electoral Reform* (1975). On the interaction between policy and the two-party system see B. Harrison, 'The Rise, Fall and Rise of Political Consensus in Britain since 1940', *History* (Apr. 1999). The three volumes of party manifestos edited by I. Dale are invaluable: published in 2000, and divided by party, they cover all party manifestos from 1900 to 1997.

For the **Conservative Party** see R. Blake's *The Conservative Party from Peel to Thatcher*; this valuable introductory textbook, first published in 1970, went through several editions before it reached its final form in 1985. A. Seldon and S. Ball (eds.), *Conservative Century: The Conservative Party since 1900* (1994) provides an ampler and collective long run-in to the subject. John Ramsden's two books on the party's history offer rich detail: *The Age of Churchill and Eden, 1940–1957* (1995) and *The Winds of Change: Macmillan to Heath, 1957–1975* (1996). The libertarian anti-statist anti-socialist stance of F. A. Hayek's *The Road to Serfdom* (1944), influential in the longer term, was comprehensively rejected at the time, but for its ongoing undercurrent on the right see R. Cockett, *Thinking the Unthinkable: Think-Tanks and the Economic Counter-Revolution 1931–1983* (1994) and R. M.Hartwell, *A History of the Mont Pelerin Society* (Indianapolis, 1995). A different (traditionalist and aristocratic) vein in anti-socialism features in James Lees-Milne's *Diaries 1946–1949* (1996), which conveniently collects his diaries published earlier as *Caves of Ice* and *Midway on the Waves*.

As for personalities, see M. Gilbert, *'Never Despair'. Winston S. Churchill 1945–1965* (1988). Lord Moran's *Winston Churchill: The Struggle for Survival, 1940–1965* (1966) offers a doctor's-eye-view with much interesting table talk; see also J. Colville, *The Fringes of Power: Downing Street Diaries* ii. *October 1941–1955* (1985). A. Seldon's *Churchill's Indian Summer: The Conservative Government 1951–55* (1981) provides a very detailed history of policy in the last Churchill government. A. Howard's biography, *RAB* (1987), complements Butler's autobiographical *The Art of the Possible* (1971). There are biographies of Eden by D. Carlton (1981), R. R. James (1986), D. Dutton (1997), and D. R. Thorpe (2003). Eden tells his own story in *The Eden Memoirs: The Reckoning* (1965) covering the years 1951–7. For Macmillan see the two volumes of A. Horne's official biography: *Macmillan: 1894–1956* (1988), and *Macmillan 1957–1986* (1989). Volumes iii–vi of Macmillan's autobiography provide rich reflective detail and quote from original sources: *Tides of Fortune 1945–1955* (1969), *Riding the Storm 1956–59* (1971), *Pointing the Way 1959–1961* (1972) and *At the End of the Day 1961–1963* (1973). *The Macmillan Diaries: The Cabinet Years, 1950–1957*, ed. P. Catterall (2003) are invaluable. For Quintin Hogg, Lord Hailsham, see his second autobiography, *A Sparrow's Flight* (1990), and G. Lewis, *Lord Hailsham* (1997). Important biographies include N. Fisher, *Iain Macleod* (1973); R. Shepherd, *Iain Macleod* (1994); S. Heffer, *Like the Roman. The Life of Enoch Powell* (1998); A. Douglas-Home, *The Way the Wind Blows* (1976); and D. R. Thorpe's *Alec Douglas-Home* (1996) and *Selwyn Lloyd* (1979). See also R. McKenzie and A. Silver, *Angels in Marble: Working Class Conservatives in Urban England* (1968) and F. Parkin's important article 'Working-Class Conservatives: A Theory of Political Deviance', *British Journal of Sociology* (Sept. 1967). M.Walker's *National Front* (1977) is an able journalist's account of political groupings further right; for a sociologist's view, energetically probing the Front's 'ideology', see N. Fielding, *The National Front* (1981).

The **Labour Party** has in the *Dictionary of Labour Biography* (12 vols., 1972–2005, and ongoing) a wonderful biographical reference work. See P. M. Williams's *Hugh Gaitskell* (1979) for an exemplary full-scale biography. For Bevan see M. Foot, *Aneurin Bevan*, ii. *1945–1960* (1973) in conjunction with P. M. Williams's critique in *Political Studies* (1979), and J. Campbell, *Nye Bevan and the Mirage of British Socialism* (1987). Hugh Dalton's *Political Diary 1918–40, 1945–60* was edited (1986) by B. Pimlott, who also published the biography, *Hugh Dalton* (1985). For Harold Wilson see his first two autobiographical volumes: *Memoirs: The Making of a Prime Minister 1916–64* (1986) and *The Labour Government 1964–1970: A Personal Record* (1971). The biographies of Wilson include those by B. Pimlott (1992), A. Morgan (1992), and P. Ziegler (1993), but see also Paul Foot's interestingly critical *The Politics of Harold Wilson* (Harmondsworth, 1968). Also valuable are J. Adams, *Tony Benn* (1992); Lord George-Brown, *In My Way* (1971); J. Callaghan, *Time and Chance* (1987) and K. O. Morgan, *Callaghan: A Life* (Oxford, 1997); P. Hollis, *Jennie Lee* (Oxford, 1997); and B. Donoughue and G. W. Jones, *Herbert Morrison: Portrait of a Politician* (1973). Roy Jenkins was well served with A. Adonis and K. Thomas (eds.), *Roy Jenkins: A Retrospective* (Oxford, 2004), and J. Campbell, *Roy Jenkins: A Biography* (1983). His *A Life at the Centre* (1991) is stylish, witty, self-critical, measured, and broad in its perspective. D. Healey in his *The Time of My Life* (1989), while not hiding his light, offers many penetrating insights.

C. A. R. Crosland's *The Future of Socialism* (1956) was the most influential and reflective study of Labour policy published in these years, but E. F. M. Durbin's *The Politics of Democratic Socialism* (1940) deserves inclusion because so influential on Labour's revisionists after its author's death in 1948. S. Crosland published the biography of her husband: *Tony Crosland* (1982); see also K. Jefferys, *Anthony Crosland* (1999). Valuably analytic from a different perspective is L. Panitch, *Social Democracy and*

Industrial Militancy: The Labour Party, the Trade Unions and Incomes Policy, 1945–1974 (Cambridge, 1976). The three strengths of *The Labour Governments 1964–1970* (2006) edited by P. Dorey are its broad policy range, its wealth of detail, and its reliance on recently released government papers.

Four Labour **diarists** offer invaluable insights into the operation of government and parliament. The first is R. H. S. Crossman, with the three richly detailed volumes covering his period as a minister (1964–70) and published in 1975–7, and his *Backbench Diaries* (1981) covering the years 1951–63; all four volumes were edited by Janet Morgan. Equally rich on ministerial experience is Barbara Castle's *The Castle Diaries 1964–70* (1984). The eight volumes of Tony Benn's diaries edited by Ruth Winstone are more personal, cover a longer time span and are less ministerial in emphasis; those relevant for this period are 1940–62 (1994), 1963–7 (1987), and 1968–72 (1988). See also P. Gordon Walker's *Political Diaries 1932–1971* (1991).

For the **Liberals** see D. Brack (ed.), *Dictionary of Liberal Biography* (1998); M. Jones, *A Radical Life: The Biography of Megan Lloyd George* (1991); J. Grimond, *Memoirs* (1979), and the inside view conveyed on *Daring to Hope: The Diaries and Letters of Violet Bonham Carter 1946–1969*, ed. M. Pottle (2000).

On **electoral behaviour**, D. Butler and D. Stokes, *Political Change in Britain: The Evolution of Electoral Choice* (1974) is the 2nd edn. of what was in the 1960s a methodologically path-breaking book. D. E. Butler has performed the remarkable feat of writing or co-writing a book on every British general election between 1951 and 2005.

10. 'THE SIXTIES'

This chapter draws on many of the sources already discussed, but the 'sixties' as a subject of study suffers generally from the irrationality so prominent among its components. Problems of interpretation are discussed in B. Harrison, 'Historiographical Hazards of Sixties Britain' in W. R. Louis (ed.), *Ultimate Adventures with Brittania* (2009). A. Marwick's huge *The Sixties: Cultural Revolution in Britain, France, Italy, and the United States, c.1958–c.1974* (Oxford, 1998) is cross-cultural in approach.

On changing **attitudes to morality** see C. Davies's two books: *The Strange Death of Moral Britain* (Brunswick, NJ, 2004) and *Permissive Britain: Social Change in the Sixties and Seventies* (1975). T. Newburn's *Permission and Regulation: Law and Morals in Post-War Britain* (1992) is valuable, and M. Jarvis covers important ground in his *Conservative Governments, Morality and Social Change in Affluent Britain, 1957–64* (Manchester, 2005). See also J. Sutherland, *Offensive Literature: Decensorship in Britain 1960–1982* (1982), and A. Aldgate, *Censorship and the Permissive Society: British Cinema and Theatre, 1955–1965* (Oxford, 1995).

There is no powerful overall analysis of the strange and prolonged **anti-system protest** in universities in the 1960s, particularly strange in Britain, but see G. Carr, *The Angry Brigade: The Cause and the Case* (1975). The anonymous *Letters of Mercurius* (1970) cast an amusingly sceptical eye on the progressive causes then being promoted in Oxford.

On **popular culture** see G. Melly's well-informed and intelligent *Revolt into Style: The Pop Arts in Britain* (1970); J. Noyce, *The Directory of British Alternative Periodicals 1965–1974* (Hassocks, 1979).

For **drugs** see B. Wootton (chairman), *Cannabis: Report by the Advisory Committee on Drug Dependence* (1968); R. Davenport-Hines, *The Pursuit of Oblivion: A Global History of Narcotics 1500–2000* (2001); and M. A. Plant, *Drugtakers in an English Town* (1975).

Index